Online Law

The SPA's Legal Guide to Doing Business on the Internet

Thomas J. Smedinghoff, Editor

Contributing Authors

Andrew R. Basile, Jr.	Ruth Hill Bro
Geoffrey G. Gilbert	Elizabeth S. Perdue
Lorijean G. Oei	Thomas J. Smedinghoff
Peter J. Strand	Jonathan E. Strouse
Larry M. Zanger	

Foreword by Ken Wasch,
President of the Software Publishers Association

Addison-Wesley Developers Press

Reading, Massachusetts • Menlo Park, California • New York
Don Mills, Ontario • Harlow, England • Amsterdam
Bonn • Sydney • Singapore • Tokyo • Madrid • San Juan
Paris • Seoul • Milan • Mexico City • Taipei

Many of the designations used by manufacturers and sellers to distinguish their products are claimed as trademarks. Where those designations appear in this book, and Addison-Wesley was aware of a trademark claim, the designations have been printed in initial capital letters or all capital letters.

The authors and publisher have taken care in preparation of this book, but make no expressed or implied warranty of any kind and assume no responsibility for errors or omissions. No liability is assumed for incidental or consequential damages in connection with or arising out of the use of the information or programs contained herein.

Library of Congress Cataloging-in-Publication Data

Online law: the SPA's legal guide to doing business on the Internet /
    Thomas J. Smedinghoff, editor.
        p.   cm.
    Includes index.
    ISBN 0-201-48980-5
        1. Computer networks—Law and legislation—United States.   2. Data
transmission systems—Law and legislation—United States.
3. Contracts—United States—Data processing.   4. Data protection—
Law and legislation—United States.   5. Computer crimes—United
States.   6. Intellectual property— United States.   I. Smedinghoff,
Thomas J., 1951– . II. Software Publishers Association.
KF390.5.C6055   1996
343.73099'9—dc20
[347.303999]   95-48894
                                                                        CIP

Sponsoring Editor: Kim Fryer
Project Manager: John Fuller
Production Coordinator: Ellen Savett
Cover design: Ann Gallager
Text design: John Fuller
Set in 10.5-point Palatino by ST Associates

3 4 5 6 7 8 9 10 MA 00999897
Third Printing, May 1997

Addison-Wesley books are available for bulk purchases by corporations, institutions, and other organizations. For more information please contact the Corporate, Government, and Special Sales Department at (800) 238-9682.

Find A-W Developers Press on the World-Wide Web at:
http://www.aw.com/devpress/

To my mother, Dorothy
and in memory of my father, John
—T.J.S.

Contents

Chapter 7   Online Payment Options   103

PART III: RIGHTS IN ELECTRONIC INFORMATION   121

Chapter 8   Understanding Electronic Property Rights   123

PART IV: REGULATING INFORMATION CONTENT   301

Chapter 19   The Role of the First Amendment Online   303

Chapter 20   Sexually Explicit Materials in a Digital World   317

Chapter 27   Contracts for Making the Online Connection   429

Preface

The purpose of this book is to provide practical, understandable, and useful information on the current state of the law as it relates to all aspects of doing business on the Internet. It is designed to help you to recognize and to deal with the legal issues you will inevitably face when engaging in online activities such as e-mail communications, electronic publishing, online advertising, and the online sale of goods and services.

This book is written both for businesses engaged in online commerce and their attorneys, and seeks to provide a comprehensive summary and explanation of the basic legal concepts and issues relevant to the variety of activities that you can undertake online. It is our intent that it will serve as a guide to making business decisions by helping readers to recognize the legal issues they face in a given situation, and to understand their options and the consequences of their actions more fully. The text is written for the nonlawyer, but extensive citations to legal authorities are provided for attorneys or other readers who would like to obtain further information.

This book is designed to be used in two ways: first, to be read cover to cover in order to gain a general understanding of the law that applies to online communications; and second, to be used as a reference book to provide answers to specific questions.

The book is organized by legal topic, primarily because that appeared to be the best way to present the material, but also because many of the legal subjects discussed in the book apply to multiple aspects of electronic commerce. Each substantive area of the law has been set forth in one or two self-contained chapters, but there is often a significant interrelationship among what may appear to be separate and distinct legal issues.

This book presents the general legal principles as they have evolved to date. However, because the applicability of the law to online communications is so new, many of the issues raised in this book are yet unresolved. Thus, if you are contemplating taking particular action in reliance on the principles set forth here, you should consult with legal counsel to determine whether the law varies in the state involved, whether the law has changed, or whether the unique facts of the particular transaction concerned will alter the outcome.

It is assumed that you are familiar with the online concepts and terms used throughout the book, such as the *Internet, Web, EDI, e-mail, computer bulletin boards,* and the like, so these are not explained in much detail. However, a glossary is provided to assist in defining these terms as well as many of the legal terms used throughout the book.

Many of the statements made throughout the book are annotated by endnotes following the text to each chapter. They are included to indicate the statute, government regulation, court opinion, or other legal authority on which the statement is based, in order to allow you or your lawyer to locate further information for the referenced statement or to provide additional information. However, the endnotes are not necessary to an understanding of the text and can be skipped.

Foreword

The world is going "net-crazy," or so it seems. The numbers of Internet domain name registrations, World Wide Web sites, and subscribers to local access providers have all skyrocketed beyond anyone's wildest expectations. The basic home computer sold today usually comes with a high-speed modem and several choices of Internet access providers, so online access is not just for work or school anymore. General circulation publications, not just computer trade press, now regularly carry stories about secure electronic payment options, digital signatures, electronic piracy, and other issues generated by the heightened interest in electronic commerce. "The Net" even seems to have replaced sports as the topic of choice at many social functions.

Online Law: The SPA's Legal Guide to Doing Business on the Internet is the first truly comprehensive guide to the legal issues involved in all facets of electronic commerce, including contracts, payment options, information security, rights, and regulating content and online conduct. Don't let this book sit on the shelf—despite scant legal precedent in this nascent field, Tom Smedinghoff has articulated sound legal principles, blended with practical advice, which make this book invaluable.

On behalf of the SPA's 1,200 member companies, we congratulate Tom and his colleagues in the Information Technology Law Department at McBride Baker & Coles for a fine job of making these complex and evolving issues easier to understand. Let's use this information to make it easier for everyone to communicate and do business online with confidence in the electronic environment.

Ken Wasch
President
Software Publishers Association
Spring 1996

About the Authors

The editor and all of the other contributing authors are members of the Information Technology Law Department of McBride Baker & Coles, a Chicago law firm, and can be reached c/o McBride Baker & Coles, 500 W. Madison Street, 40th Floor, Chicago, Illinois 60661; phone: (312) 715-5700; fax: (312) 993-9350; e-mail [lastname]@mbc.com. The McBride Baker & Coles Web site can be found at: http://www.mbc.com.

Thomas J. Smedinghoff is a partner and co-chair of the firm's Information Technology Law Department. His practice focuses on emerging information technology legal issues relating to developing topics such as electronic commerce, the Internet, multimedia, encryption, software, digital signatures, electronic publishing, data security, electronic funds transfers, digital cash, e-mail, electronic recordkeeping, computer bulletin boards, electronic licensing and distribution, and interactive online services. Mr. Smedinghoff serves as intellectual property counsel to the Software Publishers Association, and as chair of the Electronic Commerce and Information Technology Division of the American Bar Association's Section of Science and Technology. He is the author of *The Software Publishers Association Legal Guide to Multimedia* (Addison-Wesley, 1994); *SPA Guide to Contracts and the Legal Protection of Software* (Software Publishers Association, 1993); and *The Legal Guide to Developing, Protecting, and Marketing Software* (John Wiley & Sons, 1986). He is an adjunct professor of computer law at The John Marshall Law School. Mr. Smedinghoff can be contacted at smedinghoff@mbc.com.

Andrew R. Basile, Jr. concentrates his practice on all areas of information technology and intellectual property law, including patents, trademarks, and copyrights, with an emphasis on computer and electronics technologies. With an extensive technical background, Mr. Basile is a registered patent attorney, and frequently represents clients before the U.S. Patent and Trademark Office. He has substantial experience in software licensing, and has counseled clients in numerous transactions and disputes relating to intellectual property. Mr. Basile can be contacted at basile@mbc.com.

Ruth Hill Bro concentrates her practice in the information technology, copyright, and trademark areas. She is the author of "Rules to Follow to Ensure Your Faxed Signatures Are Valid," *Computing Channels*, 1995. Ms. Bro can be contacted at bro@mbc.com.

Geoffrey G. Gilbert is the former chair of the firm's litigation department. He has had extensive experience with the trial and appeal of business and intellectual property litigation, including antitrust, copyright infringement, fraud, products liability, trade secrets, and unfair competition. In recent years, Mr. Gilbert has represented numerous computer software developers in trade secret and copyright litigation in both state and federal courts. Mr. Gilbert can be contacted at gilbert@mbc.com.

Lorijean G. Oei concentrates her practice in the information technology, copyright, and trademark areas. Ms. Oei counsels businesses ranging from entrepreneurial start-ups to publicly held companies on business, technology, software publishing, and intellectual property law issues. Her recent publications include *Expanding Taxes on Computer-Related Services,* The DataLaw Report (Jan./Feb. 1995), and *Electronic-Record Storage Checklist,* 11 IEEE Software 102 (Jul. 94). Ms. Oei can be contacted at oei@mbc.com.

Elizabeth S. Perdue brings to her intellectual-, property-, and information-technology practice over twelve years of experience in corporate and transactional law. Her clients range from small businesses, to publicly held companies, to international trade associations; her practice includes mergers and acquisitions, financings, and intellectual property counseling. Ms. Perdue has been involved with the Chicago Bar Association Computer Law Committee's project on the pending revisions to Article 2 and new Article 2B of the Uniform Commercial Code. Ms. Perdue can be contacted at perdue@mbc.com.

Peter J. Strand practices primarily entertainment law, intellectual property law, and commercial litigation. He represents musicians, songwriters, authors, writers, artists, managers, independent record companies, and performers in various transactional and litigation matters in the entertainment industry. Before practicing law, Mr. Strand was a full-time musician and recorded two internationally released albums. Mr. Strand can be contacted at strand@mbc.com.

Jonathan E. Strouse is both an attorney and a certified public accountant and has practiced extensively in the areas of federal, state, and international taxation. Mr. Strouse has substantial experience in the drafting and structuring of numerous transactions that have tax, accounting, and other financial ramifications. Mr. Strouse has authored several tax-related articles that have appeared in publications such as *The Tax Lawyer, The Practical Accountant,* and the *Illinois Bar Journal.* Mr. Strouse can be contacted at strouse@mbc.com.

Larry M. Zanger is co-chair of the firm's Information Technology Law Department. A certified public accountant and winner of the Elijah Watts Sells Award, he is the immediate past chair of the Computer Law Committee of the Chicago Bar Association and writes and speaks frequently on computer law and computer business topics. For five years he was an adjunct professor of law and accounting at the University of Illinois, Chicago, College of Business. Mr. Zanger can be contacted at zanger@mbc.com.

1
Online Law: What's New and Different?

Thomas J. Smedinghoff

The advent of the global information infrastructure and the so-called digital revolution raise countless new issues and questions. Should copyright apply to digital content? How can we implement secure electronic commerce? Should we regulate the dissemination of obscenity over the Internet? Who has jurisdiction over wrongful conduct committed in cyberspace? What is the role of anonymity in the online world? How do we protect the privacy of individuals in the online environment?

Although online technology raises many new legal issues, the law available to help us resolve them, at least today, is largely based on the world as it existed before online commerce became a reality. In fact, it may be years before the law catches up to today's technology, and by then technology will have made further quantum advances, leaving the law behind, again.

Yet those who want to do business electronically today cannot wait. They need to know with some certainty the legal consequences of their online activity. Thus the challenge is to predict how these new legal issues may be resolved using the current law. That is what this book aims to do.

Of course, not every legal issue raised by online technology will matter to you. Depending upon the nature of your activities in cyberspace, some issues may be extremely important, while others will be of little or no consequence. For example, publishers worry about protecting the copyrights to their digital works, but frequently have no concern over issues such as confidentiality or online contracts. Those who buy and sell goods online have no interest in the copyrightability of their electronic records, but are generally very concerned over the security of their messages, and whether or not they have a binding and enforceable contract. Sorting through this maze of issues and identifying those that need to be addressed in a given situation can be difficult.

1.1 What's New: Issues of Online Law

The law as it exists today revolves around physical objects. Tangible goods are bought and sold. Information and content are distributed on paper, CD-ROM, film, and videotape. There is typically something tangible delivered from seller to buyer. Likewise, the medium of commerce is a tangible object—that is, paper. Contracts, purchase orders, acknowledgments, invoices, checks, order forms, and confirmations have all traditionally been embodied in paper—a medium that is both familiar and trusted. In the online world, however, paper does not exist.

In some cases, paper satisfies a legal requirement (such as a requirement that a contract be "in writing"). In other cases, paper satisfies practical business requirements (such as a background available in a paper check designed to prevent forgery, or a record that can be placed in an appropriate file for future reference). In still other cases, people simply feel more comfortable when they have paper to rely on. All of these problems must be overcome if electronic commerce is to be viable.

In addition, when information exists only in digital form, new problems are introduced. It is, for example, a trivial task to make an exact duplicate of an original electronic document and to distribute that duplicate on a massive worldwide basis, at virtually no cost. Moreover, the ability to edit, alter, or otherwise manipulate digital content in a way that is often undetectable expands the opportunities for fraud and other forms of abuse.

Current law is also territorial. That is, it is limited in application to activities or persons within the boundaries of a state or a country. Online activity, however, does not occur in any one physical location. An e-mail message sent by a company in Ohio to its supplier in Florida, for example, can pass through computers in the numerous states and other countries.

Thus, when we remove paper and the other tangible manifestations of goods and commercial activities, and remove the geographical boundaries in which the laws applicable to those activities operate, we also remove many of the premises of existing law and many of the traditional safeguards people have relied upon to make commerce work. Accordingly, if the law is to adapt to the needs of online commerce and electronic publishing, it must respond to these differences. This is starting to happen. However, it is a slow process.

1.2   Applying Old Law to a New Online World

The challenge for the law is that it must adapt to the reality of electronic communications by providing clear guidance for those who engage in online commerce. Without certainty in the legal rules, electronic commerce will not reach its commercial potential.[1]

Yet the law always lags behind technology. Our legal system is based on precedent, and new laws are not enacted as quickly as technology changes. In addition, courts often misunderstand the implications and significance of new technology. For example, in 1915, when motion pictures were a new phenomenon, the Supreme Court ruled that movies were not protected by the First Amendment, but were merely "spectacles, not to be regarded . . . as part of the press of the country or as organs of public opinion."[2] Similarly, in 1968 a federal court, noting that "the public has about as much real need for the services of a CATV system as it does for hand-carved ivory back-scratchers,"[3] held that cable television was not sufficiently "affected with a public interest" to permit local regulation.[4]

However, the law can, and in most cases does, successfully adapt to new technology. Copyright law is a prime example. As the Supreme Court has noted: "From its beginning, the law of copyright law has developed in response to significant changes in technology."[5] Authorized over 200 years ago by our Constitution, copyright law has weathered the changes brought about by new technologies such as photography, sound recording, and broadcasting; today it adequately protects works in all three of those areas.

There is, of course, a debate raging today over whether existing copyright law—or, for that matter, any other area of the law—can successfully adapt to the issues of online communications and electronic commerce. But regardless of whether existing law is a good fit for electronic publishing and online commerce, it will certainly have an impact on those who engage in this new way of conducting business. Until the law evolves to address the new issues raised by the paperless world of online communications better than it does now, the risks that businesses take, and the rights they are able to enforce, will be judged with respect to the law as it currently exists. Accordingly, those who would pioneer the new world of online commerce need to understand both the existing law and those elements of the new environment that are likely to have an impact on the way the law is applied.

1.3   Categorizing the Issues

To help put the issues in perspective, and to assist your business in addressing those of importance to its activities, this book is organized into five parts. They are:

1. **Information Security.** How can the parties to an electronic communication ensure the authenticity and integrity of the message? How do the parties "sign" an electronic document (such as a contract)? How do parties to an electronic communication ensure the confidentiality of the message? These issues of information security, and the legal role they play in facilitating electronic commerce, are addressed in Part I.
2. **Online Transactions.** How can the parties create an enforceable electronic contract online? What are the rules governing the formation and enforcement of electronic contracts? How can the vendor be paid for its goods or services online? What are the options for electronic payment? These issues are discussed in Part II.
3. **Rights in Electronic Information.** Who owns the bits and bytes that form an electronic communication? What rights does the owner have to use and control the use of that information? What rights do others have to use information that they do not own? Issues relating to rights in information—including copyrights, trademarks, trade secret rights, rights of publicity and privacy, and patent rights—are discussed in Part III.
4. **Regulating Information Content.** To what extent does the law regulate the information or content that is communicated online? What rights does government have to control the contents of the message? How do laws on obscenity, defamation, and advertising apply in the online world? Part IV considers those cases where the law regulates or controls the content of online communications.
5. **Regulating Online Conduct.** How does the law regulate conduct online? How will tax laws, export restrictions, and criminal laws be applied to this type of conduct? Is

one party liable for the actions of another online? Who has jurisdiction over disputes regarding messages that cross state or country boundaries? Part V addresses how the law regulates online conduct—from taxing it to making some forms of it a criminal offense.

Endnotes

1.   *See Intellectual Property and the National Information Infrastructure: The Report of the Working Group on Intellectual Property Rights,* Information Infrastructure Task Force, 68 (Sept. 5, 1995).

2.   *Mutual Film Corp. v. Industrial Comm'n of Ohio,* 236 U.S. 230, 244 (1915). This decision was not overturned until 1952. *Joseph Burstyn, Inc. v. Wilson,* 343 U.S. 495, 502 (1952).

3.   *Greater Fremont, Inc. v. Fremont,* 302 F. Supp. 652, 665 (N.D. Ohio 1968).

4.   *Greater Fremont, Inc. v. Fremont,* 302 F. Supp. 652, 663 (N.D. Ohio 1968), *aff'd sub nom., Wonderland Ventures, Inc. v. Sandusky,* 423 F.2d 548 (6th Cir. 1970).

5.   *Sony Corp. of America v. Universal City Studios, Inc.,* 464 U.S. 417, 430 (1984).

2

From Web Sites to Online Sales: A Road Map to the Legal Issues

Thomas J. Smedinghoff

The online world is rapidly becoming a major center of commerce. Virtually every economic and business-related activity has, or will have, an online component. For purposes of providing a road map to the online legal issues likely to be faced by businesses, online commercial activities can be broadly categorized as follows:

- **Communication.** At the heart of every commercial transaction is some form of communication between the parties involved—in person, by mail, by fax, by telephone, through agents, or, in the case of electronic commerce, through an online communication. E-mail and other forms of electronic communication are at the heart of online business transactions. In some cases the communication is designed to facilitate a transition, and may involve exchanging information, entering into a contract, or making payment. In other cases, the communication *is* the transaction, such as when software or digital content is distributed online. The issues raised by the nature and content of the communication can be quite extensive.
- **Publishing and Distributing Digital Content.** Because of their global reach, the Internet and other computer networks offer prime opportunities for publishing digital content on a worldwide scale. *Publishing* is a broad term that includes both publishing information that is intended to be read or viewed online; and electronically distributing digital content, such as software, sound recordings, movies, photographs, and databases, for use offline.
- **Advertising.** As commerce moves online, advertising follows. Internet Web sites and the commercial online services are primary forums for online advertising. But along with online advertising (just as with traditional forms) comes the obligation to comply with laws regulating advertising and the use of intellectual property.
- **Buying and Selling Goods and Services.** Tangible products cannot be distributed online, but contracts for their sale and delivery form a major part of the growing area of online commerce. Whether taking the form of electronic data interchange between large corporations or online shopping malls for consumers, the result is the same—an agreement to purchase and deliver goods. Payments for these goods can also occur online.

All of these activities can be conducted via a variety of online vehicles. Perhaps the most popular vehicle for online commerce today is the World Wide Web capability of the Internet. Another very popular vehicle is the online facilities provided by the commercial online services, such as America Online, Compuserve, the Microsoft Network, and Prodigy. But, although these two forms of online commerce have received the most attention, there are other alternatives.

For the past several years, electronic data interchange (EDI) transactions, as well as other forms of online commerce, have been accomplished through the use of private networks, sometimes referred to as *value added networks* (or *VANs*), such as Advantis and GEIS. In many cases, businesses simply set up their own private computer bulletin boards and invite prospective customers to access those boards in order to obtain the products, services, or information that it chooses to make available.

Regardless of the vehicle used, however, these activities raise a variety of legal issues, many of which are unique because they are being accomplished through electronic communications, and most of which are largely undecided.

To help put the legal issues in perspective, this chapter provides an overview, or road map, to the various legal issues that may arise when engaging in each of the various online business activities discussed above. In many respects, it functions as a checklist. As such, it identifies the key legal issues that arise, and refers you to the chapters in which those legal issues are explained and discussed. To help put some of the issues in perspective, this chapter concludes with a discussion of the legal issues involved in establishing and operating an Internet Web site.

2.1 Communication—Sending and Receiving Messages

Communication is the essence of online activity. All aspects of online commerce involve the communication of messages, which are used for many purposes. They can provide instructions to computers, convey information to humans, or serve a variety of other purposes. For example, messages can be used to negotiate and enter into contracts, make payment, publish information, or make legal demands. Moreover, messages can take a variety of forms. While e-mail is perhaps the most common form, electronic communications can also include EDI-formatted messages, electronic funds transfer payment orders, and postings to bulletin boards as well as many others.

The nature of an electronic communication, and its importance in the context in which it is made, will determine the legal concerns of the parties involved. The following sections summarize the key legal issues likely to arise with respect to electronic communications.

2.1.1 Information Security

Information security concerns are often at the forefront of the legal issues involved in electronic communications. In particular, the electronic communication of information raises questions of authenticity, message integrity, and the confidentiality or privacy of the contents of the message. These concepts are explained in Chapter 3.

Authenticity and *integrity* of online communications relating to commercial transactions are often critical. How does the recipient know that the message is from the purported sender? How does the recipient know that the message has not been altered? If a dispute develops, how can either party prove that the copy of the message that it saved is in fact the same message that was originally sent or received? Verifying the authenticity and integrity of a message is important as a business precaution taken before relying on it, and can have significant legal implications.

One particularly effective mechanism for addressing these concerns is the digital signature, a subject discussed in Chapter 4. Digital signatures provide a means, unique to online communications, for ensuring authenticity and integrity.

When messages are electronically stored, security issues also arise. For example, what should be kept, and how should it be stored, so that an electronic record will constitute reliable evidence of the facts or event it documents? Electronic record keeping is addressed in Chapter 5.

Confidentiality and *privacy* are also often important for certain messages. Sensitive contract negotiations via e-mail, patient health-care records communicated electronically, credit-card information sent over the Internet, and a company's trade secret information transmitted from one office to another are just some of the forms of electronic communication that require a high degree of privacy. In some cases, only one party to the message has a significant confidentiality concern (such as a consumer sending his or her credit-card number across the Internet to pay for goods purchased online). In other cases, privacy is an important concern to both parties (such as when an attorney communicates confidential legal advice to a client). In yet other cases, the party with the greatest concern over confidentiality is not a party to the communication at all (such as when a patient's sensitive health-care records are transmitted electronically from doctor to insurer, in which case the patient has the greatest concern over confidentiality).

The need for confidentiality can come from two sources. First, it can simply be a desire of one or both parties to the communication, such as when two parties engage in sensitive transactions or highly personal communications. In many other cases, however, an obligation of confidentiality is imposed by law or contract. In those situations, a party who fails to take appropriate steps to ensure that the contents of a message remain confidential may be exposed to liability. For example, the law requires that certain types of data (such as patient records regarding drug- and alcohol-abuse treatment) be kept confidential. (Privacy obligations are discussed in Chapter 17.) Likewise, the parties may be contractually obligated to keep information confidential, such as with the communication of a trade secret disclosed pursuant to a confidentiality agreement (see Section 12.2.2).

Threats to the confidentiality of a message come from two primary sources. The first is from those who provide the communication networks through which the message travels. Internet access providers, online services, value-added networks, other electronic communication services, and their respective employees are in the best position to intercept, read and disclose messages that travel through their facilities. The Electronic Communications Privacy Act addresses this risk, and it is discussed in Sections 17.4, 26.2.2, and 30.2.3. The right of an employer to monitor messages sent to and from its employees is discussed in Section 26.2.

The second threat comes from third parties who obtain access to the network (lawfully or otherwise) and intercept, read, and disclose the contents of a message. This risk is greatest with public networks such as the Internet, and much less with respect to secure private networks. The Electronic Communications Privacy Act also addresses this risk (see Section 17.4) as do various computer crime statutes (see Chapter 30).

In many cases, however, mere legal prohibitions or after-the-fact remedies are not sufficient. Accordingly, the parties may want to consider encryption to ensure the desired confidentiality. The use of encryption, however, raises its own set of legal issues, because the export of encryption products is highly regulated. Encryption is explained generally in Chapter 31, and its role in information security is explained in Chapter 4. Export restrictions on encryption products are discussed in Chapter 25.

2.1.2 Rights in Information

Is digital information protectible? If so, who owns information communicated online? Does an online communication infringe the rights of others? What are the rights of the recipient? How can individuals stop (or at least control) communications of data about them sent to others? These issues are introduced in Chapter 8 and discussed in detail in Chapters 9 through 17.

In many cases, the content of a message is protected by one or more valuable *intellectual property rights*. A message may, for example, consist of text, sounds, images, or data protected by copyright (discussed in Chapter 9), an individual's right of privacy (discussed in Chapter 17), or an individual's right of publicity (discussed in Chapter 16). In yet other cases, a message may contain valuable trade secrets (see Chapter 12). Moreover, each of these various rights may be owned by different persons (see Section 8.1.3).

The owner of these rights wants to ensure that they are protected. Since the sender of a message may not own all of the rights in the content comprising the message, the sender needs to ensure that it has the right to send the information. Also the recipient needs to know what rights it has to use and exploit the contents of the message. These issues are discussed in Chapters 9 through 17.

Moreover, because messages can be published through a medium, such as an online service provider or Internet access provider, issues can arise as to the liability of such provider for infringing messages communicated through their services. This is discussed in Chapter 29.

2.1.3 Regulation of Content

Can the law regulate the contents of an electronic message? In some cases, the answer is clearly "yes."

The First Amendment guarantees the right of free speech, and it protects electronic communications just as it protects other forms of speech. That does not mean, however, that anything goes. In some cases, the law regulates the content of an electronic message. These issues are introduced in Chapter 19.

Perhaps the most common situation in which the content of a message is regulated occurs when it constitutes advertising. Many online messages, especially in a business context, may be construed as advertising, even though they are not communicated in the traditional form of advertising. Advertising is heavily regulated by a variety of state and federal statutes and regulatory agencies. When do those regulations apply to online communications? How do they control and restrict the nature and content of such communications? These issues are discussed in Chapter 22.

Defamation is another concern raised by the online communication of messages. This is due, in part, to the fact that such messages can be easily and quickly published to large masses of people, often without the knowledge or consent of the original sender of the message. This makes it important to understand when and under what circumstances a message can be considered defamatory. This is discussed in Chapter 21. Likewise, because such messages are often published through an intermediary such as an online service provider or Internet access provider, issues arise as to the liability of such providers for defamatory messages communicated through their services. This is discussed in Section 29.3.

The law also regulates communications that are considered "obscene" or "indecent," or that constitute child pornography. But what is considered obscene or indecent, and whose standards apply in the global online environment? These issues are discussed in Chapter 20.

2.1.4 Regulation of Conduct

Simply sending and receiving electronic messages also raises numerous legal issues. For example, when, and under what circumstances, can an employer intercept and monitor e-mail messages to and from its employees? (See Chapter 26.) What penalties await those who seek to obtain unauthorized access to information stored on a computer? (See Chapter 30.)

The liability of individuals other than the sender of a message for damages caused by messages that infringe someone's rights, are defamatory, or are otherwise unlawful raises yet another set of issues. For example, when, and under what circumstances, is an employer liable for damages caused by e-mail messages sent by one of its employees? (See Section 26.3.) When is the online service or Internet access provider used to communicate the message liable for the damages that might result? (See Chapter 29.)

When messages are sent across national borders, additional legal controls and regulations come into play. The United States, for example, imposes export controls on the communication of technical data. (See Chapter 25.) In Europe, data protection and transborder data flow statutes must be considered. (See Section 25.5.)

2.2   Electronic Publishing and Distribution

Electronic publishing of digital content (such as text, sound recordings, images, and motion pictures) can take numerous forms. Displaying content on an online service, setting up a Web site, operating a private computer bulletin board system (BBS), or posting content to a listserv or UseNet news group are just a few examples.

Online "publishing" activities come in two basic varieties. The first involves *displaying* content to the user (such as displaying content through a Web site or online service). The user is typically free to print or download the content, but that is not necessary, as in many cases, viewing it on the screen is sufficient to meet the user's needs. With this form of publishing, the user often pays for a general right of access (such as access to the online service or Web site where the publishing occurs), rather than for the specific content involved.

The second form of publishing involves the *distribution* of content (such as text, data, sounds, images, or software) in the form of files that are downloaded by the user separate from any display, and that are normally intended to be used by the user offline at a later time. With this form of publishing, the user typically pays for the particular content involved (e.g., a specific software product downloaded). Software, sound recordings of musical works, and photographs are often distributed in this manner.

2.2.1 Rights in Information

2.2.1.1 Identifying Rights in Information. A key issue for any form of electronic publishing is the *intellectual property rights* in the content that is published. What aspects of the content are protectible? Who owns these rights? How can the owner protect these rights? Is the publisher infringing the rights of others by publishing the context? These issues are discussed in Chapters 8 through 17.

Online publishing involves the creation, collection, adaptation, combination, coordination, and/or synchronization of one or more types of content, such as text, databases, characters, musical works, sound recordings, photographs, motion pictures, and software. Each of these types of content presents several unique legal issues that need to be considered and resolved before the content is published online.

The first issue relates to the nature of the intellectual property rights that can exist in the content to be published (see Chapter 8). These property rights include copyrights (discussed in Chapters 9 through 11), trade secret rights (discussed in Chapter 12), trademark rights (discussed in Chapters 13 and 14), patent rights (discussed in Chapter 15), publicity rights (discussed in Chapter 16), and privacy rights (discussed in Chapter 17). To the extent that these rights exist in the content to be published, the publisher must ensure either that it owns them or that it obtains appropriate permission from the owner.

- **Copyright Law.** Virtually all text, databases, characters, musical works, sound recordings, photos and still images, motion pictures, and software products are automatically protected by copyright upon their creation. As a consequence, copyright protection is available for most of the content that a publisher creates, and its right to use such content created by others will be restricted by the provisions of the copyright law. Therefore, the copyright law is a factor to be considered with respect to virtually all works to be published online. Copyright law is discussed in Chapters 9, 10, and 11.

- **Trademark Law.** If the content to be published includes the trademarks of the publisher or of others, it may be necessary to consider the impact of trademark law. Trademarks of the publisher must be properly used and protected; the trademarks of others must not be used in a way that constitutes infringement or unfair competition. Note that trademarks are not limited to words and phrases. Symbols, designs, images, photographs, characters, and even sound recordings can constitute trademarks. Trademark law is discussed in Chapter 13.

- **Right of Publicity.** Use of a person's image can infringe the person's right of publicity if the image is used in a manner designed to capitalize on the person's reputation or imply endorsement. The same is true where a sound recording of a famous person, or an imitation of his or her voice, is used without permission in a manner that implies that the celebrity either created the recording or somehow endorsed or is associated with the recording. The law relating to the right of publicity is discussed generally in Chapter 16.

- **Right of Privacy.** Content that refers to an actual person (such as through use of a name, photograph, image, or voice), or contains protected data about a person, can also violate that person's right of privacy. This is particularly true if the use places a person in a false light, misappropriates a person's name or likeness for commercial purposes, discloses embarrassing private facts about the person, or otherwise intrudes upon the person's solitude. The law relating to the right of privacy is discussed in Chapter 17.

2.2.1.2 Acquiring Rights in Information. Whenever any form of content is to be published online, the publisher must own or acquire the relevant rights in the content sufficient to authorize its publication in the online forum. Some rights, such as copyrights (see Section 9.4), trade secret rights (see Section 12.2), and trademark rights (see Section 13.3), can be acquired by the publisher merely by creating the content itself. With preexisting content, owned by others, however, it is necessary to obtain some grant of permission or license to exploit the various rights inherent in the content to be published. Issues relating to licensing of content for subsequent publication are discussed in Chapter 18.

In addition, certain personal rights that might exist in content must be acquired from the individuals who, by law, will be deemed to be the owner of those rights. See Chapter 17 for a discussion of the right of privacy and Chapter 16 for a discussion of the right of publicity.

2.2.1.3 Protecting Rights in Information. Once rights are identified and secured, protecting and enforcing them become key considerations. Given the enhanced capabilities for infringement that are offered by information in digital form, content owners face real challenges in attempting to protect those rights. Chapters 9 through 17, which discuss the intellectual property rights that can be present in information, examine the ways in which each of those various rights can be perfected and protected.

2.2.1.4 Rights of Users. As with all forms of intellectual property, publishers also need to consider the rights of those who access, use, acquire, license, or buy the content they publish. For example, can a user viewing an Internet Web page print the contents of the Web page? Save the contents of the Web page to disk? Make additional copies to distribute to others? Modify portions of the content and use it in other publications? These issues take on added significance in an online context, since the digital nature of the content makes such subsequent uses extremely easy and economical.

With most forms of intellectual property, users who lawfully acquire the content from a publisher are given certain rights by law. Depending upon the nature of what is published, these rights may include the right to transfer the content to another party (see Section 11.6), and the right to make certain "fair uses" of the content (see Section 11.3). In addition, acquirers of digital content online may also have certain implied rights to make various uses of the content they have received (see Section 11.1).

In many cases it is desirable for publishers to enter into a contract (i.e., a license agreement) with those to whom content is distributed that will define the user's rights in the digital content. This allows the publisher to remove any uncertainties over the scope of the user's rights, allows the publisher to impose restrictions on the user's right to use the content, and gives the publisher an added vehicle for enforcing its rights if necessary. Online contracts that can be used to accomplish this purpose are discussed in Chapter 6.

2.2.2 Regulation of Content

Like electronic messages, the content of electronically published material is sometimes regulated by law. This is particularly true if the information published constitutes advertising (such as a Web site), or is defamatory or obscene. These issues are discussed in Chapters 19 through 22.

2.2.3 Regulation of Online Conduct

The act of electronic publishing raises several legal issues. In many cases, electronic publishing (if provided for a fee) is a transaction subject to state sales or use taxes. Accordingly, publishers need to know what taxes, if any, apply to their activities. Moreover, they need to know when, and under what circumstances, a taxing body can require a publisher located outside the jurisdiction to collect and remit taxes on transactions to the taxing body. Similar issues arise with regard to the ability of a jurisdiction to tax income derived from online transactions. These issues are discussed in Chapter 24.

Publishing certain types of content can also subject the publisher to liability for its conduct. For example, if the content published is defamatory, the publisher may be liable for the resulting damages (see Chapter 21). Or, alternatively, the publication may violate laws relating to deceptive trade practices (see Chapter 28). In fact, in many situations, a publisher can be liable for damages resulting from material it publishes, even if it was written by someone else. These issues are discussed in Chapter 29.

Finally, because content and other information can be published on a global scale, it is important for publishers to understand what states or countries might have jurisdiction over their conduct and how that jurisdiction might be enforced. Since an innocent publication in one country might constitute an illegal publication in another, this can become a very important consideration. Jurisdiction is discussed in Chapter 23.

2.3 Online Advertising

Many forms of online publishing, especially through vehicles such as the World Wide Web, will constitute advertising. This raises a host of legal issues.

All forms of advertising are governed by numerous state and federal statutes and regulations. These regulations are discussed in Chapter 22. Advertisers must also take care to avoid violating the laws relating to deceptive trade practices. These issues are discussed in Chapter 28.

Like those who publish content online, advertisers must also consider the intellectual property rights in the content to be used in the online advertising to ensure that they either own the content or have the right to publish it. (See generally, Chapters 7 through 17).

Moreover, like online publishers, advertisers must take care to ensure that the advertising material does not violate the laws governing obscenity (see Chapter 20) and does not constitute defamation (see Chapter 21).

2.4 Buying and Selling Goods and Services Online

One of the key aspects of electronic commerce is entering into transactions for the purchase and sale of goods and services, and the licensing of intellectual property. In many cases, that involves entering into online contractual agreements and making payment in an electronic form.

2.4.1 Online Contracts

How does an online vendor create an enforceable online contract? Is the so-called shrinkwrap form of contract valid in an online environment? How can each party to an electronic contract be assured that it has a valid and binding contract that the other party cannot repudiate? These and related questions are addressed in Chapter 6.

Most written contracts are signed by both parties indicating their intention to be bound. In fact, in many cases the law requires that a contract be signed in order for it to be enforceable. How do you "sign" an electronic contract and comply with other paper-based legal requirements? These issues are discussed in Section 6.3 and Chapter 4.

2.4.2 Electronic Payment

Electronic commerce involves not only creating contracts and delivering goods, but also payment. Numerous mechanisms exist to accomplish online payment. They are discussed in Chapter 7.

2.4.3 Information Security

Key to creating a binding and enforceable electronic contract is ensuring the authenticity and integrity of the messages that are used to create the contract. For example, how does the recipient know that the message is really from the purported sender? How does the recipient know that the message has not been altered? How can either party prove that the copy of the message that it saved is in fact the same as the message it originally received? Digital signatures offer one key solution to these questions. These issues of information security are discussed in Chapters 3 and 4.

Likewise, the authentication and integrity of payment-related messages is critical. If a bank receives an electronic payment instruction from someone purporting to be a customer and directing the bank to transfer money from the customer's account to a specified payee, the bank must have a means of verifying the authenticity of the sender of the message and the integrity of the message itself—for example, did the sender really mean to direct the payment of $1,000,000, or should it have been $100,000? Moreover, the bank needs to ensure that if a dispute arises, the sender cannot deny the contents of the payment message. The same is true for electronic checks, credit-card payments, and "digital cash."

For most payment-related messages, information security procedures represent a key component of the transaction and a key aspect of the recipient's willingness to rely on a message. Information security aspects of messages are discussed in Chapters 3 and 4.

The confidentiality of a payment-related message is also extremely important in several situations. For example, messages containing credit-card numbers must be kept confidential to ensure that the credit-card number is not improperly obtained and used in an unauthorized manner. Likewise, in financial EDI transactions (discussed in Section 7.3), there may be sensitive data accompanying a payment-related message. In such cases, ensuring the confidentiality of that data is also critical.

In many cases, encryption is required to ensure confidentiality of the message. Encryption is explained generally in Chapter 31, and its role in information security is explained in Chapter 4. However, export restrictions on encryption products present practical problems for online commerce. This is discussed in Chapter 25.

2.4.4 Regulation of Online Conduct

Like electronic publishing, buying and selling goods and services online results in transactions that are considered taxable in most jurisdictions. What kinds of taxes apply to these transactions? When is the vendor obligated to collect the tax from the buyer and remit it to the taxing jurisdiction? When, and under what circumstances, can a vendor located in one jurisdiction be taxed for online transactions that occur with customers in another jurisdiction? Issues relating to the taxation of online transactions are discussed in Chapter 24.

2.5 Web Sites: Putting It All Together

The World Wide Web has attracted the attention of virtually all aspects of commerce and industry. Everyone is rushing to set up a Web site and to do business on the Internet. Establishing and operating a Web site provides a good example of the legal issues that arise online. Virtually all forms of online commercial activity can be accomplished via an Internet Web site.

- A web site is a form of online publishing. Thus, we must ask: Who owns the information? How does a Web site publisher establish its legal rights in the information, and avoid violating the rights of others? How is its conduct regulated by the government?
- A web site can also constitute advertising for those that use it to promote themselves, their products, or services. Thus, we must ask whether the advertising material complies with all applicable state and federal regulations.
- Web sites are also used for buying and selling goods and services. Digital content (such as software, music, articles, photographs, and even videos) can be both sold or licensed and electronically delivered to the customer. To accomplish this, Web sites can be used to enter into contracts with others and to accept some forms of payment (such as credit card and perhaps digital cash).

Thus, an examination of the process of establishing and operating a Web site provides a good road map of the various legal issues that arise in the online business environment.

2.5.1 Before You Start: Who Owns the Domain Name?

Setting up a Web site requires a domain name—that is, an Internet address. Many people seek to obtain names tied to their business name or key trademarks (such as mcdonalds.com, mci.com, pepsi.com, and microsoft.com), since they are easy to guess and easy to remember. But what if someone's name or key trademark is already taken by someone else? Does that person have a right to that domain name? What if the person who has it is a competitor?

Alternatively, what rights does a business have in the domain name it acquires? Can it register the domain name as a trademark? Can anyone else challenge its right to the domain name? What about different companies in different industries with the same name? Who gets the domain name? For example, who has the greater right to the domain name "apple.com"—Apple Computer, Apple Records, or Apple Bank?

These and other issues relating to Internet domain names are addressed in Chapter 14. Domain names as trademarks are discussed in Section 14.2.2.

2.5.2 Building the Web Site: Rights To Use Content

Building a Web site begins with content—content will be displayed on the Web site, and other content may be published or distributed through it. Web-site content may include text, data, musical works, sound recordings, photographs, still images, motion pictures, and software. Obtaining this content raises numerous copyright issues, as well as, in certain situations, issues relating to rights of publicity, rights of privacy, defamation, and trademark law. If the content to be published is software, patent and trade secret issues may also arise.

Generally, there are three ways to obtain content for a Web site:

1. Create it.
2. Use preexisting content, choosing only those items that can be used without permission from the author.
3. Use preexisting content with permission from the owners of the rights in that content.

Each of these approaches raises its own set of legal issues.

2.5.2.1 Creating Content. Businesses that develop their own Web page content (either through their employees or by retaining an independent contractor), must understand the nature of the copyright rights that are automatically created in this process, and their impact on the proposed use of what is created. These rights are discussed in Chapter 10. This involves consideration of several important issues.

First, does the business own the copyright to the content that it created? When Webmasters create their own content, they can use employees or hire outsiders for the creative process. But regardless of whether the content consists of words, pictures, sounds, or software, businesses must take the necessary steps to ensure that they own all of the rights in the work product that others create for them (or at least the rights to use the content as planned). Merely paying someone to create content is often not sufficient to ensure ownership of the resulting copyright. In many cases, appropriate copyright assignments or work-for-hire agreements will be required. Copyright ownership is discussed in Section 9.5. A business that does not own the copyright to the content that results from its development efforts needs to ensure that it has the right to use the content to the extent necessary for its Web site (see Chapter 18).

Second, if the business does own the copyright, has it taken steps to protect its rights adequately and to preserve the value of the new asset that it has created? This includes using a proper copyright notice and registering its copyright claim. See discussion in Sections 9.4.3 and 9.4.4.

Third, if the business does not own the copyright, has it secured a license from the copyright owner that grants the rights necessary for its contemplated Web site use? Basic licensing issues are discussed in Chapter 18.

Fourth, has the process of developing the content resulted in an infringement of the copyright of anyone else? Even when work is ostensibly original, it is important to ensure that the persons creating it do not either intentionally or inadvertently infringe the copyright of any third party. Copyright rights are discussed in Chapter 10.

In addition to concerns over ownership of copyright rights, it is also important to address other rights that may exist in content to be used in a Web site, even if the content is originally created. For example, if the content incorporates the name, image, or likeness of any person, or any information about them, it may be necessary to consider whether it constitutes an infringement of that person's right of publicity or privacy. Publicity rights are discussed in Chapter 16, and privacy rights are discussed in Chapter 17.

When trademarks are included in a Web site, two sets of issues arise. If the owner of the Web site is also the owner of the trademarks, it is important to ensure that they are properly used and protected. On the other hand, if a Web site makes reference to the trademarks of others, it is important to ensure that the marks are not used in a manner that is likely to constitute trademark infringement. This could be a problem, for example, if the Web site uses someone else's trademark in a manner that implies that the Web site—or the products that it promotes or markets—are created by, associated with, or endorsed by the owner of the trademark. Trademark rights are discussed in Chapter 13.

Related to trademark law is the law of deceptive trade practices, which can have a significant impact on the way in which the content is displayed within a Web site. Problems that can arise include false endorsements, passing off, making unauthorized modifications of other peoples' works, and trade dress infringement. Deceptive trade practices online are discussed in Chapter 28.

Finally, with software, other rights may be involved as well. These include patent rights (discussed in Chapter 15), and trade secret rights (discussed in Chapter 12).

2.5.2.2 Using Content Without Permission. When using preexisting content created by others, it is important to understand the restrictions that the Copyright Act imposes on use of the work, and the extent to which it is necessary to obtain permission from the copyright owner. These issues are discussed in Chapters 11 and 18.

In some cases, it may be possible to use preexisting content developed by others without obtaining their permission. Generally, it is permissible to use content without permission of the author if:

1. It is in the public domain (see Section 11.4).
2. The use is considered a "fair use" under the Copyright Law (see Section 11.2).
3. The copying is considered *de minimis* under the Copyright Law (see Section 11.3), or
4. What is copied is not itself copyrightable, even though it comes from a copyrightable work (see Section 11.6).

However, copyright is not the only concern. There may be other rights in the work for which permission is required, such as a release of the right of publicity of any persons depicted in the content to be used (see Chapter 16).

2.5.2.3 Licensing Rights To Use Preexisting Content. To use most preexisting content on a Web site, it is necessary to obtain a license from the owner of the copyright. This process of obtaining permission involves several steps, which can be summarized as follows:

• Identify the content to be used;
• Identify the separate rights for which permission must be obtained;

- Identify and locate the owner of each right for which permission is required; and
- Negotiate and obtain the requisite form of permission.

In many cases, addressing these issues is best done by using a rights and permission professional. The issues involved in this licensing process are discussed in Chapter 18.

2.5.3 Links to and from Other Web Sites

A key feature of Internet Web sites is the ability to include links to other Web sites. A mere link, with nothing more, does not present copyright problems; nothing from the referenced Web site is copied. Going beyond a simple link, and incorporating HTML code or content from another Web site may, however, constitute copyright infringement. In addition, if a link is done in a way that improperly implies a relationship with, or endorsement by, another site, it could be a violation of unfair competition laws. These issues are discussed in Section 28.7.

2.5.4 Rights in Completed Web Sites

Once a Web site has been built, rights arise that are separate from the individual components. These include the following:

2.5.4.1 Copyrights. A Web site itself is a copyrightable work—it is usually a compilation of new and existing material. The same is true for many online publications. The creator thus has a separate copyright in the compilation. As such, it is a valuable asset worth protecting. The rights of copyright owners are discussed in Chapter 10. On the other hand, the owner's rights are limited by the rights of users who access the Web site. The rights of users with respect to Web sites and other online publications are discussed in Chapter 11.

2.5.4.2 Trademarks and Trade Dress. The name and design of the Web site or other publication may constitute a protectible trademark or trade dress, which the owner can exploit. As noted above, a Web site owner (or other publisher) also needs to be careful not to infringe on the trademarks and trade dress of others. These issues are discussed in Chapters 13 and 28.

2.5.5 Web Sites as Advertising

Most commercial Web sites are, by definition, a form of advertising. As such, they are regulated by federal and state statutes governing advertising. Both commercial and noncommercial Web sites (as well as other publishers) must avoid making false or misleading statements about their own or others' goods, services, or commercial activities. See Chapter 22 for a discussion of advertising online. In addition, if the content contains any false or misleading statements, there is a potential liability for false advertising or trade libel. These issues are discussed in Chapters 22 and 28.

2.5.6 Web Sites as Publishing

Web sites can also facilitate a form of publishing. By using the Internet and other public and private networks, publishers can achieve global distribution of content at low cost. Almost any type of content can be distributed this way, including text, sound, video, music, books, databases, software, pictures, and magazines.

Publishers face many of the same issues discussed above. Creating and obtaining rights in content, protecting the rights in their works (including copyright and trademark) and avoiding infringing on the rights of others are all concerns of publishers. In addition, because publishers often are in the business of selling or licensing their content, they will be concerned about how to create and enforce contracts with their user audience.

One area of particular importance to publishers (which may be less important to others) is the treatment of obscene and indecent material. This is discussed in Chapter 20.

2.5.7 Relationships with Customers and Users

Whether information is published on a Web site or by some other online method, it will have an audience. The audience of users may want to view, copy, or redistribute the information, or they may want to order goods and services. The rights and responsibilities of users and publishers, and how they can be limited and controlled, will be of concern to all who engage in online activities.

Users who access Web sites or otherwise view material published online may have certain implied rights to copy and use that content. These rights are discussed in Section 11.1.

Some Web site owners and other online publishers try to limit the rights of users by asking the user to enter into a general access contract. Such a contract governs users' rights with respect to the Web site. When users first sign onto the system, they are presented with an online version of a contract and asked to assent to it. Are such contracts enforceable? How do they work? This topic is discussed in Chapter 6.

2.5.8 Web Sites as Marketplaces for Buying and Selling

Web sites and other online forums can be used to buy and sell goods and services. These may be tangible goods or services that are advertised and ordered online, to be delivered offline. They may also be intangible goods, such as software and content, which are advertised, ordered, and delivered online.

From the standpoint of the online buyer or seller, the principal areas of focus will be the creation and enforceability of contracts (see Chapter 6), online payment mechanisms (see Chapter 7), and the security of messages and electronically transmitted content (see Chapter 3).

2.5.9 Payment

Many Web sites (especially those selling goods or services), need a mechanism by which to get paid. The various online payment options are discussed in Chapter 7.

2.5.10 Regulating Web Site Activity

Depending on the nature of the commercial activity undertaken via a Web site, certain other issues may arise regarding the impact of the law on the activities conducted through the Web site. These include taxation of transactions entered into via a Web site (see Chapter 24), regulations on the export of data from a Web site (see Chapter 25), and rules relating to deceptive trade practices that can occur through a Web site (see Chapter 28).

2.6 Tackling the Issues

These sections have provided only a brief outline of the issues to be considered and addressed by those who want to do business online. The following chapters explore the legal issues in detail.

PART I

INFORMATION SECURITY

3

The Legal Role of Information Security

Lorijean G. Oei

3.1 Legal Requirements for Online Communications

    3.1.1 Authenticity

    3.1.2 Integrity

    3.1.3 Nonrepudiation

    3.1.4 Writing and Signature

    3.1.5 Confidentiality

3.2 Problems Introduced by Online Communications

    3.2.1 Satisfying the Legal Requirements

    3.2.2 Real-Time Communications and Open Networks

3.3 The Solution Offered by Information Security

    3.3.1 Defining Security

        3.3.1.1 System Security

        3.3.1.2 Information Security

$\mathbf{M}$ost commerce today operates through the exchange of paper. Contracts, purchase orders, invoices, checks, receipts, and numerous other documents are usually created, exchanged, and stored on paper. That, however, is changing. Electronic commerce offers a cost-effective, efficient, and less error-prone alternative to its paper-based counterpart. Nevertheless, some businesses have been slow to embrace it. This is due in part to a perception that electronic commerce is not secure. Although electronic information has certain vulnerabilities, security measures can be taken to manage these threats.

Many businesses recognize that *information security* is a key technical and business issue, but it is important to recognize that it is also a legal issue. An electronic communication must meet certain legal requirements to be enforceable. Information security measures can play an important, even critical, role in meeting these requirements.

3.1 Legal Requirements for Online Communications

For electronic commerce to be viable from both a legal and a business perspective, the communications that are exchanged and the records of these communications that are preserved must satisfy certain legal requirements. Although not all of these requirements will apply in every situation, they generally include the following:

- Authenticity
- Integrity
- Nonrepudiation
- Writing and signature
- Confidentiality

3.1.1 Authenticity

Authenticity is concerned with the source or origin of a communication.[1] Who is the message from? Is it genuine or a forgery?

Authenticity is a practical business requirement. A party who is creating contracts, licensing information and intellectual property, or making payments online must be confident of the authenticity of the communications it receives. For example, when a bank receives an electronic payment order from a customer directing that money be paid to a third party, the bank needs to be able to verify the source of the request. The bank is faced with the problem of ensuring that it is not dealing with an impostor.[2]

Authenticity is also an important legal requirement. In the electronic payment order example, if the bank fails to take appropriate measures to verify the identity of the source of the request, the bank may be liable for any loss.

A party must also be able to establish the authenticity of its electronic transactions should there ever be a dispute. This requires a mechanism to establish the authenticity of a communication and a means of preserving an accurate record of both the communication and the means of authentication in case authenticity is ever challenged. Authentication of a record is needed in order for that record to be used as evidence in a court of law.[3]

3.1.2 Integrity

Integrity is concerned with the accuracy and completeness of the communication. Is the communication the recipient received the same as the communication that the sender sent? Is it complete? Has the communication been altered either in transmission or storage?

Integrity is a practical business requirement. A recipient needs to be confident of a communication's integrity before he or she will rely and act on it. Integrity is critical to electronic commerce when it comes to the negotiation and formation of contracts online, the licensing of digital content, and the making of electronic payments, as well as using electronic records to prove these transactions at a later date. For example, a building contractor may wish to solicit bids from subcontractors and submit its proposal to the owner online. The building contractor needs to be able to verify the accuracy of the bids upon which it will rely in formulating its proposal, and is faced with the problem of how to confirm that the bids as received are accurate.

Integrity is also a legal requirement. If the contractor ever needs to prove the amount of the subcontractor's bid, a court will first require that the contractor establish the integrity of the record he retained of that communication before that court will consider it as evidence in the case.[4] Even a communication that has been transmitted and received with its integrity intact may be accidentally or intentionally altered while in storage. Hardware that is not functioning properly or software with errors may alter the contents of an electronic record in the process of storing or retrieving it. In addition, the recipient of a communication needs some means to be able to refute a claim that he or she altered the communication.

3.1.3 Nonrepudiation

Nonrepudiation is concerned with holding the sender to his or her communication. The sender should not be able to deny having sent the communication if he or she did, in fact, send it, or to claim that the contents of the communication as received are not the same as what the sender sent if, in fact, they are what was sent. Nonrepudiation is essential to electronic commerce when it comes to a trading partner's willingness to rely on a communication, electronic contract, or funds transfer request. For example, a stockbroker who accepts buy/sell orders over the Internet would not want a client to be able to place an order for a volatile commodity, such as a pork bellies futures contract, and then be able to confirm the order if the market goes up and repudiate it if the market goes south.[5]

Nonrepudiation becomes a legal requirement when the relying party seeks to hold the other party to his or her communication. For example, when a contract is in dispute, the relying party must be able to establish the fact that the other party agreed to both the contract in general and to the specific terms of their agreement.

3.1.4 Writing and Signature

In many cases, the law requires that an agreement be both (1) documented in *"writing"*[6] and (2) *"signed"*[7] by the person who is sought to be held bound in order for that agreement to be enforceable. If two parties are entering into a contract online, these writing and signature requirements may apply. In contract law, for example, the *Statute of Frauds* provides that contracts for the sale of goods for the price of $500 or more are not enforceable unless there is a writing sufficient to indicate that a contract has been made between the parties, and that writing is signed by the party against whom enforcement is sought.[8] Thus, if a buyer sends an electronic purchase order for $800 worth of copier paper and the seller responds with an electronic acknowledgment accepting the order, the seller may believe that he or she has a contract. If the buyer later wants to back out of the deal because the seller's competitor will sell the paper for $700, the seller may not be able to enforce the contract if the electronic purchase order is not deemed to be in writing and signed. The issue, as it relates to contract enforceability, is discussed in Section 6.3.

Numerous other statutes governing other forms of transactions also require that a transaction be documented by a writing and a signature. Certain statutes regarding corporate and partnership actions prescribe writing and signature requirements. For example, a new general partner may be added to a partnership only upon the written consent of all partners in some states.[9]

In addition, federal, state, and local governments also require that certain transactions be signed and in writing. For example, federal government contracts must be in writing and executed, or signed, before the government will consider itself bound.[10] Similarly, many municipal governments have adopted the Model Procurement Code, which mandates that the purchase of supplies and services in excess of $5,000 be by formal, written contract.[11]

3.1.5 Confidentiality

Confidentiality is concerned with controlling the disclosure of information. Confidentiality may not be an issue in all situations. In some, however, it is critical. Confidentiality may be necessary to protect a property right in information, such as a trade-secret right. Information can qualify as a trade secret only if it is not generally known and reasonable security precautions are taken to maintain secrecy.[12] In addition, confidentiality may be necessary to comply with certain legal obligations, such as an obligation not to disclose patient medical records[13] or the contents of attorney-client communications.[14] Confidentiality may further be important for preventing access to and use of information that can cause harm to the owner of the information, such as credit card or bank account numbers.

Confidentiality is also concerned with controlling access to digital information. Owners of digitized intellectual property such as films, sound recordings, and literary works often want to control access to their works so they can be compensated for their creative efforts.

3.2 Problems Introduced by Online Communications

Our comfort with traditional commerce can be attributed, in part, to the sense of security that dealing with paper gives us. Although admittedly imperfect, paper-based communications have certain attributes that help them satisfy the legal requirements of authenticity, integrity, nonrepudiation, writing and signature, and confidentiality.

3.2.1 Satisfying the Legal Requirements

Many attributes of paper-based communications contribute to satisfying these legal requirements. The letterhead appearing at the top of correspondence, a company's name and logo appearing on a purchase order or invoice, and a handwritten signature are all examples of ways in which the authenticity, nonrepudiation, and writing and signature requirements can be satisfied for traditional paper-based communications. The use of watermarks, chemically treated or patterned paper or special inks, and unique printing styles or processes also provide assurance that the paper-based communication is genuine and make erasures and alterations easy to detect.

However, those attributes are lost in the move to electronic communications. Electronic records are simply patterns of volts, "ons and offs," that are represented as ones and zeros. There is nothing inherently distinctive about the ones and zeros that make up an authentic electronic communication that would distinguish them from the ones and zeros that make up a copy, a forgery, or an altered version of that electronic communication. Consequently, changes and forgeries are easy to make, but hard to detect.

Another problem with electronic communications is that it is relatively easy to "spoof" a network into sending a communication with a "return address" of someone other than the actual sender.[15] Messages can be sent anonymously or may bear several forwarding headers with abbreviated or pseudonymous user names, thus making it difficult to determine the source. Even if the authenticity of the communication can be established at the time it is received, the ease with which it could be replaced by a convincing forgery makes authenticity a continuing issue with electronic records.

Moreover, paper-based communications are unitary. That is, the message and the medium are transmitted together in a tangible, physical object. Normally, a recipient can be reasonably assured that he or she received what the sender sent. Electronic communications, by contrast, are disembodied from a tangible object. This makes them easy to alter. Compounding this problem is that the opportunity to access electronic communications is great.

Communications sent over the Internet pass through potentially dozens of forwarders and packet-switching nodes. Anyone with privileged access at any one of these transfer points can intercept, tamper with, and forward electronic information. Transmission errors can also corrupt the integrity of an electronic communication. Furthermore, a record of that communication could be easily altered while being stored on the recipient's computer system.

The ease with which electronic documents can be altered or forged and the opportunities for unauthorized access to these communications may increase the risk of repudiation. A sender, asserting that the document the recipient received is a forgery, could deny having sent a communication and thus having assented to anything. A sender, claiming that a hacker intercepted and altered the communication, or that the recipient altered it, could deny that its contents are accurate.

In paper-based transactions, meeting the requirements of a writing and signature is straightforward. With electronic communications, however, there is no writing, at least in the traditional sense of the word, and there certainly can be no traditional handwritten signature. Thus, in those situations where it is necessary (or desirable) for an electronic communication to be in writing and signed by the parties, there must be a mechanism to satisfy that requirement.

Protecting the confidentiality of electronic information can also be a problem. As digital information migrates from closed computer systems to open networks, it becomes increasingly difficult to control who can gain access to it. Thus, with electronic communications it is important that, when necessary, the parties be able to ensure the confidentiality of their communications both while they are in transit and while they are stored on either party's system.

3.2.2 Real-Time Communications and Open Networks

The speed at which electronic commerce can be transacted creates its own set of problems. Electronic commerce is conducted in real time and often contemplates one-time exchanges between parties who may have never dealt with each other before. The parties do not have the time or the opportunity to size each other up.

Most importantly, electronic commerce is increasingly conducted over open networks, such as the Internet. By definition, open networks lack rigorous access and usage controls. Just about anyone can use these networks freely to access other systems connected to the network, and to monitor and intercept communications transmitted over them. This raises concerns about the security of a communication stored on a system as well as the security of a communication once it has left that system.

Thus, the lack of paper-based indicia of trustworthiness, the speed and immediacy of electronic commerce, and the uncontrolled access to open systems raise a number of practical and legal problems for electronic commerce. Information security offers a solution to these problems.

3.3 The Solution Offered by Information Security

3.3.1 Defining Security

Security is both an end and the means to get there. The object of security is a document that meets the business and legal requirements of authenticity, integrity, nonrepudiation, writing and signature, and confidentiality. For paper documents, security is achieved through the use of letterhead, handwritten signatures, special inks, sealed envelopes, and couriers. For electronic documents, security is achieved through the use of digital signatures, encryption, acknowledgment procedures, and access controls. Like their more traditional, paper-based counterparts, these new security procedures will provide significant legal benefits if properly implemented.

Security measures can be implemented at two levels in an open computing environment: (1) system security and (2) information security.[16]

3.3.1.1 System Security. The term *system security* refers to the measures that a business itself can take to protect its own computer systems and the records and other information they contain from attack from outside (such as damage that can be caused by hackers, viruses, and natural disasters)[17] and inside (such as damage that can be caused by disgruntled, dishonest, or snooping employees).[18] System security measures include controls designed to limit access to authorized users and audit controls designed to monitor activity on the system.

Passwords are system security controls traditionally used to prevent unauthorized access. Biometric tokens, such as a retinal or hand scan, may also be used. As systems are increasingly being connected to open networks, additional access controls may be needed that are specially designed to protect systems from outside attack. One such control is the firewall.[19]

A *firewall* is hardware and software that provides a barrier between an internal network and an external network such as the Internet. Firewalls control all incoming and outgoing communications. If a user on an internal network wants to communicate with another user or server outside that network, the user's message is actually communicated to the firewall, and the firewall relays the message to the other user or server. Similarly, all outside computers communicate with the firewall, which then relays the communication to the internal network.

There are many system security measures that can be used in addition to passwords and firewalls; however, a business can employ such system security measures only on the computer systems or networks under its control. It cannot control the security of any outside network that it uses to send or receive messages (such as the Internet).

A business can, however, choose to send and receive its communications over an outside network that employs security measures commensurate with the sensitivity of those communications. There are *value-added networks* available for transmitting electronic communications that employ a variety of security measures designed to protect the information flowing through their systems. Value-added networks also limit access and usage to subscribers and are not otherwise open to the public, unlike the Internet. Thus, one approach to addressing security concerns is to send sensitive communications through value-added networks that have implemented appropriate system-security procedures.[20]

3.3.1.2 Information Security. Once digital information leaves a computer system, systemic level security measures do nothing to protect that information while it is passing through an outside network or while it resides on a computer system beyond the sender's control. Thus, perhaps the most important security strategy is to protect the information itself. Information- (or message-) level security can provide assurances that the digital information, although it can be accessed, cannot be read, copied, or modified, regardless of where it resides.

3.3.2 Using Information Security To Satisfy Legal Requirements

There are a number of information security measures that can be used to satisfy the legal requirements for electronic communications.[21] These include:
1. Digital signatures
2. Replies and acknowledgments
3. Repeat-back acknowledgments
4. The use of a process or system that produces a demonstrably trustworthy document[22]
5. Date/time stamping
6. Trusted third parties, and
7. Encryption

3.3.2.1 Digital Signatures. A handwritten signature on a paper document purporting to originate from an identified source can authenticate a communication if that signature is shown to be genuine. Of course, an electronic communication cannot bear a traditional handwritten signature, but it may bear a digital one—a cryptographic transformation of the communication. As explained in detail in Chapter 4, if a digital signature can be verified, the recipient is assured that the communication came from the sender and that the communication has not been altered since its transmission.[23] As a consequence, the sender cannot deny having sent it. Thus a digital signature can provide a means of identifying the source of a communication and verifying its integrity, thereby preventing the sender from repudiating that communication. A verified digital signature is presumed by law in certain circumstances to meet authenticity, integrity, and nonrepudiation requirements.[24]

Finally, it may also be possible to satisfy any writing and signature requirement through the use of a digital signature.[25]

3.3.2.2 Replies and Acknowledgments. Computer systems are particularly well suited to screening incoming communications and sending a return acknowledgment to the purported sender. A log showing what was received, the identified sender, the fact that an acknowledgment was sent to the sender, and that the acknowledgment was not rebuked will help verify the source of a communication. The ability to authenticate communications can thus be ensured by sending and retaining records of acknowledgments as well as any responses repudiating those acknowledgments.

A reply, when considered with the earlier communication to which it responds, tends to authenticate that reply—at least as to its contents, if not its source. For example, if a buyer sends an e-mail message offering to purchase 500 gross of #3 widgets from the seller for $1,500, and the seller returns an e-mail message counteroffering, "I will sell the #3 widgets for $1,775," the authenticity of the seller's e-mail message is supported because the reply contains specific details—for example, that the widgets are #3 widgets, not #5 widgets—that the seller would probably not know unless the seller were replying to the buyer's offer. By preserving a record of this course of correspondence, each of the e-mail messages can be authenticated.

3.3.2.3 Repeat-Back Acknowledgments. The technique of sending an acknowledgment to establish the authenticity of an electronic communication can be taken one step further to establish the integrity of a communication. With electronic communications, it is a simple matter not only to send an acknowledgment, but also to repeat the entire contents of the communication back to the purported sender. If the repeat-back acknowledgment differs from the original communication, the sender can alert the recipient. The sender will want to be sure to create and retain a record of the communication as sent, the repeat-back acknowledgment, and any repudiation of the repeat-back acknowledgment it received or a notation that none was received.

3.3.2.4 Process or System. Because electronic communications do not always have the same identifying characteristics as paper communications, it is possible to resort to other techniques for establishing authenticity that are specially suited to electronic communications. These techniques all involve the use of a computer system to perform automated record-keeping functions.[26] For example, if a company has configured its computers to automatically archive an electronic record copy of the communications it creates and receives, this may help establish that the records of those communications are genuine. The authenticity of such archival record copies can be further enhanced by adopting system security controls that limit access to archival copies. The use of such system security measures can help a company to demonstrate the integrity of its records.

Another technique is to configure the user's computers to create a log of all incoming and outgoing communications and to cross-reference this log to archived records. Log information showing the source of the record and the time of its creation or receipt provides further evidence of its authenticity.

3.3.2.5 Date/Time Stamping. A date/time stamp provides another way to verify that a communication has not been changed. A date/time stamp is issued for a *message digest* of the communication. A message digest is a condensation or summary of the communication in the form of a fixed-length, unintelligible string of characters that results from applying a mathematical function to the full-length communication. Because the message digest is derived from the communication, it is unique to that communication. Change a space or a comma in the communication and the message digest will change too. A date/time stamp fixes the content of the message digest as of a certain date. To later verify the integrity of the communication, another message digest is created for the communication. If it matches the date/time-stamped message digest, the communication has not been changed.

3.3.2.6 Trusted Third Parties. A party can establish the integrity of a communication by sending and receiving all of its electronic communications through a neutral third party that can retain a copy of each communication. Assuming that this third party is trustworthy, the parties to the communication can then rely on the third party in the event that the integrity of a record of a communication is questioned.

3.3.2.7 Encryption. If a sender wants to send an electronic communication to a recipient and keep it confidential, the sender can encrypt the communication.

3.3.3 Recognition of the Legal Effect of Security

The security measures that can be taken to help ensure that electronic communications and records satisfy the requirements of authenticity, integrity, nonrepudiation, writing and signature, and confidentiality may not yet be readily accepted, but their legal effectiveness has already been recognized. The first formal recognition of the legal effect of information security procedures occurred in 1989 with the approval of a new section to the Uniform Commercial Code (U.C.C.) known as Article 4A.[27] The U.C.C. is a model law designed to simplify, clarify, modernize, and make uniform the law governing commercial transactions.[28] Most states have adopted the U.C.C., with minor variations, as their commercial law.

Article 4A addresses the electronic transfer of funds by wire.[29] A business that wishes to transfer funds electronically from its account to the account of another can initiate the process by transmitting an electronic payment instruction, called a *payment order,* to its bank. However, that payment order cannot bear a signature or other paper-based security measure upon which the bank can rely in order to detect forgeries. The U.C.C. recognized this problem, and the reality that a bank receiving a payment order needs something objective on which it can rely in determining whether it may safely act on that order.[30] Article 4A became the first statute to provide that a party to an electronic communication could rely on information security procedures as a substitute for the traditional, time-tested requirement of a signature. Under Article 4A, an electronic message instructing a bank to transfer funds to a payee is considered valid, and the bank is authorized to transfer the funds in accordance with the order if (1) the bank's customer actually authorized the order or (2) the authenticity and integrity of the order is "verified" pursuant to a "commercially reasonable" security procedure regardless whether the order was actually authorized by that person.[31]

The bottom line is that Article 4A adopts "security procedures" rather than "signatures" as the basis for verifying transactions and apportioning legal liability. This establishes an important precedent. Other electronic transactions that employ appropriate security procedures are also likely to satisfy the various legal requirements for electronic communications.

The group responsible for Article 4A is now in the process of revising U.C.C. Article 2, which governs the sale of goods, and of writing new legislation—known as U.C.C. Article 2B—to govern transactions in software and other digital content. In addition to revising the law to address issues raised by doing business electronically, Article 2B and the revised version of Article 2 are expected to give explicit statutory recognition to the legally binding effect that can result from the use of security procedures, such as digital signatures, in electronic business relationships.[32]

Perhaps the most important recognition of the legal effect of information security measures is the Utah Digital Signature Act passed in 1995.[33] The Act provides that an electronic document that is digitally signed satisfies legal writing[34] and signature requirements[35] and that its authenticity and integrity are presumed.[36] California also has passed similar, albeit much narrower, digital signature legislation.[37] Other states are likely to follow these pioneering laws.[38]

Also likely to influence future legislation are the *Digital Signature Guidelines* prepared by an American Bar Association committee.[39] The initial draft of the Guidelines recognized that "the authentication of computer-based business information interrelates both technology and the law."[40] These guidelines build on an earlier resolution of the American Bar Association that supported government action to encourage the use of security techniques to ensure the authenticity and integrity of information in electronic form and their acceptance to satisfy legal requirements regarding a writing or signature.[41]

In the final analysis, information security provides the most reliable and effective means for satisfying the business and legal requirements for electronic communications. Given the role that information security plays in electronic commerce, one of the most promising information security measures—digital signatures—deserves mention and is considered in detail in the next chapter.

Endnotes

1.   *See* Fed. R. Evid. 901(a) (1995).

2.   *See* U.C.C. §§ 4A-202, 4A-203 & Official Comment (1989). Section 4A-202 solves this problem for a bank and its customer who has agreed to transact its banking electronically and to be subject to Article 4A. If the bank verifies the payment order through the use of a commercially reasonable security procedure, the customer will be bound even if it did not in fact authorize the payment order. U.C.C. § 4A-202(b). If, however, the customer can prove that the person sending the fraudulent payment order did not obtain the information necessary to send such order from an agent or a source controlled by the customer, the loss is shifted back to the bank. U.C.C. § 4A-203(a)(2). If the bank does not follow the security procedure and the order is fraudulent, the bank will generally have to cover the loss. U.C.C. § 4A-202(a).

     At least one bank plans to use cryptography, an information security measure, to solve the authentication problem posed by Internet banking. *See, e.g.,* Kim S. Nash & Thomas Hoffman, *Banks Hit Info Highway at Different Speeds,* Computerworld 52 (Aug. 21, 1995) (Wells Fargo Bank to permit customers to move money over the Internet subject to results of testing security methods based on 100-bit encryption).

3.   *See, e.g., U.S. v. Eisenberg*, 807 F.2d 1446 (8th Cir. 1986) (authenticity of a letter disputed); *U.S. v. Grande*, 620 F.2d 1026 (4th Cir.) (authenticity of invoice disputed), *cert. denied*, 449 U.S. 830, 449 U.S. 919 (1980).

4.   *See, e.g., Victory Med. Hosp. v. Rice*, 143 Ill. App. 3d 621, 493 N.E.2d 117 (1986).

5.   *See generally Follow the Money: A New Stock Market Arises on the Internet*, Scientific American 31 (Jul. 1995).

6.   The Uniform Commercial Code (U.C.C.) defines "writing" as "printing, typewriting or any other intentional reduction to tangible form." U.C.C. § 1-201 (46) (1995).

7.   The U.C.C. defines "signed" as "any symbol executed or adopted by a party with present intention to authenticate a writing." U.C.C. § 1-201 (39) (1995).

8.   U.C.C. § 2-201(1) (1995). *See also* U.C.C. § 1-206 (1995) (limiting enforcement of unsigned, unwritten contracts for the sale of certain personal property for $5,000 or more). Every state, except Louisiana, has adopted U.C.C. § 2-201(1) in some form. For a state-by-state listing of state statutes of frauds, see Restatement (Second) of Contracts, § 110 statutory note, at 284-85 (1982). For a discussion of the Statute of Frauds, see Section 6.3.

9.   *See, e.g.,* Uniform Limited Partnership Act § 401 (1976).

10.   *See* Pub. L. No. 97-258, 96 Stat. 927 (1982) (codified at 31 U.S.C. § 1501). Federal courts also require all documents to be filed to be signed. *See* Fed. R. Civ. Proc. 11 (1995).

11.   *See generally* Section of Public Contract Law and Section of Urban, State and Local Government Law, American Bar Association, *Model Procurement Code for State and Local Governments* § 3-204 (Feb. 1979); Section of Public Contract Law and Section of Urban, State and Local Government Law, American Bar Association, *Model Procurement Code for State and Local Governments, Recommended Regulations* R3-204.01 to .02 (Aug. 1980).

12.   *See* Section 12.2. *See also* 1 Melvin F. Jager, *Trade Secrets Law* §§ 3.03, 5.05 (1995).

13.   *See, e.g.,* Privacy Act of 1974, 5 U.S.C. § 552a (1995) (disclosure of medical and other records by government agencies); 410 ILCS 50/3(a) (1993) (patient has right to privacy and confidentiality of records).

14.   *See, e.g.,* Cal. Evid. Code §§ 950 *et seq.* (1995); American Bar Association, *Model Rules of Professional Conduct* Rule 1.6 (1992).

15.   The Computer Emergency Response Team (CERT) Coordination Center is an organization chartered to work with the Internet community to facilitate its response to computer security incidents, to raise the community's awareness of computer security, and to conduct research targeted at improving security. CERT has issued bulletins warning of such impersonation. *See* John Markoff, *Data Network Is Found Open To New Threat*, N.Y. Times, Jan. 23, 1995, at A1. These bulletins and other information by and about CERT is available on the Worldwide Web at file://info.cert.org.

16.   Information Infrastructure Task Force, NII Security: The Federal Role (Jun. 14, 1995).

17.   *See The Real SECURITY Threat: The Enemy Within*, Datamation 30 (Jul. 15, 1995).

18.   *See The Real SECURITY Threat: The Enemy Within*, Datamation 30 (Jul. 15, 1995); *New Security Glitch Could Affect Many Internet 'Hosts'*, Wall St. J., Feb. 23, 1995, at B8.

19.   *See, e.g.,* David J. Buerger, *Fire Walls Thwart Digital Vandals by Blocking Unwanted Access*, Infoworld 79 (Jun. 19, 1995).

20.   For a discussion of third-party service providers and value-added networks, see Chapter 27.

21. *See generally* Rudolph J. Peritz, *Computer Data and Reliability: A Call for Authentication of Business Records Under the Federal Rules of Evidence*, 7 Computer L.J. 23 (1986); Michael B. Keating, *Computer Evidence*, 12 Litig. 35 (Fall 1985); John H. Young, *Computer-Generated Evidence: When Is It Admissible at Trial?* 21 Trial 15 (Jan. 1985); Peter M. Storm, Comment, *Admitting Computer Generated Records: A Presumption of Reliability*, 18 J. Marshall L. Rev. 115 (1984).

22. Fed. R. Evid. 901(b)(9) (1995).

23. *See* Bruce Schneier, *Applied Cryptography: Protocols, Algorithms and Source Code in C* 37-38 (2d ed. 1996).

24. *See* Utah Code Ann. § 46-3-401 (1995); Information Security Committee, Electronic Commerce and Information Technology Division, Section of Science and Technology, American Bar Association, *Digital Signature Guidelines* § 1.33 (draft Oct. 5, 1995) [hereinafter *Digital Signature Guidelines*] Note: These guidelines are in provisional form and were published only to invite comment. A final version is expected to be published later in 1996.

25. Utah Code Ann. §§ 46-3-401(3), 43-3-402 (1995); Cal. Gov't Code § 16.5 (1995); *Digital Signature Guidelines* §§ 5.1, 5.4.

26. *See* Fed. R. Evid. 901(b)(9) (1995).

27. *See* U.C.C. Art. 4A, Funds Transfers (1989). Article 4A has been adopted in 47 states.

28. U.C.C. § 1-102(2) (1995).

29. U.C.C. Art. 4A, Prefatory Note (1989).

30. U.C.C. § 4A-203 Official Comment 3 (1989).

31. U.C.C. § 4A-202 (1989).

32. National Conference of Commissioners on Uniform State Laws, Uniform Commercial Code, Revised Article 2B, Licenses § 2B-607 (draft Dec. 1, 1995); National Conference of Commissioners on Uniform State Laws, Uniform Commercial Code, Revised Article 2, Sales § 2-212 (draft Oct. 1, 1995).

33. Utah Code Ann. §§ 46-3-101 *et seq.* (1995).

34. Utah Code Ann. § 46-3-402 (1) (1995).

35. Utah Code Ann. § 46-3-401 (3) (1995).

36. Utah Code Ann. § 46-3-401(2), (3) (1995).

37. Cal. Gov't Code § 16.5 (1995).

38. *See, e.g.,* 1995 Ore. S.B. 992 (digital signature bill taking approach similar to Utah's); 1995 Wash. S.B. 5959 (same).

39. *Digital Signature Guidelines.*

40. *Digital Signature Guidelines,* at 3.

41. American Bar Association, Resolution 115 (1992); *See also* ABA Electronic Messaging Services Task Force, Model Electronic Data Interchange Trading Partner Agreement and Commentary. 45 Bus. Law. 1645, at § 1.4, comment 1 (1990).

4

Digital Signatures

Lorijean G. Oei

Digital signatures are one of the most promising information security measures available to satisfy the legal and business requirements of authenticity, integrity, nonrepudiability, and writing and signature. To meet these requirements, however, digital signature technology must be supported by certain institutional and legal infrastructures as well as other cryptographic measures.

The *institutional infrastructure* is quickly falling into place. It includes certification authorities and repositories. Governmental and private entities are beginning to provide these services.

The legal infrastructure is being developed too, although there is not much actual "law" yet. *Legal infrastructure* includes laws that address the rights, responsibilities, and potential liabilities of those who use digital signatures, those who facilitate their use, and those who rely on them. To date, two states, Utah[1] and California[2] have passed digital signature legislation. Another important effort toward establishing the legal infrastructure is the draft *Digital Signatures Guidelines* formulated by a committee of the American Bar Association.[3] These guidelines and the Utah and California statutes are likely to shape future legislation.

Finally, cryptographic applications such as date/time stamping and encryption are available to complement digital signatures. When used in combination with digital signatures, date/time stamping and encryption meet the security concerns raised by electronic communications and open networks.

4.1 Using Digital Signatures

4.1.1 What Is a Digital Signature?

A *digital signature* is an electronic substitute for a manual signature that serves the same functions as a manual signature and more. It is an identifier created by a computer instead of a pen. In more technical terms, a digital signature is the sequence of bits that results from using a one-way hash function to create a message digest of an electronic communication. The resulting message digest is then encrypted using a public-key algorithm and the sender's private key. A recipient who has the sender's public key can accurately determine (1) whether the sequence of bits was created using the private key that corresponds to the signer's public key, and (2) whether the communication has been altered since the sequence of bits was generated.[4] Digital signatures look like an unintelligible string of alphanumeric characters. For example

```
————BEGIN PGP SIGNATURE————
Version: 2.6.2


owHtWX1sU1UUP+91G+22ysbHhDHcBeZAVmq7L9iAuNJ2UuhX2soUSpaufVsft
u8tby1kUXTGsGhAgsEY4h9b+EPBgArBGNSELGpiNEFM5A80xIzEoPiPSEiMRF
bPfR/ajW7r1BjR/ZbfO/eed9+599177j3ndS9CWlcIlqe3Df1w45vqJ85+dZ5
hPkywt6uOjb5zYvRmy2drFnZKT17a/97n/Tt11d8dNmyvqV12K7jt8Lxf

————END PGP SIGNATURE————
```

is the digital signature for the following e-mail message:

```
October 30, 1995

Dear Order Department:

We commit to purchase 10,000 widgets at your price of $175 per
hundred.

Ship to:

Industrial Products Co.
555 Retail Drive
Chicago, Illinois 60061

Sincerely,

Purchasing Department,
Industrial Products Co.
```

A digital signature is *not* a digitized image of a handwritten signature or a typed signature such as "/s/john doe." Moreover, unlike a handwritten signature, which is unique to the signer but is presumably consistent across all documents signed, a digital signature is unique for each document "signed." This is because a digital signature is derived from the document itself. As a result, any change to the document will produce a different digital signature.

A digital signature can serve the same purpose as a handwritten signature in that it may signify authorship, acknowledgment, or assent, among other things. However, a digital signature also serves important information-security purposes that handwritten signatures cannot. A digital signature allows the recipient of a digitally signed communication to determine whether the communication was changed after it was digitally signed. That is, a digital signature provides assurance about the source and integrity of the communication. Because a digital signature provides assurances as to integrity, it is to this extent superior to a handwritten signature.

4.1.2 How Is an Electronic Communication Digitally Signed?

Before a sender can digitally sign an electronic communication, the sender must first create a public-private key pair.[5] The private key is kept confidential by the sender and is used for the purpose of creating digital signatures. The public key is disclosed generally by posting the key in online databases, repositories, or anywhere else the recipient of the digitally signed communication can access it.

To digitally sign an electronic communication, the sender runs a computer program that creates a message digest (or hash value) of that communication. The program then encrypts the resulting message digest using the sender's private key. The encrypted message digest is the digital signature.[6] The sender then attaches the digital signature to the communication and sends both to the intended recipient. A digitally signed communication might look like this:

```
Subject:    Order
Author:     rqz@ipc.com
Date:       10/30/95


                    ——BEGIN PGP SIGNED MESSAGE——
Dear Order Department:

We commit to purchase 10,000 widgets at your price of $175 per
hundred.

Ship to:

Industrial Products Co.
555 Retail Drive
Chicago, Illinois 60061

Sincerely,

Purchasing Department,
Industrial Products Co.

                    ——BEGIN PGP SIGNATURE——
Version: 2.6.2

owHtWX1sU1UUP+91G+22ysbHhDHcBeZAVmq7L9iAuNJ2UuhX2soUSpaufVsft
u8tby1kUXTGsGhAgsEY4h9b+EPBgArBGNSELGpiNEFM5A80xIzEoPiPSEiMRF
bPfR/ajW7rlBjR/ZbfO/eed9+599177j3ndS9CWlcI1qe3Df1w45vqJ85+dZ5
hPkywt6uOjb5zYvRmy2drFnZKT17a/97n/Tt11d8dNmyvqV12K7jt8Lxf
                    ———END PGP SIGNATURE———
```

The digital signature process can be made very easy. With a user-friendly interface, the sender can digitally sign a communication simply by clicking on buttons with a mouse. No special technical expertise is needed. The sender should, however, appreciate the legal effects and consequences of digitally signing an electronic communication.

4.1.3 Verifying a Digital Signature

When a recipient gets a digitally signed communication, the recipient's computer runs a computer program containing the same cryptographic algorithm and hash function the sender used to create the digital signature. The program automatically decrypts the digital signature (the encrypted message digest) using the sender's public key. If the program is able to decrypt the digital signature, the recipient knows that the communication came from the purported sender, that is, the recipient has verified its authenticity. This is because only the sender's public key will decrypt a digital signature encrypted with the sender's private key.

The program then creates a second message digest of the communication and compares the decrypted message digest with the digest the recipient created.[7] If the two message digests match, the recipient knows that the communication has not been altered or tampered with, that is, the recipient has verified its integrity.[8]

4.1.4 Prerequisites for the Use of Digital Signatures

The effectiveness of the digital signature process depends upon the reliable association of a public-private key pair with an identified person. The discussion thus far has made one critical assumption: that the public-private key pair of the sender does, in fact, belong to the sender. Any assurance of authenticity would be worthless if the public key used to decrypt a digital signature belonged to an impostor and not the purported sender.

Paper signatures usually have an intrinsic association with a particular person because they are that person's own handwriting. However, public-private key pairs used to create digital signatures have no intrinsic association with anyone in particular—they are nothing more than large numbers. When a recipient obtains the public key for a digitally signed communication, how can he or she verify that the public key actually belongs to the purported sender? An impostor could have generated the public-private key pair and entered that public key in a public database under the purported sender's name.

The solution to this problem is to enlist a third party, trusted by both the sender and recipient, to perform the tasks necessary to associate a person or entity on one end of the transaction with the key pair used to create the digital signature on the other. Such a trusted third party is called a *certification authority*.

4.2 Certification Authorities

4.2.1 Function and Role

A certification authority (CA) is a trusted third person or entity[9] that ascertains the identity of a person, called a *subscriber,* and certifies that the public key of a public-private key pair used to create digital signatures belongs to that person.[10]

The certification process generally works in the following way. The subscriber:

1. Generates his or her own public/private key pair;
2. Visits the CA and produces proof of identity, such as a driver's license and passport or any other proof required by the CA; and
3. Demonstrates that he or she holds the private key corresponding to the public key (without disclosing the private key).

These three steps in the certification process are likely to vary somewhat from CA to CA. For example, one CA may require a subscriber to appear in person before the CA as part of the second step of establishing the subscriber's identity. Another CA may be willing to rely on a third party, such as a notary, to establish the subscriber's identity.[11]

Once the certification authority has verified the association between an identified person and a public key, the certification authority then *issues a certificate.*[12] A *certificate* is a computer-based record that attests to the connection of a public key to an identified subscriber.[13] A certificate identifies the certification authority issuing it and the subscriber identified with the public key. The certificate also contains the subscriber's public key and possibly other information, such as an expiration date for the public key.[14] To provide assurance as to the authenticity and integrity *of the certificate,* the certification authority attaches its own digital signature to the certificate.

The certification authority then notifies the subscriber that the certificate has been issued so as to give the subscriber an opportunity to review the contents of the certificate before it is made public.[15] It is important that the subscriber be given an opportunity to double-check the accuracy of the contents of the certificate because the subscriber may be bound by any communication digitally signed with the private key that corresponds to the public key contained in the certificate or held liable for misrepresentations to the certification authority.[16]

If the subscriber finds that the certificate is accurate, the subscriber may *publish*[17] the certificate, or direct the CA to do so, making it available to third parties who may wish to communicate with the subscriber. A certificate is published by being recorded in one or more repositories or circulated by any other means so as to make it accessible to all intended correspondents. A *repository* is an electronic database of certificates[18]—the equivalent of a digital Yellow Pages. A repository is generally available online and may be maintained by the certification authority[19] or by anyone providing repository services. Repositories are generally accessible to anyone.

Repositories contain other important information as well as certificates. If a private key is compromised or lost, such as through loss of the medium on which it is stored or accidental deletion, it is generally necessary to suspend or revoke the corresponding certificate so that others will know not to rely on communications digitally signed with that key. This information is also posted in the repository.[20]

Once a certificate has been published, the subscriber may then append the certificate to any electronic communication. If the recipient wants to verify the connection between the sender and his public key, the recipient can look to the attached certificate for some assurance.

4.2.2 Who Can Be a Certification Authority?

Certification authorities may include federal and state governmental entities, private persons or entities licensed to act as certification authorities by a state,[21] and private persons or entities acting as certification authorities for commercial purposes. For example, the U.S. Postal Service[22] has announced large-scale plans to offer services designed to facilitate electronic commerce, including functioning as an all-purpose certification authority. The USPS may be well suited to function as a certification authority: In transactions between companies or individuals, it is an objective third party with an established reputation for credibility. Through its nationwide network of post offices, the USPS can register public keys for applicants who appear in person. This will enable the USPS to provide an added level of security, such as photographs and fingerprinting, to ensure that each registered public key corresponds to a real person, not an alias or an assumed identity.

The Los Angeles County Superior Court has established a limited-purpose certification authority in connection with an electronic filing and retrieval system that will rely on digital signatures to assure the authenticity and integrity of electronic court filings. The court will act as certification authority for its own personnel. Private parties authorized by the court will act as the certification authority for attorneys and litigants.[23]

A number of private commercial certification authorities are also currently operating. These include the Net Market Company, an affiliation of shopkeepers on the Internet,[24] and VeriSign, Inc., which issues certificates and provides related services to corporations and individuals for use in digitally signing documents for any purpose.[25] Value-added networks may also serve a limited local certification authority function for subscribers to their network.[26]

4.2.3 Verifying a Certification Authority's Digital Signature

To provide assurances as to the authenticity of a certificate it issues, a certification authority digitally signs each such certificate itself. Anyone can verify the authenticity and integrity of a certificate issued by a certification authority by verifying the certification authority's digital signature using the certification authority's public key.

Note, however, that anyone who wants to verify authenticity has the same problem with the CA's public key as he or she has with any other public key. How does the person know whether the public key really belongs to the CA? The answer is that the CA has its public key certified by another, higher-level CA, which acts as a certification authority for it. That higher-level CA then digitally signs the certificate it has issued, verifying the connection between the lower-level CA and the lower-level CA's public key. The lower-level CA may then make the certificate for its key available to anyone who seeks to verify the lower-level CA's digital signature.[27]

The higher-level CA, in turn, needs to have its connection to a public key certified to by an even higher level CA, and so on and on. This process of higher and higher CAs certifying public keys is often referred to as *chaining certificates.*

Of course, the chain has to stop somewhere. Where it stops will depend on the importance of a communication to the recipient. Depending on the nature of the electronic communication, the recipient may not bother to verify the sender's signature, much less the lowest level CA's signature. If the communication is of greater importance, the recipient may trace the certificates up the chain until reaching a certificate issued by a CA he or she knows and trusts.

4.3 Protecting the Parties to the Transaction

4.3.1 Certification Practice Statements

Unless they are subject to state licensure and regulation, certification authorities generally do not adhere to any uniform standard or procedures for verifying the identities of persons for whom they issue certificates. Thus a digital signature is only as reliable as the certification authority is trustworthy in performing its functions.[28] Consequently, a party needs some way to gauge how much reliance it should place on a digital signature supported by a certificate a particular CA issued. For example, if a certification authority verifies identity based on any single piece of identification, the third party might be more cautious in its reliance than it would if the certification authority requires the subscriber to appear in person with a driver's license and passport and to be fingerprinted.

To help recipients of a digitally signed communication gauge their level of risk, the particular procedure a certification authority follows in issuing certificates may be stated in a *certification practice statement.*[29] A certification practice statement may also include information about the practices the CA follows in its operations and about the details of the security of its system.[30]

Certification practice statements may serve an important function for a certification authority as well. A certification authority that follows its announced practices may be able to avoid a claim that it was negligent in failing to do more to connect a user to a public key.[31]

4.3.2 Certificate Revocation Lists

With public-key cryptography, each person has to keep his or her private key confidential and secure. This is easier than two people trusting each other to keep a key secret, as in conventional cryptography; nevertheless, the security of private keys is a problem. It is inevitable that someone's key will be lost or compromised, either through carelessness or a successful cryptanalytic attack. In addition, there are times—such as when a person dies; a company goes out of business; or an employee quits, is fired, or transferred to a new position—when a key may no longer be needed or used. Thus, there will be times when a key needs to be revoked before it expires.

A key is revoked by revoking its certificate. The problem is how to notify people that they should no longer rely on a key. The solution to this problem is the *certificate revocation list* or *CRL*. A CRL is simply a database of certificates of keys that have been revoked before their expiration date. A CRL may be part of the repository maintained by the certification authority. If a private key is lost, compromised, or no longer used for any other reason, the corresponding public key and its certificate would be placed on the CRL.[32] Before relying on a public key, a person should verify its status by checking the CRL.

4.3.3 Certificate Expiration

It is possible for a cryptographic key to be compromised even though its holder conscientiously safeguarded it. With a little luck and a lot of motivation, keys can be broken through what is known as a *brute-force attack*. In a brute-force attack, every possible key is tried until one decrypts the ciphertext.[33] The longer the key length, the longer it takes to try all the possible keys. For example, for a key that is 56 bits long, it would take approximately 10 hours to find the key.[34] For a key that is 128 bits long, it would take 5.4 $\times$ 10^{18} years to find the key.[35]

Thus, one way to guard against a successful brute-force attack is to use a long key. Another is to change keys periodically.[36]

As with revoked keys, there must be some way to let people know when a key expires. This can be done simply by including a validity period in the certificate for a public key. Anyone who then consults the certificate for that key will know whether it has expired.

Once a key and its certificate expire, the user simply creates a new key pair and has the public key certified.

Encryption keys generally expire after a relatively short time; this raises the question of how a digital signature can be verified after the public key has expired. For example, if a company enters into a twenty-year lease, how can the integrity of the digitally signed lease be verified when the corresponding certificate has already expired?

One solution is to have the digital signature date/time stamped.[37] The date/time-stamped version of the digital signature could be used years later to enforce the original contract. The date/time stamp would establish the date and time at which the document was signed, and thus establish that at such time there was a valid certificate connecting the signer to the public key.[38]

4.3.4 Limits of Liability

A certification authority may be subject to claims for negligence in performing its functions or for misrepresentation in issuing certificates that contain false or misleading information. A certification authority's liability for such claims may be limited either by law or by contract. Utah's Digital Signature Act provides that a licensed certification authority is not liable for any loss caused by a false or forged digital signature if it complied with the requirements prescribed by that law.[39] The Act also limits a certification authority's liability to the amount of any specified reliance limit.[40] Finally, the Act provides that licensed certification authorities are not liable for punitive damages except in certain limited situations.[41]

In the absence of a statute, a certification authority may seek to limit its potential liability by specifying such a limit in its contracts with its subscribers. A certification authority may also seek to limit its potential liability to third parties who rely on certificates it has issued by notifying them of such limit in its certification practice statement. Whether such a limit would be enforceable against such a relying party depends in part on whether that party had notice of the limit.[42]

4.4 Obligations of the Parties

4.4.1 Signer

When a party to an electronic transaction uses a digital signature, that party undertakes certain obligations and makes certain representations. First, a party digitally signing a document has an obligation to do so using a private key that was generated using a trustworthy system.[43] A trustworthy system is hardware, software, and procedures that:

1. Are reasonably secure from intrusion and misuse;
2. Provide a reasonable level of availability, reliability, and correct operation; and
3. Are reasonably suited to performing their intended functions.[44]

Trustworthiness is in part a question of security. It requires, among other things, the use of system security measures such as access controls; division of duties among personnel so that a single employee could not compromise key pairs, or the system, without colluding with another employee; and audit procedures. Security measures need only be reasonable, not absolute, under the circumstances.[45]

To the extent that the public key used to verify a digital signature is the subject of a certificate issued by a certification authority, the signer has an obligation to see that all representations made to the certification authority for inclusion in the certificate or used in generating the certificate are accurate to the best of the signer's knowledge and belief.[46] If any information is false or misleading—or becomes so as a result of future events—the signer has an obligation to notify the certification authority so that it may be corrected, whether during the certification process or anytime thereafter.[47]

If a third party relies on this false information and is damaged as a result, the signer may be liable to both the relying party and the certification authority.[48] Because of this potential liability, a signer is given an opportunity to review and accept a certificate before it is published.[49]

A signer also has an obligation to retain control of the private key, protect it from being compromised, and keep it secret.[50] A signer may lose control over the key by voluntarily disclosing it to someone not authorized to sign on the signer's behalf; by losing the disk, smart card, or other object on which the key is stored; or by theft. If the signer loses control over the key, the signer may be held liable for any obligations or bills incurred by an unauthorized user.[51] A failure to safeguard the private key can thus have serious consequences.

A signer may limit his exposure by requesting that the certification authority suspend or revoke his certificate as soon as the signer learns the key has been compromised. Because a certification authority will generally have no duty or ability to monitor either the continuing accuracy of information in the certificate or events (such as loss of a key) that may warrant suspension or revocation, the signer has an obligation to request that the certificate be suspended or revoked (and to stop using the private key to create digital signatures).[52]

A signer also has an obligation to make the corresponding certificate available to the recipient of the communication if the signer expects the recipient to rely on the digital signature.[53] The signer may make the certificate available by publishing it in a repository maintained by the certification authority or a public repository, or by attaching the certificate to the communication itself.

4.4.2 Certification Authority

A certification authority's primary function is to issue a certificate that verifies the relationship between a public key and a subscriber. That third parties will rely on certificates it issues to verify digital signatures is a given.[54] Accordingly, a certification authority has an obligation to verify the identity of the person to whom it issues a certificate, and that the public key listed in the certificate corresponds to a private key held by that person.[55] Otherwise, a recipient of a digital signature who is misled by a certificate into relying on a digital signature may have a claim against the certification authority for misrepresentation.

The amount of investigation a certification authority will undertake may vary according to the purposes for which the digital signature and certificate are to be used.[56] The amount of investigation may be specified by the certification authority in its certification practice statement or by contract between the certification authority and subscriber.[57] State statutes may establish minimum requirements that cannot be lessened by contract or a certification practice statement.[58]

In order to limit the certification authority's liability stemming from representations attributed to it by the act of issuing a certificate, a certificate will normally include an expiration date.[59] This helps eliminate liability for claims of reliance on stale information. Upon expiration of a certificate, the certification authority no longer makes any representations as to the expired certificate and is discharged of its duties.[60] A person who relies on an expired certificate and is damaged will have no claim against the certification authority because it was not reasonable to have relied on the expired certificate.[61]

In addition, certification authorities may also include in a certificate other forms of limitations of their liability, such as dollar limits, which are sometimes referred to as reliance limits.[62] A *reliance limit* warns that certificates the CA issues should not be relied on for transactions in excess of a specified dollar amount. Such a reliance limit may also be specified in a certification practice statement or set by a licensing body as a limit on a certification authority's license to issue certificates.[63] If a third party who knows of the reliance limit relies on a digital signature in connection with a transaction that exceeds the limit, that third party may not be able to recover its losses from the certification authority because it was not reasonable to so rely.

Because of the importance of certificates in electronic commerce, a certification authority must promptly *suspend* a certificate at the request of the subscriber.[64] A certification authority must have a reasonable belief that the request is authorized, but may not be obligated to confirm the identity of the person requesting suspension.[65] This reflects the reality that many suspension requests will be emergencies in which there will not be time to confirm the identity of the person requesting suspension. While this may protect a subscriber from liability for unauthorized use of a key, a competitor bent on corporate sabotage could, at the same time, seriously interfere with the subscriber's business by requesting suspension.

A certification authority also has an obligation to *revoke* certificates upon request. With revocation requests, however, the certification authority must confirm the identity of the person making the request.[66] Unlike a suspension, which can be undone, a revocation is permanent and irreversible. If the subscriber has digitally signed a large number of documents, or is itself a certification authority, revoking its certificate could cause monumental problems. Consequently, a certification authority must be more cautious in revoking certificates than in suspending them.

In addition, a certification authority may have an obligation to revoke or suspend a certificate—even without the subscriber's request or consent—if it is put on notice that certain representations appearing in the certificate are false or if the certification authority's private key or trustworthy system are compromised in a manner that affects the reliability of the certificate.[67] However, the certification authority may be liable to the subscriber for an improper revocation.[68]

4.4.3 Relying Party

A recipient of a digitally signed communication, or other *relying party*, does not have prescribed obligations or duties as such. A relying party, for instance, has no duty to examine a certificate to determine whether a key is expired or not. Nor does a relying party have a duty to check a CRL to determine whether a certificate has been suspended or revoked. However, if a relying party fails to do these things or to otherwise verify the signature, the relying party assumes the risk that the digital signature is a fake, and the relying party's recourse may be limited.[69]

4.5 The Legal Effect of a Digital Signature

Although there is no generally accepted, uniform law on the subject, several states have recognized the need to provide a legal infrastructure to support the use of digital signatures.[70] Utah was the first to pass digital signature legislation.[71] Utah's Digital Signature Act establishes a scheme of optional licensure[72] and regulation[73] for certain private companies, individuals, and governmental bodies wishing to act as certification authorities. The legislation establishes minimum standards that certification authorities must meet in order to be licensed.[74] These standards include things such as minimum procedures that a certification authority must follow in issuing a certificate.[75] The legislation accords to a digitally signed communication, which has been certified by a licensed certification authority, certain legal presumptions and effects that a communication certified by a nonlicensed certification authority does not receive, such as that the communication satisfies writing and signature requirements (see Section 4.5.4).[76] The Utah Act also addresses the respective duties and liabilities of licensed certification authorities,[77] subscribers,[78] and repositories.[79]

California has also enacted digital signature legislation.[80] California's legislation, as originally introduced, was very similar to that of Utah. However, the statute that was enacted takes a more limited approach in that it applies only to communications with public entities, whereas the Utah statute applies to anyone who wishes to use digital signatures.[81]

A more comprehensive effort to address the legal effect of a digital signature has been undertaken by a committee of the American Bar Association, which is formulating *Digital Signature Guidelines*.[82] Based on these early efforts, certain conclusions can be drawn about the likely legal effect of using digital signatures.

4.5.1 Integrity

Digital signatures provide a means to verify the integrity of an electronic communication. Generally, if a digital signature can be property verified through the use of the corresponding public key, then it will be presumed that the message has not been altered since the digital signature was created.[83]

4.5.2 Authenticity

Digital signatures can also verify the source of an electronic communication. The recipient knows that the communication is authentic in that it came from the sender because only the sender's public key will decrypt a digital signature encrypted with the sender's private key. Since the public and private keys are associated with an identified signer, and are unique to each signer, the key effectively links the signer to the document.[84]

Thus, if a digital signature can be verified through the use of the sender's public key then it will be presumed that the digital signature was created by the private key corresponding to the public key. It is also presumed that the digital signature was affixed with the intention of the sender to identify him- or herself as the source of the communication.[85]

4.5.3 Nonrepudiation

When the authenticity and integrity of a communication can be established, the sender is prevented from repudiating both the contents of the communication and having sent it. The digital signature cannot be forged unless the sender loses control of his or her private key. The recipient cannot forge a document to him- or herself either. Even if the recipient were to create a digital signature using the sender's public key, the digital signature can only be decrypted using the sender's private key. The same key cannot encrypt and decrypt a single communication.

4.5.4 Writing and Signature Requirements

Like paper documents, electronic documents are governed by rules (such as the Statute of Frauds) that require certain documents to be "in writing" and "signed."[86] The general view is that the use of a digital signature will satisfy the signature[87] and any writing requirement.[88]

4.5.5 Right To Rely

If a digital signature can be verified by the recipient, then the recipient is entitled to rely generally on the communication and the sender (the person digitally signing the message) will be bound.[89] However, if the digital signature cannot be verified the recipient is not required to rely on it for identification of the purported sender, and may not be justified in doing so.[90]

4.5.6 New Paradigm Shift

With handwritten signatures, the law provides that a person is generally not liable for forgeries or other unauthorized signatures.[91] With digital signatures, especially under new and proposed legislation, a person is liable until that person revokes his or her public key.[92] A person who holds a public-private key pair has an increased responsibility similar to that of a person who signs documents using a signature machine. The person with the machine may not be able to challenge an unauthorized machine-made signature if that person has been negligent in keeping the machine secure. The signer must understand that he or she may be bound by any communication digitally signed with the private key that corresponds to the public key, and will be held liable to anyone who relies on the public key before the key was revoked and is damaged. The result is similar to that in the electronic payments context in which a person who has agreed that a bank may honor a payment order that the bank has verified through the use of commercially reasonable security procedures will bear the loss for a payment that was not in fact authorized. (See Section 3.3.3.) If this potential liability is not enough to cause a person to safeguard his or her private key, the law may impose an affirmative duty on the person to do so.[93]

4.6 What Digital Signatures Do Not Accomplish and Other Cryptographic Applications

A digital signature used alone does not provide any assurance of confidentiality. A digital signature is created by encrypting a message digest of the communication, not the communication itself. The communication may or may not be encrypted. If not, anyone who intercepts the communication can read it, or, if it is digital content, use it. Note, for example, that the text of the digitally signed letter in section 4.1.2 is readable. Digital signatures provide assurances only as to integrity and authenticity. Encrypting for confidentiality is a separate cryptographic application.[94]

4.6.1 Encryption for Confidentiality

Although digital signatures do not provide confidentiality, a communication can be encrypted so as to keep its contents confidential, and the same communication can also be digitally signed to provide assurances as to its authenticity and integrity.

To accomplish this, the communication is first digitally signed. Then the readable communication and attached digital signature are encrypted using a quick, conventional encryption algorithm and a single, secret key. To get around the perennial conventional encryption problem of how the sender and recipient can share that key—in secret and in advance over an insecure network—the single, secret key is itself encrypted using the recipient's public key. The encrypted secret key is then attached to the digitally signed document that was encrypted using conventional cryptography. Thus, when the recipient receives the communication, he or she uses his or her private key to decrypt the single, secret key, and then uses that single, secret key to decrypt the communication and digital signature.[95]

The sender need not worry about sharing the single, secret key in advance because it can be safely sent along with the communication for which it is needed. Nor does the sender need to worry about the recipient keeping the single key secret after receiving it. The single, secret key is used only for one communication. Such a one-use key is called a *session key*. A new session key is generated each time the sender wants to both digitally sign and encrypt a communication for confidentiality.

4.6.2 Date/Time Stamping

A digital signature also fails to fix a document in time since it gives no indication of when the digital signature was created. This can be very important in verifying the digital signature. It can also be important when the date a document is signed triggers the running of contractual and legal time periods. There are also times when it is important to know when a document was created or last modified. For example, an inventor who wants to establish a priority date for an invention needs some way to date drawings and related files that can be independently verified. In another example, an insured person may need to prove that he or she submitted a digitally signed objection to a denial of benefits to his or her insurer within the prescribed time period.

The author of a document could type a date into the document or rely on one supplied by his computer. However, the author could easily pre- or post-date the document. Similarly, a date or time automatically affixed by a computer system can be falsified by resetting the system's calendar/clock. Creator- or system-supplied dates are simply not independently verifiable. There must be some reliable way to date/time stamp an electronic document.

A solution is to use a date/time-stamping service. A *date/time stamp* is a digitally signed notation to a document, digital signature, or certificate indicating the date, time, and identity of the person or entity appending or attaching the notation. Digital date/time stamps work like this: Software containing a hash function creates a message digest of the electronic document. The software then sends the message digest to a third party's computer with an automatic request for a date/time stamp. The third party's computer immediately sends back a date/time stamp notation or certificate to be attached to the message digest.

The date/time stamp service then takes all the message digests it has received from different customers during some set interval, such as one minute, and hashes these together into a composite hash value called a *common validation record.* The common validation record for each interval is publicized in several different forms and locations, such as in print in the *New York Times* classified advertisements, digitally on the Internet, and on widely circulated CD-ROMs.[96] It is, therefore, not possible for the central service or anyone else to tamper with these common validation records after the fact. Anyone wanting to verify the date/time of the message digest may do so by referring to the date/time stamp certificate and the common validation record.[97]

4.6.3 Steganography: Digital Watermarks

Encryption can also be used to protect a digitized work from unauthorized disclosure. A user who pays for the right to access a digitized movie, for example, could be given the key necessary to decrypt and view the movie. The problem, however, is that once the user has decrypted the movie, there is nothing to stop that user from posting a decrypted copy of the movie on the Internet or an electronic bulletin board. A possible deterrent is to use steganography. *Steganography* is an information-security technology that scatters identifying information throughout a digitized visual or audio work. This identifying information is called a *digital watermark* because, like watermarks in paper, it helps to thwart counterfeiters and pirates and to establish the authenticity of the information on which it appears.[98]

The identifying information might include, in the case of a digitized song for example, the name of the copyright owner and information about the source and authenticity of the work. It is not possible to alter or erase the identifying information without permanently damaging the digital work.[99] It is also not possible to read the identifying information without using a cryptographic key that makes the digital watermark readable.

The digital watermark does not prevent a pirate from copying the work. It may, however, deter copying. In an online purchase, the digital watermark for the work could include the purchaser's name, along with other information about the purchaser. This would likely deter a purchaser from making and distributing copies of the work because the digital watermark would be necessarily reproduced when the purchaser made the unauthorized copies. In this way, illegal copies could be traced to the purchaser.

Endnotes

1. Utah Code Ann. §§ 46-3-101 *et seq.* (eff. May 1, 1995).

2. Cal. Gov't Code § 16.5 (enacted Oct. 4, 1995).

3. Information Security Committee, Electronic Commerce and Information Technology Division, Section of Science and Technology, American Bar Association, *Digital Signature Guidelines* (draft Oct. 5, 1995) [hereinafter *Digital Signature Guidelines*]. Note: These guidelines are in provisional form and were published only to invite comment. A final version is expected to be published later in 1996.

4. *See* Utah Code Ann. § 46-3-103(10) (1995); *Digital Signature Guidelines* § 1.9; *see also* William Stallings, *Protect Your Privacy: A Guide for PGP Users* 20 (1995). For a primer on cryptography, see chapter 31.

5. For a primer on cryptography, see chapter 31.

6. *Digital Signature Guidelines* § 1.9.

7. *See* Utah Code Ann. § 46-3-103(37) (1995); *Digital Signature Guidelines* § 1.33.

8. *See Digital Signature Guidelines* § 1.9; Michael S. Baum, Digital Signature Technical Primer in Verisign, Inc., Notarial FAQ: Frequently Asked Questions Appendix 1 (Jun. 23, 1995) (available at http://www.verisign.com).

9. *See* Utah Code Ann. § 46-3-103(5),(21) (1995); *Digital Signature Guidelines* §§ 1.5, 1.19.

10. *See* Utah Code Ann. § 46-3-103(5) (1995); *Digital Signature Guidelines* § 1.5.

11. *See, e.g.,* VeriSign, Inc., Notarial FAQ: Frequently Asked Questions (ver. 1.0e Jun. 15, 1995) (relies on notaries to verify association of subscriber to a public key) (available at http://www.verisign.com/faqs/nota_faq.htm1).

12. Utah Code Ann. § 46-3-103(14) (1995); *Digital Signature Guidelines* § 1.14.

13. Utah Code Ann. § 46-3-103(4) (1995); *Digital Signature Guidelines* § 1.4.

14. Utah Code Ann. §§ 46-3-103(4) (1995), 46-3-104; *Digital Signature Guidelines* § 1.4.

15. *See Digital Signature Guidelines* §§ 1.1 Comment 1.1.3, 1.14 Comment 1.14.3.

16. *See Digital Signature Guidelines* §§ 4.2 Comment 4.2.4, 5.6(2).

17. Utah Code Ann. § 46-3-103(24) (1995); *Digital Signature Guidelines* § 1.22.

18. Utah Code Ann. § 46-3-103(29) (1995); *Digital Signature Guidelines* § 1.24.

19. *See* Utah Code Ann. § 46-3-502 (1995).

20. *See* Utah Code Ann. § 46-3-502(1)(e) (1995); *Digital Signature Guidelines* § 1.24 Comment 1.24.1.

21. *See, e.g.,* Utah Code Ann. §§ 46-3-101 to -504 (1995). For a discussion of the efforts of several states to provide for a system of licensure through digital signature legislation, see section 4.5.

22. For general information about the U.S. Postal Service, see http://www.usps.gov.

23. *See* Joseph Kornowski, *Electronic Filing in Los Angeles Superior Court*, Los Angeles Law. 85, 87-88 (Sept. 1995).

24.   *See* Peter H. Lewis *Attention Shoppers, Internet Is Open*, N.Y. Times, Aug. 12, 1994 at D1, col.3 (late ed.-final).

25.   For more information about VeriSign's certification authority services, see http://www.verisign.com.

26.   *See* Peter H. Lewis *Attention Shoppers, Internet Is Open*, N.Y. Times, Aug. 12, 1994, at D1, col. 3 (late ed.-final).

27.   *See generally Digital Signature Guidelines* § 3.7 (availability of certification authority's certificate).

28.   Michael S. Baum, *Federal Certification Authority Liability and Policy: Law and Policy of Certificate-Based Public Key and Digital Signatures* 76 (U.S. Department of Commerce/NIST Publication No. NIST-GCR-94-654); National Technical Information Service Publication No. PB94-191-202 147-59 (1994).

29.   *See, e.g.* Utah Code Ann. § 46-3-103(6) (1995) ("certification disclosure record"); *Digital Signature Guidelines* § 1.6.

30.   *See* Utah Code Ann. § 46-3-203 (1995); *Digital Signature Guidelines* § 1.6 & Comment 1.6.1.

31.   For more information on certification practice statements, see Michael S. Baum, *Federal Certification Authority Liability and Policy: Law and Policy of Certificate-Based Public Key and Digital Signatures* 352-58 (1994). A number of interesting and vexing questions a certification authority should resolve are posed in Benjamin Wright, *The Law of Electronic Commerce* § ET1.2.5.1 (1995).

32.   *See Digital Signature Guidelines* § 3.14 & Comment 3.14.1.

33.   William Stallings, *Protect Your Privacy: A Guide for PGP Users* 13 (1995).

34.   William Stallings, *Protect Your Privacy: A Guide for PGP Users* 14 (Table 2.1) (1995) (assuming a computer that can try one million keys per microsecond).

35.   William Stallings, *Protect Your Privacy: A Guide for PGP Users* 14 (Table 2.1) (1995) (assuming a computer that can try one million keys per microsecond).

36.   Bruce Schneier, *Applied Cryptography: Protocols, Algorithms, and Source Code in C* 183-84 (1996).

37.   For a discussion of the mechanics of date/time stamping, see section 4.6.2.

38.   *See* Utah Code Ann. § 46-3-401(4)(a) (1995); *Digital Signature Guidelines* § 1.29 & Comment 1.29.2.

39.   *See* Utah Code Ann. § 46-3-308(2)(a) (1995).

40.   *See* Utah Code Ann. § 46-3-308(2)(b) (1995).

41.   *See* Utah Code Ann. §§ 46-3-308(2)(c), 46-3-204(5) (1995).

42.   *Cf. Digital Signature Guidelines* § 1.6 Comment 1.6.3.

43.   *Digital Signature Guidelines* § 4.1.

44.   *Digital Signature Guidelines* § 1.31.

45.   *Digital Signature Guidelines* § 1.31 Comments 1.31.2, 1.31.3.

46.   *See* Utah Code Ann. § 46-3-302(1)(c), (d) (1995); *Digital Signature Guidelines* § 4.2.

47.   *See Digital Signature Guidelines* § 4.4 Comment 4.4.2.

48.   *See* Utah Code Ann. § 46-3-302(4) (1995) (liable to certification authority); *Digital Signature Guidelines* § 4.2 Comments 4.2.2, 4.2.3.

49.   *See* Utah Code Ann. § 46-3-301(3) (1995); *Digital Signature Guidelines* §§ 1.14 Comment 1.14.3, 5.6(2).

50.   *See* Utah Code Ann. § 46-3-303(1) (1995) (subscriber has duty to exercise reasonable care to control private key); Cal. Gov't Code § 16.5(a)(3); *Digital Signature Guidelines* § 4.3.

51.   *See* Utah Code Ann. § 46-3-302(1)(a) (1995); U.C.C. § 4A-202(b) (1989).

52.   *See Digital Signature Guidelines* § 4.4 Comment 4.4.2.

53.   *See Digital Signature Guidelines* § 4.5.

54.   *See Digital Signature Guidelines* § 2.3 & Comment 2.3.1.

55.   *See* Utah Code Ann. § 46-3-301 (1995); *Digital Signature Guidelines* § 3.8 & Comment 3.8.1.

56.   *See Digital Signature Guidelines* § 3.8 Comment 3.8.1.

57.   *See Digital Signature Guidelines* § 3.8 Comment 3.8.1.

58.   *See* Utah Code Ann. §§ 46-3-203(1)(k), 46-3-301(1)(b) (1995); *See also Digital Signature Guidelines* § 3.8 Comment 3.8.3.

59.   *See* Utah Code Ann. § 46-3-307 (1995); *Digital Signature Guidelines* § 3.9.

60.   *See* Utah Code Ann. § 46-3-307 (1995).

61.   *See Digital Signature Guidelines* §§ 5.2(2), 5.3(1).

62.   *See* Utah Code Ann. §§ 46-3-103(26), 46-3-308 (1995); *Digital Signature Guidelines* § 3.3 Comment 3.3.1.

63.   *See* Utah Code Ann. § 46-3-308 (1995); *Digital Signature Guidelines* § 3.3 Comment 3.3.1.

64.   *See* Utah Code Ann. § 46-3-305 (1995); *Digital Signature Guidelines* § 3.11.

65.   *See* Utah Code Ann. § 46-3-305(1)(b) (1995); *Digital Signature Guidelines* § 3.11 & Comment 3.11.2.

66.   *See* Utah Code Ann. § 46-3-306(1) (1995); *Digital Signature Guidelines* § 3.12.

67.   *See* Utah Code Ann. § 46-3-306(3)(a) (1995); *Digital Signature Guidelines* § 3.13.

68.   *See* Utah Code Ann. § 46-3-306(3)(b) (1995); *Digital Signature Guidelines* § 3.13 Comment 3.13.5.

69.   *See Digital Signature Guidelines* § 5.2 & Comments 5.2.2, 5.2.3.

70.   *See, e.g.,* Utah Code Ann. §§ 46-3-101 to -504 (1995). Cal. Gov't Code § 16.5; 1995 Ore. S.B. 992 (pending); 1995 Wash. S.B. 5959 (pending).

71.   *See* Utah Code Ann. §§ 46-3-101 to -504 (1995). For a critical analysis of the Utah Digital Signature Act, see C. Bradford Biddle, Digital Signature Legislation: Flawed Efforts Will Hurt Consumers and Impede Development of a Public Key Infrastructure (unpublished manu-script, on file with the author of this chapter).

72.   *See* Utah Code Ann. § 46-3-201 (1995). Licensure is available only to an attorney or law firm, financial institution, insurance or trust company, or state governmental body. *See* Utah Code Ann. § 46-3-201(1)(a) (1995).

73.   *See* Utah Code Ann. §§ 46-3-202 to -207, 46-3-301, 46-3-304 to -306, and 46-3-307 (1995).

74.   *See* Utah Code Ann. § 46-3-201 (1995).

75.   *See* Utah Code Ann. § 46-3-301 (1995).

76.   *See* Utah Code Ann. §§ 46-3-401 to -403 (1995).

77.   *See* Utah Code Ann. §§ 46-3-202 to -207, 46-3-301, 46-3-304 to -306, and 46-3-307 (1995).

78.   *See* Utah Code Ann. § 46-3-302 (1995).

79.   *See* Utah Code Ann. § 46-3-502 to -503 (1995).

80.   Cal. Gov't Code § 16.5.

81.   *See* Cal. Gov't Code § 16.5(a).

82.   *Digital Signature Guidelines* §§ 1.1-5.7. A provisional draft of *The Guidelines* was published on October 5, 1995 only to invite comment. A final version is expected to be published in 1996.

83. *See* Utah Code Ann. §§ 46-3-103(37), 46-3-401(3) (1995); *Digital Signature Guidelines* §§ 1.33, 1.9, 5.6(2); *cf.* Cal. Gov't Code § 16.5(a)(4).

84. *Digital Signature Guidelines* § 1.9 and Comment 1.9.1.

85. *See* Utah Code Ann. § 46-3-401(3) (1995); Cal. Gov't Code § 16.5; *Digital Signature Guidelines* § 5.6.

86. For a discussion of the Statute of Frauds and its writing and signature requirements, see Sections 3.1.4 and 6.3.

87. *See* Utah Code Ann. §§ 46-3-401(3) (1995) (use of digital signature creates a presumption that the document was signed with an intent to authenticate the document and be bound by its contents); Cal. Gov't Code § 16.5 (digital signature has the same force and effect as manual signature); *Digital Signature Guidelines* § 5.1 & Comment 5.1.1 (signature requirement is satisfied by a digital signature that is affixed by the signer with the intention of signing the communication and verified by reference to a public key listed in a valid certificate); *see also* U.C.C. § 4A-202(b) (1989) (use of security procedures to verify authenticity); National Conference of Commissioners on Uniform State Laws, Uniform Commercial Code Revised Article 2. Sales. § 2-102(37) (draft Oct. 1, 1995) (same) [hereinafter Draft U.C.C.].

88. *See* Utah Code Ann. § 46-3-402(1) (1995); *Digital Signature Guidelines* § 5.4 & Comment 5.4.1; *see also* United Nations Commission on International Trade Law, Draft Model Statutory Provisions on the Legal Aspects of Electronic Data Interchange (EDI) and Related Means of Communication, Art. 6 (1994) (international EDI message satisfies the writing requirement if it is preserved and can be presented in human-readable form).

89. *See* Utah Code Ann. § 46-3-401(3) (1995); *Digital Signature Guidelines* §§ 5.2, 5.3, 5.6; *see also* U.C.C. § 4A-202; Draft U.C.C. § 2-212.

90. *See Digital Signature Guidelines* § 5.2.

91. *See* U.C.C. § 3-404 (1995).

92. *See* Utah Code Ann. § 46-3-306(5) (1995); *cf. Digital Signature Guidelines* § 5.6.

93. *See* Utah Code Ann. § 46-3-303(1) (1995); *Digital Signature Guidelines* § 4.3.

94. Encrypting for confidentiality is discussed in section 4.6.1 of this chapter.

95. *See* William Stallings, *Protect Your Privacy: A Guide for PGP Users* 26-30 (1995).

96. Charles Merrill, About Time-Date Stamping (Mar. 2, 1995) (unpublished manuscript, on file with the author of this chapter).

97. Stuart Haber, *Cryptographically Secure Digital Time-Stamping in Worldwide Electronic Commerce: Law Policy and Controls Conference Proceedings* 443 (Jan. 1994).

98. *See* Bruce Schneier, *Applied Cryptography: Protocols, Algorithms, and Source Code in C* 9-10 (1996); *see also* Denise Caruso, *Technology: Digital Commerce*, N.Y. Times, Aug. 7, 1995, at C5.

99. Information Infrastructure Task Force, *Intellectual Property and the National Information Infrastructure: The Report of the Working Group on Intellectual Property Rights* 216 (Sept. 1995).

5
Electronic Recordkeeping

Lorijean G. Oei

$\mathbf{R}$ecords serve essential business purposes. Records are, for example, vitally important when a company finds itself in a dispute with one of its trading partners or with a government agency such as the IRS. After employees leave and memories fade, records are often all that a business has to prove its version of events. But a trading partner, government agency, or court will be willing to consider records only if they are trustworthy. Although techniques exist to ensure their trustworthiness, electronic records raise special concerns. Nevertheless, with a carefully developed and conscientiously followed electronic recordkeeping system, electronic records should be accepted for any purpose.

5.1 The Need for Records

Records are critical to a successful operation. Records enable a company to document important internal business information such as which customers have paid, what sales were last year, and when the lease on its equipment expires.

In addition, a company may be required to keep records in order to comply with various legal, regulatory, and tax requirements. For example, financial institutions are required by a joint Treasury Department and Federal Reserve rule to maintain records related to domestic and international funds transfers.[1]

Finally, records are an organization's "memory" of business events and activities. Records enable a company to prove that certain events occurred or to substantiate its activities to someone outside the company. This can be important when a company wants to show that it has satisfied its obligations or to enforce its rights under a contract. For example, under an electronic publishing agreement, if the publisher claims to have paid all the royalties due and the author claims he or she was shorted, sales records and royalty reports should enable the author and the publisher to resolve their dispute. If not, the author and the publisher may need to take their dispute before a neutral third party. Records become especially critical when a business needs to prove its side of the story in court.

Thus, records serve not only a company's internal business needs, but also legal, regulatory, tax, contractual, and evidentiary purposes.

5.2 The Goals of Electronic Recordkeeping

There is no single place where you can find what "the law" says about recordkeeping. There are over 3,500 federal and thousands more state and local statutes, rules, and regulations that address issues such as the types of records that must be kept and how long they should be retained.[2] There are also countless court opinions interpreting and applying these statutes, rules, and regulations. Few of these, however, are specific to electronic records. Despite the sheer number of recordkeeping laws, the variations between them, and the lack of guidance specific to electronic records, most legal recordkeeping requirements will be satisfied by an electronic recordkeeping system designed to achieve certain basic goals.

One such goal is to ensure that all appropriate records are retained. Not every electronic communication should be kept. Only those records that *need* to be kept *should* be kept. These include internal records necessary to the day-to-day operations of the business, records that must be kept to satisfy regulatory and tax purposes, and records related to transactions and other important commercial activities.

It is also important to ensure that records are kept for as long as they are needed but no longer. How long a record should be retained will depend upon the type of record it is and the purposes for which it may be needed. Personnel records, tax returns, and contracts may have different useful lives. When a record exceeds its useful life, it should be destroyed. Records destruction is as important as records retention.

A second goal of electronic recordkeeping is to ensure that records are available whenever they are needed. If the media on which the records are stored is damaged or deteriorates, or if the electronic records cannot be retrieved, records cannot serve their essential purposes.

A third, and perhaps the most important, goal is to ensure that records are trustworthy. A business can keep all the records it wants, but if these records are not preserved in such a way that they are demonstrably authentic, accurate and complete, and reliable, trading partners will not act on them, regulatory and taxing authorities will not consider them to substantiate compliance with their requirements, and courts will not admit them as proof in a legal dispute.[3] In fact, the hesitancy of many to engage in electronic commerce is blamed in part on the perception that electronic communications and records are not verifiably trustworthy.[4]

A fourth goal is to document the electronic recordkeeping system. Such documentation should cover security policy as well as procedures to be used to implement that policy. Being able to substantiate a recordkeeping policy or procedure using such documentation is sometimes as important as the policy or procedure itself.

5.3 Record Retention

An electronic recordkeeping system should address three key issues:

1. The types and form of records to retain
2. Retention periods, and
3. Records destruction

5.3.1 Types and Form of Records To Retain

If a company does business electronically, it will still need to keep the same categories of records that it currently keeps, or would have to keep, if it conducted its business solely using paper records. In general, the types of records a company is legally obligated to keep depends on the activities and industry in which the company is engaged and where it is doing business.[5] For example, a company may be required to keep certain employment and personnel records so as to enable the government to monitor its activities and enforce compliance with laws aimed to ensure the payment of proper wages, protect the health and safety of employees, and eliminate discrimination. A company also may be required to keep records if it operates in a regulated industry, such as insurance or lending, or if it is involved in foreign trade or foreign currency transactions.

One difference with electronic recordkeeping is that a person must be more conscious about retaining electronic records. Most people intuitively follow a default practice of saving every paper record. Electronic records are often treated more casually. Perhaps due to the informality of the medium, a person using e-mail to conduct business may fail to consider whether he or she should retain copies of the electronic messages. Although that person may automatically create file copies of paper correspondence, he or she may not think to create electronic file copies of electronic correspondence.

Another difference is that for each record a business keeps electronically, it may need to keep certain additional information to help demonstrate the trustworthiness of its electronic records. These items of information may include:

- For digitally signed documents, the document itself, including the signature element, along with the signer's certificate and the software, algorithm, and hash function necessary to verify the digital signature
- Each message in a course of correspondence
- Records of acknowledgments and repeat-back acknowledgments
- Responses repudiating an acknowledgment or a record noting that no response was received
- Addressing and forwarding headers and other system-supplied information[6]
- A log of all incoming and outgoing communications
- Date/time stamp notations or certificates for date/time-stamped records

For critical business communications that are not digitally signed, it may also be a good idea to have a trusted third party retain a copy as well. This helps to prove the contents of the communications so that no one can hold a party to something it did not send, and to ensure that the record has not been changed while in storage. It also helps a recipient to prove the contents of communications it receives so that the sender cannot repudiate its communication or claim that the recipient modified it.

A related retention issue is the form in which a record of an electronic communication should be retained. Before an electronic communication may be transmitted, it is often necessary that it be translated into another format suitable for transmission. A similar translation process may also occur on the receiver's end. In addition, the sender's system and other systems through which the communication travels may attach forwarding information to the file. This raises the question of whether the record that is made of the communication should be captured in its pre- or post-translated form, or both.

Existing IRS regulations suggest that an electronic communication may be stored in either its pre- or post-translated form provided, however, that the integrity of the record can be established.[7] Thus, if a recipient chooses to create a record of a communication in its post-translated form, it should be prepared to demonstrate that its system functions reliably in performing the translation.[8]

A final retention issue is whether hard copy of electronic records should be generated and retained. Generally there is no need to print out and retain a hard copy in addition to an electronic version of a record unless a particular statute, rule, or regulation requires hard copy.[9]

If a company decides to print out its records and delete the electronic copies, however, it is important to note that a paper printout may not always be a satisfactory substitute for its electronic counterpart. Paper records may omit information that would have been reflected in the electronic record, such as time and date of origin, time and date of transmission, and who received the information and when.[10] To ensure that all pertinent information is retained, it is advisable to preserve the electronic form of a record even if a hard copy is also printed and retained. This is especially the case for important business records. If a company produces a printout, it should also be sure to print out and retain system information such as transmit and receipt logs.

5.3.2 Retention Periods

Electronic records should be retained for the same length of time as paper records are retained or, at the very least, as long as they may be material for litigation or regulatory purposes or any ongoing business transaction.[11] There is no single period specified anywhere that covers all records for all purposes. Record retention periods vary from three years to thirty years, sometimes more, depending upon the purpose for which the record is being kept.[12] Thus, a business must consider the purpose for which the record is being kept and consult the applicable statute or regulation. For example, the U.S. Department of Labor requires certain employers to retain payroll and related records for at least three years.[13] For other types of records not specifically covered by a statute or regulation, a business should consider how long it may need the record in the event of a dispute. The applicable statute of limitations may be an appropriate period to keep such a record.[14] For example, if the applicable statute of limitations for a claim based on a written contract is ten years, a party should keep a record of the contract for at least ten years from the latest date on which either party fulfilled its last obligation under the contract.

Computer systems should be configured so as to retain electronic records for as long as needed. Some e-mail software, for example, does not automatically create a permanent record of a message once it is sent. The e-mail software may place the record of the message in a temporary log, but eventually the log copy is overwritten by more recent messages. With electronic communications, a system administrator may need to configure the system to retain a permanent record of outgoing communications automatically.

5.3.3 Records Destruction

Records destruction is as important as records retention. Records have a limited useful life and should be routinely destroyed at the end of that life. However, records should be destroyed only in accordance with a systematic, well-documented procedure. In one case, for example, plaintiffs sought various records from the defendant, an aircraft manufacturer. The defendant, however, had directed its engineers to purge certain records that might be detrimental to it in future lawsuits. The defendant claimed that the records were destroyed under an established procedure, but could not produce any evidence to support its claim.[15]

The court entered a $10 million judgment against the defendant without even considering the merits of the case because it believed that the defendant selectively destroyed the records to prevent them from being used in court.[16] In fact, the defendant did have a records-retention program, and the records that were destroyed were duplicates. Another department had maintained the originals. What doomed the defendant was that it had not documented its records-destruction procedures; consequently, its claimed procedures appeared to be a sham.[17]

However, records should not be destroyed, even if they are due to be destroyed according to a records-destruction schedule, if an audit, government investigation, or litigation is imminent or pending. Otherwise, if relevant records are destroyed, the party could be liable for obstruction of justice or be sanctioned. For example, in one case, the defendant destroyed prior versions of source code despite the fact that a lawsuit was pending and the other side had made a discovery request for these versions of the source code.[18] The magistrate imposed monetary sanctions, ordered the defendant to pay the plaintiff's attorney's fees, and ruled that at trial the jury would be instructed that it could infer from defendant's actions that the source code would have revealed information adverse to the defendant's case. This is a serious consequence for a litigant; however, when the court reviewed the magistrate's ruling, it decided the ruling was not harsh enough. The court did not even let the case go before the jury, but entered judgment on the underlying claim against the defendant.[19]

The best defense is to plan well in advance for the possibility of litigation and a discovery request for electronic records by adopting an appropriate records-destruction policy. Adopting and following such a policy will help eliminate any question that records were destroyed because of their value as evidence to an opponent should a business be sued or investigated. Instructions for records disposal should be part of the design of a recordkeeping system and should address issues such as the destruction of confidential or other sensitive information.

Electronic records tend to proliferate and consequently create special records-destruction concerns. With an electronic record, multiple copies or earlier versions of the record could exist in various locations. Therefore, it is important to be sure that all copies, all backups, and any errant copies and versions are also destroyed.

5.4 Long-Term Records Availability

Electronic records should be readily accessible until they are no longer needed.[20] To ensure that electronic records remain available throughout their useful life, certain procedures should be followed systematically to create backup copies, preserve and protect the storage media so that they do not deteriorate and become unusable, and ensure that the records are logically and physically accessible.

5.4.1 Backup Procedures

An effective electronic recordkeeping system should prevent record loss by providing backup and loss recovery procedures. System backups not only provide protection in the event of hardware or software failure or accidental deletions, but also provide protection against unauthorized changes made by an intruder or disgruntled employee. Backups make it easier to restore files to their original form. Backup copies of electronic records should be maintained off-site.[21]

5.4.2 Media Integrity

An important consideration is on which medium electronic records should be stored (e.g., tape, hard disk, optical disc). In general, the medium should be reliable and "fixed" in that it has some permanency.[22] Media integrity is key to establishing the trustworthiness of an electronic record. Thus, it is advisable to:

- Use media that meet industry standards, permit easy storage and retrieval, and will last for the useful life of the records.
- Test storage media before they are used to verify that they are free from defects and are otherwise in compliance with industry standards.[23]
- Follow the media manufacturer's maintenance instructions.
- Store media in an environmentally controlled environment.[24]
- Periodically read a statistical sample of storage media to identify any loss of data. Any media for which errors are found should be replaced, and any lost data should be restored, if possible. Any other media that might have been affected by the same cause of data loss should be read and replaced. If the media are expected to deteriorate over time, the records should be copied onto new media before deterioration is likely.[25]

By ensuring media integrity, records will be available for the duration of their useful life.

5.4.3 Accessibility

Records must not only be preserved, they must also be accessible. *Accessibility* includes both physical and logical accessibility.

Records must be physically accessible. The logistics of record recovery can be troublesome and become even more so after a few years of storage. This is because the creator of a record may have used multiple versions of software over time, and the version it is currently using may not properly match the version used to create that particular record. Not only is it necessary to retain the software used to create documents, such as word processing, spreadsheet, and design software, but copies of the software containing the encryption algorithms and hash functions needed to verify the integrity of digitally signed documents must also be kept. Further complicating matters is the fact that all versions of a translation program may not be available, or all versions of the software and related hardware may not have been maintained with reliable and current documentation. Thus it is necessary either to retain all old hardware, software, and documentation, or to convert electronic records to a compatible format when upgrading or changing data-processing or electronic-communication capabilities.

If records are converted to a new system, their integrity must be checked to ensure that they were not corrupted in the conversion process. Errant characters are sometimes introduced into converted records. It is critical that conversion of preexisting electronic records be considered when planning any changes to a data-processing and electronic-communications environment.

Even if records are physically accessible, they must also be logically accessible. That is, a recordkeeping system must include some sort of indexing or retrieval system. The physical media on which records are stored must be labeled and indexed. Records should also be retrievable through descriptive file names, full or limited text searches, or document-management software. Electronically stored records are of no value if they cannot be located.

5.5 Trustworthiness

Trustworthiness is a universal requirement for keeping records. Because electronic records can be easily, and sometimes undetectably, altered through human, hardware, or software error, an electronic recordkeeping system must address the issue of system security. Otherwise it fails to provide a mechanism for ensuring the integrity of the record and for preventing an opponent from repudiating a record. If a record of a communication can be modified without detection, it has minimal evidentiary value.

To help ensure the security of an electronic recordkeeping system, a business must begin with a security policy that identifies what needs to be protected, the threats to security, critical records and data, and the strategy to be followed in carrying out the security policy. Guided by this policy, the company must then select specific security procedures to implement the policy. The goal of the policy and procedures must be to minimize the risks posed to the trustworthiness of the electronic records by humans and systems.

Security procedures may include physically securing critical communications links, important servers, and other key hardware. When that is not possible—or as an additional safeguard—limiting the number of connections to outside networks and using tools such as firewalls will minimize security breaches.

The use of access controls, such as passwords, is also important. Sophisticated smart cards are an effective alternative to traditional passwords that can be used to help identify authorized users to a system. In one such smart card system, the smart card displays a number to the user that changes over time, but is synchronized with the corresponding authentication software on the system. The user enters the number displayed by the smart card to gain access. Such smart card systems avoid the common problem of users choosing easily guessed passwords or writing passwords on notepads next to their terminals.

For critical records it is advisable to use multiple protection procedures; multiple procedures provide added security. If an access control or another security procedure fails, critical records may still be protected or, at least, alterations to the records will be detectable. For example, sensitive information can be protected from disclosure if it is stored in an encrypted form. Or, although it will not prevent alteration, a message digest of a record generated at the time the record is stored or created can be used to determine whether that record was later altered. If a new message digest generated for the record is not the same as the message digest generated when the record was originally created or stored, this means that the record has been altered.

Periodic system audits are also a useful procedure. An audit provides a means of identifying who has accessed a system (and perhaps tampered with it or a file). An audit also shows how the system is being used by authorized users and attackers as well. An audit trail can verify the security of a system, and if the system is not secure alert a business so that it may remedy discovered vulnerabilities.

Audits, together with system logs, can also show software configuration problems that may affect records. Bugs in computer software or hardware malfunctions can alter the content of electronic records. Software, especially custom software, should be tested to determine the accuracy of its operation. Similarly, a log of computer hardware operations should be routinely kept so that the fact that the hardware was functioning on the particular day when a record was received can be established.

These and many other security procedures, which are beyond the scope of this chapter, are available. Whatever security procedures are used, perhaps the most important aspect of any security program is employee awareness. If employees are not educated to appreciate the risks and trained to follow security procedures, this will seriously undermine the best security program. However, if properly implemented and documented, the use of security procedures should make records verifiably trustworthy and acceptable for any purpose.

5.6 System Documentation

An electronic recordkeeping system should be thoroughly documented. The system documentation should reflect the decisions made about which electronic records will be retained and how long those records will be retained. It should also address backup procedures, hard copy requirements, system security, and availability issues. The system documentation may also address related issues such as implementation and personnel training.

A considered and conscientiously implemented and maintained recordkeeping system will satisfy a company's own business needs for reliable records as well as legal, regulatory, tax, contractual, and evidentiary purposes.

Endnotes

1. *See* Amendment to the Bank Secrecy Act Regulations Relating to Recordkeeping for Funds Transfers and Transmittals by Financial Institutions, 60 Fed. Reg. 220 (1995). For a discussion of this and other new federal recordkeeping regulations for financial institutions, see Robert G. Ballen, Gilbert T. Schwartz & Thomas A. Fox, *Electronic Payments: The New Recordkeeping Regulations,* 112 Banking L.J. 786 (1995).

2. These statutes, rules, and regulations are collected and discussed in Donald S. Skupsky, *Legal Requirements for Business Records: Guide to Record Retention and Recordkeeping Requirements* (1995). This same information is summarized in Donald S. Skupsky, *Recordkeeping Requirements* (1994).

3. *See* Fed. R. Evid. 901 (1995).

4. Dana Blankenhorn, *Building the Tools for Web Commerce,* Interactive Age 34 (Feb. 13, 1995).

5. Donald S. Skupsky, *Recordkeeping Requirements* 9–11 (1994).

6. *See Armstrong v. Executive Office of the President,* 810 F. Supp. 335, 341–42 (D.D.C.), *aff'd in part, rev'd and remanded in part,* 1 F.3d 1274 (D.C. Cir. 1993).

7. *See* Rev. Proc. 91-59 § 5.15, 1991-43 I.R.B. 23.

8. *See* Fed. R. Evid. 901(b)(9) (1995).

9. *See, e.g.,* Rev. Proc. 91–59 § 6.03, 1991-43 I.R.B. 23 ("If hardcopy records are not produced or received in the ordinary course of transacting business (as may be the case when utilizing EDI technology) . . . hardcopy printouts of computerized records need not be created unless requested by the [IRS].") The IRS's guidelines, however, do not relieve a taxpayer of the responsibility to retain hard-copy records that are otherwise required to be retained by other laws or regulations. *See* Rev. Proc. 91-59 § 6.01, 1991-43 I.R.B. 23.

10. *See Armstrong v. Executive Office of the President,* 810 F. Supp. 335 (D.D.C.), *aff'd in part, rev'd and remanded in part,* 1 F.3d 1274 (D.C. Cir. 1993).

11. *See* International Chamber of Commerce, The Uniform Rules of Conduct for Interchange of Trade Data by Teletransmission (UNICID), ICC Pub. No. 452, Art. 10, at 19 (Jan. 1988). *Cf.* National Archives and Records Administration (NARA), 36 C.F.R. § 1234.30 (agencies should keep records for "as long as needed by the Government").

12. *See* Donald S. Skupsky, *Recordkeeping Requirements* 41–44 (1994).

13. 29 C.F.R. § 516.5 (1994).

14. This raises an interesting issue: which jurisdiction's statute of limitations is applicable? Jurisdiction is a concept tied to activities in a particular physical location; consequently, it is frequently unclear which state has jurisdiction over a particular electronic transaction. For a discussion of jurisdiction in a global, online world, see Chapter 23.

15. *Carlucci v. Piper Aircraft Corp.,* 102 F.R.D. 472 (S.D. Fla. 1984).

16. *Carlucci v. Piper Aircraft Corp.,* 102 F.R.D. 472, 486 (S.D. Fla. 1984).

17.   *But see Vick v. Texas Employment Comm'n*, 514 F.2d 734 (5th Cir. 1975) (no adverse decision or inference was drawn from the fact that the defendant had destroyed records related to the plaintiff's unemployment compensation claim; the defendant destroyed the records in accordance with its records retention program before it received notice of the plaintiff's claims).

18.   *Computer Assoc. Int'l, Inc. v. American Fundware*, 133 F.R.D. 166 (D. Colo. 1990).

19.   *Computer Assoc. Int'l, Inc. v. American Fundware, Inc.*, 133 F.R.D. 166 (D. Colo. 1990). *See also Yoffe v. United States*, 153 F.2d 570 (1st Cir. 1946) (the court inferred that discarded records contained information harmful to the defendants who were being audited by the IRS).

20.   *See* Rev. Proc. 91-59 § 5.11, 1991-43 I.R.B. 43; NARA, 36 C.F.R. § 1234.30.

21.   *See* NARA, 36 C.F.R. § 1234.28(f) ("Duplicate copies of permanent or unscheduled records shall be maintained in storage areas separate from the location of the records that have been copied."); Rev. Proc. 91-59 § 5.07, 1991-43 I.R.B. 23. ("back-up copies of machine-sensitive records retained for the [IRS] should be stored at an off-site location").

22.   *See* NARA, 36 C.F.R. § 1234.28.

23.   NARA, 36 C.F.R. § 1234.28(g). *Accord* Rev. Proc. 91-59 § 5.10, 1991-43 I.R.B. 23; Federal Acquisition Regulations (FAR), 48 C.F.R. § 4.703.

24.   *Cf.* NARA, 36 C.F.R. § 1234.28(g). *Accord* Rev. Proc. 91-59 § 5.10, 1991-43 I.R.B. 23 ; FAR, 48 C.F.R. § 4.703.

25.   *Cf.* NARA, 36 C.F.R. § 1234.28.

PART II
ONLINE TRANSACTIONS

6

Creating Contracts Online

Elizabeth S. Perdue

The ability to create and enforce contracts is essential to a commercial society. By contracting online, businesses can improve efficiencies, reduce paperwork, and streamline their operations. At the same time, however, new technologies create challenges for the legal system, which must try to apply existing law in a new context.

Take, for example, the following hypothetical e-mail exchange:

A to B: "Send us 2 dozen widgets. Usual terms. We need delivery by this Friday."

B to A: "Thanks for your order. We will deliver as requested."

Similar exchanges can occur through Web sites and online services, electronic data interchange, and other online methods.

Can the above exchange create a contract? Certainly. But several legal issues arise, many of which are the same as those encountered in traditional contracts: What are the exact terms of the contract? Is it enforceable? What happens if a message is garbled or sent in error? What if one of the messages was unauthorized or sent by an impostor? The following sections will analyze these and other contract issues as they arise in the online context.

6.1 How Can Contracts Be Formed Online?

Contracts can be formed by oral or written agreement. They can also be implied by conduct of the parties. And, with the advent of online communications, they can be formed electronically.

An *online contract* is a contract created wholly or in part through communications over computer networks.[1] Thus, contracts can be created by e-mail, through Web sites, via electronic data interchange, and other techniques.

6.1.1 Contracts Formed via E-Mail, Web Sites, and Online Services

By exchanging e-mail communications, parties can create a valid contract. Offers and acceptances may be exchanged entirely by e-mail, or they can be made by a combination of electronic communications, paper documents, faxes, and oral discussions.

Contracts may also be formed via Web sites and other online services. For example, a Web site may advertise goods or services for sale, which the customer may order by completing and transmitting an order form displayed on screen. Once the order is accepted by the vendor, a contract is formed. The goods and services may then be physically delivered offline, or in the case of software or other digital content, may be electronically delivered to the customer directly from the vendor's computer. In the case of electronic distribution, the parties may enter into a user license online, which will govern the customer's rights to use the content.

Finally, a contract can be formed by online conduct. For example, when a company offers software or other content online, and a user downloads it, it is possible for a contract to exist even without any formal agreement.

6.1.2 Electronic Data Interchange (EDI)

Electronic Data Interchange, or *EDI*, is the direct electronic exchange of routine business information between computers in a computer-processable format. The data is formatted using standard protocols so that it can be implemented directly by the receiving computer. EDI is often used to transmit standard purchase orders, acceptances, invoices, and other records. These exchanges are sometimes made pursuant to master written agreements between the parties, known as *trading partner agreements*. With or without trading partner agreements, EDI exchanges can create enforceable contracts.

EDI transactions typically are conducted by parties with a continuing business relationship, who wish to structure their commercial transactions more efficiently. For example, without EDI, a buyer generates a paper purchase order, which is mailed to the seller who then manually enters it on its computer. The seller's acknowledgment is sent and manually entered by the buyer. The process is repeated for billing and remittances. All of these steps take time, duplicate steps, create paper, and involve numerous opportunities for human error. By having computers "talk" directly to each other in the first place, these inefficiencies can be reduced.

EDI messages are composed of sets of formatted data called *transaction sets*. For example, if a buyer wishes to order goods from a seller, it initiates a purchase order transaction set with the necessary information. The data is formatted in a standardized manner previously agreed to by the parties, so that it can be processed directly by the receiving computer.[2] The transaction set can either be communicated directly to the seller's system or to a designated third party who is responsible for logging the transaction set, confirming its source, and transmitting it to the seller.

The receiving computer will usually check to see that the message was received in the proper format—for example, that all fields are completed, and that numbers and recognizable codes appear in the appropriate places. The receiving computer then confirms receipt by sending back a transaction set, known as a *functional acknowledgment*. When the purchase order itself is accepted, another transaction set will be sent, usually in the form of a purchase order acknowledgment. In some cases, for example, the seller's computer may be programmed to automatically accept certain orders, such as those within a certain dollar range. An invoice can also be transmitted electronically, completing the loop.

EDI has many uses other than buying and selling goods. For example, insurance claims, tax forms, and inventory information are often transmitted and processed electronically by direct exchange of data between computers. When EDI is combined with electronic funds transfer procedures to facilitate payment and accounting, it is referred to as *financial EDI*. Electronic payments and financial EDI are discussed in Chapter 7.

Transactions in EDI raise a number of legal and practical issues, including security issues, choice of protocols, and allocation of risks of error.[3] These are best resolved in a master trading partner agreement, which the parties enter into at the outset of the relationship. Several model trading partner agreements exist, which can be adapted to the parties' specific needs.[4] Even without a trading partner agreement, however, a contract is still formed through the electronic exchanges themselves.

6.1.3 Other Forms of Electronic Contracts

Online technology is changing rapidly, and it can be expected to accommodate a wide variety of online contracting techniques. For example, contracts may be formed through interactive telephone systems, such as orders entered through an automated Touch-Tone system.[5] Interactive television, when perfected, may also become a source of electronic contracting. Online business agencies may enable buyers and sellers to negotiate contracts online in a global forum, subject to the forum's private set of rules.[6]

The legal issues relating to these and other forms of online contracts are discussed in the following sections.

6.2 Online Offers and Acceptances

A contract may be made in any manner sufficient to show agreement, including offer and acceptance, or conduct that recognizes the existence of a contract.[7] Typically, a contract is formed when one party makes an offer that is accepted by the other party.[8]

6.2.1 Online Offers

Contract offers may be made orally, in writing, or by conduct. There is no reason why an electronically transmitted offer should be any less effective than an oral or written one.[9] To be valid, an offer must communicate to the person receiving it that, once the offer is accepted, a contract is created.[10]

For example, when a vendor advertises goods for sale to the public, the vendor is generally not considered to be making an offer, but is merely inviting others to make offers.[11] The buyer who orders goods in response to an advertisement is making the offer to buy. Until the buyer's offer is accepted, there is no contract. Otherwise a vendor could be bound by all orders it receives, which could require shipments greatly in excess of supply.

In the online context, a Web site or other online service that displays product information should be treated like a general advertisement. Once the buyer transmits an order, it must be accepted before there will be a contract.

6.2.2 Online Acceptances: E-Mail, Mouseclicks, and Other Methods

An offer may be accepted "in any manner and by any medium reasonable in the circumstances."[12] Typical offline acceptances would include written and oral communications, as well as acceptance by conduct. Their online counterparts would be acceptance by e-mail or other form of electronic message, and by conduct such as clicking on a button or downloading content.

Will the courts consider acceptance by e-mail to be a reasonable practice? If an offer is made by e-mail, one should be able to accept it by the same means.[13] But what if the offer was made by some other method, such as letter or fax? An acceptance does not necessarily have to be sent the same way as the offer.[14] However, because of the special attributes of e-mail, the courts will probably decide each case based on the circumstances.[15] To be certain, it is best to confirm the other person's customary practice before assuming that e-mail responses are appropriate for offers made via another medium.

What about conduct such as using a mouse to click on a button, entering a symbol or code, or downloading content? Will these be considered proper ways of accepting an online offer? They should be, if the offer invites acceptance in this manner. As a general rule, contracts can be created and accepted by conduct, if reasonable under the circumstances.[16] Contracts can be accepted by a nod of the head or shaking hands, sending a check, sending a purchase order, shipping goods, or the act of taking product off a shelf.[17] One can even accept a shrinkwrap license by opening the package, in some circumstances.[18] Mere silence by itself will generally not create a contract.[19] However, the types of actions typically involved in online transactions—actions such as clicking or downloading—are more deliberate than mere silence, and should be proper forms of acceptance, depending on the situation.[20]

6.2.3 Offers and Acceptances by Computer

Can the act of a computer (without human involvement) create a contract? The answer should be yes, depending on the circumstances.

A computer can generate an offer. For example, an inventory system can calculate when supplies are low, and automatically generate an electronic purchase order to the vendor. Would such an order be a binding offer? Although there are not yet any cases directly on point, one case has upheld the validity of a computer-generated insurance renewal.[21] The court, reasoning that the computer operates only in accordance with the information and directions supplied by its programmers, held that the insurance company was bound by the computer-generated renewal notice.

Under pending draft revisions to the U.C.C., computer-generated offers would be valid. Electronic messages could form a contract, even if not actually seen or reviewed by a human.[22]

Acceptances can also be generated by computer. However, they will be analyzed the same way their human-generated counterparts are analyzed—is the message an acceptance or merely an acknowledgment of receipt? In most cases the answer to this question will depend on the nature of the response. For example, in a case involving a computer order entry system, orders were placed by Touch-Tone phone and the system automatically generated a tracking number for each order. When the seller refused to fill the buyer's order, the buyer sued. The court held that no contract had been created, since the tracking number was merely for administrative convenience, and not a clear acceptance.[23]

This issue will certainly arise in EDI transactions, where a computer can automatically acknowledge receipt of an electronic purchase order by means of a functional acknowledgment. However, this type of acknowledgment means only that the computer received the message in a form it could read.[24] It does not mean that the order was accepted unless the parties have agreed to give it that effect. More typically, an EDI purchase order would be accepted by a purchase-order acknowledgment.

6.2.4 Timing of Acceptances: The Mailbox Rule

Timing of acceptances can be important in determining if there is a binding contract. That is because an offer can generally be revoked if it has not yet been accepted.[25] What happens if the person who made the offer revokes it, but the other party's acceptance is already in the mail? Under the U.S. "mailbox" rule there would be a contract. The acceptance would take effect as soon as it was out of the sender's control, if it was sent in a manner and by a medium invited by the offer.[26]

It appears that the mailbox rule will not be applied to electronic acceptances, however. The mailbox rule applies to mail and telegraph, but not to communications that are essentially instantaneous, such as telephone and telex.[27] Pending draft revisions to the U.C.C. reject the mailbox rule for electronic communications.[28]

6.3 The Requirement of a Signed Writing: The Statute of Frauds

As a general rule, contracts do not have to be in writing or signed by either party. They may be created by oral agreement, and even by conduct. However, under the statute of frauds, certain categories of contracts cannot be enforced unless they are evidenced by a signed writing.[29] These include contracts for the sale of goods valued at over $500, and contracts that are not capable of being performed within one year.[30] In addition, some contracts require all amendments and notices to be in writing; similar requirements appear in certain statutes.[31]

For contracts formed online, the traditional form of a writing (paper) and the traditional handwritten signature do not exist. So how can online contracts meet these legal requirements?

6.3.1 The Writing Requirement

When the statute of frauds applies, there must be a writing sufficient to indicate that a contract has been made between the parties.[32] As discussed in this section, electronic transmissions recorded in a tangible form should meet the writing requirement.

The definition of a *writing* is not limited to ink on paper. Rather, the essence of the requirement is that the communication be reduced to a tangible form.[33] As early as 1869, a New Hampshire court found a telegraphed contract to be a sufficient writing under the statute of frauds, stating:

> [i]t makes no difference whether that operator writes the offer or the acceptance . . . with a steel pen an inch long attached to an ordinary penholder, or whether his pen be a copper wire a thousand miles long. In either case the thought is communicated to the paper by use of the finger resting upon the pen; nor does it make any difference that in one case common record ink is used, while in the other case a more subtle fluid, known as electricity, performs the same office.[34]

The courts have also found telexes, Western Union Mailgrams, and even tape recordings to be writings under the statute of frauds.[35] Faxes have been assumed (without express decision) to be writings under the statute of frauds.[36] Magnetic recordings of data on computer disks have been held to constitute "writings" for purposes other than the statute of frauds, including under forgery statutes.[37]

Electronic transmissions recorded in a tangible medium should therefore be deemed to satisfy the writing requirement.[38] Some electronic transmissions, however, are so ephemeral that they would probably not be considered writings. These might include e-mail that is not printed out or kept in a computer log, communications on "chat lines" or electronic bulletin boards (unless printed out or kept by the systems administrator), and EDI transaction sets that are not kept in a separate log.[39] It will probably be necessary to preserve records of such communications if they are to be treated as writings.[40]

6.3.2 The Signature Requirement

Generally, a signature is "any symbol executed or adopted by a party with present intention to authenticate a writing."[41] Thus, a signature need not be ink on paper—rather, the issue is what the signer intended.

The courts have found many symbols to be signatures under the statute of frauds: names on telegrams,[42] names on telexes,[43] typewritten names,[44] names on Western Union Mailgrams,[45] and even names on letterhead.[46] Faxed signatures have been assumed to constitute effective signatures, under nonstatute of frauds cases.[47]

Thus a symbol or code on an electronic record, intended as a signature, should meet the statute of frauds.[48] Digital signatures should certainly do so. Both the draft ABA *Digital Signature Guidelines* and the Utah Digital Signature Act provide that a digital signature will meet any legal requirement for a signature.[49]

In the future, the statute of frauds may become a moot issue, at least for contracts involving sales of goods. At this writing, draft revisions to the U.C.C. Article 2 propose that the statute of frauds be eliminated. [50]

In international transactions involving the sale of goods, the statute of frauds should not apply. The major treaty governing international sales of goods specifies that no writing or signature is required.[51]

6.4 What Are the Terms of the Online Contract?

The parties to a contract do not always clearly address all of the contract terms. Terms may be missing or unclear, or the parties may have exchanged conflicting documents. In these cases, what are the terms of the contract?

6.4.1 General Principles

Generally, the terms of a contract will include:

1. The terms the parties have agreed to in their discussions and writings,
2. Terms implied by their present and past conduct,[52]
3. Terms implied by industry custom and practice,[53] and
4. Terms implied by law, such as standard U.C.C. warranties and remedies[54] (referred to as "U.C.C. gap fillers").

For example, say the parties agree that the seller will sell 100 widgets to the buyer for $100. That creates a contract. The other terms, such as delivery, warranties, and the like, can all be implied. The court may even be able to imply a missing price term.[55]

In many cases, the parties exchange form documents that may contain inconsistent or different terms. For example, a buyer sends a form purchase order, the seller accepts it with a form containing different terms, and the goods are shipped and paid for. This is the classic "battle of the forms." A contract has clearly been formed, but whose terms control? For contracts involving the sale of goods, the new terms in an acceptance will become part of the contract in some circumstances.[56] For other types of contracts, the party sending the "last shot" will prevail.[57] Pending draft revisions to the U.C.C. would modify the law on battle of the forms, both for contracts involving the sale of goods as well as for transactions in intangibles such as software and digital content.[58]

6.4.2 Examples

To illustrate the above principles in action, consider the following online contract situations:

- **Contracts Negotiated by E-Mail.** The terms of contracts negotiated by e-mail should be interpreted no differently than those in writing. If there is a dispute, a court will look to the party's writings, conduct, industry customs, and U.C.C. gap-fillers to establish the terms of the contract.
- **Contracts Via Web Sites and Other Online Services.** Many businesses sell goods and services online; the customer completes a pre-set order form and transmits it back to the seller. The contract is formed when the company accepts the order—whether by sending an acknowledgment, delivering goods, or billing the customer.

Here again, the analysis should be no different than for transactions by traditional means. The major difference is practical—the terms of the initial purchase order are within the vendor's control. The hope is that an "electronic battle of the forms" can be averted, reducing the potential for disputes. Unfortunately, there is no guarantee that businesses will stop exchanging conflicting forms.

Web sites and online services may try to impose contract terms on the user by displaying terms and conditions online, and stating that the user is deemed to accept them by continuing to use the service or access the site. Issues created by such contract terms are discussed in Section 6.4.3.

- **Contracts for Downloading Digital Content.** Vendors may offer software and other digital content to users, for immediate delivery online. Contracts governing such transactions are generally formed in one of three ways:

  1. Using one approach, the vendor can present the license terms so that the user has an opportunity to review them and must accept them affirmatively before downloading. In this case, the terms should be enforceable if accepted.
  2. Alternatively, license terms may scroll across the screen, stating that the customer is deemed to accept them by using or installing the software. This approach is similar to an online shrinkwrap license; it is discussed in Section 6.4.3.
  3. Finally, digital content may be made available for downloading without express contract restrictions of any kind.[59] Will the law imply any other terms? In these situations, courts may look to the prior course of dealing between the parties as well as to industry custom and practice. For example, if the user downloads an updated version of software that he or she had previously licensed, a court might extend the prior license terms to the update.

- **Contracts by Electronic Data Interchange.** In EDI transactions, computers exchange formatted documents such as purchase orders and acknowledgments electronically, often with little or no human intervention. While the transaction sets contain basic information such as quantity and price, they generally do not contain detailed terms such as warranties, limitations of liability, or remedies. In some cases the parties agree on such detailed terms in a trading partner agreement entered into at the outset of the relationship. The terms of the EDI contract should be those agreed to in the trading partner agreement (if any), plus those terms on which the EDI messages agree, plus U.C.C. gap-fillers.[60]

One area that may raise unique problems in EDI transactions is the use of "free text." Most EDI exchanges must occur in pre-arranged formats, which leaves little room for nonstandard terms. However, additional terms can be inserted in areas reserved for "free text." If a party adds terms using the free text fields, do they become part of the contract?

A trading partner agreement can address the issue of free text directly. However, where there is no trading partner agreement, the outcome is not clear under current law. It may depend on whether a court considers a free text entry to have been duly sent, received, and accepted.[61]

Under pending draft revisions to the U.C.C., conflicting terms would cancel each other out, unless the parties have expressly agreed to them.[62] Thus, conflicting terms added as free text in an EDI message might not be included in the contract, depending on the nature of the message.

6.4.3 Shrinkwrap and Webwrap Contracts

A shrinkwrap license is a familiar vehicle for licensing software distributed in physical form such as a diskette or CD-ROM. Typically the software is delivered in a package or envelope that contains certain license terms printed on the outside. The customer does not sign an agreement. However, the license terms state that by opening the package or using the software the customer is accepting the shrinkwrap terms.

The cases interpreting shrinkwrap licenses have generally held them to be unenforceable. This is because the license terms were not presented until after the customer had already entered into the sale contract (for example, through an accepted telephone order or off-the-shelf purchase). Thus the shrinkwrap terms were considered an unenforceable attempt by the vendor to modify the contract after the fact.[63] However the case law indicates that a properly structured shrinkwrap license can be enforceable—for example, if the shrinkwrap terms are presented before the sale is made.[64]

Under proposed revisions to the U.C.C., the current law on shrinkwrap licenses would be changed.[65] Rather than focusing on the timing of the contract, these provisions would focus on whether the user manifested assent to the terms after having had an opportunity to review them. Thus a shrinkwrap license[66] would be enforceable if (1) the user has the opportunity to review the terms,[67] (2) the terms conspicuously state what type of affirmative conduct is required for acceptance, and (3) the user manifests assent by taking such conduct after having the opportunity not to do so.[68] What type of "affirmative conduct" will be sufficient to manifest assent? It seems clear that, under the draft rules, hitting a return key or entering code would constitute assent, but merely retaining possession would not.[69]

Shrinkwrap concepts will also be relevant in many online transactions. For example, an online publisher of software or other digital content may want to impose restrictions on its users. To do this, the publisher may display terms and conditions on screens along with the content, stating that the user is deemed to accept the terms by using or downloading the content. Similarly, a number of Web sites contain a statement at the bottom of the homepage screen, or even on a separate screen that is linked to the homepage, setting forth certain restrictions, such as limitations on liability, terms and conditions of access and use of the Web page, and disclaimers of warranties.[70]

These types of online shrinkwrap contracts (sometimes referred to as "webwraps")[71] would be enforceable under proposed U.C.C. revisions as currently drafted, as long as they are properly structured.[72] The terms should be presented in a manner designed to call the user's attention to them, and the user must be required to take some sort of affirmative conduct to indicate acceptance. For example, license terms or warranty disclaimers should not be hidden away behind obscure hypertext links or file names. Rather, they should be conspicuously referenced, and the user should be conspicuously notified that a specific action (such as hitting a return key) constitutes assent to the terms. If a Web site has multiple pages, the license or other terms should be referenced on each page. Ideally a user should be required to view the terms and click on an "accept" button before proceeding.

Until the pending U.C.C. revisions are finalized, some courts may continue to apply the analysis used in previous shrinkwrap license cases. Under that analysis, enforceability would turn, at least in part, on whether the shrinkwrap or webwrap terms were presented before or after a contract was made. Thus, some contracts that might pass muster under the pending U.C.C. revisions may not be enforced under the present case law, and vice versa.

6.4.4 Warranties

Businesses that engage in selling goods should already be familiar with the concept of implied warranties. Basically, any contract for the sale of goods contains certain implied warranties. These include a warranty that the goods are fit for their ordinary purposes and will pass without objection in the trade (known as the "warranty of merchantibility")[73] and a warranty that the goods are fit for the buyer's purposes, where the seller has reason to know those purposes and that the buyer is relying on the seller's judgment (known as the "warranty of fitness for a particular purpose").[74] These implied warranties will continue to apply to online contracts for sales of goods.

In addition to implied warranties, a seller can make express warranties by making statements about its products or services and how they will perform.[75] A warranty can exist even if the word "warranty" is not used. Thus, businesses should be careful about the statements made on their Web sites or other online information, to either avoid making unrealistic warranties or to disclaim them properly. A seller who provides a sample or demonstration copy may be deemed to warrant that the goods will conform to the sample.[76] Those who provide demonstration or evaluation copies of software or other digital content should be aware of the warranties they are making by such activity.

To exclude or limit implied and express warranties, they must be disclaimed in a conspicuous manner.[77] Standards for conspicuousness in contracts made online are discussed in the following section.

Contracts involving intangibles, such as rights in digital content and information, may soon be subject to implied warranties as well. Under draft Article 2B to the U.C.C., new implied warranties are being proposed, including a warranty of the licensor's right to license intangibles, a warranty that computer programs will comply with written specifications or will be merchantible, and a warranty of reasonable care and workmanlike effort in collecting and providing data and services relating to intangibles.[78]

6.4.5 Conspicuousness

Certain types of contract terms must be "conspicuous" to be effective. For example, in contracts for the sale of goods, warranty disclaimers must be conspicuous.[79]

Under pending draft revisions to the U.C.C., a term is conspicuous if it is so displayed or presented that a reasonable person would likely have noticed it. Language that is in capital letters, larger or contrasting type, or contrasting color would be considered conspicuous.[80]

The draft U.C.C. revisions also make allowance for devices such as Web page hypertext links and other cross references. Thus, for example, if a Web page included a conspicuous reference to "WARRANTY DISCLAIMER," and the text of the disclaimer were available by clicking on the word, that should meet the conspicuousness requirement.[81] However, if a warranty disclaimer were hidden behind a link entitled "additional product information," it would probably not be conspicuous.

Finally, the draft U.C.C. revisions provide a separate definition of conspicuousness for an electronic message intended to evoke a response without the need for review by a human. This would apply in most EDI exchanges. In those cases, a term is conspicuous if it is in a form that would enable the recipient or the recipient's computer to take it into account or react to it without human review.[82] Thus, for example, a warranty disclaimer included in a free text segment of an EDI transaction set might not be sufficiently conspicuous.

6.5 Mistakes in Electronic Communications

Mistakes in electronic transmission can occur because of (1) physical problems in networks and other communications systems, (2) programming errors, or (3) human errors. A flaw in a computer program, or environmental or faulty conditions in a network, can result in the recipient receiving information that is different from the information the sender sent. On the human side, the person entering information may make a typographical error, or may unintentionally click on the wrong button. Given the speed and ephemeral nature of electronic communications, it may be more difficult to catch such errors than it is in traditional paper transactions.

For example, consider a buyer who intended to order 1,000 widgets. Due to a typographical error in sending an e-mail, the buyer orders 10,000 widgets. In such a case, was a contract ever formed? Who bears the risk of mistakes?

The law regarding the role of mistakes in contracts is complex. Historically, courts tried to differentiate between mutual mistakes (where both parties are mistaken) and unilateral mistakes (where only one party is mistaken).[83] However, most courts now recognize that it is difficult to categorize mistakes this way. In addition, it is not always fair to penalize one party for a mistake when the result would be a windfall for the other.

Thus, the treatment of mistakes will depend on (1) how far along the parties are in the transaction, (2) whether it would be oppressive to hold the mistaken party to the contract, and (3) whether the other party would be unduly harmed if the contract were not enforced.[84] For example, if the above buyer discovered his or her mistaken widget order before the seller relied on it, the court would be likely to cancel the contract rather than giving the seller a windfall. However, if the shipment had already been sent, the contract would be likely to stand unless the seller knew of the error.

Errors may be made by intermediaries. For example, in one case a telegraph company transmitted the wrong price term by dropping a digit.[85] The court enforced the correct price, because the other party had reason to know of the error. The majority of courts have placed the risk of error on the sender unless the other party had reason to know of the error.[86]

The pending draft revisions to the U.C.C. specifically address the risk of an intermediary's error in an electronic communication. The risk would be placed on the sender, unless the recipient should have discovered the error by the exercise of reasonable care, or unless the recipient failed to use an agreed-upon authentication system.[87]

The parties can and should contractually allocate risks of error between themselves. One approach might be to define a commercially acceptable security procedure and place the risk of mistake on the party that fails to follow it. This is the approach taken in U.C.C. Article 4A, which governs electronic funds transfers.[88]

6.6 Impostors and Persons Without Authority

Everyone is concerned about identity and authority in electronic communications. Reports of fraudulent computer schemes make headline news. For example, a 15-year-old boy was apparently able to bilk $10,000 out of Internet users by establishing an online account under a false name, taking orders, and arranging for empty boxes to be delivered COD.[89] However, fraud and lack of authority exist in traditional transactions as well. Online technology may create new opportunities for misuse, but it also provides new tools to combat it.

Issues of identity and authority generally fall into two categories: (1) Impostors who fraudulently pose as someone else (or as a fictitious person), and (2) Individuals who lack actual authority to bind their employers. These issues are discussed separately below.

6.6.1 Impostors

When contracting electronically, it is important to know the true identity of the party on the other end of the message. A user can easily adopt a pseudonym online. Someone can also send electronic messages and make them appear to come from someone else.[90]

For those who want to engage in online contracting, two major issues arise: (1) How can you be sure that the person with whom you are communicating is the person he or she claims to be? and (2) Can an impersonator bind you to an electronic contract?

The first issue—confirming identity—is not new to online communications. Impostors operate in paper transactions, and even in face-to-face ones. A related concern, of course, is whether the other party is creditworthy and able to perform. That is why for large transactions, businesses rely on tried and true techniques for verification, including personal references, business and credit references, corporate certificates, and notarized documents. These techniques will no doubt continue, depending on the size of the transaction.

What is different about online transactions? The principal difference is the ease by which the technology permits impostors to operate without extensive investment. But the same technology also provides verification techniques that surpass those available on paper. For example, a digital signature can provide assurance that the communication was sent by a known party and not an impostor[91] (see Chapter 4). As an added benefit, the recipient also knows that what it received is what was sent, without alteration.

The second issue—whether an innocent party can be bound by an impostor's electronic communication—is of particular interest to those considering electronic commerce. And the electronic rules may differ from the traditional ones. Under present law, for example, the signature of a forger will not bind the impersonated party; it will bind only the forger.[92] Exceptions exist if the innocent party ratifies the signature, or if its negligence substantially contributed to the forgery.[93] For example, if someone is negligent in maintaining security for his or her automated signature machine, that person may be bound if the machine is misused.

Pending draft revisions to the U.C.C. would allocate risks of forgery in electronic communications using rules similar in part to those now used for electronic fund transfers. If adopted, the rules would permit the recipient of an electronic message to attribute it to the party shown as the sender, if:

1. The recipient followed an agreed-upon security procedure, and based on that procedure concluded that the message came from the person shown as the sender, or
2. The impostor had a relationship with the impersonated party, which enabled the impostor to gain access to and use the method that the impersonated party uses to identify data messages as its own.[94]

Thus, if this proposal is adopted, one could be bound by an unauthorized message in some circumstances. For example, if an employee or former employee had access to a company's e-mail system and its passwords and generated messages purporting to come from the company president, the company could be bound by these messages, perhaps even without any showing of negligence.[95]

6.6.2 Persons Without Authority To Contract

Although stories of forgery and impostors make good press, they are still the exception rather than the norm. More often, businesses will face the issue of having negotiated a contract only to find out that the person they were dealing with on the other side did not have the proper authority. For example, a contract may be signed by a representative on behalf of a company, and the company may later claim not to be bound because the representative lacked authority. Similar issues will arise in online contracts.

How can a business verify that the person it is dealing with online has actual authority to bind a company? That business can apply the same techniques that are used with paper contracts now. Verifying authority occurs through personal and business contacts, reviewing public information, and requiring corporate certificates and resolutions. This can be costly and time consuming, however, and is not warranted in most smaller transactions, be they online or off.

Even if a person lacks actual authority, a contract may still exist if he or she had "apparent authority." *Apparent authority* means that a person has been vested by the entity with sufficient "indicia" of authority that others would reasonably believe that he or she does indeed have authority.[96] For example, if a company provides a representative with company business cards and letterhead, the company switchboard directs calls to that person, and the company's literature refers to the person as Director of Purchasing, the person has the apparent authority to purchase goods. Even if the person does not have actual authority, the company will be bound by his or her purchase orders. It may not be reasonable, however, to assume that the same person has authority to negotiate a corporate merger.

What indicia will create apparent authority in purely online transactions? This is not clear. If no business cards, letterhead, phone calls, or personal visits are exchanged, the only indicators of someone's authority may be the fact that he or she purports to have a corporate e-mail address, and purports to hold the title of president. This may not suffice. However, other actions may clothe the person with apparent authority. For example, information on a Web site or in other company communications may clothe the person with apparent authority.[97] In addition, digital signatures may, under some systems, provide an opportunity for verification of the message sender's authority as well as his or her identity. For example, depending on the scope of a certification, a certification authority may be able to certify not only the identity of the person holding the designated public key, but also that person's title and capacity.[98]

6.7 Whose Law Applies?

The above discussion focuses on general principles of U.S. law. However, the laws applicable to the formation and enforcement of contracts vary from state to state and from country to country. If a dispute arises under a contract between citizens of different states or countries, and if the pertinent law is not the same in both places, whose law will the court apply to resolve the dispute? The answer to this question falls within the scope of a body of law known as "conflict of laws" or, simply, "choice of law."

The analysis of choice of law issues arising out of contracts entered into online is not likely to differ greatly from the analysis that applies to more conventional contracts. As a result, established choice of law principles should suffice in most cases.

The parties can avoid uncertainty over this issue by specifying in the contract whose law will control in the event of a dispute. Such a choice of law provision will be enforced by a U.S. court unless (1) the law chosen "has no substantial relationship to the parties or the transaction" or (2) application of the law of the chosen state "would be contrary to a fundamental policy of a state which has a materially greater interest" in the resolution of the dispute and whose law would control in the absence of an agreement otherwise.[99] However, in consumer leases of tangible property, a choice of law provision will not be enforced unless it specifies the state of the lessee's residence.[100] In addition, pending drafts of new Article 2B to the U.C.C. would apply a different choice of law rules, including rules more favorable to consumers.[101]

The law selected by the parties to a commercial transaction will usually meet the "substantial relationship" requirement, and will rarely interfere with a truly fundamental policy of another interested state.[102] As a result, in a dispute between U.S. citizens arising out of a commercial transaction it is unusual for the agreed law not to be applied.[103] A choice of law agreement will also be enforced by U.S. courts in disputes between U.S. and foreign citizens, although the chance of the party's agreement being rejected on public policy grounds is probably greater in that context than it is in the context of a purely domestic transaction.[104] As noted above, however, consumer transactions may be treated differently in some cases.

If the parties have not agreed on a choice of law, a court will make the decision for them. As a general rule, the law of the jurisdiction that has the "most significant relationship to the transaction and the parties" with respect to the issue in dispute will control.[105] The jurisdiction having the "most significant relationship" is determined based on an analysis of a variety of factors, including:

- the place of contracting[106]
- the place the contract was negotiated[107]
- the place of performance[108]
- the location of the "subject matter" of the contract, and
- the domicile, residence, nationality, place of incorporation and place of business of the parties.[109]

A similar analysis is applied by U.S. courts when a transaction is international. Thus, for example, a U.S. court applied French law to a contract when two of the contracting parties were French and all of the negotiations occurred in France.[110] But a U.S. court refused to apply Liberian law to a contract between a California company and a Liberian company, where there was no showing that application of Liberian law would further the interests of the foreign state.[111]

What happens if a foreign court is making the decision about choice of law? The U.S. conflict of laws principles will not apply; rather, the foreign court will apply its own rules. However, many transactions involving the international sale of goods are governed by the Convention on the International Sale of Goods, which can greatly lessen the risk of conflict.[112] The CIGS is not a panacea, however, and U.S. citizens who engage in international transactions are well-advised to obtain advice from competent legal counsel regarding ways the foreign country's laws could affect the resolution of a dispute, and, as with purely domestic transactions, to include choice of law provisions in their agreements whenever possible.

Endnotes

1. Some articles on "electronic contracts" use the term to refer solely to electronic data interchange (EDI), described later in this section. This book treats EDI as only one of many forms of electronic contracting.

2. The formats may be established under a trading partner agreement between the parties, or by adoption of an agreed-upon standard. Typical EDI standards include the ANSI X12 Standard, developed by the American National Standards Institute, the EDIFACT Standard, developed by the United Nations, and the NIST Standard, developed by the National Institute of Standards and Technology.

3. For further discussion of EDI, see ABA Electronic Messaging Services Task Force, *The Commercial Use of Electronic Data Interchange—A Report and Model Trading Agreement*, 45 Business Lawyer 1645 (June 1990)("ABA Model"); Wright, *The Law of Electronic Commerce* (2d Ed. 1995); Baum and Perritt, *Electronic Contracting, Publishing and EDI Law* (1991).

4. *See, e.g.,* ABA Electronic Messaging Services Task Force, *The Commercial Use of Electronic Data Interchange—A Report and Model Trading Agreement*, 45 Business Lawyer 1645 (June 1990); EDI Association of the United Kingdom, *Standard Electronic Data Interchange Agreement*, 6 Computer Law & Practice No. 2 at 65 (1989); International Chamber of Commerce, *Uniform Rules of Conduct for Interchange of Trade Data by Teletransmission* (1988).

5. *See Corinthian Pharmaceutical Systems, Inc. v. Lederle Labs*, 724 F. Supp. 605 (S.D. Ind. 1989); *Electronic Marketplace*, Electronic Com. Bull. 8 (Oct. 1992); *Fax Pump Melds Fax, Call Processing Capabilities*, Network World, May 27, 1991, at 29, col. 2.

6. *See On-Line Service to Assist Global Trade*, Wall St. J., Sept. 26, 1995 at B10 611 (AT&T, Dun & Bradstreet, and others forming a joint venture for a virtual business agency.)

7. U.C.C. § 2-204. The principal statute in the United States relating to contracts is Article 2 of the Uniform Commercial Code ("U.C.C."), which applies to transactions in sales of goods. It has also been generally applied to sales and licenses of software. See cases cited at National Conference of Commissioners on Uniform State Laws, Draft U.C.C. Article 2B at v, note 7 (Dec. 1, 1995 draft). Because it is a good statement of general contract law, the U.C.C. is also often referred to in non-goods cases.

    Article 2 of the U.C.C. is currently being revised to reflect changes in business practices and to add provisions relating to electronic communications. A new article 2B is also being proposed that will cover licensing of software and other digital content. Presently the revisions are in the drafting stage, for consideration by the National Conference of Commissioners on State Uniform Laws (N.C.C.U.S.L.). The draft revisions to Article 2 dated October 1, 1995, and the draft of Article 2B dated December 1, 1995 are the ones referenced in this book. Once revisions are approved by the N.C.C.U.S.L. they will become effective only when adopted into law at the state level.

8. The other basic element required to create an enforceable contract is consideration—something of value, which need not be money, must be given or promised.

9. Draft U.C.C. §§ 2B-204 and 2B-205 (February 2, 1996 draft) and draft U.C.C. § 2-208 (October 1, 1995 draft) all expressly provide for contracts formed by electronic communications.

10. *See Restatement (Second) of Contracts* § 24 (1979).

11. *See Mesaros v. United States*, 845 F.2d 1576 (Fed. Cir. 1988) (United States Mint's advertisement of commemorative coins not an offer, but an invitation for offers), and authorities cited therein.

12. U.C.C. § 2-206(1)(a).

13.	It is well established that an acceptance may properly be sent by the same means as the offer, unless the offer says otherwise. *See Restatement (Second) of Contracts* § 65 (1979).

14.	*See, e.g., Market Development Corp. v. Flame-Glo, Ltd.,* 1990 WL 116319 (E.D. Pa. 1990) (mailed offer accepted by fax).

15.	For example, if the parties have regularly corresponded in the past by e-mail, an e-mail acceptance will probably be effective. However, in some cases a person may have an e-mail address that he or she rarely uses or does not monitor. In that case, it may not be appropriate to send an acceptance to that person by e-mail when the offer was made via a different medium.

16.	U.C.C. § 2-203; *Restatement (Second) of Contracts* § 19 (1979).

17.	*Cargill Inc. v. Wilson,* 16 U.C.C. Rep. Serv. 615 (Mont. 1975) (sending check); *Mead Corp. v. McNally-Pittsburg Mfg. Corp.,* 654 F.2d 1197 (6th Cir. 1981) (sending purchase order); *Dubrofsky v. Messer,* 31 U.C.C. Rep. Serv. 907 (Mass App. Div. 1981) (shipping goods); *Fender v. Colonial Stores, Inc.,* 19 U.C.C. Rep. Serv. 402 (Ga. App. 1976) (taking product off shelf).

18.	*Arizona Retail Systems, Inc. v. The Software Link, Inc.,* 831 F. Supp. 759 (D. Ariz. 1993) (where no prior contract existed, opening a software package can constitute acceptance of terms on outside of package). See Section 6.4.3 for a discussion of shrinkwrap issues.

19.	*South Hampton Co. v. Stinnes Corp.,* 733 F.2d 1108, 1119 (5th Cir. 1984). In some cases a merchant's silence may constitute acceptance of additional terms to a contract, or may act to confirm a written summary of a verbal contract. *See* U.C.C. §§ 2-207, 2-201(2).

20.	See Section 6.4.3.

21.	*State Farm Mutual Auto. Ins. Co. v. Bockhurst,* 453 F.2d 533 (10th Cir. 1972).

22.	Draft U.C.C. § 2-208 (October 1, 1995 draft) would provide that if an electronic message, initiated by one party, evokes an electronic response, a contract is created when the initiating party receives a message signifying acceptance. The counterpart of this section in draft Article 2B is § 2B-205, which currently takes a more detailed approach. It includes as a form of acceptance the act of delivering digital information or access, if appropriate.

23.	*Corinthian Pharmaceutical Systems v. Lederle Labs,* 724 F. Supp. 605 (S.D. Ind. 1989). The seller's other correspondence stated that orders were not effective under accepted by the seller.

24.	*See* Section 6.1.2. The ABA Task Force on Electronic Messaging Services has stated that functional acknowledgments are particularly inappropriate as evidence of contract acceptance. *See ABA Model,* 45 Business Lawyer at 1673 n. 116.

25.	*Restatement (Second) of Contracts* § 42 (1979). However, "firm offers" may not be revoked early. A *firm offer* is one that is in writing and is specified as remaining open for a certain time. The offer may not be revoked before the time stated. *See* U.C.C. § 2-205 (relating to offers by merchants).

26.	*Restatement (Second) of Contracts* § 63 (1979). An offeror can avoid the mailbox rule by stating that acceptances will only be effective upon receipt. *Id.*

27.	*Restatement (Second) of Contracts* § 64 (1979). Although electronic messages are transmitted very quickly, they are not instantaneous. In many systems, messages are routed through networks and administrators and can be delayed for a matter of hours or even days.

28.	Draft U.C.C. § 2-208 (October 1, 1995 draft) provides that an electronic acceptance is effective on receipt, not transmission. *Also see* Raymond T. Nimmer, *Electronic Contracting, Legal Issues* (Paper presented at the American Bar Association Science and Technology Section Meeting, August 6, 1995). The ABA model for EDI trading partner agreements also rejects the mailbox rule. *ABA Model,* 45 Business Lawyer 1645, 1678 (June 1990).

29. The reasons generally cited for requiring a signed writing are twofold: (1) the act of writing and signing is considered to be deliberate and serious, ensuring that a party gives due consideration to the matter, and (2) evidence of a signed writing is considered more trustworthy and less susceptible to fraud than mere human memory or testimony.

30. Other contracts that must be in writing and signed are: (1) contracts by executors and administrators, (2) contracts of suretyship, (3) agreements in consideration of marriage, and (4) contracts for sale of real property. See citations for state statutes of fraud listed at *Restatement (Second) of Contracts*, ch. 5, Statutory Notes at 282 (1979).

31. *See, e.g.,* U.C.C. § 8-319 (writing required for sale of securities); 31 U.S.C. § 1501 (writing required for U.S. government obligations). Many written contracts provide that all amendments must be in writing and signed.

32. *See* U.C.C. § 2-201. There is a great deal of case law regarding how detailed the signed writing must be. Those issues will be no different for online contracts. For example, in one case, a handwritten (unsigned) memo, plus signed payroll cards, were together deemed to be a sufficient signed writing to evidence a contract. *Crabtree & Evelyn v. Elizabeth Arden Sales Corp.,* 305 N.Y. 48, 110 N.E.2d 551 (1953).

33. U.C.C. § 1-201(46) defines "written" or "writing" as "printing, typewriting or any other intentional reduction to tangible form."

34. *Howley v. Whipple,* 48 N.H. 487 (1869). One commentator has noted that "the Whipple opinion was a bit eccentric in its metaphors, to be sure, but was not maverick in its results." Note, *The Statute of Frauds Online: Can a Computer Sign a Contract for the Sale of Goods?* 14 Geo. Mason U. L. Rev. 637 (Summer 1992).

35. *Joseph Denunzio Fruit Co. v. Crane,* 79 F. Supp. 117 (S.D. Cal. 1948)(telex is a writing); *McMillan Ltd. v. Warrior Drilling & Eng. Co.,* 512 So.2d 14 (Ala. 1986) (mailgram is a writing); *Ellis Canning Co. v. Bernstein,* 348 F. Supp. 1212 (D. Colo. 1972) (tape recording is a writing). But *see Roos v. Aloi,* 127 Misc. 2d 864, 487 N.Y.S.2d 637 (Sup. Ct. 1985) (tape recording is not a writing).

36. *See Bazak International Corp. v. Mast Industries, Inc.,* 73 N.Y.2d 113, 7 U.C.C. Rep. Serv. 2d 1380 (1989)(faxes assumed without discussion to be writings under U.C.C. § 2-201). In *American Multimedia Inc. v. Dalton Packaging, Inc.,* 143 Misc. 2d 295, 540 N.Y.S.2d 410 (Sup. Ct. 1989), a faxed purchase order was assumed to be a writing for purposes of a federal arbitration statute.

37. *People v. Avila,* 770 P.2d 1330 (Colo. Ct. App. 1988) (recording on computer disk was a "writing" for purposes of the forgery statute). *See also Clyburn v. Allstate Insurance Co.,* 826 F.Supp. 955 (D.S.C. 1993).

38. *See* Wright, *The Law of Electronic Commerce,* § 16.4.5 (2d Ed. 1995). The draft U.C.C. revisions to Article 2 and 2B have virtually eliminated all references to "writings" and substituted the term "records," to encompass electronic messages. *See* Draft U.C.C. Article 2B at xvii (December 1, 1995 draft). The current draft revisions also contemplate repealing the statute of frauds entirely for transactions in sales of goods and transactions in intangibles.

39. Because EDI transaction sets are automatically exchanged between computers, there is flexibility in how the information can be recorded. It is thus possible for both the sending and receiving computers to dump the information into a general database without keeping more than a momentary record of each separate transmission. Trading partner agreements often require that separate logs be kept of all transactions.

40. As discussed in Chapter 5, it is advisable to keep records of such electronic communications in any case.

41. U.C.C. § 1-201(39).

42. *Hillstrom v. Gosnay*, 188 Mont. 388 (614 P.2d 466 (1989). *Contra, Pike Industries, Inc. v. Middlebury Associates*, 398 A.2d 280 (Vt. 1979); *aff'd on other grounds*, 436 A.2d 725 (Vt. 1980), *cert denied*, 455 U.S. 947 (1992). *See* note, *The Statute of Frauds Online: Can a Computer Sign a Contract for the Sale of Goods?* 14 Geo. Mason U. L. Rev. 637 (Summer 1992).

43. *Joseph Denunzio Fruit Co. v. Crane*, 79 F. Supp. 117 (S.D. Cal. 1948), *vacated*, 89 F.Supp. 962 (1950), *reinstated*, 188 F.2d 569 (9th circ), *cert denied*, 342 U.S. 820 (1951).

44. In *Watson v. Tom Growney Equip. Inc.*, 721 P.2d 1302 (N.M. 1986), a name typed on a purchase order was found to be a sufficient signature, since the signatory had deliberately filled out other details on the form. A typewritten signature on a U.C.C. financing statement was found to satisfy the signature requirement of the statute of frauds in *Matter of Save On Carpet of Arizona, Inc.*, 545 F.2d 1239 (9th Cir. 1976), but not in *In re Carlstrom*, 3 U.C.C. Rep. Serv. 766 (Bk. D. Me. 1966).

45. *Hessenthaler v. Farzin*, 388 Pa. Super. 37 (1989)(focus on intent to authenticate); *McMillan, Ltd. v. Warrior Drilling & Eng Co.*, 512 So. 2d 14 (Ala. 1986).

46. In *Kohlmeyer & Co. v. Bowen*, 126 Ga. App. 700, 192 S.E.2d 400 (1972), a securities brokerage firm's name was printed on a confirmation statement for the sale of securities. The court found the printed name was intended as authentication, and met the signature requirement under the statute of frauds. *Also see Associated Hardware Supply Co. v. Big Wheel Distrib. Co.*, 355 F.2d 114 (3d Cir. 1966) (letterhead).

47. In *Beatty v. First Exploration Fund 1987 and Co. Limited Partnership*, 25 B.C.L.R.2d 377 (1988), a British Columbia case, faxed signatures on proxy documents were sufficient to meet the signature requirements under a limited partnership agreement. In *Gilmore v. Lujan*, 947 F.2d 1409 (9th Cir. 1991), the court upheld an agency's determination that a fax did not meet the regulation's strict requirement that a document be "holographically signed in ink," but criticized the agency for its narrow-minded approach. In *Madden v. Hegadon*, 565 A.2d 725 (N.J. Super. 1989), *aff'd*, 571 A.2d 296 (N.J. 1989), a faxed signature was deemed effective for filing a nomination petition.

48. *See* discussion in Wright, *The Law of Electronic Commerce*, § 16.4.5 (2d Ed. 1995); Lowry, *Does Computer Stored Data Constitute a Writing for the Statute of Frauds and the Statute of Wills?* 9 Rutgers Computer & Tech. L.J. 93 (1982). However, some commentators have noted the difference between electronic communications and more conventional means such as telegraph and telex, and noted also that there should be some requirement to evidence a connection between the signature and the signatory. One commentator proposes that such a connection could exist if it were shown that the electronic communications system uses commercially reasonable security measures. Baum, *Analysis of Legal Aspects in EDI and the Law* 129 (1989).

49. *See* Section 46-3-402 of the Utah Digital Signature Act. See Chapter 4 for a discussion of digital signatures. The wording of Draft U.C.C. § 2-102(a)(37) (October 1, 1995 draft) also supports the status of digital signatures as effective signatures. Digital signatures serve both of the purposes underlying the statute of frauds: they evidence deliberateness and seriousness by the signer, and are reliable proof of what was said.

50. Draft U.C.C. § 2-201 (October 1, 1995 draft).

51. The United Nations Convention on Contracts for the International Sale of Goods (CISG), Article 11. The CISG, to which the United States and many other countries are signatories, applies to transactions in sales of goods. It governs when the buyer and seller have their places of business in different countries, and both countries are parties to the treaty. However, the parties may specify in their contract that they do not wish the CISG to govern.

52. The parties' course of performance (performance of the contract in question) and course of dealing (their past conduct) will be relevant in interpreting the contract. U.C.C. §§ 2-208; 1-205.

53. "Usage of trade," which refers to recognized practices in the industry, will be relevant in interpreting a contract. U.C.C. § 1-205.

54. *See* U.C.C. § 2-314 (implied warranty of merchantability); § 2-315 (implied warranty of fitness for particular purpose); § 2-701 *et. seq.* (remedies).

55. U.C.C. § 2-305.

56. Under U.C.C. § 2-207, an acceptance that contains new or different terms from the offer can still create a contract. Between merchants, the additional terms are made part of the contract unless (1) the offer expressly limits acceptance to the terms of the offer, (2) the additional terms materially alter the contract, or (3) the other party objects to the additional terms within a reasonable time. In consumer transactions, the additional terms are not made part of the contract unless expressly agreed to; the original offer would thus control.

57. Under the common law "mirror image" rule, if the acceptance contains terms different from the terms of the offer, it is not a true acceptance, but a counteroffer. Once the other party performs (such as by delivering goods or making payment), it has accepted the terms of the counteroffer. Thus, the terms of the party whose form is the "last shot" would prevail. *See* White and Summers, *Uniform Commercial Code* § 1-3 (3d Ed. 1988).

58. Draft U.C.C. §§ 2-207 (October 1, 1995 draft), 2B-309 (February 2, 1996 draft).

59. Of course, copyright restrictions will apply. One interesting issue is whether the user is entitled to the benefits of Section 117 of the Copyright Act, which permits *owners* of *copies* of software to make backup copies, and to load the software onto RAM. It is not clear that the downloader will be the "owner" of a copy of software downloaded online.

60. If it becomes generally understood in the online community that downloading software subjects the user to certain terms, a court might imply the industry understanding into the contract. However, industry custom may be difficult to show for online transactions; the level of user sophistication and knowledge varies widely.

61. For example, U.C.C. § 1-201(26) states that a person "receives" a notice when "(a) it comes to his attention, or (b) it is duly delivered at the place of business through which the contract was made or at any other place held out by him as the place for receipt of such communications."
     U.C.C. § 1-201(27) states that a notice is effective for a particular transaction from the time it is brought to the attention of the individual conducting that transaction, or from the time it would have been brought to his attention if the organization had exercised due diligence.
     Draft U.C.C. § 2-208 (October 1, 1995 draft) provides that electronic messages are deemed received when the message enters the recipient's designated information system, or if no system is designated, when it enters any information system of the recipient.

62. Draft U.C.C. §§ 2-207 (October 1, 1995 draft), 2B-310 (February 2, 1996 draft).

63. *Step-Saver Data Systems v. Wyse Technology*, 939 F.2d 91 (3d Cir. 1991)(shrinkwrap license in package delivered after telephone contract was not part of the contract); *Arizona Retail Sys., Inc. v. Software Link, Inc.*, 831 F. Supp. 759 (D. Ariz. 1993)(shrinkwrap license was enforceable where there had been no prior agreement, but was not enforceable where there was a prior telephonic agreement); *ProCD, Inc. v. Zeidenberg*, 1996 WL 10068 (W.D. Wis. 1996) (shrinkwrap license in package not visible at time of sale was unenforceable). *Also see Vault Corp. v. Quaid Software Ltd.*, 847 F.2d 255 (5th Cir. 1988)(state statute authorizing shrinkwrap licenses was preempted by federal law. The lower court had held that the shrinkwrap license would be an invalid contract of adhesion, were it not for the statute.)

64. In *Arizona Retail*, n. 63 supra, the court enforced one shrinkwrap license and not another, based on its analysis of two different fact patterns. Under the first fact pattern, the buyer received an evaluation copy of the software, along with a separate "live" copy in a shrinkwrap package. It was entitled to return both copies if it was not satisfied with the

demonstration. Once the buyer elected to keep the software and opened the shrinkwrap, the court held a contract had been formed and the shrinkwrap terms were part of the contract. By contrast, in the second fact pattern, the sale contract had been formed over the telephone, and the shrinkwrap package was an unenforceable attempt to modify a preexisting contract.

65. *See* Draft U.C.C. §§ 2B-307 and 2B-308 (December 1, 1995 draft), and comments to those sections. These provisions would apply to transactions in intangibles such as software and digital content.

66. The relevant provisions apply to standard form licenses and mass market licenses. Draft U.C.C. §§ 2B-307 and 2B-308 (December 1, 1995 draft). Mass market licenses are defined as standard form licenses for intangibles which are frequently used in transactions with the general public, and which are not altered for the transaction. Draft U.C.C. § 2B-102(a)(29).

67. The user has an "opportunity to review" the terms if they are made available, in a manner designed to call the user's attention to them, either before delivery of the software or digital content, or during the course of initial use or preparation to use the software or digital content. Draft U.C.C. § 2B-102(a)(32) (December 1, 1995 draft).

68. Similar provisions would apply to standard form contracts for the sale of goods. Certain terms may be unenforceable, such as those that a reasonable licensor should know most licensees would not accept. Draft U.C.C. § 2B-308 (February 2, 1996 draft); draft U.C.C. § 2-206.

69. Draft U.C.C. §§ 2B-115 and 2B-307, n. 5 (February 2, 1996 draft).

70. *See,* for example, http://www.mci.com.

71. See Kennedy and Davids, *Web-Site Agreements Do Not Wrap Up IP Rights,* The National Law Journal at C3 (Oct. 23, 1995).

72. Note, however, that certain terms of the contract might still be unenforceable. See discussion at n. 68, supra.

73. U.C.C. § 2-314.

74. U.C.C. § 2-315.

75. U.C.C. § 2-313.

76. *Id.*

77. U.C.C. § 2-316.

78. Draft U.C.C. §§ 2B-401, 2B-403, 2B-404 (February 2, 1996 draft).

79. U.C.C. § 2-316. Under pending draft revisions to the U.C.C., warranty disclaimers in transactions involving software and digital information must also be conspicuous. Draft U.C.C. § 2B-406 (February 2, 1996).

80. Draft U.C.C. § 2-102(a)(9); draft U.C.C. § 2B-102(a)(8) (February 2, 1996). The present U.C.C. language is not tailored to online transactions, and provides that a term is conspicuous when it is "so written that a reasonable person against whom it is to operate ought to have noticed it." U.C.C. § 1-201 (10). The draft revisions to the U.C.C. attempt to eliminate all references to "writings" and "documents," and substitute language referring to "records" that will accommodate electronic transactions as well as traditional paper documents.

81. Draft U.C.C. §§ 2-102(a)(9)(iii), 2B-102(a)(8)(iii) (February 2, 1996 draft).

82. Draft U.C.C. §§ 2-102(a)(9), 2B-102(a)(8) (February 2, 1996 draft).

83. *Restatement (First) of Contracts* § 503 (1932).

84. 3 *Corbin on Contracts* § 608 (1960).

85. *Germain Fruit Co. v. Western Union Telegraph Co.,* 137 Cal. 598, 70 P. 658 (1902).

86.   This is the majority position. See Calamari & Perillo, *The Law of Contracts*, § 2-24; 1 *Williston on Contracts* § 94 (Third Ed.) (1959). Courts following the minority position would hold that no contract exists.

87.   Draft U.C.C. §§ 2B-322 (February 2, 1996 draft), 2-213 (October 1, 1995 draft).

88.   *See* U.C.C. § 4A-202. Also see Draft U.C.C. § 2B-322, comment 8.

89.   *Computerworld*, p. 12, (May 8, 1995).

90.   *Boardwatch*, p. 8 (April 1995).

91.   Of course, digital signatures will not ensure that the other party is creditworthy, trustworth, or able to perform; that function will continue to be performed independently from the medium used, just as it is now.

92.   U.C.C. § 3-404.

93.   *See* U.C.C. § 3-404, and comments 3 and 4.

94.   Draft U.C.C. § 2-212. A different version is presented in draft U.C.C. § 2B-114 (February 2, 1996 draft). Also see U.C.C. §§ 4A-202, 4A-203 (relating to funds transfers).

95.   Draft U.C.C. § 2-212 (October 1, 1995 draft); draft U.C.C. § 114 (February 2, 1996 draft).

96.   3 *Am. Jur. 2d Agency* § 71 (1986); *Restatement (Second) of Agency* § 8A (1958).

97.   Thus, if a company's Web page says "To place your order, contact our Director of Sales, John Doe, at doe@company.com," it has clothed John Doe with apparent authority to accept orders. However, if the Web page itself is not legitimate, that might not be the case.

98.   See Chapter 4 for a discussion of digital signatures and certification authorities.

99.   *Restatement (Second) of Conflict of Laws*, § 187(2)(a) and (b) *(1971). Also see* UCC § 1-105 (parties' choice of law will be respected if it bears a reasonable relationship to the transaction).

100. U.C.C. § 2A-106.

101. Draft U.C.C. § 2B-107 (February 2, 1996 draft). The current draft proposes a rule that would only enforce a choice of law provision if it specifies the law of the state where the consumer resides, or the law of the state where the licensor of intangibles is located. If a copy of intangibles is to be delivered (other than by electronic transmission), the law of the state where the copy is delivered would govern.

102. *Restatement (Second) of Conflict of Laws*, § 187 (1971), comments f and g.

103. However, this is not always the case. For example, in *United Counties Trust Co. v. Mac Lun, Inc.*, 643 F.2d 1140 (5th Cir. 1981), *rehearing denied*, 647 F.2d 1123, the court refused to apply the parties' choice of New York law. The parties were Kentucky and New York corporations, the contract related to equipment in Georgia, and there was no relationship with New York.

104. Application of choice of law principles in this context is discussed generally at 15A *C.J.S. Conflict of Laws* §§ 3 and 4(10) (1967 and 1985 Supp.).

105. *Restatement (Second) of Conflict of Laws*, § 188 (1971). Note, however, the different choice of law rules under Articles 2A of the U.C.C. (relating to leases), and under the current draft of new Article 2B of the U.C.C. (relating to transactions in intangibles). *See* n. 100 *supra*.

106. The "place of contracting" is the place where the "last act necessary . . . to give the contract binding effect" occurred, which is, in most cases, given relatively little weight. *Id.*, comment e. The little weight afforded to the "place of contracting" is not likely to change in the online world where contracts can be formed by a mouse click.

107. The place of negotiation is believed to be a more significant contract than the place of contracting, but only if the negotiations occur in one state, which is not likely to be the case with transactions conducted online. *Id.*

108. The place of performance will be given significant weight in the choice of law analysis if a contract is to be performed entirely within the boundaries of a given state; otherwise not. *Id.* Absent a compelling reason to do something else, the law that controls is the local law of the state where the seller is to deliver the merchandise, or where the services, or most of the services, are to be physically performed. *Id.*, § 191, 196.

109. *Id.*, § 188(2)(a)–(e).

110. *Transatlantic Cement, Inc. v. Lambert Freres et Cie,* 462 F. Supp. 363 (S.D.N.Y. 1978).

111. *Diamond Mining and Management, Inc. v. Globex Minerals, Inc.,* 421 F. Supp. 70 (N.D. Cal 1976).

112. *See, supra,* n. 51.

7

Online Payment Options

Thomas J. Smedinghoff

$\mathbf{A}$ key issue for electronic commerce is how to make payment electronically in a manner that is efficient, reliable, and secure. In the paper world, payments are accomplished via cash, checks, credit and debit cards, money orders, and other mechanisms. In the online world, the electronic equivalent of these payment mechanisms is also available or under development.

7.1 Introduction to Payment Mechanisms

Understanding electronic payment options begins with an understanding of the basics of money. Specifically, it begins with understanding how money can be represented and how it can be transferred.

Money can be represented in one of two basic forms. The most familiar form is through the use of a *token*. That is, a physical object that does not in itself have intrinsic value is used to represent money. The most common forms of tokens are paper (such as dollar bills), and metal (such as coins). Money can also be represented *notationally*, that is, as a number or other entry in a record book (which often resides on a computer). Most money held by the major banks exists in this form. Thus, for example, when the First National Bank of Chicago transfers money to BankAmerica, it does not physically transfer the tokens (such as the dollar bills and the coins). Rather, the specified sum is simply subtracted from the computer records of the First National Bank of Chicago and added to the computer records of BankAmerica.

There are also two basic ways that money (or the value it represents) can be exchanged between buyer and seller. The first, and most common, is through the *direct exchange of tokens*—that is, for the buyer to simply hand to the seller the tokens representing the agreed-upon sum of money. In other words, there is a physical transfer. In this scenario, only two parties are involved.

Alternatively, money can be transferred by means of an *instruction* from the buyer directed to a third party instructing that third party to pay the seller. In many cases, the instruction is in the form of a document that the buyer gives the seller and the seller in turn redeems with the third party. Examples of this kind of instruction include checks and executed credit card charge slips. Alternatively, the buyer might issue the instruction directly to the third party (such as an instruction to a bank to initiate an electronic funds transfer).

Not surprisingly, both modes of payment (i.e., transferring tokens or generating instructions to third parties) are available in online transactions. Instructional modes of payment can be accomplished through the use of electronic funds transfers, online credit and debit card transactions, and electronic checks. And, although still in the experimental stage, many organizations are working on schemes to provide for the direct transfer of tokens representing money. These tokens exist in a digital rather than paper or metallic form, and are often referred to as digital cash.

This chapter first reviews various instructional modes of electronic payment, including electronic funds transfers, electronic checks and credit cards. A discussion of digital cash follows.

7.2 Electronic Funds Transfers

Electronic funds transfer (*EFT*) is a term generally applied to the movement of funds from one bank account to another, by means of electronically communicated payment instructions.

Functionally, electronic transfers of funds include two principal categories: credit transfers and debit transfers. With a *credit transfer*, the buyer instructs its bank (via a payment order) to transfer funds to the seller's bank for credit to the seller's account—that is, the instruction to pay is given by the person making the payment. A *debit transfer* occurs when the seller instructs its bank (via a payment order) to collect funds for it by debiting the buyer's bank account at the buyer's bank—that is, the instruction to pay is given by the person receiving payment.[1] Insurance payments, health club dues, and utility bills are frequently deducted from consumer checking accounts via debit transfers.

The concept of an electronic funds transfer is not complex, although some transfers can in practice be rather intricate. The following illustrates the process for a credit EFT transfer.

A credit electronic funds transfer typically involves five participants: the originator of the payment, the originator's bank, a funds-transfer system, the beneficiary of the payment, and the beneficiary's bank. A typical credit transfer is initiated by the *originator* (for example, a buyer wishing to pay its supplier).[2] The originator sends a payment order to its bank instructing the bank to cause a payment to be made to the *beneficiary* (for example, the supplier to be paid)[3] by deposit to the beneficiary's bank account.[4] The mechanics by which the originator issues payment orders to its bank are usually the subject of an agreement between the originator and its bank,[5] and (for commercial transactions) are governed by the provisions of U.C.C. Article 4A "Fund Transfers."[6]

The *payment order* sent by the originator to its bank serves many of the same purposes as a check. It is an instruction to the bank to pay, or to cause another bank to pay, a sum of money to the beneficiary.[7] It typically includes the name and routing number of the beneficiary's bank, the name of the beneficiary to be paid, the beneficiary's account number at the beneficiary's bank into which the funds are to be deposited, the dollar amount to be paid, and the requested payment date.

The originator's bank accepts and processes the payment order on receipt, and executes the originator's payment order by sending another payment order to the beneficiary's bank.[8] In EFT transactions, the payment order of the originator's bank, and any subsequent payment orders, are communicated electronically to the beneficiary's bank, as is the originator's payment order to its bank. A *funds-transfer system* is normally used to communicate payment orders from the originator's bank to the beneficiary's bank, and for effecting a settlement of funds between the two banks in order to complete the funds transfer.[9]

The following funds-transfer systems are available for effecting payments electronically in the United States:[10]

- **Automated Clearing House.** The Automated Clearing House (ACH) Network is a nationwide electronic payments system used by more than 22,000 participating financial institutions, over 160,000 corporations, and millions of consumers.[11] The ACH system tends to be the funds-transfer system of choice among businesses making electronic payments to vendors because it is economical and can carry considerable amounts of remittance information in standardized, computer-processable data formats. The ACH system is also the primary system used for consumer EFT debit transactions (such as payment of insurance bills, utility bills, and health club dues by deduction from a consumer's checking account), as well as for direct deposit and other similar payments to a consumer's checking account. The National Automated Clearing House Association (NACHA) was formed in 1974 as the regulatory body for the ACH Network.

- **Fedwire.** Fedwire is the funds-transfer system owned and operated by the Federal Reserve Banks.[12] Fedwire provides for the transfer of funds between banks using their reserve or clearing accounts with Federal Reserve Banks. Fedwire is typically used for transactions requiring immediate settlement and finality. However, each transaction can carry only limited administrative or remittance information. Fedwire fees are high compared with those of ACH and other electronic payment mechanisms.

- **Clearing House Interbank Payments System.** The Clearing House Interbank Payments System (CHIPS) is a funds-transfer system owned and operated by the New York Clearing House Association, whose members are the 12 New York money center banks, and in which some 125 banks participate. A CHIPS payment can carry only limited remittance information. CHIPS processes primarily international funds transfers among its members.[13]

- **Society for Worldwide Interbank Financial Telecommunications.** The Society for Worldwide Interbank Financial Telecommunications (S.W.I.F.T.) is a messaging system operated by a consortium of more than 1,700 banks in more than 80 countries. S.W.I.F.T. is not a financial settlement system; rather, it is a communications system by which payment orders and other messages are communicated among its members. Settlements are then executed through either Fedwire, CHIPS, bilateral correspondent bank arrangements, or check.

The funds-transfer process is completed when the beneficiary's bank accepts the payment order for the benefit of the beneficiary.[14] The beneficiary's bank is then obligated to pay the beneficiary (by crediting the beneficiary's account),[15] and the originator's obligation to the beneficiary for that payment is discharged.

A *funds transfer*, then, is a series of transactions involving discrete payment orders, such as the payment order from the buyer to its bank and the payment order from the buyer's bank to a seller's bank, made for the purpose of paying a seller.[16] Although we often refer to this process as an "electronic" funds transfer, a payment order can be transmitted orally or in writing as well as electronically.[17]

In a business context, funds transfers rely heavily on security procedures, rather than on traditional signatures, to establish the authenticity and integrity of an electronic payment order. The Uniform Commercial Code defines a *security procedure* as a procedure established by agreement between a customer and its bank for the purpose of (1) verifying that a payment order is that of the customer, or (2) detecting errors in the transmission or the content of the payment order.[18] Although a security procedure could involve the use of a digital signature, the statute indicates that it can also be based on the use of algorithms or other codes, identifying words or numbers, encryptions, call-back procedures, or other security devices.

The significance of using a security procedure for electronic funds transfers (at least in a business context) is that the parties establish the rules for authentication. If a bank and its customer have agreed on a security procedure for authenticating a payment order issued to the bank in the name of the customer, then a payment order received by the bank is effective as the order of the customer, *whether or not it was authorized by the customer*, if (1) the security procedure is a commercially reasonable method of providing security against unauthorized payment orders, and (2) the bank proves that it accepted the payment order in good faith and in compliance with the security procedure.[19] Thus, for example, if a customer's payment orders were signed with a digital signature, and the bank verified that digital signature, then the bank would be acting properly by making payment in accordance with the payment order even if the payment order was not in fact authorized by the customer.

This is contrary to traditional legal principles, which provide that an unauthorized signature is ineffective except as the signature of the unauthorized signer.[20]

7.3 Business-to-Business EFT: Financial EDI

Business-to-business electronic funds transfers are governed by U.C.C. Article 4A and the rules of the funds-transfer system used to effect the transaction. One key form of business-to-business electronic payments involves a combination of electronic data interchange and electronic funds transfers, and is known as *financial EDI*.

Electronic data interchange (*EDI*) is widely recognized as "the exchange of routine business transactions in a *computer-processable* format, covering such traditional applications as inquiries, planning, purchasing, acknowledgments, pricing, order status, scheduling, test results, shipping and receiving, invoices, payments, and financial reporting."[21] Computer-processability is a key attribute and benefit of EDI—it means that the communicated information, such as a purchase order,

1. Can be read by a computer without human processing or interpretation,
2. Is electronically storable and retrievable, and
3. Can be used in other applications without having to reenter or reformat it manually.[22]

EDI can be combined with EFT to forge a powerful commercial tool. That is, an electronically communicated payment order (discussed in the previous section) can be associated with electronically communicated remittance information. This information typically indicates the amount of the payment, the invoices to which the payment should be applied, the buyer's account number, and other relevant information that, if received electronically, can be processed automatically by the seller and integrated into the seller's accounts receivable computer system. When these are transmitted in a computer-processable (i.e., EDI) format, the process is often referred to as *financial EDI.*[23]

Thus, from the perspective of the online trading partners (the buyer and the seller), a financial EDI transaction typically has two components: (1) the payment of funds (for example, an electronic instruction to "pay ABC Co. $100 on December 15, 1997"), and (2) the electronic communication of remittance information associated with the payment (for example, "this pays invoice number 12345"). Both payment and remittance information components are typically in machine-processable form and travel electronically rather than via paper, although they are usually intended for different destinations. The payment component is destined for the seller's bank, with instructions to credit the seller's bank account. The remittance information component is ultimately destined for the seller, for processing in the seller's accounts receivable system.

The buyer can communicate the remittance information associated with a payment order to the seller via several alternate routes. The remittance information can be bundled with the payment order, transferred through the funds-transfer system to the seller's bank,[24] and ultimately communicated by the seller's bank (assuming it has appropriate processing capabilities) to the seller. Alternatively, the remittance information can be communicated separately from the payment order, either directly from the buyer to the seller, or from the buyer through one or more third-party service providers (or the Internet) to the seller.

The authenticity and integrity of information communicated in a financial EDI transaction is important to its effectiveness and legal efficacy.[25] Information security procedures can provide the requisite reliability and control. These are discussed in Chapters 3 and 4.

7.4 Consumer-Based EFT

Consumer-based electronic funds transfers (i.e., any EFT transaction involving a consumer) are governed by the Electronic Fund Transfer Act.[26] The EFT Act is the primary federal law governing consumer rights in EFT transactions. It requires that the electronic-funds service provider give the consumer initial and periodic disclosure statements,[27] and imposes limitations on consumer liabilities.[28]

The EFT Act is implemented by Regulation E, which is promulgated by the Federal Reserve Board.[29] Regulation E is the principal regulation between banks and their customers for electronic transfer in and out of consumer asset accounts, including ATM card transactions, point-of-sale transactions, and ACH deposit and debit transactions. Consumer smartcard transactions may also, at some point, become governed by Regulation E. The EFT Act, as implemented by Regulation E, is fundamentally a consumer-protection law. It is much more protective of bank customers than the equivalent Article 4A provisions, which reflect a more balanced allocation of risks among the parties.

Under Regulation E, a consumer's liability for unauthorized electronic funds transfers is limited to $50 so long as the unauthorized transfer is promptly reported. Negligence by the consumer, such as in writing his or her access code on the ATM card and leaving it where it can be found, cannot be taken into account to impose greater liability. Thus, the consumer will not be bound when his or her electronic signature is used to effect a transfer, unless the consumer actually used or authorized it.[30] This differs substantially from the security procedure approach for business EFT transactions taken under Article 4A of the Uniform Commercial Code (described in Section 7.2).

7.5 Online Credit-Card Payment

Payment for goods or services ordered or obtained online can readily be accomplished using ordinary credit cards. The buyer communicates his or her credit card number to the seller, electronically, in a manner analogous to making a credit-card purchase by phone or through the mail. Transactions of this type have become very common in certain electronic environments, particularly those environments with a consumer orientation.

Credit cards operate under a number of limitations that apply both to face-to-face as well as to online transactions. For example, credit cards are not anonymous. The use of credit-card numbers allows detailed information to be compiled about the cardholder's buying habits and purchasing history—the use or sale of which information would be considered by many to be an invasion of their privacy. Credit cards are also not practical for low-value transactions, as the transaction cost is simply too high. Credit-card transactions are also not appropriate for transactions between individuals. Only merchants who are registered with the appropriate credit-card issuer may accept payment via credit cards. Finally, credit cards have credit limits that may have to be verified before the vendor will proceed with the transaction.

When credit cards are used online, they are also subject to significant security risks (see, generally, Chapter 3). Specifically, depending upon the level of security provided by the electronic medium, there is a risk that the number can be intercepted by third parties and used for unauthorized purposes. This is a particular concern with the transmission of credit-card numbers via the Internet, which is not designed for secure communications. In addition, buyers may be somewhat wary over the identity and integrity of vendors with whom they are dealing only in an online relationship, especially if they have never heard of the vendor before, or if the vendor is new and has no established physical location. At the same time, vendors need some assurance that they are dealing with the true owner of the credit card, and not merely with someone who has obtained the card number.

In other words, online credit-card transactions must be both secure and nonrefutable. The credit-card owner must be able to protect his or her credit-card number from unauthorized interception and use. The vendor must have a way to verify its authenticity (i.e., to verify that the credit-card number is being used by its true owner); its integrity (i.e., to verify that the number has not been altered in transmission or otherwise); and its nonrepudiation (i.e., to verify that the sender cannot deny having authorized the transaction). Thus, for widespread acceptable implementation of credit-card payment online, it is necessary to implement a mechanism that will allow the following:

1. A customer to present his or her credit-card information (along with an authenticity signature) securely to the merchant;
2. The merchant to validate that it is dealing with the true owner of the credit-card account, and that it has received the proper number;
3. The merchant to relay the credit-card information and signature to its bank;
4. The bank to relay the information to the customer's bank for authorization; and
5. The authorization information to be communicated to the merchant so the transaction can proceed.

Most attempts to promote the use of credit cards in an electronic-commerce transaction have focused on this issue of security—that is, the problem associated with communicating a credit-card number over a potentially insecure communications medium. Two general approaches have been developed.

7.5.1 Secure Credit-Card Payment

The first approach has focused on the development of a secured credit-card payment system. This typically involves the use of encryption technology to encrypt a credit-card number while in transit over the Internet or other communications network, in order to protect the privacy of the credit-card number. This is combined with use of a digital signature to authenticate the transaction (see Chapter 4 regarding digital signatures). Systems of this type are being developed by a number of banks and credit-card processors.

Generally, the components necessary for secure payment transactions are privacy, integrity, and authentication (see Chapter 3). Secure payment protocols that implement these components will make it possible for individual transaction information (such as credit-card information) to be sent through the Internet without concerns over disclosure of sensitive information. In addition, the authentication provided by digital signatures will allow merchants to certify the consumer as the legitimate owner of a card; and the consumer will receive verification that the processing bank has accepted the card for payment.

7.5.2 Registry Credit-Card Payment

An alternative approach is to group sellers together in an affiliation with a central office that handles credit-card services for all of the members. A buyer would then register his or her credit-card number with the central office and obtain a group-specific account number back. This account number could then be used in lieu of the credit-card number when the buyer deals with any member of the group. This avoids the need to communicate credit-card information online. A problem with this approach, however, is that both the buyers and the sellers must subscribe to the same service in order to complete a purchase transaction.

First Virtual Holdings, Inc. has developed such a system to allow consumers to use credit cards over the Internet without fear that their account numbers will be misappropriated.[31] Their card numbers are stored on a protected computer system at First Virtual Holdings, and never pass over the Internet. Instead, consumers register with First Virtual and receive ID numbers in exchange for their card numbers. When they want to buy something electronically, they simply supply their ID number to the merchant, who then supplies the information to First Virtual to start the billing process.

In another approach, CyberCash, Inc. has developed a technology that enables consumers to encrypt their credit-card information at their personal computer using software provided for free by CyberCash.[32] When the information is transmitted to the merchant, it is in encrypted form: the merchant never sees the number, only the encrypted version of the data. Thus, if a hacker were to break into a merchant's server, he or she would obtain only useless encrypted data.

To order goods over the Internet, a customer encrypts the credit-card number using the Cybercash software, establishes a link with the merchant, and then places an order using the encrypted information. The merchant then adds additional data and forwards the transaction over the Internet to CyberCash. CyberCash performs error checking and forwards all the information to the normal, trusted credit-card authorization and settlement networks. To complete the transaction, CyberCash returns an electronic receipt with credit-card authorization data to the merchant who then finalizes the transaction with the consumer. The complete process takes less than a minute from the time the consumer clicks on "Pay."

7.6 Electronic Checks

In mid-1995, several major banks and technology companies announced plans to develop an electronic check-payment system for use over the Internet and other online services.[33] This system would enable businesses and consumers to make online payments to anyone, for any purpose, using so-called electronic checks delivered via e-mail. The recipient of the electronic check could then deposit it in a bank, also via e-mail.

The concept of an electronic check is modeled on the paper check, and will contain all the information that is currently included on a paper check. But the information will exist in an electronic format rather than a paper one. It will use digital signatures (see Chapter 4) for signing and endorsing and, to authenticate the payer, the payer's bank and bank account. Delivery will be by e-mail or other communications options, such as the World Wide Web. Functionally, however, electronic checks will be used by businesses and consumers like paper checks, and will be processed through existing interbank clearing systems.

Thus, electronic checks can be sent directly by the payer to the intended recipient via e-mail without going through a bank (as would be required for electronic funds transfers). An electronic check, like a paper check, would represent authorization to withdraw money from the check writer's bank account. It would not guarantee, however, that there was money in the account. Thus, as with paper, an electronic check could bounce.

7.7 Digital Cash

If paper documents (like checks) can be represented electronically, why not do the same with paper money—that is, why not convert it to electronic form? That is exactly the theory behind the much discussed development of so-called digital cash.

As its name implies, *digital cash* is nothing more than a way of representing money (dollar bills and coins) in a digital form on an electronic medium. Digital cash is, in essence, an electronic token. The money (i.e., the value) is represented by a series of numbers that are digitally signed by an issuing bank and that can be stored on a variety of media. For example, digital cash can be stored on a credit-card–size piece of plastic with an imbedded microchip (known as a *smartcard*) that one can "load" up with digital cash purchased with traditional currency or withdrawn from one's bank account. Alternatively, the coins and dollars comprising digital cash can be downloaded over phone lines from a bank (or other digital-cash issuer) and stored on a PC or in an electronic "wallet," a palm-sized device used to store and transmit digital cash. The money represented by the digital token can be exchanged directly online between remote transacting parties.

In many respects, the trillions of dollars that are transferred each day by banks, other financial institutions, and government clearing houses are already a form of digital cash. No dollar bills or coins are physically transferred between the many banks participating in electronic funds transfers. Instead, credit points are simply subtracted from one bank account's computer records and added to another's by clearing houses such as the Federal Reserve. Digital cash would simply extend this concept to the individual level.

Under most models, digital cash will be issued by banks and secured with digital signatures created by the issuing bank with its private keys (see Chapter 4). Obtaining digital cash typically involves withdrawing funds from a bank account—much like what occurs through an Automatic Teller Machine. For example, users might connect to their bank from their computer through the Internet and request the amount of digital cash they want to withdraw, just as if they were doing it in person. The bank would then authenticate the requester and verify that adequate funds are in the requester's account. But instead of delivering cash, the bank will send a stream of data representing the digital cash that the requester stores on the hard disk of his or her computer. Each coin representing the digital cash typically contains a unique serial number (to allow the bank to be sure it never accepts the same coin twice) and is digitally signed by the bank to ensure authenticity.

With digital cash, it is possible to transmit payment (that is, actual money) from any personal computer to any other personal computer, via e-mail, the Internet, or any other electronic computer network system. Using digital cash, buyers can shop online and transmit the money for purchases directly to a merchant over the Internet. Similarly, digital cash can be used to facilitate online transactions such as paying for access to a database; paying to receive today's news; paying for access to articles, papers, magazines, movies on demand, and other information published over the Internet; paying to play a game over the Internet; paying money owed to another individual; ordering a pizza; and other similar items.

This functionality highlights two of the key advantages that digital cash offers over credit-card payments. First is the ability to accomplish peer-to-peer (e.g., person-to-person) payment. With credit cards, by contrast, a buyer is able to pay only a seller who has registered with a credit-card issuer. Second is the ability to facilitate transactions for very small dollar amounts. The transaction costs involved in credit cards are not suited to small-dollar transactions that are likely to be prevalent in some online environments (such as transactions for certain types of digital content like articles or songs that may involve fractions of a cent). Thus, for a certain segment of the online economy, digital cash may be a preferred form of payment.

In addition, digital cash can also be programmed to do things that paper money never could, such as earmarking it for special purposes, with conditions on where or how it can be spent. For example, digital cash could be issued to employees of a business for use in a petty-cash account to buy office supplies. Any other unauthorized use, such as buying lunch at a local restaurant, would not be possible. Similarly, parents could send to a college student digital cash that is designated for tuition, books, or room and board. It could not be used for any other purpose.

Although the concept is still developing, there are generally two types of digital cash: *online digital cash* and *offline digital cash*. With *online digital cash*, it is necessary to interact with a bank (via its computer) in order to complete a transaction with a third party. With *offline digital cash*, on the other hand, transactions are conducted only between the payer and the receiver of the cash.

Each form of digital cash can be either "identified" or "anonymous." *Identified digital cash* typically includes some information about the identity of the person who originally withdrew the money from a bank account in the form of digital cash. Thus, the flow of that particular digital cash through the economy can be traced. *Anonymous digital cash*, on the other hand, is much more analogous to the use of paper money. That is, it can be spent or otherwise transferred to another party in a manner that is generally untraceable.

Implementation and use of digital cash introduces a number of new issues that need to be addressed. These include: who should be allowed to issue digital cash, and how it will be regulated; how digital cash transactions will be taxed (since they can transcend physical boundaries); who will set standards for digital cash; how users of digital cash ensure that payments made over the Internet are secure; how consumers will be protected; and how regulatory agencies will police money laundering and counterfeiting on private networks. Consider the following:

- **Terms of Issuance.** What are the terms of the legal relationship between the entity issuing and/or redeeming digital cash on the one hand and the merchants and consumers who are utilizing digital cash on the other? Is the relationship a contractual one or is it one governed by federal or state law regulation?
- **Retrievability.** Digital-cash coins and tokens must be (1) storable on computer systems, smartcards, and the like, and retrievable by their owners; (2) accessible—the process of using digital cash must be quick and easy to effect; and (3) reliable—users of digital cash must feel confidence in the process and be assured that it will operate properly regardless of component failures or system load conditions.
- **Security.** Digital cash must be difficult to counterfeit, forge, or otherwise tamper with. This includes preventing or detecting duplication and double-spending. Users must be assured that their digital cash (and the storage device on which it is maintained, such as a smartcard or computer disk) cannot be easily forged or altered, and that if it is altered, evidence of this tampering will be immediately apparent. Likewise, the recipient of a digital cash payment must be able to verify that the digital cash received is authentic.

Paper money contains a number of built-in deterrents to forgery—primarily through a design that makes counterfeiting difficult. Digital cash, on the other hand, is nothing more than a series of digits that are readily duplicated. Accordingly, it is necessary to design a digital-cash system that somehow prohibits the copying (i.e., double-spending) of the data representing the money.

Digital cash relies heavily on cryptography[34] (see Chapter 31). In the digital-cash schemes being implemented and under consideration, security is accomplished primarily through a combination of encryption and either online verification by the issuing bank or detection of double-spending after the fact, in a manner designed to deter such conduct.

In online digital-cash systems, double-spending is controlled by requiring the recipient to contact the issuing bank's computer with every transaction. The issuing bank maintains a database of all of the "digital coins" issued and spent, and thus is in a position to indicate to the recipient of digital cash whether the specific coins being transferred are still "spendable." Thus, if a bank indicates that the digital cash in question has already been spent, the merchant would refuse the transaction, much the same as it would with a credit-card transaction where the issuer indicated that the card was no longer valid.

Offline digital-cash systems, on the other hand, address the problem of double-spending through the use of cryptographic protocol that will allow the issuing bank to identify the double-spender at least by the time the digital cash makes its way back to the bank. The theory here is that if users know they will get caught, they will be less likely to attempt any double-spending.

- **Protected.** Users of digital cash must be assured that they cannot be easily duped, swindled, or falsely implicated in a fraudulent transaction. They must be protected against eavesdroppers and counterfeiters.
- **Regulation.** Whether digital-cash schemes are, or should be, subject to any federal or state law or regulation is a subject of much debate. At present there are no government regulations that apply directly to digital cash. However, there is much discussion over whether Uniform Commercial Code Articles 3 and 4 or the Federal Electronic Fund Transfer Act and its associated Regulation E will (or should) govern the issuance and use of digital cash. There is also concern that Regulation E will be applied to consumer stored-value cards containing digital cash. Because these cards are used primarily for low-value transactions, it may not be practical or cost efficient to comply with all of its consumer protection requirements.
- **Anonymity.** Another very controversial issue surrounding digital cash is the question of whether digital cash should be anonymous. In essence, there is a rather significant controversy between those who believe that digital-cash transactions should be conducted anonymously, like paper money transactions, and those who believe that digital-cash transactions must be traceable for purposes of criminal law enforcement and national security.

  One digital cash company, Digicash,[35] has developed "blinding" encryption technology that lets the issuing bank certify an electronic note without tracing to whom it was issued. The result is that the digital cash is as anonymous as paper cash.

  What information regarding the issuance and use of digital cash will be maintained, and by whom? What rights does the holder of this information have to use it, and does the user of digital cash have a right to a reasonable expectation of privacy? If so, to what extent? Are there any exceptions?
- **Crime Issues.** Law enforcement officials are concerned that the widespread use of truly anonymous digital cash could greatly hamper their efforts to deal with crimes such as money laundering, drug trafficking, and terrorism. Particularly worrisome is the prospect of large quantities of digital cash being moved around the Internet—where identities are easy to conceal, communications are instantaneous, and national borders mean nothing. Digital cash can easily be sent in and out of a country undetected, facilitating money laundering on a grand scale. Tax evasion is also a significant problem. Moreover, there is a concern that counterfeiters could easily replicate the series of digits that constitute digital cash. Of course, governments would be hard pressed to monitor or control stateless digital cash.

- **Risk of Loss.** Numerous other transaction-based issues must also be considered. Who bears the financial risk in a system of electronic money on the Internet? Who will establish the laws for online commerce based on digital cash? Who has jurisdiction over a transaction—the laws of the purchaser in our country or the seller in another? Who bears the risk in an international transaction where digital cash is transferred, but the merchant fails or refuses to perform? What if the merchant becomes insolvent and is unable to fulfill its obligations? What if the consumer loses his or her digital cash, or it is destroyed by a disk crash or erasure?

7.8 The Role of Information Security

Although the options for online payment are, to a large extent, still being developed, one thing is clear: they all rely heavily on the use of information-security techniques, particularly encryption and digital signatures. Payment orders issued to banks directing the transfer of funds electronically are often digitally signed so that the receiving bank can verify their authenticity and integrity, and can rely on them under applicable law. Online credit-card transactions are typically encrypted (to ensure privacy of the credit-card number), and frequently these are digitally signed so that the parties can authenticate the sender and verify the integrity of the message. Digital cash, by its very nature, relies heavily on digital signatures to establish the authenticity and validity of the data representing the cash. Electronic checks, like EFT payment orders, utilize digital signatures so that a bank can assure itself that it is authorized to rely on the instruction contained in the form of a check.

Information security is discussed in Chapters 3 and 4.

Endnotes

1. Credit transfers between businesses are governed by Uniform Commercial Code (U.C.C.) Article 4A. Debit transfers between businesses are outside the scope of Article 4A. Consumer credit and debit transfers are covered by the Electronic Fund Transfer Act of 1978, 15 U.S.C. § 1693 *et. seq.*

2. The *originator* of a credit transfer is the person initiating a funds transfer, usually a buyer or a lessee who seeks to pay its seller or lessor. *See* U.C.C. Article 4A § 104(c) "Originator."

3. The *beneficiary* is the person for whom the payment is intended. Typically funds are transferred to the beneficiary's bank for deposit directly into the beneficiary's account. *See* U.C.C. Article 4A § 103(a)(2) "Beneficiary."

4. U.C.C. § 4A-104(a) (1989).

5. For an explanation of the electronic funds transfer issues arising between a commercial customer and its bank, and a model agreement designed to address that relationship (with extensive commentary), see "Model Funds Transfer Services Agreement and Commentary," Working Group on Electronic Financial Services, Subcommittee on Electronic Commercial Practices, Uniform Commercial Code Committee, Business Law Section, American Bar Association (1994). Copies can be obtained from the American Bar Association, 750 North Lake Shore Drive, Chicago, IL 60611.

6.   Consumer transactions are governed by the Electronic Fund Transfer Act of 1978, 15 U.S.C. § 1693 *et. seq.,* and Regulation E, 12 C.F.R. § 205.

7.   U.C.C. § 4A-103(a)(1) (1989).

8.   In more complex transactions there are one or more additional banks known as *intermediary banks* between the originator's bank and the beneficiary's bank. In such a funds transfer, the instruction contained in the originator's payment order to its bank is carried out by a series of payment orders by each bank in the transmission chain to the next bank in the chain until the beneficiary's bank receives a payment order to credit the beneficiary's account. *See* U.C.C. Article 4A, Prefatory Note at 2, and § 104(b) "Intermediary Bank."

9.   U.C.C. § 4A-105(a)(5) (1989).

10. In contrast to check-based payments, the originator may specify the funds-transfer system to be used by the originator's bank to communicate payment to the beneficiary's bank. Selection of a funds-transfer system may be desirable because of the wide variation in cost among the differing funds-transfer systems and options available to the parties—such as immediate versus next day settlement, the ability to warehouse payment orders, and the ability to have remittance information accompany payment. If the originator does not select a funds-transfer system, the originator's bank may, in its discretion, select a funds-transfer system. U.C.C. § 4A-104(a) (1989).

11. National Automated Clearing House Association, *1995 ACH Rules: A Complete Guide to the Rules & Regulations Governing the ACH Network* (1995) at i. There are 40 ACHs in the United States, including 11 private ACHs operated by banks for their own account and 29 regional ACHs operated by associations of financial institutions.

12. *See* Subpart B of Regulation J of the Federal Reserve Board, 12 C.F.R. § 210.26(e)(19) (hereinafter "Reg. J"); *see generally,* Reg. J §§ 210.25-210.32.

13. *See* New York Clearing House Association, *Clearing House Interbank Payments System* (1992) at 2 ("CHIPS users also include many other commercial banks headquartered in New York, over 95 New York branches or agencies of foreign banks," among others). Participating banks are required to have offices in New York City and clearing accounts with the New York Federal Reserve Bank. *Id.*

14. U.C.C. § 4A-104(a) (1989).

15. U.C.C. § 4A-404(a) (1989).

16. U.C.C. § 4A-104(a) (1989).

17. U.C.C. § 4A-103(a)(1) (1989).

18. U.C.C. § 4A-201 (1989).

19. U.C.C. § 4A-202(b) (1989).

20. *See* U.C.C. Article 3 § 403.

21. Data Interchange Standards Association, *Introduction to Electronic Data Interchange* (Alexandria, Va., 1991) at 7. For a general discussion of the law relating to EDI, *see* Baum & Perritt, *Electronic Contracting, Publishing and EDI Law* (Wiley, 1991); Wright, *The Law of Electronic Commerce* (Little, Brown, 1995); Baum, *EDI and the Law,* EDI Forum (1989) at 78–83, and *EDI and the Law* (Walden, *ed.*) (Blenheim, 1989).

22. EDI standards define commonly used business transactions in a formal, structured manner called *transaction sets.* A transaction set is typically the electronic analog of a business document (such as a purchase order, invoice, or remittance advice). Much of the information included in a transaction set parallels that contained in a corresponding paper document. The information is typically organized in a preordered structured format. See Chapter 6 for further discussion of EDI.

23. The term *financial EDI* is defined here to encompass a combination of electronic data interchange and electronic funds transfers. However, the term *financial EDI* is sometimes applied to a variety of other financial-related transactions, such as purely administrative information transfers between trading partners that are unrelated to specific payments. Such administrative information may include periodic reports and statements sent between a bank and its customer via EDI. *See* Hill & Ferguson, *Introduction to EFT and Financial EDI,* EDI Forum (EDI Publications, Inc. 1989) at 26.

24. Not all funds-transfer systems can accommodate the communication of remittance information.

25. *See, e.g., Delbrueck & Co. v. Manufacturers Hanover Trust Co.,* 609 F.2d 1047, 1051 (2d Cir. 1979) (which notes in detail a funds-transfer systems verification procedure and states that "[t]he practices associated with banking transactions can be conclusive evidence of the legal effect of those transactions.").

26. The Electronic Fund Transfer Act is found at 15 U.S.C. § 1693.

27. See 15 U.S.C. §§ 1693(c), 1693(d)(c), and Regulation E at 12 C.F.R. §§ 205.7 and 205.9(b).

28. 15 U.S.C. §§ 1693(g), 1693(i); Regulation E at 12 C.F.R. §§ 205.5 and 205.6.

29. 12 C.F.R. Part 205.

30. 12 C.F.R. § 205.6.

31. http://www.fv.com

32. http://www.cybercash.com

33. The project is being undertaken by the Financial Services Technology Consortium (FSTC). FSTC is a consortium of financial services providers, national laboratories, universities, and government agencies who sponsor and participate in noncompetitive collaborative research and development on interbank technical projects. For more information, see http://www.llnl.gov/fstc/index.html

34. For more information on the use of encryption for digital cash, see Bruce Schneier, *Applied Cryptography* (John Wiley & Sons 1996).

35. http://www.digicash.com

PART III

RIGHTS IN ELECTRONIC INFORMATION

8
Understanding Electronic Property Rights

Thomas J. Smedinghoff

The world of the Internet and other online forms of electronic communication is a world of digital information. The "content," "data," or "information"[1] that inhabits this world includes many of the things that we know in a tangible form—numbers and letters, text and data, messages, sound recordings, images and graphics, photographs, motion pictures, and software. Yet, when digitally represented, all of these things take on an identical form—a series of ones and zeros recorded in a machine-readable format.

There is no question that this information can have considerable value. The enormous revenues of the publishing, advertising, music recording, motion picture, and computer software industries underscore the fact that ownership of this information has significant economic consequences.

Who owns this information? What does ownership mean? What rights do the owners have? What can non-owners do? Does the digitized form of online information affect these rights? How do the traditional laws dealing with the ownership of information apply in cyberspace? Is it appropriate to talk about property rights in digital information communicated via global networks such as the Internet?

"Ownership" of information is not a simple unitary concept. Instead, it involves the interplay among a variety of different rights—including copyright, trademark, trade secret, patent, publicity, and privacy rights. Although each of these rights has different characteristics and limitations, they also share a number of common themes when applied to digital information. This overview addresses some of those common themes.

Specifically, to provide a foundation for understanding the various electronic property rights discussed in the following chapters, this chapter addresses two fundamental concepts:

1. The nature of information as property—that is, what does it mean to "own" information; and
2. The impact of digitization on rights of ownership in information.

8.1 What Does It Mean to "Own" Information?

The law is clear that property rights exist in information; that is, information can be "owned."[2] To varying degrees, all of the intangible intellectual property rights discussed in the following nine chapters can be owned, and they can also be transferred by the owner to others.[3] But ownership of information is very different from ownership of tangible personal property such as a car, computer, or refrigerator.

This section will examine some of the key characteristics shared by information property rights, and the ways that they differ from tangible property rights. The individual property rights themselves (copyright, trade secret, trademark, patent, publicity, and privacy), and the ownership issues discussed in this section, are explained in the subsequent chapters.

8.1.1 Ownership Is Not Equated With Possession

Information cannot be "possessed" in the same way that a tangible good (such as a car, computer, or refrigerator) can be possessed. Unlike a car, which can be possessed by only one person, the same information can be simultaneously possessed by multiple persons.

This is because rights in information exist separately from any copy of the information. In other words, although information normally exists on a tangible medium such as paper, film, tape, disk, or CD-ROM,[4] its existence as a property right is independent of any particular medium. Information does not necessarily exist in one place, nor is it tied to any one medium. The rights to the story *Gone With the Wind,* for example, exist independently of whether the work is embodied in a paper book, a movie on film or videotape, or a disk or CD-ROM. Thus, when we consider rights in information, we cannot focus on possession of any particular tangible medium on which a copy of the information may happen to reside. "Owning" the rights in information is unrelated to ownership of any tangible copy or medium. For example, when you buy a book at a bookstore, or a compact disc at a music store, you become the owner of the copy embodying the information contained on it. You do not, however, become the owner of the information contained on that copy.[5]

Thus, unlike the instance with tangible goods, you can transfer information to a second party, but also still retain it. When an automobile dealer sells you a car, it parts with possession of the car and cannot sell that same car again to someone else. When an electronic publisher sells you a copy of today's news, or a software publisher sells you a copy of its latest product, the result is that both you and the publisher now have the information. The publisher does not part with what it has sold you, and remains free to sell the same thing—the information—to others. Unlike tangible goods, information can be "used" without using it up and "sold" without giving it up.[6]

8.1.2 Ownership Involves Multiple Legal Rights

The ownership of information is not a single, indivisible right. Rather, it is a composite or "bundle" of rights. Owning information means controlling the right to do one or more things with that information, including the following:

- The right to control *access* to the information,
- The right to control *disclosure* of the information,

- The right to control *use* of the information,
- The right to control *copying* of the information,
- The right to control *alteration* or *destruction* of the information,
- The right to control *distribution* of the information, and
- The right to control the *public performance or display* of the information.

The existence of these ownership rights does not come from a single statute, but rather from a variety of different sources. The primary sources of these rights are copyright law, trade secret law, trademark law, patent law, and the law relating to the individual rights of privacy and publicity.[7] These are discussed in the following chapters in this section of the book.

Not all of these rights will exist with respect to all forms of information. A magazine article in digital form, for example, is most likely to be protected by copyright law, thereby providing its owner with the right to control copying, alteration, distribution, and public display of the article. However, it is unlikely that the rights granted under the trade secret or patent laws will be relevant in such an instance. On the other hand, information consisting of a computer program may be simultaneously protected by copyright, trade secret, and patent law. Thus, ownership of information involves controlling one or more of several different rights.

8.1.3 Ownership May Be Split Among Multiple Persons

Because the ownership of information involves a bundle of several different rights, it follows that these rights in information may be owned by several different persons. One person (such as the author of an article) may own the right to control copying of the information, whereas another person (such as an online service provider) may own the right to control access to the information. The fact that property rights in information may be owned by several persons means that, in many cases, no single person's rights are absolute.

For example, a photographer may own copyright rights in a photograph he took of Elvis Presley. However, Elvis Presley's estate separately owns Elvis's right of publicity. Consequently, the photographer does not have the absolute right to copy, use, modify, or distribute his copyrighted photograph for all purposes; his rights are limited to uses that avoid infringing the right of publicity. Elvis Presley's estate has the right to control commercial uses of his image; but it cannot copy the copyrighted photograph without the photographer's permission.

Similarly, when an author's copyrighted content is made available via an online service such as Compuserve, Prodigy, or America Online, the rights inherent in the copyright are owned by the author, whereas the right to control access to the information belongs to the provider of the online service. Further, if the work that is published via an online service contains the image or likeness of an individual, or certain types of information about an individual, that individual may (in some cases) control the right to alter and/or distribute that information.

In addition, ownership of any single right in information can usually be subdivided among multiple persons. For example, the rights to publish a book might be divided by the medium of publication. Thus one publisher may obtain the right to publish the work in hard-copy form, another publisher may obtain the right to publish the work in paperback form, and yet a third publisher may obtain the right to publish the work in electronic form. The manner in which rights may be divided depends, to a certain extent, on the industry involved. In some cases, rights are divided along geographical lines (such as North American distribution rights, European distribution rights, etc.), or by language (English and foreign-language editions), a fact that presents its own unique problems for online distribution.

When setting up a Web page, for example, a business may want to include content from brochures or other forms of marketing literature that were prepared for it by an advertising agency or other creative talent. If the ad agency retained the copyright in the material and granted the business a right to publish and distribute that material in paper form only, the business may find it is not authorized to put its own advertising material on its Web site in electronic form—at least not without obtaining additional permission, and perhaps paying an additional fee.

Thus, one may "own" certain rights in information, while others may own different rights in the same information.

8.1.4 Ownership Is Limited in Scope

Regardless of who owns any of the various rights in information, it is also important to understand that each of those rights is limited in scope by the law from which it is obtained. Unlike the ownership of tangible goods, where ownership is typically exclusive, ownership of rights in information does not always mean that an individual can control all use of that information by others. The scope of any given right is typically limited. For example, the right to control copying of a book (which comes from the copyright law), does not extend to the right to control copying of the ideas or facts contained in the book. Rather, it is limited to a right to control copying of the particular words (that is, the expression) that the author has chosen to express those ideas. Likewise, the right to control the access to, use of, and disclosure of information (a right that trade secret law grants inventors and discoverers of valuable information), is limited to information that is, in fact, secret. It does not protect the same information when it is independently discovered by someone else. Nor does it protect the information if it is not kept secret by the original discoverer or inventor.

Thus, when evaluating ownership rights in information, it is important to look at each right separately and determine the scope of each right granted. As discussed in the next several chapters, there is a wide variation in the scope of each of the various information property rights.

8.1.5 Ownership Is Subject to Numerous Exceptions

In addition to limitations on the scope of the rights granted in information, each of the rights granted is subject to numerous exceptions. Under these exceptions, the law will permit non-owners to exercise rights in the information, even without the owner's permission. There are different exceptions for the different types of rights, as discussed in the following chapters.

For example, the copyright law grants an author the exclusive right to control copying of his or her work; however, under the fair use exception, others may also copy the work in certain circumstances. Copyright owners also have the exclusive right to distribute their works; however, under the first sale doctrine, someone who buys a copy of the work is free to resell or transfer that particular copy. Likewise, although the owner of a trade secret has the right to control the use and disclosure of the information, others are still free to use the same information if they discover it independently. The right to control the distribution of information about one's self that flows from the right of privacy is subject to exceptions flowing from the First Amendment right of free speech, which normally allows the use of such information when it is newsworthy. Thus, in evaluating the scope of one's ownership in information, it is important to take into account the rights of non-owners to use the information under the applicable exceptions.

The limits on the scope of each of the rights that comprise online property rights, and the exceptions to each of the online property rights, define the rights of non-owners to make use of the information. Thus, when considering the enforcement of "online property rights," it is important to determine who owns each of the relevant rights, and to examine the scope of the rights involved and the limitations that apply to those rights. As discussed in the next several chapters, each of these factors can have a profound impact on the ability to enforce an online property right.

8.1.6 An Example

An example may help to put the foregoing principles in perspective. Consider the rights to the information consisting of a picture of basketball star Michael Jordan printed on a box of Wheaties cereal, or displayed on a General Mills Web site to promote their cereal. What property rights are involved in this picture? Who "owns" these rights? What can the owners do? What can non-owners do? As discussed above (and explained in detail in the following chapters):

- The rights in the photo exist separately from any tangible medium, such as the film, print, negative, cereal box, or Web server on which the photo appears. Someone who buys a box of Wheaties does not own any rights in the photo itself.[8]
- There are at least two legal rights in the photo—a copyright and a right of publicity. Moreover, these rights are presumably owned by separate persons—the photographer usually owns the copyright in the photo that allows him or her to control what others do with that photo (for example, the photographer can prevent others from copying that photo), and Michael Jordan owns a right of publicity in

his image that allows him to control certain uses of that photo, even by the photographer who owns the copyright in the photo.

- The individual types of rights may also be subdivided. Thus, the cereal company (General Mills) may have the permission of the photographer and Jordan to use the photo on a cereal box or Web page, but not on a book or a game.

- Each person's rights are limited in scope. For example, the photographer has the right to control copying and distribution of the photo of Jordan, but he or she cannot prevent anyone else from taking a picture of Jordan, nor does the photographer have a monopoly on the idea of using a picture of a basketball player on a box of cereal or a Web page. Michael Jordan himself can only control uses of the photo that would infringe his right of publicity. Thus, he can stop use of the photo for promotional purposes on a cereal box without his permission, but he cannot stop use of that same photo in a newspaper story about his performance in an NBA championship game. Moreover, neither the photographer nor Jordan can stop a purchaser of a box of Wheaties from reselling that box with Jordan's picture.

- Finally, the rights are subject to exceptions. For example, anyone can copy the photo (notwithstanding the photographer's wishes to the contrary), in cases where the copying is deemed to be fair use. In addition, the photographer can publish the photo (notwithstanding Michael Jordan's wishes to the contrary), in cases where its use involves news or freedom of the press.

8.2 Impact of Digital Form on Ownership Rights

In addition to the foregoing characteristics of information property rights, it is important to focus on the impact of representing information in digital form. In many cases, this form is likely to increase the risk that the owner's rights can be violated, and could make these rights harder to enforce.

Computer technology has had an enormous impact on the creation, reproduction, and dissemination of all forms of information. Any two-dimensional work can readily be "digitized"—that is, translated into a computer-readable series of zeros and ones. In such a digital form, information possesses a number of characteristics not found in information represented in tangible form. These characteristics include the following:

- Digital information can be more easily and quickly copied, and the copies are virtually indistinguishable from the original (both the first and the hundredth generation are virtually identical). As one commentator has noted, "the Internet is the world's biggest copying machine."[9] The owner's legal rights may thus be more easily violated and harder to enforce.

- Digital information can easily be edited, manipulated, and combined with other information, without detection. Again, this ease of manipulation means that more violations are likely to occur, and enforcement can be difficult. Also, alterations and distortions raise the risks that the integrity of the original work and the author's reputation will be damaged.

- Digital information can now be distributed worldwide, virtually instantaneously on a massive scale by almost anyone. Printing presses, complex distribution systems, and warehouses used to store hard copies are no longer needed. These factors greatly increase the risk of violations. In addition, it is far more difficult to identify, locate, and prosecute electronic "pirates" than it is to prosecute traditional infringers. Finally, a pirate's customers can continue to redistribute the work electronically, thus potentially multiplying the infringement many times over.

As one commentator has pointedly asked, "If our property can be infinitely reproduced and instantaneously distributed all over the planet without cost, without our knowledge, without its leaving our possession, how can we protect it?"[10]

There is no question that a digital environment creates problems for those who seek to enforce their rights in information. On the other hand, at least one aspect of digital technology may increase an owner's remedies and reduce a user's rights. In order to read, view, hear, or otherwise consume digital information, one must technically "copy" it in the RAM of a computer. Thus, the mere act of reading or viewing the work can technically constitute copyright infringement, under traditional principles. (See Section 10.1.) By contrast, merely reading a printed book is not infringement.

This aspect of computer and online technology creates a dilemma for the law—how can it be illegal merely to read (or use) something on a computer in the intended manner? Recognizing this unfairness (in the context of software) and the need to adapt the law to changing conditions, Congress amended the copyright law in 1980 to permit certain limited "copying" of computer software. The *owner* of a *copy* of a software program may use that copy in its intended fashion by copying it into RAM, and may make a limited number of backup copies. However, this Copyright Act exception is not worded broadly enough to address concerns relating to online transmissions (since the receiver does not obtain a tangible copy), or to media that comprise leased or licensed copies (since the reader does not "own" the physical copy).

Thus, the nature of digital technology can pose increased risks to owners and users alike. Under current law and technology, information owners may face more infringement with fewer practical ways to combat it. Users face the prospect that, by merely viewing or consuming digital information in the intended manner, they could be violating the law. This dilemma can be resolved only by further understanding and advances in the field of law and technology.

In the meantime, existing legal principles will govern our rights and obligations in online transactions. The challenge for rights owners is to determine how to protect their rights in information that can be infinitely reproduced and instantaneously distributed worldwide, at no cost and without their knowledge. The challenge for those who wish to use information is to determine the rules that govern their conduct and that define their rights to use, adapt, and distribute that information. The following chapters will discuss these issues in more detail.

8.3 Two Perspectives: Owners and Users

Finally, it is important to note that everyone needs to address rights in information from two perspectives: (1) as an *owner* of rights in information, and (2) as a *user* of information owned by someone else.

Electronic communication of information is a two-way street. An individual sends information that he or she owns to another, and worries about controlling its subsequent use. But that same person also receives information from someone else, and wonders what he or she can do with it.

Owners of rights in information want to know the scope of their rights, how to protect those rights when the information is made available online, and how to exploit the value of their information online. Conversely, persons using information owned by others want to know what use they can make of it (short of getting permission) without infringing the rights of the owner.

Thus, when considering the issue of rights in online information, it is important to address it from both perspectives. That is, both the owners of information and those who do not own the information have certain rights to the use (or to control the use) of the information. The ultimate goal, of course, is to address three categories of issues that are important with respect to using information in an online environment: *ownership*, *rights of owners*, and *rights of users*. In other words:

1. Who owns the information?
2. If the information is mine, what rights do I have in it, how do I protect it when it is available online, and how do I exploit its value online? and
3. If the information is not mine, how is my conduct restricted, and what use can I make of the information (short of getting permission) without infringing the rights of the owner?

These issues, as they apply to each of the specific ownership rights in information, will be addressed in the remaining chapters in Part III of this book.

Endnotes

1.   Terms such as *data, content* and *information* are frequently used to describe the "things" that can reside on a computer or in a machine-readable form. In some cases the words are used interchangeably; in other cases they are intended to mean different things. For purposes of this book, we will use these terms interchangeably to mean anything that can be digitally represented in the machine-readable storage devices used by computer. That is, these terms will refer to anything that can be represented by ones and zeros, such as letters, numbers, words, sounds, images, video, software, and the like.

2.   *See Ruckelshaus v. Monsanto Co.*, 467 U.S. 986, 1002-04 (1984); *Carpenter v. United States*, 484 U.S. 19, 25-27 (1987).

3.   *See, e.g.*, 17 U.S.C. § 201 (copyrights); 1 Roger M. Milgrim, *Milgrim on Trade Secrets*, § 2.01[2], at 2–11 (1993) (trade secrets); 35 U.S.C. § 261 (patents).

4. In fact, some forms of information (such as a secret formula, your opinion of a presidential candidate, or the location of a buried treasure) could also exist only in your mind.

5. You do, however, obtain certain limited rights, such as the first sale right to further transfer that copy. See Section 11.5.

6. It is, of course, possible to own a tangible good without possessing it. Leases are a good example—that is, the lessor of a car owns the car, but does not have possession. However, the lessor always has a right to possession, such as upon termination of the lease or a default by the lessee. Conversely, the owner of rights in information need not possess a copy of, nor even have the right to possess, any existing copy.

7. The copyright law, for example, grants to owners of a copyrighted work the right to control copying, alteration, distribution, public performance, and public display of the work. Trade secret law governs the right to control access to and the use and disclosure of information. Patent law grants the right to control the manufacture and use of the patented item. The rights of privacy and publicity allow the owners of those rights some measure of control over the alteration and distribution of certain information about themselves. Criminal laws allow persons to control access to information.

8. However, they do acquire the right to resell that particular copy of the photo pursuant to the first-sale doctrine. See Section 11.5.

9. *Policing Cyberspace,* U.S. News & World Report, (Jan. 23, 1995) (quoting Marybeth Peters, Register of Copyrights).

10. John Perry Barlow, *The Economy of Ideas,* Wired, March 1994 at p. 85.

9

Copyrights in Digital Information

Thomas J. Smedinghoff

Endnotes

9.1 What Is a Copyright?

A copyright is a form of protection provided by the laws of the United States (and most other countries) to those who create what the law refers to as "original works of authorship."[1] It is, in essence, a grant of certain exclusive rights to authors in order to allow them commercially to exploit their works. These rights are discussed in Chapter 10.

Whether in digital form or in print, most information is automatically protected by copyright from the moment it is created. The author is not required to use a copyright notice, register with the U.S. Copyright Office, or, for that matter, take any action whatsoever. The protection applies automatically. Consequently, copyright is one of the key "rights" in information.

Because copyright protection is automatic, its impact must be considered whenever a copyrightable work is created, used, or encountered online. Copyright owners need to understand the nature and scope of the rights they have, and everyone else needs to understand the rules that govern their use of those copyrighted works. Key questions include: Who owns the copyright in information? What rights are granted to copyright owners? How do you ensure that your use of information owned by others is lawful?

9.2 Applicability of Copyright to Online Communications

9.2.1 Digital Forms of Information Protected

Copyright protection applies to most works regardless of the form in which the work exists or the media on which it is recorded, so long as the work can be perceived, reproduced, or communicated directly by humans or indirectly with the aid of a machine.[2] Information that exists in a traditional form, such as on paper, does not lose its copyright protection when it is converted into a digital form. Likewise, works that are originally created in a digital machine-readable form (and that exist only in such a form), obtain all of the same copyright protections as those granted to works originally created in a more traditional form (such as paper).

Thus, for example, an e-mail message is protected by copyright just as if the same message were handwritten, typed, or printed in the form of a letter on paper.[3] Similarly, a story is protected by copyright regardless of whether the words are printed on paper, recorded in a magnetic form on a computer disk, or in an optical form on a CD-ROM disc. Likewise, a photograph is protected in both a printed and digital form.

9.2.2 Online Conduct Always Implicates Copyright

Not only is most digital information protected by copyright, but all forms of online conduct also involve rights protected under the copyright law. In other words, it is impossible to do anything online with copyrighted information that does not involve one or more of the rights granted to the copyright owner. For example, viewing a copy of an Internet Web page involves making a copy of its copyrighted content (i.e., the copyrighted text and images comprising the Web page are copied to the user's computer, where they are displayed for viewing). Thus, the user viewing the Web page is making a copy, and the owner of the Web site is making a public display of the copyrighted content. If the user prints the contents of the Web page, or saves it to disk, an additional copy is made. Moreover, in such a case, the owner of the Web site may be engaged in the distribution of copyrighted content. All of these actions—copying, displaying, and distributing—involve rights exclusively granted to the copyright owner (the rights are discussed in detail in Chapter 10). In fact, something as simple as sending an e-mail message typically involves the copying and distribution of copyrighted material.

These far-reaching implications will, of course, have a profound impact on the ability of the copyright owner to protect its rights, as well as in the liability of the user for its online conduct.

9.2.3 Digital Challenges to Copyright Owners

When content exists in digital form, it is a trivial task to make a copy that is indistinguishable from the original, to modify that copy in a manner that cannot be detected, and instantaneously to distribute that copy worldwide at virtually no cost. As a consequence, it has become very easy for almost anyone to infringe the copyright of another on a massive scale. Moreover, it is often very difficult for the copyright owner to detect the infringement and to identify and prosecute the infringer.

The digital world of online communications poses perhaps the greatest challenge to the scheme of copyright protection that has served us so well for over 200 years. When copyrighted works are written on paper, chiseled in stone, or set in cement, the time and expense involved in duplicating, modifying, or distributing copies of these works; the ease of detecting infringement; and the relative ease of identifying and prosecuting infringers combined to allow the law to protect adequately the rights of authors. But when these barriers are removed, as they are in the online world, these rights become more difficult to enforce.

Some copyright owners have chosen to respond to these challenges by adopting new business models that place less emphasis on enforcement of rights in content, or models that use content as a loss leader for other purposes.[4] For example, many publishers on the World Wide Web provide their content for free as a form of open advertising to induce readers to purchase their other goods or services. Others provide content for free but charge sponsors for advertising space. Yet several recent cases indicate that, notwithstanding the problems of enforcement, copyright protection remains viable as a form of protection for online works.

9.2.4 Digital Challenges to Copyright Users

Copyright also presents special challenges for online users of digital content owned by others. Although most digital information is copyrightable, the traditional rules seem inappropriate in many cases. For example, e-mail messages are copyrightable, yet they are routinely copied by recipients and forwarded to others. Likewise, a great deal of copyrighted content is electronically published on numerous online services, yet these same services provide interface software products that include the capability to copy this material to a printer or to a disk for further use. Online users of copyrighted content owned by others need guidance to determine when their conduct constitutes infringement and when it is permissible. These issues are discussed in Chapter 11.

9.2.5 Copyright on Global Information Networks

When information is published online, the publication takes on a global nature. But what protection does a U.S. publisher have when its content is copied and further distributed by someone in another country?

There is no such thing as an international copyright. Copyright laws are territorial, and apply only to acts of infringement that occur within a country's borders. However, several international treaties link together major nations and establish both minimum standards for protecting each other's copyrighted works and the basis upon which such protection is to be extended. The Berne Convention is the principal copyright treaty. As of July 1995, 114 countries have signed the Berne Convention.

One of the key elements of the Berne Convention is the principle of "national treatment." This principle obligates all of the countries that have signed the Berne Convention to extend the protection of their copyright law to foreigners whose works are infringed within the borders of their country. Thus, for example, if a work created by a German author were infringed in the United States, the author would be able to turn to the U.S. copyright law to punish the infringers. Likewise, if a copyrighted work created by a U.S. author were infringed in France, a French court would extend the protection of French copyright law to the U.S. author.

9.3 Information Protected by Copyright

The Copyright Act[5] protects virtually all types of information available online. Works that qualify for copyright protection include literary works, databases, characters, musical works, sound recordings, pictorial and graphic works, video and motion pictures, software; compilations and multimedia works.[6]

- **Literary Works.** All types of text-based works are typically copyrightable. This includes literary works such as books, plays, poems, articles, and the like, as well as other works expressed in words, numbers, or other symbols.[7] The majority of all works currently available on the Internet and other computer networks are literary works. E-mail messages; many forms of online advertisements; marketing literature; product descriptions; essays; catalogs; dictionaries; documentation; online help files; textual information posted on Internet Web sites, FTP sites, and gopher sites; and messages posted to listservs, UseNet groups, and other public and private discussion groups are all literary works protected by copyright.

- **Data.** Pure data, such as names and addresses, part numbers, stock quotes, price lists, temperature readings, and so forth, are facts, and as such do *not* qualify for copyright protection.[8] As a general rule, facts by themselves can never be copyrightable. This is true of all facts—scientific, historical, biographical, and news of the day. They are part of the public domain available to every person.[9] Thus, for example, a person's name, address, and telephone number is an uncopyrightable fact, as is their birth date, and the populations of each of the cities and towns in the United States. Similarly, Internet domain names,[10] URL addresses for Internet Web sites, and public-private key pairs used for public key encryption and digital signatures (see Chapters 4 and 31) are not copyrightable.

- **Databases.** Collections of data (such as databases), however, are normally copyrightable as compilations.[11] This is true for databases comprised of copyrightable components (such as a database of news articles), as well as for databases comprised of uncopyrightable components (such as a database of names and addresses, a database of part numbers, or a database of URL addresses for Internet Web sites). However, the scope of protection provided by copyright law for databases of uncopyrightable facts is much less than that provided for databases of copyrighted materials. It protects only the selection, coordination, and arrangement of the information by the author. It does not prevent copying of the facts themselves. Moreover, some databases of uncopyrightable components do not qualify for copyright protection due to a lack of originality; an example is a database consisting of the white pages of a standard phone book (see Section 9.4.2).[12]

- **Characters.** Fictional characters can exist in a visual form (e.g., Mickey Mouse and Superman); in a literary form, such as in the text of a story (e.g., Sherlock Holmes, the Hardy Boys, or James Bond); or as represented by actors in a motion picture or television program (e.g., James Bond, E.T., Darth Vader, or Superman). In each of these cases the character can be entitled to copyright protection.[13] They are most readily protectable when they exist in some sort of pictorial or graphic form, as occurs with cartoon characters such as Mickey Mouse, Donald Duck, Superman, and Peanuts.[14] Characters that exist only in the words of a book or play can also be copyrightable, separate and apart from the text containing the story in which they appear. However, whether or not they are protected by copyright depends upon the degree to which they are developed in the story. The less developed the characters, the less likely it is that they will be copyrightable.[15]

- **Musical Works.** Musical works are copyrightable.[16] Copyright protection for musical works extends to both the words and the music.[17] Even if the music alone or the lyrics alone are in the public domain, the combination may be original enough to qualify.[18] Thus, musical instrument digital interface (MIDI) files are presumably protected by copyright.[19]

- **Sound Recordings.** A sound recording is a work that results from the recording of a series of musical, spoken, or other sounds. It can be embodied in any physical medium, such as CD-ROM discs, diskettes, or audio tapes.[20] Sound recordings are copyrightable regardless of the nature of the sounds recorded.[21] Common examples of a copyrightable sound recording include a recording of a performance of a musical work (whether or not the music is copyrighted); a recording of spoken words, such as a drama or a speech (whether or not the words are copyrighted); a recording of sounds of nature (for example, birds chirping, waves crashing onto the shore, etc.); special sound effects (for example, a door slamming, cars crashing together, etc.); or virtually any other sound that can be recorded.[22] Thus, sound recordings captured in digital form, such as WAV files, are copyrightable works.

- **Photographs and Still Images.** Pictorial and graphic works are copyrightable.[23] These include advertisements, cartoons, charts, comic strips, diagrams, drawings, paintings, designs, games, puzzles, maps, mosaics, patterns, photographs, photomontages, prints and art reproductions, technical drawings, architectural drawings or plans, blueprints, diagrams, and mechanical drawings.[24] There is no implied criterion of artistic taste, aesthetic value, or intrinsic quality necessary for copyrightability.[25] Thus, GIF files of any of these items typically represent copyrightable information. In one case, for example, when photographs from *Playboy* magazine were scanned into digital GIF format without permission and uploaded to a computer bulletin board where they were made available for downloading by subscribers, such conduct constituted copyright infringement.[26]

- **Motion Pictures and Other Audiovisual Works.** Motion pictures, video, and other audiovisual works are copyrightable.[27] Audiovisual works are works that consist of a series of related images that are intrinsically intended to be shown by the use of machines or devices such as televisions, computers, or other electronic equipment, together with accompanying sounds, if any.[28] Thus, audiovisual works include a film, a videotape, a videodisc, a television news broadcast,[29] and a videogame.[30] Whether viewed through a television via a broadcast or cable transmission, or viewed on a computer connected to the Internet, such audiovisual works are copyrightable.

- **Software.** Software is copyrightable.[31] Software, like other copyrightable works, can be dedicated to the public domain. However, when initially created, virtually all software qualifies as a copyrightable work.

- **Compilations and Derivative Works.** Copyright protection is also available for compilations and derivative works. A *compilation* is "a work formed by the collection and assembling of preexisting materials or of data that are selected, coordinated or arranged in such a way that the resulting work as a whole constitutes an original work of authorship."[32] Examples of compilations include catalogs, databases, directories, magazines, and anthologies. A *derivative work* is "a work based upon one or more preexisting works, such as a translation, fictionalization, motion picture version, sound recording, art reproduction, abridgment, condensation, or any other form in which a work may be recast, transformed, or adapted."[33] Examples of derivative works include the translation of a book from English to French, a movie based on a book, a new version of a computer program, and a new sound recording that is based on a copyrighted musical composition. Even a new version of a work in the public domain can constitute a derivative work.[34]

- **Multimedia Works.** Multimedia works are generally works that combine two or more of the foregoing categories into a single medium.[35] Multimedia works are clearly copyrightable, often comprising compilations or derivative works.

9.4 Acquiring and Perfecting a Copyright

9.4.1 Automatic Protection

Copyright protection applies automatically to any work of authorship that qualifies.[36] As soon as the work is created, it is protected by federal copyright, even if the author has not included a copyright notice, registered with the U.S. Copyright Office, or taken any other steps to assert a copyright claim.[37] For that matter, authors may initially be unaware of the applicability of copyright protection for their works. But as long as the work is one of the types protected by copyright and meets the requirements to qualify for copyright protection (discussed in the next section), the protection applies automatically.

This rule has two important implications. First, almost all digital content that an individual creates will automatically be protected by copyright. Therefore, it is important to determine who owns that copyright (see Section 9.5), and to understand that the work is a potentially valuable asset that the owner may want to exploit, preserve, and protect against exploitation by others. Second, it is important to understand that virtually all preexisting information created by someone else will also be the subject of copyright protection. Accordingly, to use, copy, modify, or distribute any such material (such as on a Web page) will require the permission of the copyright owner, unless the use qualifies under one of the exemptions provided by the Copyright Act (discussed in Chapter 11). The absence of a copyright notice or the failure of the copyright owner to register his or her work does not mean that it is safe to use the work.[38]

9.4.2 Requirements To Qualify

The Copyright Act sets forth only two minimal requirements that must be met in order for a work to qualify for copyright protection. The work must be *original* and it must be *fixed in a tangible form*.[39] The originality requirement is easily met; however, the fixation requirement presents some issues for works that exist in a computer-readable form.

9.4.2.1 Originality. The quantum of originality required to support a copyright is minimal. *Original* means only (1) that the work was "independently created" by the author and (2) that it possesses at least some minimal degree of "creativity."[40]

In most cases, the originality standard is easily met. Thus, for example, a painting of a U.S. flag on the side of a motorcycle is sufficiently original to meet the requirement for copyrightability.[41] Likewise, electronic messages such as simple e-mail messages, postings to listservs, UseNet news groups, chat lines, and other online discussion forums will all presumably meet the requirement for sufficient originality to support copyrightability.

Although the standard is very low, there are works that fail to meet the minimal standard of originality, and thus do not qualify for copyright protection. Online fact-based data may fall into this category, since the Supreme Court has held that facts are not copyrightable and that collections or compilations of facts (such as databases) are copyrightable only to the extent that the selection and arrangement of the data includes the requisite originality (see the discussion at Section 11.6.2). Other examples of works that do not show evidence of the requisite level of originality include the white pages of a phone book;[42] words and short phrases such as names, titles, and slogans; familiar symbols or designs; mere listings of ingredients or contents; blank forms, such as address books, report forms, order forms and the like, which are designed for recording information and do not in themselves convey information; and works consisting entirely of information that is common property, such as standard calendars, height and weight charts, schedules of sporting events, and lists or tables taken from public documents or other common sources.[43]

In light of the foregoing, it is clear that Internet domain names and URL Web addresses are not copyrightable, as they are nothing more than an address on the Internet. (They may, however, raise trademark issues. See Chapter 14.) Likewise, electronic messages that consist of nothing more than formatted data (such as EDI transaction sets, digital cash "coins," and e-mail addresses) are not copyrightable. Keys used for encryption and digital signatures (such as public-private key pairs) are likewise not copyrightable.

9.4.2.2 Fixation. Originality is not enough to ensure copyright protection. Copyright also requires the existence of a tangible object—that is, to be copyrightable, a work must be *fixed* in a tangible medium from which it can be perceived, reproduced, or otherwise communicated, either directly or with the aid of a machine or device.[44] Thus, copyrighted works are printed on paper, painted on canvas, chiseled in stone, recorded on film, copied onto disks, and so forth. It makes no difference what the form, manner, or medium of fixation may be, so long as the information can be read, heard, or viewed directly or through the use of a machine or device such as a computer, VCR, or CD-player.[45] By contrast, something that exists only in someone's mind, or statements that someone makes orally to other people, are not "fixed" in a tangible medium of expression, and thus are not copyrightable unless and until they are written down on paper, recorded in some fashion, or otherwise fixed in a form that allows the thoughts or words to be reproduced or otherwise communicated.

Information fixed in a digital form on computer disk, tape, or CD-ROM meets the fixation requirement necessary for copyrightability (as does the same information fixed on paper, microfilm, or some other medium). A computer program or other digital content residing in the memory of the central processing unit of a computer also meets the fixation requirement.[46] According to one court, even if a computer program resides in the RAM of a computer for only a millisecond, it is sufficiently fixed to meet the requirement of the Copyright Act.[47] In other words, all information created for placement on an electronic database, Web site, or FTP site, or for transmission through the Internet or other online network, will likely be "fixed" in a manner that requires its protection by copyright.

An online transmission of information, however, is not, by itself, a fixation. While a transmission may result in a fixation, a work is not fixed by virtue of the transmission alone. Therefore, works transmitted "live" via the Internet will not meet the fixation requirement, and will be unprotected by the Copyright Act unless the work is being fixed at the same time as it is being transmitted.[48] However, the work being transmitted meets the fixation requirement "if a fixation of the work is being made simultaneously with its transmission."[49] Thus, electronic network transmissions from one computer to another, such as e-mail, which only reside on each computer in RAM (random access memory), are sufficiently fixed to be copyrightable.[50]

9.4.3 Copyright Notice

Although most information is automatically protected by federal copyright law as soon as it is created, there are two other steps a copyright owner should take to obtain the full benefit of the protection provided by the copyright law: include a proper copyright notice on the information, and register the copyright with the U.S. Copyright Office.

A copyright notice is not required to obtain copyright protection in most countries, including the United States.[51] However, it is strongly recommended that copyright owners use a copyright notice, as it is the best way to advise others of their copyright claim. In addition, if a proper copyright notice is used, infringers will not be able to reduce their liability of damages by arguing that their infringement was "innocent."

The copyright notice must contain three basic elements:[52]

1. The symbol © (the letter *c* in a circle), or the word *Copyright*, or the abbreviation *Copr.*
2. The year of first publication of the information.[53]
3. The name of the owner of the copyright in the work, or an abbreviation by which the name can be recognized, or a generally known alternative designation of the owner.

Thus, for a digital copyrighted work first published in 1997, any of the following would constitute a proper copyright notice:

Copyright 1997 [name of owner of copyright]
Copr. 1997 [name of owner of copyright]
© 1997 [name of owner of copyright]
Copyright © 1997 [name of owner of copyright]

The year in the copyright notice should be the year in which the copyrighted work was first published, which may not necessarily be the year in which it was created.

Publication is a term of art under the Copyright Act. Generally, publication occurs when copies of a copyrighted work are distributed to the public by sale or other transfer of ownership, or by rental, lease, or lending. Publication also occurs when the owner offers to distribute copies of the work to a group of persons for purposes of further distribution. Note, however, that any form of dissemination in which a material object containing the work does not change hands is not a publication no matter how many people are exposed to the work.[54] Thus, a work that is only displayed or performed via the Internet (such as on a Web site) would not be considered published, no matter how many people have access to the display or performance, because a material object—such as a disk containing a copy of the work—does not change hands.

Nonetheless, it is a good idea to include copyright notices on Web sites and on all content published online. In some cases it can be a very effective deterrent, and it costs nothing to include it.

9.4.4 Copyright Registration

Copyright registration is a formal procedure that makes a public record of a copyright with the U.S. Copyright Office. It enables a copyright owner to sue infringers, helps to prove ownership of a valid copyright, and allows for the recovery of certain damages and attorneys fees in the event of litigation against infringers. Registration is not a condition of copyright protection.[55] However, the copyright law is designed to encourage registration. The advantages of registration can be summarized as follows:

- Registration establishes a public record of the copyright claim.
- Registration is necessary before the copyright owner can file an infringement suit.[56]
- If the work is registered within five years of publication, registration will establish *prima facie* the validity of the copyright and of the facts stated in the certificate of registration (for example, name of copyright owner, date of first publication, and so forth).[57] This is important because it makes the copyright owner's burden of proof in a lawsuit easier and because it increases the likelihood of obtaining a preliminary injunction against an infringer.
- If the copyrighted work is registered prior to an infringement (or within three months of publication if such infringement occurs after publication), statutory damages (see Section 10.6.1.4) and attorneys' fees will be available to the copyright owner in court actions relating to such infringement. Otherwise, only actual damages may be recovered.[58]

At present, the Copyright Office is not set up to handle registrations electronically, although it plans to do so in the near future. Thus, even though the content to be registered may exist only in a digital form, the registration process must be handled through more traditional means.

When registering a digital copyrighted work, the following three items must be sent to the Copyright Office in the same envelope or package:

1. A properly completed application form,
2. The filing fee, and
3. A deposit of the work being registered.

The address is: Register of Copyrights, Library of Congress, Washington, D.C. 20559

The Copyright Office uses a variety of different application forms, depending upon the copyrighted item being registered. The appropriate form for registration depends on the nature of the copyrighted work.

The filing fee is currently $20.[59] The fee should be paid by check or money order payable to the Register of Copyrights.

A deposit of the work being registered must accompany each application for registration. The deposit requirement varies according to the type of work being registered, and whether or not the work has been published. Copyright Office regulations specify the deposit requirements of each type of work. These requirements are also set forth in Copyright Office Circulars, which are available through the Internet at gopher://marvel.loc.gov:70/11/copyright/circs.

To order forms and circulars, call the Copyright Office forms and circulars hotline at (202) 707-9100, or write to U.S. Copyright Office, Publications Section, LM-455, Library of Congress, Washington, D.C. 20559. Instructions for filling out each of the forms are also available from the same source.

9.5 Who Owns the Copyright?

Since copyright rights in a work arise automatically, the next logical question is: who owns the copyright? By law, the copyright in a work is initially owned by the *author* of the work.[60] But who is the author? The answer to that question depends on the circumstances.

As a general rule, the author (and thus, the owner of the copyright) is the person who actually creates the work; that is, the person who translates an idea into a fixed, tangible expression entitled to copyright protection.[61] Thus, the author is the person who wrote the e-mail message, the photographer who took the picture, the recording artist who performed the musical work, the sound engineer who performed the task of capturing and electronically processing sounds, the person who compiled and edited recorded sounds or visual images, the person who compiled the foregoing content into a Web page, and so forth.

But this is not always true. In some cases, the copyright law considers the author to be the person who commissioned the work and who paid for the time and materials necessary to create it, rather than the person who actually did the creative work. In other cases, however, the person who paid for the work to be created has no rights in the resulting product, regardless of the price paid. In either case, it is important to understand that there may be multiple authors.

When someone creates a work individually, with no assistance from anyone else, and creates it outside the scope of any employment obligations, there is no question that he or she is the author of the work, and consequently the owner of the copyright.[62] This is the easiest case to deal with.

When one party hires someone to create a work for them, however, the rules become somewhat more complicated. In that case, the identity of the author of the work is determined by the nature of the hiring party's relationship with the person who created the work. Specifically, if the work is a *work made for hire*, then the person for whom the work was prepared is considered the author, and hence the owner of the copyright.[63] The person(s) who actually created the work will have no rights in the copyright. However, if it is not a work made for hire, then the person(s) who actually created the work will own the copyright.

The Copyright Act provides two mutually exclusive ways for works to acquire work-for-hire status: one for cases where the work is created by *employees* and the other for cases where the work is created by *independent contractors* by special order or commission.[64] Consequently, in order to determine whether there is a "work for hire" relationship between the person developing a copyrighted work and the party that hired them, it is necessary to determine whether they are performing the work as employees or independent contractors.[65]

9.5.1 Works Created by Employees

If the persons hired are considered to be "employees," any copyrightable work product prepared by them within the scope of their employment is considered to be a "work made for hire."[66] As a consequence, the employer (rather than the employees who actually created the work) is considered to be the "author" of the work, and will own all of the rights comprised in the copyright.[67] The employees who created the work will not have any rights in the copyright whatsoever, unless their employer expressly grants rights to them in a written document signed by both of them.[68]

Thus, for example, work-related e-mail messages or Web site HTML documents created by employees on the job are copyrighted works owned by their employer. As a consequence, the employer, rather than the employee, controls the right to copy and distribute such e-mail messages and HTML documents.

But note that only works created by employees within the scope of their employment will be governed by the "work made for hire" doctrine. Work done outside the normal scope of employment will not normally be covered.

9.5.2 Works Created by Independent Contractors

The reality of the business world is that very frequently the persons that a business commissions to develop a copyrightable work are not its employees (in the literal employee/employer sense). Independent contractors and freelance talent abound in most industries, and companies both large and small frequently use independent contractors to develop a copyrightable work product for them. Examples include Web pages, photographs, logos, articles, software, advertising materials, technical manuals, catalogs, and marketing materials. This raises the troublesome question of who owns the copyright to the resulting work—an issue that is frequently not even discussed between the parties.

Generally, because independent contractors are not employees, when they create a copyrightable work for a client, their work is not considered to be a "work made for hire." Consequently they will own the copyright in any copyrightable works that they develop for a client.

Businesses that want to own the copyright in works created for them by independent contractors have two options. First, they can obtain a written assignment of the copyright from the independent contractor. Second, they can enter into a written work-for-hire agreement, provided that the nature of the project is one that the copyright law considers to be eligible for work-for-hire treatment.[69]

Under the Copyright Act, two criteria must be satisfied before the work of an independent contractor will be considered a work made for hire:[70]

1. The work must be specially ordered or commissioned for use as one of the following:
   - A contribution to a collective work,[71]
   - Part of a motion picture or other audiovisual work,[72]
   - A translation,
   - A supplementary work,[73]
   - A compilation,[74]
   - An instructional text,
   - A test,
   - Answer material for a test, or
   - An atlas; *and*
2. The parties must expressly agree in a written instrument signed by both of them that the work will be considered a work made for hire.

It is important to note that unless *both* of these requirements are fulfilled, the work will not be considered a "work made for hire" and the business will not own the copyright in the work created by the independent contractor it hired. Thus, merely signing a contract with an independent contractor specifying that a work is to be deemed a "work made for hire" (the second of the two requirements) will not necessarily deprive the independent contractor of his or her copyright. The work must also fulfill the first requirement by falling within one of the nine categories listed above.

Even if the work performed by a consultant meets the first part of the two-part test, it is important to remember that the Copyright Act also requires a written agreement between the parties specifically stating that the work to be created by the consultant is a "work made for hire." The agreement must be signed by both parties.[75]

If work performed by an independent contractor cannot be fitted within the "work made for hire" doctrine, but the hiring party nonetheless wants to obtain the copyright ownership in the resulting product, the only alternative is to have the independent contractor execute a written assignment of his or her copyright.

Endnotes

1. 17 U.S.C. § 102(a). See Section 9.4.2.

2. 17 U.S.C. § 102(a) ("copyright protection subsists . . . in original works of authorship fixed in any tangible medium of expression, now known or later developed, from which they can be perceived, reproduced, or otherwise communicated, either directly or with the aid of a machine or device").

3. *See, e.g., Salinger v. Random House, Inc.,* 811 F.2d 90, 94 (2d Cir. 1987) (letters are copyrightable), *cert. denied,* 484 U.S. 890 (1987).

4. *See, e.g.,* Esther Dyson, *Intellectual Value,* Wired, 136 (Jul. 1995).

5. 17 U.S.C. §§ 101 *et. seq.*

6. 17 U.S.C. §§ 101, 102(a).

7. 17 U.S.C. § 101 (definition of "literary works").

8. *Feist Publications, Inc. v. Rural Tele. Serv. Co.,* 499 U.S. 340, 111 S. Ct. 1282 (1991).

9. *Feist Publications, Inc. v. Rural Tele. Serv. Co.,* 499 U.S. 340, 111 S. Ct. 1282, 1287, 1288, 1289, 1290, and 1293 (1991).

10. Note, however, that domain names may be protectable as trademarks. See Chapter 14.

11. A compilation is any work formed by the collection and assembling of preexisting materials that are selected, coordinated, or arranged in such a way that the resulting work as a whole constitutes an original work of authorship. 17. U.S.C. §§ 101 (definition of "compilation") and 103(a).

12. *Feist Publications, Inc. v. Rural Tele. Serv. Co.,* 499 U.S. 340, 111 S. Ct. 1282 (1991).

13. *See Walt Disney Productions v. Air Pirates,* 581 F.2d 751 (9th Cir. 1978) ("Mickey Mouse," "Donald Duck," and several other Disney characters); *Detective Comics, Inc. v. Bruns Publications, Inc.,* 111 F.2d 432, 433–434 (2d Cir. 1940) ("Superman" character); *United Feature Syndicate, Inc. v. SunRise Mold Co.,* 569 F. Supp. 1475, 1480 (S.D. Fla. 1983) ("Peanuts" characters); *Eden Toys, Inc. v. Florelee Undergarment Co.,* 697 F.2d 27 (2d Cir. 1982) ("Paddington Bear," a character in a series of children's books); *Nichols v. Universal Pictures Corp.,* 45 F.2d 119, 121 (2d Cir. 1930) (discussing copyrightability of literary characters), *cert. denied,* 282 U.S. 902 (1931); *Filmvideo Releasing Corp. v. Hastings,* 509 F. Supp. 60, 66 (S.D.N.Y. 1981) ("Hopalong Cassidy" character developed in a series of books was sufficiently lineated, developed and well known to the public to be copyrightable), *aff'd,* 668 F.2d 91 (2d Cir. 1981).

14. *See Walt Disney Productions v. Air Pirates,* 581 F.2d 751, 755 (9th Cir. 1978) ("while many literary characters may embody little more than an unprotected idea . . . , a comic book character, which has physical as well as conceptual qualities, is more likely to contain some unique elements of expression").

15. *Nichols v. Universal Pictures Corp.,* 45 F.2d 119, 121 (2d Cir. 1930), *cert. denied,* 282 U.S. 902 (1931).

16. 17 U.S.C. § 102(a)(2).

17. *See Mills Music, Inc. v. Arizona,* 187 U.S.P.Q. 22, 31 (D. Ariz. 1975), *aff'd,* 591 F.2d 1278 (9th Cir. 1979).

18. *Plymouth Music Co. v. Magnus Organ Corp.,* 456 F. Supp. 676, 679 (S.D.N.Y. 1978).

19. *See, e.g., Frank Music Corp. v. CompuServe, Inc.,* No. 93 Civ. 8153 (S.D.N.Y. filed December 1993). This class-action lawsuit was filed on behalf of more than 140 owners of musical compositions against CompuServe. The suit alleged that the uploading to, storage by, and downloading from CompuServe of musical instrument digital interface (MIDI) files constituted an infringement of the copyrights in the musical compositions owned by the plaintiffs. MIDI files are computer files that contain instructions controlling how and when devices such as digital synthesizers

produce sound. They can be stored in digital form on computer-readable media and later recalled to play back the musical work that is the subject of the MIDI recording. The suit alleged that CompuServe, by allowing its users to upload and download MIDI files, had permitted, facilitated, and participated in the recording and distribution of performances of several copyrighted musical compositions. The suit was settled on October 25, 1995 by the payment of $568,000 to the plaintiffs, and an agreement by CompuServe to require its forum managers to obtain licenses, as needed, for the future online distribution of music at a license rate of 6.95 cents per download.

20. 17 U.S.C. § 101 (definition of "sound recordings"). However, a sound recording does not include any sounds accompanying a motion picture or other audiovisual work. In that case, the sound is treated as part of the motion picture or audiovisual work that it accompanies. *Id.*

21. 17 U.S.C. § 102(a)(7).

22. *See Innovative Concepts in Entertainment, Inc. v. Entertainment Enterprises, Ltd.*, 576 F. Supp. 457, 461 (E.D.N.Y. 1983) (sound recording of crowd noises from an actual hockey game was copyrightable).

23. 17 U.S.C. § 102(a)(5).

24. 17 Copyright Office Cir. 40, Copyright Registration for Works of the Visual Arts 2 (1990).

25. H.R. Rep. No. 1476, 94th Cong., 2d Sess. 54 (1976), *reprinted in* 1976 U.S.C.C.A.N. 5659, 5667.

26. *Playboy Enterprises, Inc. v. Frena*, 839 F. Supp. 1552 (M.D. Fla. 1993).

27. 17 U.S.C. § 102(a)(6).

28. 17 U.S.C. § 101 (definition of "audiovisual works").

29. *See WGN Continental Broadcasting Co. v. United Video, Inc.*, 693 F.2d 622, 626 (7th Cir. 1982).

30. *See Midway Mfg. Co. v. Artic Int'l, Inc.*, 704 F.2d 1009, 1011 (7th Cir.), *cert. denied*, 464 U.S. 823 (1983).

31. 17 U.S.C. §§ 101 (definition of "computer program") and 117. *See e.g., Computer Assocs. Int'l. Inc. v. Altai, Inc.*, 982 F. 2d 693 (2d Cir. 1992) ("it is now well settled that the literal elements of computer programs, i.e., the source and object codes, are the subject of copyright protection").

32. 17 U.S.C. § 101 (definition of "compilation").

33. 17 U.S.C. § 101 (definition of "derivative work").

34. *See, e.g., Alfred Bell & Co., v. Catalda Fine Arts, Inc.*, 191 F.2d 99 (2d Cir. 1951); *SAS Institute, Inc. v. S&H Computer Systems, Inc.*, 605 F. Supp. 816 (M.D. Tenn. 1985).

35. Thomas J. Smedinghoff, *The Software Publishers Association Legal Guide to Multimedia* at p. 4 (1994).

36. 17 U.S.C. § 102(a). "Works of authorship" that can be protected by copyright are discussed in Section 9.3.

37. The rules are somewhat different for works created prior to January 1, 1978, the effective date of the current copyright law.

38. Under the Copyright Act of 1909, publication of a work without a copyright notice injected the work into the public domain. Under the Copyright Act of 1976, publication of a work without a notice also generally resulted in a loss of the copyright, but the law was not as unforgiving. There were a number of remedial provisions that the copyright owner could take to retain his or her copyright. Effective as of March 1, 1989, however, a copyright notice is no longer required on any copy of a copyrighted work published after that date. Also, under the Copyright Act of 1976, registration of a copyright has always been optional (although it is required as a condition of bringing a lawsuit).

39. 17 U.S.C. § 102(a).

40. *Feist Publications, Inc. v. Rural Telephone Service Co.*, 499 U.S. 340, 111 S. Ct. 1282, 1287 (1991).

41. *INT-Elect Engineering, Inc. v. Clinton Harley Corp.*, 27 U.S.P.Q. 2d 1631, 1633 (N.D. Cal. 1993).

42. *Feist Publications, Inc. v. Rural Telephone Service Co.*, 499 U.S. 340, 111 S. Ct. 1282, 1291–1293 (1991) (white pages of phone book not protectable by copyright).

43. 37 C.F.R. §§ 202.1(a), (c) and (d).

44. 17 U.S.C. § 102(a).

45. H.R. Rep. No. 1476, 94th Cong., 2d Sess. 52 (1976), *reprinted in* 1976 U.S.C.C.A.N. 5659, 5665.

46. *MAI Systems Corp. v. Peak Computer, Inc.*, 991 F.2d 511, 518 (9th Cir. 1993), *cert. dismissed*, 114 S. Ct. 671 (1994); *Advance Computer Services of Michigan, Inc. v. MAI Systems Corp.*, 845 F. Supp. 356 (E.D. Va. 1994); *Triad Systems Corp. v. Southeastern Express Co.*, 1994 U.S. Dist. LEXIS 5390 (N.D. Cal. March 18, 1994); *Stern Electronics, Inc. v. Kaufman*, 669 F.2d 852, 855 (2d Cir. 1982) (putting work in "memory devices" of a computer "satisfies the statutory requirement of a 'copy' in which the work is 'fixed'").

47. *Triad Systems Corporation v. Southeastern Express Co.*, 31 U.S.P.Q. 2d (BNA) 1239, 1243 (N.D. Cal. 1994) ("the Copyright Law is not so much concerned with the temporal 'duration' of a copy as it is with what that copy does, and what it is capable of doing, while it exists. 'Transitory duration' is a relative term that must be interpreted and applied in context. This concept is particularly important in cases involving computer technology where the speed and complexity of machines and software is rapidly advancing, and where the diversity of computer architecture and software design is expanding at an ever-increasing rate. *Contu Report* at 22–23").

48. *Intellectual Property and the National Information Infrastructure: The Report of the Working Group on Intellectual Property Rights,* Information Infrastructure Task Force, Sept. 5, 1995 at 32. Unfixed broadcasts are not within the subject matter of federal copyright law.

49. 17 U.S.C. § 101 (definition of "fixed"); *see also Intellectual Property and the National Information Infrastructure: The Report of the Working Group on Intellectual Property Rights,* Information Infrastructure Task Force, Sept. 5, 1995 at 32; *Baltimore Orioles, Inc. v. Major League Baseball Players Association*, 805 F.2d 663, 668 (7th Cir. 1986) (telecasts that are videotaped at the same time that they are broadcast are fixed in tangible form), *cert. denied*, 480 U.S. 941 (1987).

50. *Intellectual Property and the National Information Infrastructure: The Report of the Working Group on Intellectual Property Rights,* Information Infrastructure Task Force (Sept. 5, 1995) at 33; *Advanced Computer Services of Michigan, Inc. v. MAI Systems Corp.*, 845 F. Supp. 356, 363 (E.D.Va. 1994) (concluded that program stored only in RAM is sufficiently fixed is confirmed, not refuted, by argument that it "disappears from RAM the instant the computer is turned off"; if power remains on (and the work remains in RAM) for only seconds or fractions of a second (the resulting RAM representation of the program arguably would be too ephemeral to be considered fixed"); *Triad Systems Corp. v. Southeastern Express Co.*, 31 U.S.P.Q. 2d (BNA) 1239, 1243 (N.D. Cal. 1994) ("copyright law is not so much concerned with the temporal 'duration' of a copy as it is with what that copy does, and what it is capable of doing, while it exists. 'Transitory duration' is a relative term that must be interpreted and applied in context").

51. 17 U.S.C. § 401(a). This rule applies to works first published after March 1, 1989.

52. 17 U.S.C. § 401(b).

53. In the case of modified versions of previously published information or content, the year of first publication of the modified version is sufficient. 17 U.S.C. § 401(b)(2). In the case of compilations or derivative works incorporating previously published material, the year date of first publication of the compilation or derivative work is sufficient.

54. *See* 17 U.S.C. § 101 (definition of "publication"); H.R. Rep. No. 1476, 94th Cong. 2d Sess. 138 (1976), *reprinted in* 1976 U.S.C.C.A.N. 5659, 5754.

55.   17 U.S.C. § 408(a).

56.   17 U.S.C. § 411.

57.   17 U.S.C. § 410(c).

58.   17 U.S.C. § 412.

59.   Copyright registration fees are adjusted at five-year intervals, based on changes in the Consumer Price Index.

60.   17 U.S.C. § 201(a). The author can, of course, always assign ownership of the copyright to someone else.

61.   *Community for Creative Non-Violence v. Reid*, 490 U.S. 730, 109 S. Ct. 2166, 2171 (1989).

62.   17 U.S.C. § 201(a).

63.   17 U.S.C. § 201(b).

64.   17 U.S.C. § 101 (definition of "work made for hire"); *Community for Creative Non-Violence v. Reid*, 490 U.S. 730, 109 S. Ct. 2166, 2176 (1989).

65.   *Community for Creative Non-Violence v. Reid*, 490 U.S. 730, 109 S. Ct. 2166, 2178 (1989). Unfortunately, it is not always easy to determine whether an individual is an "employee" for purposes of the work-made-for-hire doctrine, or an "independent contractor" (in which case a different set of work-for-hire rules apply—see Section 9.5.2. Generally, whether someone is an employee or an independent contractor is determined using principles of the general common law of agency. This requires consideration of the hiring party's right to control the manner and means by which the product is created. *Id.* at 2172–2173, 2178.

66.   17 U.S.C. § 101 (definition of "work made for hire").

67.   17 U.S.C. § 201(b).

68.   17 U.S.C. § 201(b).

69.   Note that, by contrast, all work performed by employees for their employers within the scope of their employment are considered works for hire. With independent contractors, however, only nine specially enumerated categories of work can qualify for work-for-hire treatment. 17 U.S.C. § 101 (definition of "work made for hire").

70.   17 U.S.C. § 101 (definition of "work made for hire").

71.   A *collective work* is a work, such as a periodical issue, anthology, or encyclopedia, in which a number of contributions, constituting separate and independent works in themselves, are assembled into a collective whole.

72.   *Audiovisual works* are works that consist of a series of related images that are intrinsically intended to be shown by the use of machines or devices such as projectors, viewers, or electronic equipment, together with accompanying sounds, if any. 17 U.S.C. § 101 (definition of "audiovisual works").

73.   A *supplementary work* is a work prepared for publication as a secondary adjunct to a work by another author for the purpose of introducing, concluding, illustrating, explaining, revising, commenting upon, or assisting in the use of the other work, such as forewords, afterwords, pictorial illustrations, maps, charts, tables, editorial notes, musical arrangements, answer material for tests, bibliographies, appendices, and indexes. 17 U.S.C. § 101 (definition of "work made for hire").

74.   Compilation is a work formed by the collection and assembling of preexisting materials or of data that are selected, coordinated, or arranged in such a way that the resulting work as a whole constitutes an original work of authorship. The term *compilation* includes collective works.

75.   *Schiller & Schmidt, Inc. v. Nordisco Corp.*, 969 F.2d 410, 412 (7th Cir. 1992) (statutory language requires that writing be signed "by both parties, and it means what it says").

10

Online Rights of Copyright Owners

Thomas J. Smedinghoff

The Copyright Act grants the owner of the copyright in a work[1] certain rights to control the use of the work. Whether the work is available in a digital form online or in a traditional paper form, the copyright owner is given the exclusive rights to do the following:[2]

- Make copies of the work (the *reproduction right*);
- Prepare derivative works based upon the work (the *adaptation right*);
- Distribute copies of the work publicly by sale, rental, lease, or lending (the *distribution right*);
- Perform the work publicly (the *public performance right*);[3] and
- Display the work publicly (the *public display right*).[4]

When someone other than the copyright owner, or a person acting with the owner's permission, performs one of those acts, it is an infringement of the copyright unless it comes within an exception provided by the law.[5] (These exceptions, which define the rights of users of the work, are discussed in Chapter 11). The following sections will explain each of these rights.

10.1 Reproduction Right

The Copyright Act gives the copyright owner the exclusive right to reproduce, and to authorize others to reproduce, the copyrighted work—that is, to make copies.[6] A *copy* is any material object (such as a disk, tape, or random access memory) in which the work is fixed, and from which the work can be perceived, reproduced, or otherwise communicated, either directly or with the aid of a machine or device.[7]

United States case law has taken a rather strict interpretation with respect to copying digital content. "Copying," for purposes of copyright law, occurs whenever any copyrightable digital content is transferred to a permanent storage device (such as a disk or CD-ROM), or into a computer's random access memory.[8]

In other words, recording a work on a diskette, hard disk, CD-ROM disc, tape, computer chip, or any other computer-readable media constitutes making a copy. Likewise, loading a copy of a digital work into the random access memory of a computer for viewing, listening, or execution constitutes making a copy.

Because of the nature of computer-to-computer communications, such reproduction of digital information will occur with virtually all interactions of a user with the information. Whenever a computer user accesses a document resident on another computer, the image on the user's screen exists—under contemporary technology—only by virtue of the copy that is reproduced in the user's computer memory. Thus, the following acts each constitute making a copy:

- Simply browsing a document resident on another computer (since it involves the creation of a copy in the user's computer memory in order to display an image of the document on the user's screen)
- Uploading or downloading information from one computer to another[9]
- Transferring a file online from one computer network user to another[10]
- Using a high-resolution scanner to create a digital copy of a photograph[11]
- Digitally sampling a copyrighted sound recording and using it[12]
- Loading and executing a program resident on the hard disk of a computer (i.e., the software is "copied" from the hard disk to the memory of the computer even though such use is temporary)[13]

As these examples illustrate, it is virtually impossible to do anything online with digital information that does not involve making a copy. In the absence of permission from the copyright owner, or an excuse recognized by the copyright law, such acts constitute copyright infringement.[14]

Not all online copying of digital information constitutes copyright infringement, however, and therein lies one of the challenges of applying the copyright law to the world of digital online information. Traditional copyright law provides several exceptions to the reproduction right—that is, several defenses—to a claim of copyright infringement made by the copyright owner. These exceptions include, for example, assertions that the copying constitutes "fair use," or that the copying was authorized by an "implied license" from the copyright owner (these exceptions are discussed in Chapter 11). In addition, many argue that certain forms of copying that would otherwise be considered unlawful are nonetheless acceptable in a digital online context. A good example is e-mail. E-mail messages are routinely copied and forwarded to additional recipients. Although this conduct meets the traditional test of copyright infringement, many would argue that custom and usage in the online world justifies such conduct nonetheless.

10.2 Adaptation Right

The Copyright Act gives the copyright owner the exclusive right to prepare a derivative version of his or her work.[15] A *derivative work* is a new work that is based on the preexisting work. It could be a revision of the original version, a translation from one language to another, or any other form in which the original work can be recast, transformed, or adapted.[16] A French translation of an English novel, a movie based on a book, a book that tells the story of copyrighted choreography (for example, a ballet) in photographs,[17] a "colorized" black-and-white motion picture,[18] a revised version of a software product, and a digitally altered photograph are all examples of derivative works. Transforming a work, such as an audiovisual work, into an interactive work also constitutes the preparation of a derivative work.

The *adaptation right*—the right to create derivative works—can be a critical issue for works in an online environment because of the ease with which they can be digitally altered, modified, or incorporated in other works and the fact that such alterations can be done in a manner that defies detection. This has important implications both for those who would modify the works of others, and for those who seek to protect the integrity of the works they have created and seek to be compensated for the use of their works incorporated into derivative works.

Modifying, adapting, and revising a copyrighted work, like copying, constitutes copyright infringement, unless authorized by the copyright owner or one of the statutory exceptions, such as fair use, discussed in Chapter 11. Such modifications might include, for example, editing a work; morphing two or more pictures; splitting or combining sound recordings or images; translating text into another language; or otherwise rewriting, revising, or modifying copyrighted information for use in another work.

10.3 Distribution Right

The Copyright Act gives the copyright owner the exclusive right to distribute the copyrighted work.[19] The concept of *distribution* includes the right to sell copies of the copyrighted work, as well as the right to rent, lease, and lend copies of the work. Thus, virtually any situation in which information is communicated from one computer to another would appear to involve a distribution of the digital content. Examples include forwarding an e-mail message; making a file available on a computer bulletin board, Web site, or FTP site; or simply sending digital information to another person via the Internet or other online network. In one case, a court held that making copyrighted photographs available in digital form on a computer bulletin board for downloading by subscribers constitutes infringement of the copyright owner's exclusive right to distribute the work.[20]

An interesting example of an online claim based on both the reproduction and distribution right was raised in a December 1993 class action lawsuit filed on behalf of over 140 owners of musical compositions against CompuServe. The suit involved the uploading to, and downloading from, CompuServe of musical instrument digital interface (MIDI) files that comprised performance of the plaintiffs' copyrighted musical compositions. MIDI files are computer files that contain instructions controlling how and when devices such as digital synthesizers produce sound. They can be stored in a digital form on computer-readable media such as disks and CD-ROMs and later recalled to play back the musical work that is the subject of the MIDI recording.

The plaintiffs alleged that CompuServe, by allowing its subscribers to upload and download MIDI files, permitted, facilitated, and participated in the infringing, recording, and distribution of performances of several copyrighted musical compositions. CompuServe settled the case in 1995 by making a $568,000 payment to the plaintiffs, and agreeing to have its forum managers purchase licenses, as needed, for each future online distribution of music.[21]

The distribution right normally covers the right to convey a possessory interest in a tangible copy of the work (such as a diskette or CD-ROM). In the online environment, however, where one party downloads a file from, or transfers a file to, another party, the recipient ends up possessing a copy of the transferred file, but no physical media has been transferred. Thus, it is not clear whether the sender "distributed" that file or whether the recipient "reproduced" it.

Determining whether an online file transfer constitutes a "reproduction" or a "distribution" can have a significant consequence. If the transfer is characterized as a distribution (rather than a reproduction), then the copyright owner has no right to control further disposition of *that copy* by the purchaser.[22] Thus, for example, when a customer buys a copy of a book in a bookstore or a CD in a music store, it is not a copyright infringement to sell[23] that copy to someone else (as long as the customer does not make any additional copies as well). This is known as the *first-sale doctrine*. Under this doctrine, the copyright owner's right to distribute a particular copy is limited to the first time he or she sells or otherwise disposes of that specific copy.[24] Once the owner parts with a particular copy or phonorecord, the new owner then has the right to sell or otherwise transfer it. This is discussed further in Section 11.5.

10.4 Public Performance Right

Owners of most copyrighted works also have the exclusive right to perform their works publicly.[25] This right is available to all types of "performable" works—literary, musical, dramatic, and chronographic works, pantomimes, motion pictures, and other audiovisual works—with the exception of most sound recordings. It is limited, however, to public performances. It does not apply to private performances. Thus, understanding the scope of the public performance right requires consideration of what it means to perform a work, and when such performance is considered to be done publicly.

To *perform* a work means to recite, render, play, dance, or act it, either directly or by means of any device or process or, in the case of a motion picture or other audiovisual work, to show its images in any sequence or to make the sounds accompanying it audible.[26] A performance may be accomplished either directly (e.g., a live performance on a stage) or by means of any device, such as equipment for reproducing or amplifying sounds or visual images, any sort of transmitting apparatus, or any type of electronic retrieval system.[27]

Thus, for example, a singer is performing when he or she sings a song; a broadcasting network is performing when it transmits the singer's performance (whether simultaneously or from records); a local broadcaster is performing when it transmits the network broadcast; a cable television system is performing when it retransmits the broadcast to its subscribers; and an individual is performing whenever he or she plays a compact disc containing the performance or communicates the performance by turning on a radio.[28]

In an online environment, it has been argued that the communication of a copyrighted work such as music or motion pictures should be characterized as a performance. The debate centers around the issue of whether there is a distinction between a transmission of a copy of a work and a performance of the work. When a copy of a work is transmitted from one computer to another in digital form so that it may be captured in a user's computer, without the capability of simultaneous "rendering" or "showing," the general view is that it has not been performed. Thus, for example, a file comprising the digitized version of a motion picture might be transferred via the Internet without constituting a performance of the motion picture. When, however, the motion picture is literally "rendered"—by showing its images in sequence—so that users with the requisite hardware and software might watch it with or without copying the performance, then, under the current law, a performance has occurred. If that performance is "public" then the public performance right of the copyright owner is implicated.[29]

The performance of a work is done *publicly* in two types of situations.[30] First, a performance is considered to be "public" if it occurs at a place open to the public or in any place where a substantial number of persons outside a normal circle of a family and its social acquaintances is gathered.[31]

Second, the concept of a public performance includes acts that transmit or communicate a performance of the work to the public by means of any device or process, such as radio and television broadcasting.[32] It is also worth noting that a performance made available by transmission to the public at large is considered "public" even though the recipients are not gathered in a single place, and even if there is no proof that any of the potential recipients was operating his or her receiving apparatus at the time of the transmission.[33] Thus, a performance that occurs over the Internet will be considered "public" even if it is viewed by only one person at a time, each from a separate location, and each at a different time, such as by accessing a Web site.

10.5 Public Display Right

Owners of most copyrighted works also have an exclusive right to display the copyrighted work publicly.[34] This right relates to works that can be seen (such as photographs) as opposed to works containing only sounds that can be heard. Like the public performance right, this right is limited to public displays. The copyright owner has no right to prohibit private display of the copyrighted work.

The concept of display covers any showing of a copy of the work, either directly or by means of a film, slide, television image, or any other device or process, such as by a computer.[35] The term *display* includes the projection of an image on a screen or other surface by any method, the transmission of an image by electronic or other means, and the showing of an image on a cathode ray tube or similar viewing device connected with any sort of information storage and retrieval system.[36] Thus, whenever a user of a publicly available online system or service visually "browses" through copies of works accessible on the system, a display occurs. The same is true of a Web site. In one case, a court held that allowing subscribers of a computer bulletin board system to look at copyrighted pictures stored on the system constituted a display.[37]

The display of a work is considered public on the same terms as a performance is considered public. As a consequence, virtually all online displays of copyrighted work will probably be considered to be a "public display." Displaying a work on the Internet, such as on a Web Site, would clearly qualify as a public display, since it is accessible to anyone who cares to retrieve it.

In one case, a court held that making digital versions of copyrighted pictures available on a computer bulletin board system for viewing by subscribers without authorization of the copyright owner constituted infringement of the public display right, since the subscribers to the board consisted of a substantial number of persons outside of the normal circle of family and its social acquaintances.[38] This is true even though most displays of the images are done privately (say, at a user's home).

10.6 Remedies Available to Copyright Owners

Anyone who violates any of the exclusive rights of the copyright owner is an infringer of the copyright.[39] Copyright infringement is determined without regard to the intent or the state of mind of the infringer. Even those who infringe a copyright innocently are liable to the copyright owner.[40] The making of even a single unauthorized copy may constitute an infringement.[41]

There are a variety of remedies available to the copyright owner who can prove that its copyright has been infringed. The law allows for both civil and (in some cases) criminal remedies.

10.6.1 Civil Remedies

Copyright infringement claims brought by copyright owners against alleged infringers are filed as civil (rather than criminal) claims. The Copyright Act allows the copyright owner a potentially impressive array of sanctions to bring against a copyright infringer. These include an injunction to stop the infringement, impoundment and destruction of all infringing copies, compensation for damages, and, in some cases, reimbursement of attorneys' fees.

10.6.1.1 Injunction. The first goal of the copyright owner is to stop the infringement. This is accomplished by obtaining a court-ordered injunction prohibiting the defendant from continuing to copy, and (where appropriate) from continuing to market the infringing copies of the plaintiff's work. If the copyright owner can demonstrate that it is likely to prevail on its claim of infringement, the court has the power to issue a temporary injunction at the beginning of the lawsuit that will remain in effect while the case is being decided.[42] At the conclusion of the lawsuit, if it is determined that the defendant has infringed the copyright owner's rights, the court has the authority to make the injunction permanent[43] and to provide the other relief discussed in the following sections.

Injunctions are routinely granted in cases involving copyright infringement of digital works. In one case involving distribution of digital copies of *Playboy* photographs by a computer bulletin board, the court entered an injunction prohibiting the defendant operator of the bulletin board from continuing to make such photographs available for distribution.[44] In another case, the court issued an injunction against the operator of a computer bulletin board from copying or distributing any of Sega's copyrighted computer video games.[45]

10.6.1.2 Impoundment of Infringing Copies. The Copyright Act authorizes the court to order the impoundment of all allegedly infringing copies of the copyrighted work at any time during the pendency of a copyright infringement lawsuit.[46] This is done to ensure that all infringing copies of the work can be destroyed at the conclusion of the lawsuit if the plaintiff prevails. Thus, for example, in one case involving a computer bulletin board that made infringing copies of computer games available for distribution, the court ordered that the software and data, along with the computers and other equipment used to facilitate such infringement, be impounded during the pendency of the litigation.[47]

10.6.1.3 Destruction of Infringing Copies. At the conclusion of the lawsuit, if the court determines that the defendant has infringed the plaintiff's copyright in its work, it may, as part of the final judgment or decree, order the destruction or other reasonable disposition of all copies of the work found to have been made or used in violation of the copyright owner's exclusive rights, as well as all disks, tapes, masters, or other articles by means of which such copies may be reproduced.[48]

10.6.1.4 Damages. A copyright owner whose work has been infringed is also entitled to an award of money damages as compensation for the financial injury caused by the misappropriation. Generally, two alternative damage measures are available: (1) damages measured by the sum of the copyright owner's actual losses and the defendant's profits, or (2) statutory damages.

The copyright owner has the right to recover any damages that it suffered as a result of the infringement, plus any profits made by the infringer.[49] Actual damages may include lost profits as well as the reduced market value of the work caused by the unauthorized distribution of infringing copies. In addition, the copyright owner may recover the profits made by the defendant on the marketing of the infringing work to the extent they are not taken into account in calculating the plaintiff's actual damages.[50]

Alternatively, the copyright owner may elect, at any time during the lawsuit, to recover "statutory damages," in which case there is no need to prove actual loss. Under the Copyright Act, the court may award statutory damages to the copyright owner of $500 to $20,000.[51] If the court finds that the defendant acted willfully, it may increase the award of statutory damages to as much as $100,000.[52] The option to take statutory damages is not available, however, unless the work has been registered within the time period required by the statute (see Section 9.4.4).[53]

10.6.1.5 Costs and Attorneys' Fees. The Copyright Act also allows the court to award the costs of the litigation, including reasonable attorneys' fees, to the prevailing party.[54]

It is important to note, however, that attorneys' fees are available to the prevailing party only if the work has been registered within the time period required by the statute (see Section 9.4.4).[55]

10.6.2 Criminal Penalties

In certain cases, persons who infringe a copyright may be liable for criminal as well as civil penalties. The copyright law makes it a criminal offense to infringe a copyright "willfully and for purposes of commercial advantage or private financial gain."[56] Penalties include up to five years in prison and $250,000 in fines if the offense consists of the reproduction or distribution, during any 180-day period, of at least 10 copies or phonorecords, of one or more copyrighted works, with a retail value of more than $2,500.[57]

10.6.2.1 Willfulness. In order for infringement of a copyright to be criminal, the infringement must be committed "willfully."[58] To establish willfulness, most courts require a showing of bad purpose or evil motive in the sense that there is an intentional violation of a known legal duty.[59]

10.6.2.2 Profit Motive. The term *commercial advantage or private financial gain* as used in the criminal provision of the U.S. Copyright Act refers essentially to the requirement of a profit motive. It is irrelevant whether the hope of a profit is realized or not. It is necessary only that the activity be for the *purpose* of financial gain or benefit.[60]

A problem with the financial gain requirement arose in the case of *United States v. LaMacchia*.[61] In that case, a 21-year-old student at Massachusetts Institute of Technology was accused of setting up a computer bulletin board service (BBS) on the Internet for the purpose of making unauthorized copies of computer software available for downloading. It was estimated that over $1 million worth of commercial copyrighted software was downloaded from this BBS, but there was no evidence that LaMacchia sought or derived any personal benefit from this activity. Accordingly, he could not be charged with criminal copyright infringement. In late 1995, legislation was introduced in Congress to subject such conduct to the criminal provisions of the Copyright Act, notwithstanding the lack of a profit motive.

The government was more successful in the case of *United States v. Kenadek*.[62] This case, the first criminal copyright action involving a computer bulletin board, was directed against the Davy Jones Locker BBS located in Milbury, Massachusetts. The defendant made copyrighted software available on his BBS for downloading by users, but only to users who first paid a fee for access to the copyrighted files. Thus, showing a profit motive was not a problem. The defendant was charged with criminal copyright infringement in September, 1994, and plead guilty in December, 1994. He was sentenced in March 1995 to two years' probation, including six months of home detention and three months with an electronic monitor. He was also fined $2,000.

Endnotes

1. The identity of the "owner" of the copyright is a key issue. This is discussed in Section 9.5.

2. 17 U.S.C. § 106.

3. This right applies only to literary, musical, dramatic, and choreographic works, pantomimes, and motion pictures and other audiovisual works, and certain digital audio transmissions. It does not apply to other forms of sound recordings or to pictorial, graphic, or sculptural works.

4. This right applies only to literary, musical, dramatic, and choreographic works, pantomimes, and pictorial, graphic, or sculptural works, including the individual images of a motion picture or other audiovisual work. It does not apply to sound recordings.

5. 17 U.S.C. § 501(a).

6. 17 U.S.C. § 106(1).

7. 17 U.S.C. § 101 (definition of "copies").

8. *MAI Systems Corp. v. Peak Computer, Inc.*, 991 F.2d 511, 518 (9th Cir. 1993) *cert. dismissed*, 114 S.Ct. 671 (1994) (the loading of plaintiff's copyrighted operating system software into the memory of a computer by turning it on constitutes copyright infringement when done by someone other than an authorized licensee); *Vault Corp. v. Quaid Software, Ltd.*, 847 F.2d 255, 260 (5th Cir. 1988) ("the act of loading a program from a medium of storage into a computer's memory creates a copy of the program"); *Advanced Computer Services v. MAI Systems Corp.*, 845 F. Supp. 356 (E.D. Va. 1994); *Triad Systems Corp. v. Southeastern Express Co.*, 31 U.S.P.Q.2d (BNA) 1239 (N.D. Cal. 1994); *Final Report of the National Commission on the New Technological Uses of Copyrightable Works*, at 13 (1978) ("the placement of a work into a computer is the preparation of a copy"); *Id.* at 40 ("the introduction of a work into a computer memory would, consistent with the [current] law, be a reproduction of the work, one of the exclusive rights of a copyright proprietor").

9. *See Playboy Enterprise, Inc. v. Frena*, 839 F. Supp. 1552 (M.D. Fla. 1993); *Sega Enterprises, Ltd. v. Maphia BBS*, 30 U.S.P.Q.2d (BNA) 1921 (N.D. Cal. 1994).

10. For example, if an author transfers a file (such as a manuscript) to a publisher with an Internet account, copies will typically, at a minimum, be made (a) in the author's Internet server, (b) in the publisher's Internet server, (c) and the publisher's local area network server, and (d) in the editor's microcomputer.

11. *See, e.g., Playboy Enterprises, Inc. v. Frena*, 839 F. Supp. 1552 (M.D. Fla. 1993).

12. *Grand Upright Music, Ltd. v. Warner Bros. Records, Inc.*, 780 F. Supp. 182 (S.D.N.Y. 1991); *Jarvis v. A & M Records*, 827 F. Supp. 282, 27 U.S.P.Q.2d 1812 (D.N.J. 1993); *Tin Pan Apple, Inc. v. Miller Brewing Co.*, 30 U.S.P.Q.2d (BNA) 1791 (S.D.N.Y. 1994) (noting that "it is common ground that if defendants did sample plaintiff's copyrighted sound recording, they infringe that copyright . . .").

13. *See MAI Systems Corp. v. Peak Computer, Inc.*, 991 F.2d 511, 518 (9th Cir. 1993) ("copying" for purposes of copyright law occurs when a computer program (or any digital content) is transferred from a permanent storage device (such as a disk or CD-ROM) into a computer's random access memory); *Advanced Computer Services of Michigan, Inc. v. MAI Systems Corp.*, 845 F. Supp. 356 (E.D. Va. 1994).

14. *MAI Systems Corp. v. Peak Computer, Inc.*, 991 F.2d 511, 518 (9th Cir. 1993); *Advanced Computer Services of Michigan, Inc. v. MAI Systems Corp.*, 845 F. Supp. 356 (E.D. Va. 1994).

15. 17 U.S.C. § 106(2).

16. 17 U.S.C. § 101.

17.   *Horgan v. MacMillan, Inc.*, 789 F.2d 157, 163 (2d Cir. 1986).

18.   See Copyright Registration for Colorized Versions of Black and White Motion Pictures. Notice of Proposed Rulemaking, Docket No. RM86-1A (June 11, 1987); Copyright Registration for Colorized Versions of Black and White Motion Pictures, 52 Fed. Reg. 23443 (1987).

19.   17 U.S.C. § 106(3).

20.   *Playboy Enterprises, Inc. v. Frena*, 839 F. Supp. 1552, 1556 (M.D. Fla. 1993). But *see, Religious Technology Center v. Netcom On-line Communications Services, Inc.*, No. C-95-20091, 1995 U.S. Dist. LEXIS 18173 (N.D. Cal. Nov. 21, 1995).

21.   *Frank Music Corp. v. CompuServe, Inc.*, 93 N. Civ. 8153 (S.D.N.Y., filed Dec. 1993).

22.   17 U.S.C. § 109.

23.   However, this exception does not apply to the *rental* of sound recordings or computer programs. That is, although someone who purchases a copy of a sound recording or a computer program has the right to resell that particular copy, the rental or leasing of that copy constitutes copyright infringement if done without permission from the copyright owner. 17 U.S.C. § 109(b). See *Central Point Software, Inc. v. Global Software & Accessories, Inc.*, 880 F. Supp. 957 (E.D.N.Y. 1995).

24.   17 U.S.C. § 109.

25.   17 U.S.C. § 106(4). The performance right does not apply to certain sound recordings. *See* 17 U.S.C. § 114(a). By its nature, it also does not apply to pictorial or graphic works. 17 U.S.C. § 106(4).

26.   17 U.S.C. § 101.

27.   H.R. Rep. No. 1476, 94th Cong., 2d Sess. 63–64 (1976), *reprinted* in 1976 U.S.C.C.A.N. 5659, 5677). Thus, for example, using a CD player and an amplifier to play a song recorded on a CD at a seminar or conference is just as much a "performance" as standing on a stage at a public auditorium and singing the same song "live" for the assembled audience.

28.   H.R. Rep. No. 1476, 94th Cong., 2d Sess. 63–64 (1976), *reprinted in* 1976 U.S.C.C.A.N. 5659, 5677.

29.   *Intellectual Property and the National Information Infrastructure: The Report of the Working Group on Intellectual Property Rights*, Information Infrastructure Task Force (Sept. 5, 1995) at 82.

30.   17 U.S.C. § 101.

31.   H.R. Rep. No. 1476, 94th Cong., 2d Sess. 64 (1976), *reprinted in* 1976 U.S.C.C.A.N. 5659, 5677–78.

32.   H.R. Rep. No. 1476, 94th Cong., 2d Sess. 64 (1976), *reprinted in* 1976 U.S.C.C.A.N. 5659, 5677–78.

33.   H.R. Rep. No. 1476, 94th Cong., 2d Sess. 64-65 (1976), *reprinted* in 1976 U.S.C.C.A.N. 5659, 5678.

34.   17 U.S.C. § 106(5). The display right does not apply to sound recordings. *See* 17 U.S.C. § 114(a). With respect to motion pictures and other audiovisual works, the public display right applies to individual images, as opposed to showing the motion picture itself, which would constitute a performance rather than a display. *See* 17 U.S.C. § 106(5).

35.   17 U.S.C. § 101 (definition of "display"). With respect to motion pictures and other audiovisual works, it is a display (rather than a performance) to show their "individual images non-sequentially."

36.   H.R. Rep. No. 1476, 94th Cong., 2d Sess. 64 (1976), *reprinted in* 1976 U.S.C.C.A.N. 5659, 5677–78.

37.   *Playboy Enterprises, Inc. v. Frena*, 839 F. Supp. 1552 (M.D. Fla. 1993).

38.   *Playboy Enterprises, Inc. v. Frena*, 839 F. Supp. 1552 (M.D. Fla. 1993). *See also Thomas V. Pansy Ellen Products, Inc.*, 672 F. Supp. 237, 240 (W.D. N.C. 1987) (display at a trade show was public even though limited to members); *Ackee Music, Inc. v. Williams*, 650 F. Supp. 653, 655–656 (D. Kan. 1986) (performance of copyrighted songs at defendant's private club constitute a public performance).

39.   17 U.S.C. § 501(a).

40.   But the innocence or willfulness of the infringing activity may be relevant with regard to the award of statutory damages. *See* 17 U.S.C. § 504(c).

41.   *See* House Report at 61, *reprinted* in 1976 U.S.C.C.A.N. 5674.

42.   17 U.S.C. § 502.

43.   17 U.S.C. § 502.

44.   *Playboy Enterprises, Inc. v. Frena*, 839 F. Supp. 1552 (M.D. Fla. 1993).

45.   *Sega Enterprises, Ltd. v. Maphia*, 30 U.S.P.Q.2d (BNA) 1921, 1929 (N.D. Cal. 1994).

46.   17 U.S.C. § 503.

47.   *Sega Enterprises, Ltd. v. Maphia*, 30 U.S.P.Q.2d (BNA) 1921, 1929 (N.D. Cal. 1994).

48.   17 U.S.C. § 503(b).

49.   17 U.S.C. §§ 504(a) and (b).

50.   17 U.S.C. § 504(b).

51.   17 U.S.C. § 504(c)(1).

52.   17 U.S.C. § 504(c)(2).

53.   *See* 17 U.S.C. § 412.

54.   17 U.S.C. § 505. *See also Fogerty v. Fantasy, Inc.*, 114 S. Ct. 1023 (1994).

55.   *See* 17 U.S.C. § 412.

56.   17 U.S.C. § 506.

57.   18 U.S.C. §§ 2319 and 3571ff.

58.   17 U.S.C. § 506(a). The term *willfully* is not defined in Section 506 of the Act, nor is a definition provided in the legislative history of that section.

59.   *United States v. Moran*, 757 F. Supp. 1046, 1048 (D. Neb. 1991); *United States v. Cross*, 816 F.2d 297, 300 (7th Cir. 1987); *United States v. Heilman*, 614 F.2d 1133 (7th Cir. 1980), *cert. denied*, 447 U.S. 922, 100 S. Ct. 3014 (1980); *United States v. Gottesman*, 724 F.2d 1517, 1522–1523 (11th Cir. 1984); *United States v. Wise*, 550 F.2d 1180 (9th Cir. 1977), *cert. denied*, 434 U.S. 929, 98 S. Ct. 416 (1977), *reh'g denied*, 434 U.S. 977, 98 S. Ct. 542 (1977); *United States v. Rose*, 149 U.S.P.Q. 820 (S.D.N.Y. 1966). A minority view defines "willfully" to require only an intent to copy and does not require proof of an intent to infringe. *United States v. Backer*, 134 F.2d 533, 535 (2d Cir. 1943); *United States v. Taxe*, 380 F. Supp. 1010 (C.D. Cal. 1974); *aff'd in part, rev'd in part*, 540 F.2d 961 (9th Cir. 1976), *cert. denied*, 429 U.S. 1040, 97 S. Ct. 737 (1977), *reh'g denied*, 429 U.S. 1124, 97 S. Ct. 1163 (1977).

60.   *United States v. Cross*, 816 F.2d 297, 301 (7th Cir. 1987); *United States v. Moore*, 604 F.2d 1228, 1235 (9th Cir. 1979) (it is irrelevant whether there was an exchange for value so long as there existed the hope of some pecuniary gain). *See also United States v. Shabazz*, 724 F.2d 1536, 1540 (11th Cir. 1984) (holding that it was not necessary to show that the defendant actually made a profit; the only requirement was that he engaged in business "to hopefully or possibly make a profit").

61.   *United States v. LaMacchia*, 871 F. Supp. 535 (D. Mass. 1994).

62.   *United States v. Kenadek*, No. 94-10221 (D. Mass. 1994).

11

Online Rights of Copyright Users

Thomas J. Smedinghoff

Practically all online activity implicates copyright law for two reasons. First, most communications involve copyrightable material. As discussed in Chapter 9, most forms of information are automatically protected by federal copyright, even in the absence of a copyright notice or registration. As a consequence, most of the text, images, sounds, and software communicated online consist of copyrighted material. Second, as discussed in Chapter 10, most online activity involves one or more of the copyright owner's exclusive rights of reproduction, adaptation, distribution, performance, or display. Viewing the contents of a Web page or computer bulletin board, forwarding an e-mail message, uploading and downloading content, and printing the contents of an online publication or saving it to disk all involve copying by the user and distribution, public performance, or public display by the publisher. In what circumstances do these activities, when undertaken without express permission from the copyright owner, constitute copyright infringement?

A copyright owner's rights in information are not absolute. Although they are often referred to as "exclusive" rights, there are numerous exceptions and limitations on the rights granted by the Copyright Act. As a consequence, there are many cases where copyright-protected digital information (or parts of it) may be used by non-owners without obtaining permission from the copyright owner.

Generally, it is permissible to use digital information without permission from the copyright owner if

1. There is an "implied license" to use the information,
2. The use is considered a "fair use" under the copyright law,
3. The copying is considered *de minimis* such that it does not constitute infringement,
4. It is in the public domain, or
5. What is used is not itself copyrightable, even though it comes from a copyrightable work.

11.1 Implied Licenses

With permission from the copyright owner a user can, of course, do certain things, such as copy and distribute a copyrighted work, that would otherwise constitute copyright infringement. Permission from the copyright owner can come in a variety of forms.

In some cases, for example, permission from the copyright owner might simply take the form of a statement at the end of a Web page such as "Permission is granted to copy and distribute this document provided proper attribution and copyright notice is included." In other cases, permission comes in the form of a more traditional license agreement—that is, a contract between the copyright owner and the user authorizing the user to exercise rights that are normally reserved to the copyright owner. The contract might be reduced to writing and signed by both parties; it may be an oral agreement between the parties; or, as in the case of software, it might be a shrinkwrap agreement that accompanies the software and is accepted by the user through the conduct of opening the package.

All of these forms of permission have one thing in common—they represent an *express license* by the copyright owner that authorizes a user to do something with the copyrighted work. Unfortunately, however, in many online situations the issue of the rights of users is not even addressed, much less the subject to any express agreement from the copyright owner.

In many cases, however, it is likely that some limited form of permission is available to the user via an *implied license.* An implied license to use a copyrighted work is a binding contract that is implied as a result of some act or conduct on the part of the copyright owner.[1] The parties have not expressly agreed on the contract; rather, the agreement is implied from their conduct.

Courts have found the existence of an implied license to make certain uses of a copyrighted work on the basis of a variety of fact patterns.[2] Depending on the situation, there are at least three key factors in the online world that seem to support the existence of implied licenses in some cases to make at least some uses of online digital works:

11.1.1 Necessity

Virtually all forms of online conduct somehow implicate the rights of copyright owners (e.g., they involve copying, adaptation, distribution, performance, or display of the copyrighted work—see Chapter 10). Therefore, it seems logical that copyright owners must be presumed to impliedly consent to the conduct that is required for the online use of their works that they intend. Sending an e-mail message via the Internet, for example, involves numerous acts of copying that occur automatically as the message passes through the various aspects of the network.[3] By sending the message, the sender arguably consents to the necessary copying.

Likewise, when copyrighted material, such as a photograph, is incorporated into a Web site, it cannot be used by others in the manner in which it is intended unless an act of copying occurs. Specifically, in order to view the Web page it is necessary to copy its contents onto the RAM of the user's computer in order to display it on the screen. Since this conduct constitutes making a "copy," and thus constitutes at least a technical copyright violation, it must be presumed that the author who posted material on the Web site granted an implied license to make such copies. In other words, when the copyright owner delivers a copy of copyrighted material (such as the content of an Internet Web site) this is one factor that may be relied upon in determining that an implied license has been granted.[4]

The problem arises, in large part, because copying is such a necessary part of online conduct, but is not required at all for the analogous conduct with paper products. For example, consider the many magazines, newspapers, product brochures, catalogues, and other printed material that are distributed in paper form. People can readily view and use this information without having to make an additional copy. But in order to view the same information at an Internet Web site, the viewer must copy the material to his or her computer to the extent necessary to display it on the screen, even if for a temporary duration.

This problem is analogous to that addressed by Congress in 1980 with respect to computer software. There, Congress determined that copyright protection should prohibit the unauthorized copying of computer programs, but should not inhibit the rightful use of these works.[5] Because any placement of any copyrighted work into a computer is the preparation of a copy, and thus, a potential copyright infringement, Congress added Section 117 to the Copyright Act to make clear that the owner of a copy of a computer program has the right to copy that program onto a computer for purposes of using it for its intended purpose.[6] In other words, Congress recognized that when a user purchases a computer program at a local computer store it is impossible to use that program for its intended purpose unless that program were copied from the diskette or CD-ROM on which it was originally acquired onto the hard disk and memory of a computer. Congress made clear in Section 117 that such copying does not constitute copyright infringement.

Congress has not yet extended the copyright law in this manner to any other copyrighted digital works. However, it may be argued that courts should treat other works in a similar manner, or alternatively, that the law should be modified accordingly. Whether this will happen, however, remains to be seen.

11.1.2 Custom and Usage and Functionality

In many cases, well-recognized online customs and practices have been established that, while not necessary to the primary use of a digital work, are so prevalent that copyright owners might be presumed to understand them and agree to them in certain cases. In some cases the custom or usage is implemented in the functionality of a particular online system that is, or should be, understood by those who use them. Posting an e-mail message to a listserv is an example. Since the author of the copyrightable message knows that the listserv will automatically copy and redistribute the message to all the subscribers of the listserv, the author presumably grants an implied license for such copying.

Other customs are not automated, but are part of so-called accepted online practice. E-mail is perhaps a good example, as many would argue that there is a well recognized custom of copying e-mail messages and forwarding them to others, sometimes with additional annotations. Technically speaking, this conduct of copying, modifying, and distributing copyrighted material constitutes copyright infringement. But if "everyone does it" all the time, and everyone knows that others do it all the time, does this provide a basis for finding the practice to be noninfringing?

To date, there is not much law with respect to interpreting the copyright law in light of custom and practice. However, there is some possible support for such a theory.

Perhaps the best example is the Sony Betamax case involving a practice of home taping of copyrighted movies from televisions.[7] In the *Sony* case, the court recognized that there was a common practice whereby individuals would tape movies off their televisions primarily because they were not at home when the movie was originally shown but desired to have it available for viewing later. The court concluded that this practice, which it characterized as "time-shifting," constituted fair use (discussed in Section 11.2). As a consequence, it validated the practice of home taping.

11.1.3 Copyright Owner Conduct

Certain online actions by the copyright owner are, by definition, an invitation to make a copy, and thus appear to involve an implied license to use a copyrighted work. Posting a file on an ftp site, which exists for the purpose of making files available for downloading, is a good example of conduct that clearly gives rise to an implied license to make a copy.

11.1.4 Scope of License

Even when there is no question that an implied license exists, the difficulty comes in defining the scope of that implied license. Those who set up Web sites on the Internet impliedly consent to the copying of their material in the memory of the computers of those who view the Web site. But what about printing that material or saving it to disk? Does their consent include such additional copying? Does the fact that the Web browser that an individual uses to access the Web site contains a print and save-to-disk option have an impact on this issue? Even if such printing and copying to disk is included within the scope of the implied license, is it limited to the personal use of the individual involved, or can that individual make additional copies to pass around the office, to clients and friends, or to use as part of his or her own Web page? These, of course, are unanswered questions that will require further definition from the courts.

Because an implied license is nonexclusive, and does transfer ownership of the copyright, the licensor can still bring suit for copyright infringement if the licensee's use of the work exceeds the scope of the nonexclusive license.[8]

The scope of the implied license, like any contract term, turns on the parties' intent. In the absence of express intent, a court will look to the surrounding circumstances and the parties' conduct.[9] However, the question of the scope of the implied license is one of fact. Thus, in many cases it is not likely to be resolved in advance of trial.[10]

11.2 Fair Use

Portions of a copyrighted work may, in some situations, be copied, adapted, and distributed without permission of the copyright owner pursuant to the doctrine of *fair use*. But determining when the fair-use doctrine applies can be a rather difficult task. There is no bright line test; there are no hard and fast rules. Instead, each case must be decided on the basis of its unique facts and circumstances.[11]

11.2.1 The Fair-Use Factors

The Copyright Act sets forth four factors to be considered in determining whether an act that would otherwise constitute an infringement is permitted by the doctrine of fair use:[12]

1. The purpose and character of the use, including whether the use is of a commercial nature or is for nonprofit educational purposes—that is, commercial uses are less likely to be fair use; nonprofit educational uses are more likely to qualify as fair use.
2. The nature of the copyrighted work—that is, copying from factual works is tolerated more than copying from more creative fictional works.
3. The amount and substantiality of the portion used in relation to the copyrighted work as a whole—that is, the more that is copied, or the more significant the portion that is copied (regardless of the quantity), the less likely that fair use will apply.
4. The effect of the use upon the potential market for or value of the copyrighted work—that is, if the use has an adverse impact on the market for the original work, it will not constitute fair use.

The Copyright Act itself does not specify how each of these factors is to be weighed. No single factor is dispositive, although courts tend to consider the fourth factor to be the most important.[13]

Online conduct, such as forwarding e-mail messages, downloading content from Web pages, trading files, sampling a song, or scanning and uploading copyrighted pictures is common, but is it "fair use"? Many people mistakenly believe that fair use applies so long as the resulting product is not marketed commercially, but this is not necessarily true. Thus questions abound as to when, if ever, the online copying of digital information constitutes fair use. Cases have had very little opportunity to consider "digital" fair use issues in an online environment. However, it is reasonable to expect that courts will approach claims of fair use online just as they do in traditional environments.

The following summary of how the courts analyze each of the four fair use factors is likely to apply in the digital world as well.

11.2.1.1 The Purpose and Character of the Use. First, courts look at the purpose and character of the use of the copyrighted work. In doing so, they normally consider two factors: (1) whether the copying is for a noncommercial use, as opposed to a commercial purpose; and (2) whether the copying involves a transformative use of the original. A *transformative use* is one in which the copied material is incorporated into another work that has a different purpose or different character from that of the original, such as a work that adds new expression, meaning, or message to the material copied from the original work. Copying in an attempt to duplicate the original and multiply the number of copies is not a transformative use.[14]

Generally, if the copying is for commercial or profit-making purposes, there is a presumption that the copying is not fair use.[15] But where the copying is of a transformative nature, that is, the matter taken from the copyrighted material is used for some new objective or purpose, the presence of profit motivation will not be considered as important as it would be if the copying were not of a transformative nature.[16] However, when the copying merely duplicates the original, the presence of a commercial purpose will weigh heavily against a finding of fair use.

11.2.1.2 The Nature of the Copyrighted Work. The second factor in the fair-use test is the nature of the copyrighted work from which the material was copied. Courts look at two issues when addressing this factor: (1) whether the copyrighted work is published or unpublished,[17] and (2) whether the copyrighted work is factual or creative.

If the copyrighted work has not previously been published, courts are less likely to conclude that copying is fair use.[18] Likewise, courts are less likely to find fair use if the work copied is more creative in nature.[19] For example, copying from a motion picture is less likely to be fair use than copying from a news broadcast.[20]

11.2.1.3 The Amount and Substantiality of the Portion Used. The third factor looks to the amount and substantiality of the portion used in relation to the copyrighted work as a whole. As a general proposition, the greater the portion of a work that is copied, the less likely it is that the copying will be considered fair use. Where an entire copyrighted work is copied, such as a complete software product, sound recording, or photograph, the copying is unlikely to qualify as fair use.[21]

The quantity of material copied is not the only issue. Courts also examine the copied material from a qualitative perspective. In one case, for example, a magazine copied only approximately 300 words out of President Ford's memoirs, but in ruling that this was not fair use, the court emphasized the significance of the quotations by noting that they amount to "the heart of the book," the part most likely to be newsworthy and important in licensing serialization rights.[22]

In some cases, however, it is possible that copying an entire copyrighted work may qualify as fair use. In 1984, for example, the Supreme Court sanctioned the videotaping of television programs for home use. In that case, the Court recognized that the copying was not transformative and took the entirety of the copyrighted work, and acknowledged that these facts argued against a finding of fair use. However, the Court justified a finding of fair use by the fact that the copying, (1) was private, (2) was noncommercial, (3) was done to permit the consumer one viewing at a convenient hour of copyrighted material that was offered to him free of charge, and (4) caused no appreciable loss of revenue to the copyright owner.[23]

11.2.1.4 The Effect of the Use on the Potential Market for the Copyrighted Work. The fourth fair-use factor is often considered to be the most important.[24] If copying a portion of another's copyrighted work has no demonstrable effect upon the potential market for, or the value of, the copyrighted work, it may be considered a fair use.[25] On the other hand, if the copying could have a potential impact on the market for the work from which the copy was taken, it is very likely that the copying will not be considered to be fair use.[26]

Thus, in one case a court held that the market for the copyrighted work (the letters of J. D. Salinger) was impaired by the copying, despite the fact that Salinger had no immediate plans to publish the letters.[27] The court held that Salinger had the right to protect his *opportunity* to sell the letters.[28] Although the defendant's work would not displace the market for the published letters, the fact that the defendant had copied the "most interesting" parts made it likely that the market for the letters themselves would be impaired.

11.2.2 Fair Use Online

As the foregoing discussion makes clear, determining whether a particular act of copying from the copyrighted information of another is fair use is not necessarily a simple analysis.

Three cases involving online copyright infringement illustrate the application of the four fair-use factors. The first case, brought by Playboy Enterprises against the operator of a computer bulletin board, was based on allegations that the bulletin board contained a number of *Playboy* photographs that had been uploaded by subscribers and that were available to subscribers for downloading.[29] Playboy claimed that such practice infringed its copyrights in the photographs. The defendant argued that it was fair use to make the copyrighted photographs available on his BBS, but the court rejected this argument.

With respect to the first factor, the court found that the defendant's use was clearly commercial since access to the bulletin board was available to those who paid $25 per month or who purchased products from the defendant. This, the court held, clearly weighed against the finding of fair use. With respect to the second factor, the court found that the photographs were in the category of fantasy and entertainment, and therefore entitled to broader protection than factual works.

With respect to the third factor, the amount and substantiality of the portion of the copyrighted work used, the defendant argued that the photographs were only a small portion of the magazine from which they were taken. The court, however, disagreed, noting that it "is not implying that people do not read the articles in [Playboy's] magazine. However, a major factor to [Playboy's] success is the photographs in its magazine. By pirating the photographs for which [Playboy] has become famous, Defendant Frena has taken a very important part of [Playboy's] copyrighted publications."[30] Finally, with respect to the fourth factor, the effect of the use on the potential market for or value of the copyrighted work, the court also found against a finding of fair use. As the court pointed out, if this type of conduct became widespread it would adversely affect the potential value for the copyrighted work.

A similar case involved the uploading of copyrighted Sega games to a computer bulletin board known as Maphia, which games were then made available to subscribers for downloading.[31] In that case the sysop also argued that his conduct constituted fair use. There the court reviewed the four fair-use factors, and found against the defendant on each one.

With respect to the first factor, the court pointed out that when copying is for the purpose of making multiple copies of the original, and thereby saving users the expense of purchasing additional authorized copies, this militates against a finding of fair use. Because users of the Maphia bulletin board were likely to and encouraged to download Sega games to avoid having to buy video game cartridges from Sega, to the profit of the operator of the bulletin board, the commercial purpose and character of the unauthorized copying weighs against a finding of fair use.

With respect to the second fair-use factor—the nature of the copyrighted work—the court noted that video game programs are for entertainment uses and involve fiction and fantasy, facts that weigh against a finding of fair use.

With respect to the third fair-use factor, the court noted that the entire game programs were copied, a fact that weighed against a finding of fair use. Finally, with respect to the fourth factor, the court noted that it is obvious that should the unauthorized copying of Sega's video games by defendants and others become widespread, there would be a substantial and immeasurable adverse effect on the market for Sega's copyrighted video games. Accordingly, the court denied the defense of fair use.

The third case involved an individual who posted to the Internet copyrighted documents consisting of the writings of L. Ron Hubbard, the founder of the Church of Scientology.[32] Although he claimed that his postings were done for purposes of criticism, and thus constituted fair use, the court disagreed.

With respect to the first factor, the court concluded that the copying was not commercial in nature, and was done for the purpose of criticism or comment—for example, to evoke discussion of various Scientology philosophies. This, the court felt, weighed in the defendant's favor. However, the court did note that the copying was only minimally transformative since, unlike the typical critic, the defendant added little new expression to the Church's works.

With respect to the second factor, the court concluded that the unpublished nature of the works weighed against fair use. Likewise, because the defendant "copied all or almost all of many of the works," the third factor weighed heavily in the plaintiff's favor.

Finally, with respect to the fourth factor, the plaintiff contended that posting its copyrighted works over the Internet, where more than 25 million subscribers could access them, would have a potentially detrimental effect on the market for its works. However, the court held that the demand of those seeking out the teachings of the Church would not be met by the defendant's postings, and thus concluded that it was unlikely to diminish the sale of the plaintiff's works.

Nonetheless, in balancing these factors, the court concluded that the large percentage of the works copied, combined with the minimal added criticism or commentary, negated a finding of fair use.

11.3 *De Minimis* Copying of Copyrighted Information

In some cases, a *de minimis* rule has been applied to allow the literal copying of a small and usually insignificant portion of a copyrighted work.[33] However, determining whether the portion copied qualifies as *de minimis* requires considerations of both the quantity and quality of the portion used in relation to the whole of the copyrighted work. That is, the rule considers how much of the copyrighted work has been copied and how important the copied portion is to the work as a whole.[34]

Copying a small portion of a copyrighted work may still be infringing if it is *qualitatively* important to the work as a whole.[35] In other words, copying a small amount of qualitatively nonessential material may not constitute infringement, but if the material copied is qualitatively essential, then a court is likely to find copyright infringement.

Thus, being careful to copy only a small part of qualitatively essential material does not necessarily prevent a finding of appropriation.[36] The practical problem is determining when material is "qualitatively essential." Unfortunately there is no easy rule. The qualitative importance of a given quantity of material varies depending upon the type of work in question and in its relation to the rest of the copyright owner's work.

In the case of music, courts often look to see whether the small portion that has been copied is the distinctive or "catchy" musical phrase or lyric that gives a song its appeal,[37] the part that "is pleasing to the ears of lay listeners,"[38] or the part that makes "it popular and valuable."[39] In other words, if the portion copied is commercially important to the original work, the copying is most likely to constitute copyright infringement. In one case, for example, the defendant copied four notes of a 100-measure jingle and the words "I Love" from the lyric "I Love New York." The court held that although on its face the taking was relatively slight, on closer examination "the musical phrase that the lyrics 'I Love New York' accompany, is the heart of the composition."[40] In a 1991 case involving digital sampling, a court concluded that the use of three words was enough to constitute an infringement of the copyright law.[41]

In the case of motion pictures, "borrowing" bits and pieces of a film or television clip may also be copyright infringement. In one case, for example, the defendant used various clips of a number of Charlie Chaplin films averaging less than 1 minute in length. Despite the fact that the portions used were quantitatively small, the court held that the use infringed the copyright because the use was "qualitatively substantial" in that "each of the scenes [the defendant] used was among Chaplin's best . . . and . . . each such excerpt was central to the film in which the portion used was intimately tied to the story and was a main source of comedy for the motion picture as a whole."[42]

11.4 Public Domain

To the extent that information is in the public domain, it may be freely used, copied, adapted, distributed, and displayed without fear of copyright infringement. But making this determination is frequently more difficult than it appears.

11.4.1 When Is a Work "Public Domain"?

Copyrightable information is in the public domain generally only if

1. The original copyright has expired,
2. The copyright has been abandoned by the copyright holder, or
3. The work was created by the federal government.

11.4.1.1 Copyright Has Expired. Determining if a copyright has expired requires determining when the work was first created, and, in some cases, when it was first published.[43]

For works created after January 1, 1978, the rules are rather simple and straightforward. Copyright protection in a work created after January 1, 1978, begins as soon as the work is created. If the individual who created the work was also the original owner of the copyright, the copyright protection lasts for the life of the author plus 50 years.[44] If the individual who created the work did so under a work-for-hire relationship (e.g., as an employee), the copyright lasts for 75 years after the year of first publication, or 100 years after the year of creation, whichever comes first.[45] (The concept of a "work for hire" is explained in Section 9.5). As a consequence, no work created after January 1, 1978, can enter the public domain until 2029 at the earliest.

Works created before January 1, 1978, were originally governed by the Copyright Act of 1909. Under that act, copyright protection was granted for a term of 28 years, with a one-time right to renew that protection for an additional 28-year term. When the Copyright Act of 1909 was superseded by the Copyright Act of 1976, certain adjustments were made to the remaining term of protection applicable to copyrighted works created prior to January 1, 1978 (the effective date of the Copyright Act of 1976). Those adjustments depend, however, on whether the work was copyrighted under the Copyright Act of 1909, and if so, whether the work is in its first or second 28-year term of copyright protection. Consequently, the rules for determining the terms of copyright protection applicable to works created before January 1, 1978, can be somewhat complex and confusing. As a general rule, however, if the work was published prior to January 1, 1978, the maximum term of copyright protection allowed under the new copyright law was 75 years.[46] Works published prior to 1922 are now clearly in the public domain.

11.4.1.2 Copyright Has Been Abandoned. A copyright can be intentionally abandoned by its owner. This is often the case with public domain software (although it is not the case with shareware).

In addition, a copyrighted work may enter the public domain before the copyright expires if it was first published before March 1, 1989, without a copyright notice. Works first published after this date, however, need not bear a copyright notice.[47]

If a work created prior to January 1, 1978 (i.e., a work governed by the Copyright Act of 1909) was published without a proper copyright notice, then the work automatically entered the public domain.[48] However, for works created after January 1, 1978 (i.e., works governed by the Copyright Act of 1976), the law was not as unforgiving. For works in this category, publication without a notice would *not* invalidate the copyright if:

1. The notice was only omitted from a relatively small number of copies,
2. Registration of the work was made within 5 years after publication without notice and a reasonable effort to add the notice to all copies was made after the omission was discovered, or
3. The notice was omitted in violation of an express requirement in writing as a condition of the copyright owner's authorization of the public distribution of the work.[49]

Accordingly, any work created after January 1, 1978, and published without a notice prior to March 1, 1989, *may* be in the public domain. However, you can not necessarily be sure of this conclusion, unless you can rule out the applicability of all three of these special cases.

Effective March 1, 1989, a copyright notice is *not* required at all on any copyrighted work. Accordingly, the omission of a copyright notice from any work published after March 1, 1989, has no impact whatsoever on the copyright status of the work. As a consequence, the lack of a copyright notice does not mean that the work is in the public domain. In other words, there is a risk in copying from a work published after March 1, 1989, that does not bear a copyright notice, as mere lack of a notice does not mean that the work is not copyrighted.

This is, of course, the situation with most information communicated online. That is, the information often bears no copyright notice, but because it was first published after March 1, 1989, it retains all of its copyright protection. Thus, nothing can be inferred about the copyright status of a work solely by virtue of the fact that it contains no copyright notice. In fact, it is often best to assume that any content available online is protected by copyright unless otherwise noted.

11.4.1.3 Work Was Created by the Federal Government. If a work was created by the federal government or as work for hire for the federal government, the work is also treated as public-domain material. By law, the federal government holds no copyright in works created by it or in works created for it as work for hire.[50] Thus, information obtained from government Web sites, FTP sites, bulletin boards, and the like (such as copies of statutes, proposed legislation, committee reports, opinions of courts and administrative agencies, speeches by public officials, proposed government regulations, weather reports, maps, satellite photographs, and other government documents), are all in the public domain, and may be freely copied, adapted, distributed, performed, and displayed, as applicable.

However, this rule applies only to the U.S. federal government. Works created by other governmental entities, such as state, municipal, and local governments, as well as foreign governments, may be protected by copyright.[51] Moreover, the federal government is not precluded from receiving and holding copyrights transferred to it by assignment, bequest, or otherwise.[52] Thus, the fact that a document, map, survey, or photograph is published by the government does not necessarily mean it is not protected by copyright. The Copyright Act does not prohibit copyright protection in works prepared under government contract or grant. Instead, the terms of the grant or the contract in each case will determine whether the works created will be treated as government works not subject to copyright, or whether the creator of the works will be allowed to retain a federal copyright.[53] Only if the work was created by a government employee, or if it was created by an independent contractor for the government pursuant to a work-for-hire arrangement, will the work be in the public domain.

Thus, as the foregoing makes clear, the mere fact that a work owes its origin to, or is otherwise related to, the federal government, does not necessarily mean that no copyright protection applies. Some further investigation may be necessary.

11.4.2 Risks in Using Public-Domain Information

Determining that a copyrightable work is in the public domain does not end the inquiry. There are a number of other issues that may still prevent use of the information without permission.

First, to the extent that the work is protected by copyright in more than one country, frequently the duration of the copyright will vary from country to country. For example, if a work is considered to be in the public domain because the term of copyright protection in the United States has expired, it is still very possible that the term of copyright protection in another country has not expired. Thus, use of the information in such other country (such as making it available via an Internet Web site) may still constitute infringement in that particular country (even though it will not constitute infringement in the United States). Similarly, if the work was published without a copyright notice in the United States before March 1, 1989, this may result in the work being in the public domain in the United States, but will have no effect on its copyright status in another country that does not require such formalities. Accordingly, it may not be copyright infringement to copy and distribute the work in the United States, but foreign distribution may nonetheless be prohibited by the continuing foreign copyrights.

Second, it is important to understand that frequently a single work consists of a number of overlapping copyrights. Thus it is possible that a work now in the public domain may incorporate (with permission) copyrighted materials that are not in the public domain. A recording of a song, for example, includes a copyright in the underlying musical composition, and a separate copyright in the sound recording. If the copyright in the sound recording enters the public domain, but the copyright in the musical composition does not, copying the sound recording will still result in infringement of the copyright in the underlying musical composition. In one case, for example, the court found that copying and distributing a sound recording of a *Lone Ranger* radio program that was not protected by copyright still constituted infringement of the underlying radio scripts on which the sound recording was based.[54]

Finally, it is also important to note that a new work based on a public-domain work may itself be the subject of copyright protection. Thus, a photograph of a public-domain painting is protected by copyright, as is a movie based on a public-domain work, such as one of Shakespeare's plays. Although the underlying public-domain work may be copied, the copy may not be made from the new work based on it (such as the photograph or the movie in the foregoing examples).

11.5 First-Sale Doctrine

The Copyright Act gives the copyright owner the exclusive right to distribute the copyrighted work (see Section 10.3).[55] Although this right is one of the exclusive rights granted to the copyright owner, it is subject to an important limitation. After the copyright owner has sold a particular copy of the work (i.e., made the "first sale" of that copy), it has no right to control further disposition of that copy by the purchaser.[56] Thus, for example, when you buy a copy of a book in a bookstore or a CD in a music store, it is not copyright infringement to sell your copy to someone else (as long as you do not make any additional copies as well).

This principle is known as the *first-sale doctrine*. Under this doctrine, the copyright owner's right to distribute a particular copy is limited to the first time he or she sells or otherwise disposes of *that specific copy*.[57] In other words, the distribution right is limited to the exclusive right to sell a copy *once*, because once the copyright owner parts with a particular copy, the recipient then has the right to sell or otherwise transfer it. The copyright owner's exclusive right to distribute copies of the work is "extinguished" with respect to that copy.[58]

There is a question, however, as to whether the first-sale doctrine should apply to the online transmission of digital content (as opposed to the distribution of the content on tangible media such as diskettes or CD-ROMs). An online transmission of the content involves both the reproduction of the work and the distribution of the reproduction. Yet the copyright owner who uses a particular copy of the work for the transmission does not "dispose of the possession of *that copy*" as required to trigger the first-sale rule. That copy of the work remains with the copyright owner and the recipient of the transmission receives only a reproduction of the work. Accordingly, it has been suggested that the first-sale provisions of the Copyright Act be amended to make clear that they do not apply to the sale of other disposition of the possession of a copy by online transmission.[59] If this position is adopted, the purchaser of a copyrighted work who obtains it by online communication (e.g. by downloading it) would not have any right to transfer that copy to anyone else.

On the other hand, if the electronic online communication of a copyrighted work from the copyright owner to a recipient is considered to be a "distribution," then, under the first-sale doctrine, the recipient will have the right to sell or otherwise transfer possession of that copy to someone else without the copyright owner's permission. But the right to transfer the copy is still limited.

This is because the first-sale doctrine restricts only the copyright owner's distribution right; it in no way affects the reproduction right. Thus, the first-sale doctrine does not allow the original recipient to make a subsequent online transfer of a copy of a work because, under current technology, the transmitter retains the original copy of the work while the new recipient of the transmission obtains a reproduction of the original copy (i.e., a *new* copy), rather than the copy owned by the transmitter. The language of the Copyright Act, the legislative history, and case law make clear that the first-sale doctrine applies only to those situations where the owner of a particular copy disposes of the physical possession of that particular copy.[60]

If the owner of a particular copy transmits a copy to another person without authorization, such a transmission would involve an unlawful reproduction of a work, and the first-sale doctrine would not shield the transmitter from liability for the reproduction nor for the distribution. Under the first-sale doctrine, the owner of a particular copy of a copyrighted work may distribute it but may not reproduce it.[61] Therefore, the transmission would constitute infringement of the copyright owner's reproduction right.[62]

A narrow exception to the first-sale doctrine applies to copies of sound recordings and computer programs. Purchasers of copies of sound recordings and computer programs may not rent, lease, or lend a copy to others without getting permission to do so from the copyright owner.[63]

11.6 Noncopyrightable Aspects of a Work

Regardless of the copyright status of a work, the law is clear that anyone is free to copy "noncopyrightable" elements of that work. Determining what constitutes a noncopyrightable aspect of a work is often easier in theory than in fact. However, it should not be overlooked.

11.6.1 Facts

Facts by themselves can never be copyrightable.[64] This is true of all facts—scientific, historical, biographical, and news of the day. They are part of the public domain available to every person.[65] Thus, for example, the names, towns, and telephone numbers of the persons living in a certain geographic area and listed in a phone book are uncopyrightable facts.[66] Likewise, Internet domain names and URLs are simply addresses that do not qualify for copyright protection.

Anyone is free to use the facts contained in another's copyrighted publication or database, as long as they take only facts, and not the expression used by the author to communicate those facts.[67] No matter how much original authorship the work displays, the facts and ideas it exposes are free for the taking. The very same facts and ideas may be divorced from the context imposed by the author, and restated and reshuffled by second comers, even if the author was the first to discover the facts or to propose the ideas.

11.6.2 Databases of Facts

Even though facts are not, by themselves, copyrightable, it is important to understand that a compilation (e.g., a database) of such noncopyrightable elements may itself be copyrightable.[68] Thus, for example, even though facts (such as domain names and

URLs) are not copyrightable, compilations of facts (such as in a list of the 50 "hottest" Web sites) *may* be copyrightable.[69]

The key to understanding how a collection of uncopyrightable facts can achieve copyrightable status lies in the copyright requirement of originality. The author of the compilation typically chooses which facts to include, in what order to place them, and how to arrange the collected data so that they may be used effectively by readers. These choices as to selection and arrangement, if made independently by the compiler with at least a minimum degree of creativity, are sufficiently original to be copyrightable. Thus, even a directory that contains absolutely no copyrightable elements, only facts, meets the requirements for copyright protection if it features an original selection or arrangement.[70]

But although compilations of facts *can* be copyrightable, they are not copyrightable *per se*.[71] Something more than mere "collection and assembling" is required. The fact that someone has expended a great deal of time, effort, and money to create the compilation has no bearing on its copyrightability.[72] The "sweat of the brow" expended by the compiler in gathering and compiling data does not constitute the requisite originality necessary to qualify the compilation for copyright.[73]

In determining whether a fact-based work is copyrightable, courts focus on the manner in which the collected facts have been *selected, coordinated, and arranged*. Facts are never original, so the compilation author can claim originality, if at all, only in *the way the facts are presented*. Thus, the principal focus of courts is on whether the selection, coordination, and arrangement are sufficiently original to merit protection.[74]

The originality requirement is not particularly stringent. It merely calls for independent creation, not novelty. Thus, a compilation of facts can qualify for copyright protection even though it is similar to a work previously produced by others, and hence is not novel.[75]

A compiler may settle upon a selection or arrangement that others have used. Originality requires only that the author make the selection or arrangement independently (i.e., without copying that selection or arrangement from another work), and that it display some minimum level of creativity. The vast majority of compilations will pass this test, but not all will. There remains a narrow category of works in which the creative spark is utterly lacking or so trivial as to be virtually nonexistent.[76] The selection and arrangement of facts cannot be so mechanical or routine as to require no creativity whatsoever. The standard of originality is low, but it does exist.[77]

Thus, for example, the Supreme Court has held there is nothing remotely creative about arranging names alphabetically in a white pages telephone directory. It is an age-old practice, firmly rooted in tradition and so commonplace that it has come to be expected as a matter of course.[78] In other words, it is a selection and arrangement of facts that is so mechanical or routine as to require no creativity.[79]

Even if a compilation of noncopyrightable data qualifies as a copyrightable compilation, it receives only limited protection. Copyright protects only the author's original contributions (i.e., the selection, coordination, and arrangement)—not the facts or information conveyed. The copyright in a compilation extends only to the material contributed by the author of such work, as distinguished from the preexisting material employed in the work, and does not imply any exclusive right in the preexisting material.[80]

In other words, the copyright in a factual compilation is "thin." Notwithstanding a valid copyright, a subsequent compiler remains free to use the facts contained in another's publication to aid in preparing a competing work, as long as the competing work does not feature the same selection and arrangement.[81] No matter how much original authorship the work displays, the facts and ideas it exposes are free for the taking. The very same facts and ideas may be divorced from the context imposed by the author, and restated and reshuffled by others, even if the author was the first to discover the facts or to propose the ideas.[82] Thus, for example, in one case the defendant was free to copy the subscriber information in the Illinois Bell Telephone directory and rearrange the information into phone number or street order, notwithstanding that the telephone directory "as a whole" was copyrightable because it contained some copyrightable text and yellow pages advertisements.[83]

Accordingly, with a database of uncopyrighted facts, the only thing that can be protected by copyright is the selection, coordination, and arrangement of the permission database. The facts themselves can be freely copied without a license (as long as they are divorced from the copyrightable expression added by the person who created the database).

11.6.3 Ideas

Similarly, "ideas" cannot be protected by copyright.[84] Protection is available only for the "expression" of an "idea."[85] Accordingly, if a given idea is reduced to a tangible form of expression (which any work must be in order to be eligible for copyright), only the form of expression will be protected; the underlying idea may be freely adopted and copied by others. Thus, for example, although a particular version of the "map" conveying "a New Yorker's view of the country" is copyrightable, the "idea" of creating such a distorted map is not.

11.6.4 Words, Phrases, and Titles

There are also certain limited aspects of the text that comprises a literary work that are not copyrightable. Specifically, individual words and short phrases, such as names, titles, and slogans are not copyrightable.[86] Even if a name, title, or short phrase is novel, distinctive, or lends itself to a play on words, it cannot be protected by copyright.[87] Likewise, the title of a book, movie, play, poem, or other work of authorship is generally not entitled to copyright protection.[88] Presumably domain names, URLs, and HTML tags (i.e., hypertext links) are themselves not copyrightable either.

Endnotes

1.   3 Melville B. Nimmer & David Nimmer, *Nimmer on Copyright* § 10.03[A], at 10-18 (1994).

2.   *See, e.g., Effects Associates, Inc. v. Cohen*, 908 F.2d 555 (9th Cir. 1990) (moviemaker had an implied license to incorporate special effects footage into a movie where moviemaker paid $56,000 for the development of the footage, since to hold otherwise "would mean that plaintiff's contribution to the film was of minimal value, a conclusion that can't be squared with the fact that $56,000 was paid for the footage"); *Oddo v. Ries*, 743 F.2d 630, 634 (9th Cir. 1984) (plaintiff partner who contributed to the partnership a manuscript based on his preexisting articles gave partnership implied license to use preexisting articles as used in manuscript otherwise his contribution to the partnership would have been of minimal value); *MacLean Assoc., Inc. v. Wm. M. Mercer-Meidinger-Hansen, Inc.*, 952 F.2d 769, 779 (3rd Cir. 1991) (defendant had implied nonexclusive license to use software developed by independent contractor on behalf of defendant for a particular client of defendant; however, defendant exceeded scope of that license by marketing the software to other clients); *Irwin v. American Interactive Media, Inc.*, No. 93-1403 (N.D. Cal. Apr. 14, 1994) (developer and producer of CD-I system had implied, nonexclusive license to use composer's music in promotional campaign), *reported in Current Developments: Proprietary Rights/CD-I Marketer May Sue Under Copyright or Contract*, 11 The Computer Lawyer 35 (Jul. 1994); *Pamfiloff v. Giant Records, Inc.*, 794 F. Supp. 933, 939 (N.D. Cal. 1992) (recording agreement giving record producer limited recording rights in copyrighted musical compositions necessarily contained implied nonexclusive license to use the underlying compositions); *Ladas v. Potpourri Press, Inc.*, 846 F. Supp. 221, 225 (E.D.N.Y. 1994) (implied, nonexclusive license to market items incorporating plaintiff's copyrighted artwork was created through course of dealings and understanding that the items would be marketed for several years after artwork was delivered in light of fact that it took several years to bring a design to market).

3.   *See, e.g., Religious Technology Center v. Netcom On-Line Communication Services, Inc.*, No. C-95-20091, 1995 U.S. Dist. LEXIS 18173 (N.D. Cal. November 21, 1995) (noting that when someone posts a message to an Internet Usenet newsgroup it is automatically copied onto numerous computers on the Usenet).

4.   *Effects Associates, Inc. v. Cohen*, 908 F.2d 555, 559 (9th Cir. 1990).

5.   *Final report of the National Commission on New Technological Uses of Copyrighted Works* 12 (1978) ("CONTU Report").

6.   17 U.S.C. § 117.

7.   *Sony Corp. of America v. Universal City Studios, Inc.*, 464 U.S. 417, 104 S. Ct. 774 (1984).

8.   *MacLean Assoc., Inc. v. Wm. M. Mercer-Meidinger-Hansen, Inc.*, 952 F.2d 769, 779 (3rd Cir. 1991); *Interqual, Inc. v. Parkside Health Management Corp.*, 1993 U.S. Dist. LEXIS 10248 (N.D. Ill. July 23, 1993).

9.   *See Vail v. Board of Educ. of Paris Union School Dist. No. 95*, 706 F.2d 1435 (7th Cir.), *aff'd*, 104 S. Ct. 2144 (1983); 3 *Nimmer on Copyright* § 10.08, at 10-71 (principles of contract law are generally applicable in the construction of copyright licenses).

10.   *See, e.g., Pytka v. Van Alen*, 1992 U.S. Dist. LEXIS 11855 (E.D. Pa. Aug. 10, 1992) (finding implied license, but denying summary judgment in light of factual dispute as to scope of that license).

11.   *Campbell v. Acuff-Rose Music, Inc.*, 114 S. Ct. 1164, 1170; *Harper & Row Publishers, Inc. v. Nation Enterprises*, 471 U.S. 539, 549, 105 S. Ct. 2218, 2225 (1985); *see also American Geophysical Union v. Texaco, Inc.*, 802 F. Supp. 1 (S.D.N.Y. 1992), *aff'd* 37 F.3d 881 (2d Cir. 1994), for an excellent discussion of the law relating to fair use.

12. 17 U.S.C. § 107.

13. *Harper & Row Publishers, Inc. v. Nation Enterprises*, 471 U.S. 539, 566, 105 S. Ct. 2218, 2233 (1985).

14. *Campbell v. Acuff-Rose Music, Inc.*, 114 S. Ct. 1164, 1171 (1994); *American Geophysical Union v. Texaco, Inc.*, 802 F. Supp. 1, 12 (S.D.N.Y. 1992), *aff'd* 37 F.3d 881 (2d Cir. 1994).

15. *Sony Corp. of America v. Universal City Studios*, 464 U.S. 417, 449, 104 S. Ct. 774, 793 (1984). The key issue is not whether the copier's sole motive for the use of the copyrighted material is monetary gain, but whether it stands to profit from exploitation of the copyrighted material without paying the customary price. *Harper & Row Publishers, Inc. v. Nation Enterprises*, 471 U.S. 539, 562, 105 S. Ct. 2218, 2231 (1985). Thus, even if one does not directly profit in the sense of a monetary gain, a profit-making purpose can be found in cases where money is saved by copying rather than buying or licensing the required copies. *See Television Digest, Inc. v. United States Tele. Ass'n*, 841 F. Supp. 5, 9 (D.D.C. 1993). Moreover, the fact that you are a nonprofit organization does not compel a finding of fair use. *Marcus v. Rowley*, 695 F.2d 1171, 1175 (9th Cir. 1983).

16. *See, K. Campbell v. Acuff-Rose Music, Inc.*, 114 S. Ct. 1164, 1171 (1994) (2 Live Crew rap song that parodied Roy Orbison's "Pretty Woman" qualified as fair use notwithstanding its commercial nature); *Salinger v. Random House, Inc.*, 811 F.2d 90, 96 (2d Cir. 1987), (a biographer's use of copyrighted letters written by J.D. Salinger to enrich his biography of Salinger was fair use even though he expected to earn profits on the biography) cert. denied, 484 U.S. 890 (1987); *New Era Publications Int'l ApS v. Carol Publishing Group*, 904 F.2d 152 (2d Cir.) (author's use of quoted material "to enrich" his highly critical biography of the founder of the Church of Scientology is a protected fair use, "notwithstanding that he and his publisher anticipate profits"), *cert. denied*, 498 U.S. 921, 111 S. Ct. 297 (1990); *Consumers Union of United States, Inc. v. General Signal Corp.*, 724 F.2d 1044, 1049 (2d Cir. 1983) ("although the purpose of [the] use undoubtedly is commercial, this fact alone does not defeat a fair use defense . . . almost all newspapers, books and magazines are published by commercial enterprises that seek a profit") cert. denied, 469 U.S. 23 (1984); *Rosemont Enterprises, Inc. v. Random House, Inc.*, 366 F.2d 303, 307 (2d Cir. 1966) ("whether an author or publisher reaps economic benefits from the sale of a biographical work, or whether its publication is motivated in part by a desire for commercial gain . . . has no bearing on whether a public benefit may be derived from such a work." Moreover, the district court, in emphasizing the commercial aspects of the Hughes biography, failed to recognize that "all publications presumably are operated for a profit"), *cert. denied*, 385 U.S. 1009 (1967); *American Geophysical Union v. Texaco, Inc.*, 802 F. Supp. 1, 12–13 (S.D.N.Y. 1992 *aff'd* 60 F.3d 913 (2d Cir. 1995).

17. *Harper & Row Publishers, Inc. v. Nation Enterprises*, 471 U.S. 539, 553, 105 S. Ct. 2218, 2226–27 (1985).

18. *Harper & Row Publishers, Inc. v. Nation Enterprises*, 471 U.S. 539, 551, 105 S. Ct. 2218, 2226 (1985).

19. *Harper & Row Publishers, Inc. v. Nation Enterprises*, 471 U.S. 539, 563, 105 S. Ct. 2218, 2232 (1985).

20. *See Sony Corp. of America v. Universal City Studios*, 464 U.S. 417, 455 n. 40, 104 S. Ct. 774, 795 n. 40 (1984).

21. *Sony Corp. of America v. Universal City Studios*, 464 U.S. 417, 450, 104 S. Ct. 774, 792 (1984).

22. *Harper & Row Publishers, Inc. v. Nation Enterprises*, 471 U.S. 539, 564-66, 568, 105 S. Ct. 2218, 2232–33, 2234–35 (1985).

23. *American Geophysical Union v. Texaco, Inc.*, 802 F. Supp. 1, 22 (S.D.N.Y. 1992), *aff'd* 60 F.3d 913 (2d Cir. 1995).

24. *Harper & Row Publishers, Inc. v. Nation Enterprises,* 471 U.S. 539, 566, 105 S. Ct. 2218, 2233 (the fourth factor, effect on the market, is "undoubtedly the single most important element of fair use"). Not all courts agree, however, that this is the effect of the Supreme Court's language. *See American Geophysical Union v. Texaco, Inc.,* 802 F. Supp. 1, 21 (S.D.N.Y. 1992), *aff'd* 60 F.3d 913 (2d Cir. 1995). Moreover, in *Sony* the Court noted that if the use by the defendant of the copyrighted work is for commercial gain, the likelihood of harm to the market for the copyrighted work may be presumed. *Sony Corp. of America v. Universal City Studios,* 464 U.S. 417, 451, 104 S. Ct. 774, 793 (1984).

25. *Sony Corp. of America v. Universal City Studios,* 464 U.S. 417, 450, 104 S. Ct. 774, 792–793 (1984).

26. *Campbell v. Acuff-Rose Music, Inc.* 114 S. Ct. 1164, 1177 (1994) (the fourth fair-use factor "requires courts to consider not only the extent of market harm caused by the particular actions of the alleged infringer, but also whether unrestricted and widespread conduct of the sort engaged in by the defendant . . . would result in a substantially adverse impact on the potential market for the original").

27. *Salinger v. Random House, Inc.,* 811 F.2d 90 (2d Cir. 1987), cert. denied, 484 U.S. 890 (1987).

28. Diminution of market value in plaintiff's works "is not lessened by the fact that their author has disavowed the intention to publish them during his lifetime. . . . He is entitled to protect his *opportunity* to sell his letters. . . ." *Salinger v. Random House, Inc.,* 811 F.2d 90, 99 (2d Cir. 1987) (emphasis in original); *see also Pacific and Southern Co. v. Duncan,* 744 F.2d 1490, 1496–97, (11th Cir. 1984) (where defendant copied news stories broadcast on plaintiff television station, court found injury to the plaintiff's potential market even though plaintiff had not yet sold videos of its broadcasts), *cert. denied,* 471 U.S. 1004 (1985); and *Meeropol v. Nizer,* 560 F.2d 1061, 1070 (2d Cir. 1977) (fact that copyrighted letters have been out of print for 20 years does not necessarily mean that they have no future market that can be injured).

29. *Playboy Enterprises v. Frena,* 839 F. Supp. 1552 (M.D. Fla. 1993).

30. *Playboy Enterprises v. Frena,* 839 F. Supp. 1552, 1558 (M.D. Fla. 1993).

31. *Sega Enterprises Ltd. v. Maphia,* 30 U.S.P.Q. 2d 1992 (N.D. Cal. 1994).

32. *Religious Technology Center v. Newtcom On-Line Communications Services, Inc.,* No. C-95-20091, 1995 U.S. Dist. LEXIS 16184 (N.D. Cal. September 22, 1995).

33. *Warner Bros., Inc. v. American Broadcasting Cos., Inc.,* 720 F.2d 231, 242 (2d Cir. 1983); *G.R. Leonard & Co. v. Stack,* 386 F.2d 38 (7th Cir. 1967); *Werlin v. Reader's Digest Ass'n,* 528 F. Supp. 451, 463–464 (S.D.N.Y. 1981).

34. *Atari, Inc. v. North Am. Philips Consumer Elec. Corp.,* 672 F.2d 607, 619 (7th Cir.) ("it is enough that substantial parts were lifted"), *cert. denied,* 459 U.S. 880 (1982); *see also Vault Corp. v. Quaid Software, Ltd.,* 847 F.2d 255, 267 (5th Cir. 1988) (copying 30 characters out of 50 pages of source code is *de minimis*); *Smith v. Little, Brown & Co.,* 245 F. Supp. 451, 458 (S.D.N.Y. 1965).

35. *Henry Holt & Co. v. Liggett & Myers Tobacco Co.,* 23 F. Supp. 302, 304 (E.D. Pa. 1938) (copying three sentences from a book not *de minimis*); *Iowa State Univ. Research Found., Inc. v. American Broadcasting Cos.,* 463 F. Supp. 902, 904–905 (S.D.N.Y. 1978), *aff'd,* 621 F.2d 57 (2d Cir. 1980) (defendant's broadcast of one 12-second segment and one 2½-minute segment of plaintiff's film held to infringe); *Roy Export Co. Establishment, etc. v. Columbia Broadcasting Sys., Inc.,* 503 F. Supp. 1137 (S.D.N.Y. 1980), *aff'd,* 672 F.2d 1095 (2d Cir.) (segment of film lasting 1 minute and 15 seconds infringed), *cert. denied,* 459 U.S. 826 (1982); *Nikanov v. Simon & Schuster, Inc.,* 246 F.2d 501, 503–504 (2d Cir. 1957) (while the material copied was a relatively small portion of total text, it was an integral part and of real importance to the book as a whole).

36. *See, e.g., Harper & Row Publishers, Inc. v. Nation Enterprises,* 471 U.S. 539, 564–566, 105 S. Ct. 2218, 2233 (1985) (finding that 300 words taken from plaintiff's 200,000-word manuscript was infringing); *Henry Holt & Co. v. Liggett & Myers Tobacco Co.,* 23 F. Supp. 302, 304 (E.D. Pa. 1938) (copying three sentences from a book can constitute infringement); *Dawn Assocs. v. Links,* 203 U.S.P.Q. 831, 835 (N.D. Ill. 1978) (defendant that copied one sentence from advertisement appropriated protected expression).

37. *Bright Tunes Music Corp. v. Harrisongs Music, Ltd.,* 420 F. Supp. 177 (S.D.N.Y. 1976), *modified,* 722 F.2d 988 (2d Cir. 1983); *see also Baxter v. MCA Inc.,* 812 F.2d 421, 425 (9th Cir. 1987) (finding that taking as few as six notes can constitute copyright infringement).

38. *Arnstein v. Porter,* 154 F.2d 464, 473 (2d Cir.), *aff'd on reh'g,* 158 F.2d 795 (2d Cir. 1946).

39. *Johns & Johns Printing Co. v. Paull-Pioneer Music Corp.,* 102 F.2d 282, 283 (8th Cir. 1939).

40. *Elsmere Music, Inc. v. National Broadcasting Co.,* 482 F. Supp. 741, 744 (S.D.N.Y.), *aff'd,* 623 F.2d 252 (2d Cir. 1980). However, the court concluded that the parody of the song was entitled to the fair-use defense.

41. *Grand Upright Music Ltd. v. Warner Bros. Records, Inc.,* 780 F. Supp. 182 (S.D.N.Y. 1991) (in that case, a rap artist named Biz Markie had used a three-word phrase and its accompanying music from the song "Alone Again (Naturally)").

42. *Roy Export Co. Establishment, etc. v. Columbia Broadcasting Sys., Inc.,* 503 F. Supp. 1137, 1145 (S.D.N.Y. 1980), *aff'd,* 672 F.2d 1095 (2d Cir.), *cert. denied,* 459 U.S. 826 (1982).

43. *Publication* is a term of art under the Copyright Act. Generally, publication occurs when a copy of a copyrighted work is distributed to the public by sale or other transfer of ownership, or by rental, lease, or lending. Publication also occurs when the copyright owner offers to distribute copies of the work to a group of persons for further distribution.

44. 17 U.S.C. § 302(a).

45. 17 U.S.C. § 302(c).

46. 17 U.S.C. § 304.

47. 17 U.S.C. § 401.

48. *Stewart v. Abend,* 495 U.S. 207, 110 S. Ct. 1750, 1766 (1990).

49. 17 U.S.C. § 405.

50. 17 U.S.C. § 105.

51. However, certain works by state and local governments may be found not copyrightable for public policy reasons. For example, *see Building Officials & Code Adm. v. Code Technology, Inc.,* 628 F.2d 730, 733–735 (1st Cir. 1980).

52. 17 U.S.C. § 105.

53. H.R. Rep. No. 1476, 94th Cong., 2d Sess. 59 (1976), *reprinted in* 1976 U.S.C.C.A.N. 5659, 5672–73.

54. *Lone Ranger Television, Inc. v. Program Radio Corp.,* 740 F.2d 718, 722 (9th Cir. 1984).

55. 17 U.S.C. § 106(3).

56. 17 U.S.C. § 109.

57. 17 U.S.C. § 109(a).

58. *T.B. Harms Co. v. Jem Records, Inc.,* 655 F. Supp. 1575, 1582 (D. N.J. 1987); *Columbia Pictures Industries, Inc. v. Aveco, Inc.,* 612 F. Supp. 315, 319–320 (M.D. Pa. 1985) *aff'd* 800 F. 2d 59 (3d Cir. 1986).

59.   *Intellectual Property and the National Information Infrastructure: The Report of the Working Group on Intellectual Property Rights,* Information Infrastructure Task Force (Sept. 5, 1995) at pp. 106–109, 245–250.

60.   *Intellectual Property and the National Information Infrastructure: The Report of the Working Group on Intellectual Property Rights,* Information Infrastructure Task Force (Sept. 5, 1995) at 106.

61.   House Report at 79, reprinted in 1976, U.S.C.C.A.N. 5693 (under the first-sale doctrine, "the owner of the physical copy or phono record cannot reproduce or perform the copyrighted work publicly without the copyright owner's consent").

62.   *Intellectual Property and the National Information Infrastructure: The Report of the Working Group on Intellectual Property Rights,* Information Infrastructure Task Force (Sept. 5, 1995) at 107.

63.   17 U.S.C. § 109(b). *See Central Point Software, Inc. v. Global Software & Accessories, Inc.,* 880 F. Supp. 957 (E.D.N.Y. 1995).

64.   *Feist Publications, Inc. v. Rural Tele. Serv. Co.,* 499 U.S. 340, 111 S. Ct. 1282, 1287, 1288, 1289, 1290, 1293 (1991); *Harper & Row Publishers, Inc. v. Nation Enterprises,* 471 U.S. 539, 547, 105 S. Ct. 2218, 2224 (1985) ("no author may copyright facts or ideas").

65.   *Feist Publications, Inc. v. Rural Tele. Serv. Co.,* 499 U.S. 340, 111 S. Ct. 1282, 1288–1289 (1991).

66.   But even though facts are not, by themselves, copyrightable, it is important to understand that a compilation (e.g., a database) of such noncopyrightable elements may itself be copyrightable. 17 U.S.C. § 103(a). A *compilation* is defined as "a work formed by the *collection and assembling of* preexisting materials or of data that are *selected, coordinated, or arranged* in such a way that the resulting work as a whole constitutes an original work of authorship" 17 U.S.C. § 101 (emphasis added). Thus, for example, notwithstanding that facts (such as the names of cities and streets) are not copyrightable, compilations of facts (such as in a list of the 50 "most livable" cities in the United States) *may* be copyrightable. *Feist Publications, Inc. v. Rural Tele. Serv. Co.,* 499 U.S. 340, 111 S. Ct. 1282, 1289 (1991).

67.   *Feist Publications, Inc. v. Rural Tele. Serv. Co.,* 499 U.S. 340, 111 S. Ct. 1282 (1991).

68.   *Feist Publications, Inc. v. Rural Tele. Serv. Co.,* 499 U.S. 340, 111 S. Ct. 1282, 1289 (1991). *In Harper & Row Publishers, Inc. v. Nation Enterprises,* 471 U.S. 539, 105 S. Ct. 2218 (1985), for example, the Supreme Court held that President Ford could not prevent others from copying bare historical facts from his autobiography, although he could prevent others from copying his subjective descriptions and portraits of public figures.

69.   *Feist Publications, Inc. v. Rural Telephone Service Co.,* 499 U.S. 340, 111 S. Ct. 1282, 1289 (1991).

70.   *Id.*

71.   *Id.* at 1293.

72.   *Id.* at 1290–1292.

73.   *Id.* at 1292. *See Suid v. NewsWeek Magazine,* 503 F. Supp. 146, 147–148 (D.D.C. 1980) (research to discover quotations from unpublished letters does not justify copyright to the discoverer of those quotations). However, the Supreme Court has noted that "[p]rotection for the fruits of such research . . . may in certain circumstances be available under a theory of unfair competition."

74.   *Feist Publications, Inc. v. Rural Telephone Service Co.,* 499 U.S. 340, 111 S. Ct. 1282, 1294 (1991).

75.   *Originality* means only that the work owes its origin to the author, that is, it is independently created, and not copied from other works. *Alfred Bell & Co. v. Catalda Fine Arts, Inc.,* 191 F.2d 99, 102 (2d Cir. 1951); *Wihtol v. Wells,* 231 F.2d 550, 553 (7th Cir. 1956). Originality is discussed in Section 9.4.2.1.

76.   *Feist Publications, Inc. v. Rural Telephone Service Co.,* 499 U.S. 340, 111 S. Ct. 1282, 1294 (1991).

77.   *Id.* at 1296.

78.   *Id.*

79.   *Id.*

80.   *Id.* at 1294–1295.

81.   *Id.* at 1295.

82.   *Id.* at 1289.

83.   *Illinois Bell Telephone Co. v. Haines & Co. Inc.,* 932 F.2d 610 (7th Cir. 1991).

84.   17 U.S.C. § 102(b); *Harper & Row Publishers, Inc. v. Nation Enterprises,* 471 U.S. 539, 547, 105 S. Ct. 2218, 2224 (1985) ("no author may copyright facts or ideas").

85.   Specifically, the Copyright Act provides: "In no case does copyright protection for an original work of authorship extend to any idea, procedure, process, system, method of operation, concept, principal, or discovery, regardless of the form in which it is described, explained, illustrated, or embodied in such a work." 17 U.S.C. § 102(b). *See also* 37 C.F.R. § 202.1(b).

86.   37 C.F.R. § 202.1.

87.   Copyright Office Cir., No. 34, Copyright Protection Not Available for Names, Titles, or Short Phrases (1990).

88.   *See* 37 C.F.R. § 202.1(a); *Duff v. Kansas City Star Co.,* 299 F.2d 320, 323 (8th Cir. 1962); *Becker v. Loews, Inc.,* 133 F.2d 889, 891 (7th Cir. 1943), *cert. denied,* 319 U.S. 772 (1943) ("the copyright of a book or play does not give the copyright owner the exclusive right to the use of the title"); *Warner Bros. Pictures, Inc. v. Majestic Pictures, Corp.,* 70 F.2d 310, 311 (2d Cir. 1934); *Arthur Retlaw & Assocs., Inc. v. Travenol Laboratories, Inc.,* 582 F. Supp. 1010, 1014 (N.D. Ill. 1984) ("one cannot claim copyright in a title"). But the mere fact that words and short phrases are not protectable by copyright does not necessarily mean that they are free for the taking. In certain situations, names and short phrases may be protectable as trademarks, or under the law of unfair competition. *Leeds Music, Ltd. v. Robin,* 358 F. Supp. 650, 660 (S.D. Ohio 1973) (title of the rock opera *Jesus Christ Superstar* could not be used for a motion picture or television production).

12
Protecting Trade Secrets Online

Thomas J. Smedinghoff

In some cases, information communicated online may be a trade secret. Although such information may also be protected by copyright, the real value presumably lies in the secret it contains. Thus, realizing the benefits of online communications with respect to one's trade secrets involves understanding the requirements for obtaining and preserving trade secret rights, and how those can be implemented when trade secrets are communicated electronically.

12.1 What Is a Trade Secret?

A trade secret is any information that (1) is secret, and (2) has economic value by virtue of the fact that it is kept secret.[1]

Almost any information can be a trade secret. Formulas, customer lists, databases,[2] computer software,[3] product designs, manufacturing processes, business plans, algorithms, and the like have all been protected as trade secrets as long as they possess the minimum qualifications.

Technical information, such as the composition or design of a product, a manufacturing method, or the know-how necessary to perform a particular operation or service, has been a traditional category of information protected as trade secrets.[4] One of the best-known examples of a trade secret is the formula for Coca-Cola.[5]

But it is important to understand that many other categories of information can also qualify as trade secrets. Examples include production-related information (such as production schedules, cost data, machinery requirements, and time requirements); supplier and customer information (such as pricing, key contacts, and other valuable purchase and sales information); sales and marketing information (such as forecasts, marketing plans, competitive intelligence information, customer needs and buying habits, and market reports and studies); financial information (such as budgets, forecasts, costs, margins, and profits); and general administrative information (such as business plans and the identity of decision makers). Information about new "and as of yet unreleased" products (such as product design, features, capabilities, and release dates) can also qualify as trade secrets prior to release of the product, even though the information will become readily known and thus lose its trade secret status after the product is released.

Theoretically, trade secret protection can last forever, but the protection can also be lost in an instant. This is because a trade secret is protected only as long as it is kept a secret and so long as no one else duplicates it by legitimate, independent research or reverse engineering.[6] But, as in the case of the Coca-Cola formula, if proper steps are taken to preserve secrecy, trade secret protection can last indefinitely.

12.2 Acquiring and Preserving Trade Secret Rights

Trade secret protection for information, like copyright protection, applies automatically to information that qualifies.[7] No legal formalities, such as notice or registration, are required. However, as discussed below, there is a general obligation to take steps that are appropriate under the circumstances to keep the information secret.

12.2.1 Requirements To Qualify

The trade secret laws will not protect all information. To qualify as a trade secret, information must have two basic characteristics: it must be secret, and it must provide its owner with economic value—such as an advantage over competitors who do not have it.

12.2.1.1 Secrecy Requirement. The secrecy requirement may be somewhat obvious, but is also of critical importance. In the absence of secrecy, there is no trade secret protection.[8] The concept of "secrecy" is really a term of art; it has two elements: (1) the information must *be* secret, that is, not known generally to the industry, and (2) the information must be *treated as* and *kept* secret. The first element is generally not controllable by the owner, but the second element is.

12.2.1.1a Not Generally Known. Whether the information *is secret* is determined by whether persons in the industry also possess the same information. Information that is general knowledge within an industry cannot be a trade secret even though it may not be known to most people. For example, a data compression technique used for the storage and retrieval of data comprising digital images may be unknown to most people. However, if it is generally known to persons designing and using compression techniques within the industry, then it will not qualify as a trade secret. Conversely, a new application for well-known information (such as a secret method for using publicly available information about particular stocks or bonds to predict their future performance) may constitute a trade secret.

Generally, to determine whether information is protectable as a trade secret, it is necessary to examine the extent to which it is known to anyone other than its owner, and the ease or difficulty with which the information could properly be acquired or duplicated by others.[9] Absolute secrecy, however, is not required. When a business discovers or develops information that it considers to be a secret, it may disclose the information to persons legally obligated to keep it secret, such as employees, and to persons who expressly agree to keep it secret, such as persons who sign a confidentiality agreement, without compromising its trade secret protection. As long as the disclosure is made in confidence, and is so understood by both parties, the veil of secrecy will not be deemed to have been broken.

12.2.1.1b Keeping It Secret. In addition to the requirement that the information be secret within the industry, the law also requires that the trade secret owner take *reasonable steps to maintain its secrecy.* In essence, the owner must act as if it is a valuable secret and guard it accordingly. Otherwise, protection may be lost. In one case, for example, a court held that software used in the design and manufacture of class rings was not a trade secret because, among other things, the plaintiff never proved that it intended to keep the relevant information secret.[10] This conclusion was based in part on the fact that when the software was installed, no policy was established to keep it secret, and that the plaintiff had allowed one of its employees to write an article explaining the system to other experts in the field.

Depending on the circumstances, fulfilling this obligation to maintain secrecy may require the owner to take affirmative steps designed to ensure that the information will remain secret.[11] This may include steps such as restricting access to persons having a "need to know," using passwords and key codes, encrypting sensitive data, employing physical security measures such as locked file cabinets, and requiring employees and others to sign confidentiality agreements.[12] When trade secret information is communicated electronically, it may be necessary to require the use of secure networks or, alternatively, to require that the information be encrypted so that any unauthorized persons who are able to access the message will be unable to read its contents. Trade secret information that is stored in a digital form should be kept on a secure system and/or in encrypted form.

12.2.1.2 Economic Value Requirement. In addition to being a secret, the information must provide its owner with economic value or an advantage over its competitors who do not have the information. Otherwise, there really is not anything worth protecting.

Courts sometimes analyze the economic value of a trade secret by looking at the time and effort that has gone into its development. The time and money spent on developing technology, know-how, a customer list, or other information frequently can give its owner a big "head start" over any competitor who is only beginning the same process. In essence, trade secret law protects the value of this head start by requiring competitors to spend their own time and money to create a competing product. In this way, the law protects the trade secret owner's investment in the product.[13]

Other attributes of value include the willingness of others to pay for access to the information, use of the trade secret information in the operation of a business, and the existence of tangible benefits obtained through the use of the information.[14]

12.2.2 Establishing a Confidential Relationship Online

In many cases, disclosure of trade secrets is a necessary part of the normal course of business. Depending on the circumstances, disclosure to employees, consultants, joint venturers, suppliers, and in some cases customers may be required to accomplish a business objective. The information will still be protected as a trade secret, however, as long as the disclosure is "in confidence"—that is, under circumstances such that the recipient is legally obligated to keep it secret.

Thus, establishing a confidential relationship with everyone who will be authorized to have access to trade secret information is critical. Trade secret law prohibits the recipient of a trade secret from using or disclosing the trade secret without the consent of the owner only when it is done in violation of a confidential relationship.[15] When there is no confidential relationship between the owner of a trade secret and someone who learns of it legitimately, the latter is free to use it in any way he or she desires. Thus, independent development of the same secret, and reverse engineering of products purchased on the open market, are perfectly proper.[16]

A disclosure of the secret is made "in confidence" when (1) the person to whom the secret is disclosed expressly promises to keep it secret, such as by signing a confidentiality agreement acknowledging that the material is secret and that he or she will not disclose it to others, or (2) it is disclosed in the context of a relationship in which the law will imply an obligation of confidentiality.[17]

The best example of an implied obligation of confidentiality occurs in the employer-employee relationship. In most states, employees are automatically bound not to disclose or use for their own benefit the trade secrets disclosed to them by their employer, so long as they have notice of the confidential nature of the information. No written contract is necessary to create this obligation.[18]

When a trade secret is disclosed to a customer, joint venture partner, or other potential business partner, however, there is usually no obligation of confidentiality implied by law. Thus, to establish a relationship of confidentiality that will preclude the recipient from disclosing or exploiting the trade secret, it is normally necessary to enter into a confidentiality agreement to this end.

The online communication of trade secret information to a person bound by an obligation of confidentiality will not result in a waiver of trade secret protection, so long as the communication is done securely. However, where a trade secret owner desires to communicate confidential trade secret information to a party with whom it does not have a preexisting confidential relationship, it will be necessary to establish such a relationship prior to the communication. Although this can be done through the use of a standard written confidentiality agreement, it can also be accomplished through the use of an online confidentiality agreement. In such a situation, however, it is important to establish the identity of the person to whom the information is to be disclosed, and to ensure that the recipient enters into a binding agreement that cannot be repudiated. This can perhaps best be done through the use of an electronic non-disclosure agreement secured through the use of digital signatures. Digital signatures are discussed in Chapter 4, and online contracting is discussed in Chapter 6.

12.2.3 Provide Notice of Trade Secret Claim

Even when trade secrets are disclosed in confidence, the recipient must be put on notice that the disclosed information constitutes a valuable trade secret. Someone who is truly unaware that particular information constitutes a trade secret will be more difficult to prosecute for misappropriation.

Whether a trade secret is disclosed on paper or via an online communication, the information should be clearly marked as "confidential." The primary goal is to be sure that everyone who comes into contact with the information is aware of its trade secret status. This will encourage them to treat it as a trade secret, and will make it easier for a court to punish anyone who improperly discloses it.

12.2.4 How Trade Secret Rights Can Be Lost

Unlike copyright protection, which normally lasts for the life of the author plus 50 years, or patent protection, which lasts for twenty years after the application is filed, trade secret protection can last forever. That is why, for example, Coca-Cola chose trade secret protection for its formula. However, trade secret protection is also very fragile. It is automatically lost whenever the secret is disclosed or becomes generally known within the industry. This can happen through independent discovery or unrestricted disclosure.

12.2.4.1 Independent Discovery. Trade secrets are protected only as long as competitors fail to duplicate them by legitimate independent research.[19] Once someone independently discovers a trade secret, that person is free to use or disclose it.

Independent discovery can occur in two ways. First, another person can serendipitously happen onto the same idea or solution, or can do the work and spend the money necessary to develop it independently. Second, with respect to trade secrets that relate to the way a product is designed, another person can purchase a product, take it, study it, and figure out how it works. This latter process is known as *reverse engineering* and is perfectly legal once a product is sold on the market.[20] However, a trade secret owner obtains some practical protection against reverse engineering to the extent that the process is too costly or time consuming for a competitor to undertake.

12.2.4.2 Unrestricted Disclosure. Unrestricted disclosure of trade secret information—that is, disclosure to persons who are not subject to any obligation of confidentiality—will result in the loss of trade secret protection.[21] This frequently occurs through simple carelessness on the part of the trade secret owner. In one case, for example, trade secret protection was lost when a company allowed one of its employees to publish an article explaining its system to other experts in the field. The court found that the information in the article was sufficient to enable an experienced engineer to duplicate the product without too much difficulty.[22]

Courts have held that an unrestricted disclosure also occurs when trade secret information is posted to the Internet.[23] As one court has pointed out:

> one of the Internet's virtues, that it gives even the poorest individuals the power to publish to millions of readers, can also be a detriment to the value of intellectual property rights. The anonymous (or judgment proof) defendant can permanently destroy valuable trade secrets, leaving no one to hold liable for the misappropriation. Although a work posted to an Internet newsgroup remains accessible to the public for only a limited amount of time, once that trade secret has been released into the public domain there is no retrieving it.[24]

Unrestricted disclosure can also occur through marketing. Any product that has been sold on the market is generally open to duplication by skilled engineers.[25] If the product is sold outright instead of being licensed, and if the trade secret can be determined by an inspection of the product itself, the trade secret will be lost when that occurs. If the product (such as software or other technology) is licensed, however, and the licensee is contractually bound to keep it confidential, this will constitute a protected disclosure and trade secret protection will not be waived. In other words, the party to a confidentiality agreement will not be permitted to obtain rights in the trade secret, even by reverse engineering.

12.3 Protecting Trade Secrets Communicated Electronically

In many cases, valuable and confidential trade secret information is best kept locked away in a safe or under armed guard. But this can defeat the very purposes for which a trade secret is held—that is, to use it in one's business and obtain the economic advantages that flow from it.

In reality, to obtain the benefits of a trade secret, businesses typically need to communicate the secret information to trusted employees, current and potential business partners, and, in some cases, suppliers and customers. Although such communications have typically been made orally or by delivery of paper or some other tangible product, much trade secret information will increasingly be stored, used, and communicated electronically. As a consequence, it is important for the trade secret owner to consider how best to implement electronic communications of trade secrets where appropriate. Likewise, it is important for those who obtain access to the secrets of others via online communications to understand their rights and obligations with respect to the information involved.

Communicating trade secret information electronically creates numerous security risks that may jeopardize trade secret protection. The mere fact that the information exists in a digital form, a form that is easily copied and widely distributed, is itself a security risk. If the formula for Coca-Cola, for example, is typed on a single sheet of paper and kept in a vault at the company headquarters, it is by definition much more secure (although perhaps not very useful) than if the same information were stored in digital form and transmitted via e-mail to persons who needed access to it.

Communication of trade secret information over public networks, such as the Internet, also raises a host of security risks. These range from the possibility of unauthorized interception to the risk that a message may be inadvertently sent to the wrong recipient. Generally, communication of trade secret information electronically requires consideration of two elements:

1. Maintaining secrecy through the communication channel (i.e., protecting the information from disclosure as a result of intentional or inadvertent interception, the viewing by access providers or others who may be on the network, and so forth); and

2. Controlling the disclosure to the recipient by imposing sufficient legal obligations on the recipient's use and disclosure of the information.

Protecting the secrecy of the information during the communication process may require encryption or other security techniques designed to prevent unauthorized access and to render the information useless to unauthorized viewers. Protecting the information once it has been received by the recipient normally requires imposing a legal obligation on the recipient not to use or disclose the information except as expressly authorized.

Whether trade secret owners will communicate their trade secrets electronically will largely depend on the extent that they believe that the secrecy of the trade secret will not be compromised by such a distribution. Thus, if electronic communication networks are going to be used for disseminating trade secrets to those that need access, adequate security measures must be used to ensure that trade secret information remains secret. Alternatively, the message itself must be protected by information security methods such as encryption.

12.4 Rights of Trade Secret Owners

Owners of trade secret rights in information essentially acquire three basic rights. These are the rights to control (1) access to the information; (2) use of the information; (3) disclosure of the information.

12.4.1 Right To Control Access

The owner of a trade secret has the right to control access to the information comprising the secret. Anyone who acquires the information (that is, obtains access to it) by "improper means," is liable for trade secret misappropriation.[26]

Improper means of acquiring the trade secret of another includes theft, bribery, and breach of an obligation of confidentiality. In addition, the unauthorized interception of electronic communications of trade secret information has also been expressly recognized as a way in which the trade secret can be acquired by improper means.[27]

It is important to understand, however, that a trade secret owner's right to control access to the information is not the same as an exclusive right to possess the information. The owner is protected only against a wrongful or "improper" acquisition of the trade secret information.[28] Moreover, the trade secret owner's right to control access to the information is not absolute. As noted in Section 12.2.4, there are several ways that trade secret information can be acquired legally, notwithstanding the intentions of the trade secret owner. These methods include independent discovery of the information and reverse engineering of the information from publicly available products.[29]

12.4.2 Right To Control Use

In situations where the owner of a trade secret has disclosed it to someone under an obligation of confidentiality, any actual use of the trade secret information by the recipient without (or in excess of) the consent of the trade secret owner constitutes misappropriation.[30]

Use of a trade secret means any exploitation of the information that either helps the recipient or hurts the owner of the trade secret. This includes using the trade secret information in the production of goods or performance of services, as an aid to research and development, to respond to business or marketing activities of the trade secret owner, to solicit customers, and so forth.[31] The bottom line is that any use, in any way, for any purpose, that either helps the recipient's business or hurts the business of the trade secret owner, will constitute misappropriation unless the trade secret owner has consented to the use.

12.4.3 Right To Control Disclosure

Where the owner of a trade secret has disclosed it to someone under an obligation of confidentiality, any further disclosure of the trade secret information by the recipient without the consent of the trade secret owner also constitutes misappropriation.[32]

An unauthorized disclosure of trade secret information can occur in a variety of ways. Mere disclosure of the information, to the public or to a competitor, would clearly be improper. In addition, if the recipient embodies the trade secret in products and physically markets them, that could also be an improper disclosure.

12.5 Rights of Non-Owners of Trade Secret Information

Trade secret law does not prohibit the acquisition, use, or disclosure of another's trade secrets *per se*. Thus the mere fact that someone acquires, uses, or discloses trade secret information does not necessarily mean that the owner of the trade secret can successfully bring a lawsuit for misappropriation. The law only prohibits the acquisition of trade secrets by *improper means,* or the *unauthorized* use or disclosure of a trade secret that was acquired by improper means or pursuant to an obligation of confidentiality.[33]

If a person's possession, use, or disclosure of another's trade secret does not fall into one of these categories, then he or she has done nothing wrong. For example, if information is publicly available on the Internet, further use of it should not constitute infringement.[34] Likewise, if an individual obtains a copy of a publicly marketed product (such as by purchase), he or she is free to try to reverse engineer that product in order to learn the secret of how it works, and then use that information or disclose it to others.[35] Of course, anyone who discovers a trade secret on his or her own through independent work is free to do whatever they would like with it.

It is the improper conduct in obtaining, using, or disclosing a trade secret that gives rise to liability for misappropriation. In many cases, the improper conduct will relate to the way in which the trade secret was obtained. Theft of trade secret information, fraud, and inducing an employee or other person to disclose the information in breach of an obligation of confidence are obvious examples. Generally, anyone who acquires a trade secret by "improper" means is liable for misappropriation.[36] In addition, it is now recognized that the unauthorized interception of communications constitutes an improper means of acquisition of the trade secrets of another.[37] Of course, trade secrets discovered by proper means, such as independent discovery, or reverse engineering, do not constitute misappropriation.

More often than not, however, the trade secret will have been obtained legitimately. For example, it may be disclosed to an employee on the job or to a customer who has signed a confidentiality agreement. In this case, liability for trade secret misappropriation occurs only if the employee or the customer uses or discloses the trade secret in a way that breaches the obligation of confidentiality. This might occur for example, if either of them used the trade secret to assist in starting a competing business, or gave it away to a third party. Posting the secret information on the Internet (such as in a publicly accessible discussion group) would clearly constitute an improper disclosure if done in violation of an obligation of confidentiality.

If someone wrongfully obtains a trade secret, or uses or discloses a trade secret in violation of a confidential obligation, he or she will be liable to the owner of the trade secret for damages regardless of the way in which the trade secret was used. Thus, for example, if someone improperly obtains information relating to a new trade secret digital data compression algorithm and then modifies or improves it for a use that is totally unrelated to the original product, he or she will still be liable for misappropriation of the original trade secret. Improper "use" of a trade secret does not require precise duplication or copying. Modifications or improvements to the original trade secret will still subject one to liability if the secret of the original owner is substantially involved.[38]

Additionally, if a trade secret was obtained wrongfully, neither the fact that it *could* have been discovered by legitimate means, nor that it *might* have been independently developed, is a defense. It is the improper conduct that is the key to liability in a misappropriation case.[39]

The form in which the information is taken is also irrelevant. A trade secret can be appropriated by intercepting an electronic communication, taking a physical disk, tape, or copy of a document, or by memorizing it. Individuals may be able to memorize algorithms, plans, techniques, formulae, and the like, but this does not mean that they can claim the information as their own knowledge. It is as much a breach of confidence to reproduce trade secrets from memory as to copy them onto tangible media.

In one case, for example, the court found that a group of employees had over the years actually memorized their employer's plans and drawings, so that they actually had a mental picture of these trade secrets. This, the court held, was no different from having a copy or picture on paper. Since these "mental pictures" were obtained by the employees while working for their employer, the court concluded that "to carry them away in this manner was [as much] a violation of a confidence reposed in them by their employer, as if they had made copies or photographs and carried them away."[40]

It should also be noted that an unauthorized user of a trade secret can also be held liable for misappropriation, even in the absence of a confidential relationship with the owner, if he or she knew that the trade secret had been obtained in violation of an obligation of confidentiality, or was subsequently informed of that fact.[41] The application of this principle is illustrated by a case involving a customer of a data processing service bureau.[42] There, the service bureau customer had requested a backup copy of the software being run on its behalf because it doubted the ability of the service bureau to remain in business. An employee of the service bureau provided such a copy, but, unbeknownst to the customer, this was done in violation of company policy. Before the customer could use the software, however, it was put on notice by the service bureau that the programs were its exclusive property. This notice, the court held, subjected the customer to trade secret liability for its subsequent use of the software for which it had paid no money. When the customer ignored the notice and used the software, it was held liable for trade secret misappropriation.

12.6 Trade Secrets in Other Countries

In light of the global nature of electronic communications, trade secret owners need to consider the availability of trade secret protection for information transmitted to countries outside of the United States. Generally, although trade secret rights are not as universally recognized as copyright rights, they are fairly well respected throughout much of the industrialized world. The North American Free Trade Agreement (NAFTA), signed by the United States on December 8, 1993, obligates member countries (United States, Canada and Mexico) to protect trade secrets from unauthorized acquisition, disclosure, or use.[43] Likewise, the General Agreement on Tariffs and Trade (GATT), executed on April 15, 1994 among the major industrialized nations of the world, obligates member countries to protect "undisclosed information" that has commercial value, that is not in the public domain, and that is subject to reasonable steps to maintain its secrecy.

Finally, many countries have existing laws designed to provide protection for trade secrets. These include the United Kingdom, France, Germany, Italy, Japan (where a national trade secrets law was enacted in 1991), India (where protection was added in 1991), China (where protection was added in 1993), and Korea (which provided protection for trade secrets in 1991).

Endnotes

1.   *See* Uniform Trade Secrets Act § 1(3); *Restatement (First) of Torts* § 757, Comment b (1939); *Restatement (Third) of Unfair Competition* § 39 (1995). The Uniform Trade Secrets Act, which has now been adopted in 40 states, defines a trade secret as "Information, including a formula, pattern, compilation, program, device, method, technique or process, that: (i) derives independent economic value, actual or potential, from not being generally known to, and not being readily ascertainable by proper means by other persons who can obtain economic value from its disclosure, and (ii) is the subject of efforts that are reasonable under the circumstances to maintain its secrecy."

2.   *MAI Systems Corp. v. Peak Computer, Inc.*, 991 F.2d 511, 521 (9th Cir. 1993), *cert. dismissed* 114 S. Ct. 671 (1994) (holding that a customer database qualifies as a trade secret).

3. *Avtec Sys., Inc. v. Peiffer,* 21 F. 3d 568, 30 U.S.P.Q.2d 1365, 1370 (4th Cir. 1994) ("there is no difficulty in finding the existence of a trade secret in the source or object codes to computer programs. . . ."); *MAI Systems Corp. v. Peak Computer, Inc.,* 991 F.2d 511, 522 (9th Cir. 1993), *cert. dismissed,* 114 S. Ct. 671 (1994); *Atari Games Corp. v. Nintendo of America, Inc.,* 975 F.2d 832 (Fed. Cir. 1992); *Computer Assocs. Int'l, Inc. v. Altai, Inc.,* 23 U.S.P.Q.2d. 1241 (2d. Cir. 1992), *amended,* 982 F.2d 693 (2d. Cir. 1992); *Trandes Corp. v. Guy F. Atkinson Co.,* 798 F. Supp 284, 288 (D. Md., 1992), *aff'd in part and rev'd in part,* 996 F.2d 655 (4th Cir. 1993), cert. denied 114 S. Ct. 443 (1993); S.O.S., Inc. v. Payday, Inc., 886 F.2d 1081, 1089–90 (9th Cir. 1989).

4. *See Restatement (Third) of Unfair Competition* § 39 Comment d (1995).

5. *Coca-Cola Co. v. Hy-Po Co.* 1 F. Supp. 644, 645 (E.D.N.Y. 1932); *Coca-Cola Bottling Co. v. Coca-Cola Co.,* 107 F.R.D. 288, 289 (D. Del. 1985).

6. *University Computing Co. v. Lykes-Youngstown Corp.,* 504 F.2d 518, 534 (5th Cir. 1974), *reh'g denied,* 505 F.2d 1304 (5th Cir. 1974).

7. *See* Uniform Trade Secret Act § 1(4). According to the *Restatement (Third) of Unfair Competition* § 39 (1995), "A trade secret is any information that can be used in the operation of a business or other enterprise and that is sufficiently valuable and secret to afford an actual or potential economic advantage over others."

8. *Avtec Systems, Inc. v. Peiffer,* 21 F.3d 568, 30 U.S.P.Q.2d 1365, 1370 (4th Cir. 1994) ("the hallmark of a trade secret is not its novelty but its secrecy"); *Dionne v. Southeast Foam Converting & Packaging, Inc.,* 397 S.E.2d 110, 113, 17 U.S.P.Q.2d 1565, 1567 (Va. 1990).

9. Note, however, that "the theoretical ability of others to ascertain the information through proper means does not necessarily preclude protection as a trade secret. Trade secret protection remains available unless the information is readily ascertainable by such means." *Restatement (Third) of Unfair Competition* § 39 Comment f (1995).

10. *Jostens, Inc. v. National Computer Systems, Inc.,* 318 N.W.2d 691, 700 (Minn. 1982).

11. *Amoco Prod. Co. v. Lindley* 609 P.2d 733, 743 (Okla. 1980).

12. Steps that can be taken to ensure protection of trade secrets are described in Section 12.3.

13. *See, e.g., Integrated Cash Management Services, Inc. v. Digital Transactions, Inc.,* 920 F.2d 171, 172 (2d Cir. 1990) (noting plaintiff's investment of "millions of dollars" in research and development costs). *But see Pressure Science, Inc. v. Kramer,* 413 F. Supp. 618, 628 (D. Conn. 1976), aff'd, 551 F.2d 301 (2d Cir. 1976) (noting that expenditure of a great deal of effort and several thousand dollars "cannot convert known concepts into trade secrets").

14. *Restatement (Third) of Unfair Competition* § 39 Comment e (1995).

15. *See* Uniform Trade Secret Act § 1(2); Restatement (Third) of Unfair Competition § 40 (1995).

16. *See, e.g.,* Cal. Civ. Code § 3426; 765 ILCS. 1065/2. *See also Restatement (Third) Of Unfair Competition* § 43 (1995).

17. *See Restatement (Third) of Unfair Competition* § 41 (1995).

18. *See, e.g., Integrated Cash Management Services, Inc. v. Digital Transactions, Inc.,* 732 F. Supp 370 (S.D.N.Y. 1989) *aff'd,* 920 F.2d 171 (2d Cir. 1990); *Engineered Mechanical Services, Inc. v. Langlois,* 464 So. 2d 329 (La. Ct. App. 1st Cir. 1984) *cert. denied* 467 So. 2d 531 (La. 1985). *See also Restatement (Third) of Unfair Competition* § 42 Comments b and c (1995). It is often wise, however, to have employees sign confidentiality agreements in which they expressly acknowledge that the confidential information to which they have access is considered to be the employer's trade secret, and that they will not improperly use or disclose it. An employee confidentiality agreement serves to demonstrate that the employer considers its developments to be secret and

valuable. It is also the most persuasive possible evidence that employees were informed from the outset that they would not be permitted to use their employer's software and other trade secrets except in the course of its business.

19. *University Computing Co. v. Lykes-Youngstown Corp.*, 504 F.2d 518, 534 (5th Cir. 1974).

20. Cal. Civ. Code § 3426.1(a) ("reverse engineering or independent derivation alone shall not be considered improper means"); 765 ILCS § 1065/2(a) ("reverse engineering or independent development shall not be considered improper means"). *See also Atari Games Corp. v. Nintendo of America, Inc.*, 975 F.2d 832, 24 U.S.P.Q.2d 1015 (Fed. Cir. 1992) ("Reverse engineering object code to discern the unprotectable ideas in a computer program is a fair use"); and *Sega Enterprises, Ltd. v. Accolade, Inc.*, 977 F.2d 1510 (9th Cir. 1992) ("where disassembly is the only way to gain access to the ideas and functional elements embodied in a copyrighted computer program and where there is a legitimate reason for seeking such access, disassembly is a fair use of the copyrighted work, as a matter of law"). *See also Restatement (Third) of Unfair Competition* § 43 (1995) ("Independent discovery and analysis of publicly available products or information are not improper means of acquisition").

21. *See, e.g., Advanced Computer Services of Michigan, Inc. v. MAI Systems Corp.*, 845 F. Supp. 356, 370 (E.D. Va. 1994) ("trade secret rights do not survive when otherwise protectable information is disclosed to others, such as customers or the general public, who are under no obligation to protect its confidentiality"); *Secure Services Technology, Inc. v. Time and Space Processing, Inc.*, 722 F. Supp. 1354, 1361 (E.D. Va. 1989).

22. *Jostens, Inc. v. National Computer Systems, Inc.*, 318 N.W.2d 691, 700 (Minn. 1982).

23. *Religious Technology Center v. Netcom Online Communications Services, Inc.*, No. C-95-20091, 1995 U.S. Dist. LEXIS 16184 (N.D. Cal. Sept. 22, 1995) (holding that when plaintiff's alleged trade secrets were posted on the Internet, they lost their status as secrets). *See also Religious Technology Center v. F.A.C.T. NET, Inc.*, No. 95-B-2143, 1995 U.S. Dist. LEXIS 13892 (D. Colo. Sept. 15, 1995); *Religious Technologies Center v. Lerma*, 897 F. Supp. 260 (E.D. Va. 1995).

24. *Religious Technology Center v. Netcom Online Communications Services, Inc.*, No. C-95-20091, 1995 U.S. Dist. LEXIS 16184 (N.D. Cal. Sept. 22, 1995).

25. *Analogic Corp. v. Data Translation, Inc.*, 358 N.E.2d 804, 807 (Mass. 1976).

26. *See* Uniform Trade Secrets Law § 1(1) (1979) (definition of "improper means"); *Restatement (Third) of Unfair Competition* § 43 (1995) (definition of "improper").

27. *See, e.g.,* Uniform Trade Secrets Law § 1(1) (1979) ("'improper means' includes . . . espionage through electronic or other means"); *Restatement (Third) of Unfair Competition* § 43 (1995) ("'improper' means of acquiring another's trade secret . . . include . . . interception of communications. . . .").

28. *Restatement (Third) of Unfair Competition* § 43 Comment a (1995).

29. *See, e.g., Restatement (Third) of Unfair Competition* § 43 (1995) ("independent discovery and analysis of publicly available products or information are not improper means of acquisition"). *See also Bonito Boats, Inc. v. Thunder Craft Boats, Inc.* 489 U.S. 141, 109 S. Ct. 971 (1989); *Kewanee Oil Co. v. Bicron Corp.* 416 U.S. 470–92 S. Ct. 1879 (1974). *See also* Commissioner's Comment to Uniform Trade Secrets Act § 1 (1979) (indicating that "proper means" includes independent invention, discovery by reverse engineering, observation of items in public use or on public display and obtaining the trade secret from published literature).

30. *See* Uniform Trade Secrets Law § 1(2)(ii) (1979); *Restatement (Third) of Unfair Competition* § 40(b) (1995).

31. *Restatement (Third) of Unfair Competition* § 40, Comment c (1995).

32. *Restatement (Third) of Unfair Competition*, § 40(b) (1995); Uniform Trade Secrets Law § 1(2)(iii) (1979).

33. See Uniform Trade Secrets Act §§ 1(1), 1(2) (1979); *Restatement (Third) of Unfair Competition* §§ 40, 43 (1995).

34. *Religious Technology Center v. Lerma*, No. 95-1107-A, 1995 U.S. Dist. LEXIS 17833 (E.D. Va. November 28, 1995) (noting that "[a]lthough the person who originally posted a trade secret on the Internet may be liable for trade secret misappropriation, the party who merely down loads Internet information cannot be liable for misappropriation because there is no misconduct involved in interacting with the Internet."). *See also Religious Technology Center v. Netcom Online Communications Services, Inc.*, No. C-95-20091, 1995 U.S. Dist. LEXIS 16184 (N.D. Cal. Sept. 22, 1995); *Religious Technology Center v. F.A.C.T. Net, Inc.*, No. 95-B-2143, 1995 U.S. Dist. LEXIS 13892 (D. Colo. Sept. 15, 1995); *Religious Technology Center v. Lerma*, 897 F. Supp. 260 (E.D. Va. 1995).

35. *See Atari Games Corp. v. Nintendo of America, Inc.*, 975 F.2d 832, 24 U.S.P.Q.2d 1015 (Fed. Cir. 1992) and *Sega Enterprises, Ltd. v. Accolade, Inc.*, 977 F.2d 1510 (9th Cir. 1992).

36. Uniform Trade Secrets Act, § 1(2); *Restatement (Third) of Unfair Competition* § 40 (1995).

37. *Restatement (Third) of Unfair Competition*, § 43 (1995). *See also Kewanee Oil Co. v. Bicron Corp.* 416 U.S. 470, 94 S. Ct. 1879, (1974) (identifying wiretapping as an example of an improper means of acquisition).

38. *Restatement (Third) of Unfair Competition* § 40 Comment c (1995); *M. Bryce & Assocs., Inc. v. Gladstone*, 215 U.S.P.Q. 81, 319 N.W.2d 907, 912 (Wis. App. 1982), *cert. denied*, 459 U.S. 944 (1982); *Digital Dev. Corp. v. International Memory Systems*, 185 U.S.P.Q. 136, 141 (S.D. Cal. 1973).

39. *Telex Corp. v. International Business Machines Corp.*, 510 F.2d 894, 929–930 (10th Cir. 1975), *cert. dismissed*, 423 U.S. 802 (1975).

40. *Schulenburg v. Signatrol, Inc.*, 33 Ill. 2d 379, 212 N.E.2d 865, 868 (1965), *cert. denied* 383 U.S. 959 (1966).

41. *Restatement (Third) of Unfair Competition* § 40(b)(3) (1995). *See also* Uniform Trade Secrets Act § 1(2)(c).

42. *Computer Print Systems, Inc. v. Lewis*, 281 Pa. Super. 240, 422 A.2d 148, 155 (1980).

43. North American Free Trade Agreement, § 1711.

13
Trademark Rights

Andrew R. Basile, Jr.

Trademarks—or what many people call *brand names*—can be found in virtually every avenue of commerce and advertising, and they are essential to the proper functioning of our consumer-based market economy. As commerce has migrated to the Internet and the online services, trademarks have followed. Web site owners and electronic publishers are all making extensive use of trademarks.

The special nature of cyberspace (in particular, its lack of geographic boundaries) is leading to conflicts among trademark owners. Already there have been a number of well-publicized disputes over use of trademarks online, including disputes over the rights to Internet *addresses* (or *domain names*). In this contentious environment, companies must be vigilant to protect their trademark rights and to avoid infringing on the rights of others. This chapter provides a basic understanding of trademark law and the special issues that arise when trademarks are used in connection with the Internet or other channels of electronic commerce.

13.1 Trademark Fundamentals

Trademarks are words, symbols, or other devices used to distinguish the goods or services of one person from those of another.[1] Examples include *Ford* for automobiles and *IBM* for computers. Trademarks that are used in connection with services are called *service marks*. Examples include *American Airlines* for air transportation and *Kmart* for retail services.[2]

Any number of items can constitute a trademark. The most commonly used forms of trademarks are:

- **Words and Phrases.** Examples include *Xerox, Kodak, Don't Leave Home Without It,* and *You Deserve a Break Today.*
- **Pictures and Symbols.** Examples include the Windows icon used by Microsoft and the Nike "swoosh."
- **Numerals and Letters.** Examples include *IBM,* and television and radio station call letters.[3]
- **Abbreviations and Nicknames.** Examples include *Coke* for Coca-Cola.[4]
- **Colors.** Colors can be trademarks if they become closely associated with a product. An example of a color trademark is the color pink for Owens Corning insulation.[5]

209

- **Sounds and Music.** Examples include advertising jingles and television program themes.
- **Internet Domain Names.** An Internet domain name can qualify as a trademark, so long as it is used to indicate the source or origin of goods and services (see Chapter 14).

The owner of a trademark has the exclusive right to use the mark in a particular market on particular kinds of goods or services.[6] Because this right is exclusive, trademarks provide consumers with a reliable indication of source. For example, Crest brand toothpaste is manufactured by Procter & Gamble. Although many consumers do not know this, they nevertheless believe (correctly) that all toothpaste bearing the *Crest* trademark originates from the same source, and they expect that the next tube they purchase will be of the same high quality as the last tube. Under the trademark law, this expectation is fulfilled because only a single company—Procter & Gamble—has the right to apply the mark *Crest* to toothpaste.

The trademark law also provides manufacturers with a property interest in the good reputations (or *"goodwill"*) associated with their trademarks. This concern for reputation in turn encourages manufacturers to strive for consistency and quality.

13.2 The Role of Trademarks Online

13.2.1 Cyberspace: Media and Marketplace

From a marketing perspective, *media* are means of mass communication and, in particular, vehicles for developing brand recognition through advertising. The Internet and other digital networks are often described as *new media* because, like TV and radio, they provide an avenue for the widespread dissemination of advertising and other marketing communications.

But the Internet and its kin are more than media. They are also becoming marketplaces, where buyers and sellers can interact, negotiate and consummate sales transactions.

The best example of cyberspace as media and marketplace is the World Wide Web.[7] Many businesses have elaborate Web sites to advertise and promote their products and services. As communications media, these sites provide the buying public with information in the form of text and graphics, and will soon offer CD-quality audio and full-motion video. As marketplaces, many Web sites provide an opportunity for interactive buying and selling. For example, many Web sites are virtual stores offering products ranging from wine to flowers. Moreover, Web sites can function as distribution channels with respect to services that can be performed online or digital goods that can be transmitted online (such as software, photographs, video, and sound recordings).

13.2.2 Use of Trademarks in Cyberspace

Trademarks play the same crucial role in cyberspace as they do in conventional media and marketplaces. There are at least four ways that trademarks are used in online environments:

- **Advertising.** Many Internet Web sites and storefronts available through online services function like computerized billboards or television commercials. For example, a frequently visited Web page might have a prominent legend extolling viewers to "Drink Acme Brand Cola!" In some ways, advertising online is no different from advertising in a newspaper. It raises the same trademark, unfair competition, and other legal concerns. See Chapter 22 for more information about advertising online and Chapter 28 regarding unfair competition.
- **Product Identification.** Web sites and other online channels that function as marketplaces use trademarks to identify the products and services offered for sale.
- **Online Services.** Trademarks are used to identify services that are actually offered and provided in cyberspace. For example, there are a number of vendors whose only customer outlets are Web sites. These include the Yahoo search page (http://yahoo.com), the Music Boulevard online music store (http://www.musicblvd.com) and the NewsPage news service (http://newspage.com). The trademarks associated with these services are prominently displayed when a user views the services' Web sites.
- **Domain Names.** Trademarks are often used on the Internet as the *address* or *domain names* of Web sites themselves. For example, in the World Wide Web, Microsoft's domain name is microsoft.com. This topic is discussed further in Chapter 14.

Each of the items listed above involves either the use of a traditional trademark as part of content transmitted online (for example, a Web site advertising Ford cars), or the creation and use of trademarks to identify online-specific goods and services (for example, information retrieval services).

13.3 Acquiring Trademark Rights Online

13.3.1 Overview

There are two scenarios where trademark rights can be obtained through online use. In the first, the initial and/or only use of the mark is online. In the second, the mark is initially used in a conventional manner (that is, offline) but is later brought into an online environment. In either case, the trademark owner has an opportunity to acquire rights in new trademarks and expand the scope of rights in existing ones. This section explains the process of securing new or expanded rights through proper trademark selection, use, and registration.

Unfortunately, trademark law is a double-edged sword. As a company focuses on developing the strongest possible trademark rights, it also needs to ensure that a new or expanded use does not infringe on the rights of prior users. Section 13.5 deals with avoiding such trademark disputes.

13.3.1.1 Marks First and/or Exclusively Used Online. In some cases, a mark may be adopted specifically for use online. Eventually, the mark may also be used offline (such as on physical goods or in print advertising). In the meantime, however, the owner will want to secure the legal right to prevent others from infringing the mark—online or otherwise.

This involves:

- Selecting a "strong" trademark (see Section 13.3.2),
- Ensuring that the mark will not infringe a prior user's rights (see Section 13.5.1),
- Using the mark online in a manner that establishes trademark rights (see Section 13.3.3),
- Registering the mark in the United States and foreign countries, as necessary (see Sections 13.3.4 and 13.3.5),
- In appropriate cases, registering the mark as an Internet domain name (see Section 14.2.1).

13.3.1.2 Marks First Used in Ordinary Commerce. When a trademark owner has already established rights to a trademark in ordinary commerce, using the mark online may represent an expansion to new territories or trade channels. For example, if an existing mark is used to identify a Web page or products advertised at a Web site, consumers all over the world could be exposed to that mark. This may constitute an expansion (in geographic terms) of the mark's original use. The mark owner needs to consider how this expanded use translates into new trademark rights, and how those rights can be protected. This process involves following the same basic steps outlined above for new marks, including clearance, proper use, and registration.

13.3.2 Selecting a Strong Trademark

The process of selecting a new mark is the easiest and least expensive opportunity to secure strong trademark rights and avoid conflict with others. Once you have begun using and investing in a trademark, you will have charted a course that may be difficult—and expensive—to change.

The key to selecting a trademark is to pick a name that is (1) easily protected (or "strong"), and (2) does not infringe on the rights of a prior user. This section outlines the principles of trademark strength. Section 13.5.1 explains how to avoid infringing on the rights of prior users.

Trademark *strength* (or *distinctiveness*) refers to the capacity of a mark to distinguish the goods or services of one provider from those of another. Trademark strength is rated (from strongest to weakest) on the following scale:[8]

- **Fanciful or Coined.** Marks that have no recognized meaning at the time they are adopted. Examples include *Exxon, Xerox,* and *Kodak.*
- **Arbitrary.** Marks that have a recognized meaning that does not relate to the product with which they are used. Examples include *Apple* as applied to computers and *Yahoo* as applied to online services.
- **Suggestive.** Marks that suggest (but do not explicitly describe) a feature of the product. Examples include *Leggs* for pantyhose and *Obsession* for perfume.

- **Descriptive.** Marks that merely describe a feature of the product. Examples include *Computerland* for computer stores and *Quik-Print* for printing services.
- **Generic.** Words that are common names for the products to which they are applied. Examples include *aspirin* for pain reliever and *beer* for alcoholic beverages.

Fanciful marks such as *Kodak* and *Exxon* are very strong marks because they have no recognized English meaning, and, therefore, purchasers assume they are indications of source rather than descriptions of products. Similarly, arbitrary marks such as *Apple* for computers, are strong because they have no recognized meaning in the context of the goods to which they are applied.

Suggestive and descriptive marks, on the other hand, are weaker because they relate to the quality or function of the product.[9] Thus, it may not be apparent to consumers that these marks are functioning as sources of origin. Suggestive marks are stronger than descriptive marks because reference to the products' qualities is indirect. That is, a purchaser must exercise some imagination or thought to reach a conclusion about the goods or services from the suggestion raised by the mark.

Marks may be descriptive in various ways. Typically, descriptive marks are adjectives that explain or praise the product or service, such as *Quik-Print* for printing services. Other types of descriptive marks include surnames such as *Smith,* and geographic terms such as *American.* A descriptive term is still descriptive even if misspelled, hyphenated, abbreviated, linked with other terms, or used with *Company, Inc.,* or similar words.

Fanciful, arbitrary, and suggestive marks are considered inherently distinctive and are entitled to trademark protection as soon as they are adopted.[10] In contrast, descriptive marks are not inherently distinctive and do not qualify for protection until they have gained public recognition as trademarks. This recognition is called *acquired distinctiveness* or *secondary meaning.*[11] Under federal law, five years of continuous and exclusive use is presumed sufficient to develop secondary meaning, although less time may be required with extensive advertising and promotion.[12]

Acquired distinctiveness has allowed descriptive surname marks such as *Ford* for automobiles and *McDonald's* for restaurant services to become protected trademarks.[13] In fact, even the most descriptive marks can acquire such a high degree of secondary meaning that they become as strong as arbitrary or fanciful marks. Examples include famous airlines (*American* and *United*), and car lines (*Chrysler* and *Chevrolet*).

The following formatives are frequently used with computer-related marks, and in many cases are descriptive. If a proposed mark contains one of these formatives, it may be descriptive. Of course, a descriptive prefix or suffix may be combined with other elements in a way that avoids descriptiveness.

cyber	*data*	*soft*	*system*
page	*com*	*pro*	*net*
Web	*master*	*inter*	*base*

At the bottom of the strength hierarchy are generic terms. A generic term is an ordinary word that identifies a type of product by describing "what it is" rather than "whose it is." Thus, terms such as *apple* for fruit or *beer* for beverage are considered generic. Generic terms do not distinguish one brand from another and are not entitled to trademark protection.

From a legal perspective, the best marks are fanciful, arbitrary, or suggestive. If your marketing strategy will enable you to select those types of marks, you will find that they are easier to protect and register. Also, because fanciful and arbitrary marks tend to be unique, their use is less likely to cause infringement problems with prior users.

13.3.3 Meeting Use Requirements

13.3.3.1 General Requirements. In the United States, a person acquires trademark rights by *using* a trademark in commerce to distinguish his or her goods or services from those of others.[14] No government registration is necessary to acquire trademark rights. However, registration (discussed in Section 13.3.4) can considerably expand those rights.

The first party to use a mark is said to have "priority" over second comers, at least in the particular market where the mark is used. If a conflict arises between multiple users of the same or similar marks, the party having priority prevails.[15] However, priority may be measured with respect to a particular territory or channel of trade. Thus it is possible for two parties to each have priority with respect to the same mark in different territories.[16] One problem with using trademarks online is that cyberspace transcends geographic territories. Thus, parties who use the same mark in different locales may be in conflict when they both go online.

13.3.3.2 Tangible Goods. With tangible goods, the "use" required to establish trademark ownership includes placing the mark directly onto the goods or their packaging.[17] If a mark is used only online, it obviously cannot be placed directly onto physical goods, although the mark can be used to advertise and promote the goods online. However, mere online use will not be sufficient to obtain a federal registration of a trademark for physical goods.[18] As discussed in Section 13.3.3.4, service marks are treated differently.

Also, once rights are established by physical application on goods in at least one part of the country, online use may expand those rights to distant geographic locales even though physical goods are not shipped to those areas. For example, suppose a manufacturer of soft drinks distributes its product only in Colorado and Utah but advertises extensively in all 50 states via a Web page ("The next time you're in Colorado, buy a six pack of Acme brand cola"). Application of the mark to physical goods in Utah and Colorado is sufficient to establish a protectable trademark in those states. Advertisement of the mark throughout the United States is then sufficient to expand those trademark rights to the entire country.

13.3.3.3 Digital Goods. Some goods, such as software, movies, magazines, and other content are capable of being digitized and distributed online. With these "digital goods," it should be possible to obtain broad trademark rights through purely online use. The following strategies should help manufacturers of digital goods to establish trademark rights:

• Present the mark to users at the time they purchase the digital good.

- Use the mark as the name of the files containing the digital goods (such as naming a file *acme.exe* for a computer program sold under the mark *Acme*).[19]
- Encode the mark into the digital good so that it is displayed at least once each time the user views or uses the digital good (such as on the boot screen of a software program).

If the digital good is also distributed in tangible media (such as on paper or in a computer diskette), the mark should be applied to the tangible form as well. However, tangible distribution of digital goods is not required to establish trademark rights.

13.3.3.4 Services. With services, sufficient "use" would include placing the mark on brochures or advertisements promoting the service.[20] Service marks need not be physically associated with a tangible item or good. Therefore, service mark rights can be established purely through online promotional use, regardless of whether the services themselves are rendered online (such as an information retrieval service) or offline (such as an airline).

13.3.4 Obtaining Federal Registration

13.3.4.1 Overview of Registration. Registration is available for trademarks and service marks used in interstate or foreign commerce. Trademarks can be registered with federal, state,[21] and foreign authorities. In the United States, trademark registration is optional because trademark rights arise from use, not registration. In addition, an application for registration can be filed prior to actual use, under the "intent-to-use" provision of the Lanham Act.[22] Under this provision, applicants with a bona fide intention to use a mark can reserve it ahead of time.

Federal registration is relatively inexpensive and bestows many valuable benefits. For example, registration gives the registrant nationwide priority to its mark as of the date the application to register is filed.[23] This is particularly important for smaller businesses that may have only a limited geographical reach in their early years. Registration also makes enforcement of trademark rights easier and less expensive by according favorable presumptions to the registrant.[24] It allows the trademark owner to sue in federal court and to obtain attorney fees, triple damages, and destruction of infringing articles in certain cases.[25] A registrant can also have U.S. Customs stop the infringing goods at the border—before they enter the United States.[26]

Generally, any mark may be federally registered provided that (1) it is distinctive of the goods or services to which it is applied, and (2) it has been used in interstate or foreign commerce. This "used-in-commerce" standard is fairly stringent. With respect to goods, it generally requires that the mark be placed on the goods, their containers, labels or tags affixed to the goods, or the displays associated with the goods, and that the goods be sold or transported in commerce. With respect to services, it means that the mark must be used or displayed in the sale or advertising of services that are rendered in commerce.[27]

13.3.4.2 Marks Used Only Online. As with marks used in offline commerce, it is a good idea to register marks federally that are used online whenever practicable. Generally, registration will be available in these circumstances:

- **Online Services.** Marks used in connection with services rendered online (such as an online database) may be federally registered.
- **Services Advertised Online.** Marks for services rendered offline (such as airline services) can be registered even if the marks are used only online to promote or advertise these services.
- **Digital Goods.** A trademark used in connection with digital goods should be registrable, even if the mark is used only online. As explained above, digital goods are software, music, pictures, or other content that is digitized and distributed online.

13.3.4.3 Marks Used in Both Regular and Online Commerce. Many trademarks will be used both online and offline. If you have already registered a mark for regular goods and services, it may not be necessary to file anything new when you use it online. However, a new registration should be considered in the following situations:

- **New Products or Services.** If online use involves new products or services delivered online, an additional federal registration may be advisable. For example, a Web site that sells Vintage brand wines might also offer an online database about wines. Such a new use of an existing trademark could qualify for a separate registration.[28]
- **New Channels of Distribution or Modes of Use.** The existing registration may be narrow in scope if it focuses on a specific channel of distribution. Going online may merit a new, broader registration. For example, suppose a market research firm has registered its service mark for "conducting telephone market research interviews for others." If that firm begins conducting its research interviews online, it may want to obtain a registration broader than "telephone" interviews.
- **Interstate Commerce.** Some marks do not qualify for federal registration because they are not used in interstate or foreign commerce. This is often true of marks used by local businesses. However, once such marks are used on the Internet they may reach customers in other states or countries and therefore may qualify for federal registration.[29]

13.3.5 Foreign Registration

A registration in the United States will not adequately protect a mark in other countries. Thus, trademark owners who sell products in Canada, Mexico, Europe, or elsewhere should consider registering their trademarks abroad. In certain countries, trademark rights are available only by registration, and there is little or no protection for unregistered marks.[30] In other words, trademark rights may stop at the U.S. border unless foreign registrations are obtained.

Because digital networks frequently cross national boundaries, the online use of trademarks poses difficult problems for global trademark management. Short of registration in multiple jurisdictions, it may be difficult to secure rights to a mark in the many nations where the mark may be "used." Thus, a U.S. mark owner could develop a loyal customer base in a particular foreign country through online sales, only to discover that another party has—by virtue of earlier registration—acquired superior rights in that country.

13.3.6 Proper Trademark Notice

Under U.S. law, a trademark owner may give notice of a claim to a trademark by placing a notice symbol next to the mark. Although notice is not required, mark owners who fail to give notice may be unable to collect damages or profits in a dispute.[31] The proper notice for marks registered with the U.S. Patent and Trademark Office is to place the symbol ® next to the mark.[32] If the mark is not registered, use the symbol "TM" for trademarks and "SM" for service marks. Do not use the ® symbol for unregistered marks. Where a mark appears numerous times in a document or on a package, the notice symbol need only be used once.

Notice procedures in an online environment are fairly straightforward. The mark should be displayed with proper notice at least the first time it is presented to the user. If the mark is used in connection with the online distribution of digital goods (that is, software or other content), the notice should be displayed when the material is used or viewed by the end-user (such as on a boot screen display).

13.4 Enforcing Trademark Rights Online

13.4.1 Trademark Infringement

A trademark owner has the exclusive right to use the trademark in a given market, in connection with a particular kind of goods or services. Violation of this right is called *trademark infringement* and is established by showing that the accused infringer is:

- Using a mark that is the same as or similar to the trademark,
- Using that mark in connection with the sale or advertising of goods or services, and
- Using the mark in a way that is likely to cause confusion as to the source, origin, sponsorship, or approval of goods or services.[33]

The key to establishing infringement is showing that the accused infringement creates a likelihood of consumer confusion.[34] A nonconfusing use of a mark is not infringement (although it may be unlawful dilution, as discussed in Section 28.10). When two parties are using identical marks on the same type of goods, in the same markets, there is a clear likelihood of confusion, and the unauthorized user is guilty of trademark infringement. In such cases, the crucial question is: Which party has prior rights in the mark? These kinds of disputes are sometimes called *priority contests.*

In many other instances, however, infringement (that is, likelihood of confusion) is not clear-cut. For example, infringement may be found even if the marks differ, so long as they are confusingly similar.[35] In assessing similarity of word marks, courts compare their appearance, sound, meaning, and connotation.[36] Courts also consider other factors, including:

- Sophistication of relevant consumers,[37]
- Similarity of the goods on which marks are used,[38] and
- Defendant's good faith in adopting its mark.[39]

The following are examples of marks that have been found confusingly similar:

Supercuts (hair salon)	and	*Superclips* (hair salon)[40]
Apple (computers)	and	*Pineapple* (computers)[41]
Black Label (beer)	and	*Black Label* (cigarettes)[42]
Godiva (chocolates)	and	*Dogiva* (dog biscuits)[43]

By comparison, the following marks have been found not to create a likelihood of confusion:

Wheaties (for cereal)	and	*Oaties* (for cereal)[44]
Swatch (watches)	and	*T-watch* (watches)[45]

Under the Lanham Act, the test for likelihood of confusion encompasses different types of confusion, including confusion as to source, sponsorship, affiliation, or connection. Thus, trademark law affords the trademark owner "protection against use of its mark on any product or service that could reasonably be thought by the buying public to come from the same source" or be affiliated with, approved by, or sponsored by the trademark owner.[46] Thus, owners of a mark for airplanes may prevent unauthorized use of the mark in connection with airline services.

Trademarks can be infringed through a variety of online activities, including use of infringing names for Web sites or for products offered online. For example, when a bulletin board operator distributed unauthorized copies of Sega games online, trademark infringement was found. The court held that the public was likely to be confused into believing the games came from Sega.[47]

13.4.2 Limitations of Trademark Owners' Rights

The trademark law does not grant the trademark owner a monopoly to use a particular term. Rather, the owner's rights are limited to preventing *confusing use* of the term. Thus, using another party's mark is not infringement unless the use creates a likelihood that consumers will be confused as to source or sponsorship, although unauthorized use of famous marks may constitute unlawful dilution.[48] There are at least five situations in which unauthorized use of a trademark may be permissible.

13.4.2.1 Unrelated Goods or Services. In most cases, the scope of trademark rights is limited to the particular kind of goods or services with which the trademark is used.[49] For example, the owners of the mark *Domino* for sugar were unable to prevent another party from using the mark *Domino's* for pizza, because sugar and pizza are not sufficiently *"related."*[50] Goods and services are "related" if they are the type that consumers would expect to come from the same source or be sponsored or approved by the trademark owner.[51] For example, personal computers and printers would in many cases be "related goods."

One of the benefits of choosing or developing a strong mark (see Section 13.2.2) is that it affords a wider range of protection over a wider range of goods. For example, the owner of the strong mark *K2,* used on skis, was able to stop the same mark from being used on a totally different product, cigarettes, while the owner of the mark *Mustang* for campers was unable to prevent its use on a similar product, automobiles.[52]

13.4.2.2 Use Other Than as a Trademark. Mere references to a trademark do not amount to infringement if the references do not create any likelihood of confusion. For example, a guidebook of used car prices that merely lists various makes (such as Ford, Chevrolet, and Chrysler) does not infringe the trademark rights in those names.

A fair, descriptive use of a trademark is also permissible. For example, a computer manufacturer can refer to its computer as "IBM compatible," so long as the reference to IBM does not lead consumers to believe the computer is sponsored or approved by IBM.[53] Thus, a prominent, unauthorized display of the IBM logo in connection with the phrase "IBM compatible" would probably constitute infringement.

Similarly, a business may also use a word or phrase in its ordinary dictionary sense without committing trademark infringement. For example, the owner of the trademark *FISH-FRI* could not prevent others from using the ordinary term *fish fry* in a descriptive manner.[54]

13.4.2.3 Remote Geographic Territories. An important rule in trademark law is that each trademark (as applied to particular goods or services) may have only a single owner in a particular market. If multiple owners were allowed, then the trademark could not function as a reliable indicator of source.

With local or regional businesses, however, different people in different areas may own rights to the same mark. For example, there are over 100 service stations in the United States named *Ray's.* As long as these rights are cultivated in separate locales, each owner has exclusive rights to the trademark in his or her particular town.[55] If two owners expand into the same territory, there will be a dispute over which one has priority. The party with priority will have the exclusive right to use the mark in the disputed territory.

The phenomenon of multiple remote users can exist on a global scale. As explained in Section 13.4.3, online use of trademarks can evoke new disputes between remote parties who have been peacefully coexisting with the same mark for years.

13.4.2.4 Different Channels of Trade. The owner of a mark—particularly a weak mark—may not be able to prevent use of a similar mark in a different channel of trade. For example, a mark used in business-to-business marketing might not cause confusion with a similar mark used in retail stores, because business and retail are different channels of trade with different buyers.

13.4.2.5 Parody. Parodies and satires occupy a special position under the law, because they are entitled to a certain degree of privilege under the First Amendment's right of free speech. When legal rights under federal and state laws come into conflict with the First Amendment protection for free speech, the courts balance the rights to be protected. In situations involving noncommercial expression or political commentary, such as news stories, satires, and documentaries, the determination is often in favor of free speech. In situations involving commercial expression, however, the First Amendment protection is more limited.[56]

Parodies of well-known trademarks are likely to be very popular online, in part due to the "nonconformist" nature of many participants in the online community. Unfortunately, it is difficult to state a rule governing when a parody mark will be permitted and when it will be considered an infringement; the courts have not been consistent in their analyses.[57] It appears that courts are more likely to permit a parody trademark if it is used for a literary or media work, the courts will more likely permit it than it will for other works. For example, parodies of *Cliffs Notes* and the L.L. Bean catalog were found noninfringing.[58] Thus, using a parody mark for an online magazine may have a better chance of surviving attack than a parody mark for a product sold online.

On the other hand, when a parody mark is used to sell products or services, the courts have been less sympathetic. For example,

- *Garbage Pail Kids* for stickers was an infringement of *Cabbage Patch Kids*,[59] and
- *Mutant of Omaha* on T-shirts was an infringement of *Mutual of Omaha*.[60]

However,

- *Bagzilla* was not an infringement of *Godzilla*,[61] and
- *Lardashe* was not an infringement of *Jordache*.[62]

As one commentator has noted, whether a court will find infringement by a parody may depend on whether or not the court was amused.[63] Given the inconsistency in the court decisions, the decision to use a parody mark online should be given careful consideration.

13.4.3 Online Infringement Problems

Trademark rights can be infringed online, just as they can in any other medium or marketplace. Indeed, the following features of online commerce make it particularly conducive to trademark infringement disputes.

13.4.3.1 Conflict Between Previously Remote Users. Because trademark rights are territorial, different parties have traditionally been able to use the same mark on the same goods or services in different locations. But when those same marks are used online, the notion of territorial separation begins to break down. By using the Internet, a seller in Montana can now do business with a customer in Mongolia as easily as he or she can do business with someone in neighboring North Dakota.

This global market promises to lead to conflict as formerly remote users go online. The logical approach to resolving these conflicts is to grant the first (or "senior") user of the mark the right to use the mark online. However, there are two difficulties with this approach. First, under current law, the junior user of the mark has priority in its territory, even over the senior user. If the senior user is given the right to use the mark in cyberspace, then the senior user's online activities will eventually reach persons located in the junior user's territory. Moreover, if future business conditions require that the junior user go online, awarding cyberspace rights to the senior user may, in practical effect, divest the junior user of its right to use its mark even in its own territory.

Unfortunately, there is no easy resolution to these conflicts—except of course to avoid them when adopting a new mark by carefully searching for prior users.

13.4.3.2 Global Scale of Networks. The remote user question becomes even more complex when one considers that different parties in different countries may have rights to the same mark. Such parties are bound to collide when they begin using their respective marks on the Internet, or on another global network. In many cases it is not clear which party is entitled to use the mark online. Moreover, the laws of different nations may be in conflict on this point. Assuming that one party has the superior right, how does it enforce that right against an infringer in a distant country? These are difficult questions without clear resolution at the present time.

13.4.3.3 Blurring of Trade Channels. Many users of similar marks are able to coexist peacefully in the everyday world because they operate in different channels of trade. In contrast, the online environment is a seamless web of information resources in which concepts such as channels of trade may be difficult to apply. For example, suppose two separate entities use a similar mark, the first with wholesale customers, and the second with retail customers. In ordinary commerce, wholesale and retail channels may be sufficiently distinct so that the parties' mutual use of a similar mark creates no likelihood of confusion. In an online environment, however, distinctions such as wholesale and retail begin to break down because both types of customers have easy access to the parties' Web pages and other online offerings.

13.4.3.4 Conflict with Information Providers. Some mark owners may find themselves in conflict with other companies that use similar marks in the computer, communications, and information services industries.

For example, consider a restaurant called the Uptown Cafe. Being in food service, the Uptown Cafe has never conducted a trademark search with respect to the computer industry, or, for that matter, any other industry unrelated to food. Uptown Cafe obtains the domain name "uptown.com" to establish an Internet Web page. It is promptly sued by Uptown Electronics, which owns a federal registration for the mark Uptown in connection with computers. The theory asserted by Uptown Electronics is that any trademark use of *Uptown* on the Internet is inherently a use in connection with electronics, and is therefore an infringement of its trademark.

Although this example may strike some as preposterous, a suit based on a similar situation has already erupted in California.[64] The implication of this case, which has not yet been decided, is that all trademark users—particularly those outside the computer industry—should check existing computer-industry marks before taking a mark online. This is especially true for companies that have nothing to do with computers, as they are more likely to be unaware of potential conflicts with computer-industry mark owners.

13.4.3.5 Domain Names. *Domain names* are alphanumeric addresses used to locate resources on the Internet. Many companies use their trade names or trademarks as domain names. This practice has led to a number of trademark-related disputes over the right to use particular domain names, including mcdonalds.com, mci.com, and mtv.com. Domain names are discussed in detail in Chapter 14.

13.4.4 Remedies for Trademark Infringement

If the trademark owner can prove infringement, a court can issue an order (an *injunction*) forcing the infringer to stop using the mark, conduct a remedial advertising campaign, or take other actions. The court can also award the mark owner actual damages, as well as any profits earned by the infringer. Under the federal statute, the court may triple these damages, and in "exceptional cases" may award attorney fees to the winning party if the owner has registered its trademark and provided the proper trademark notice.[64]

13.5 Avoiding Trademark Disputes

13.5.1 Clearing Marks for Use Online

Before going online with a new trademark, you should conduct a trademark availability search. A trademark search is a computer-assisted review of existing marks. Although it is not foolproof, a search should reveal existing uses of the same or similar marks. It will help avoid a possible infringement action in the future and it will help determine if the mark can be protected. A search does not wholly eliminate the risk that someone else is using the mark, as it is likely to miss recently adopted marks.

In conjunction with these searches, you should investigate whether the mark is being used online. This can be accomplished by using a public search tool such as Yahoo (http://yahoo.com).

Clearance searches are advisable not only for new marks, but also for existing marks that are being expanded into online uses. As discussed in Section 13.4.3, this new foray could provoke a dispute with a heretofore unknown prior user. A search can help identify such a risk.

13.5.2 Consent and Concurrent Use Arrangements

The trademark law allows only one party to own a trademark for particular goods and services in a particular market. When multiple parties are using the same or similar marks, they can establish consent or concurrent use arrangements to avoid conflict, clarify their respective rights and obligations, and ensure that they are complying with the one-owner rule.

13.5.2.1 Consent Agreements. In a consent agreement, the senior user consents to a junior user's adoption of the same or similar trademark.[65] The underlying premise of a consent agreement is that the parties' mutual use of the same mark will not cause any confusion in the marketplace. The parties usually agree to take necessary steps to rectify confusion if it does arise.[66] Typically, the parties to a consent agreement sell different goods that, at first blush, seem as though they could be related but on closer examination turn out to be unrelated because of channels of distribution, advertising orientation, price, or other factors.[67]

As you adopt marks for use online, consider establishing a consent agreement to resolve potential conflicts before they become costly headaches. Be aware, however, that many of the consent agreements commonly used today might not be effective in an online environment. For example, a typical consent agreement includes restrictions on channels of trade that cannot easily be applied to cyberspace. Consent agreements should expressly speak to online commerce, and should specify which party is allowed to use its respective marks online, such as in a Web page or as a domain name. If both parties will be using their respective marks online, the consent agreement should also state (and explain why) that use will not cause consumer confusion.

13.5.2.2 Concurrent Use Registration. A *concurrent use registration* is a registration issued by the U.S. Patent and Trademark Office to two or more parties who use the same or similar marks on the same or related goods. To avoid confusion, the parties' rights are restricted to separate territories. Concurrent use registrations involve a special proceeding before the Trademark Trial and Appeal Board.[68]

The basis of a concurrent use registration is that unrestricted use of the mark in question by multiple parties is likely to create confusion, and therefore the parties are consigned to different geographic areas. In contrast, the basis of a consent agreement is that use of a mark by multiple parties is not likely to create confusion, and therefore mutual use within the same territory is acceptable.

Concurrent use registrations are very problematic in cyberspace because of their premise that geographic separation will eliminate potential consumer confusion. There is no geographic separation in cyberspace, and therefore the concurrent use arrangement breaks down if either party (or both) attempts to go online. This is obviously a sticky problem whose solution will be as much technical as it is legal. One possibility may be for the parties to adopt a joint plan for directing online inquiries to the proper party. Which party would be the "proper" one would depend on the locale from which the inquiry originates.

Endnotes

1. Trademarks are governed by state law as well as by a federal statute known as the Lanham Act, 15 U.S.C. § 1051 *et seq.*

2. In this chapter, the term *trademark* will be used to refer to both trademarks and service marks unless the context otherwise requires.

3. *Pathfinder Communications Corp. v. Midwest Communications Co.*, 593 F. Supp. 281 (N.D. Ind. 1984).

4. *Coca-Cola Co. v. Busch*, 44 F. Supp. 405, 410 (E.D. Pa. 1942).

5. *Qualitex Co. v. Jacobson Prods. Co.*, 115 S. Ct. 1300, 34 U.S.P.Q.2d 1161 (1995).

6. 15 U.S.C. § 1114.

7. The *World Wide Web* is a nickname for a collection of information resources (both commercial and noncommercial) available on the Internet using the http protocol. These resources (or *Web sites*) contain text, graphic, audio, and video files organized using a set of instructions called *hypertext mark-up language* ("html"). Web sites can be accessed by Internet users who have the proper software (or *browser*).

8. *Abercrombie & Fitch Co. v. Hunting World, Inc.*, 537 F.2d 4, 189 U.S.P.Q.2d 769 (2d Cir. 1976).

9. *Trademark Manual of Examining Procedure* § 1209.01.

10. *Two Pesos v. Taco Cabana, Inc.*, 112 S. Ct. 2753, 23 U.S.P.Q.2d 1081 (1992).

11. *Vision Center v. Optiks, Inc.*, 596 F.2d 111 (5th Cir. 1979).

12. 15 U.S.C. § 1052(f).

13. The marks *McDonald's* and *Ford* were descriptive when they were adopted because they are surnames, but they later acquired strength through promotion and customer recognition.

14. Under the intent-to-use provisions of the Lanham Act, a person who intends to use a trademark can acquire limited rights prior to actually using a mark. 15 U.S.C. § 1051(b).

15. Thomas J. McCarthy, *McCarthy on Trademarks and Unfair Competition* § 16.02.

16. *Hanover Star Milling Co. v. Metcalf*, 240 U.S. 403 (1916); *United Drug Co. v. Theodore Rectanus Co.*, 248 U.S. 90 (1918).

17. 15 U.S.C. § 1127.

18. However, such advertising use may establish common law priority in the mark if within a reasonable time it is then physically applied to the goods.

19. Digital file names have been recognized as trademarks, at least when used by an infringer. See cases discussed at footnote 47.

20. 15 U.S.C. § 1127; *See McCarthy on Trademarks*, § 16.01 *et seq.*

21. Each of the 50 states has its own trademark laws. If a trademark is federally registered, however, there is usually no need for state registration. State registration may be a good option if a mark does not qualify for federal registration.

22. 15 U.S.C. § 1051(b).

23. 15 U.S.C. § 1057.

24. 15 U.S.C. § 1115(a).

25. 15 U.S.C. §§ 1117, 1118.

26. 15 U.S.C. § 1124.

27. 15 U.S.C. § 1127.

28. These new services may qualify for a federal service mark registration if they are sufficiently distinct from activities involved in the sale of goods or performance of other services. For example, a grocery store cannot obtain a separate service mark registration for bagging groceries, because that service is part of the store's primary grocery business. Thus, one must consider whether the services offered online are sufficiently distinct from offline products and services to support a separate registration. *Trademark Manual of Examining Procedure* § 1301.01(a).

29. *See, e.g., Larry Harmon Pictures Corp. v. William's Restaurant Corp.*, 929 F.2d 662 (Fed. Cir. 1991).

30. L. Horwitz et al., *Intellectual Property Counseling and Litigation*, § 40.02(2)(d).

31. 15 U.S.C. § 1111.

32. *Id.*

33. 15 U.S.C. § 1114(a).

34. *Polaroid Corp. v. Polarad Elecs. Corp.*, 287 F.2d 492 (2d Cir. 1961).

35. Thomas J. McCarthy, *McCarthy on Trademarks*, § 23.03(2).

36. *Franklin Mint Corp. v. Master Mfg.*, 667 F.2d 1005 (C.C.P.A. 1981).

37. *Bristol-Meyers Squibb v. McNeil-P.P.C.*, 973 F.2d 1033 (2d Cir. 1992).

38. *Merriam-Webster, Inc. v. Random House, Inc.*, 35 F.3d 65 (2d Cir. 1994).

39. *Polaroid Corp. v. Polaroid Electronics Corp.*, 287 F.2d 492 (2d Cir. 1961).

40. *Supercuts, Inc. v. Super Clips*, 18 U.S.P.Q.2d 1378 (D. Mass. 1990).

41. *Apple Computer, Inc. v. Formula Int'l, Inc.*, 725 F.2d 521 (9th Cir. 1984).

42. *Carling Brewing Co. v. Phillip Morris, Inc.*, 277 F. Supp. 326 (N.D. Ga. 1967).

43. *Grey v. Campbell Soup Co.*, 650 F. Supp. 1166 (C.D. Cal. 1986).

44. *Quaker Oats Co. v. General Mills, Inc.*, 134 F.2d 429 (7th Cir. 1943).

45. *Swatch Watch S.A. v. Taxor, Inc.*, 785 F.2d 956 (11th Cir. 1986).

46. Thomas J. McCarthy, *McCarthy on Trademarks*, § 24.03(2).

47. *Sega Enterprises, Inc. v. Maphia*, 857 F. Supp. 679 (N.D.Cal. 1994). *See also Playboy Enterprises, Inc. v. Frena*, 839 F. Supp. 1552 (M.D. Fla. 1993).

48. For example, the use of a mark on different goods or in a distant territory might not constitute infringement because of an absence of a likelihood of confusion.

49. However, famous marks such as *Kodak* and *Exxon* are entitled to additional protection under state law anti-dilution rules, as well as the recently enacted Federal Trademark Dilution Act of 1995.

50. *Amstar Corporation v. Domino's Pizza, Inc.*, 615 F.2d 252 (5th Cir. 1980).

51. *Dwinell-Right Co. v. National Fruit Products Company*, 140 F.2d 618 (1st Cir. 1944).

52. *Philip Morris, Inc. v. K-2 Corp.*, 555 F.2d 815, 816 (C.C.P.A. 1977); *Westward Coach Mfg. Co. v. Ford Motor Co.*, 388 F.2d 627, 634–635 (7th Cir.) *Cert. denied*, 392 U.S. 927 (1968). In this case, the *Mustang* mark was considered weak because it had already been used by different persons on a wide variety of items.

53. Of course, the claim must be true to avoid liability for false advertising. See Chapter 22.

54. *Zatarains, Inc. v. Oak Grove Smokehouse, Inc.*, 698 F.2d 786 (5th Cir. 1983).

55. *See Hanover Starr Milling Co. v. Metcalf*, 240 U.S.403 (1916); *United Drug Co. v. Theodore Rectanus Co.*, 248 U.S. 90 (1918).

56.   *See Board of Trustees of State University of New York v. Fox*, 492 U.S. 469, 477–480 (1989).

57.   For a good discussion of how courts should (but may not) balance trademark law and the First Amendment, see Arlen Langvardt, Trademark Rights and First Amendment Wrongs: Protecting the Former Without Committing the Latter, 83 The Trademark Reporter 633 (Sept./Oct. 1993).

58.   *See Cliffs Notes, Inc. v. Bantam Doubleday Dell Publishing Group, Inc.*, 886 F.2d 490 (2d Cir. 1989); *L.L. Bean, Inc. v. Drake Publishers, Inc.*, 811 F.2d 26 (1st Cir. 1987). But *see Dallas Cowboys Cheerleaders, Inc. v. Pussycat Cinema, Ltd.*, 604 F.2d 200 (2d Cir. 1979) (in which the use of cheerleader uniforms in a pornographic movie was found to be infringement).

59.   *Original Appalachian Art Works, Inc. v. Topps Chewing Gum, Inc.*, 642 F.Supp. 1031 (N.D. Ga. 1986) (preliminary injunction granted).

60.   *Mutual of Omaha Ins. Co. v. Novak*, 836 F.2d 397 (8th Cir. 1987).

61.   *Toho Co. v. Sears Roebuck & Co.*, 645 F.2d 788 (9th Cir. 1981) (garbage bags).

62.   *Jordache Enterprises, Inc. v. Hogg Wyle Ltd.*, 828 F.2d 1482 (10th Cir. 1987) (jeans).

63.   *McCarthy on Trademarks and Unfair Competition*, § 31. 38(1) (1993).

64.   P. Lewis, *Technology: Online*, N.Y. Times, August 14, 1995, at D5.

65.   *In re E. I. DuPont DeNemours & Co.*, 476 F.2d 1357 (C.C.P.A. 1973).

66.   *Trademark Manual of Examining Procedure*, § 1207.01(c)(viii).

67.   *Id.*

68.   15 U.S.C. § 1052(d); *Trademark Manual of Examining Procedure*, § 1207.04(b).

14
Rights to Domain Names

Andrew R. Basile, Jr.

14.4 Reverse Domain-Name Hijacking

Endnotes

A series of legal battles has erupted over rights to use Internet *domain names*. Primarily, these disputes involve trademark owners who believe that their trademarks are being improperly used by third parties as domain names. This chapter explores the relationship between trademark law and domain names, and explains how both trademark owners and domain-name users can protect their rights.

14.1 Understanding Domain Names

14.1.1 What Is a Domain Name?

The Internet is a network of computers interconnected for electronic communication. Every computer connected to the Internet is assigned a numeric address, which the other computers on the network use to route messages to that computer. A typical numeric Internet address is 200.98.102.23. These addresses are difficult for humans to remember, so the Internet authorities also assign alphanumeric addresses, or *domain names.* Examples of domain names include "whitehouse.gov" or "microsoft.com."

Initially, businesses gave little thought to domain names. Domain names were like telephone numbers—as long as each one was unique, they allowed the Internet to function. Apart from this primary function, domain names had little significance and were often chosen by technical personnel who paid little or no attention to marketing considerations.

All this changed with the advent of the World Wide Web as an advertising media and marketplace. Because people use domain names to locate Web resources, companies doing business online want domain names that are easy to remember and that relate to their products, trade names, or trademarks. For example, a florist might find the domain name "flowers.com" very valuable. Likewise, owners of famous trademarks such as Microsoft usually register those trademarks as domain names (e.g., "microsoft.com").

14.1.2 Domain-Name Conflicts

The format for Internet domain names is relatively simple. Typically, it consists of a word or mnemonic followed by ".com" for commercial entities, ".gov" for governmental entities, ".edu" for educational institutions, and ".mil" for military agencies. This practice presents a problem for commercial entities in particular, since many unrelated companies in different lines of business share similar names that they would like to use as part of an Internet domain name. Consider, for example, Apple Computer and Apple Records—which one has the right to use the domain name apple.com? Or consider United Airlines and United Van Lines; which one gets the domain name united.com?[1] Also, numerous companies are known primarily by the name *American* or *First*. Which ones are entitled to the domain names american.com and first.com? This problem carries the potential for serious conflicts, especially as many companies discover that "their" trade name or trademark is being used by others as an Internet domain name.

Many such cases result from legitimate conflicts between two businesses that use a similar name. Other cases, however, are sparked when a particular mark is reserved as a domain name by a competitor or an individual hoping to profit when the rightful owner of the mark decides to do business on the Internet and is forced to purchase rights to the domain name. Some trademark owners have characterized these practices as "domain grabbing" or "domain hijacking."[2] The common theme of these cases is that the so-called hijacker had no legitimate purpose for obtaining the domain name, other than to harass or hold up a trademark owner. Recent disputes in this category include:

- **McDonald's v. Quittner.** Joshua Quittner is a journalist who published an article about the fact that the owners of many famous trademarks had failed to register their marks as domain names. In connection with this article, he obtained the domain name mcdonalds.com, and began taking e-mail at ronald@mcdonalds.com. When McDonald's objected, Quittner surrendered the name in exchange for a $3,500 donation to a grade school.[3]
- **MTV v. Curry.** Adam Curry was a disc jockey at MTV Networks. In 1993, he approached MTV about starting a Web page under the domain name "mtv.com." Curry claimed that MTV told him he was free to develop the site at his own expense. For the next year, Curry operated mtv.com as a Web site featuring information about rock music. In January 1994, however, MTV demanded that Curry surrender the domain name mtv.com. When Curry refused, MTV filed suit, alleging trademark infringement and unfair competition. The parties have since settled, with MTV apparently in control of the mtv.com domain name.[4]
- **Stanley Kaplan v. Princeton Review.** Stanley Kaplan and Princeton Review are competitors in the test preparation business. In 1994, Princeton Review obtained the domain name kaplan.com allegedly to taunt arch rival Kaplan. Princeton Review operated a Web page at this address featuring advertisements that promoted Princeton Review and belittled Kaplan. When faced with Kaplan's initial demand to cease using kaplan.com, Princeton Review reportedly offered to surrender the domain name in exchange for a case of beer. Not amused, Kaplan sued

for trademark infringement. The suit was ultimately resolved through binding arbitration in Kaplan's favor.[5] Afterwards, Princeton Review's president remarked that Kaplan had "no sense of humor, no vision and no beer."[6]

- **MCI v. GTE.** It was reported that GTE's Sprint temporarily acquired mci.com as a domain name.[7] Sprint and MCI are, of course, competitors in the field of long-distance communication.
- **Better Business Bureau v. Mark Sloo.** The Council of Better Business Bureaus (BBB) filed a trademark lawsuit against Mark Sloo, who had obtained a domain name bbb.com.[8] According to BBB's complaint, Mr. Sloo acquired the domain name with the intent of trading on the goodwill associated with the BBB mark. Allegedly, Mr. Sloo had told BBB that he acquired the domain name because "he was interested in establishing a consumer complaint system on the Internet."[9]

14.2 Acquiring Rights in a Domain Name

A domain name can be valuable property in cyberspace. This section outlines steps for acquiring rights to use a domain name.

14.2.1 Obtaining a Domain Name

The first step in acquiring the right to use a domain name is to contact Network Solutions, the government subcontractor responsible for assigning domain names in the United States.[10] Network Solutions assigns domain names on a first-come, first-served basis, and many names have already been assigned. Thus, the longer one waits to apply, the greater the chance that one's choice of domain names will not be available.

In assigning a domain name, Network Solutions performs certain technical procedures that allow computers on the Internet to recognize the new domain name. Although these procedures are necessary for creating a new domain name, they do not bestow the legal right to use that domain name. Thus, persons who acquire a domain name from Network Solutions can still be sued for using that domain name by another party who believes that the domain name violates its trademark or other rights.

A business that plans to acquire a new domain name should first conduct a trademark search to determine whether anyone else is already using the proposed domain name as a trademark. This precaution is equally important for a business that already uses the proposed domain name as a trademark, because use of its trademark as a domain name may represent an expanded use of the mark with new services (the service of providing information), in new territories (the global reach of the Internet), or via new channels of trade (online communication). This expanded use could provoke a dispute with another user of the same mark.

For example, Frenchy Frys Catering, a distributor of French fry vending machines, was recently sued by Fry's Electronics, a computer and electronics retailer, for using the domain name frys.com. Fry's Electronics asserted that even though Frenchy Frys may be entitled to use the term *frys* in its French fry business, the use of *frys* in an online (i.e., "electronic") environment is a use in the field of computers and therefore a violation of Fry's rights.[11]

A search is also important because Network Solutions requires each applicant for a domain name to represent and warrant that:

- It has the right to use the requested domain name,
- It intends to use the name on a regular basis,
- It will not use the name for any unlawful purpose, and
- Its use of the name will not violate any third party's rights in any jurisdiction.[12]

The applicant must also agree to defend and indemnify Network Solutions for any claim or expense resulting from the applicant's use of the domain name.[13] This indemnity could result in significant expense if a third party sues Network Solutions in a dispute over the applicant's choice of domain name.

14.2.2 Protecting a Domain Name as a Trademark

The next step in protecting a domain name is to acquire trademark rights with respect to the name. A trademark, as explained in Chapter 13, is a word or symbol used to indicate the source or origin of particular goods or services. Thus, merely obtaining a domain name from Network Solutions does not create trademark rights in that name.

A domain name may be protected as a trademark, however, if it is used in commerce to indicate the source or origin of goods or services.[14] In the case of goods, this usually means the domain name must be applied to the goods, their containers or the displays associated with the goods.[15] In the case of services, the mark must be displayed in the sale or advertising of the services.[16] For example, the domain name for an online store could be a service mark for the service of retail sales.

Those who use an existing trademark as a domain name do not need to worry about acquiring trademark rights in the domain name *per se*. For example, if the maker of *Pepsi* brand soft drinks acquires the domain name pepsi.com, its trademark rights in *Pepsi* already exist by virtue of its use in ordinary commerce.

By comparison, companies that do not use a domain name as a trademark in ordinary commerce can still develop trademark rights in the name if they offer online services or digital products (see Section 13.3.3) in connection with the domain name. For example, a service called *NewsPage* offers news information to Internet users. Its domain name, newspage.com, functions as a service mark because it indicates the source of the services offered at that Internet address. By analogy, the domain name functions as a service mark in the same way that radio station call numbers or telephone number mnemonics can develop trademark significance.[17]

An Internet domain name may be eligible for trademark registration in the U.S. Patent and Trademark Office ("PTO") if its owner uses it (or intends to use it) as a trademark or service mark. When the PTO considers an application to register a domain name, it generally disregards the Internet suffixes such as .com.[18] Thus, the base domain name by itself must be sufficiently distinctive (that is, not generic or descriptive) to support a registration. See Section 13.3.2 for a discussion of distinctiveness (or *strength*).

Consequently, there is little benefit in obtaining a separate federal registration of a previously registered mark simply because the registered mark is used as a domain name, with Internet address suffixes. For example, if a company has a registered trademark for *Acme* on trucks, it does not need a separate registration for acme.com simply because it has obtained acme.com as a domain name. See Section 13.3.4 for cases where online use of marks may warrant additional registrations, however.

14.3 Preventing Use of a Mark as a Domain Name

As explained above, many trademark owners, including McDonald's and MCI, have found that competitors and others have "hijacked" their trademarks for use as Internet domain names. To date, the equities in most of these cases seem lopsided in favor of the trademark holders. However, many future domain name disputes are likely to be much less clear cut, with courts finding that both parties have a legitimate claim to the name at issue.

For example, several organizations use the term *united*, including United Airlines, United Way, and United Van Lines. Does any one of these entities have a superior right to the domain name united.com? If one of these mark holders obtains the domain name united.com., do any of the others have the right to object?

The probable answer in this case is that each owner of a "United" trademark has an equal right to use the domain name united.com. The reason for this is that trademark law does not confer a monopoly to use a particular word such as *united*. Rather, a trademark right protects its owner from unauthorized use of the mark *in a manner that is likely to cause confusion* among the purchasing public. Use of the same mark by different parties on unrelated goods usually does not lead to confusion. Thus, each party's rights are limited to the use of the mark on its respective goods.

So long as the public is not confused, some trademark owners may find that they cannot prevent others from using their trademarks as domain names. Notwithstanding this cautionary note, there are a number of strategies trademark owners can pursue against other parties who use trademarks as domain names.

14.3.1 Network Solutions' Dispute Resolution Procedure

Network Solutions' official position is that it "cannot act as an arbiter of [trademark] disputes arising out of the registration and use of domain names."[19] Unfortunately, Network Solutions and other Internet service providers have been caught in the middle of the fight between trademark owners and other parties who have used their trademarks as domain names.[20] In an effort to stave off litigation, Network Solutions has adopted certain procedures for handling trademark disputes.[21]

Under these procedures, the owner of a trademark registration in the U.S. or abroad can file an objection with Network Solutions if another party is using the trademark as a domain name.[22] The domain-name user must show within 30 days that it also has a trademark registration (in any country) for the contested domain name, and must post a bond (payable to Network Solutions) sufficient to cover any damages sought by the complaining party.[23]

If the domain-name user cannot post bond or produce a trademark registration, then the domain name is suspended (or placed into a "hold status") until the dispute is resolved by court order, arbitration judgment, or settlement agreement.[24]

If the domain-name user has a trademark registration for the disputed name, Network Solutions will not suspend its domain name.[25] In that case, the complaining party will have to work out a settlement or go to court with the domain-name user. In cases where both parties have trademark registrations for the disputed mark, the complaining party might not have a case of "hijacking." In fact, the domain-name user may have a legitimate—and perhaps even superior—claim to use the name at issue.

14.3.2 Lanham Act Remedies

Trademark owners can also pursue legal action in the courts against domain-name users. Such suits will typically be brought under sections 32 and 43(a) of the Lanham Act.[26] As explained above, trademark infringement under section 32 is grounded on a showing that the defendant: (1) is using the mark in commerce,[27] and (2) that such use is likely to cause confusion or deception. Section 43(a) offers additional remedies for confusion relating to affiliation, sponsorship, or approval. The following examples illustrate fact patterns where a likelihood of confusion may exist.

14.3.2.1 Similar Goods or Services. A likelihood of confusion may exist where the defendant is using its domain name in connection with the same type of goods or services as the trademark owner. For example, consider a hypothetical trademark *Acme Airlines*. Because *Acme* is a fairly common mark, the owner of the *Acme Airlines* mark might not be able to prevent another party from using the domain name acme.com in connection with, for example, soft drinks. However, it probably could prevent others from using acme.com in connection with air travel. The difference is that use of the term *acme* in connection with air travel may create a likelihood of confusion. In some cases, consumers may believe that the infringing domain name is actually operated by Acme Airlines. In other cases, they may believe that the domain name is somehow sponsored or approved by Acme Airlines. In either case, the domain-name user could be violating the Lanham Act.

14.3.2.2 Trademark Relates to Computers. A likelihood of confusion may also exist when the allegedly infringed trademark is used in connection with computers, communications, or information services. Arguably, these marks could be infringed on by any similar domain name (regardless of how the domain name is used), because an Internet domain name is inherently used in connection with computers, information, and communication.

For example, *Wired* (a magazine about the Internet and digital technology) recently objected to the use of the domain name wire.net by WIRE, a group devoted to women's issues. In the end, WIRE (the women's group) changed its name to Women's Wire.[28] The apparent strength of *Wired* magazine's position was that its mark *Wired* is used in close connection with the Internet, and arguably, therefore, any use of *wire* as a domain name necessarily posed a risk of consumer confusion.[29]

14.3.2.3 Defendant Shows Bad Faith. A trademark owner's case will be particularly strong where the domain-name user has adopted a domain name in bad faith—that is, with the intent of deriving benefit from the trademark owner's reputation. Bad faith may exist, for example, when a company adopts one of its competitor's trademarks as a domain name. This type of bad faith is found in the classic domain-name hijacking cases discussed in Section 14.1.2, and will weigh strongly against the domain-name user in litigation.

14.3.2.4 Mark Is Very Strong. One theory espoused by owners of famous marks is that unauthorized use of such marks as a domain name is inherently a use in commerce that is likely to cause confusion. For example, if someone obtains a domain name for mcdonalds.com (or another famous trademark), he or she might draw a substantial number of McDonald's hamburger customers who would mistakenly attribute that Web page (or lack thereof) to McDonald's Corporation. Although this position has not been tested by the courts, it would seem to have particular strength in connection with highly distinctive and unique marks.

14.3.3 Dilution Claims

Using a state law dilution theory, owners of very strong marks may be able to prevent unauthorized use of the marks as domain names. Dilution rights protect holders of famous marks such as *Coca-Cola* and *Big Mac* from having others use their marks even if there is no likelihood of confusion. For example, a party who uses the domain name exxon.com could be subject to a dilution claim by the owners of the famous *Exxon* trademark.

14.4 Reverse Domain-Name Hijacking

Domain-name hijacking is obviously a concern for companies of all sizes. However, smaller and mid-sized companies should also focus on the risk that they might be accused of domain-name hijacking by an overzealous trademark owner.

Under Network Solutions' current policy, this risk has some teeth. Anyone with a federal registration that reads on a domain name can request Network Solutions to suspend the domain name. Unless the domain-name user has a federal or foreign registration covering the same name, Network Solutions may do just that.[30]

Losing a domain name could be a disaster for a business that is built around a Web page. This problem is especially acute for new businesses because it may take a year or longer to obtain a trademark registration. In the meantime, someone who has a registration for the same mark—even in a wholly different industry—can ask Network Solutions to take away the new company's domain name.

For example, suppose a company known as Stellar Limited develops Web pages and other online promotions. Its portfolio is on the Web at stellar.com, and at great expense it has advertised its domain name in various trade publications. One day, Stellar, Inc., a maker of industrial valves and owner of a federal trademark registration for *Stellar*, files a complaint with Network Solutions, demanding that Stellar Limited's domain name be revoked. Under its current policy, Network Solutions may pull the domain name unless Stellar Limited presents a trademark registration within 30 days. Because Stellar Limited cannot afford to lose its domain name, and does not have a trademark registration, it may be forced to pay Stellar, Inc., a hefty sum in settlement of its claim.

Based on this hypothetical case, it seems that Network Solutions' new policy may actually invite "reverse domain-name hijacking," whereby someone with a trademark registration holds up a domain-name—even if the parties are in completely different industries and the name in question is as common as rain.

It is likely that Network Solutions' policy will evolve over time to deal with these types of problems. In the meantime, however, domain-name users should consider taking two steps.

First, conduct a careful trademark search for any proposed domain name. If the search reveals other parties who own registrations (or applications to register) for the same mark (but on different goods), consider entering into a consent agreement with the other owners before committing resources to the domain name. Of course if another party is using the *same* mark on the *same* goods as the domain-name user there is probably a serious conflict and the advice of a trademark attorney should be sought.

Second, apply for a federal registration for any mark that is also used as a domain name and is not already registered. Because the registration may take well over a year to obtain, the application should be filed as soon as possible.

Endnotes

1.   In reality, "united.com" is registered to a business known as *United Video*.

2.   A. Brunel, *Billions Registered, But No Rules: The Scope of Trademark Protection for Internet Domain Names*, 7 Journal of Proprietary Rights 2.

3.   *Id.*

4.   *MTV Networks v. Curry*, 867 F. Supp. 202 (S.D.N.Y. 1994).

5.   D. Burk, *Trademarks Along the Infobahn: A First Look at the Emerging Law of Cybermarks*, Richmond Journal of Law and Technology, Feb. 4, 1995, http://www.urich.edu/jolt

6.   J. Quittner, *Making a Name on the Internet*, Newsday, Oct. 7, 1994, at A4.

7.   International Trademark Association (INTA) Bulletin, *Registration of Internet Domain Names in the USPTO*, February, 1995.

8.   Hamilton, *Trademarks on the Internet: Confusion, Collusion or Dilution*, Presented at the University of Texas School of Law Conference on the Emerging Law of Computer Networks (May 18th and 19th, 1995).

9.   *Id.*

10. Its telephone number is (703) 742-4777. Network Solutions assigns domain names in North America. Other organizations assign domain names in different parts of the world. Names assigned by these foreign organizations have suffixes that indicate their country of origin, such as ".uk" for the United Kingdom, and ".au" for Australia. Independent international bodies such as APNIC and RIPE coordinate these activities, at least on a regional basis. However, no one government or organization has worldwide authority over the assignment of domain names.

11. P. Lewis, *Technology: Online*, N.Y. Times, Aug. 14, 1995, at D5.

12. Network Solutions, Inc. Domain Dispute Resolution Policy Statement, dated July, 1995 (ulr ftp://rs.internic.net/policy/internic/internic-domain-4.txt) (hereinafter, the NSI Policy Statement).

13. NSI Policy Statement, § 4.

14. In examining an application for registration of a domain name, the PTO follows the same policy it applies to applications for registration of alphanumeric telephone number marks, such as 1-800-FLOWERS. INTA Bulletin, *supra*.

15. K. Klesh, *Internet Domain Names and the USPTO: An Interview*, Thomson & Thomson Client Times, August, 1995, at 4.

16. *Id.*

17. Some commentators have addressed the trademark significance of domain names by drawing an analogy with broadcast designators and telephone mnemonics. *See* D. Burk, *supra*.

18. INTA Bulletin, *supra*; K. Klesh, *supra*.

19. NSI Policy Statement, § 6(b).

20. P. Lewis, *Technology: Online*, N.Y. Times, Aug. 14, 1995, at D5.

21. NSI Policy Statement, § 6.

22. If the dispute does not involve a federally registered trademark, then the user of the domain name can continue its use until a court order or arbitrator's judgment to the contrary is received by Network Solutions. NSI Policy Statement, § 6(b).

23. NSI Policy Statement, § 6.

24. *Id.*

25. *Id.*

26. Section 32 provides remedies for the infringement of federally registered trademarks. Section 43(a) provides remedies for false designation and descriptions (that is, unfair competition).

27. Although merely obtaining a domain name may not be sufficient "use in commerce" to establish trademark rights, it may be a sufficient "use" for purposes of establishing a Lanham Act violation. In *Brach Van Houten Holding v. Save Brach's Coalition*, 856 F. Supp. 472 (N.D. Ill. 1994), plaintiff Brach's prevented a protest group from using plaintiff's famous candy logo on the group's literature criticizing plaintiff's decision to close a factory on the West Side of Chicago. Although this case did not involve online activity, it demonstrates how noncommercial "use" of a mark can trigger infringement liability.

28. Brunel, *supra*, at 5.

29. *See also* P. Lewis, *supra* (discussing dispute over fry.com between catering company and Fry's Electronics).

30. NSI Policy Statement, § 6(c)(2).

15

Role of Patents Online

Andrew R. Basile, Jr.

Patents touch virtually all aspects of commerce, and the online world of electronic commerce is no exception. There are three ways that patents may have an impact on doing business electronically.

First, every company that engages in electronic commerce will use software, protocols, and equipment that may be covered by patents. To the extent that patents cover techniques used to conduct online commerce, it may be necessary to pay license fees for the privilege of using that technology. Thus it is said that the information highway may become a tollway, with its motorists paying license fees and royalties to the holders of certain key patents.[1]

Second, companies that develop technology used in conducting online commerce may want to consider ways in which that technology can be protected through patents.

Third, companies that distribute software online (or otherwise) will find that software—regardless of its purpose—may be covered by patents, and the unauthorized distribution of patented software could lead to claims of patent infringement.

15.1 Patent Fundamentals

15.1.1 What Is a Patent?

A *patent* is a right granted to an inventor by the federal government to exclude others from making, using, selling, or importing an invention.[2] Patents are available throughout the world, and are issued on a country-by-country basis. Patents are obtained in the United States by filing a patent application with the federal Patent and Trademark Office (PTO), pursuant to the Patent Act of 1952.[3]

In the United States, most patents expire 20 years after a patent application is filed.[4] Patent protection begins when the patent issues, so the patent's life lasts 20 years less the time that the application is pending. Patents filed before June 8, 1995, expire the later of 17 years from the date of issuance or 20 years from the date of filing.

15.1.2 Types of Patents

The United States grants three types of patents:

1. **Utility Patents** (for machines and other useful inventions),
2. **Design Patents** (for ornamental designs), and
3. **Plant Patents** (for distinct and new varieties of plants).[5]

Utility patents are granted for new and useful processes, machines, articles of man-ufacture, or compositions of matter.[6] Most things that people think of as inventions—such as light bulbs and telephones—are covered by utility patents. Software may be the subject of a utility patent.

Design patents are granted for new, original, and ornamental designs.[7] Unlike util-ity patents, their term lasts 14 years from the date of issuance. A design patent covers a design as applied to an article of manufacture. Designs in the abstract are not patentable. Typical subject matter for design patents includes the shape of products, such as auto-mobiles and toys. In recent years, design patents have been granted for icons displayed on computer screens.[8]

15.1.3 Patent Claims

At the end of every patent are numbered sentences called *claims*. Claims are the legal definitions of the patented invention. For example, a patent might include a claim reciting:

A computer network for conducting online transactions, including:

1. A first computer adapted for entering a sales order,
2. A second computer adapted for receiving the sales order, and
3. A communication means for transmitting the sales order from the first computer to the second computer via a *microwave signal*.

Such a claim would cover any network that included each of the three recited ele-ments, even if the network included additional computers or other elements not recited in the claim. However, the claim would not cover a network that lacked one or more of the recited elements. For example, if the network had a communication link, but the link connected the computers via a fiber optic signal (as opposed to a microwave signal), then it would not fall within the literal scope of the claim.[9]

This example illustrates an important but counterintuitive principle in patent law: the more elements in a claim, the narrower the claim's coverage. The reason is that, to infringe on the claim, an accused device must have each of the recited elements.

A patent may have many claims, and each stands as a separate definition of the invention. Thus, a patent covers any device or method that falls within the scope of at least one of the patent's claims, even if the device or method is not covered by any of the other claims.

15.1.4 Patent Infringement

A patent grants its owner the exclusive right to make, use, sell or offer for sale, and import the patented invention. Patent infringement occurs when another person or organization performs one of these acts without the patent owner's permission.

A patent is "literally" infringed on by the unauthorized use, manufacture, or sale of a device or process (the "accused device") that falls within the literal scope of any of the patent's claims. A patent may also be infringed under the "doctrine of equivalents" if the accused device includes every claim element or its equivalent, and it performs the same function as the claimed invention in the same manner to achieve the same result.[10]

The *doctrine of equivalents* is a judicial extension of literal infringement. Its purpose is to provide the patentee with a remedy when a defendant has appropriated the essence of the invention, but in some minor way has avoided the technical, literal limitations of the patent claim.[11]

15.1.5 Assignment and License

A patent is a property right that may be assigned or licensed. Patent assignments must be recorded in the PTO within 3 months.[12] Failure to record an assignment leaves the purchaser's title vulnerable to competing claims of ownership from other parties. Patent licensing is discussed in Chapter 18.

15.2 What Can Be Patented?

Patent protection is available for any invention that is:

1. Patentable subject matter,
2. Useful,
3. New, and
4. Nonobvious.

15.2.1 Patentable Subject Matter

The patent statute defines *patentable subject matter* as any "process, machine, article of manufacture, or composition of matter."[13] The Supreme Court has interpreted this language broadly, holding that patent protection is available for "anything under the sun that is made by man."[14]

However, the patent law does not protect every kind of idea or innovation. In particular, discoveries of the laws of nature, physical phenomena, or abstract ideas by themselves cannot be patented.[15] If there is anything patentable from such discoveries, it is the application of the law, phenomenon, or idea to some new and useful end. For example, Einstein could not have patented his theory of relativity. He could, however, have patented a spacecraft based on the theory of relativity.

15.2.2 Utility

The requirement that an invention be "useful" means that it function as described and that it fulfill some purpose.[16] Almost anything worth building meets the requirement of utility. Typically, the U.S. PTO rejects inventions as "lacking utility" only if it believes they are impossible to practice.[17] For example, a patent application directed to a time machine or perpetual motion machine would be rejected as lacking utility, unless the inventor could demonstrate that the machine worked as described.

15.2.3 Novelty

The requirement that an invention be *new* (or *novel*) means that the claimed invention, at the time it was invented, was not "known or used by others in this country, or patented or described in a printed publication in this or a foreign country."[18] The universe of knowledge existing at the time of the invention is called the *prior art*. Generally, an invention is novel unless it is identically disclosed by the prior art, in which case it is said to be *anticipated* by the prior art.

15.2.4 Nonobviousness

The requirement that an invention be *nonobvious* means that the invention cannot simply be a trivial variation of the existing art. Legally speaking, an invention is "obvious" when the invention, although not identically disclosed by the prior art, differs from the prior art in such a minor way that the invention as a whole would have been obvious to a person skilled in the art at the time the invention was made.[19]

For example, suppose the prior art discloses red, blue, and yellow sailboats, and also that green paint is a good substitute for blue paint. The claimed invention of a green sailboat is, strictly speaking, novel because the existing art only discloses sailboats that are red, blue, and yellow. However, the invention as a whole is probably obvious to one skilled in the art of sailboat making because the prior art suggests substituting green paint for blue paint.

Obviousness is a tricky concept because, like the solution to a riddle, many good inventions seem obvious in hindsight. Thus, in evaluating obviousness, one must consider only the information and understanding that was available at the time of the invention. Nonobviousness may be established by reliance on "secondary considerations," such as the commercial success of the invention or the existence of a long-standing but unsolved problem.[20]

15.2.5 Software

There has been much debate in recent years as to whether computer software is or should be patentable. Despite the controversy, the PTO and the courts have concluded that software is patentable.[21] Many software-related patents have already been granted. Well-known examples include the Compton's multimedia patent and the Unisys patent that reportedly covers data compression in accordance with the GIF standard.[22]

The controversy surrounding software patents relates to the rule that patents are not available for abstract ideas or algorithms. Because software programs are inherently algorithmic, it was thought for many years that they could not be protected by patents. During the 1970s, the two software-related patents considered by the U.S. Supreme Court were both held unpatentable.[23]

The tide began to turn in 1981 with the case of *Diamond v. Diehr*.[24] That case involved a method for operating a rubber molding press. In accordance with the claimed method, a computer program used a formula to determine how long the rubber should be allowed to cure. The court held that the method was patentable because it was primarily directed to a physical process, namely curing rubber, to which the mathematical formula was applied.

This ruling and the decisions that followed it led the PTO to adopt a rule that software-related inventions were patentable, but only if they were applied to some physical process or thing.[25] For example, a claimed computer program might involve using a digital signal-processing algorithm to filter a heartbeat signal on a noisy electrode applied to a human chest. The electrode and the heartbeat signal are physical things, and their inclusion in the claim means that the claimed method comprises more than just a mere algorithm.

In a 1994 case, *In re Alappat*, the Court of Appeals for the Federal Circuit went even further by suggesting that any claim reciting a *programmed computer* would be patentable subject matter.[26] After all, the court reasoned, a computer is a machine, and the patent statute says that machines are patentable subject matter.[27]

After *Alapat*, it appeared that one need only couch a software invention in terms of a computer programmed in accordance with the software. A more recent case, *In re Lowry*, seems to allow even greater latitude.[28] *Lowry* involved a claim to data structures. Data structures are essentially schemes for organizing data in a computer. The court held that the claimed invention was patentable because, in addition to the data structure, the claims recited computer memory. Memory is a "thing," and, therefore, the claim was directed to patentable subject matter.

The PTO has responded to these decisions by issuing proposed examination guidelines.[29] Under these proposed guidelines, the following types of inventions are presumed to be patentable subject matter (the classes of patentable subject matter include machines, processes, and articles of manufacture):

- A computer whose actions are directed by software is a "machine."
- Computer-readable memory that can be used to direct a computer to function in a particular manner is an "article of manufacture."
- A series of steps to be performed on a computer is a "process."

Under these guidelines, a diskette containing a computer program could be patented. However, a diskette merely encoded with data representing creative or artistic expression (such as a music CD) cannot be patented.[30] Also, a compilation or arrangement of data independent of any physical element cannot be patented, nor can a process that does nothing more than manipulate abstract ideas or concepts.

15.3 The Role of Patents in Electronic Commerce

By its very nature, electronic commerce is technology intensive. Many aspects of electronic commerce can be the subject of patents. This section reviews specific examples of online patents and discusses how those patents affect end-users and manufacturers.

15.3.1 Patents That Touch Online Commerce

15.3.1.1 Interfaces. An *interface* is a connection between two devices or between a device and a person. For example, user interfaces are the graphics and command structures presented to users of software. Interfaces also exist between hardware and software. For example, an *application program interface* (API) is a set of commands used by software applications to communicate with other software.

Interface schemes can be patented in two ways. First, the graphic symbols of user interfaces can be the subject of design patents.[31] Second, the logical structure of the interface itself can be patented. For example, one patent that was issued to Apple Computer claims a user-interface method for allowing a user to traverse a hypertext database.[32]

In online commerce, some interface between the contracting parties is necessary. For example, if a business sponsored an online storefront, it would need to provide an interface to enable its customers to browse through the available merchandise and place orders. To that extent, patents on interfaces may be applicable.

The use of intellectual property rights—either patents or copyrights—to protect interface specifications is somewhat controversial.[33] Some commentators argue that if the interface of a popular program is protected, it may be impossible for other programs to be "interoperable" with the popular program. This in turn may thwart free competition to an extent not intended by intellectual property laws.

15.3.1.2 Communications Protocols. A *communications protocol* is a prearranged set of formats and procedures that computers use to exchange data.[34] For example, the Internet is a set of protocols known as *TCP/IP*.[35] These protocols enable thousands of networks connected to the Internet to exchange data.

Protocols can be used to specify matters relating to the mechanics of computer communication (such as speed, security, and error detection), as well as matters relating to the substance of the communication (such as which field of a record corresponds to quantity, and which field corresponds to price). Fundamentally, electronic commerce (as well as the entire online world) is grounded on protocols. All of the software and systems that you use to conduct online commerce will be built around a number of protocols.

Many protocols are in the public domain. However, it is possible to patent a protocol, so online activities could easily involve use of patented protocols. For example, U.S. Patent No. 5,450,425 claims a protocol for fault-tolerant communication of a data packet.

15.3.1.3 Data Compression. *Data compression* is a technique for reducing the size of data files by eliminating redundancy (such as strings of blank characters). Compression is useful for saving disk storage space, but its real value is in facilitating the online transmission of files containing digitized audio and video signals. Such files range from very large to enormous. Many communications links (such as the common telephone/ modem connection) are slow relative to the size of these files. Data compression reduces a file's size to manageable levels, allowing users to access multimedia content online without suffering inordinate delays as the content is downloaded. Compression technologies also promise real-time exchange of audio and video data, allowing computers to be used as telephones or televisions.

Although online commerce does not require data compression, as a practical matter most online traders will want to offer their customers or trading partners access to video, audio, and image files. For example, a seller may publish an online catalog featuring pictures of its products. For the time being, these multimedia offerings will require the use of data compression.

The key to mass application of data compression is standardization. Everyone must have the capability to compress and decompress images in accordance with predetermined algorithms. Accordingly, several compression formats have gained wide following, including Graphics Interface Format (GIF) and Tag Image File Format (TIFF).

Data compression techniques are patentable. One patent (the LZW patent), held by Unisys, is widely thought to cover data compression in accordance with the GIF and TIFF standards.[36] Since the LZW patent was issued in 1985, Unisys has been quietly enforcing it against developers of data compression software. In the meantime, CompuServe, a large online service provider, had been promoting GIF as a public standard for compressing images. Many developers had built GIF into their software, which was in turn used by many companies to provide online visual content on CompuServe and other networks.

In 1993, Unisys demanded that CompuServe take a license for its use of GIF. As an accommodation to the many third parties who had developed GIF-based offerings through CompuServe, the CompuServe license included a special provision whereby CompuServe had the authority to sublicense the LZW patent to those developers. In 1994, CompuServe announced that the sublicense was available—but for a fee.[37] Predictably, this infuriated developers, who felt they had been misled to believe that GIF was an open standard.[38]

Unisys has instituted a licensing program for developers of Web browsers, viewers, servers, and other software that uses GIF or TIFF compression techniques.[39] To minimize the impact of licensing on developers who may have believed GIF was a public-domain format, Unisys has publicly stated that it will not seek damages from any publisher of GIF-capable software that was distributed before 1995.[40] Moreover, publishers of such software can continue to sell products initially distributed before 1995. However, publishers cannot sell updated versions or modifications without a license.[41]

15.3.1.4 Encryption and Security Procedures. As explained in Chapter 31, encryption is a technique for encoding online messages so that they can only be read by someone having the proper code (or key). There are two popular forms of encryption—*secret key* and *public key*. The leading secret key system is DES, which is endorsed by the U.S.

government as an official standard.[42] The leading public key system is RSA, which takes its name from its inventors, Ron Rivest, Adi Shamir, and Leonard Adleman.[43]

As discussed in Chapters 4 and 31, public key encryption is a revolutionary technology that allows secure online transactions. It not only preserves the secrecy of transmissions (such as credit-card numbers), but also provides a way of verifying both the identity of the person who sent a particular message (such as purchase or payment orders) and the integrity of that message. It is no exaggeration to say that without public key encryption, online commerce over public networks such as the Internet would be unworkable.

Encryption techniques are patentable. The basic idea of public key encryption was patented in 1980, and the RSA system was patented in 1983.[44] Rights to these patents are held by Public Key Partners of Sunnyvale, California, an affiliate of RSA Data Security, Inc. (RDSI). They are widely licensed to Microsoft, Lotus, Novell, and many other major developers of tools for online communications. RDSI also offers qualified users a limited, free license to use a version of its patented encryption technique.[45]

15.3.1.5 Electronic Sales Systems. There are a number of logistical problems in selling content (such as books, software, and music) online. Many of these issues concern security—that is, ensuring that only paying customers receive the content. The technology for solving these problems may be patented.

For example, in April 1995, Interactive Gift Express, a small publicly traded marketer of flowers and gift baskets, announced that it had acquired U.S. Pat. No. 4,526,643, directed to a method for electronic distribution of information products such as software and music.[46] The patented method involves providing an authorization code to enable the software or music to be reproduced in a physical object at the point of sale. In August, 1995, the company filed suit for patent infringement against a dozen firms involved in electronic commerce.[47]

15.3.1.6 Information Processing and Retrieval. The online world is a computer environment, and as such it necessarily involves information processing, storage, and retrieval. These technologies can be patented. For example, in 1993, Compton's NewMedia announced that it had obtained U.S. Pat. No. 5,241,671 directed to a technique for searching and retrieving information from a multimedia database.[48] The announcement provoked an uproar from the multimedia industry, which believed that Compton's patent was too broad—that is, that it claimed techniques that were already known in the art.[49] The furor prompted the PTO to order a reexamination of the patent. This time, the PTO rejected Compton's claims.[50]

The subject matter of Compton's patent touches online commerce because online environments are increasingly multimedia. Apart from that, however, the patent illustrates how a new technique for information processing and retrieval—multimedia or otherwise—can be patentable.

15.3.2 Impact on End-Users

The term *end-user* for purposes of this topic means a company that trades online but does not develop the software and equipment that make online commerce possible.

In many cases, patents are drafted in such a way that they are infringed by end-users. For example, the Unisys LZW patent is infringed at the time an image is compressed or viewed. Thus, end-users themselves could be directly liable to patent owners for infringement.

In most cases, however, this infringement results from use of software or equipment purchased from a developer or other supplier. Many sales and license contracts include a provision whereby the supplier warrants to the end-user that the supplier's product does not infringe on the rights of any third party.[51] Thus, as a practical matter, it is the suppliers who are primarily concerned with, and responsible for, patent infringement. Of course, when the end-user has developed its own software or other technology, it may be solely responsible for infringement.

Accordingly, many patentees often ignore end-users and instead focus their enforcement efforts on suppliers. For example, with respect to the LZW patent, Unisys issued a press release stating:

> Organizations introducing a World Wide Web server and home page to the Internet are not expected to license the [patented] technology if they used a third-party software application to develop their server offering. Only the commercial third-party developer in that case should secure a license.[52]

Although this statement may not amount to a blanket release of end-user liability, it evidences a strategy on Unisys's part to confine its enforcement efforts to developers.

Thus, end-users who trade online using commercially available software can, as a practical matter, usually rely on the vendors either to obtain the appropriate licenses or to pay damages in the event of a patent infringement lawsuit. There are some exceptions, however.

First, large end-users should not overlook the possibility that in a dispute, they may be the "deep pocket" defendant that the patentee pursues, especially if the original vendor is defunct or unable to pay substantial damages. When such users are concerned about a specific patent (such as the LZW patent), it would be an appropriate precaution to ask a software provider to document that it has secured a suitable license from the patentee.

Second, end-users should also remember that they may be treated as developers to the extent that they produce their own infringing software or are involved in the redistribution of infringing software. Along these lines, some patents may be infringed by techniques devised by the end-user itself. In those instances, there may be no responsible vendor against which the end-user can seek indemnification.

15.3.3 Impact on Developers

Unlike end-users, developers are on the front line of patent disputes. Developers, for purposes of this discussion, would include companies who make browsers, viewers, servers, computers, and other software and equipment used in online commerce, as well as the numerous service providers who supply the communications and other infrastructure used in online commerce.

Unfortunately, developers usually learn of a potential patent problem after a product has been bought to market. If an infringement problem arises, it can often be resolved by taking a license from the patentee. Licensing is discussed in Chapter 18. In many cases, it will also be possible to redesign products so that they do not infringe.

One problem that confounds developers occurs when standards (such as protocols) that are thought to be in the public domain turn out to be covered by patents.[53] This situation apparently arose in connection with the GIF compression standard and the Unisys LZW patent, as discussed in Section 15.3.1.3. The difficulty here is that the market probably will not accept a product that does not adhere to the standard. Thus, it may be impossible to design around the patent, and therefore infringement will be inevitable.

Adverse patents held by a competitor are another problem facing developers. A competitor may be unwilling to license its patents, and instead may simply demand that the developer stop selling the infringing product. For this reason, a business may want to track its competitors' patent activity carefully to avoid infringement problems. This tracking is easily accomplished by using computerized patent databases.

On the bright side, developers should not overlook the possibility that their technology is entitled to patent protection.

15.3.4 Impact on Software Distributors

Patents affect software distributors in that software—regardless of its purpose—may be patented. The unauthorized sale or license of patented software may constitute patent infringement. Of course, this risk applies regardless of whether software is distributed by mail, online, or through retail stores.

15.4 Enforcing Patent Rights Online

15.4.1 Scope of Patentee's Rights

The patent statute allows the patentee to prevent others from making, using, selling or offering to sell, or importing any patented invention.[54] As explained above, the *patented invention* is the invention defined by the patent's claims. These rights enable a patentee to proceed against either a manufacturer (for making and selling the infringing product) or its customers (for using it). The patent owner may, under certain conditions, also prevent the importation of a product that was made outside the United States using a process patented in the United States.[55]

A person who makes, uses, sells, or imports a patented invention without permission is a *direct infringer.* The patentee can also prevent others from inducing or contributing to that direct infringement.[56] Inducement cases typically involve patents that are infringed by end-users at the encouragement or suggestion of a vendor. For example, suppose a vendor sells an instruction manual that explains how users can modify the vendor's software. If this modification infringes a patent, the end-users are the direct infringers, but the vendor is possibly liable for inducing infringement.

Contributory infringement may arise when (1) a defendant sells or imports a component that constitutes a material part of a patented invention knowing the component to be especially made or adapted for use in infringing the patent, and (2) the component is not a staple article or commodity of commerce suitable for substantial noninfringing use.[57] For example, suppose a patent claims a method of encryption that is only directly infringed by end-users. A vendor who sells security software that uses the patented method is probably contributorily liable for the end-users' infringement, unless the software has substantial noninfringing uses.

Theories of inducing infringement and contributory infringement are quite valuable in enforcing patents in an online environment because they target developers and other providers who often are more easily located and sued than direct infringers.

15.4.2 Remedies for Patent Infringement

When a patent is infringed, the patent owner can recover money damages and attorney fees, and can obtain a court order (or *injunction*) prohibiting further infringement.[58]

Damages for patent infringement can include the profits that the patentee has lost as a result of the infringement. With software-related inventions, these damages can be significant because, in calculating lost profits, only the variable costs are deducted from gross receipts.[59] Of course, the primary cost of software is the sunk development costs. The variable costs of each copy (especially with online distribution) are usually low. Thus, in some cases, lost profits of software approach the full price of the software.

Even if the patentee cannot establish its entitlement to lost profits, it may at least recover a reasonable royalty for the infringing activity.[60] In appropriate cases, these money damages can be multiplied up to three times.[61] Also, in "exceptional cases," the patentee can recover its attorney's fees.[62]

Although money damages in patent cases can be significant, an injunction can be particularly devastating because it can wipe out investments made to produce or market a product. In one dramatic case, Kodak was forced to close its entire instant photography business after it lost a patent infringement suit to Polaroid.[63]

15.4.3 Limitations of Patent Rights

There are a number of important limitations on patent rights, which, in effect, carve out the permissible uses of patented technology.

- **Claim Scope.** The principal limitation of patent rights is that they cover only the invention defined in the claims. In many cases, claim coverage is far more narrow than suggested by the patent's specification. The public is free to practice anything disclosed in the specification that is not claimed (assuming the subject matter is not claimed in another patent). Be aware, however, that in certain circumstances, patents can be reissued with broader claims. Assessments as to the scope of any potentially adverse patent should be made in consultation with a qualified patent attorney to determine whether there are other pertinent patents that should be considered.

- **Validity.** In some cases, the PTO issues patents for inventions that are not, in fact, new and nonobvious. This can occur in the online commerce field, for example, because the area is so new that it has been difficult for the PTO to accumulate a complete database of existing computer technology.[64] If challenged in court, such patents may be held invalid. Invalidity is often a successful defense against a claim of patent infringement. But a defendant has the burden of proving invalidity by clear and convincing evidence.
- **Expiration.** A utility patent expires 20 years after the date it is filed in the PTO, and a design patent expires 14 years after it is issued. Except in special circumstances, a patent term cannot be extended. Once a patent expires, the claimed invention enters the public domain.[65] However, even after a patent expires, a patented article may be protected by other rights. For example, a patented design may be protected by trademark law even after the design patent expires; likewise, a computer program that embodies a patented invention may be protected by copyright law, even after the patent for the invention expires.[66]
- **First-Sale Doctrine.** Although a patent owner has the right to exclude others from selling an invention, this right is extinguished with respect to a particular article once the article is sold. In other words, the original buyer is free to resell the article. Many technologies used online are embodied in software, the use of which typically is licensed as opposed to sold. In a software license, the first-sale doctrine does not apply, and the patentee can retain control over the disposition of the patented software.
- **Implied License.** A patent owner may be deemed to have granted implied licenses to practice a patented invention. For example, the sale of a patented article grants the original and subsequent purchasers an implied license to use the article.

15.4.4 Geographic Scope of Patent Monopoly

Online networks are typically global, and it is possible that infringements of U.S. patents may occur worldwide. As a general rule, however, a U.S. patent is enforceable only in the United States and its territories and possessions.[67] Use of the patented invention in Canada, for example, does not infringe a U.S. patent. To protect the invention in Canada or other foreign countries, the patentee must procure patents in each separate country.

There are, however, cases where a U.S. patent can reach activities outside of the United States. In particular, a U.S. patent could be infringed by a company that induces or contributes to the direct infringement of others, even if this direct infringement takes place outside the United States.[68] Such liability may apply in these cases if:

1. The defendant supplies components of a patented invention from the United States,
2. The components are combined outside the United States in a manner that would infringe the patent if such combination occurred within the United States, and
3. The defendant actively induces or knowingly contributes to the combination.[69]

For example, suppose a vendor distributes software online to persons outside the United States. The software, when loaded onto a computer, causes the computer to fall within the scope of a machine claim of an issued U.S. patent. Under these facts, the vendor could be liable for contributory infringement, even though its customers are in foreign countries.

This same theory is equally applicable to persons outside the United States who induce or contribute to infringement in the United States. For example, suppose the software from the preceding illustration is provided by a German vendor from an Internet server located in Germany. Liability for contributory infringement can arise from the importation of a component especially adapted for use in an infringement. Arguably, the German vendor is doing exactly that by transmitting the software to a location inside the United States.[70]

15.5 Obtaining a Patent

Patent rights are acquired in the United States by filing a patent application in the PTO within the one-year statutory bar period. Patents in foreign countries are similarly obtained by filing in each specific country.

15.5.1 Qualified Applicant

In the United States, a patent application can be filed only in the name of the actual inventor or inventors, and they must each sign the patent application.[71] Unless the patent application is expressly assigned by the inventors, it will be issued as a patent in the name of the inventors, who own the patent jointly. An application cannot be filed without an inventor's signature, except under special circumstances such as when the inventor is missing, dead, or refuses to cooperate with an employer or other party who is entitled to have the application filed.[72]

15.5.2 Patent Application Process

The application process begins by submitting to the PTO an application including a description (or *specification*) illustrating the best known example (or *embodiment*) of the invention, drawings, and proposed claims. Once filed, the application is assigned to an examiner, who reviews the application to determine whether it complies with applicable rules and whether the claimed invention is patentable. If the examiner rejects the application (as often happens), the applicant has at least one opportunity to amend the claims and submit arguments to overcome the rejection. The whole process takes about two years on average.

Although the law does not require that a lawyer prepare and file a patent application, the preparation and prosecution of a patent application is a difficult task subject to many complex laws and rules, and, therefore, should normally be done by a qualified patent attorney. The drawings that typically are included in the application should be drafted by a professional familiar with the legal requirements of patent drawings.

Including government filing fees and attorney fees, the preparation and prosecution of a patent application can typically cost between $5,000 and $10,000. Difficult or complex cases can be substantially more expensive. In addition, maintenance fees ranging from $480 to $2,900 must be paid 3.5, 7.5, and 11.5 years after the patent is issued.

15.5.3 Statutory Bar: Loss of Rights

Even if an invention is new and nonobvious at the time it is invented, the right to a patent will be lost forever if an application is not filed within one year after the invention is first: (1) in public use or on sale in the United States, or (2) patented or described in a printed publication anywhere in the world.[73] This deadline is called the one-year *statutory bar*. The events that trigger the bar—use, sale, patenting, and publication—are interpreted broadly by the courts. For example, placing a new software product onto the Internet for use or downloading by the public could in many cases constitute a triggering event with respect to any invention embodied in the software.

The right to a patent may also be lost if the inventor "abandons" the invention, although this rule is rarely invoked.[74]

The statutory bar rules in foreign countries are more stringent because they offer no one-year grace period. There, patent rights are generally lost if the application is not filed before the first public use or publication of the invention. However, in most countries, it is sufficient that the application was at least filed in the United States before the first public use, provided that the application is then filed in the foreign country within 12 months.

The bottom line is that patent applications should be filed as early as possible because, in many cases, the one-year statutory bar may be triggered without the inventor's knowledge. Thus, the longer one waits to file an application, the greater the chances that the statutory bar may expire.

15.5.4 Obtaining Patents in Foreign Countries

With limited exceptions (discussed in Section 15.4.4), a U.S. patent can be used only to protect an invention in the United States. To reach activities in other countries, one needs to file a patent application in each separate country. There are international treaties that facilitate this.[75] Under these treaties, applications filed abroad receive the benefit of an earlier U.S. filing date if they are filed within a specified time. In most cases, this specified time is 12 months after the U.S. filing date. This time may be considerably longer for applications filed under the Patent Cooperation Treaty (PCT).

Applications may be filed abroad after the 12-month deadline, but they will not have the benefit of the earlier U.S. filing date. Consequently, events (notably sales of the invented item) occurring after the U.S. filing date can be used by the foreign patent offices as a basis for denying an application. Thus, as a practical matter, the 12-month foreign filing period is often the inventor's only opportunity to obtain patent protection abroad.

15.6 Ownership of Patent Rights

The general rule is that inventors own the rights to their inventions until such time as they assign them. In some cases, inventors may be obligated to assign their patent rights, just as, for example, a homeowner may be obligated to sell his or her home once he or she accepts an offer. However, the obligation to assign a right is different from the actual assignment.

15.6.1 Inventions by Contractors

Many companies use independent contractors to develop technology. If the contractors do not assign the patent application to the contracting company, then the contractor—not the company—will have legal title to the issued patent. In some cases, the company may have the right to compel an assignment, but this right may require costly litigation to enforce.

To reduce this risk, some companies insist on having agreements with their contractors specifying that the company owns any inventions made by the contractors in connection with their performance of the contract. Such agreements usually require the contractors to execute any patent applications or assignments necessary to vest title in such invention in the company. When the contractor is a corporation or other entity, the contracting company should ensure that the contractor's employees and subcontractors are also similarly obligated to assign their inventions.

15.6.2 Inventions by Employees

Whether an employer owns the inventions of its employees varies from state to state. Generally speaking, the employer owns inventions made within the scope and purpose of the employee's employment.[76] Ownership is less clear when the invention is made outside the scope and purpose of employment, such as on the employee's own time. Often, employers have written agreements with their employees delineating which inventions belong to which party. Some states, such as Illinois and California, regulate the content of such agreements to prevent employers from overreaching.[77]

If an employee uses any time, material, or facilities of the employer in developing an invention, then the employer may have, at a minimum, a *shop right*.[78] A shop right is a nonexclusive, nontransferable license to the employer to use the employee's invention. The extent of shop rights also varies from state to state.

As explained earlier, the employer's claim to ownership of an invention is not the same thing as actual ownership. The employer must secure an assignment of each patent or patent application made in the name of its employees. Otherwise, legal title to the patent remains with the employee, and the employer may have to sue to acquire good title.

Endnotes

1. Los Angeles Times, April 17, 1994, at D1.

2. 35 U.S.C. § 271.

3. 35 U.S.C. § 1 *et seq.*

4. 35 U.S.C. § 154(a)(2); as discussed below, some types of patents have different terms.

5. Plant patent protection is available for the invention or discovery of a distinct and new variety of plant. The right granted by having a plant patent is the right to prevent others from asexually reproducing the plant or selling or using the plant so reproduced.

6. 35 U.S.C. § 101.

7. 35 U.S.C. § 171.

8. *See, e.g.,* U.S. Pat. Nos. D295,765 and D295,635.

9. Depending on the circumstances, however, the network could fall within the scope of the claim under the doctrine of equivalents. See Section 15.1.4.

10. *See Graver Tank & Manufacturing Co. v. Linde Air Products Co.* 339 U.S. 605, 85 U.S.P.Q. 328 (1950); *Pennwalt Corp. v. Durand-Wayland, Inc.,* 833 F.2d 931, 4 U.S.P.Q.2d 1737 (Fed. Cir. 1987).

11. For example, if a claim to a machine recited "screws" and the defendant's machine used "bolts," the defendant's machine would not literally infringe. However, a court could, depending on the circumstances, find infringement under the doctrine of equivalents.

12. 35 U.S.C. § 261.

13. 35 U.S.C. § 101.

14. *Diamond v. Chakrabarty,* 447 U.S. 303, 309 (1980).

15. *Id.*

16. *Moleculon Resp. Corp. v. CBS, Inc.,* 793 F.2d 1261 (Fed. Cir. 1986).

17. *Manual of Patent Examining Procedure* (MPEP) § 706.03(p).

18. 35 U.S.C. § 102(a).

19. 35 U.S.C. § 103.

20. *Graham v. John Deere Co.,* 383 U.S. 1 (1966).

21. *Patents in Cyberspace: Impact of Recent Federal Circuit Decisions,* The Computer Lawyer, January, 1995, at 1.

22. See Section 15.3.1.3.

23. *Gottschalk v. Benson,* 409 U.S. 63, 175 U.S.P.Q. 673 (1972); *Parker v. Flook,* 437 U.S. 584, 198 U.S.P.Q. 193 (1978).

24. *Diamond v. Diehr,* 450 U.S. 175, 209 U.S.P.Q. 1 (1981).

25. The test, known as the *Freeman-Walter-Abele* test, has two steps. Step one is to determine whether the claim recites a mathematical algorithm. If an algorithm is found, step two is to determine whether or not the algorithm is applied to physical elements or process steps. If so, then the claim is directed to patentable subject matter.

26. *In re Alappat,* 33 F.3d 1526, 31 U.S.P.Q.2d 1545 (Fed. Cir. 1994)(en banc).

27. The invention in *Alappat* was a technique used to smooth waveforms on an oscilloscope display screen. The technique was essentially to perform a series of mathematical calculations on the displayed data. The court ruled that the claim was patentable because it was directed to a "machine," which produced a useful, concrete, and tangible result.

28. *In re Lowry,* 32 F.3d 1579, 32 U.S.P.Q.2d 1031 (Fed. Cir. 1994).

29. Request for Comments on Proposed Examination Guidelines for Computer-Implemented Inventions, Patent and Trademark Office (Docket Number 95053144-5144-01) (May 30, 1995).

30. *Id.*

31. *See, e.g.,* U.S. Pat. Nos. D295,765 and D295,635.

32. U.S. Pat. No. 5,408,655; *see also* U.S. Pat. Nos. 5,448,695 and 5,347,658.

33. *See* J. Band and M. Katoh, *Interfaces on Trial* (Westview Press, 1995).

34. H. Hahan and R. Stout, *The Internet Complete Reference* (Osbourne McGraw-Hill, 1994), at 30.

35. *Id.*

36. U.S. Pat. No. 4,558,302.

37. P. Lewis, *Software Companies Upset by Demands for Royalties,* New York Times, Jan. 5, 1995, at D1.

38. *Id.*

39. *Unisys Clarifies Policy Regarding Patent Use in On-line Service Offerings,* Unisys Press Release dated January 6, 1995.

40. *Id.*

41. *Id.*

42. National Institute of Standards and Technology (NIST), FIPS. Publication 46-1: Data Encryption Standard, January 22, 1988.

43. *Answers to Frequently Asked Questions About Today's Cryptography,* RSA Data Security, Inc., Oct. 5, 1993, p. 7.

44. U.S. Patent Nos. 4,200,770, 4,218,582, and 4,405,829.

45. *Ciphertext,* RSA Data Security, Inc., Summer 1994, Vol. 2, No. 1, at 12.

46. Business Wire, April 27, 1995.

47. New York Times, Aug. 28, 1995, at D1.

48. New York Times, Nov. 28, 1993, at 3-10.

49. J. P. Milliot, *USPTO Again Rejects Compton's Patent Claims,* Forbes ASAP, Nov. 7, 1994, at 15.

50. M. Giarratena, *Compton's New Media Patent Prompts Multimedia Patent Scrutiny and Changes at the Patent Office,* Multimedia and Technology Licensing Law Report, Feb., 1995, at 4.

51. *See, e.g.,* Uniform Commercial Code § 2-312.

52. Unisys Press Release, *supra* note 39.

53. H. Beck, *Patent Issues in Establishing Technological Standards,* Computer Law Strategist, July, 1995, Vol. 8, No. 3, p. 1.

54. 35 U.S.C. § 271.

55. 35 U.S.C. § 271(g).

56. 35 U.S.C. §§ 271(b) and 271(c).

57. 35 U.S.C. § 271(c).

58. 35 U.S.C. § 283.

59. *Paper Converting Mach. Co. v. Magna-Graphics Corp.,* 745 F.2d 11, 223 U.S.P.Q. 591 (Fed. Cir. 1984).

60. 35 U.S.C. § 284.

61.   35 U.S.C. § 284; generally, enhanced damages are awarded only in cases of willful infringement.

62.   35 U.S.C. § 285; exceptional cases include cases of willful infringement and cases involving inequitable conduct by the patentee in obtaining the patent.

63.   Forbes ASAP, March 27, 1993, at 58.

64.   T. Riordian, *A Consultant Singles Out for Scorn Two Patents Recently Granted to Big Computer Companies*, N.Y. Times, March 20, 1995, at D2.

65.   *Kohler Co. v. Moen, Inc.*, 12 F.3d 632, 29 U.S.P.Q.2d 1993 1241 (7th Cir.); utility patents issued before June 8, 1995 expire the later of 20 years after their filing date or 17 years after issuance.

66.   *Id.*

67.   35 U.S.C. § 271; but *see* 35 U.S.C. § 105 ("any invention made, used or sold in outer space on a space object or component thereof under the jurisdiction or control of the United States shall be considered to be made, used or sold within the United States for the purposes of this [statute]. . . .").

68.   35 U.S.C. § 271(f).

69.   Specifically, under 35 U.S.C. 271(f), this requires either that: (i) the defendant supplies at least a substantial portion of the components of the invention and actively induces the combination, or (ii) the defendant supplies a component that is especially made or adapted for use in the invention and not a staple article of commerce suitable for substantial noninfringing use.

70.   35 U.S.C. § 271(c). In an online environment it may be debatable which party—the U.S. customer or the German vendor—is "importing" the software into the United States.

71.   35 U.S.C. §§ 111, 115.

72.   35 U.S.C. §§ 117, 118.

73.   35 U.S.C. § 102(b).

74.   35 U.S.C. § 102(c).

75.   Paris Convention for the Protection of Industrial Property; Patent Cooperation Treaty.

76.   *Arachnid, Inc. v. Merit Indus., Inc.*, 939 F.2d 1574, 19 U.S.P.Q.2d 1513 (Fed. Cir. 1991).

77.   *See, e.g.,* Illinois Patent Act, 765 I.L.C.S. 1060/2.

78.   *McElmurry v. Arkansas Power & Light Co.*, 995 F.2d 1576, 27 U.S.P.Q. 2d 1129 (Fed. Cir. 1993).

16
Right of Publicity

Elizabeth S. Perdue

Whenever digital content includes a person's identity, such as a name, image, or voice, right of publicity issues will arise. The right of publicity exists separate and apart from copyright rights. Thus, individuals have certain rights to control how their identity is used in a work, even if someone else owns the copyright. Those who operate in the online world must become knowledgeable about the right of publicity if they are to avoid liability.

16.1 What Is the Right of Publicity?

Every person has the right to control and profit from the commercial value of his or her own identity. This is the right of publicity. Thus, if an online communication uses a person's identity for commercial purposes, that person may be able to object.

Technically, all individuals have a right of publicity, although, for the most part, celebrities are the ones who invoke it. There are several rationales behind the right of publicity:

1. It protects the financial interests of those whose livelihoods are based on their fame.
2. It allows them to protect their reputations, by helping them prevent unauthorized endorsements and other misuses.
3. It prevents unauthorized people from unfairly profiting from the efforts and reputations of others.

The right of publicity arises under state law, which differs from state to state.[1] This chapter discusses general legal principles; for specifics, refer to the law of the appropriate state.

The right of publicity protects against the unauthorized use of a person's identity or persona in a way that is likely to cause harm to its commercial value. Protected types of "identities" and "personas" include: names (including nicknames, professional names, or group names), images (photographs and videos), likenesses (portraits and drawings), voices, imitations, or impersonations (including soundalikes).

For example, courts have found infringement in the following types of cases:

- Printing baseball players' photographs on chewing gum cards.[2]
- Using the phrase "Here's Johnny" as part of a name for a portable toilet.[3]
- Using a Jackie Onassis lookalike in a Christian Dior ad.[4]
- Using advertising posters of the defendants photographed so as to look as much as possible like members of the rock group The Beatles.[5]
- Using rock stars' names on T-shirts.[6]
- Combining the head of Cary Grant with the body of a model, as part of a fashion article.[7]
- Imitating Groucho Marx's "persona" in a play.[8]
- Using a soundalike of singer Tom Waits in a Frito-Lay commercial and of Bette Midler in a car commercial.[9]
- Running an ad showing a robot dressed in a wig and costume resembling Vanna White, posed next to a game board like the Wheel of Fortune.[10]

Thus, anyone who engages in online publishing or advertising, be it through a Web site or distribution of information or publications online, must be sensitive to the right of publicity. It is relatively easy to convert an article, photograph, or video into digital form and transmit it online. However, unless appropriate permission is obtained, such use may constitute an infringement with respect to the persons depicted or identified.

16.2 First Amendment Exception

Like all other property rights in information, an individual's right of publicity is not absolute. A person's identity may be used in some cases, even if technically for commercial purposes. This exception is based on the right of free expression under the First Amendment of the U.S. Constitution. News, political commentary, satire, and other communications of public interest enjoy this privileged status. That is why newspapers, as well as magazines such as *People* or the *National Enquirer,* are able to publish photographs and other personal details without permission and without infringing rights of publicity.[11]

To determine whether a work is "privileged" under the First Amendment, the courts apply a balancing test to the specific facts and circumstances, weighing the competing interests of the individual's right of publicity against the benefits to society of news dissemination and free expression. Whether the use is acceptable depends upon where it falls in the spectrum ranging from "news" (such as current events and political commentary) and "public interest" (such as fiction and satire) to "commercial speech" (such as advertising).

In determining where a work falls in the spectrum, courts ask: What is the work's primary "message"? If the message is "buy" (for example, using a picture of basketball star Michael Jordan on a box of Wheaties or a Web site promoting the cereal), the work is commercial speech and entitled to little protection. In other words, the publishers must get Michael Jordan's permission.

If the message is "news" in the sense of political and current events (for example, using a picture of Michael Jordan in an online news account of his return to the Chicago Bulls), the work is entitled to a higher, almost total, degree of protection. No permission is required.[12]

If the message is "public interest" (for example, a *People* magazine story about Michael Jordan), the work is also entitled to a high degree of protection. "Public interest" is an expansive category and has been defined in broad and far-reaching terms. It is not limited to the dissemination of news, but includes all types of factual, educational, and historical data, or even entertainment and amusement, of interest to the public.

There is, however, one important caveat: to fall within the First Amendment's protection, there must be a reasonable relationship between the identity of a person and the subject of the story. The use must be legitimately related to the story's information value and may not be a mere disguised commercialization of a person's identity.

Using a person's name or photograph in an advertisement may also be protected as long as it is reasonably related to news or other matters of public interest. In one case, for example, Delphi Internet Services Corporation was allowed to use an outlandish, bare-butt photograph of controversial radio talk show celebrity Howard Stern in an advertisement for an online bulletin board service. Delphi had set up the bulletin board to debate Stern's own political candidacy for governor.[13] The court acknowledged that Stern's name and photograph were used without his permission and for advertising purposes. However, the court held that Delphi's service was analogous to that of a news vendor or book store. The incidental use of Stern's photograph in an advertisement by a news disseminator did not violate his right of publicity or privacy. As the court pointed out, "it is the purpose of the advertisement that determines whether it is protected, not whether the defendant has permission to use the likeness. The newsworthy use of a private person's name or photograph does not give rise to a cause of action . . . as long as the use is reasonably related to a matter of public interest."[14]

16.3 Who Is Protected by the Right of Publicity?

The right of publicity is most often asserted by celebrities. This is because the right of publicity relates to the commercial value of a person's identity. A noncelebrity's name, likeness, or voice will be likely to have little commercial value.[15] However, even a relatively unknown person's identity can have economic value and be protected.

In one case, for example, the plaintiff was the father of eight children, who had secured a home using the defendant's real estate services. When the real estate firm used his name and story in an advertisement without permission, he sued and won.[16]

Generally, corporations or other entities do not have a right of publicity.[17] However, individuals sometimes transfer or license their publicity rights to a corporation, which will then be able to enforce those rights.[18] Moreover, the right of publicity has been extended to musical groups that have a "persona."[19]

16.4 Does the Right of Publicity Continue After Death?

If the right of publicity ended with a celebrity's death, it would be easy to avoid problems by using only names or pictures of the departed. Unfortunately, the law in this area differs from state to state. In some states, the right survives death; in others it does not.[20]

In the majority of states, the right of publicity continues after death. The length of time it survives also differs from state to state: time periods range from 10 years to 100 years to forever. In at least one state, the right survives only if the person exploited his or her identity while alive.[21]

The minority position is that a person's right of publicity does not survive death.[22] In states applying that rule, once a person dies, others are free to use his or her identity without violating any right of publicity.

While the right of publicity differs from state to state, most online communications transcend state boundaries. To be safe it may be necessary to follow the law of the most restrictive state.

Endnotes

1. Twenty-four states recognize a right of publicity. Eleven of those states protect it by common law: Connecticut, Georgia, Hawaii, Illinois, Michigan, Minnesota, Missouri, New Jersey, Ohio, Pennsylvania, and Utah. Nine states protect it by statute: Kentucky, Massachusetts, Nebraska, Nevada, New York, Oklahoma, Rhode Island, Tennessee, and Virginia. Four states have both statutes and common law: California, Florida, Texas, and Wisconsin.

2. *Haelan Laboratories, Inc. v. Topps Chewing Gum, Inc.,* 202 F.2d 866 (2d Cir.), *cert. denied,* 346 U.S. 816 (1953).

3. *Carson v. Here's Johnny Portable Toilets, Inc.,* 498 F. Supp. 71 (E.D. Mich. 1980), *aff'd and rev'd in part,* 698 F.2d 831 (6th Cir. 1983).

4. *Onassis v. Christian Dior-New York, Inc.,* 472 N.Y.S.2d 254 (N.Y. Sup. Ct. 1984), *aff'd,* 110 A.D.2d 1095 (N.Y. App. Div. 1985).

5. *Apple Corp., Ltd. v. A.D.P.R., Inc.,* 843 F. Supp. 342, 30 U.S.P.Q.2d 1372, 1376 (M.D. Tenn. 1993), relying on *Onassis v. Christian Dior-New York, Inc., supra.*

6. *Bi-Rite Enterprises, Inc. v. Button Master,* 555 F. Supp. 1188 (S.D.N.Y. 1983).

7. *Grant v. Esquire, Inc.,* 367 F. Supp. 876 (S.D.N.Y. 1973) (remanded for review of First Amendment issues).

8. *Groucho Marx Prods. v. Day & Night Company,* 523 F. Supp. 485 (S.D.N.Y. 1981), *rev'd on other grounds,* 689 F.2d 317 (2d Cir. 1982). The case was dismissed on appeal because under California law at the time, the right of publicity did not survive Groucho Marx's death. See Section 16.4.

9. *Waits v. Frito-Lay, Inc.,* 978 F.2d 1093 (9th Cir. 1992); *Midler v. Ford Motor Co.,* 849 F.2d 460 (9th Cir. 1988). Until the Midler case, soundalikes were not traditionally protected under the right of publicity.

10. *White v. Samsung Electronics America, Inc.,* 971 F.2d 1295 (9th Cir. 1992), *reh'g denied en banc,* 989 F.2d 1512 (9th Cir. 1993), *cert. denied,* 113 S. Ct. 2443 (1993).

11. Of course, if a magazine published a photograph without obtaining the copyright rights from the photographer, there could be a separate copyright violation.

12. Again, copyright rights may require separate permission from the photographer.

13. *Stern v. Delphi Internet Services Corp.,* 626, N.Y.S.2d 694, N.Y. Misc. LEXIS 197 (N.Y. Sup. Ct. 1995).

14. *Id.* at 698.

15. But see Section 17.2.2 regarding invasion of one's right of privacy by misappropriation of a name or likeness for commercial purposes.

16. *See, e.g., Canessa v. J.I. Kislak, Inc.,* 233 A. 2d 62 (N.J. 1967).

17. *See Rouch v. Hite,* 5 Media L. Rptr. 2069, (N.Y. Sup. Ct. 1979); *Eagles Eye, Inc. v. Ambler Fashion Shop, Inc.,* 627 F. Supp. 856 (E.D. Pa. 1985).

18. *See, e.g., Bi-Rite Enterprises, Inc. v. Button Master,* 555 F. Supp. 1188 (S.D.N.Y. 1983); *Cepeda v. Swift & Co.,* 415 F.2d 1205 (8th Cir. 1969). A New York court has also held that one person's right of publicity may be marital property, subject to equitable distribution on divorce. *Elkus v. Elkus,* 572 N.Y.S.2d 901 (N.Y. App. Div. 1991) (Opera singer Fredericke von Stade). *See also Apple Corps., Ltd. v. A.D.P.R., Inc.,* 843 F. Supp. 342, 30 U.S.P.Q.2d 1372 (M.D. Tenn. 1993) (noting that the rights of publicity of the Beatles music group and of its former members individually are owned by plaintiff Apple Corps., Ltd.); *Factors Etc., Inc. v. Pro Arts, Inc.,* 652 F.2d 278, 279 (2d Cir. 1981) (noting that Elvis Presley formed a corporation and assigned it exclusive ownership of all rights to use for commercial purposes his name and likeness).

19. *See, e.g., Bi-Rite Enterprises, Inc. v. Button Master,* 555 F. Supp. 1188 (S.D.N.Y. 1983); *Apple Corps., Ltd. v. A.D.P.R., Inc.,* 843 F.Supp 342, 20 U.S.P.Q.2d 1372, 1375–1376 (M.D. Tenn. 1993) [holding that the stage name of a group of individuals——in that case the Beatles——is entitled to the same protection as the name of one of the individuals that composed that group, and concluding that defendant's use of the name "The Beatles" in its advertising and promotion materials violated the Tennessee Personal Rights Protection Act, Tenn. Code Ann. § 47-25-1105(a)].

20. See generally Bangman, *A Descendable Right of Publicity: Has the Time Finally Come for a National Standard?* 17 Pepperdine L. Rev. 933 (1990).

21. The "exploitation during life" requirement was applied at various times in a number of states, but was later rejected in most, by statute or case law.

22. At this writing, Ohio and New York appear to be the only jurisdictions rejecting the survival of rights of publicity. *Reeves v. United Artists,* 572 F. Supp. 1231 (N.D. Ohio 1983), *aff'd,* 765 F.2d 79 (6th Cir. 1985) (federal court interpreting Ohio law); *Pirone v. MacMillan, Inc.,* 894 F.2d 579 (2d Cir. 1990).

17
Right of Privacy

Thomas J. Smedinghoff

Publishing content that includes a person's identity—such as a name, image, or voice—or communicating information about an individual, may raise right of privacy issues. Generally, persons have certain rights to control the use of information about them and the use of their identity, even if someone else owns the copyright to the work in which the information appears. Thus, in many situations the right of privacy has an important impact on online communications.

17.1 The Many Aspects of Privacy

The right of privacy is a concept that is used in a variety of ways to mean a variety of different things. Moreover, some aspects of privacy are protected or regulated by law, whereas others are not. Thus, it is important to understand the different things that can be discussed in the name of "privacy," and how they affect one's right to use, or control the use of, online information.

Generally, the following aspects of an individual's right of privacy are important in the context of rights in electronic information:

- **Privacy of a Person's Persona.** Certain privacy rights attach to a person's persona—that is, a person's name, identity, photograph, voice, and so forth. Any misuse of that persona can constitute an invasion of that right of privacy.
- **Privacy of Data About a Person.** Privacy rights can also attach to information about a person that is collected and used by others. This might include, for example, information about a person's spending habits, medical history, religious or political affiliations, tax records, employment records, insurance records, criminal records, and the like. Misuse of this information by collecting organizations or their customers has often been a source of controversy, and most recently has been the subject of a new Directive issued by the European Union.
- **Privacy of a Person's Communications.** There is also, in certain situations, a right of privacy with respect to online communications sent to or from an individual. Thus, in certain circumstances, monitoring or disclosing the contents of an electronic communication by anyone other than the sender or the intended recipient can constitute an invasion of privacy.

- **Anonymity.** Finally, there is the ultimate form of privacy—anonymity. Anonymity often plays an important role in online electronic communications. The extent to which anonymity is a right, and ought to be respected, is also the subject of much controversy.

17.2 Privacy of a Person's Persona

The right of privacy with respect to a person's persona is a common-law right based on the general principle that each person has the "right to be let alone."[1] In some states, it is also protected by statute. In either case, the rules regarding this right of privacy will vary from state to state.

Essentially, there are four types of right of privacy violations with respect to one's persona:[2]

- Publicity that places a person in a *false light*,[3]
- *Misappropriation* of a person's name or likeness for commercial purposes,[4]
- Public disclosure of embarrassing *private facts*,[5] and
- *Intrusion* upon a person's solitude.[6]

This aspect of the right of privacy is in some ways similar to the right of publicity (see Chapter 16), but it differs in one vital respect. The right of privacy generally protects against personal embarrassment and intrusion, while the right of publicity protects a person's commercial interests in his or her identity. The right of privacy also differs from defamation (see Chapter 21) in that it can be violated by the publication of true information, while defamation typically involves false information. Truth is a defense to defamation, but not to a violation of rights of privacy or publicity.

17.2.1 False Light

The first type of invasion of privacy involves a publication that places a person in a *false light* in a manner that is highly offensive to a reasonable person.

This can occur in a variety of ways, including adding false material to a true report, distorting facts or images, omitting relevant details, or by attempting to fictionalize a recognizable person. The following are examples of cases where courts have found right of privacy violations based on placing a person in a false light:

- Using stock footage of a Mardi Gras parade, with recognizable people, as incidental background to an adult film.[7]
- Publishing a book that contained a fictionalized (but recognizable) portrayal of a psychologist who conducted nude encounter sessions.[8]
- Using the photograph of a woman to illustrate an article about a mother who abandoned her child.[9]
- Using the photograph of a woman in conjunction with two newspaper articles on the subject of neighborhood prostitution, when in fact the woman had no connection with prostitution.[10]

- Televising a report on "arson for profit" that implicated an apartment building's manager by displaying his knowledge of arson schemes, but omitting the context of his remarks.[11]

Because of the nature of digital information—which allows the combination of different images, sounds, and information in creative or unusual ways—there is great potential for creating works or images that place someone in a false light. For example, combining a person's face with an offensive picture of another's body, or combining a person's picture with an offensive setting or with offensive sounds, could be privacy violations. In combining or creating images, it is important to view the creation from the point of view of the person depicted: If the person is placed in an offensive or false light, and the newsworthiness does not outweigh the individual's interests,[12] it could be a violation of the right of privacy.

17.2.2 Misappropriation

Another type of right of privacy violation involves *misappropriation* of a person's name or likeness, usually for commercial purposes. This also is similar to the right of publicity (discussed in Chapter 16), but protects against injuries to a person's feelings or dignity, while the right of publicity protects the commercial value of a person's identity.[13] In particular, whereas the right of publicity protects an individual's right *to profit from* commercial use of his or her name or likeness, the right of privacy protects an individual's interest *in avoiding* the public limelight.

There are three elements to a misappropriation claim:

1. That the defendant appropriated the plaintiff's name or likeness for the value associated with it, and not in an incidental manner or for a newsworthy purpose;
2. That the plaintiff can be identified from the publication; and
3. That there was some advantage or benefit to the defendant.[14]

The following are examples of cases where misappropriation existed:

- Use of a person's photograph to advertise insurance[15]
- An advertisement for Christian Dior using a Jackie Onassis lookalike[16]
- Inclusion of a person's name in a printed advertisement stating that he was a satisfied user of defendant's photocopiers[17]
- Unauthorized use of plaintiff's nickname "Crazylegs" on a product[18]

17.2.3 Private Facts

An individual's privacy rights can also be violated by the disclosure of private facts about a person, if the information disclosed would be highly offensive to a reasonable person. Truth is not a defense.[19] As one court has noted, "even people who have nothing rationally to be ashamed of can be mortified by the publication of intimate details of their life."[20] Where the information is publicly available, however, courts generally find there is no invasion of privacy.[21]

Likewise, if the information is newsworthy, courts will balance the offensiveness of the activity against the newsworthiness of the facts revealed. If the public's interest in the news outweighs the damage to the individual, there is no privacy violation.[22]

17.2.4 Intrusion

The right of privacy also includes the right not to have others intrude on one's solitude or private affairs, if the intrusion would be highly offensive to a reasonable person.[23] Generally, cases involving intrusion relate to improper news gathering practices, such as illegal surveillance or trespass. For example, a reporter who uses fraud to obtain access to someone's home to take photographs,[24] or who violates federal or state laws against wiretapping[25] or interception of electronic communications (discussed in Section 17.4) may be liable for an invasion of privacy.

Intrusive invasion of privacy may also occur through the use of information in violation of the conditions of an individual's consent, if the result is an intrusion into the subject's private affairs. For example, if a person permits the use of a photograph based on the condition that the image be shown only in a certain way, there could be an invasion of privacy if the publisher does not comply with the conditions. In one case, for example, an AIDS patient gave permission to use his image in unidentifiable silhouette; violation of this condition was a privacy violation.[26] Similarly, in a case involving Jackie Onassis, invasion of privacy was found when a photographer violated a court ordered restriction on the distance from which he could photograph her.[27]

An interesting example of a claim for invasion of privacy by intrusion was a class action suit brought by American Express cardholders against American Express Company.[28] The case was based on a practice by American Express of categorizing and ranking its cardholders based on spending habits, and then renting this information to participating merchants as part of a targeted joint marketing and sales program. Apparently American Express would analyze where its cardholder members shop and how much they spend, and also consider behavioral characteristics and spending histories. It would then offer to create a list of cardholders who would most likely shop in a particular store and rent that list to the merchant. It also offered to create lists that target cardholders who purchase specific types of items, such as fine jewelry.

The cardholders alleged that this practice intruded into their seclusion and thus constituted an invasion of their right of privacy. The court dismissed the claims, however, on the ground that there was no unauthorized intrusion or prying into the plaintiff's seclusion. The alleged wrongful actions involved American Express's practice of renting lists that it compiled from information contained in their own records. As the court pointed out, "by using the American Express card, a cardholder is voluntarily, and necessarily, giving information to defendants that, if analyzed, will reveal a cardholder's spending habits and shopping preferences. We cannot hold that a defendant has committed an unauthorized intrusion by compiling the information voluntarily given to it and then renting its compilation."[29]

17.3 Privacy of Data About a Person

Data about individuals is collected by numerous government agencies and private organizations. Government agencies collect extensive information about individuals through military records, social security records, medicare payments, tax payments, and the like. Similarly, private entities such as banks, credit-card companies, stores, insurance companies, and credit-reporting agencies maintain extensive databases of information about individuals. Computer technology enhances not only the collection and storage of this information, but also its compilation and cross referencing. Moreover, with the advent of online communications, this information is readily communicated both to those who have a legitimate need to know it, and to others who may misuse it.

In the United States, there is no single statute or regulation that governs the collection, communication, and use of all types of information about individuals. To the extent that individuals have a right of privacy with respect to this information, it is usually provided by a limited statute that applies to a specific entity (such as the government) or to specific industries (such as the banking industry, credit-reporting industry, etc.). Thus, the legality of the online collection and communication of personal data must be evaluated in the context of any such limited law that may exist.

17.3.1 Privacy Act of 1974

The Privacy Act of 1974 imposes limits on the collection and use of personal information by federal government agencies.[30] It does not apply to the collection of personal information by private entities.

The Privacy Act imposes on government agencies the responsibility to "collect, maintain, use, or disseminate any record of identifiable personal information in a manner that assures that such action is for a necessary and lawful purpose, that the information is current and accurate for its intended use, and that adequate safeguards are provided to prevent misuse of such information."[31]

Essentially, the Privacy Act seeks to give individuals a certain degree of control over the use of information that the federal government possesses about them. Thus, although there are a number of exceptions, the Privacy Act generally prohibits any government agency from disclosing any record relating to an individual without the individual's consent.[32] In other words, the individual who is the subject of data maintained by the federal government retains certain rights to control the use, by the federal government, of that data. There are, of course, numerous exceptions in the statute that allow government the use and disclosure of data without consent. Nonetheless, the general principle involves a statutory recognition that individuals have certain rights with respect to personal data held by the federal government.

17.3.2 Financial Information

Extensive financial information about individuals is routinely gathered and disseminated by many types of financial institutions. This includes banks, credit-card companies, credit-reporting agencies, mortgage holders, savings and loan associations, credit-card authorization services, debt collection agencies, and electronic funds transfer systems (such as automated teller machines, point-of-sale systems, check guaranty systems, telephone transfers, and home banking systems).

This information can often provide a rather detailed profile about an individual. As one Supreme Court Justice has noted:

> In a sense a person is defined by the checks he writes. By examining them [one] gets to know his doctors, lawyers, creditors, political allies, social connections, religious affiliation, educational interests, the papers and magazines he reads, and so on *ad infinitum*. . . . [T]he banking transactions of an individual give a fairly accurate account of his religion, ideology, opinions, and interests.[33]

As a general matter, there are not any universal limitations on the use of this information. However, there are some statutes regulating certain uses of information by certain entities. For example, the Fair Credit Reporting Act[34] regulates the collection and use of personal data by credit-reporting agencies. The Equal Credit Opportunity Act[35] prohibits creditors from gathering certain types of information from credit applicants—such as sex, race, color, religion, national origin, birth control practices, or child-bearing plans.[36] The Federal Right to Financial Privacy Act of 1978[37] limits the ability of financial institutions to disclose customer information to agencies of the federal government.

Several states have also enacted legislation addressing limited aspects of financial privacy.[38] For example, several states have bank records statutes that prohibit financial institutions from disclosing financial records of a customer to a third party without the customer's consent.

17.3.3 Health and Medical Records

Records relating to the physical and mental health of individuals are collected by numerous health-care professionals, including physicians, dentists, nurses, hospitals, and other health-care workers and institutions. The information is compiled for, or used by, insurers, employers, schools, credit agencies, and numerous other entities. In many cases, the information can be quite sensitive. Its use is governed by some federal, state, and local statutes, ordinances, and regulations. However, there are currently no comprehensive laws regarding medical records privacy, and the laws that do exist do not generally prohibit collecting, sharing, and selling private medical information.

Generally, medical records about an individual are owned (at least in a physical sense) by the doctor, dentist, or hospital that produced them.[39] Courts have also recognized that, although the subject of a medical record may have a right of access to that information, he or she does not own the actual record.[40] But although it is generally true that medical records are owned by the person or institution that recorded them,[41] it is also clear that the subject of the record has a legal interest in it. This interest apparently allows the subject to control disposition of the record, at least for as long as the health information is useful. It may include, for example, the right to limit the dissemination of information from the record, and the right to control, within limits, where the physical record will be sent.[42]

Several states also have medical records statutes that allow individuals to have access to their medical records. Some of these statutes limit the use and disclosure of medical or mental health records. There is also a federal health research data statute that prohibits disclosure of data collected by the National Centers for Health Services Research and for health statistics in any way that would identify an individual.

17.3.4 Insurance Records

The insurance industry collects, maintains, and uses a vast amount of information about persons with whom it does business. As a general rule, the use of this information is not heavily regulated. However, some states have enacted insurance records statutes that require insurers to provide general information about their personal data collection, use, and dissemination practices to applicants and policyholders, and regulate or prohibit the disclosure of information collected about individuals.

17.3.5 Employment Records

Employers maintain numerous forms of information regarding their employees. Maintenance of some information is required by law (e.g., equal employment reporting data); other information is maintained to meet specific needs of the employer. In addition to basic personal information, salary history, educational background, and medical history, such records may include drug and alcohol testing, AIDS testing, and psychological testing. Again, although the collection and use of some of this information is regulated by statute (for example, specific statutes relating to the use of AIDS-related information), for the most part, employer use of this information is unregulated by privacy statute or regulation (although its use may be subject to sanction via the law of defamation, invasion of privacy rights, or some other legal theory).

17.3.6 Other Privacy Legislation

Several other federal and state statutes have been enacted to provide limited privacy rights in specific situations. For example, the Federal Cable Communications Policy Act prohibits a cable television company from using its cable system to collect personal information about its subscribers without their consent, and generally bars the cable operator from disclosing such data. It also requires cable television operators to inform their subscribers about the nature of the personal data collected, data disclosure practices, and subscriber rights to inspect and correct errors in such data.

The Family Educational Rights and Privacy Act permits a student or the parent of a minor student to inspect and challenge the accuracy and completeness of educational records which concern the student. It also prohibits schools receiving public funds from using or disclosing the contents of a student's records without the consent of the student or the parent of a minor student.

The Video Privacy Protection Act prohibits video tape sale or rental companies from disclosing customer names and addresses, and the subject matter of their purchases or rentals for direct marketing use.

17.3.7 European Privacy Directive

In Europe, privacy rights in information about individuals has received much broader protection than it has in the United States. Moreover, this protection applies not only to the collection, maintenance, and use of information about individuals, but also to the electronic communication of such information across national borders (see Section 25.5).

In October 1995, the Council of the European Union formally adopted a Directive on "the Protection of Individuals with regard to the Processing of Personal Data and on the Free Movement of Such Data." This Directive, which member countries have three years to implement formally through appropriate legislation, seeks to protect individual privacy by prohibiting the improper collection, use, and communication of data relating to individuals. In doing so, the Directive seeks to protect certain fundamental rights of individuals, while at the same time ensuring the free flow of personal data within countries comprising the European Union.

The provisions of the Directive are rather broad and encompass virtually any information about an identifiable individual. It regulates all forms of processing of personal data, including data collection, recording, storage, adaptation, retrieval, use, making data available, or destruction of data. Accordingly, it is clear that the online electronic collection of data, recording of data, retrieval of data, dissemination of data, and so forth, are covered by the provisions of the Directive.

Persons who collect and maintain personal data (*data controllers*) must abide by four key areas of responsibility: *data quality, lawful processing, sensitive data,* and *notification.* With respect to *data quality,* a data controller must ensure that personal data is processed fairly and lawfully; that it is collected and processed only for specified, explicitly legitimate purposes; that what is collected is not excessive in relation to the purpose for which it was collected; that the data is accurate and kept up to date; and that it is kept no longer than necessary for the purpose for which it was collected.

The obligation to *process data lawfully* means the data may be processed only

1. If the data subject has consented,
2. If it is necessary in relation to entering into performance of a contract, or
3. If it is necessary in the pursuit of the legitimate interest of the person controlling the data.

The processing of sensitive data is generally forbidden. *Sensitive data* includes that relating to racial or ethnic origin, political opinions, religious or philosophical beliefs, trade-union membership, health information, or sexual-related information. There are, however, exceptions, including consent, vital interests, health care, and so on.

Finally, the data controller is obligated to provide the subject of the data with *notice* of

1. The identity of the data controller,
2. The intended purposes of the processing, and
3. Any other information that may be necessary to ensure that the obtaining and processing is fair (e.g., who will receive the data and what rights the data subject has).

Individuals about whom data is collected have three fundamental rights. First, they have a right of access—that is, the right to know whether or not data about them is being processed, communication in an intelligible form of the data processed, and knowledge of the logic involved in the automatic processing of data relating to them. Second, they have a right to correct or erase incomplete, inaccurate, or unlawfully processed data; and a right to require the data controller to notify any third party to whom the data has been disclosed of any such correction. Finally, where a person has a compelling and legitimate ground, he or she may object to the processing of personal data. A data subject may also object to the processing of personal data for the purposes of direct marketing.

In each European Union member state, a supervisory authority will be responsible for monitoring the application of national data protection laws.

A key provision of the data protection Directive relates to transborder data flow. According to Article 25 of the Directive, personal data may not be transferred to a country outside of the EU unless the country to which the data is sent ensures an adequate level of protection. This is discussed in Section 25.5.

17.4 Privacy of a Person's Online Communications

The prior sections have discussed the right of privacy as it relates to information about a person or the use of his or her persona. These rights, to the extent that they exist, restrain the ability of people or entities to communicate information relating to another person.

In addition, however, there is a right of privacy that protects a person's own online electronic communications, regardless of the subject matter. This right is provided through the federal Electronic Communications Privacy Act (ECPA).[43]

The ECPA protects all forms of electronic communications—telephone voice communications as well as computer-to-computer digital communication such as e-mail and messages stored in electronic bulletin boards. It was enacted to address "the growing problem of unauthorized persons deliberately gaining access to, and sometimes tampering with, electronic or wire communications that are not intended to be available to the public."[44]

The ECPA applies both to the government and private persons and entities. It is relatively complex, and includes a variety of exceptions. The two key issues that it addresses, however, are (1) interception and disclosure of electronic communications, and (2) unlawful access to stored electronic communications.

17.4.1 Interception of Electronic Communications

The ECPA generally prohibits any person from intentionally intercepting an electronic communication, or from disclosing the contents of any intercepted electronic communication.[45] This prohibition applies not only to those who seek to break into an electronic communications system (such as hackers), but also to those who own and operate such systems (such as an Internet access provider, a private network operator, the sysop of a computer bulletin board, and the like).

However, this prohibition does not prohibit an employee or agent of a provider of an electronic communication service from intercepting, disclosing, or using the communication in the normal course of his or her employment while engaged in any activity that is necessarily incident to the rendition of the service or to the protection of the rights or property of the provider of that service.[46] This has significant implications for employer monitoring of e-mail, which are discussed in Section 26.2.

17.4.2 Accessing Stored Electronic Communications

The ECPA also prohibits any person from unlawfully and intentionally accessing a stored electronic communication without authorization.[47] The legislative history makes clear that if an authorized user of an electronic communications service exceeds the scope of his or her authorized access, that will also constitute a violation of the statute.[48]

The ECPA also prohibits any person or entity who provides an electronic communication service to the public from divulging the contents of any communication stored on the system (other than to the intended addressee, and other limited exceptions).[49] But the ECPA does not provide users of a system with a right of privacy as against the operator of the system, at least with respect to stored messages. Stored messages can be reviewed, but not disclosed, by the system operator. This too has significant implications for employer monitoring of e-mail, which are discussed in Section 26.2.

17.5 Anonymity of Communications

Online communications, particularly those conducted on the Internet, afford individuals the opportunity to communicate anonymously. Through the use of anonymous remailer services, individuals can post messages stripped of any identifying characteristics of source.

According to the Supreme Court, the right to speak anonymously is protected by the First Amendment.[50] In doing so, the Court identified several valuable purposes served by anonymous speech. It noted, for example, that the First Amendment promotes literature and the arts by allowing authors to produce works under assumed names, recognizing that authors may desire anonymity due to fear of economic or official retaliation, concern about social ostracism, or merely a desire to preserve as much of one's privacy as possible. The Court also noted that anonymous speech has played an important role throughout history in allowing individuals to criticize oppressive practices and laws where such criticism would otherwise be suppressed. Finally, the Court noted that anonymity allows individuals who may be personally unpopular to ensure that readers do not prejudge their message simply because they do not like the proponent.[51]

On the other hand, online anonymity does present numerous practical problems. It allows those who infringe the electronic property rights of others to escape detection. It allows persons to engage in fraudulent electronic commerce, harassment, and defamation. It facilitates numerous other forms of criminal conduct.

Moreover, while the right to speak anonymously may be protected by the First Amendment, the Supreme Court has also suggested that there may be limits on this right. In one case, for example, the Supreme Court upheld a statute compelling disclosure to the Federal Election Commission of the names of contributors who donated to the campaigns of candidates for federal office.[52] In another case, the Supreme Court stated that "identification of the source of advertising may be required as a means of disclosure, so that the people will be able to evaluate the arguments to which they are being subjected."[53] And in a recent California Supreme Court decision, the court upheld a state statute forbidding anonymous mass political mailings by political candidates.[54] Thus, there is certainly argument for the proposition that many of the forms of anonymity possible in the online world (including, perhaps, anonymous digital cash—see Section 7.7), will be subject to government regulation.

Endnotes

1. *Garner v. Triangle Publications, Inc.*, 97 F. Supp. 546, 548 (D. N.Y. 1951); *Diaz v. Oakland Tribune, Inc.*, 188 Cal. Rptr. 762, 139 Cal. App. 3d 118 (1st Dist. 1983).

2. *See* William L. Prosser, *Privacy*, 48 Cal. L. Rev. 383 (1960); *Restatement (Second) of Torts*, §§ 652A–652I (1977). *See also Haynes v. Alfred A. Knopf, Inc.*, 9 F.3d 1222, 1229 (7th Cir. 1993).

3. *See, e.g., Time, Inc. v. Hill*, 385 U.S. 374, 391–394, 87 S. Ct. 534, 544–545 (1967).

4. *See, e.g., Carson v. Here's Johnny Portable Toilets, Inc.*, 698 F.2d 831 (6th Cir. 1983); *Martin Luther King, Jr. Center For Social Change, Inc. v. American Heritage Products, Inc.*, 250 G. 135, 296 S.E.2d 866 (2d Cir. 1953), *cert. denied* 346 U.S. 816 (1953); 346 U.S. 816 (1953); *Douglass v. Hustler Magazine, Inc.*, 769 F.2d 1128, 1138–1139 (7th Cir. 1985).

5. *See, e.g., Haynes v. Alfred A. Knopf, Inc.*, 8 F.3d 1222, 1229–1235 (7th Cir. 1993); *Daily Times Democrat v. Graham*, 276 Ala. 380, 162 So. 2d 474 (Ala. 1964); *Barbara v. Time, Inc.*, 348 Mo. 1199, 159 S.W.2d 291 (Mo. 1942); *Diaz v. Oakland Tribune, Inc.*, 139 Cal. App. 3d 118, 188 Cal. Rptr. 762, 767–778 (1st Dist. 1983); *Banks v. King Features Syndicate, Inc.*, 30 F. Supp. 352 (S.D. N.Y. 1939).

6. *See, e.g., Dietemann v. Time, Inc.*, 449 F.2d 245 (9th Cir. 1971); *Nader v. General Motors Corp.*, 255 N.E.2d 765, 770–771 (N.Y. 1970).

7. *Easter Seal Society for Crippled Children & Adults v. Playboy Enterprises, Inc.*, 530 So. 2d 643 (La. Ct. App.), *cert. denied*, 532 So. 2d 1390 (La. 1988).

8. *Bindrim v. Mitchell*, 92 Cal. App. 3d 62, 155 Cal. Rptr. 29 (Cal. Ct. App. 1979), *cert. denied*, 444 U.S. 984 (1979).

9. *Prystash v. Best Medium Publishing Co.*, 157 Conn. 507, 254 A.2d 872 (1969); *see also Restatement (Second) of Torts* § 652E, illustrations 6–9.

10. *Parnell v. Booth Newspapers, Inc.*, 572 F. Supp. 909 (W.D. Mich. 1983).

11.   *Cantrell v. American Broadcasting Cos.*, 529 F. Supp. 746 (N.D. Ill. 1981).

12.   News reports, documentaries, and other newsworthy portrayals may be protected to a certain extent by the First Amendment. In some cases, courts have found a person's interest in privacy can be outweighed by the public's interest in obtaining the news, *even if* the person is portrayed in a false light. *See Leopold v. Levin*, 45 Ill. 2d 434, 259 N.E. 2d 250 (1970) (documentary novel and motion picture using a fictionalization of a famous murder were protected by the First Amendment).

13.   *See Zacchini v. Scripps-Howard Broadcasting, Co.*, 433 U.S. 562, 573, 97 S. Ct. 2849, 2856 (1977) (noting the differences between the rights of privacy and publicity).

14.   *Matthews v. Wozencraft*, 15 F.3d 432, 437 (5th Cir. 1994).

15.   *Pavesich v. New England Life Ins. Co.*, 122 Ga. 190, 50 S.E. 68 (1905).

16.   *Onassis v. Christian Dior-New York, Inc.*, 472 N.Y.S.2d 254 (1984) (a public figure does not forfeit right of privacy).

17.   *Fairfield v. American Photocopy Equipment, Co.*, 138 Cal. App. 2d 82, 87, 291 P.2d 194, 197 (2d Dist. 1955); *see also National Bank of Commerce v. Shaklee Corp.*, 207 U.S.P.Q. 1005 (W.D. Tex. 1980) (unauthorized use of name of famous columnist to imply an endorsement of defendant's products).

18.   *Hirsch v. S.C. Johnson & Son, Inc.*, 90 Wis. 2d 379, N.W.2d 129 (1979).

19.   *See Haynes v. Alfred A. Knopf, Inc.*, 8 F.3d 1222, 1230 (7th Cir. 1993) (this branch of privacy law "is not concerned with . . . the accuracy of the private facts revealed. It is concerned with the propriety of stripping away the veil of privacy with which we cover the embarrassing, the shameful, the tabooed, truths about us"); *Cox Broadcasting Corp. v. Cohn*, 420 U.S. 469, 1 Media L. Rptr. 1819 (1975); *Time, Inc. v. Hill*, 385 U.S. 374, 1 Media L. Rptr. 1791, (1967).

20.   *Haynes v. Alfred A. Knopf, Inc.*, 8 F.3d 1222, 1229 (7th Cir. 1993).

21.   *See Cox Broadcasting Corp. v. Cohn*, 420 U.S. 469, 492, 95 S. Ct. 1029, 1044–45 (1975) (rape victim's name available from court records); *Florida Star v. B.J.F.*, 491 U.S. 524, 532–33, 109 S. Ct. 2603, 2608–2609 (1989) (publication of rape victim's name obtained from a police report that was not a public document); *Haynes v. Alfred A. Knopf, Inc.*, 8 F.3d 1222, 1231–1232 (7th Cir. 1993) ("the First Amendment creates a privilege to publish matters contained in public records even if publication would offend the sensibilities of a reasonable person").

22.   *See Haynes v. Alfred A. Knopf, Inc.*, 8 F.3d 1222, 1232 (7th Cir. 1993) ("the First Amendment greatly circumscribes the right even of a private figure to obtain damages for the publication of newsworthy facts about him, even when they are facts of a kind that people want very much to conceal. . . . The possibility of an involuntary loss of privacy is recognized in the modern formulations of this branch of the privacy tort, which require not only that the private facts publicized be such as would make a reasonable person deeply offended by such publicity but also that they be facts in which the public has no legitimate interest").

23.   *See Restatement (Second) of Torts* § 652B.

24.   *Dietemann v. Time, Inc.*, 449 F.2d 245 (9th Cir. 1971).

25.   *Boddie v. American Broadcasting Cos.*, 731 F.2d 333 (6th Cir. 1984).

26.   *See Anderson v. Strong Memorial Hosp.*, 140 Misc. 2d 770 (N.Y. Sup. Ct. 1980).

27.   *Gallella v. Onassis*, 487 F.2d 986 (2d Cir. 1973).

28.   *Dwyer v. American Express Company*, 652 N.E.2d 1351 (Ill. App. 1 Dist. 1995).

29.   *Dwyer v. American Express Company*, 652 N.E.2d 1351, 1354 (Ill. App. 1 Dist. 1995).

30.   Codified in major part at 5 U.S.C. § 552a.

31. Privacy Act at § 2(b)(iv).

32. 5 U.S.C. § 552a(b).

33. *California Bankers Association v. Schultz,* 416 U.S. 21, 85, 94. S. Ct. 1494, 1529 (1974) (Douglas J. dissenting).

34. 15 U.S.C. § 1681, *et seq.*

35. 15 U.S.C. § 1691, *et seq.*

36. Reg. B, 12 C.F.R. §§ 202.5(d)(iii)–(v).

37. 12 U.S.C. § 3401, *et seq.*

38. *See* 1 George Trubow, Editor, *Privacy Law and Practices,* § 3.03(iv)(d) at pp. 3–82.

39. *See, e.g.,* Tennessee Code Annotated, § 68-11-304 (1983).

40. *See, e.g., In Re: Culbertson's Will,* 57 Misc. 2d 391, 292 N.Y.S.2d 806 (N.Y. Sup. Ct. 1968).

41. *See Gotkin v. Miller,* 514 F.2d 125 (2d Cir. 1975), *aff'g* 379 F. Supp. 859 (E.D. N.Y. 1974).

42. *See Estate of Finkle,* 90 Misc. 2d 550, 395 N.Y.S.2d 345 (N.Y. Sup. Ct. 1977).

43. 18 U.S.C. § 2701 *et. seq.*

44. Sen. Rep. No. 541, 99th Cong., 2d Sess.1 (1986), *reprinted in* 1986 U.S.C.C.A.N. at 3589, 3590.

45. 18 U.S.C. § 2511(1).

46. 18 U.S.C. § 2511(2)(a).

47. 18 U.S.C. § 2701(a).

48. Sen. Rep. No. 541, 99th Cong., 2d Sess. 1 (1986), *reprinted in* 1986 U.S.C.C.A.N. at 3589, 3590.

49. 18 U.S.C. § 2702.

50. *McIntyre v. Ohio Elections Commission,* 115 S. Ct. 1511, 1516 (1995).

51. *McIntyre v. Ohio Elections Commission,* 115 S. Ct. 1511, 1516–17 (1995).

52. *Buckley v. Valeo,* 424 U.S. 1, 60-84(1976).

53. *First National Bank of Boston v. Bellotti,* 435 U.S. 765, 792 fn. 32 (1978).

54. *Griset v. Fair Political Practices Commission,* 884 P.2d 116, 126 (Cal. 1994).

18
Licensing Rights in Information Owned by Others

Andrew R. Basile, Jr.

In many cases, a person will want to use or distribute software and digital content owned by others. Licensing is the mechanism for accomplishing this. This chapter provides an overview of licensing, and explains the circumstances where licensing may be required. It also discusses special issues that arise when material is licensed for use or distribution online.

18.1 Understanding Licensing

18.1.1 What Is a License?

A *license* is a contract in which a party with proper authority (the "licensor") grants permission for another party (the "licensee") to do something that would otherwise be prohibited. In effect, the license is an agreement by the licensor not to enforce its legal rights. A license is usually memorialized in a written agreement, although in many cases licenses can arise by operation of law or be implied by the conduct of the parties.[1]

The subject matter of most license agreements involves intellectual property rights—that is, copyrights, trademarks, patents, and trade secrets, as well as rights of publicity and privacy.

Licenses are the legal mechanisms that allow owners of these rights (such as movie studios, programmers, songwriters, and authors) to exploit their works commercially. For example, the owner of the copyright in a movie generates substantial revenue by licensing theaters to show the movie publicly.[2]

18.1.2 License versus Sale

In a sale, title to a particular article is transferred to a customer, who is then able to use it in any manner he or she desires—free from any restrictions imposed by the seller, and subject only to the copyright, patent, and trademark laws.

In contrast, a license does not transfer ownership of the article to the customer. Rather, the customer merely obtains the right to use the article, subject to the restrictions imposed by the license.

Software developers in particular prefer to license (rather than sell) copies of their programs because licensing allows them to restrict the customer's resale rights, prohibit disassembly of the software, and limit their warranty obligations and other liabilities.

18.1.3 How Does Licensing Relate to Online Commerce?

In the physical world, many forms of intellectual property can be exploited without licensing. For example, no license is directly involved when someone purchases a book. The buyer owns a copy of the book and can do with it what he or she pleases, so long as the author's copyright is not violated (such as by copying the book or publicly performing the story it tells).[3]

However, a book that is placed on a public network (such as the Internet) can be read only by displaying it on, or loading into, a user's computer. Either scenario involves a reproduction and/or display that may infringe on the copyright in the book, unless the copyright owner has granted permission (that is, a license) for the other party to conduct these activities (see Sections 10.1 and 10.5).[4]

18.1.4 What Rights Must Be Licensed?

The basic operating assumption behind a license agreement is that the licensor has enforceable legal rights that the licensee's proposed activity will infringe. These rights, as discussed in Chapters 8 through 17, include:

- Copyrights
- Patent rights
- Trademark rights
- Trade secret rights
- Privacy rights
- Publicity rights

In order to use particular technology or content, the licensee must license (or otherwise "clear") those rights that its proposed use might infringe. In most cases, only some of the foregoing rights will be involved. For example, patent rights would be of no concern when licensing a song.

For each of the major types of content, the following list sets forth the rights that frequently apply:

- **Text.** Copyright, trade secret, trademark, and privacy rights.
- **Databases.** Copyright, trademark, and privacy rights.
- **Musical Works.** Copyright.
- **Sound Recordings.** Copyright and rights of publicity.
- **Images.** Copyright and rights of publicity and privacy.
- **Audiovisual Works.** Copyright and rights of publicity and privacy.
- **Software.** Copyright, patent, and trade secret.

Where content is protected by multiple forms of intellectual property, these rights are often held by more than one person. For example, a movie could be subject to a copyright held by the producer, as well as to rights of publicity held by individual actors. Moreover, a particular type of intellectual property right may be divided and held by multiple parties. For example, an author may own the U.S. copyright to a book but may have sold the French copyright to a book publisher.

Complexities of multiple ownership are magnified by the fact that online content is often multimedia—that is, it often incorporates a variety of textual, audio, and video works. Ownership issues must be considered with respect to each constituent work. With a movie, for example, the script may be based on a book, the copyright of which is owned by the original author, while the soundtrack may include musical works owned by the original composers. Clearing the rights to use content can be a daunting task, and in some cases a professional rights clearing agency should be retained.

18.1.5 When Is a License Required?

A license is required when the proposed use of technology or content would violate one of the licensor's intellectual property rights (that is, copyright, patent, trademark, trade secret, and publicity, or privacy rights). For example, the following activities will generally require some sort of license.

18.1.5.1 Distribution of Content Online. Digital networks such as the Internet are a tremendous medium for distribution of content, including online newspapers and magazines, movies, and recorded music. In most cases, online distribution consists of the transmission of a copy to a user's computer, where the copy is stored in the computer's memory or on its disk drive.[5] Online distribution of copyrighted subject matter requires a license, because it may infringe on one or more of the copyright owner's exclusive rights to reproduce,[6] distribute,[7] and publicly display[8] the content (see Sections 10.1, 10.3, and 10.5). Other rights such as trademark and rights of publicity may also be implicated. In sum, online distribution of content owned by others requires a license.

18.1.5.2 Online Performance of Content. As bandwidth and processing power have increased, it has become possible to transmit music and videos over the Internet and other public networks so that the music and videos may be heard or viewed by computer users in real time (much like radio and television). Such transmissions typically require a license because they will infringe on the copyright owner's exclusive right of public performance. For example, a Web page that enables users to play copyrighted music or videos on demand would require a performance license from the copyright owners. There is a subtle distinction between the *distribution* of content online and the public performance of content online. With mere distribution, content is transmitted to the user without capability of simultaneous showing or rendering. With performance, the content is transmitted for users to watch or listen to in real time.[9]

However, online distribution and public performance are not mutually exclusive. If a transmission of content transfers a copy of the content to the user's computer and also allows the user to hear or watch the content as it is being transmitted then the transmission is both a distribution and a performance.[10]

The distinction between distribution and public performance is important when dealing with music because songwriters frequently authorize the Harry Fox Agency of New York to license distribution (or "mechanical") rights, and other rights agencies (such as ASCAP and BMI) to license public performance rights. While this division may have worked smoothly in the past (when distribution and performance were easily distinguished), it creates a problem online, where the line between distribution and performance may be thin. Unfortunately, companies that want to use music online may face competing claims from both mechanical and performance rights agencies, with each agency asserting that almost any type of online transmission of music falls within its bailiwick. In effect, distributors of online content may be forced to pay both distribution and performance royalties each time a musical work is transmitted.

Whether a transmission of a song is characterized as a distribution or a performance may also determine whether a license must be acquired from the owner of the copyright in the sound recording. As explained in Section 9.3, music and sound recordings are distinct works, although a song typically embodies both. Copyrights in music are initially held by the composers who record the music. Copyrights in sound recordings are initially held by singers and other artists who record a performance of the music. Traditionally there has been no right of public performance accorded to sound recordings, although this has changed with the recent enactment of the Digital Performance Right in Sound Recordings Act of 1995. Thus, mere performance of sound recordings (such as by a radio station) does not require a license, although a license is required from the owner of the copyright in the underlying music. Online, however, an additional license will now be required if the transmission falls within the scope of the new act or constitutes a distribution.

18.1.5.3 Public Display of Content. Public display of online content typically occurs with Web sites, which allow users to browse through displays of text, graphics, and other content, such as online magazines and database services.

Although this type of "browsing" might not always constitute a distribution or performance it will still infringe the copyright owner's rights of reproduction and public display. Consequently, a license is required.[11]

18.1.5.4 Use and Distribution of Software. Software can be protected by copyright, trade secret and patent laws. The use or distribution of protected software infringes these various rights, and requires a license.

18.1.6 When Is a License Not Required?

Not every use of technology or creative content requires a license. Companies that may need to use others' technology or content should first assess what major property rights—that is, copyright, patent, trademark, trade secret, publicity, and privacy rights—protect that technology or content. Then, for each major property right, the determination should be made whether the proposed activity actually constitutes an infringement. If the proposed activity does not infringe on a particular right, then no license is required with respect to that right.

For each major property right, there are a number of permissible uses for which a license might not be required. They are as follows:

18.1.6.1 Copyright. Online publishers and others doing business online can use someone else's copyrighted material without permission when the proposed use:

- Is a "fair use" (see Section 11.2).
- Is a *"de minimus use"* of the material (see Section 11.3).
- Appropriates only the ideas expressed in the material, not the expression itself (see Section 11.6).
- Involves a copyright that has expired, or a work that has otherwise fallen into the public domain (see Section 11.4).

18.1.6.2 Patent. A product developer or other party can make, use, and sell the technology described in a patent when:

- The technology is not covered by the patent's claims, either literally or under the doctrine of equivalents (and the developer has obtained the advice of a patent lawyer to this effect) (see Section 15.4.1).
- The patent has expired (see Section 15.4.3).
- The patent is invalid (but note that taking the position that a patent is invalid can be risky) (see Section 15.4.3).

18.1.6.3 Trademark. Online vendors and other parties may be able to use a term that is incorporated in a trademark when it is used:

- Simply as a word, not as a trademark (for example, using the term *apple* in connection with fruit but not computers) (see Section 13.4.2.2).
- In a good-faith, descriptive sense that is not likely to cause confusion (such as the references in this book to trademarked terms) (see Section 13.4.2.2).
- As a mark on unrelated goods and in a manner that is not likely to cause confusion (see Section 13.4.2.1). (Under anti-dilution rules, famous trademarks like *Coke* cannot be used without permission, even if the use is on unrelated goods.)
- As a parody (see Section 13.4.2.5).

18.1.6.4 Trade Secrets. Product developers and others may be able to use someone's trade secret if:

- The secret, through no fault of the developer, has become publicly known (see Section 12.5).
- The developer acquires knowledge of the secret through its own, independent research (see Section 12.5).
- The developer acquires knowledge of the secret through reverse engineering that was not in violation of an enforceable agreement (see Section 12.5).

18.1.6.5 Rights of Publicity. Advertisers, publishers, and other parties communicating online may be able to use someone's name and likeness if the use is:

- Not a "commercial exploitation" of the name (see Section 16.1).
- Privileged under the First Amendment because it deals with news, commentary, satire, or other communications of public interest (see Section 16.2).

18.1.6.6 Rights of Privacy. The disclosure of information concerning an individual may be permissible (even without a license) if:

- It relies on publicly available facts (see Section 17.2).
- It is protected by the First Amendment because it deals with matters of public interest (see Section 17.2).

18.2 Special Issues in Online Licensing

The novelty of online commerce means that rules of law and existing license structures may be difficult to apply, creating the four concerns discussed below. The first two concerns (obtaining proper rights and sublicenses) apply to both software and creative content. The second two concerns (new media and ownership) are more pertinent to creative content.

18.2.1 Obtaining the Rights You Need

A licensee's goal is to acquire permission to use intellectual property (such as copyrights) belonging to another party. However, because online commerce is relatively new, there is some uncertainty as to how intellectual property rights relate to particular online activities. This means licensees must carefully consider whether their license agreements actually grant them the right to engage in the activities necessary to accomplish their online objectives.

For example, the copyright statute grants copyright owners certain exclusive rights, including the right of public distribution and the right of public performance (see Sections 10.3 and 10.4). As explained in Section 18.1.5.2, there is some question as to whether certain online transmissions of copyrighted works constitute a *performance*, a *distribution*, or both.[12] Thus, a licensee who obtains only the right to *distribute* copyrighted material may find that its proposed activity also constitutes a performance, in which case the licensee would not have all of the rights it needed to conduct the desired activity.

Licensees can ensure that they have acquired the appropriate rights by obtaining license provisions that speak not only in terms of the statutory rights (such as distribution and performance), but also specifically to the licensee's proposed activity. For example, if the licensee wants to place a photograph on a Web page, the license should expressly state that the licensee may do this.[13]

At the same time, the rights acquired under the license should be broad enough to accommodate changes in technology. Licensees must ensure that any limitations on their rights (for example, restrictions relating to media or geography) do not hamper or interfere with their intended use of the software or content.

This consideration is particularly important in an online environment, where vast technical changes can occur overnight. For example, consider a license to use a photograph on an "Internet Web page" site. Despite its current popularity, the Web may one day be replaced with an even more advanced protocol, much as Web sites have supplemented Gopher protocol sites. A scope-of-use clause limited to the Web could prevent the licensee from migrating its offering to a different protocol if the Web falls out of favor.

18.2.2 The Right to Sublicense

Licensees who acquire the right to distribute content online may also need to obtain the right to sublicense content to their end-users. For example, suppose a licensee obtains a license to distribute a novel online. To view the novel, the licensee's customers will have to copy it—either onto their computer's memory or in the form of a printout. This copying may constitute copyright infringement unless the customer has a sublicense to copy.

In licensing content for online use, licensees should determine what rights their customers or end-users will need in order to use that content. Licensees should then ensure that they obtain the right to sublicense rights sufficient to permit their customers' intended use, especially if the end customer is to have the right to make copies of content. However, if a license does not include a sublicense provision, a court may still find that such a right is implied by the circumstances of the license. This is particularly true if the license specifically recites that the licensee had permission to distribute content to end-users. Nevertheless, the most prudent approach is to ensure that the license specifically provides a right to sublicense if necessary to achieve the licensee's objective.

18.2.3 The New Media Problem

Many content licenses contain limitations about the type of media with which the content may be used. Media limitations will affect licensing activities in two ways. First, on a going-forward basis, licensees may have to negotiate carefully media limitations in future license agreements they enter into (this is discussed in Section 18.3.4.1). Second, licensees may have to determine the impact of media limitations on licenses that have already been granted. This second type of problem is the focus of this section.

Media-limitation clauses raise issues whenever a new media technology becomes available. The basic question is whether or not the licensee can use the content on the new medium. For example, suppose that in 1985 you obtained the rights to show a movie over "television." At that time, it was not contemplated that a movie could be distributed over digital networks such as the Internet. Now, in 1996, the Internet allows online transmission of real-time video (i.e., "television") programming. Does your license entitle you to distribute the movie over the Internet?

In resolving these types of questions, courts apply general contract law principles and attempt to determine the intent of the parties. In so doing, the courts consider a variety of factors, including:

- Whether the new media technology was known or anticipated at the time of the license grant.[14]

- Whether the license specifically contemplated use of the content with technology not yet known or developed.[15]
- Whether the governing jurisdiction follows the rule that all rights not specifically granted are reserved to the licensor.[16]

Generally, where the grant of rights is very broad with respect to media, the courts have no trouble concluding that the license includes media not necessarily contemplated by the parties at the time they entered into the license. In contrast, where the language used in the contract is not so broad, the courts take a more restrictive approach.

18.2.4 Identifying the Proper Owner

Media and other license limitations may also make it difficult to identify the person who owns the rights that need to be licensed.[17] Often the apparent owners of content hold only rights for particular media (such as paper or television). They may not have the authority to grant a license to use the content online.[18]

This problem has arisen with regard to the online re-publication of newspapers and magazines. For example, newspaper publishers, such as *The New York Times*, licensed online service providers such as LEXIS/NEXIS to provide back issues online. Many of the articles in those back issues, however, were written by freelance journalists. As independent contractors, these journalists retained ownership of the copyright interest in the articles. The newspapers were merely licensees that acquired the right to publish the journalists' stories. In 1993, a group of writers sued the newspapers and the online service providers, alleging copyright infringement. These writers, along with the National Writers Union, contend that the licenses granted to the newspapers were limited to print media.[19] By placing the newspapers and magazines online, the journalists argue, the publishers have exceeded the scope of their licenses, and have thereby violated the journalists' copyrights.

Because the arrangements between publishers and journalists were often poorly documented, it is difficult to ascertain the scope of the licenses granted by the journalists to the newspapers and whether the newspapers had the right to distribute the stories online.[20]

In sum, online publishers should not assume that an apparent rights holder (such as an author, newspaper publisher, or movie producer) has the authority to license particular content for online distribution. The rights holder may have never acquired electronic rights, or he or she may have had the electronic rights but transferred them to someone else.[21] Most troubling, many older transactions between rights holders did not contemplate the emerging digital revolution. Those transactions are laden with media restrictions and other terms that make it very difficult to determine which owner or owners have the right to use the content online.

When this kind of ambiguity exists, licensees should seek a warranty from the licensor that it has the authority to grant electronic rights, and strong indemnification should this prove not to be the case.

18.3 Structuring the License

Once a prospective licensee has identified what rights it needs and who owns those rights, the licensee will need to reach a definitive license agreement. This section outlines the major provisions found in a typical license agreement and addresses (to the extent applicable) the implications of licensing technology or content for use online.

18.3.1 Subject Matter

Central to any license agreement is a clear definition of the licensed subject matter. The definition should be sufficiently specific so that an objective observer (such as a judge in a future dispute) can determine which specific portions of a book, film, sound recording, and so forth are the subject of the agreement.

18.3.2 Exclusivity

Most content licenses are nonexclusive, thereby leaving the owner free to license the same content to others. However, in certain situations it may be appropriate to seek an exclusive license. Exclusive licenses are usually more expensive because they deprive the licensor of the opportunity to relicense the same content to other parties. Exclusive licensees can expect greater royalty expense, specified marketing commitments, guaranteed minimum royalties, and automatic conversion to a nonexclusive license if certain royalty projections are not met.

18.3.3 Scope of Rights Granted

18.3.3.1 General Scope. Besides defining the licensed subject matter, a license needs to set forth the scope of the license—that is, exactly what the licensee is entitled to do with the licensed material. The trick to licensing (from the licensee's perspective) is to acquire exactly the rights needed to pursue the desired activity, without paying for rights that are not required.

Often, scope-of-rights provisions have two sections, one setting forth which activities are permitted, and another setting forth which activities are prohibited. If a licensee exceeds the scope of the rights granted, he or she becomes a mere infringer, and is then subject to an injunction and money damages.[22]

The scope of a license can be crafted many ways. Subject to antitrust considerations, a licensor can prescribe whatever conditions or restrictions it desires on use of the licensed subject matter. For example, a copyright holder can limit the licensee's right to use the licensed content to a specific medium (for example, CD ROM). The licensee may not then use the license in a different medium (for example, online).

18.3.3.2 Rights Relating to Copyright. Many of the rights that are licensed in an online environment are derived from copyrights. With respect to these rights, licensees will want, at a minimum, to have reproduction rights, adaptation rights, distribution rights, and the right to publicly display and/or perform the content.[23] Each of these rights, to the extent they are necessary, should be clearly set forth in the license agreement.

- **Right to Copy.** The right to copy the licensed content is the most fundamental right that a licensee must have with respect to the content being licensed (see Section 10.1). Any content used online will be copied repeatedly simply by the very nature of computer networks.[24] Also, licensees may need the freedom to place copies of the content on multiple servers. To avoid liability for each of these copies, licensees will need a license that grants them the right to copy. When software is licensed, licensees may also need the rights to make back-up and archive copies.
- **Right to Adapt.** In any situation where licensed content will be modified in any respect, it is important that the license authorize the licensee to adapt the content—that is, to prepare a derivative work based on the content. Often transferring content from one media to another involves making an adaptation. Thus, licensees for online applications must at a minimum have the right to digitize content that is not provided in digital form. In addition, the use of content by computers is dynamic and may involve run-time, user-driven alterations. If applicable, this situation should also be covered by the license.
- **Right to Distribute.** The distribution right is separate and distinct from the right to copy. Merely having the right to copy does not authorize a licensee to publicly distribute those copies. In many cases, it will be impossible for a licensee to use content in an online environment without a distribution right, because the transmittal of content over a network will constitute a public distribution[25] (see Section 10.3).
- **Right to Publicly Perform.** The public performance right may be required if the licensed content will be performed online. For example, an audiovisual work that can be viewed in real time on the Internet's World Wide Web is operated in a public setting (comparable to a movie theater), and is therefore publicly performed. As explained in Section 18.1.5.2, there is a subtle distinction between performing a work online and using online channels to distribute a work that can be used to effect a performance in private. Licensees may want to secure both online performance and distribution rights to avoid this question altogether.
- **Right to Transmit.** Any online transmission of content necessarily involves making at least a temporary copy of the content at the receiving computer. Online transmission may also involve public performance and distribution. To ensure that they have all rights necessary to distribute or perform content online, licensees should seek a "right to transmit" content online, preferably in both a distribution format (that is, a format wherein the content cannot be perceived as it is being transmitted, but rather is stored for later rendition) and a performance format (that is, a format wherein the content can be perceived as it is being transmitted). Securing a right to transmit is now particularly important when licensing sound recordings in view of the recent Digital Performance Rights in Sound Recordings Act of 1995. See Section 10.6.
- **Right to Publicly Display.** Transmission of content online will usually involve public display. For example, a photograph on the Internet that can be downloaded or viewed using a Web browser is publicly displayed (see Section 10.5). Accordingly, licensees should ensure that they have the right to publicly display the content.

18.3.3.3 Rights Relating to Patents.

- **Right to Make and Use.** Unlike the case in copyright law, in patent law, the patentee's exclusive rights to make and use a patented invention are not limited to public activity. Any use or manufacture of a patented invention—public or private—is an infringement. Licensees will need to consult with patent counsel to understand how a particular patent's claims might affect their proposed activities. In some cases, a patent may be worded so that it is only infringed by the end user. However, a party that provides software enabling end-users to infringe may be liable to a patentee for contributory infringement or inducing infringement (see Section 15.4.1). Therefore licensees also need to think about how their customers' activities may relate to particular patent claims.
- **Right to Sell, Offer for Sale, and Import.** The right to sell and import under the patent law corresponds to the right to distribute under the copyright law. For example, in an online environment, any distribution of patented software will require a right to sell.[26]
- **Right to Sublicense.** Patents can cover both devices and methods. In the online environment, licensees may find that they are not so much "selling" a patented device as encouraging others to practice a patented method. In that case, it may be appropriate to secure a right to sublicense, so that the licensee can authorize its end-users to perform the patented method.

18.3.4 Restrictions on Use

18.3.4.1 Media. Content is frequently licensed for use only in a particular medium, such as print, phonorecording, film, videotape, broadcast television, cable television, and so forth. With the advent of online digital networks, and the convergence of telephone, television, and other media, the boundaries between traditional media are becoming blurred. It will soon be possible for many to receive "television" and "radio" programming on computers via digital networks such as the Internet. In this environment, traditional restrictions regarding media formats may be difficult to apply.

With respect to the Internet and other online environments, the question of media is especially difficult due to the rapid nature of online media evolution. In contractually defining such media, parties are tempted to use terms such as *online, network,* or *Internet.* Unfortunately, in the fluid world of digital communications, these words have a chameleon quality and mean different things in different contexts.

The risk this presents to the licensee is that a media restriction will be interpreted in such a way as to prevent migration of the licensee's project to the next generation of digital technology. For example, suppose you want to license the likeness of Elvis Presley for use on a Web page. A media restriction that limited your use of Elvis to the World Wide Web, or even to the Internet, could be very risky. As technology develops and communications channels integrate, concepts such as the Internet may no longer be relevant. A media limitation such as "the Internet" could hamstring you as you attempt to keep your offerings in mainstream communications channels.

We may find that the idea of a media limitation is simply not workable in a world where traditionally separate media are melded together in a seamless digital environment. In the meantime, savvy licensees will attempt to negotiate flexible terms. From the licensee's perspective, it might be advantageous to limit use to *digital media,* which could then be broadly defined in the agreement as "any communications channel where content is transmitted in a digital or other format suitable for computational machine processing, including computer networks such as the Internet."

A better tactic traditionally used by licensees is to incorporate very broad and expansive language into the contract, authorizing them to exploit the content "by any present or future method now known or hereafter developed." Although only a handful of courts have analyzed language of this type, most have held that it authorizes the licensee to use the content on later-developed technology not contemplated by the parties at the time the license was issued.[27]

Even if proposed media restrictions seem acceptable at a first glance, licensees should also carefully consider whether incidental uses in other media may be necessary. For example, suppose you license copyrighted photographs for display on a Web page. You may find that it would be desirable to promote your Web page through print advertising that includes the copyrighted photographs. To accomplish this, you will need media rights that include not only the Internet but also newspapers and magazines.

18.3.4.2 Territories. It is important to consider where distribution will take place. Content licenses frequently limit use and distribution to a specific geographical area, such as the United States and/or selected other countries. In an online environment, territorial restrictions are inherently problematic because content placed on the Internet, for example, is available worldwide. Thus, it may be appropriate that a license to publish or distribute content or software on the Internet be worldwide in scope.

In negotiating for worldwide rights, licensees should keep in mind that different people may own rights to the same work in different countries. Thus, the owner of the U.S. copyright in a particular movie may have sold the French copyright in the same movie. Consequently, a particular licensor may not have the authority to grant worldwide rights.

18.3.4.3 Term. Many licenses are for a specified term. Once the term of the license expires, the licensee cannot continue to exploit any product that contains the licensed subject matter. In some agreements, the license may be subject to early termination for reasons such as the event of default. Depending on how easily termination can be triggered, these provisions may create great risk for the licensee.

18.3.5 Rights of Other Parties

In some situations, obtaining a license to use content from the copyright holder may not be sufficient. Additional permissions may also be required from persons who have contractually reserved certain rights in the content, as well as persons who may have rights of publicity or privacy with respect to the content.[28] The license agreement should address who is responsible for obtaining the appropriate permission or release and who is responsible for paying any resulting fees.

18.3.6 Credits

The copyright holder may want to be given credit in the work in which the licensed material will be used. Many licenses will specify the wording of the credit, and, in some cases, the location of the credit, the size and prominence of the display of the credit, and other similar information. Requirements for displaying credits can present serious logistical problems when using works on a computer or online environment and should not be accepted lightly.

18.3.7 Delivery

A *deliverable* is something tangible (such as a document or diskette) that the licensor is required to provide to the licensee. Typically this would be a copy of the licensed content if the licensee does not already have one. The license should specify when delivery will take place and exactly what deliverables, if any, the content owner has agreed to provide.

18.3.8 License Fees and Royalties

The license fees, royalties, or other charges used in a content license vary greatly but are usually based on some quantifiable metric, such as time, number of copies, or licensee's gross receipts. One difficulty with licensing software or other material for use or distribution online is that metrics normally used in computing royalties—such as the number of copies made—may be impossible to measure in an online environment. Thus, in certain online applications, a flat fee approach may be appropriate.

18.3.9 Warranties

Licensees typically ask a licensor to warrant that it has the right, power, and authority to grant the license, and that the licensed subject matter will not infringe rights of a third party. Since online environments tend to be global, licensees should seek a warranty of noninfringement that is worldwide in scope.

18.3.10 Limitation of Liability

Licensors may seek to establish a limit on the scope of their liability for any damages that licensees suffer, particularly when their licensed subject matter is software. Limitations on liability are typically structured as either:

1. A limit on the total damages the licensee is entitled to recover;
2. An exclusion of certain types of damages, such as consequential damages; and/or
3. A limitation of the time period for bringing suit or revoking acceptance of deliverables.

18.3.11 Indemnification

In addition to obtaining appropriate warranties, licensees should seek an indemnification from the licensor. An indemnification clause is somewhat like an insurance policy in case the licensed subject matter violates the rights of a third party. In that event, the licensor must indemnify (that is, pay for) the licensee's legal expenses and other costs associated with a third-party claim. Of course, the indemnity is only as good as the licensor's creditworthiness. If the licensor goes out of business or is insolvent, the indemnity is worthless.

18.3.12 Right To Assign

An *assignment* is a transaction in which one party to a contract transfers all of its rights and obligations to someone else. Licensors often insist on a clause prohibiting or limiting the licensee's rights to transfer. These restrictions can present serious problems if the licensee is merged into or purchased by another company, and the license agreement should expressly permit transfer in those situations.

Endnotes

1. *See, e.g., Bandag, Inc. v. Al Bolser's Tire Stores, Inc.,* 750 F.2d 903, 223 U.S.P.Q. 982 (Fed. Cir. 1984).

2. Under the Copyright Act, one of the copyright owner's exclusive rights is that of public performance. Hence, a movie theater or other venue needs a license to exhibit a film publicly. On the other hand, private viewings (such as at home) are not public, and therefore do not require licenses.

3. See Section 11.6.

4. *See Playboy Enterprises, Inc. v. Frena,* 839 F. Supp. 1552, 1156 (M.D. Fla. 1994) (availability of photographs on BBS constituted unauthorized public display); *Sega Enterprises Ltd. v. Maphia,* 30 U.S.P.Q.2d 1921, 1926 (downloading of computer games from bulletin board to user's computer constituted unauthorized copying).

5. *Intellectual Property and the National Information Infrastructure,* The Report of the Working Group on Intellectual Property Rights (1995) (hereinafter, "NII Report"). Arguably, a transmission does not constitute a distribution unless it is in a format where the user is able or likely to retain a permanent copy. For example, some online dissemination of music is really in the nature of a public performance (as opposed to a distribution) because it is transmitted in a stream of bytes that are simply used to generate the song in real time and are quickly discarded. Granted, a determined user could capture the byte stream as it is transmitted, and store it for future playback. By the same token, however, a listener could tape a song as it is broadcast over the radio. That the listener has such capability does not transform a radio broadcast from a performance into a distribution.

6. The reproduction occurs because a copy of the work is placed onto the user's computer. *See Sega,* 30 U.S.P.Q.2d at 1926. See Section 10.1.

7. The distribution occurs because a copy of the work is transmitted to the user. *See Playboy,* 839 F. Supp. at 1556; *but see NII Report, supra* note 5, at 245 (stating that "it is not clear under the current law that a transmission can constitute a distribution of copies. . . .").

8. Under the Copyright Act, a *display* includes "the transmission of an image by electronic or other means, and the showing of an image on a cathode ray tube, or similar viewing apparatus connected with any sort of information storage and retrieval system." *Playboy,* 839 F. Supp. at 1556 [quoting H.R. Rep. No. 1476, 94th Cong., 2d Sess. 64 (Sept. 3, 1976)]. Under this broad definition, both the transmission to the user and the display on the user's screen constitute an infringing "display." The requirement that a display be "public" is easily met when the transmission takes place on the Internet or other public network. *Playboy,* 839 F. Supp. at 1557 (transmission to BBS customers held public display). See Section 10.5.

9. *NII Report supra* note 5, at 82.

10. *NII Report, supra* note 5, at 246 n.536.

11. The right of reproduction is infringed on because a copy of the content is transmitted to the user's computer. Also, as explained in note 8, this transmission and the display of the content on the user's computer both infringe on the content owner's exclusive right of public display.

12. *NII Report, supra* note 5, at 245.

13. A suitable provision would be "Licensor grants licensee the right to prepare and place a digitized copy of the picture onto one or more servers connected to the Internet or other computer network, and to make the copies of the picture available to the public via electronic distribution or transmission originating from said servers in accordance with the hypertext transfer protocol (http) or any other protocol."

14. *See Ettore v. Philco Tele. Broadcasting Corp.,* 229 F.2d 481, 488 (3rd Cir. 1956); *Cohen v. Paramount Pictures Corp.,* 845 F.2d 851, 853 (9th Cir. 1988).

15. *Wexley v. KTTV, Inc.,* 108 F. Supp. 558, 559 (S.D. Cal. 1952), *aff'd* 220 F.2d 438 (9th Cir. 1955).

16. *See Rey v. Lafferty,* 990 F.2d 1379, 1387–88 (1st Cir. 1993).

17. This issue is usually not a concern in a commercial software or patent licensing agreement. Licensees in these cases generally rely on the licensor's warranty that it has authority to grant the license.

18. *Simon & Schuster, Inc. v. Quintex,* 1990 U.S. Dist. LEXIS 1997; 1991 U.S. Dist. LEXIS 20330 (author of book assigned "electronic rights" to plaintiff, and licensed "television rights" to defendant; plaintiff sued when defendant tried to distribute soundtrack of television show on audiotape).

19. *Tansini v. New York Times Co.,* No. 93 Civ. 8678 (S.D.N.Y. filed Dec. 16, 1993); *Freelance Writers and Online Commerce,* National Writers Union Position Paper, May 30, 1995.

20. *Comment: Don't Put My Article Online!: Extending Copyright's New-Use Doctrine to the Electronic Publishing Media and Beyond,* 143 U. Pa. L. Rev. 899, 905 (Jan. 1995).

21. See note 18.

22. *See, e.g., Marshall v. New Kids on the Block Partnership,* 780 F. Supp. 1005 (S.D.N.Y. 1991).

23. In practice, many licenses do not expressly refer to these rights. Rather, a license may specify that the licensee has the "right to put content onto a Web page for transmission to users on the Internet." From such a grant, one can infer the rights of copying, display, and distribution that are subsumed by the right to "put content on a Web page." However, such shorthand notation may fail to define the licensee's rights with sufficient precision to avoid dispute, particularly in the technologically fluid world of cyberspace.

24. For example, suppose that without seeking permission, someone posts a magazine article onto the Internet (such as on a newsgroup or Web page). This posting involves making a number of infringing copies. The first copy is made when the article is typed or scanned from a magazine into a computer. The second is made when the article is uploaded from the computer to a network server. Additional infringing copies are likely to be made as other users download the article from the server. Still more copies may be made if those users print the downloaded article.

25. *Playboy*, 839 F. Supp. at 1556.

26. 35 U.S.C. 271.

27. *See, e.g., Rooney v. Columbia Pictures Indus, Inc.*, 538 F. Supp. 211 (S.D.N.Y.) *aff'd* 714 F.2d 117 (2d Cir. 1982).

28. For example, well-known actors, actresses, and recording artists may have reserved certain rights to control the use of the film and/or sound recordings of their performances. In many cases, unionized talent may have certain rights pursuant to a collective bargaining agreement.

PART IV

REGULATING INFORMATION CONTENT

19

The Role of the First Amendment Online

Ruth Hill Bro

Virtually all online activity involves conduct that can be characterized as "speech" or as publishing. From e-mail communications to more sophisticated forms of online publishing, the so-called global information infrastructure has facilitated an unprecedented worldwide exchange of ideas, information, and content. It has been praised for facilitating the revolutions rejecting communism in Eastern Europe as well as the student uprising in China. It has also been condemned for enabling massive dissemination of pornography and other forms of content offensive to the morals of our society.

As a consequence, the debate has raged over whether some controls should be placed on the information disseminated electronically. From calls for censorship at one extreme to cries of free speech at the other, the debate is often emotionally charged.

This chapter, and the other chapters in Part IV, discuss the current law regarding "free speech" as it pertains to publishers, advertisers, and others who desire to communicate or publish electronically. These chapters also explain when and under what circumstances the content of online communications can be regulated.

19.1 The Guarantees of the First Amendment

The First Amendment to the Constitution of the United States provides that "Congress shall make no law . . . abridging the freedom of speech, or of the press. . . ." The First Amendment right of free speech is perhaps the primary safeguard for rights in communicating online. It confers broad powers to communicate with others without government interference.

The right of freedom of speech is far reaching. It includes the right to speak and the right to receive speech.[1] It also includes the right not to speak.[2] Moreover, in keeping with the tradition that the founders of this country established in debating public issues, it includes the right to speak anonymously.[3] In fact, political expression—discussion of public issues, governmental affairs, and qualifications of candidates for public office—receives the broadest First Amendment protection in order "to assure unfettered interchange of ideas for the bringing about of political and social changes desired by the people."[4] Ultimately, the First Amendment means that "government has no power to restrict expression because of its message, its ideas, its subject matter, or its content."[5]

The First Amendment right to speak can take many forms, including written text (books, pamphlets, and written messages on clothing), the spoken word, motion pictures, radio and television broadcasts, videotape recordings, music, drama, dancing, gestures, and so on.[6] The First Amendment also protects online communications.[7]

It is important, however, to understand that the First Amendment prohibits only the "government" from interfering with one's speech or publishing activities. Its language specifically says that "*Congress* shall make no law. . . ." Although Congress is the lawmaking arm of the federal government, the guarantees of the First Amendment apply to the states through the Fourteenth Amendment.[8] The First Amendment does not, however, limit private employers who seek to restrict speech and publishing activities by their employees within the scope of their employment. It also does not limit online services (such as America Online, CompuServe, and Prodigy) who may want to censor messages published by their members or take further action, such as denying services to those whose speech and publishing activities they deem objectionable.

In order for the First Amendment to apply, some sort of "state action" must be involved. "State action" occurs when the government acts directly through its executive, legislative, or judicial branches. State action can also occur indirectly: (1) when a private entity performs acts that traditionally constitute an exclusively governmental function,[9] or (2) when the government requires, significantly encourages, or otherwise profits from private activity.[10] For example, if Congress attempted to impose certain requirements on online access providers that directly limited free speech, there might be sufficient state action to trigger the provisions of the First Amendment.

Even as it relates to government action, however, the First Amendment right of free speech does not absolutely protect all forms of communication. Although the language of the First Amendment states that "Congress shall make *no law*," the Supreme Court has not interpreted the First Amendment literally.[11] Instead, the Supreme Court has held that government may restrain speech "for appropriate reasons."[12]

For example, falsely yelling "fire!" in a theater is not protected under the First Amendment.[13] At best, the enjoyment of the film for all involved would be greatly diminished; at worst, people could be injured or killed in the stampede to escape from what turns out to be nonexistent danger. In such a situation, courts have held that the government has an interest in protecting public safety that outweighs the individual's right to say anything he or she pleases. In other words, in certain cases an individual's interests in free speech, as protected by the First Amendment, must be balanced against the interests of the government in regulating speech.

Generally, governmental regulation of speech and press activity falls into three categories:

1. Regulation based on the conduct of the speaker,
2. Regulation based on the content of the speech, and
3. Regulation based on the medium by which the speech is communicated.

19.2 Regulating Speech-Related Conduct

Conduct-based regulations govern conduct associated with speaking, such as the times a public speech may be given, the places appropriate for such speeches, and the permissible sound levels for such speeches. The breadth of the government's power with respect to such time, place, and manner restrictions, as they are often called, depends upon the forum in which the speech or assembly will occur.

In traditional public forums, such as streets, parks, and sidewalks, government regulation is permitted only if it is not based on content (that is, if it is viewpoint neutral and subject-matter neutral), is narrowly tailored to serve a significant state interest (such as preventing excessive noise in residential areas), and leaves open ample alternative channels of communication.[14] The primary question in determining content neutrality is whether or not the government has adopted the speech regulation because it disagrees with the message communicated.[15] For instance, an ordinance that allows peaceful labor picketing of any school involved in a labor dispute but prohibits all other peaceful picketing within 150 feet of a school is invalid because it is content based.[16] Similarly, a law that prohibits signs within 500 feet of a foreign embassy only if they criticize the policies of the foreign government is content based and thus invalid.[17]

In nonpublic forums (government forums not traditionally linked to speech and assembly, such as public schools, government office buildings, public libraries, military bases, jails, and buses), government regulation is permitted only if it is reasonable and viewpoint neutral (that is, the regulation must not suppress expression just because the government opposes the speaker's view).[18] For example, a court permitted a school district's practice of providing one labor union access to a school mail system while prohibiting access to all other labor unions because access was not based on the viewpoints of the unions but rather on their status (the union with access was the exclusive representative of all of the school's teachers, while the union without access had no official responsibility to the school district).[19] The interschool mailing system that was used to send messages within a school was not a public forum and thus was not subject to that more stringent test; because the restrictions were reasonable and not viewpoint based, they were valid.[20]

19.3 Regulating the Content of Speech

Content-based regulations of speech prohibit communication of certain ideas and thus are held to a higher level of scrutiny. To be valid, content-based restrictions on speech must (1) be necessary to achieve a *compelling* (not just a *significant*) government interest; and (2) use the least restrictive means available that will still achieve the government's objective.[21] The regulation must not unnecessarily interfere with First Amendment freedoms.[22] For example, the government has a great interest in regulating indecent speech to prevent minors from being exposed to it. Although completely banning all such speech would meet the government's objective of protecting minors, such a solution would be too broad and would place an undue burden on free speech.[23] Instead, the government could achieve its purpose without unduly restricting free speech by prohibiting the distribution of indecent material to minors.

Some categories of speech have been held to have so little value that they are not protected at all under the First Amendment—that is, they may be banned altogether. As the Supreme Court noted, these types of speech "are no essential part of any exposition of ideas, and are of such slight social value as a step to truth that any benefit that may be derived from them is clearly outweighed by the social interest in order and morality."[24] Although the Supreme Court initially identified obscenity, profanity, defamation, and fighting words as unprotected, it has modified its position over the years and has acknowledged that in some contexts such speech may be protected under the First Amendment.[25] A discussion of these categories of speech, as well as advertising (which is subject to significant regulation), follows.

19.3.1 Obscenity and Child Pornography

Obscenity and child pornography are not protected under the First Amendment.[44] Because these types of speech present significant liability issues for online publishers, they are discussed at length in Chapter 20.

19.3.2 Defamatory Speech

Defamatory communications, whether written (libel) or spoken (slander), that injure another's reputation or good name are not protected under the First Amendment.[45] Defamation is a significant issue for online publishers. It is discussed in more detail in Chapter 21.

19.3.3 Inciting Lawless Action

The First Amendment does not protect speech if it creates a clear and present danger of imminent lawless action.[46] The threatened lawless action must be imminent or almost immediate, and there must be some evidence of an intent to produce, and a likelihood of producing, imminent disorder.[47] Mere advocacy of violence, however, is not incitement to imminent lawless action and thus is protected under the First Amendment.[48]

For example, a conviction for disorderly conduct was upheld because the accused passed the bounds of argument and undertook to incite a riot.[49] Because of concerns that a fight was about to break out, the police asked the speaker to break up the crowd and finally asked the speaker to stop speaking; he repeatedly refused and was ultimately arrested. Conversely, the statement, "We'll take the fucking street later [or again]," yelled at an antiwar demonstration as a sheriff and deputies were attempting to clear the street, does not indicate an intention to produce imminent lawless action.[50]

In the online context, an American man sent a series of private electronic mail messages to a Canadian recipient in which he described rape and murder fantasies and the possible means of carrying them out with the other man. Because the messages were not seen as directed to inciting or producing imminent lawless action, they were protected under the First Amendment.[51]

19.3.4 Fighting Words

Speech can be restricted if it constitutes *fighting words* (that is, words likely to cause a fight).[52] Fighting words are offensive or abusive language that, by its very nature, judged by the probable reaction of a person of common intelligence, is likely to produce a violent reaction.[53] Merely annoying or derisive words do not constitute fighting words.[54]

The Supreme Court, however, has not upheld any conviction based upon this fighting-words doctrine for over 50 years.[55] Instead, the Court has tended to declare laws targeting fighting words, especially those that are designed to punish certain viewpoints, unconstitutional because such statutes tend to be overbroad or vague.[56]

Even if the fighting-words doctrine retains some validity, it is highly unlikely to arise in the online context. Unlike the typical fighting-words scenario, in which there is face-to-face speech,[57] online communication is largely removed from physical contact. For example, a person in New York who is the target of abusive words fired off by a person in California via e-mail would have to travel (by plane, train, or automobile) to reach the speaker in order to respond physically. Any physical reaction to speech online will not be immediate unless the speaker and recipient are in close physical proximity (for example, their offices are right next door to one another).

19.3.5 Advertising and Other Commercial Speech

The First Amendment protects commercial speech if it concerns lawful activity and is truthful (that is, not misleading or fraudulent).[26] Yet commercial speech is subject to more stringent regulation than noncommercial speech.[27]

Commercial speech has been defined as speech that "does no more than propose a commercial transaction."[28] Advertising is the prime example of commercial speech. The mere fact, however, that the speech in question is an advertisement[29] or refers to a specific product[30] does not necessarily mean that it is commercial speech. Otherwise, an article reviewing the safety and efficacy of a particular product would constitute commercial speech. Likewise, having an economic motive for distributing the speech in question is not enough by itself to turn the material into commercial speech.[31] If that were not the case, all novels or newspapers written for profit would be considered to be commercial speech.

For example, although the contestants in a labor dispute have interests that are primarily economic, the First Amendment protects both the employer and the employee when they express their views to influence the outcome; they do not need to discuss the merits of unions in general or any subject beyond the dispute at hand to prevent their expression from being characterized as commercial speech.[32] The combination of some or all of the aforementioned characteristics, however, may provide strong support that the speech in question is commercial speech.[33]

Two features of commercial speech permit regulation of its content: (1) commercial speakers know both their market and their products and thus are well-situated to assess the accuracy of their messages and the legality of the underlying activity, and (2) commercial speech is hardy because it is "the offspring of economic self-interest" and thus is not particularly susceptible to being crushed by overbroad regulation.[34] Speech proposing commercial transactions, an area that traditionally has been subject to government regulation, thus differs from other protected forms of expression.[35]

The threshold question is whether the commercial speech at issue concerns lawful activity and is not misleading. If the answer is No, then the speech is unprotected. If the answer is Yes, the speech is entitled to some protection under the First Amendment. Nevertheless, it may still be regulated so long as the regulation

1. Serves a *substantial* government interest (not the more difficult to establish *compelling* interest required for other content-based restrictions on speech),
2. Directly advances that interest, and
3. Is not more extensive than is necessary to serve that interest.[36] It should be noted, however, that this last requirement of "narrow tailoring" does not mean that the government must choose the least restrictive means of advancing its interest;[37] it is enough if there is a reasonable fit between the interest and the restriction chosen.[38]

For example, the Supreme Court upheld a State University of New York (SUNY) resolution barring commercial enterprises from operating in university facilities; when a houseware company representative attempted to sell her goods in "Tupperware"-type parties in SUNY student dorm rooms and refused the campus police request that she leave, she was arrested and charged with trespass, loitering, and soliciting without a permit.[39] The Supreme Court upheld the university resolution because it promoted a substantial interest (promoting security and an educational atmosphere, preventing commercial exploitation of students, and preserving residential tranquility), it reasonably fit the interest to be served, and directly advanced that interest.[40]

The Supreme Court, however, refused to uphold a government ban on beer labels displaying the true alcohol content of the beer, because the regulation violated the First Amendment.[41] Although the government had a substantial interest in ensuring the public's health, safety, and welfare by preventing brewers from competing on the basis of alcohol strength, the government failed to prove that the proposed regulation would directly advance that interest.[42] Moreover, the regulation was not narrowly tailored to achieve the objective: numerous less-restrictive (and perhaps more effective) alternatives—including directly limiting the alcohol content of beers, banning advertising that emphasizes high alcohol strength, or limiting the ban to malt liquors (which have higher alcohol content)—could have been used to achieve the government's interest.[43]

The regulation of online advertising is discussed in Chapter 22.

19.4 Regulating Speech Based on the Medium: Where Will Online Communications Fit In?

Each medium of expression presents special First Amendment problems.[58] Broadcasting media such as television and radio are regulated differently than print media such as newspapers. For example, broadcasters can be sanctioned for airing indecent speech that would not be sanctioned if it were published in printed form.[59] Moreover, although the First Amendment protects publishers such as newspapers from being required to print the responses of those they criticize,[60] broadcasters are not similarly protected and instead must give free air time to provide a "right of reply."[61] Similarly, federal law prohibits the advertisement of cigarettes and little cigars on any medium of electronic communication subject to the jurisdiction of the Federal Commerce Commission,[62] but permits such advertisements in print media.[63]

One reason cited by the Supreme Court for such differential treatment is that print media do not require government-issued licenses to operate, while both television and radio broadcasters operate on frequencies assigned to them through a government license. Because there are only a limited number of frequencies, receiving a government license for such a scarce public resource is a privilege with strings attached: broadcasters must accept government regulation that ensures that they operate in the public's interest.[64]

The Supreme Court has also noted that such differential regulation is justified because radio and television patrons become a captive audience to whatever is broadcast before the channel can be changed, just as someone who answers an obscene call suffers some harm before he or she is able to hang up.[65] In upholding such regulations, the Supreme Court has noted that unlike other media, radio and other broadcast media are (1) *uniquely* pervasive and (2) *uniquely* accessible to children.[66] For example, after discovering that warnings on cigarette labels were not discouraging smoking, particularly among the young, federal regulations banned cigarette advertising on commercial broadcasts because younger people were far more influenced by, and exposed to, broadcasting messages.[67] The federal statute prohibiting such advertising in broadcasting but not elsewhere was justified because there are significant differences between broadcasting and print media: "Written messages are not communicated unless they are read, and reading requires an affirmative act. . . . It is difficult to calculate the subliminal impact of this pervasive propaganda, which may be heard even if not listened to, but it may reasonably be thought greater than the impact of the written word."[68]

Other sources of speech are less intrusive. Unwanted access to adult movie theaters or bookstores can be controlled: unwilling adults can avoid exposure by not frequenting such places (the nature of the places is evident from the outside of the building), and distribution to minors can be limited by age restrictions. Moreover, those who receive unsolicited mailings that offend them are not a captive audience: they can simply avert their eyes and throw the objectionable material away.[69] They can also request that their names be removed from such mailing lists.[70] Mail is considered much less intrusive and much more controllable than radio or television broadcasts; parents exercise a high degree of control over the disposition of mail in their mailboxes.[71] Because suitable remedies are not similarly available in the broadcast media, courts have reasoned, the transmission itself must be regulated.

Courts also consider telephone services to be far less intrusive than broadcasters and thus subject to less restrictive regulation. Because users of a dial-a-porn service, for example, must take affirmative steps (dial a specific number, provide proof of age, and so on) in order to receive the communication, indecent private commercial telephone communications cannot be banned altogether or even restricted to certain hours of the day, as would occur in a broadcasting scenario.[72] Yet telephone services also differ from newspaper publishers. Because telephone service providers are classified as common carriers, they must provide public access to phone services in a nondiscriminatory way (no individualized decisions whether and under what terms to deal) and must not censor or otherwise edit messages communicated over their lines.[73]

The question of where online communications fit into this picture is a difficult one. Part of the problem is that online communications are not uniform: the World Wide Web differs from computer bulletin boards, which, in turn, differ from electronic mail. It might be argued that the World Wide Web is somewhat like radio and television broadcasting in its accessibility to everyone and its pervasiveness. Yet, more affirmative steps must be taken to access a Web site than to merely turn on a radio or television. Moreover, Web sites are not subject to licensing as broadcasters are: such sites are not a scarce commodity that must be carefully monitored to further the public interest. The information at the Web sites, like unsolicited mail, is more controllable; if a Web visitor doesn't like what he or she sees on a Web site, the visitor can avoid that Web site or that part of the Web site in the future. In fact, increasing numbers of Webmasters are using disclaimers and warnings regarding the content of their Web sites to alert more sensitve browsers to stay away. Taking their cue from adult theaters and 900 number businesses, such Webmasters are imposing barriers that browsers must affirmatively overcome to gain entrance to possibly objectionable material.

Adult computer bulletin board services perhaps most closely resemble the dial-a-porn services. Most sexually explicit materials, which are the focus of recent legislative efforts to regulate online communications, are accessible only through a computer bulletin board service that requires payment of a fee and proof of age in order to gain access to the offered depictions (although the descriptions themselves, which do not require payment of a fee or proof of age, might be indecent). Still, such services are not "uniquely pervasive" and "uniquely accessible" as the broadcast media are. A series of affirmative steps must be taken to be exposed to such services; they do not appear simply by turning on the computer.

Private electronic mail messages, which are sent from one specific entity to another, function more like private U.S. mail communications that are not subject to government interference. Electronic mail messages posted to an entire Internet listserv more closely resemble unsolicited mail: if the recipient does not want it, he or she can simply deposit it in an electronic trash receptacle.

It is too soon to tell how online communications will be classified,[74] but one thing is certain: the way they are classified will determine the way they are regulated and how much First Amendment protection they will receive. Of all the communications media, broadcasting has been given the most limited First Amendment protection because of the finite number of licenses available, its sheer pervasiveness, and the ease with which children can access it. Although computers can be accessed by most children with ease (indeed, many children are far more adept in accessing computers than their less technologically up-to-date parents), online communications differ from broadcasting in key ways: there is no licensing of online communications, and they are not uniquely pervasive. Unlike broadcasters and print publishers (such as newspapers and magazines), there is no organizing or unifying force determining what will be presented online on any given day. It is the online user who determines what he or she will sample that day by selecting from a virtually unlimited array of menus.

However online communications will be classified, they will be protected to some degree by the First Amendment. Those doing business online can help to protect themselves from liability by being aware of the various laws that govern different types of speech, particularly sexually explicit materials (see Chapter 20), defamation (see Chapter 21, and commercial speech (see Chapter 22).

Endnotes

1. *Martin v. City of Struthers*, 319 U.S. 141, 143 (1943).

2. *West Virginia State Bd. of Educ. v. Barnette*, 319 U.S. 624 (1943) (enjoined enforcement of regulation requiring public school students to salute and pledge allegiance to the U.S. flag).

3. *McIntyre v. Ohio Elections Comm'n*, 115 S. Ct. 1511 (1995).

4. *Roth v. United States*, 354 U.S. 476, 484 (1957). *See also McIntyre v. Ohio Elections Comm'n*, 115 S. Ct. 1511, 1518-1519 (1995).

5. *Police Dep't of the City of Chicago v. Mosley*, 408 U.S. 92, 95 (1972).

6. *See, e.g., Schad v. Borough of Mount Ephraim*, 452 U.S. 61, 65 (1981).

7. *United States v. Baker*, 890 F. Supp. 1375 (E.D. Mich. 1995); *Cubby, Inc. v. CompuServe Inc.*, 776 F. Supp. 135 (1991).

8. *See Gitlow v. New York*, 268 U.S. 652, 666 (1925).

9. *Marsh v. Alabama*, 326 U.S. 501, 506–508 (1946) (town owned by a private corporation had sufficient characteristics of a municipality to constitute a public place, and thus Jehovah's Witness who distributed religious literature on a company-owned sidewalk could not be convicted under state trespass law criminalizing entering or remaining on the premises of another after being warned otherwise). *See also Hudgens v. N.L.R.B.*, 424 U.S. 507, 516–521 (1976) (emphasizing narrowness of Marsh decision).

10. For example, private use of government property can constitute state action. *See Burton v. Wilmington Parking Auth.*, 365 U.S. 715, 725–726 (1961) (state action occurred when a private restaurant leasing space in building owned and operated by a state agency refused to serve a black person). *But see Rendell-Baker v. Kohn*, 457 U.S. 830, 840–844 (1982) (receipt of public funds or extensive government regulation, by themselves, do not necessarily constitute state action).

11. *Gitlow v. New York*, 268 U.S. 652, 666 (1925); *Chaplinsky v. New Hampshire*, 315 U.S. 568, 571 (1942); *Cohen v. California*, 403 U.S. 15, 19 (1971).

12. *Elrod v. Burns*, 427 U.S. 347, 360 (1976).

13. *Schenck v. United States*, 249 U.S. 47, 52 (1919).

14. *Ward v. Rock Against Racism*, 491 U.S. 781, 791 (1989).

15. *Id.*

16.   *Police Dep't of the City of Chicago v. Mosley*, 408 U.S. 92, 97–98 (1972).

17.   *Boos v. Barry*, 485 U.S. 312, 319 (1988).

18.   *Perry Educ. Ass'n v. Perry Local Educators' Ass'n*, 460 U.S. 37, 46 (1983); *Lehman v. City of Shaker Heights*, 418 U.S. 298, 304 (1974).

19.   *Perry Educ. Ass'n v. Perry Local Educators' Ass'n*, 460 U.S. 37, 49 (1983).

20.   *Id*. at 47.

21.   *Sable Communications of California, Inc. v. F.C.C.*, 492 U.S. 115, 126 (1989).

22.   *Id*.

23.   *See, e.g., Butler v. Michigan*, 352 U.S. 380, 383 (1957).

24.   *Chaplinsky v. New Hampshire*, 315 U.S. 568, 572 (1942).

25.   For a modification of the Supreme Court's view in *Chaplinsky*, see *Cohen v. California*, 403 U.S. 15 (1971) (the words "Fuck the Draft" on the back of a jacket worn in a public courthouse were protected).

26.   *See, e.g., Central Hudson Gas & Electric Corp. v. Public Service Comm'n of New York*, 447 U.S. 557, 563–564 (1980) (First Amendment protection of commercial speech is based on the informational function of advertising; commercial messages that do not accurately inform, that mislead, or that are related to illegal activity have no informational value); *Virginia State Bd. of Pharmacy v. Virginia Citizens Consumer Council, Inc.*, 425 U.S. 748, 770 (1976) (government cannot suppress dissemination of truthful information about a lawful activity — such as pharmacist advertisements of the retail prices of prescription drugs—because of a fear of the information's effect on its recipients).

27.   *Virginia State Bd. of Pharmacy v. Virginia Citizens Consumer Council, Inc.*, 425 U.S. 748, 770 (1976).

28.   *Pittsburgh Press Co. v. Pittsburgh Comm'n on Human Relations*, 413 U.S. 376, 385 (1973).

29.   *New York Times Co. v. Sullivan*, 376 U.S. 254, 265-266 (1964) (full-page advertisement criticizing police conduct in Montgomery, Alabama, not commercial speech).

30.   *See Bolger v. Youngs Drug Products Corp.*, 463 U.S. 60, 66 (1983), *citing Associated Students for Univ. of California at Riverside v. Attorney General of the United States*, 368 F. Supp. 11, 24 (C.D. Cal. 1973).

31.   *See Bolger v. Youngs Drug Products Corp.*, 463 U.S. 60, 66 (1983), *citing Bigelow v. Virginia*, 421 U.S. 809, 818 (1975).

32.   *Virginia State Bd. of Pharmacy v. Virginia Citizens Consumer Council, Inc.*, 425 U.S. 748, 762–763 (1976).

33.   *Bolger v. Youngs Drug Products Corp.*, 463 U.S. 60, 66-67 (1983).

34.   *Central Hudson Gas & Electric Corp. v. Public Service Comm. of New York*, 447 U.S. 557, 564, n. 6 (1980), *citing Bates v. State Bar of Arizona*, 433 U.S. 350, 381 (1977).

35.   *Bolger v. Youngs Drug Products Corp.*, 463 U.S. 60, 64-65 (1983).

36.   *Central Hudson Gas & Electric Corp. v. Public Service Comm. of New York*, 447 U.S. 557, 566 (1980); *Rubin v. Coors Brewing Co.*, 115 S. Ct. 1585, 1589 (1995).

37.   *Board of Trustees of State Univ. of New York v. Fox*, 492 U.S. 469, 476-481 (1989).

38.   *Id*. at 480.

39.   *Id*. at 471–472.

40.   *Id*. at 475–481.

41.   *Rubin v. Coors Brewing Co.*, 115 S. Ct. 1585 (1995).

42.   *Id*. at 1592.

43. *Id.* at 1593.

44. *New York v. Ferber,* 458 U.S. 747, 764 (1982).

45. *Chaplinsky v. New Hampshire,* 315 U.S. 568, 572 (1942).

46. *Schenck v. United States,* 249 U.S. 47, 52 (1919) (introduced the first formulation of the clear and present danger test: "[t]he question in every case is whether the words used are used in such circumstances and are of such a nature as to create a clear and present danger that they will bring about the substantive evils that Congress has a right to prevent.").

47. *Hess v. Indiana,* 414 U.S. 105, 109 (1973).

48. *Brandenburg v. Ohio,* 395 U.S. 444, 448-449 (1969).

49. *Feiner v. New York,* 340 U.S. 315 (1951).

50. *Hess v. Indiana,* 414 U.S. 105, 107 (1973).

51. *United States v. Baker,* 890 F. Supp. 1375, 1382 (E.D. Mich. 1995), *citing Brandenburg v. Ohio,* 395 U.S. 444, 447 (1969). Baker was the first to be prosecuted for an online violation of the federal anti-threat law, 18 U.S.C.A. § 875(c), which prohibits the transmission in interstate or foreign commerce of any communication containing a threat to kidnap or injure the person of another.

52. *Chaplinsky v. New Hampshire,* 315 U.S. 568, 573 (1942).

53. *Id.*

54. *Id.*

55. Geoffrey R. Stone, *et al., Constitutional Law* 1100 (2d ed. 1991).

56. *See, e.g., Gooding v. Wilson,* 405 U.S. 518 (1972), where the Supreme Court held that an antiwar demonstrator who called a police officer "son of a bitch" and threatened him with bodily harm (choking to death, cutting to pieces) could not be convicted under the overbroad Georgia statute prohibiting "opprobrious words or abusive language, tending to cause a breach of the peace." *See also Terminiello v. City of Chicago,* 337 U.S. 1 (1949), where the Supreme Court held unconstitutional a breach of the peace statute that restricted speech that stirs the public to anger, invites dispute, causes unrest, or creates a disturbance; the Court noted that an audience's unfavorable response (a heckler's veto) does not justify denial of the right to speak.

57. *Chaplinsky v. New Hampshire,* 315 U.S. 568, 573 (1942).

58. *Joseph Burstyn, Inc. v. Wilson,* 343 U.S. 495, 503 (1952).

59. *F.C.C. v. Pacifica Foundation,* 438 U.S. 726, 748 (1978).

60. *Miami Herald Publishing Co. v. Tornillo,* 418 U.S. 241, 256-257 (1974).

61. *Red Lion Broadcasting Co. v. F.C.C.,* 395 U.S. 367, 392 (1969).

62. 15 U.S.C.A. § 1335 (1982).

63. *Capital Broadcasting Co. v. Mitchell,* 333 F. Supp. 582 (D.C. 1971), *aff'd,* 405 U.S. 1000 (1972).

64. *Red Lion Broadcasting Co. v. F.C.C.,* 395 U.S. 367, 394 (1969); *Capital Broadcasting Co. v. Mitchell,* 333 F. Supp. 582, 586 (D.C. 1971), *aff'd,* 405 U.S. 1000 (1972).

65. *F.C.C. v. Pacifica Foundation,* 438 U.S. 726, 748-749 (1978).

66. *Id.*

67. The court noted that "[a] pre-school or early elementary school age child can hear and understand a radio commercial, or see, hear and understand a television commercial, while at the same time be substantially unaffected by an advertisement printed in a newspaper, magazine or appearing on a billboard." *Capital Broadcasting Co. v. Mitchell,* 333 F. Supp. 582, 586 (D.C. 1971), *aff'd,* 405 U.S. 1000 (1972).

68. *Id., citing Banzhaf v. F.C.C.,* 405 F.2d 1082, 1100-1101 (D.C. Cir. 1968), *cert. denied,* 396 U.S. 842 (1969).

69. *Bolger v. Youngs Drug Products Corp.,* 463 U.S. 60, 72 (1983) ("[T]he 'short, though regular, journey from mail box to trash can . . . is an acceptable burden, at least so far as the Constitution is concerned.'"), *quoting Lamont v. Comm'r of Motor Vehicles,* 269 F. Supp. 880, 883 (S.D.N.Y.), *summarily aff'd,* 386 F.2d 449 (2d Cir. 1967), *cert. denied,* 391 U.S. 915 (1968).

70. *Bolger v. Youngs Drug Products Corp.,* 463 U.S. 60, 72 (1983).

71. *Id.* at 73–74.

72. *Sable Communications of California, Inc. v. F.C.C.,* 492 U.S. 115, 127–128 (1989).

73. *F.C.C. v. Midwest Video Corp.,* 440 U.S. 689, 701 (1979).

74. As this book goes to press, the new telecommunications bill (S. 652), which includes the Communications Decency Act of 1996 (CDA), was signed into law on February 8, 1996. The CDA allows the federal government for the first time to regulate the Internet and online services and prohibits the use of computer networks to transmit sexually explicit and other indecent materials to minors. The constitutionality of the CDA has already been challenged.

20
Sexually Explicit Materials in a Digital World

Ruth Hill Bro

20.1 Introduction

Computer-based forms of online communication have become the newest medium for creating and transporting sexually explicit materials. Both the Internet and private computer bulletin board systems (BBSs) make available sexually explicit images and text and provide forums for discussing sexually explicit topics.

These innovations have not gone unnoticed by the public, legislators, and law enforcement. Sweeping morality judgments about what is and is not fit to be transmitted by computers over telephone lines are fast replacing the Wild West mentality, in which anything goes—including obscenity and child pornography—that has long been associated with the information superhighway. This new era is characterized by new legislation regulating the content of what is transmitted (the Communications Decency Act of 1996) as well as sting operations by law enforcement to expose and prosecute "adult" BBSs and others who peddle or display obscenity or child pornography.[1]

The current laws governing the right to communicate sexually explicit materials, and any changes spawned by the current debate over the subject, will have a significant impact not only on those who seek to sell or otherwise communicate sexually explicit materials, but also on businesses engaged in unrelated activities who might nonetheless use sexually explicit materials on their Web site or in other forms of online advertising.

Sex sells, and perhaps no one knows that better than Calvin Klein, who has long used sexual images and innuendo in his advertising to sell designer clothing and fragrances. Beginning with his 1980 ad in which the 15-year-old Brooke Shields claimed that nothing came between her and her Calvins, Klein's advertisements have increasingly courted controversy. His summer 1995 ad campaign prompted an FBI investigation into whether his ads featuring provocatively posed teen-looking models, some wearing only underwear, constituted child pornography.[2] The ads lack Calvin Klein's usual glossy finish, opting instead for an amateur, shot-in-the-basement look reminiscent of cheap porn films. The television spots feature a male, disembodied voice asking nervous teenagers standing against a backdrop of cheap paneling to answer questions and take off pieces of clothing.[3] The print ads feature anything from spread-legged shots with glimpses of underwear from under skirts or shorts (using a centerfold approach in one photo) to a young-looking female wearing a vest and jeans and touching her breasts.[4]

This is the first time that a mainstream advertiser has been accused of using child pornography to sell his wares.[5] It probably will not be the last. One writer has described the advertising of Calvin Klein, and countless other advertisers, as "pyro-marketing," which seeks to "intentionally inflame public opinion with incendiary imagery for the specific purpose of cashing in."[6] It remains to be seen, however, whether Calvin Klein will be cashing in this time: he was forced to pull the plug on the multimillion dollar ad campaign after only a few weeks. Although the controversy generated millions of dollars worth of free advertising, it is not clear whether the ads or the controversy itself have fueled demand for his designer clothing. Klein's potential loss may not have been just financial if the Justice Department had concluded that any of the images constituted child pornography. Because minors were not used in those photos deemed objectionable, the Justice Department decided that none of the ads violated federal child pornography laws.[7]

Although Calvin Klein's ads were limited to billboards, television commercials, magazine spreads, and mass transit posters, they could just as easily have appeared on a Web site. As businesses use the latest wave in communications technology to reach new customers, they will inevitably use one of the tried-and-true methods of advertising: sexual images and innuendo. To avoid liability and multimillion dollar mistakes, those doing business online must be aware of the potential legal minefields.

As noted in Chapter 19, although the First Amendment generally protects all forms of speech, there are exceptions for certain forms of sexually explicit materials. The dissemination of obscenity and child pornography may be completely prohibited.[8] Conversely, the communication of material that is considered "indecent" may be regulated, but may not be completely banned.[9] In general, such regulations must be narrowly tailored to achieve the government's objective and burden no more speech than necessary. The level of regulation will also depend upon the medium in which the speech occurs: rules suitable for broadcasting may not be suitable for printed media. This chapter therefore discusses the law regarding material that is considered to be obscene, indecent, or child pornography.

20.2 Obscenity

The U.S. Constitution does not protect obscene materials[10] regardless of whether they appear in a magazine mailed to a purchaser's home or are transmitted to a user's computer screen through the Internet or a commercial bulletin board service. Such materials are considered to have so little social value that society's interest in order and morality outweighs any benefit derived from them.[11] Indecent materials, however, are protected under the First Amendment, although subject to some forms of regulation.[12]

20.2.1 Defining Obscenity

Material is not necessarily obscene merely because it concerns sex: "sex and obscenity are not synonymous."[13] Supreme Court Justice Stewart once observed that he could probably never adequately define hard-core pornography, but that he knew it when he saw it.[14] Unfortunately, those who do business on the Internet need a more concrete definition of what sexually explicit materials are unprotected if they are to avoid criminal liability.

In 1973, the Supreme Court fashioned a three-part test that constitutes the current legal definition of obscenity:

1. Would the "average person, applying contemporary community standards" find that the work, taken as a whole, appeals to "the prurient interest?"
2. Does the work depict or describe, in a "patently offensive" way, sexual conduct that is specifically defined by the applicable state law?
3. Does the work, taken as a whole, "lack serious literary, artistic, political, or scientific value?"[15]

If the answer to all three questions is yes, then the work is obscene and unprotected by the First Amendment—that is, the distribution of such material may be prohibited.

Many states[16] have patterned their own obscenity legislation after this language. Understanding this three-part test can be crucial to avoiding liability under both state and federal law. Unfortunately, although the test sounds simple enough, problems can arise in defining some of the terms it uses—especially the concept of *community standards* when considered in the context of communicating online.

20.2.1.1 Appeals to Prurient Interest Under Contemporary Community Standards. The first step in determining whether sexually explicit material is obscene is to evaluate whether the work appeals to the prurient interest when judged by the applicable contemporary community standards. Thus, it becomes important to understand what is meant by *contemporary community standards* and what constitutes *prurient interest.*

20.2.1.1a Contemporary Community Standards. Determining whether content is obscene based on *community standards* presents a significant issue for material that can be accessed and downloaded electronically throughout the world. In cyberspace, geography is irrelevant: a person can access information on Internet Web sites and computer bulletin board systems from anywhere in the world. Moreover, unlike a conventional publisher that can determine the communities to which its printed materials will be sold or mailed, an online publisher typically has no control over the location from which someone accesses the information. Thus, the phrase *contemporary community standards* raises unique issues when applied in an online context.

In formulating its test for obscenity, the Supreme Court rejected a national community standard, emphasizing that the people of Maine or Mississippi should not be forced to accept the public depiction of conduct tolerated in Las Vegas or New York City.[17] Although the sexually explicit material transmitted will not be judged by standards appropriate for the 1950s, "contemporary community standards" in some locales may well seem very uncontemporary compared to those of other communities. Yet the federal obscenity statute is not unconstitutional merely because federal judicial districts will apply standards that vary from community to community rather than uniform national standards of obscenity: various states can prosecute distributors of obscenity for different degrees of criminal liability based on violations of state obscenity statutes.[18] If a distributor's audience for sexually explicit materials comprises different communities with different local standards for obscenity, the distributor bears the burden of complying with each community's prohibitions.[19]

In determining the common conscience of a particular community, the community as a whole—young and old, educated and uneducated, religious and nonreligious, men, women, and children—should be considered.[20] In basing a decision on contemporary community standards, a jury must consider the entire community, not the reactions of a sensitive or callous minority, and not simply the jurors' own subjective reactions.[21]

Yet online communications are not (and often cannot be) limited to a single county or state or even country, but instead are available throughout the world. If a computer user in Los Angeles, California, makes sexually explicit digitized images available to a computer user in Cedar Rapids, Iowa, which locale's community standards apply?

Electronic publishers bear the risk of being subject to the more restrictive community standards of those who access their materials. In obscenity cases involving the U.S. mail, in which the sender mails materials from one state to a recipient in another state, prosecutors have great discretion in selecting the applicable "community" as long as it has some connection to the facts of the case.[22] Generally, prosecutors may use the community standards of the sending jurisdiction or the receiving jurisdiction.[23] For example, courts have held that dial-a-porn services must tailor their messages to different local standards if they want to avoid obscenity charges.[24]

Similarly, when film distributors voluntarily conspired to distribute an obscene film in interstate commerce, the court held that the conspirators forfeited any right they may have had to be judged according to the community standards of the locales in which they had centered their operations.[25] The court rejected the conspirators' argument that they had not received a fair trial because they were tried in Memphis, Tennessee, where their guilt was determined by "puritanical" standards that would not have been the yardstick used in several other areas where the conspirators had displayed their film.[26]

There is, of course, a difference between mailing obscene materials to a specific recipient in a designated community and making the same materials available on a bulletin board or Internet site without any knowledge of or control over the locations from which individuals can access, view, and copy such materials. Nonetheless, at least one case suggests that a bulletin board operator can be criminally liable for allowing sexually explicit materials to be accessed from a community where they are considered to be obscene.[27]

In 1994, Robert and Carleen Thomas operated a San Francisco–based bulletin board called Amateur Action, which allowed paid subscribers to view and download sexually explicit images. They were convicted of interstate transportation of obscene materials via phone lines after those materials were downloaded by a Tennessee postal inspector. The Thomases were judged not by the community standards of San Francisco, but rather by the arguably more conservative community standards of Memphis, Tennessee.[28]

If the courts, in fact, take this approach with respect to obscenity online, the most conservative communities in the United States could well be dictating what is or is not obscene for the rest of the country.[29] This is precisely the sort of national standard that the Supreme Court sought to avoid in formulating the above test by which the affected local community would judge the appropriateness of the material.

This sort of national standard for online obscenity also raises a new question regarding jurisdiction. When and under what circumstances may a person be subjected to the laws of states or countries outside the one in which he or she is located? This issue is discussed in Chapter 23.

20.2.1.1b Prurient Interest. Material that beckons to a "shameful or morbid interest in nudity, sex, or excretion, and . . . goes substantially beyond limits of candor in description or representation of such matters"[30] appeals to the "prurient interest." Conversely, material that on the whole merely arouses a "good, old fashioned, healthy interest in sex" does not appeal to the prurient interest.[31] What some communities regard as a "healthy interest in sex," however, can differ markedly from the views of other communities.

In gauging whether particular material appeals to the prurient interest, a court considers the material's effect on a *normal* person: its effect "not upon any particular class, but upon all those whom it is likely to reach . . . [i]n other words, . . . its impact on the average person in the community."[32] In determining whether material appeals to a person's prurient interest, courts do not focus on a particular segment of society, such as the most sensitive person or the least sensitive person.[33] If, however, the material is targeted to a particular deviant group—such as sadomasochists—the material will be judged as to how it would appeal to the prurient interest of members of that group, not how it would affect the average or normal person.[34] Materials that may not appear to be sexually stimulating to average adults may be highly stimulating to a deviant group; if judged according to normal standards, many such deviant materials would escape regulation.

Descriptions or advertisements designed to lure potential downloaders of visual images can be used as evidence that the work in question is designed to appeal primarily to the prurient interest. For example, a publisher's own evaluation of a book, as demonstrated by advertising that stresses sexual arousal and is obviously designed to appeal to the prurient interest, can be taken at face value by a court in declaring the whole work obscene, despite evidence that the work may have had some value in the scientific community.[35] Moreover, a pedophile's own handwritten descriptions, such as "15 year old shows nipple," or "13 year old flashes" followed by "hot," on videotapes containing child pornography have been held to demonstrate that the accused knew that the videotapes contained sexually oriented material designed to sexually arouse a pedophile.[36] Such descriptions or advertisements, however, are only one factor to be considered and do not by themselves determine the outcome.

20.2.1.2 Patently Offensive. In establishing the second element of its three-part test, the Supreme Court gave examples (not mandates) of the kinds of patently offensive materials that states could prohibit: patently offensive representations of normal or perverted ultimate sex acts, whether actual or simulated; masturbation; excretory functions; and lewd exhibition of the genitals.[37] The Court perceived such depictions as hard-core pornography as opposed to expression protected by the First Amendment.

Patently offensive does not, however, refer to all types of offensiveness, such as offensiveness traceable to the political content of the speech or to its satire of contemporary attitudes.[38] The applicable state law defining "patently offensive" materials includes both the statute itself and its authoritative construction by the courts.[39] For example, Illinois's obscenity statute defines *patently offensive material* just as the Supreme Court did, except that it also includes sadomasochistic sexual acts in its definition.[40]

20.2.1.3 Lacks Serious Value. The third part of the Supreme Court's test for obscenity asks whether the work, taken as a whole, *lacks serious literary, artistic, political, or scientific value.* Unlike the first part of the test (which asks whether the work appeals to the prurient interest), the third prong is not decided in reference to what value an ordinary member of a given community would assign the work when judged against contemporary community standards.[41] Instead, the proper inquiry is whether a reasonable person would find literary, artistic, political, or scientific value in the work when taken as a whole.[42]

If a sexually explicit work, *taken as a whole,* has any serious literary, artistic, political, or scientific value, then the work is not obscene. The taken-as-a-whole test has a couple of implications. If an entire work is obscene, but throws in a quotation or two from Voltaire, the work lacks serious value.[43] A work need not be proven to be "utterly" without redeeming social value.[44] Conversely, the taken-as-a-whole test ensures that a prosecutor—who bears the burden of proving that the work as a whole lacks any serious value—cannot take a few lines or images of a work out of context and thereby mischaracterize the entire work as obscene.

Patently offensive sexual material that appeals to the prurient interest will be protected by the First Amendment if it has serious literary, artistic, political, or scientific value. For example, medical books containing graphic depictions and descriptions of the human anatomy have serious scientific value because they are used to educate physicians and other medical personnel.[45]

20.2.2 Possession versus Distribution

An adult's mere possession in his home of obscene material that depicts adults is not a crime. As the Supreme Court observed, "[i]f the First Amendment means anything, it means that a State has no business telling a man, sitting alone in his own house, what books he may read or what films he may watch. Our whole constitutional heritage rebels at the thought of giving government the power to control men's minds."[46] The Supreme Court later emphasized, however, that this limited right to possess obscene materials did not depend "on any First Amendment right to purchase or possess obscene materials, but on the right to privacy in the home."[47]

The right to possess obscene material in the privacy of one's own home does not create a correlative right to receive, transport, or distribute such material (whether selling it or giving it away).[48] Moreover, the government's power to regulate exposure to obscene materials is not limited to juveniles and nonconsenting adults.[49] States can ban or otherwise regulate the display of obscene material in local commerce and areas of public accommodation, such as theaters and bars, even though all those wishing to attend are consenting adults.[50] Likewise, the federal government has prohibited the knowing use of the U.S. mail system to deliver obscene material[51] and has banned the importation of obscene materials into the United States from any foreign country.[52]

Thus, it appears that the State can tell a man sitting alone in his own house in front of his computer terminal that he cannot transmit obscene material to, or receive such material from, others on the Internet and similar online forums. Even if certain materials are not obscene in another country and are downloaded by someone in the United States, such "importation" via computer may be illegal.

Most states prohibit the promotion or dissemination of obscene material. For example, Michigan broadly defines the "dissemination" of obscene material to include "manufacture, sell, lend, rent, publish, exhibit, or lease, to the public for commercial gain, or to offer to or agree to any of the foregoing."[53] Although Michigan's statute does not specifically refer to computer promotion or dissemination, there is no reason that this statute would not apply in the online context. Obscene material can certainly be sold, rented, published, or exhibited online.

20.2.3 Obscenity in the Online World

The prosecution of the Thomases on computer-related obscenity charges is not unique. Others have been prosecuted, both at the state and federal level, for obscenity offenses that were facilitated by a computer.[54]

The Thomases argued on appeal to the Sixth Circuit that computer transmissions are not included within the terms "transporting obscene material in interstate or foreign commerce."[55] Yet the Sixth Circuit rejected this argument by citing the decision of another court, which held that the federal statute's use of such terms as *transports, distribution, picture, image,* and *electrical transcription* clearly indicates that computer transmissions constitute transportation in interstate commerce and that Congress intended to stem such transportation regardless of the means used.[56] In this 1995 case, a military officer was convicted of violating two federal statutes in connection with his transmission and possession via computer of child pornography and other obscene matter.[57]

More and more states are amending their obscenity and child pornography statutes to include specific references to computer technology.[58] Even in those states that have not amended their statutes, the creation, possession, and distribution of obscenity are crimes regardless of the medium used. Moreover, a computer-related offense could result in the seizure and forfeiture of any computer equipment used to commit the offense.[59]

20.3 Special Rules for Child Pornography

Child pornography, like obscenity, is not protected by the First Amendment. It is a crime to create it,[60] to disseminate it,[61] and to possess it in the privacy of your own home.[62] Unlike the three-part test for obscenity discussed in Section 20.2.1, there is no requirement that child pornography appeal to the prurient interest of the average person, that the sexual conduct be portrayed in a patently offensive way, or that the work be considered as a whole.[63] Community standards are irrelevant in child pornography cases. Nonobscene materials depicting children engaging in sexual conduct can be prohibited by state law.[64]

The distribution of such depictions can be banned because they contribute to the sexual abuse of children in at least two ways: (1) the materials provide a permanent record of the child's participation that increases the harm to the child when circulated, and (2) continued distribution (including advertising and selling) of such material contributes to the demand for production of material that requires the sexual exploitation of children.[65] Typically, the sellers and promoters are the ones held accountable for such materials, because they are much easier to identify than the creators of child pornography.[66]

Although it is clear that child pornography is illegal, it is not so clear what exactly constitutes child pornography. At the federal level, *child pornography* is defined as any *visual depiction* involving the use of a minor engaging in sexually explicit conduct.[67] Although the child pornography laws of some states, such as Indiana, define a minor as someone under the age of 16, federal law defines a minor as someone under the age of 18.[68]

Contrary to what one might think, all nude photographs of minors are not child pornography, and all child pornography does not necessarily depict nude children. For example, a parent's photo of their little one naked on a bear rug (suitable for the family photo album) is not child pornography. A photo of a scantily clad child posed in a lascivious or lewd way is child pornography.[69] Moreover, a pedophile's possession of an otherwise innocent nude photo of a child does not transform that photo into child pornography.[70]

It should be noted that some states specifically refer to nudity in their child pornography statutes. For example, under Missouri's statute, a "prohibited sexual act" means "nudity, if such nudity is to be depicted for the purpose of sexual stimulation or gratification of any individual who may view such depiction."[71] Yet a minor need not be completely unclothed in order to be "nude;" being inadequately or partially clothed especially so as to be socially unacceptable is sufficient to constitute being "naked" or "nude."[72] A Missouri court held that a 14-year-old girl who was photographed wearing only a G-string was "nude" for purposes of the statute.[73] Likewise, a child wearing a T-shirt with no cover over the genital or pubic area would also be considered nude.[74]

Even a photograph of fully clothed minors has been classified as child pornography under federal law. The federal child pornography statute prohibits the use of minors engaging in any "sexually explicit conduct,"[75] which is defined as including "lascivious exhibition of the genitals or pubic area of any person."[76] For example, videotapes showing minor female subjects, clad in very tight leotards or bathing suits and shown dancing or gyrating in a fashion indicative of adult sexual relations, have been held to constitute the sexually explicit conduct prohibited by federal law.[77]

Child pornography statutes increasingly refer specifically to the use of computers. For example, under federal law, it is a crime to knowingly transport in interstate commerce, including by computer, visual depictions of minors engaging in sexually explicit conduct.[78] Illinois recently amended its statute to prohibit the creation, distribution, and sale of child pornography using a computer.[79]

One of the newest forms of child pornography is computer-simulated images. Under federal law, electronic splicing of photographs of children's faces onto electronically altered adult bodies is not expressly prohibited.[80] Instead, federal law prohibits the *use* of a minor engaging in sexually explicit conduct for the purpose of producing any visual depiction of such conduct.[81] If no minor has been used, no crime has been committed. Although federal law permits depictions of "simulated" minors engaging in sexually explicit conduct, it does not permit depictions of real minors engaging in simulated sexual conduct.[82]

The Supreme Court has also acknowledged that it would be permissible to produce sexually explicit materials using young-looking adults to portray children.[83] The Court noted that "the distribution of descriptions or other depictions of sexual conduct, not otherwise obscene, which do not involve live performance or photographic or other visual reproduction of live performances, retains First Amendment protection."[84] Moreover, the Court observed that "if it were necessary for literary or artistic value, a person over the statutory age who perhaps looked younger could be utilized. Simulation outside of the prohibition of the statute could provide another alternative."[85]

Most state statutes likewise do not yet ban simulation of child pornography.[86] To avoid constitutional overbreadth, a Georgia court narrowed the phrase "depicts a minor" to mean "any photographic representation that was made of a human being who at that time was a minor. . . ."[87] Missouri's child pornography statute specifically provides that "child pornography" does not include material that is not the visual reproduction of a live event.[88] Yet in interpreting that statute, a Missouri court held that photographs of photographs that were made of live events qualified as visual reproductions of a live event.[89] Under the terms of the statute, "creating" child pornography is not restricted to taking the original photographs.[90] To rule otherwise, the court reasoned, would allow clever pornographers to avoid prosecution by photographing original photos and then discarding them, using the reproductions instead.[91]

Both Arizona[92] and Virginia[93] have recently enacted laws that prohibit simulated child pornography (computer-generated composite photographs). The constitutionality of these statutes, however, has not yet been tested.

20.4 Indecent Material

If sexually explicit material is not considered obscene under the test outlined in Section 20.2.1, it may nonetheless still be considered "indecent." *Indecent materials* is a catchall phrase for sexually explicit materials that are not obscene.

Although indecent materials cannot be prohibited, they can be—and usually are—regulated by state and federal law. The government's exercise of such regulatory power does not depend upon a showing that the material in question is obscene.[94] Nonetheless, because such laws involve regulation of content, the government must assert a compelling interest in regulating the material and use "narrowly drawn regulations designed to serve those interests without unnecessarily interfering with First Amendment freedoms."[95] For example, a Michigan statute prohibiting the sale or distribution of all materials "tending . . . to the corruption of the morals of youth" was invalidated by the Supreme Court for not being narrowly enough drawn to address the evil identified by the state.[96] The statute, in effect, "reduce[d] the adult population of Michigan to reading only what is fit for children."[97]

One of the most common types of regulation of indecent material prohibits distribution to minors. That is, the State can shield minors (defined in most states as those under the age of 18 years old) from the influence of indecent literature even though it is not obscene by adult standards.[98] Although laws vary from state to state, and from community to community, most states prohibit the sale, distribution, or provision to children of material that is "harmful" to minors.[99] The predominant appeal to the prurient interest will not be judged with reference to an average adult, but rather with reference to average children of the same general age of the child to whom the material was provided.[100]

Typically, to be guilty of such an offense, one must either know that the person is a child or fail to exercise reasonable care in determining the true age of the child.[101] For example, a clerk in a convenience store can exercise reasonable care in selling *Playboy* magazine by demanding proof of age. Unlike in-person transactions, it is hard to judge someone's age online.[102] It is not clear what "reasonable care" means for commercial BBSs, network service providers, and even those with Web sites sporting racy advertisements. Posting indecent material to a bulletin board that is open to people of all ages could constitute a violation of the duty to take reasonable care in distributing materials that are harmful to minors. Moreover, even when BBSs and others take precautions, teenagers can easily borrow someone else's driver's license or credit card and gain access to sexually explicit materials online with no danger of a face-to-face confrontation.

Using state statutes that ban distribution of harmful materials to minors, states can prosecute BBSs for providing access to sexually explicit materials. For example, Georgia now specifically prohibits dissemination of harmful materials and advertisements to a minor through a computer or computer network.[103] Although Illinois' statute does not specifically refer to computers, it broadly defines "material" as "any writing, picture, record or *other representation or embodiment*."[104] Those doing business online should take care in choosing what materials they place on their Web sites and in controlling access to those Web sites if any of their materials could possibly be construed as being harmful to minors. Even though state regulations cannot reduce the adult population to reading only what is fit for children, state regulations can require that persons take reasonable care in ensuring that indecent materials do not fall into the hands of minors.[105]

The scope of the State's power to regulate indecent material is determined in large part by the medium in which it is expressed.[106] Of all the communication media, broadcasting has been given the least First Amendment protection because of its sheer pervasiveness and the ease with which children can access it and become a captive audience to whatever is broadcast.[107] For over 60 years, censors have determined what is suitable and decent in radio and television. For example, the Supreme Court upheld the power of the federal government to regulate a radio broadcast containing a 12-minute monologue by comedian George Carlin that both discussed and liberally used language that was indecent but not obscene.[108] Analogizing the regulation to the law of nuisance, which focuses more on channeling behavior than prohibiting it, the court observed that " 'a nuisance may be merely a right thing in the wrong place . . . like a pig in the parlor instead of the barnyard' . . . when the Commission finds that a pig has entered the parlor, the exercise of its regulatory power does not depend on proof that the pig is obscene."[109] Government can prohibit broadcasters from making indecent materials available to children and may do so by a requirement that such materials air only at a time when children would not be likely to hear them.[110]

This captive-audience rationale has been extended to the school environment. The Supreme Court upheld a school disciplinary rule that prohibited the use of obscene language and gesture and other conduct that materially and substantially interferes with the educational process; the student in question had delivered a nomination speech filled with sexual innuendo and lewd references to the male anatomy to a room full of children required to attend the student government assembly.[111]

Yet adult bookstores, theaters, and nightclubs are not regulated as restrictively as broadcasters are. Typically such sources of indecent materials are regulated through zoning ordinances, which control, for example, how close such facilities can be located to residential areas, churches, parks, schools, or other adult-only facilities.[112] Although the Supreme Court has upheld zoning ordinances that constitute merely time, place, and manner restrictions (see Section 19.2 for a discussion of such provisions), it has struck down ordinances that completely prohibit indecent material. For example, the Court held that a community's zoning ordinance that banned *all* live entertainment, including nonobscene nude dancing, violated First Amendment rights.[113]

Regulation of indecent language on dial-a-porn phone lines has not been held to the same high standard as broadcasting. In that context, other controls—such as access codes, credit cards, and scrambling devices—can be used instead to restrict children's access.[114] Moreover, the captive-audience theory does not work quite the same way in the phone sex context; such calls require affirmative action on the part of the caller.[115] Such services are allowed to engage in the business of indecent language so long as they comply with the procedures outlined in the Code of Federal Regulations for indecent telephone message services.[116] Federal law makes it clear, however, that the use of *obscene language* through telephone lines and the making of any *indecent* communication to a minor are strictly prohibited and may result in a stiff fine and imprisonment.[117]

The regulation of indecent material in the online context dramatically changed on February 8, 1996, when the Communications Decency Act of 1996 (CDA) was signed into law as part of the Telecommunications Act of 1996 (S .652). The CDA (Sections 501 through 509 of the Telecommunications Act) prohibits the use of interactive computer services to make "indecent" material available to minors. Many fear that the new legislation will reduce the Internet to what is only fit for children and that words judged to be "indecent" in broadcasting (the "seven dirty words")[118] will suddenly subject their online users to criminal penalties that include up to two years imprisonment and up to $250,000 in fines, thereby having a chilling effect on Internet speech.[119] Others fear that serious works of redeeming value, such as Michelangelo's David or Salinger's *The Catcher in the Rye*, could be effectively eliminated from online discussions and postings because they could be characterized as "indecent."[120] Although the statute makes exceptions for access providers and those who have restricted the access of minors by using such controls as credit cards or adult personal identification numbers (similar to measures used by dial-a-porn services) or by taking in good faith "reasonable, effective, and appropriate actions under the circumstances," the average user (who participates in chat groups or sends e-mail messages via listservs) appears to be unprotected. As this book goes to press, the constitutionality of the CDA has already been challenged.[121]

Those doing business online can help to protect themselves by attempting to ensure that any materials they display or transmit that could be regarded as indecent are not made accessible to minors. It should go without saying that online users should avoid obscenity and child pornography in all their forms.

Endnotes

1. On September 13, 1995, the FBI arrested 12 people and raided over 120 homes and offices nationwide as they concluded a two-year undercover investigation, called "Innocent Images," into the use of computer networks to distribute child pornography and arrange sex with children. *Arrests Made in Computer Child Porn*, Chicago Tribune, Sept. 14, 1995, § 1, at 6.

2. Nancy Millman, *F.B.I. Examines Klein Jeans Ads; An Investigation of Whether Child Pornography is Involved*, Chicago Tribune, Sept. 9, 1995, at 1 [business section].

3. *See* Barbara Karkabi, *Latest Klein Ads Criticized as Kiddie Porn*, Houston Chronicle, Aug. 19, 1995, at 1; Sharon Graydon, *Nothing Comes Between Us and Our Calvins Except Good Taste*, Vancouver Sun, Sept. 2, 1995, at A15; Gary Arnold, *Shameless Sleaze Takes a Bath at Nation's Box Offices, and Klein Ad Bites the Dust*, Washington Times, Sept. 17, 1995, at D5.

4. Barbara Karkabi, *Latest Klein Ads Criticized as Kiddie Porn*, Houston Chronicle, Aug. 19, 1995, at 1.

5. Nancy Millman, *F.B.I. Examines Klein Jeans Ads; An Investigation of Whether Child Pornography is Involved*, Chicago Tribune, Sept. 9, 1995, at 1 [business section].

6. Bob Garfield, *Come On, Calvin, Light My Fire; Pyro-Marketing Burns Us All*, Washington Post, Sept. 10, 1995, at C01.

7. *Provocative Ads Not Porn: U.S.*, (Washington, Associated Press) Chicago Daily Law Bulletin, November 16, 1995, at 1.

8. *N.Y. v. Ferber*, 458 U.S. 747, 764 (1982).

9. *Butler v. Michigan*, 352 U.S. 380, 383 (1957).

10. *Chaplinsky v. New Hampshire*, 315 U.S. 568, 571–572 (1942); *Roth v. United States*, 354 U.S. 476, 484–485 (1957); *Paris Adult Theatre I v. Slaton*, 413 U.S. 49, 69 (1973).

11. *Chaplinsky v. New Hampshire*, 315 U.S. 568, 572 (1942).

12. *Sable Communications of California, Inc. v. F.C.C.*, 492 U.S. 115, 126 (1989).

13. *Roth v. United States*, 354 U.S. 476, 487 (1957).

14. *Jacobellis v. Ohio*, 378 U.S. 184, 197 (1964) (Stewart, J., concurring).

15. *Miller v. California*, 413 U.S. 15, 24 (1973). *See also United States v. Thomas*, 1996 U.S. App. LEXIS 1069 (6th Cir. January 29, 1996), in which the Sixth Circuit applied the *Miller* test to sexually explicit materials online.

16.   *See, e.g.,* 720 I.L.C.S. § 5/11-20(1)(b) (Michie 1993) (Illinois); Ind. Code Ann. § 35-49-2-1 (Burns 1994) (Indiana); Mich. Comp. Laws § 752.363 (1991) (Michigan).

17.   *Miller v. California,* 413 U.S. 15, 32 (1973).

18.   *Hamling v. United States,* 418 U.S. 87, 106 (1974).

19.   *Sable Communications of California, Inc. v. F.C.C.,* 492 U.S. 115, 125–126 (1989).

20.   *Roth v. United States,* 354 U.S. 476, 490 (1957).

21.   *Smith v. United States,* 431 U.S. 291, 305 (1977).

22.   *United States v. Sandy,* 605 F.2d 210 (6th Cir. 1979), *cert. denied,* 444 U.S. 984 (1979); *Hamling v. United States,* 418 U.S. 87 (1974).

23.   *United States v. Langford,* 688 F.2d 1088, 1094 (7th Cir. 1982), *cert. denied,* 461 U.S. 959 (1983). *See also United States v. Thomas,* 1996 U.S. App. LEXIS 1069 (6th Cir. January 29, 1996), in which the court emphasized that venue for federal obscenity prosecution lies in any district from, through, or into which the material moves.

24.   *Sable Communications of California, Inc. v. F.C.C.,* 492 U.S. 115, 125–126 (1989).

25.   *United States v. Sandy,* 605 F.2d 210, 217 (6th Cir. 1979), *cert. denied,* 444 U.S. 984 (1979).

26.   *Id.* at 217-218.

27.   *United States v. Thomas,* No. 94-CR-20019 (W.D. Tenn. July 28, 1994), *aff'd* 1996 U.S. App. LEXIS 1069 (6th Cir. January 29, 1996).

28.   *Id.* The Sixth Circuit rejected the Thomases' many grounds for appeal, including their argument that the use of computer technology requires a new definition of "community;" the court avoided the question by noting that the defendants knew, and controlled, which jurisdictions had access for downloading because membership was necessary and applications were submitted and screened before passwords and material were distributed.

29.   Given the greater odds of winning in a community with stricter standards, both plaintiffs and prosecutors may be tempted to engage in "forum shopping," which occurs "when a party attempts to have his action tried in a particular court or jurisdiction where he feels he will receive the most favorable judgment or verdict." *Black's Law Dictionary* 655 (6th ed. 1990).

30.   *Roth v. United States,* 354 U.S. 476, 487, n.20 (1957).

31.   *Brockett v. Spokane Arcades, Inc.,* 472 U.S. 491, 499 (1985) [clarifying *Roth v. United States,* 354 U.S. 476 (1957)].

32.   *Roth v. United States,* 354 U.S. 476, 490 (1957).

33.   *Id.*

34.   *Mishkin v. New York,* 383 U.S. 502, 508 (1966). *See also Hamling v. United States,* 418 U.S. 87 (1974); *Ward v. Illinois,* 431 U.S. 767 (1977).

35.   *Ginzburg v. United States,* 383 U.S. 463, 473–475 (1966).

36.   *United States v. Knox,* 32 F.3d 733, 754 (3d Cir. 1994), *cert. denied,* 115 S. Ct. 897 (1995).

37.   *Miller v. California,* 413 U.S. 15, 25 (1973).

38.   *F.C.C. v. Pacifica Foundation,* 438 U.S. 726, 745–746 (1978).

39.   *Ward v. Illinois,* 431 U.S. 767, 771 (1977).

40.   *See, e.g.,* 720 I.L.C.S. § 5/11–20(b) (Michie 1993).

41.   *Pope v. Illinois,* 481 U.S. 497, 500–501 (1987).

42.   *Id.* at 501.

43.   *Miller v. California,* 413 U.S. 15, 25, n.7 (1973), *citing Kois v. Wisconsin,* 408 U.S. 229, 231 (1972).

44.   *Miller v. California,* 413 U.S. 15, 24–25 (1973).

45.   *Id.* at 26.

46. *Stanley v. Georgia*, 394 U.S. 557, 565 (1969).

47. *United States v. 12 200-Ft. Reels of Super 8mm. Film*, 413 U.S. 123, 126 (1973).

48. *United States v. Orito*, 413 U.S. 139, 141–142 (1973) (there is no "zone of constitutionally protected privacy" that follows obscene material once it is moved beyond the home area); *United States v. 12 200-Ft. Reels of Super 8mm. Film*, 413 U.S. 123, 128–129 (1973); *Paris Adult Theatre I v. Slaton*, 413 U.S. 49, 66 (1973). *See also United States v. Thomas*, 1996 U.S. App. LEXIS 1069 (6th Cir. January 29, 1996), in which the Court noted that the "[d]efendants went beyond merely possessing obscene GIF files in their home. They ran a business that advertised and promised its members the availability and transportation of the sexually explicit GIF files they selected."

49. *Paris Adult Theatre I v. Slaton*, 413 U.S. 49, 57 (1973).

50. *Id.*

51. *United States v. Reidel*, 402 U.S. 351, 352 (1971), *citing* 18 U.S.C. § 1461.

52. *United States v. 12 200-Ft. Reels of Super 8mm. Film*, 413 U.S. 123, 124–125 (1973), *citing* 28 U.S.C. § 1252; *United States v. Thirty-Seven (37) Photographs*, 402 U.S. 363, 375–376 (1971). *See also* U.S. Const. Art. 1, § 8, cl. 3 (giving Congress broad, comprehensive powers to "regulate Commerce with foreign Nations. . . .").

53. Mich. Comp. Laws § 752.362(2) (1991).

54. *See, e.g., United States v. Maxwell*, 42 M.J. 568, 1995 CCA LEXIS 129 (U.S.A.F. C.C.A. 1995) (violation of federal laws); *State ex rel. Macy*, 891 P.2d 600 (Okla. Ct. App. 1994) (in violation of Oklahoma law, defendant sold CD-ROM discs containing obscene materials and ran a network allowing individuals to dial in and access obscene materials; the defendant's computer equipment, which was used to distribute the obscene material, was seized).

55. Brief of the Appellant at 17 (April 17, 1995), *United States v. Robert Alan Thomas* (No. 94–6648).

56. *United States v. Maxwell*, 42 M.J. 568, 1995 CCA LEXIS 129 (U.S.A.F. C.C.A. 1995).

57. *Id.* Colonel Maxwell was convicted of violating 18 U.S.C. § 2252, for receiving or transporting visual depictions of minors engaged in sexually explicit conduct, and 18 U.S.C. § 1465, for transporting in interstate commerce, for the purpose of distribution, obscene visual depictions.

58. *See, e.g.,* 720 I.L.C.S. § 5/11-20.1(f)(5) (1995).

59. *See, e.g., State ex rel. Macy*, 891 P.2d 600 (Okla. Ct. App. 1994).

60. 18 U.S.C. § 2252 (West 1995).

61. *Id.*

62. *Osborne v. Ohio*, 495 U.S. 103, 108–110 (1990).

63. *N.Y. v. Ferber*, 458 U.S. 747, 764 (1982).

64. *Id.* at 749–751 (films showing young boys masturbating were not obscene, but could be banned under state law without constitutional problems).

65. *Id.* at 759–760.

66. *Id.* at 760.

67. 18 U.S.C. § 2252 (1995).

68. 18 U.S.C. § 2256(a) (1995).

69. *United States v. Knox*, 32 F.3d 733, 747 (3d Cir. 1994), *cert. denied*, 115 S. Ct. 897 (1995). *United States v. Weigand*, 812 F.2d 1239, 1244 (9th Cir. 1987), *cert. denied*, 484 U.S. 856 (1987).

70. *United States v. Villard*, 885 F.2d 117, 122 (3d Cir. 1989).

71. *Missouri v. Foster*, 838 S.W.2d 60, 68 (Mo. Ct. App. 1992), *citing* Mo. Rev. Stat. § 568.060.2.

72. *Missouri v. Foster*, 838 S.W.2d 60, 68 (Mo. Ct. App. 1992).

73. *Id.*

74.   *Id.* (example provided by the court).

75.   18 U.S.C. § 2251(a) (1995).

76.   18 U.S.C. § 2256(2)(E) (1995).

77.   *United States v. Knox,* 32 F.3d 733, 747 (3d Cir. 1994), *cert. denied,* 115 S. Ct. 897 (1995) (court held that even though no one of these factors was dispositive, the totality of the factors suggest that the children were engaged in conduct that would appeal to the lascivious interest of an audience of pedophiles).

78.   18 U.S.C. § 2252 (1995).

79.   720 I.L.C.S. § 5/11-20.1 (Michie 1995) (using the phrase "or other similar visual reproduction or depiction by computer" throughout statute).

80.   *See* 18 U.S.C. § 2251 *et seq.* (1995).

81.   18 U.S.C. § 2251 (1995).

82.   18 U.S.C. §§ 2251, 2256 (1995).

83.   *New York v. Ferber,* 458 U.S. 747, 763 (1982).

84.   *Id.* at 764–765.

85.   *Id.* at 763.

86.   *See, e.g., Aman v. Georgia,* 409 S.E.2d 645, 646 (Ga. 1991), *citing* Ga. Code Ann. § 16-12-100(b)(8).

87.   *Aman v. Georgia,* 409 S.E.2d 645, 646 (Ga. 1991).

88.   *Missouri v. Foster,* 838 S.W.2d 60, 63–64 (Mo. Ct. App. 1992), *citing* Mo. Rev. Stat. § 573.010(1).

89.   *Missouri v. Foster,* 838 S.W.2d 60, 64 (Mo. Ct. App. 1992).

90.   *Id.*

91.   *Id.*

92.   Under Arizona law, it is a Class 1 misdemeanor "for any person depicted in a visual or print medium or live act as a participant in sexual conduct to masquerade as a minor." It is also a crime to produce, record, film, photograph, develop, duplicate, distribute, transport, exhibit, sell, purchase, or exchange any visual or print medium that "depicts a participant in sexual conduct as a minor even though any such participant is an adult." Ariz. Rev. Stat. Ann. § 13-3554 (1995).

93.   Under Virginia law, a person will be guilty of a Class 5 felony if he or she creates, produces, sells, gives away, distributes, displays, or electronically transmits "sexually explicit visual material which utilizes *or has as a subject* a person less than eighteen years of age. . . . [emphasis added]." *Va. Code Ann.* § 18.2-374.1 B (1995). "Sexually explicit visual material" under this section includes a "digital image," [see subsection A], and prohibited production includes "computer-generated reproduction" that uses or has as a subject a person less than eighteen years of age [see subsection B3]. Virginia also prohibits the use of any communications system, including computers, computer networks, and bulletin boards, and any other electronic means to promote the use of a minor in violation of section 18.2-374.1. *Va. Code Ann.* § 18.2-374.3 (1995).

94.   *F.C.C. v. Pacifica Foundation,* 438 U.S. 726, 750–751 (1978).

95.   *Sable Communications of California, Inc. v. F.C.C.,* 492 U.S. 115, 126 (1989).

96.   *Butler v. Michigan,* 352 U.S. 380, 381 (1957).

97.   *Id.* at 383.

98.   *Ginsberg v. N.Y.,* 390 U.S. 629, 636 (1968) (Supreme Court upheld New York statute prohibiting the sale of "girlie magazines" to minors even though the material was entitled to First Amendment protection with respect to adults).

99. For example, Illinois provides that material is harmful "if, to the average person, applying contemporary standards, its predominant appeal, taken as a whole, is to prurient interest, that is a shameful or morbid interest in nudity, sex, or excretion, which goes substantially beyond customary limits of candor in description or representation of such matters, and is material the redeeming social importance of which is substantially less than its prurient appeal." 720 I.L.C.S. § 5/11-21(b)(1) (Michie 1993).

100. 720 I.L.C.S. § 5/11-21(c) (Michie 1993).

101. 720 I.L.C.S. § 5/11-21(a) (Michie 1993).

102. In fact, the convenience store clerk has been virtually eliminated online. Anyone, regardless of age, can browse Playboy's Website and view nude photographs of Playboy Playmates.

103. *See* Ga. Code Ann. § 16-12-100 *et seq.* (Michie 1995). Georgia is not alone: Oklahoma and Virginia have both recently expanded their laws to protect minors from sexually explicit online transmissions, Montana has enacted legislation regulating online content, and several other states—including Alabama, California, Connecticut, Illinois, Maryland, New York, Oregon, and Pennsylvania—have recently considered or are considering such legislation. Ellen Mesmer, "Cyberspace Is a Free-Fire Zone on the Free Speech Battlefield," *Network World,* June 5, 1955, at 64.

104. 720 I.L.C.S. § 5/11-21(b)(2) (Michie 1993) (emphasis added).

105. *Butler v. Michigan,* 352 U.S. 380, 383 (1957).

106. As the Supreme Court has observed, "each medium of expression presents special First Amendment problems." *F.C.C. v. Pacifica Foundation,* 438 U.S. 726, 748 (1978).

107. *Id.* at 748–749.

108. *F.C.C. v. Pacifica Foundation,* 438 U.S. 726 (1978).

109. *Id.* at 750–751.

110. *Id.* at 749–750, n.28.

111. *Bethel School Dist. No. 403 v. Fraser,* 478 U.S. 675 (1986).

112. *See, e.g., City of Renton v. Playtime Theatres, Inc.,* 475 U.S. 41 (1986); *Young v. American Mini Theatres, Inc.,* 427 U.S. 50, 52 (1976).

113. *Schad v. Borough of Mount Ephraim,* 452 U.S. 61 (1981).

114. *California v. LaRue,* 409 U.S. 109, 117 (1972).

115. *Id.* at 118.

116. *Sable Communications of California, Inc. v. F.C.C.,* 492 U.S. 115, 128 (1989).

117. *Id.* at 127–128. *See also* Philip Elmer-DeWitt, *Cyberporn,* Time, July 3, 1995, at 40 (private adult BBSs typically require a driver's license for proof of age, are off-limits to minors, and require significant computer skills to transform binary files into full-color images; random access is extremely unlikely).

118. *F.C.C. v. Pacifica Foundation,* 438 U.S. 726 (1978) (George Carlin and the "Seven Dirty Words").

119. John Schwartz, *Language on 'Indecency' Sparks Telecommunications Bill Protest,* Washington Post, Feb. 5, 1996, at A08.

120. *Id.*

121. The U.S. is not alone in attempting to control online decency: in Germany, CompuServe was forced to block access for its all 4 million of its users to sex-oriented areas of the Internet; in Japan, a man was arrested for distributing pornography on his home page. David Hipschman, *Telcom Act Endangers Free Speech,* Santa Fe New Mexican, Feb. 6, 1996, at D-1. In Saudi Arabia, e-mail accounts can be inspected at will by the ministry of the interior, and ordering something like a Playboy centerfold could lead to imprisonment for dealing in pornography. Jon Auerbach, *Fences in Cyberspace; Governments Move to Limit Free Flow of the Internet,* Boston Globe, Feb. 1, 1996, at 1.

21
Defamation Online

Ruth Hill Bro

21.1 Defamation in an Online World

Electronic publishing, e-mail, and other forms of online communication involve the exchange of facts, ideas, and opinions expressed through words, images, and sounds. Thus, like any other form of communication, an online communication has the potential to defame.

The culture of free expression that exists in many online environments, the enhanced ability one has to send messages to millions of users worldwide within a matter of seconds, and the low access and distribution costs in the online world can greatly magnify the opportunities to defame. It is very easy, for example, to post a message to a bulletin board on America Online that can potentially reach millions of other subscribers within a few seconds at virtually no cost. To distribute the same message in the real world, one would have to mail it (huge postage, reproduction, and staffing costs), be quoted in a newspaper or magazine or on a television or radio broadcast (no control over access or the content of what is printed), hand out leaflets (huge reproduction and staffing costs), or perhaps make the comment in a public speech (a limited audience, amplification costs, and publicity costs). Moreover, the ability to make such comments anonymously is greatly facilitated in the online context.

Defamation is a broad term for two specific torts: (1) *libel* (written and visual defamation), and (2) *slander* (oral and aural defamation). Laws prohibiting defamation protect individuals and entities from damage to their reputations caused by false statements. This chapter outlines the basic principles of defamation law, which the courts are just beginning to apply to the escalating number of lawsuits stemming from derogatory online communications.

The law of defamation varies from state to state. Typically, when an allegedly defamatory statement is published nationwide, courts tend to apply the law of the state where the victim resides, because it is presumed that the victim is injured most in his home state.[1] A defamation lawsuit, however, can be filed in any jurisdiction in which the defamatory remarks were published,[2] which in the online context could be anywhere in the world. Such jurisdictional questions are examined in Chapter 23.

21.2 What Is Defamation?

The following elements are generally required to file either a libel or slander lawsuit:

1. A false and defamatory communication,
2. Of and concerning the plaintiff,
3. That is published to a third party,
4. With some degree of fault, and
5. That results in injury to the plaintiff.[3]

As the following discussion explains, each of these elements is complicated by a number of related considerations.

21.2.1 False and Defamatory Communication

A *defamatory communication* is one that is both false and injurious to the reputation of another. Put another way, defamation is that which tends to injure 'reputation' in the popular sense; to diminish the esteem, respect, goodwill or confidence in which the plaintiff is held, or to excite adverse, derogatory or unpleasant feelings or opinions against him.[4] Merely annoying, hurtful, embarrassing, or unflattering statements, however, will generally not be considered defamatory.[5]

Defamation may occur directly or through inference, insinuation, sarcasm, and even statements made in jest (unless clearly not meant, or taken, seriously). The court, or the jury, will determine whether a statement would be reasonably understood to be defamatory when taken in context. For example, to say someone is a "scab" may or may not be defamatory depending upon whether it is meant (and understood) to communicate that the plaintiff is a "scoundrel" (defamatory) or unwilling to participate in a labor strike (nondefamatory).[6]

It is often thought that stating an opinion is not defamatory if it is clearly denoted as such. Unfortunately, the law is not so clear-cut and will depend on how the communication is reasonably interpreted.[7] Merely inserting the phrase, "in my opinion," before all statements will not protect a statement from being construed as defamatory.[8] If a statement couched as an opinion gives rise to an inference that it is based upon fact, whether because of the wording or the context, it can be defamatory.[9]

In Illinois, for example, courts consider four factors to determine whether a statement of opinion implies factual allegations:

1. Whether the statement has a precise core of meaning or whether the statement is indefinite and ambiguous,
2. Whether the statement is verifiable,
3. Whether the literary context would influence the average reader's readiness to infer factual content, and
4. Whether the broader social context or setting in which the statement appears signals a usage of either fact or opinion.[10]

For example, an Illinois court held that the following statement that was posted as a notice on the Prodigy computer network was not defamatory because it was a statement of opinion: "I don't foresee a very bright future for your company and I have no wish to be sucked into the financial maelstrom. . . ."[11] Conversely, the speaker's claim that the plaintiff "exhibit[ed] all the classic symptoms of Paranoia" was not an opinion (and thus was actionable as defamation), because "the statement clearly contains factual allegations of want of integrity that are subject to verification—that [the plaintiff] is a compulsive liar, that he blames others for his mistakes, and that he feels everyone is out to get him."[12]

Quoting a statement made by someone else will not usually defame the person quoted if the quotation is accurate and is made in context. Slight alterations are also not actionable, unless they result in a material change in the meaning of the quoted statement.[13] Because it is easy to alter or manipulate written or oral statements in online communications, however, one should be careful in using quotations, their attributions, and context.

Like words, a photograph or image can defame.[14] This is particularly true if the picture makes a false or misleading statement about the subject or casts him or her in a false light. For example, an advertisement for bed sheets used a photograph of a female model that was juxtaposed with a picture of an elderly man holding a book widely known to be vulgar and offensive; the combination was defamatory because it improperly implied that the model was "a willing call girl waiting to be used by a stranger whetting his sexual appetite."[15] A photograph was defamatory when published in a magazine story about gangs, because the individuals in the photograph were not connected with gangs or with the story.[16] In another case, the *Saturday Evening Post* was liable for publishing a satirical article on taxicab drivers that included a picture of a cab driver, because the combination incorrectly implied that she was one of the cab drivers described in the story.[17]

In general, the use of a photo or image can be defamatory if (1) it does not accurately reflect the image originally sought to be captured, or (2) it is displayed in a context (for example, in conjunction with other photographs, captions, or text) that suggests a defamatory "fact" about the person depicted.[18]

Obviously, online technology creates enormous potential for defamation liability based upon altered images, sounds, or misleading combinations. This is especially true because digital technology makes it impossible to distinguish an altered image from the original. Liability for contextual defamation is also possible given the ease with which text and images may be combined to communicate defamatory "facts."

21.2.2 Of and Concerning the Plaintiff

The second element of a defamation claim requires that the defamatory statement be about, or of and concerning, the plaintiff.[19] Courts considering this issue look to what a reasonable person in the audience would conclude, rather than what was intended—that is, "not who is meant but who is hit."[20]

Generally, any living person can be defamed, as can a corporation or other entity capable of having a reputation. Because a defamation action is personal to the plaintiff, however, neither the dead nor their survivors have a case unless the survivors are independently defamed.

Only individuals or entities, not groups, can sue for defamation. If a statement is made about a group, a question arises as to whether the statement is sufficiently "of and concerning" the individual members to justify a defamation action. No individual is defamed if the group is so large that "there is no likelihood that a reader would understand the article to refer to any particular member. . . ."[21] As the size of the group increases, it becomes more and more difficult for the plaintiff to show that he or she was the target of the article. Thus, recovery typically has been allowed only in cases involving numbers of 25 or fewer.[22]

21.2.3 Publication to a Third Party

The third element of a defamation action requires that the objectionable material be published to at least one third party. This means that someone other than the plaintiff and defendant must see, hear, or read the communication.[23] Publication need not be intentional. Indeed, a defamatory communication could be negligently published. For example, someone could leave a written document in a place where a third party is likely to read it, or could speak so loudly that it is likely a third party will overhear.[24]

In the online context, where messages are so easily and quickly forwarded, there is a great danger of publication. It is just as easy to send a message to a thousand people as it is to send it to one. It therefore may be difficult in the online context to argue that a message was not published to at least one third party.

Merely reprinting or forwarding defamatory material that was produced by someone else does not insulate a person from a charge of defamation. "[O]ne who republishes a libel is subject to liability just as if he had published it originally, even though he attributes the libelous statement to the original publisher, and even though he expressly disavows the truth of the statement."[25] Nonetheless, because defamation requires some level of fault (discussed below), one who republishes a defamatory statement made by someone else in a totally innocent and nonnegligent manner may avoid liability, assuming that the person who republished the statement has taken adequate steps to verify the truth of the publication.[26] Ideally, however, when republishing materials created by others, it is important to get both a warranty from the source that the content is not in any way defamatory as well as indemnification (a promise to reimburse) against possible liability.

21.2.4 Fault

The degree of fault a plaintiff must prove is one of the most complicated issues in defamation law, because it is so intertwined with First Amendment free speech considerations. Essentially, the degree of fault required depends upon the status of the defamed person.

If the defamed person is a public figure or a public official, then a statement about him or her will be considered defamatory only if it was published with "actual malice"—that is, with knowledge that it was false or with reckless disregard as to whether or not it was false.[27] *Actual malice* is *not* negligence, mere ill will, animosity, or even a failure to investigate or to act as a reasonably prudent person.[28]

This rule is primarily intended to safeguard freedom of speech and freedom of the press, both of which are guaranteed by the First Amendment. Moreover, the public figure—unlike the private person—theoretically has access to the media to repudiate the libel, although this justification is weaker in the Internet context in which virtually anyone has the means to communicate with millions at a time. Accordingly, there is greater freedom in reporting about, and criticizing the activities of, public figures and public officials. The proliferation of rumor-mongering tabloids at the supermarket indicates how difficult it is for a public figure to successfully sue the news media for defamation.

A person may be a public figure in either of two ways. First, the individual may achieve such pervasive fame or notoriety that he or she becomes a public figure for all purposes and in all contexts. More commonly, however, an individual voluntarily injects himself or herself into, or is drawn into, a particular public controversy, and thereby becomes a public figure for a limited range of issues.[29]

Private persons—those who are not public figures—have an easier standard for proving defamation. Generally, each state's law will set the appropriate level of "fault" required, which is usually negligence.[30]

The distinction between public and private figures has already begun to be tested in the online context. In one case, for example, a company that relied upon e-mail for direct marketing sued an Internet-distributed newsletter publisher that claimed that the company engaged in direct-marketing scams.[31] The publisher argued that because the company had distributed its e-mail on the Internet, the company should be treated as a public figure and therefore be required to show actual malice on the part of the publisher. The parties reportedly settled for a small sum because the company could not prove injury stemming from the publicity—sales had actually soared following the newsletter report. Yet, this case raises the interesting issue of how far the "public figure" concept can be stretched in the online context: if someone regularly posts commentary to an online chat group, does that person thereby become a "public figure" subject to all kinds of commentary so long as comments are made without malice? At least one court has suggested that the ability to command attention in the press is, without more, not reason enough to be classified as a public figure.[32]

21.2.5 Injury and Damages

Injury to the defamed person is an essential element of the defamation claim. In some cases, however, injury will be presumed and need not be proven. This presumption arises when a communication is within one of the four categories deemed to be "defamatory per se." Statements are considered *defamatory per se* if they impute to another person

1. A criminal offense,
2. A loathsome and communicable disease,

3. Conduct tending to injure a person in his or her business, trade, profession, or office, or

4. In some states, unchastity in a woman.[33]

In these cases, no proof of injury is required because the subject matter is considered so clearly defamatory that injury is presumed. With other types of statements, the injurious effect on reputation must be specifically shown.

In one case, for example, a court held that various statements posted as notices on the Prodigy computer network by the defendant's agent (whom he had recruited to conduct a campaign of public disparagement against his former software licenser) were actionable as defamation per se.[34] Claims that the licenser made shipments late and did not fulfill obligations to customers imputed to the licenser a lack of ability in his profession. Other claims, that the licenser was under investigation by the State of Texas and that federal mail fraud and customer charges were pending, imputed criminal offenses to the licenser and implied a lack of integrity.

If the plaintiff succeeds in his or her claim, the court or jury may award damages. These can include

1. Compensatory or actual damages caused by the defamation, such as loss of a contract or a job, mental anguish, or humiliation,[35]

2. Presumed damages, and

3. Punitive damages.

Presumed damages and punitive damages usually require a showing of actual malice.[36]

In the first Australian case concerning defamation on the Internet, the Western Australian Supreme Court awarded $40,000 in damages to an Australian professor for comments made by the defendant on an anthropology bulletin board in which he attacked the professor's academic competence and implied misconduct; the court held both kinds of comments to be defamatory.[37]

21.3 Who Is Liable?

One who originally publishes a defamatory statement with the requisite degree of fault is, of course, liable for his or her conduct. Likewise, in most cases, one who repeats or otherwise republishes a defamatory statement is subject to liability as if he or she had originally published it.[38] In contrast, however, distributors such as bookstores and libraries may be liable for defamatory statements of others only if they knew or had reason to know of the defamatory statement at issue. A distributor or deliverer of defamatory material is considered a passive conduit and will not be found liable in the absence of fault.

Thus, the question arises whether an online service provider or the operator of a computer bulletin board is more like a bookstore, library, or newsstand (which has no liability for distributing defamatory material without knowledge), or a newspaper or other publisher (which is liable for any defamatory content it publishes). In 1991, a court held that CompuServe was an "electronic news distributor" that was more like a bookstore or public library; because CompuServe had exercised no editorial control and did not know or have reason to know about the defamatory comments posted by a subscriber, the court absolved it of liability.[39]

In 1995, however, a court ruled that another online service provider, Prodigy, could be held liable for libelous statements made by one of its subscribers because Prodigy exercised "sufficient control over its computer bulletin boards to render it a publisher with the same responsibilities as a newspaper."[40] The securities investment banking firm of Stratton Oakmont, Inc. sued Prodigy for $200 million for comments made by an unidentified person who had posted a message to Prodigy's Money Talk bulletin board claiming that the firm and its president had acted fraudulently and criminally in regard to an initial public offering of stock. Because Prodigy had a policy of systematically monitoring messages submitted to the forum, and had pledged to be a family-oriented computer network that would bar or remove objectionable messages, the court held that Prodigy was responsible for the posting.

In so ruling, the court noted that a distributor or deliverer of defamatory materials—such as a bookstore or library—is considered to be a "passive conduit" that will not be held liable unless it knew or had reason to know of the defamatory statement at issue. Conversely, publishers—such as newspapers—are more than passive conduits for news, commentary, and advertising. Increased liability comes with editorial control.

The court also emphasized that Prodigy could be held liable for the actions of its Board Leaders, who Prodigy hired to enforce its guidelines, despite Prodigy's characterization of such individuals as independent contractors who were not acting as Prodigy's agents. The court noted that Prodigy exercised control over the Board Leaders and could be held liable for their actions or inaction in running Prodigy's online discussion forums. After these publisher and agency arguments were resolved, however, Stratton Oakmont agreed to drop its libel suit in exchange for Prodigy's public statement that it was "sorry" (though Prodigy in no way acknowledged fault). Stratton Oakmont also agreed not to oppose Prodigy's motion for a rehearing on the issue of whether it can be held liable for defamation as a publisher, an issue that has significant implications for all online access providers. In December 1995, the Court denied Prodigy's motion, citing the need for precedent in this area as well as Prodigy's failure to explain why its "new" facts (regarding the true extent of its editorial control) were not included in the original opposing papers.

This decision was legislatively overruled on February 8, 1996, when the Communications Decency Act of 1996 (CDA) was signed into law as part of the Telecommunications Act of 1996 (S .652). Section 509 of the CDA (47 U.S.C. § 203(c)(1)) helps to shield access providers such as Prodigy from defamation liability in a section called "Protection for 'Good Samaritan' Blocking and Screening of Offensive Material." That provision states that "no provider or user of an interactive computer service shall be treated as the *publisher* or speaker of any information provided by another information content provider" (i.e., any person responsible for the creation of information provided through the service). It also states that no provider of an interactive computer service shall be held liable on account of any voluntary action "taken in good faith to restrict access to or availability of material that the provider or user considers to be obscene, lewd, lascivious, filthy, excessively violent, harassing or otherwise objectionable." It is still too early to tell, however, how broadly or narrowly this provision will be interpreted by the courts.

Although this provides some protection for interactive computer services, significant liability issues remain for persons responsible for the creation of information. Those doing business online can still protect themselves by understanding the full range of liability associated with defamatory comments and measure their business-related communications against such yardsticks. This issue of secondary liability for defamation is discussed further in Section 29.3.

21.4 Defenses to Defamation

There are a number of defenses to defamation, but these differ from state to state. In most cases, truth is an absolute defense to defamation, even if the statement causes injury or is published with malicious intent.[42] Indeed, the Supreme Court has held that the plaintiff has the burden of proving falsity, rather than the defendant being required to prove truth.[43] Of course, if a statement is literally accurate but leaves a false impression, there may be defamation.[44]

Statements made in certain situations are privileged and may not be the subject of a defamation action. For example, statements made in a judicial or legislative proceeding are privileged, at least if they have some reasonable relationship to the case.[45] Reporting these types of statements may also be privileged in some states, but, as noted above, care must be taken with accuracy, attribution, and avoidance of defamatory inference or innuendo.

There is also a defense for communications considered to be "fair comment." The First Amendment protects comments on legitimate matters of public interest, as long as they are not made with actual malice.

Finally, parodies may also enjoy First Amendment protection, at least with respect to public figures. Most parody cases, however, have involved situations where the material was so clearly a parody that no one could reasonably have believed it to be based on fact.

21.5 Product Disparagement

Closely related to the concept of defamation is *product disparagement*, otherwise known as *trade libel*. While defamation focuses on injury to a person's reputation or character stemming from another's false statements, product disparagement focuses on pecuniary loss stemming from false statements about a competitor's product.[46] Basically, product disparagement is a statement about a competitor's goods that is false or misleading and that is made to influence others not to buy the competitor's goods.[47] Product disparagement is similar to false advertising, except that it involves misrepresentations about someone else's products, services, or commercial activities.

Disparagement claims may be asserted under both state and federal law.[48] Because laws on disparagement vary from state to state, one should always consult the applicable state law. See Section 28.3 for further discussion of product disparagement.

Endnotes

1. *Hanley v. Tribune Publishing Co.*, 527 F.2d 68, 70 (9th Cir. 1975). *See also Restatement (Second) Conflict of Laws* § 150(2) (1971).

2. R. Timothy Muth, *Defamation and Jurisdiction in Cyberspace*, Wisconsin Lawyer, Sept. 1995, at 56.

3. *See Restatement (Second) of Torts* § 558 (1977).

4. W. Page Keeton et al., *Prosser and Keeton on the Law of Torts* § 111 at 773 (5th ed. 1984) and cases cited therein. *Restatement (Second) of Torts* § 559 (1977) defines a *defamatory statement* as one that "tends so to harm the reputation of another as to lower him in the estimation of the community or to deter third persons from associating or dealing with him."

5. *Gordon v. Lancaster Osteopathic Hosp. Ass'n Inc.*, 489 A.2d 1364, 1369 (Pa. Super. Ct. 1985); *Pierce v. Capital Cities Communications, Inc.*, 576 F.2d 495, 503-504 (3d Cir.), *cert. denied*, 439 U.S. 861 (1978).

6. *Wozniak v. Local 1111 of the United Elec., Radio & Mach. Workers of America*, 57 Wis. 2d 725, 205 N.W.2d 369 (Wis. 1973). *See also Zinda v. Louisiana Pacific Corp.*, 149 Wis. 2d 913, 440 N.W.2d 548, 552 (Wis. 1989)("[I]f the statements are capable of a nondefamatory as well as a defamatory meaning, then a jury question is presented as to how the statement was understood by its recipients.").

7. *Gertz v. Robert Welch, Inc.*, 418 U.S. 323 (1974). *See also National Ass'n of Gov't Employees, Inc. v. Central Broadcasting Corp.*, 396 N.E.2d 996 (Mass. 1979).

8. *Milkovich v. Lorain Journal Co.*, 497 U.S. 1, 19 (1980). *See also Unelko v. Rooney*, 912 F.2d 1049 (9th Cir. 1990).

9. *Milkovich v. Lorain Journal Co.*, 497 U.S. 1, 19 (1990).

10. *Tamburo v. Calvin*, 1995 U.S. Dist. LEXIS 3399 (N.D. Ill. March 15, 1995).

11. *Id.*

12. *Id.*

13. *Masson v. New Yorker Magazine, Inc.*, 501 U.S. 496 (1991).

14. *Regan v. Sullivan*, 557 F.2d 300, 308–309 (2d Cir. 1977) (showing plaintiff's picture as part of a "rogues gallery" may be libel; it was a jury question as to whether such exhibition implied the person was a criminal).

15. *Russell v. Marboro Books*, 18 Misc. 2d 166, 183 N.Y.S.2d 8, 17 (N.Y. Sup. Ct. 1959).

16. *Metzger v. Dell Publishing Co.*, 207 Misc. 182, 136 N.Y.S.2d 888 (N.Y. Sup. Ct. 1955).

17. *Peay v. Curtis Publishing Co.*, 78 F. Supp. 305 (D.D.C. 1948).

18. *Roskos v. New York News, Inc.*, 4 Media L. Rep. 2148 (N.Y. Sup. Ct. 1979).

19. *Auvil v. CBS "60 Minutes,"* 800 F. Supp. 928, 933 (E.D. Wash. 1992).

20. *Camer v. Seattle Post-Intelligencer*, 45 Wash. App. 29, 723 F.2d 1195, 1201 (1986), *quoting* P. Ashley, *Say it Safely* 30 (3d ed. 1966).

21. *Golden North Airways, Inc. v. Tanana Publishing Co.*, 218 F.2d 612, 618–620 (9th Cir. 1954).

22. *Restatement (Second) of Torts* § 564A, Comment b 797–798 (1977).

23. W. Page Keeton et al., *Prosser and Keeton on the Law of Torts* § 113, at 797–798 (5th ed. 1984).

24. *Geraghty v. Suburban Trust Co.*, 238 Md. 197, 208 A.2d 606 (Md. 1965); *Great Atlantic & Pacific Tea Co. v. Paul*, 256 Md. 643, 261 A.2d 731 (Md. 1970).

25. *Hoover v. Peerless Publications, Inc.*, 461 F. Supp. 1206, 1209, (E.D. Pa. 1978).

26. *See Cubby, Inc. v. CompuServe Inc.*, 776 F. Supp. 135, 140 (S.D.N.Y. 1991) (where CompuServe was found not to be liable for republication of defamatory material uploaded to CompuServe by a third party without any knowledge on the part of CompuServe that the contents were defamatory).

27. *New York Times Co. v. Sullivan*, 376 U.S. 254, 279-280 (1964).

28. *Proctor & Gamble Mfg. Co. v. Hagler*, 880 S.W.2d 123, 126 (Tex. Ct. App. 1994).

29. *Gertz v. Robert Welch, Inc.*, 418 U.S. 323, 351 (1974).

30. *Id.* at 347.

31. *Suarez Corp. v. Meeks*, Case No. 267513 (Cuyahoga Cty., Ohio C.P.). *See also Executive Update CEO Briefing*, Investor's Business Daily, March 8, 1995, at A4.

32. *Time, Inc. v. Firestone*, 424 U.S. 448, 454, n.3 (1976).

33. *Restatement (Second) of Torts* §§ 570, 574 (1977).

34. *Tamburo v. Calvin*, 1995 U.S. Dist. LEXIS 3399 (N.D. Ill. March 15, 1995).

35. *Abofreka v. Alston Tobacco Co.*, 288 S.C. 122, 341 S.E.2d 622 (S.C. 1986).

36. In *Dun & Bradstreet, Inc. v. Greenmoss Builders, Inc.*, 472 U.S. 749 (1985), which involved a false credit report, the Supreme Court held that presumed damages and punitive damages were available to non-public-figure plaintiffs despite lack of actual malice, when there was no "public concern" content in the defamation.

37. Francis Auburn, *Usenet News and the Law,* Web Journal of Current Legal Issues (1995).

38. *Stratton Oakmont, Inc. v. Prodigy Services Co.*, No. 31063/94 (N.Y. Sup. Ct. May 24, 1995).

39. *Cubby, Inc. v. CompuServe Inc.*, 776 F. Supp. 135, 140 (S.D.N.Y. 1991).

40. *Stratton Oakmont, Inc. v. Prodigy Services Co.*, No. 31063/94 (N.Y. Sup. Ct., May 24, 1995).

41. *See Restatement (Second) of Torts* §§ 581, 612 (1977).

42. *Curtis Publishing Co. v. Butts*, 388 U.S. 130, 151 (1967). In some states, however, truthful statements published with malicious intent may be actionable. For example, in West Virginia, good faith is required for publishing truthful statements in print, while truth is an absolute defense for oral defamation. *Burdette v. FMC Corp.*, 566 F. Supp. 808 (S.D. W. Va. 1983).

43. *Philadelphia Newspapers, Inc. v. Hepps*, 475 U.S. 767, 775–776 (1986).

44. *Coughlin v. Westinghouse Broadcasting and Cable, Inc.*, 603 F. Supp. 377, 385 (E.D. Pa. 1985), *aff'd*, 780 F.2d 340 (3d Cir. 1985), *cert. denied*, 476 U.S. 1187 (1986).

45. *See Hagendorf v. Brown*, 699 F.2d 478, 480 (9th Cir. 1983).

46. *Auvil v. "CBS 60 Minutes,"* 800 F. Supp. 928, 932-933 (E.D. Wash. 1992).

47. *Aerosonic Corp. v. Trodyne Corp.*, 402 F.2d 223, 231 (5th Cir. 1968).

48. *See* § 43(a) of the Lanham Act.

22
Advertising Online

Peter J. Strand

22.1 Introduction

Online advertising is part of the brave new world of information technology. Traditional advertising—product or service promotion through broadcast commercials and print ads—can now be supplemented, or even replaced, by information at Web sites and on electronic bulletin boards. It is this ability to distribute an electronic "brochure" to every potential customer that makes online advertising so enticing, and perhaps even necessary to remain competitive.[1]

Many forms of traditional advertising are used in the online world. In many respects, however, online advertising is new both in format and in its method of reaching its audience and attracting consumers. It can be a "narrowcast" rather than broadcast because it can be designed for one-on-one contact with potential customers. Furthermore, online advertising can be designed so that the customer seeks the ad rather than the ad seeking its audience. An online advertisement will not have to be all things to all people, seek the broadest audience, or appeal to the lowest common denominator as ads in other media often do.

Although the medium is obviously new, less about it is new than first appears: the aim is the same—to sell products or services—and so are the restrictions and limitations imposed by the various state and federal agencies, regulations, and statutes discussed later in this chapter.

There is no doubt that the rules and regulations of the several federal agencies, the law of false advertising, and the various consumer fraud protection statutes that influence the content and the form of traditional advertising apply also to commercial speech online.

In most cases, a commercial enterprise that intends to be active online should assume that its online activities are subject to regulation. Therefore, to maximize the enormous potential benefit of going online, businesses must be aware of the legal restrictions on methods and content of commercial speech. Without a clear understanding of these restrictions, a business runs the risk of violating the law.

22.2 What Is Advertising?

For any commercial enterprise contemplating going online, there are several obvious questions: what is advertising?, what forms of advertising are regulated?, and is what I'm doing subject to regulation?

There is no specific legal definition of advertising. However, advertising may generally be defined as any action intended to draw the attention of the public to a product, service, person, or organization.[2] Thus, almost any use of information can constitute advertising, even if the person publishing it does not consider himself an advertiser in the traditional sense. For example, there is no question that a Web site providing information about a business, or its products or services, constitutes advertising. In addition, the method by which information is presented online often blurs traditional distinctions between advertising and editorial content. Often there are no obvious breaks in the flow of the content: no beginnings and ends, no physical page breaks, no commercial breaks.

22.3 Regulation of Advertising

Advertising is speech. Therefore, it is protected by the First Amendment (see Section 19.3.5). However, the protection of commercial speech, including advertising, is limited,[3] and untruthful commercial speech is not protected at all.[4] As discussed in Chapter 19, noncommercial speech, such as news and commentary, is strongly protected from regulation by the First Amendment. However, when editorial content and advertising blend together, the whole may be considered commercial speech subject to a higher level of regulation. The content and format of commercial speech, especially advertising, are subject to rules, regulations, and restrictions that do not apply to other speech.

Advertising is regulated in the United States at the federal level by the Federal Trade Commission (FTC), the Food and Drug Administration (FDA), the Bureau of Alcohol, Tobacco, and Firearms (ATF), and even the Department of Transportation (DOT). Federal statutes governing advertising include the Lanham Act,[5] the Federal Trade Commission Act (FTC Act),[6] and the Federal Food, Drug, and Cosmetics Act (FDA Act),[7] as well as various agency regulations.[8] Advertising is regulated at the state level by the individual state's attorneys general and consumer protection agencies and through public and private enforcement of consumer protection, unfair competition, and deceptive trade practices statutes.

Many advertising regulations are general in scope and apply regardless of the medium used. For example, the federal Lanham Act prohibits false or misleading statements in commercial advertising or promotion. State and federal agencies regulate product or service statements, claims, and representations to ensure fair competition and to protect consumers from false claims and representations. The essence of all regulation of advertising is that fair competition requires accurate information upon which consumers can rely.

In addition, there are a number of medium-specific restrictions. For example, television advertising is subject to special industry rules and practices, including prohibitions on cigarette ads,[9] network screening of ads for "offensiveness," and voluntary agreements by certain manufacturers not to run ads on television. It is not yet clear whether the same forces that inspired such practices on television will also move to regulate online practices.

Although the net cast by advertising regulations is broad, there are limits. For example, the Lanham Act prohibits false and misleading statements made in "commercial advertising and promotion." These terms are not defined; however, one case has defined *advertising* for these purposes as statements made for the express purpose of influencing consumers to buy the goods or services represented.[10] Thus, for example, a "disparaging" business reference made to a potential client was not actionable because it was not "made in commerce or in the context of commercial advertising and commercial promotion."[11] On the other hand, "informational" brochures, reports, and films prepared for purposes of selling, price lists, sales memoranda, and even individual telephone calls and letters have all been held to constitute commercial advertising subject to the Lanham Act.[12]

The "commercial advertising" limitation was intended to ensure that political advertising, editorial content, and statements of opinion were not restricted.[13] As already noted, however, in the online context, these distinctions can become blurred. Therefore, the cautious user will treat all online statements relating to any type of commercial activity as "advertising" subject to the reach of the Lanham Act.

Statements must also be publicly disseminated to be actionable. There is a general notion that advertising for Lanham Act purposes necessarily involves public dissemination of information.[14] This suggests that private noncommercial communications are not advertising under the Lanham Act.

Online activity conducted through Web sites or online services such as America Online or Prodigy will, by definition, involve public dissemination of advertising content. Private e-mail messages, on the other hand, might not meet this requirement. However, unlike traditional communications, e-mail can be easily retransmitted by the recipient to the public, and often is. Thus, care should be taken even in private messages.

22.4 The Regulators

As noted above, several federal and state agencies police advertising and have the authority to investigate advertising claims, bring judicial and administrative actions against misleading or false advertising, and even impose penalties for advertising violations. The federal agencies that regulate advertising include the FTC, FDA, FCC, ATF, and DOT.

22.4.1 Federal Trade Commission

The FTC is the dominant government force in the regulation of advertising. It regulates unfair methods of competition and is empowered to prevent the use of unfair or deceptive acts or practices.[15] The FTC's authority comes from the FTC Act which makes it unlawful to "disseminate, or cause to be disseminated, any false advertisement in commerce *by any means.*"[16]

The FTC has published several advertising guidelines and issued regulations concerning advertising content. The framework of the FTC's regulation of advertising is in three policy statements: *FTC's Policy Statement on Deception; FTC's Policy Statement on Advertising Substantiation;* and *FTC's Policy Statement on Unfairness.*

The *FTC's Policy Statement on Deception* (Deception Policy)[17] sets forth the FTC's policy on deceptive and unfair trade practices. The Deception Policy provides a detailed interpretation by the FTC of Section 5 of the FTC Act, under which "unfair methods of competition in or affecting commerce and unfair or deceptive acts or practices in or affecting commerce, are declared unlawful."[18] Under the Deception Policy, an act or practice is deceptive if it has a tendency or capacity to mislead a substantial number of consumers in a material way.[19]

Under the *FTC's Policy Statement on Advertising Substantiation* (Substantiation Policy),[20] advertisers, and advertising agencies, must have a reasonable basis for all claims made in advertisements before the advertisements are disseminated. The FTC considers the failure to "possess and rely on a reasonable basis for objective claims" to be an unfair and deceptive practice in violation of Section 5 of the FTC Act.

Any claim, express or implied, must be substantiated before the ad is run. The advertiser must be able to substantiate all claims such as "tests prove," "studies show," "recommended by," "longer lasting," "faster acting," or "new and improved." In other words, the advertiser must have the tests or the surveys that back up its claims, and claims not supportable by empirical data must be supported by other reasonable grounds. With respect to implied claims, the FTC expects advertisers to be aware of all ways their claims might reasonably be interpreted, and to be able to substantiate each interpretation.

The amount of support required depends on the type of claim, the product advertised, the benefits of a truthful claim, the consequences of a false claim, the difficulty in substantiating the claim, and on the opinions of experts in the field.[21]

Claims that are clearly opinions, such as general statements about a product's superiority, may not be required to be substantiated. However, the prudent advertiser will ensure that all of its claims can be substantiated in one way or another.

The *FTC's Policy Statement on Unfairness* (Unfairness Policy)[22] addresses injury caused by an unfair practice. The Unfairness Policy requires that the injury be substantial. That is, it must be not merely trivial or speculative; it must not be outweighed by the countervailing benefits to consumers or to competition that the practice produces; and it must be an injury that consumers themselves could not have avoided easily.[23]

The FTC has also issued policy statements covering various specific advertising topics including using testimonials and endorsements,[24] pricing,[25] advertising mail-order merchandise,[26] advertising warranties and guarantees,[27] consumer-lending and consumer-leasing advertising,[28] bait advertising[29] and advertising energy consumption of home appliances[30] and advertising guides covering a wide variety of products, including metallic watch bands, mirrors, hosiery, jewelry, luggage, tires, fallout shelters, shell homes, and shoes.[31] Any online advertiser of services or products must consult the FTC regulations to ensure compliance.

In addition to its own investigative work, the FTC also receives information and investigates reports from the National Advertising Division of the Council of Better Business Bureaus, which monitors postings on online services and in online newsgroups. If it finds a defective claim, which the advertiser refuses to stop making, the Better Business Bureau will refer the case to the FTC.

The FTC's Web page address is http://www.ftc.gov.

22.4.2 Food and Drug Administration

The FDA Act[32] gives the FDA authority to regulate advertising and labeling with respect to food and drugs. The FDA Act does not specifically define advertising; however, the federal regulations provide that advertising with respect to food and drugs includes promotional material in a separate medium from the product package.[33] Thus, information posted online regarding any products regulated by the FDA will be subject to the FDA labeling and advertising regulations.

The FTC and the FDA have a Liaison Agreement that specifies each agency's responsibility and jurisdiction.[34]

The FDA's Web page address is http://www.fda.gov.

22.4.3 Bureau of Alcohol, Tobacco, and Firearms

The ATF shares jurisdiction with the FTC over the regulation of advertising alcoholic beverages. Federal law mandates certain statements in connection with advertising of distilled spirits, and no advertisement of alcohol may be disseminated unless the statements are included in the ad.[35] For example, advertisements must provide adequate information to identify the product, the alcoholic content of the product, and the advertiser.

22.4.4 Federal Communications Commission

The FCC was created to regulate interstate and foreign commerce in communication by wire and radio.[36] The FCC has authority over all communications that are broadcast or transmitted by wire. The FCC and FTC entered into a liaison agreement that gave the FTC primary jurisdiction over the regulation of unfair and deceptive advertising in the media, including broadcast media. The FCC has not yet asserted jurisdiction over online activity.

The FCC's Web page address is http://www.fcc.gov.

22.4.5 Department of Transportation

The DOT polices advertising by entities that generally are subject to its regulatory control, such as airlines, bus companies, and other carriers.

The DOT's Web Page address is http://www.dot.gov.

22.4.6 States

Each state seeks to protect consumers against false advertising. All fifty states and the District of Columbia have statutes that, like Section 5 of the FTC Act, prohibit unfair methods of competition including false, misleading, or confusing advertising. A number of state statutes incorporate reference to the FTC Act and specifically refer to the FTC for guidance and direction in defining unfair trade practices.[37]

Several states have adopted the Uniform Deceptive Trade Practices Act (UDTPA). The UDTPA defines deceptive practices as the course of a business, vocation, or occupation that: causes likelihood of confusion or is false or a misrepresentation of the source, sponsorship, approval, certification, ingredients, condition, quality, characteristics, or geographic origin of goods or services; false or misleading advertising; or disparagement of another's goods or services by false or misleading representations.[38]

22.5 Principles of Advertising Regulation

The regulation of advertising in the United States, regardless of the medium, is governed by a very simple principle that can be summarized in very familiar words: Tell the truth, the whole truth, and nothing but the truth. This principle is the essence of the various federal and state statutes and regulations that affect advertising. In general, if you follow these principles for online activity, you will not run afoul of the "advertising police."

22.5.1 Tell the Truth

In general, if you tell the truth in advertising (and remember the broad definition of advertising) you will avoid liability for misleading advertising. Most of the federal and state statutes concerning advertising focus on false advertising. For example, the most important statute with respect to advertising is the Lanham Act, which prohibits false or misleading representations of the nature, characteristics, or qualities of goods, services, or commercial activities; made in commerce; in the context of commercial advertising or commercial promotion; that injure or are likely to injure someone.[39]

The Lanham Act's coverage is very broad; it covers virtually any false or misleading statement made about a product or service, whether one's own or a competitor's.[40] (Another section of the act prohibits other types of unfair competition, including trademark infringement, trade-dress infringement, and false endorsements. These are discussed in Chapters 13 and 28.[41])

The truth is also required by the FTC Act, which prohibits false and misleading statements. Under Section 5 of the act, an advertisement is "misleading" if it fails to reveal facts that are material in light of the representations made, or with respect to the consequences that may result from use of the product.[42] For example, a representation that "anyone could qualify for credit" was false and misleading because the credit card company had minimum requirements, and not anyone could qualify.[43]

Advertising on the Internet is subject to the same requirements. The DOT became one of the first federal agencies to police online advertising when it imposed a $14,000 civil penalty against Virgin Atlantic Airways for advertising a fare on the Internet that was no longer available.[44] The fare expired before Virgin updated its Web page, which listed various available fares.

22.5.2 The Whole Truth

Sometimes it is not enough to tell just the truth. Even completely true statements can be misleading if they are incomplete or fail to disclose material information. Advertisers are required to tell the whole truth.

The whole truth, according to the FTC, is often more than accurate and truthful statements or representations. The truth is what is stated, what is missing, and what is implied. The FTC will actively challenge advertising that it considers to be misleading, even where the statements made are true, if the FTC finds that the ads have misleading implications.

For example, the FTC challenged an advertising campaign that Kraft ran in print and broadcast media to support its Kraft Singles American Cheese. The ads stated that each Kraft Single was made from five ounces of milk and focused on the calcium content of Kraft Singles due to a growing public concern about adequate calcium in the diet. The FTC took issue with the ad campaign and filed a complaint against Kraft alleging that the advertisements were deceptive and likely to mislead consumers because the ads *implied* that each Kraft Single contained the same amount of calcium found in five ounces of milk. Although it was true that Kraft used five ounces of milk in making each Kraft Single, the implication that the calcium content in the cheese slice was equal to that in five ounces of milk was misleading because thirty percent of the calcium is lost during processing. The misleading implications in the ads violated the FTC Act.[45]

True facts presented in a misleading fashion or that falsely imply qualities or characteristics are also actionable if they are not the whole truth.[46] Statements, descriptions, claims, or representations that are misleading (even if literally true), confusing, or having a tendency to deceive,[47] as well as innuendo, indirect intimation, and ambiguous suggestions[48] are prohibited. Examples of violations for telling less than the whole truth include:

- Misrepresentations of test results. The ad cited a survey of nine hundred "women" that included three hundred girls under the age of eighteen.[49]
- Misleading comparisons. "In shampoo tests with over nine hundred women like me, Body on Tap got higher ratings than Prell for body." The test participants made no direct comparisons; they only rated shampoos in several categories.[50]
- Product disparagement. A TV commercial showing a polar bear throwing a can of Coca-Cola in a garbage can marked "Keep the Arctic Pure" disparaged the purity of Coke.[51] Product disparagement is advertising that disparages another person's goods, services, or commercial activities. Comparative advertising is permitted if statements regarding a competitor's product or services are true.[52]
- Visual images without text. A commercial that showed an orange being squeezed directly into a carton of orange juice, when the juice was not fresh but pasteurized.[53] A television commercial that shows a bottle of aspirin being replaced by a tube of topical analgesic is deceptive because it implies that the analgesic contains aspirin.[54]

- Implied representation. A record album cover featuring the name and likeness of a famous performer, when he performed only as a background musician on the recording.[55]
- Omissions of material information. The failure of a credit card company to disclose a deposit requirement and application fee in a television commercial violated the FTC Act because the omissions were likely to mislead consumers.[56]
- Implied claims. A claim that a topical analgesic puts the "strong relief of aspirin right where you hurt" where there was no aspirin in the product was unfair and deceptive.[57]

The anonymity of advertising online creates potential for advertiser-based deception and consumer fraud. For example, a consumer interested in a certain product manufactured by several competitors can send a request for information on those products relating to performance durability, economy, and so on of the product. Since the responses would be anonymous, it is possible that, rather than reports from genuine satisfied or dissatisfied customers, the product provider in the guise of a consumer could provide false information or self-serving information about the product.

22.6 International Consequences

The Internet connects the entire world. Online activity recognizes no borders. Content posted online in Shenandoah, Iowa can be accessed in New York, London, Tokyo, or Tehran. This global access raises several questions: Is an online advertiser subject to the regulations of the jurisdiction where the ad is posted, everywhere it is received, or every location that has access to the ad? Jurisdictional issues are discussed generally in Chapter 23. The cautious online advertiser will consider the rules and regulations (and perhaps the mores and customs) of each country in which the advertiser does, or hopes to do, business.

Borderless markets already exist in advertising within the United States. State laws vary with respect to permitted advertising. For example, games of chance and games that require the purchase of a product to participate are illegal in some states. National television, radio, and print advertisers have addressed this problem by using disclaimers stating that residents of certain states are not eligible to participate or that the offer is void in certain states.

It may be necessary to employ such a device for international advertising online. Certainly it would be prudent to become aware of advertising restrictions and regulations for the product or service advertised on a global basis. Each country where the online message is received will have laws and regulations regarding advertising. For example, Nazi symbols may be banned in Germany, comparative ads may be strictly regulated in some countries, ads for certain products may be forbidden in some countries, and there may even be restrictions on spokespeople. Further investigation should be undertaken to determine whether disclaimers are adequate where any particular kind of advertising may be illegal.

There are some international advertising and marketing standards proposed. The International Standards Organization has generated proposed environmental marketing guides for advertisers making claims about the environmental features of the goods or services. The goal is to create private sector voluntary marketing standards that, if met, would ensure compliance with the laws of various countries.

Another organization concerned with the transnational scope of online advertising is the International Marketing Supervision Network. Founded in 1992, it is an organization of criminal and civil law enforcement agencies from around the world that has the responsibility of protecting consumers against fraud. The United States, Australia, New Zealand, Canada, Mexico, Japan, and the European community are all members. The organization is essentially a clearinghouse for information about fraud perpetrated over international borders.

22.7 Intellectual Property Issues

Protection of intellectual property for online advertising involves many of the same issues that arise in advertising in other media: ads may be copyrighted; they may contain trademarks, trade names, or trade dress; and they have the potential to violate rights of privacy and publicity.

Intellectual property is more complicated online because of the nature of the transmission, that is, digital information that is not manifested in a hard, tangible copy. Nevertheless, the online advertiser should be aware of its, and other's, intellectual property rights. Issues of concern include obtaining permission to use the intellectual property of others and securing and protecting the rights in the ads created by or for the advertiser. Because of the multimedia possibilities for online advertising, there is an even greater risk of infringing on another's copyright, and a commensurate greater need to clear all rights.

There are multiple rights that may need to be cleared for a single ad online. For example, an advertiser that uses the image or photograph of a baseball player in a stadium full of people will need to obtain use rights from the owner of the photograph (the copyright), the baseball player to use his likeness (right of publicity), permission of every recognizable face in the crowd (right of privacy), the team or the league if a team name or logo is identifiable (trademark), and the owner of any recognizable building or structure, including the stadium (privacy). If the ad incorporates audio, the music and the recording must be cleared as well as the content of any spoken audio, including the permission of the performers (publicity/voice) and the creator of the audio contents (copyright).

A brief outline of intellectual property issues facing online advertisers follows. These issues are discussed in greater detail in Chapters 8 through 18.

22.7.1 Copyright

Online advertisers must take care both to avoid infringing on another's rights and to protect their own rights in advertisements. Copyrights are an essential element of advertising.

Each element of the ad, that is the ad copy or text, the music (both the composition and the recording), and the visual images (film, photograph, video), may be a copyrightable work protected under the Copyright Act[58] (see Section 9.3 regarding works protected by copyright). The advertiser will own the copyright in the completed ad if it either creates the ad itself or engages another to create the ad under a work made for hire agreement (see Section 9.5).

If any elements of the ad are imported from an outside source or are preexisting works, the right to use each element must be obtained before the ad is disseminated. For example, to incorporate a music video created by someone else without infringing on any of the various copyrights connected with the video, the advertiser must obtain permission to use three different copyrights: the copyright in the video (i.e., the visual images), the copyright in the song, and the copyright in the recording. Failure to obtain any of these three rights could render the advertisement an infringing work (see Chapter 18 regarding licensing rights to use content).

The flip side of clearing rights is owning them. Material put online may be copyrightable. The advertiser's ad copy, photo images, music, order forms, and so forth, if original, are each proper matter for copyright. It may also be appropriate to undertake the registration of the copyright with the United States Copyright Office to protect the copyright owner's rights with ads (see Section 9).

22.7.2 Trademarks

There are three major areas of concern regarding trademarks and online advertising. First, the advertiser will be likely to use its own trademark to identify its goods and services. Therefore, the advertiser will want to take the appropriate steps to secure its rights in the trademark it uses (see Chapter 13 on trademark use and registration).

The second major area of concern is the use of another's trademark in online advertising. For example, an advertiser may want to provide information that allows the consumer to compare a competitor's products with its own. Use of the competitor's product name and/or logo may involve the use of a registered trademark. Such use is permissible if the representation of the other's mark is truthful, accurate, does not mislead, and does not disparage or dilute the other's trademark (see Chapter 13 on trademark infringement and dilution).

Finally, unfair competition laws prohibit a broad range of deception practices, including trade name infringement, false endorsements, and trade dress infringement. Online advertisers should become familiar with these prohibitions to avoid liability (see Chapter 28 on deceptive trade practices).

22.7.3 Publicity and Privacy

In addition to the copyright and trademark clearances that must be obtained, the online advertiser must be aware of the rights of publicity and privacy of any persons depicted in the ads. These rights may also need to be cleared.

The right of publicity gives an individual the right to control the use of his or her voice, likeness, image, signature, photograph, and persona (see Chapter 16). Publicity rights are often descendible and can be controlled by the individual's estate or heirs.

The right of privacy may be less of a concern, but it will arise most often in the context of individual testimonials or large group photos where an individual is clearly recognizable. In most cases, the advertiser must obtain a release from each individual whose image or likeness appears in the photograph (see Chapter 17).

Endnotes

1. The conventional wisdom is that there are about 30 million online users, and that $1.5 billion was spent on online advertising in the United States. Wall Street Journal, April 14, 1995.

2. George Eric Rosden & Peter Eric Rosden, 2 *The Law of Advertising*, § 17.02[2] (1995).

3. *Bates v. State Bar of Arizona*, 433 U.S. 350, 387 (1977).

4. *In re: R.M.J.*, 455 U.S. 191, 203 (1982).

5. 15 U.S.C. § 1125(a).

6. 15 U.S.C. § 45 et seq.

7. 21 U.S.C. § 301 et seq.

8. See 16 C.F.R. §§ 1-999 (FTC); 47 C.F.R. §§ 1-100.5, (FCC); and 21 C.F.R. §§ 1-299 (FDA).

9. *The Federal Cigarette Labeling and Advertising Act*, 15 U.S.C. § 1331 *et seq.* (1965); *Capital Broadcasting v. Mitchell*, 333 F. Supp. 582 (D. D.C. 1971) aff'd 405 U.S. 1000.

10. *Event Media International, Inc. v. Time, Inc.*, 1992-2 Trade Cases ¶ 70,029 (CCH), (S.D.N.Y. 1992).

11. *Id.*

12. *Mylan Laboratories, Inc. v. Pharmaceutical Business, Inc.*, 808 F. Supp. 46, 458 (D. Md. 1992) (drug package inserts); *National Artists Management Co. v Weaving*, 769 F. Supp. 1224 (S.D.N.Y. 1991) (private statements made on telephone to induce sales); *Mobius Management Systems, Inc. v. Fourth Dimension Software, Inc.*, 880 F. Supp. 1005, 1020 (S.D.N.Y. 1994) (letter to customer disparaging competitor); *Glenn v. Advertising Publications, Inc.*, 251 F. Supp. 889 (S.D.N.Y. 1966) (reports and films for selling); *U.S. Meyer, Inc. v. Ira Green, Inc.*, 326 F. Supp. 338 (S.D.N.Y. 1971) (price lists); *PPX Enterprises v. Audio Fidelity Enterprises*, 818 F.2d 266 (2d Cir. 1987) (record labels); *William Electronics v. Bally Mfg. Corp.*, 568 F. Supp. 1274 (N.D. Ill. 1983) (internal sales memoranda distributed to product distributors).

13. *Groden v. Random House, Inc.*, 61 F.3d 1045, 1051 (2d Cir. 1995).

14. *Garland Company v. Ecology Root Systems*, No. 95-2092-JWL, 1995 U.S. Dist. LEXIS 10951, at *3 (D. Kan. July 13, 1995).

15. 15 U.S.C. § 45.

16. 15 U.S.C. § 52 (Emphasis supplied).

17. 45 Anti-Trust and Trade Reg. Report, (BNA) 689 (1983).

18. 15 U.S.C. § 45(a).

19. 45 Anti-Trust and Trade Reg. Report, (BNA) 689 (1983).

20. *FTC's Policy Statement on Advertising Substantiation*, 48 Fed. Reg. 10,471 (1983).

21. *In Re: Thompson Medical Co.*, 104 F.T.C. 648, 821 (1984), *aff'd* 791 F. 2d 189 (D.C. Cir. 1986), *cert. denied*, 479 U.S. 1086 (1987).

22. *See Appendix to In Re: Harvester,* 104 F.T.C. 949, 1070 (1980). The FTC's Policy on Unfairness has been incorporated into the 1994 Amendments to the FTC Act.

23. *Id.*

24. *FTC's Guides Concerning Use of Endorsements and Testimonials in Advertising,* 16 C.F.R. § 255.0(a) *et. seq.* (1987).

25. *FTC's Guides Against Deceptive Pricing,* 16 C.F.R. § 1.5 (1990).

26. *The FTC's Mail Order Merchandise Rule,* 16 C.F.R. §435 (1995).

27. *FTC's Guides for the Advertising of Warranties and Guarantees,* 16 C.F.R. §§ 239.1-239.5 (1995).

28. 15 U.S.C. §§ 1601 *et. seq.* (1990).

29. 16 C.F.R. § 238 (1995).

30. 16 C.F.R. § 305 (1995).

31. *See* 16 C.F.R. §§ 19-24 and §§ 228-255.

32. 21 U.S.C. § 353 *et. seq.*

33. 21 C.F.R. § 202.1(1)(1).

34. 36 Fed. Reg. § 18,539.

35. 27 U.S.C. § 205(f).

36. Communications Act of 1934, 47 U.S.C. § 151.

37. For example, *see* Consumer Fraud and Deceptive Business Practices Act, 815 ILCS 505/2 (1993).

38. Uniform Deceptive Trade Practices Act, § 2.

39. *National Artists' Management Company, Inc. v. Weaving,* 769 F. Supp. 1224, 1230 (S.D.N.Y. 1991).

40. *Truck Components, Inc. v. K-H Corp.,* 776 F. Supp. 405, 409 (N.D. Ill. 1991).

41. The Lanham Act is drafted in two "prongs." The prong relating to false advertising is discussed in this section. The prong relating to false or misleading designations of source, including trademark infringement, false endorsements, and trade dress infringement is discussed in Chapter 13.

42. 15 U.S.C. § 55.

43. *F.T.C. v. American Standard Credit Systems,* 874 F. Supp. 1080, 1088 (C.D. Cal. 1994).

44. *Virgin Atlantic Internet Penalty,* New York Times, November 21, 1995.

45. *Kraft, Inc. v. Federal Trade Commission,* 970 F.2d 311 (7th Cir. 1992).

46. *Vidal Sassoon, Inc. v. Bristol-Myers Co.,* 661 F.2d 272, 274 (2d Cir. 1981).

47. *Tacquino v. Teledyne Monarch Rubber,* 893 F.2d 1488, 1500 (3d Cir. 1990).

48. *Vidal Sassoon, Inc. v. Bristol-Myers Co.,* 661 F.2d 272, 277 (2d Cir. 1981).

49. *Vidal Sassoon, Inc. v. Bristol-Myers Co.,* 661 F.2d 272, 274 (2d Cir. 1981).

50. *Id.*

51. *Polar Corp. v. Coca-Cola Co.,* 871 F. Supp. 1520 (D. Mass. 1994).

52. *Gordon & Breach Science Publishers v. A.I.P.,* 859 F. Supp. 1521, 1531 (S.D.N.Y. 1994).

53. *Coca-Cola v. Tropicana Products, Inc.,* 690 F.2d 312, 318 (2d Cir. 1982).

54. *Thompson Medical Company v. F.T.C.,* 791 F.2d 189, 197 (D.C. Cir. 1986).

55. *PPX Enterprises v. Audio Fidelity Enterprises,* 818 F.2d 266, 272 (2d Cir. 1987).

56. *F.T.C. v. American Standard Credit Systems,* 874 F. Supp. 1080, 1088 (C.D. Cal. 1994).

57. *Thompson Medical Company v. F.T.C.,* 791 F.2d 189, 197 (D.C. Cir. 1986).

58. 17 U.S.C. § 101 *et seq.*

PART V

REGULATING ONLINE CONDUCT

23
Who Has Jurisdiction?

Geoffrey G. Gilbert

The online world has no territorial boundaries; it is as easy for a person in New York to do business online with someone in California as with someone in India. However, the laws that govern our rights and responsibilities online tend to be territorial, a reflection of their origin in a pre-electronic age. States and countries, and their courts, are limited in the extent to which they can enforce laws and render judgments against people outside their boundaries. If a business in Florida sets up a Web site, will it be subject to suit in California? If an individual in Canada defames a U.S. resident over the Internet, can suit be brought in the U.S. courts? These questions turn on what court has jurisdiction both over the matter in dispute and over the parties.

23.1 Jurisdiction: The Key to Enforcing Rights

Ultimately, a government's ability to enforce its laws depends on whether it can seek redress from a court when they are broken. The same is true of an individual's ability to enforce his or her rights against others. Both types of claimants must find a court that has both (1) *subject-matter jurisdiction* (the power to decide the particular type of dispute before it) and (2) *personal jurisdiction* (the power to make the wrongdoer obey its orders). Otherwise, the court will be unable to enforce its decision, and the claimant will have no remedy.

Subject-matter jurisdiction refers to a court's power to decide the particular dispute at hand. For example, only federal courts have subject-matter jurisdiction over copyright and patent cases. On the other hand, only a state court has subject-matter jurisdiction over contract cases between citizens of its state.

In general, the rules for subject-matter jurisdiction are very clear, and the question is rarely disputed. Personal jurisdiction, however, is more complex. The remainder of this chapter, therefore, focuses on the rules governing personal jurisdiction.

23.2 Territorial Limits of Personal Jurisdiction

Even if a court has jurisdiction over the subject matter of a controversy, it must also have "personal" jurisdiction over the defendant. For a court to have personal jurisdiction over a defendant, the defendant must either (1) be a resident of the state in which the court is located, or (2) have submitted him- or herself, or itself, to the jurisdiction of courts in that state by his or her, or its, actions.

23.2.1 Jurisdiction over Residents

In general, individuals and entities are subject to the laws of their states of residence, and are subject to being sued there. In other words, the courts in a state have general jurisdiction over that state's residents.

For natural persons, residency is normally easy to determine. One is a resident of the state in which one lives, works, votes, and so on. Entities can be residents of multiple states. They are residents of their state of organization (the state of incorporation for corporations), and also of every state in which they are "doing business" (i.e., where they are engaged in continuous and systematic activity).[1] Thus, for example, a Texas corporation is a resident of Texas, and is also a resident of every state in which it has a branch office or otherwise regularly conducts its affairs. A corporation is also likely to be a resident of every state where its employees (including "telecommuters") live and regularly work.[2]

Residents can be sued in courts in their state(s) of residence on any type of claim: the claim need not have any relation to the state.[3] Thus, for example, a resident of California who commits trademark infringement on the Internet could be sued in California federal court. Personal jurisdiction would exist even if the defendant was not in California at the time the infringement occurred, and even if neither the plaintiff nor the injury had any connection with California. The mere fact of residence is enough, by itself, to confer personal jurisdiction over the defendant in the courts of that state.

23.2.2 Jurisdiction over Nonresidents

Most disputes over personal jurisdiction concern defendants who are admittedly *not* residents of the state in which the suit has been filed (the "forum state"), but who are nevertheless alleged to have submitted themselves to the jurisdiction of courts in that state by virtue of some act that is alleged to have given rise to the claim being asserted. It is this type of jurisdiction that is of particular interest in the online world, and the balance of the discussion in this chapter, therefore, pertains to the assertion of personal jurisdiction over nonresidents with respect to causes of action that are alleged to have arisen in the forum state. (The court in which such an action is filed will be referred to as the *forum court.*)

Jurisdiction over nonresidents is usually based on state statutes, called *long-arm statutes.* Although these statutes vary from state to state,[4] all of them are subject to and limited by the two due process clauses in the United States Constitution.[5] Thus, if it would be a violation of due process to assert jurisdiction over a defendant, there is no jurisdiction, no matter what the forum state's long-arm statute says.

Questions of personal jurisdiction ultimately turn on concepts of due process that are characteristically imprecise. Thus, personal jurisdiction issues are analyzed in terms of the *minimum contacts rule:* did the defendant have sufficient contacts with the forum state so that jurisdiction over him or her will not "offend traditional notions of fair play and substantial justice?" Courts also ask whether the defendant's contacts were such that he or she "should reasonably anticipate being haled into court in the forum state?" Or, stated another way, did the defendant so "purposefully avail himself" of the privilege of conducting activities in the forum state that he should be on notice that he could be subject to suit there?[6]

The minimum-contacts rule is intended to ensure both fairness to the defendant and the "orderly administration of the laws."[7] Not surprisingly, however, there is much uncertainty over how these principles should be applied in a given case, and a recent Supreme Court opinion in this area was decided by a vote of 5 to 4.[8]

What types of activity will subject a nonresident to the jurisdiction of the courts in the forum state? At a minimum, a nonresident is subject to being sued on a claim arising directly from his or her actions while physically present in that state.[9] Thus, a traveling salesperson of consumer products must comply with the consumer protection laws of every state in which he solicits business. If he violates those laws, if he injures someone while driving his car, or if he skips town without paying his motel bill, he can be sued in the state where the violation occurs, regardless of whether he is still there when the suit is filed. Similarly, if the salesperson makes a sale and his employer delivers a defective product, the company will be subject to a breach of contract suit in the customer's home state.

However, personal jurisdiction over nonresidents is not limited to claims arising out of their actions while they are physically within the state's borders. Nonresidents are also subject to personal jurisdiction with respect to claims arising out of other types of contact with the forum state that do not include presence within the state.[10] Nevertheless, the procedure is essentially the same in all cases of long-arm jurisdiction. First, the court must decide whether the claim arose out of a type of conduct specified in the forum state's long-arm statute. The specified conduct typically fall into one of the following two categories: (1) the *transaction of business* in the forum state, or (2) the *commission of a tortious act* there. If the conduct fits one of the specified categories, the court must then ensure that asserting jurisdiction over the defendant in the particular case before it will not violate the defendant's right to due process.[11]

23.2.2.1 Transaction of Business. In order to prove that a claim arises out of the transaction of business in the forum state, the plaintiff must show that the defendant engaged in some conduct by which it knowingly or purposefully availed itself of the right to do business in the forum state. In general, telephone solicitations, direct mail, and advertising can satisfy the test, provided that some part of the performance due by the defendant under the contract occurred (or was to have occurred) in the forum state. In other words, if the nonresident can be said to have initiated the transaction, and if its performance of all or part of the resulting agreement took place in the forum state, jurisdiction will be upheld in a suit that arises out of that transaction filed against the nonresident by a forum state resident.[12]

The following example will illustrate. Imagine an Internet Web site resident on a server in Oklahoma that is used by an Oklahoma company to sell Old West memorabilia. When items are ordered, they are shipped free on board (FOB) Tulsa, Oklahoma, which means that the vendor's performance under the contract, delivery of the merchandise, takes place in Oklahoma, not the forum state. On these facts, an Illinois customer would not be able to sue the Oklahoma vendor for breach of contract in an Illinois court because the Oklahoma vendor had not purposefully directed its activities to Illinois residents, and no part of its performance had occurred there. In this example, the seller had done nothing more than make it possible for Illinois residents who wished to do business with it in Oklahoma to do so.[13]

However, what if the Web site software for the Oklahoma business resided on a server located at the Illinois office of an Internet access provider? In that case, the court would first have to decide if merely using the access provider's Illinois server constituted "doing business" in Illinois, such that the Oklahoma vendor would be subject to suit there generally.[14]

If the court were to decide that simply using a server located in a state did not constitute doing business there, it would then have to determine whether the cause of action being asserted against the Oklahoma business arose out of (or was somehow "connected" to) the server's presence in Illinois. If the claim was merely that merchandise ordered from the Web page was defective, it should not give rise to long-arm jurisdiction in Illinois.

The location of a file server was deemed irrelevant by a Florida court in a case involving a database leased to a New York company.[15] The court held that the fact that the database was in Florida did not create sufficient contacts with that state to support jurisdiction over the New York company in a collection suit filed by the database provider. The court reasoned that if the location of the database in the forum state were enough for jurisdiction, users of online services could be haled into court in the state where the supplier's billing office and database happened to be located, even if the customers had been solicited and serviced entirely in their home states. The court felt such a result would violate due process.[16]

The decision of an Ohio court in a case involving CompuServe provides additional insight into how online jurisdiction issues are likely to be resolved.[17] CompuServe, based in Ohio, sued a Texas CompuServe member in federal court in Ohio. CompuServe claimed that the defendant had submitted himself to the jurisdiction of that court by signing up for membership and by offering software for sale on a CompuServe BBS. The court disagreed, however, concluding that the relationship between CompuServe's customers and the State of Ohio is too attenuated to support the exercise of personal jurisdiction over an out-of-state member.[18] Although the court acknowledged that physical entry into the state was not necessary for jurisdiction, the connection between the defendant's activities and the state had to be more than incidental.[19]

As a general proposition, therefore, the more passive a nonresident is with respect to a transaction, and the fewer things that "happen" in the forum state, the less likely a court is to find that the claim arose out of the transaction of business within the forum state.[20] Decisions in this area thus frequently turn on the following factors:

- Whether the transaction was initiated by the defendant purposefully directing his or her activities toward residents of the forum state.[21]
- Whether the defendant visited the forum state in connection with the negotiations that preceded execution of the agreement.[22]
- Whether the agreement was executed by the defendant while he or she was physically present in the forum state.[23]
- Whether all or any part of the performance called for by the agreement was rendered by the defendant in the forum state.[24]
- Whether the agreement created continuing relationships and obligations between the plaintiff and the defendant.[25]

No list of relevant factors in this area can do more than suggest broad categories, and the way personal jurisdiction disputes are decided depends heavily on the facts of each case.[26] As a result, persons who enter into transactions online, such as vendors who advertise and process orders for merchandise via a Web site, are at risk of being sued by their customers just about anywhere. Vendors can reduce the risk (but also their sales) by avoiding direct solicitations to consumers (whether by e-mail or regular mail). Providing for deliveries FOB the vendor's place of business, instead of to the customer's home or business, will eliminate one type of contact with the customer's home state. Vendors can also include a forum selection clause in contracts entered into online. Such a clause designates a court or courts to the exclusion of all others in which any dispute arising out of the transaction must be filed. If the forum selected bears a close relation to the deal, and is adequately disclosed in advance, it stands a good chance of being enforced in a true arm's-length transaction.[27]

23.2.2.2 Commission Of Tortious Acts.

23.2.2.2a Negligence. In a famous case, the Illinois Supreme Court decided that Illinois courts had personal jurisdiction over the Ohio manufacturer of a safety valve that was installed in a water heater in Pennsylvania and sold to a customer in Illinois.[28] Suit was brought by an Illinois consumer for personal injuries attributed to a defect in the valve. The court stated that it was unable to separate the alleged negligence in manufacturing the safety valve from the resulting injury, and concluded, therefore, that "the tort was committed in Illinois." Due process requirements were deemed satisfied by the fact that businesses in foreign states that manufacture products for the Illinois market benefit from the enforcement of its laws, albeit indirectly. The court concluded that the use of such products in the ordinary course of commerce was "sufficient contact with this State to justify a requirement that [the defendant] defend here."[29]

It is not enough, however, for the defendant simply to be able to foresee that its products may be carried by the stream of commerce into the forum state.[30] Thus, in a recent case involving a defective part that was made in Japan, incorporated into a finished product in Taiwan, and then exported for sale in California, the Supreme Court decided that the Japanese manufacturer was not subject to suit in California.[31] The California plaintiff argued that the defendant had knowingly delivered its product into the stream of international commerce with the knowledge that it would ultimately be sold in California, and, therefore, was subject to being sued there. The Supreme Court held, however, that simply putting the part into the stream of commerce with the knowledge that it might reach California was not enough. What was required, the Court's majority held, was "an action of the defendant purposefully directed toward the forum state."[32]

Like the defendants in the two cases just discussed, the operator of a bulletin board or a Web site on the World Wide Web can be said to have introduced whatever appears there into the stream of commerce with the knowledge that it might be accessed and acted upon by "consumers" from just about anywhere in the world. Should, therefore, that operator be subject to suit anywhere a negligence claim may arise out of that publication? Except in cases involving personal injuries, merely transmitting information, or making it accessible, via the Internet should not be sufficient to subject the publisher to a negligence suit filed outside its state of residence.[33] Personal injury claims arising out of the sale of merchandise, however, will depend on the nature and extent of the vendor's contact with the injured plaintiff's state. For example, the sale of component parts to a manufacturer will be much less likely to trigger jurisdiction in a suit brought by an injured end-user than a sale of finished goods made directly to the end-user. The result in such a case is likely to be the same, however, whether the merchandise is ordered online, by telephone, or through the mail.

23.2.2.2b Intentional Torts. Fraud, defamation, and misappropriation of trade secrets are examples of what are sometimes referred to as *intentional torts*.[34] Not surprisingly, a person who knowingly causes injury to another will be subject to suit in the victim's home state almost without exception. Courts are not sympathetic to the defendant's complaints about the burden of litigating in the victim's home state.

Thus, a California court took jurisdiction over the author of a libelous article that had been published in the *National Enquirer*.[35] The author had no contact with California. Nevertheless, California was where the person defamed in the article lived. On appeal, the U.S. Supreme Court held that the author had properly been sued in California because she had knowingly caused injury to a person in that state. Where and how the article was published was irrelevant, and the Court's analysis suggests that the result would have been the same if the libel had been posted on a computer bulletin board in Timbuktu.[36]

In another California case, the court sustained jurisdiction over a Vermont corporation in a suit that alleged intentional interference with prospective economic advantage, slander of title, libel, and unfair competition.[37] These claims arose out of two sets of communications that had been made by the defendant to potential purchasers of the plaintiff's product. In one set of communications, allegedly false statements about the plaintiff's product were included in letters and telephone calls to California residents. In the second set of communications, the statements were published on a computer bulletin board and read by three potential customers of the plaintiff, none of whom was based in California.

The court acknowledged that merely transmitting information through the use of interstate communication facilities would not alone be enough to establish jurisdiction over the sender. However, communications that are "purposely directed" toward a resident of another state will support the exercise of jurisdiction by courts in that state. In the case before it, the court concluded that the defendant's tortious statements, although made to third persons outside California, were expressly calculated to have an effect, that is, to cause injury, within California. The key factor was that the defendant was accused of acting intentionally, as opposed to having committed acts of untargeted negligence, the result of which fortuitously injured plaintiff."[38]

The cases arising out of intentional wrongs demonstrate how far long-arm jurisdiction can reach. As a general proposition, the more egregious the wrong, the longer the reach. Conversely, the less serious the alleged misconduct and the less focused it is on the claimed victim, the less likely a court is to find that the defendant has submitted to the jurisdiction of a distant forum.

23.3 Criminal Jurisdiction

The rules of criminal jurisdiction are similar to those that apply to intentional torts. As a result, a crime committed online will subject the perpetrator to prosecution, both in the state in which he or she was physically present when the crime was committed, and in the state or states in which the victim or victims of the crime reside.[39] In fact, any state in which an essential part of a crime has been committed has jurisdiction to try the offense.[40] Thus, a theft of funds caused by fraudulent wire transfers can be prosecuted where the bank is located as well as in the perpetrator's home state.

A more intriguing question is whether or not the operator of an online service that complies with the laws of the state or country in which the service is located can nevertheless be prosecuted for violating the laws of each other state or country from which the service is accessible via the Internet. The State of Minnesota has tried to address this question in the context of off-shore gambling.

Minnesota's general criminal jurisdiction statute provides that a person may be convicted and sentenced under the law of Minnesota if that person "being without the state, intentionally causes a result within the state prohibited by the criminal laws of this state."[41] It is far from clear, however, that the operator of a gambling site in the Bahamas, accessible via the Internet, would intentionally have caused a result in Minnesota simply by making the site accessible from that state.

Minnesota law enforcement officials have apparently anticipated this possible defense, and have argued that persons who provide services to the gambling site also risk exposing themselves to criminal liability as accomplices. Such persons potentially include Internet access providers and credit-card companies "that continue to provide services to gambling organizations after notice that the activities of the organizations are illegal. . . ."[42] Although it is also unclear that the Attorney General's position on this point would be accepted by a court, its warning is not likely to be ignored by credit-card companies and Internet service providers who receive official notice that they are violating Minnesota's criminal law.[43] Moreover, it is reasonable to expect that the position taken by Minnesota authorities against online gambling will be followed elsewhere, and that it will be extended to activities besides gambling.

A similar case that has gone to trial involved a California-based BBS devoted to sexually explicit material. A U.S. postal inspector in Tennessee signed onto the BBS, downloaded certain images and ordered others through the mail. These online transactions resulted in the BBS operators being prosecuted in federal court in Tennessee for the crime of transporting obscene images by a "facility or means of interstate commerce" in violation of federal law.[44] There was substantial evidence that the defendants had knowingly dealt with Tennessee residents through the mail and by telephone, in addition to via their BBS. On these facts, it is not at all surprising that a court decided the defendants could be tried in Tennessee. Nevertheless, future obscenity prosecutions are likely to arise out of the operation of online services where jurisdiction is predicated solely on the fact that allegedly illegal subject matter has been made accessible via the Internet.[45]

23.4 Jurisdiction over International Transactions

Treaties control the exercise of jurisdiction and the enforcement of judgments between sovereign nations. Where treaties do not exist, comity among nations has established a practice "by which the final judgments of foreign courts of competent jurisdiction are reciprocally carried into effect under certain regulations and restrictions which vary in different countries."[46]

A discussion of bi-lateral treaties and the comity doctrine is beyond the scope of this work. In general, however, the rules of personal jurisdiction are applied by U.S. courts in much the same way in international transactions as they are in interstate transactions.[47] Thus, foreign defendants can be sued in the United States on claims arising out of the "transaction of business" or the commission of "tortious acts" in this country.

Moreover, judgments entered against U.S. citizens by foreign courts are enforceable in this country, provided the U.S. citizen was either a resident of the foreign country at the time, or had, by his or her actions, submitted him- or herself to the jurisdiction of its courts.[48]

Thus, for example, if a European accesses a database in California and downloads a copyrighted computer program or trade secret to a computer in Sweden without the owner's consent,[49] the European, who has committed an intentional act of wrongdoing in this country, will be subject to suit in a U.S. court. By the same token, if a U.S. citizen, while sitting at a terminal in California, breaks into a European computer and steals trade secrets, he or she is subject to being sued in the European jurisdiction whose citizens have been injured by those wrongful acts.[50] A U.S. resident is also subject to prosecution in this country for violations of U.S. criminal laws, even though the violations occurred while he or she was abroad.[51]

Under the circumstances, there is understandable concern on the part of Internet Web site and BBS operators that they may inadvertently run afoul of both the civil and the criminal laws of foreign states. A public BBS may risk suit in Germany, for example, by sponsoring a dialogue that would be protected in the United States by the First Amendment. The operator of a U.S. Web site featuring sexually oriented material that is lawful in this country risks prosecution in a country with much stricter obscenity laws, just as the operator of a Web site in a more liberal European country might risk prosecution in one of the United States.

Eventually, as legislation is enacted and new treaties are approved, online operators may gain protection from suits in jurisdictions, both foreign and domestic, to which their message is not "purposefully directed." In the meantime, prudent "residents" of the Internet, particularly those with assets and personnel abroad, will do their best to make sure that they do not publish material that violates foreign law on systems that are accessible to citizens of other countries. The bottom line is that, until the laws are more well developed in the area of nonresident personal jurisdiction over claims arising out of events occurring online, users of this powerful new medium are well advised to err on the side of caution in conducting their business affairs.

Endnotes

1. Charles A. Wright and Arthur R. Miller, 4 Federal Practice & Procedure, § 1069, p. 358 (1987).

2. See Chapter 24, § 24.2.1.2.

3. *Helicopteros Nacionales de Columbia, S.A. v. Hall*, 466 U.S. 408, 414, n. 9 (1984).

4. A discussion of the various long-arm provisions is beyond the scope of this chapter. See, generally, however, E. H. Schopler, Annotation, *Construction And Application of State Statutes or Rules of Court Predicating In Personam Jurisdiction over Nonresidents or Foreign Corporations on the Commission of a Tort within the State*, 24 A.L.R. 3d 532 (1969); and E. H. Schopler, Annotation, *Validity as a Matter of Due Process, of State Statutes or Rules of Court Conferring In Personam Jurisdiction over Nonresidents or Foreign Corporations on the Basis of Isolated Business Transaction Within State*, 20 A.L.R.3d 1201 (1968).

5. U.S. Const. Art. IV, § 1; 28 U.S.C. § 1738; *Hanson v. Denckla*, 357 U.S. 235 (1958).

6. *See International Shoe Co. v. Washington*, 326 U.S. 310 (1945).

7. *World-Wide Volkswagen Corp. v. Woodson*, 444 U.S. 286 (1980).

8. *Asahi Metal Industry Co. v. Superior Court of California*, 480 U.S. 102 (1987) (holding that jurisdiction by California court over Japanese corporation would be unreasonable and unfair).

9. *Burnham v. Superior Court of California*, 495 U.S. 604 (1990).

10. *Burger King Corp. v. Rudzewicz*, 471 U.S. 462 (1985).

11. This two-part procedure is used in most states, and is clearly described in *CompuServe, Inc. v. Patterson*, 1994 U.S. Dist. LEXIS 20352 (S.D. Ohio 1994), *aff'd on reh'g* 1995 U.S.Dist. LEXIS 7530 (S.D. Ohio 1995). In other states, such as California, the long-arm statute "confers jurisdiction coextensive with that permitted by the Due Process Clause," which makes a two-part analysis unnecessary. *California Software, Inc. v. Reliability Research, Inc.*, 631 F. Supp. 1356, 1359, n. 4 (C.D. Cal. 1986).

12. *Arthur Young & Company v. Bremer*, 197 Ill. App. 3d 30, 554 N.E.2d 671, 676 (1st Dist. 1990).

13. This example is derived from the facts in *Excel Energy Co., Inc. v. Pittman*, 239 Ill. App. 3d 160, 606 N.E.2d 637 (4th Dist. 1992).

14.   *See* discussion of general jurisdiction in Section 23.2.1.

15.   *Pres-Kap, Inc. v. System One, Direct Access, Inc.,* 636 So.2d 1351 (Fla. App. 3d Dist. 1994).

16.   *Id.,* p. 1353.

17.   *CompuServe, Inc. v. Patterson,* 1994 U.S. Dist. LEXIS 20352 (S.D. Ohio 1994), *aff'd on reh'g* 1995 U.S.Dist. LEXIS 7530 (S.D. Ohio 1995).

18.   *Id.,* 1994 U.S.Dist. LEXIS 20352, at *20-21.

19.   *Id.,* 1994 U.S.Dist. LEXIS 20352, at *11, quoting from *CompuServe, Inc. v. Trionfo,* 91 Ohio App. 3d 157, 631 N.E.2d 1120 (Franklin Cty. 1993).

20.   Only the acts of the defendant can be considered in determining whether or not business was actually transacted in the forum state; that is, it is the defendant who must purposefully avail him- or herself of the privilege of doing business in a particular state in order to become subject to suit there. *Hanson v. Denckla,* 357 U.S. 235, 253 (1958), *In-Flight Devices Corp. v. Van Dusen Air, Inc.,* 466 F.2d 220, 226 (6th Cir. 1972).

21.   *Keeton v. Hustler Magazine, Inc.,* 465 U.S. 770 (1984), *Roth v. Garcia Marquez,* 942 F.2d 617 (9th Cir. 1991); *Hagar v. Zaidman,* 797 F. Supp. 132 (D. Conn. 1992).

22.   *A.S.C. Leasing, Inc. v. Porter,* 651 F. Supp. 384 (D. Md. 1987); *Intermar Overseas, Inc. v. Argocean SA,* 117 App. Div. 2d 492, 503 N.Y.S. 2d 736 (1st Dept. 1986).

23.   *Sunbelt Corp. v. Noble, Denton & Associates,* 5 F.3d 28 (3rd Cir. 1993); *Watral v. Murphy Diesel Co.,* 358 F. Supp. 968 (E.D. Wis. 1973); *Trans-continent Refrigerator Co. v. A Little Bit Of Sweden, Inc.,* 658 P.2d 271 (Colo. CT. App. 1982).

24.   *Radiation Researchers, Inc. v. Fisher Industries, Inc.,* 70 F.R.D. 561 (W. D. Okla. 1976); *Cavalier Label Co. v. Polytam, Ltd.,* 687 F. Supp. 872 (S.D. N.Y. 1988); *Wells American Corp. v. Sunshine Electronics,* 717 F. Supp. 1121 (D.S.C. 1989).

25.   *Burger King Corp. v. Rudzewicz,* 471 U.S. 462, 473 (1985), and *Travelers Health Association v. Virginia,* 339 U.S. 643, 648 (1950).

26.   See cases cited in notes 21–25.

27.   *See Burger King Corp. v. Rudzewicz,* 471 U.S. 462, 472, n. 14 (1985); and *Carnival Cruise Lines, Inc. v. Shute,* 499 U.S. 585 (1991).

28.   Gray v. American Radiator & Standard Sanitary Corp., 22 Ill.2d 432, 176 N.E.2d 761 (1961). *See also* E.H. Schopler, Annotation, A.L.R. 3d 24 *supra,* n. 4, for a discussion of numerous cases applying this rule.

29.   *See also Mann v. Frank Hrubetz & Co.,* 361 So.2d 1021 (Ala. 1978); *Bradley v. Cheleuitte,* 65 F.R.D. 57 (D. Mass. 1974); *Catalono v. BRI, Inc.,* 724 F. Supp. 1580 (E.D. Mich. 1989); *Britton v. Cann,* 682 F. Supp. 110 (D.N.H. 1988); and *Tokyo Boeki (USA), Inc. v. S.S. Naverinio,* 324 F. Supp. 361 (S.D.N.Y. 1971).

30.   *See,* for example, *World-Wide Volkswagen Corp. v. Woodson,* 444 U.S. 286 (1980), *supra,* n. 7.

31.   *Asahi Metal Industries Co. v. Superior Court of California,* 480 U.S. 102 (1987).

32.   *Asahi, supra,* n. 31, 480 U.S., p. 112.

33.   *California Software, Inc. v. Reliability Research, Inc.,* 631 F. Supp. 1356, 1359, n. 4 (C.D. Cal. 1986).

34.   *Markarian v. Garoogian,* 767 F. Supp. 173, 178 (N.D. Ill. 1991) (fraud); *Calder v. Jones,* 465 U.S. 783 (1984) (defamation); *Sybron Corp. v. Wetzel,* 46 N.Y.2d 197, 385 N.E.2d 1055, 1058 (1978) (trade secrets). *See also North American Philips Corp. v. American Vending Sales, Inc.,* 35 F.3d 1576 (Fed. Cir. 1994 (patent infringement).

35.   *Calder v. Jones,* 465 U.S. 783 (1984). *See also Holmes v. TV-3,* 141 F.R.D. 692 (W.D. La. 1991).

36. *See generally* Michael J. Yaworsky, Annotation, *In Personam Jurisdiction, In Libel And Slander Action, Over Nonresident Who Mailed Allegedly Defamatory Letter From Outside State*, 83 A.L.R. 4th 1006 (1991), and the following cases, which involve libels arising out of telephone interviews: *Ticketmaster-New York v. Alioto*, 26 F.3d 201 (1st Cir. 1994), and *Madara v. Hall*, 916 F.2d 1510 (11th Cir. 1990).

37. *California Software Inc. v. Reliability Research, Inc.*, 631 F. Supp. 1356 (C.D. Cal. 1986).

38. *Id.*, at 1361.

39. *See also Blackmer v. United States*, 284 U.S. 421 (1932) (U.S. citizen residing abroad is subject to punishment in U.S. court for violations of U.S. laws through conduct abroad); *Rivard v. United States*, 375 F.2d 882 (5th Cir. 1967) (U.S. court has jurisdiction to try Canadian nationals for conspiracy to smuggle heroin into the U.S.).

40. 21 Am. Jur. 2d, *Criminal Law*, § 345 (1981 & Supp. 1995). *See* B.C. Ricketts, Annotation, *Jurisdiction To Prosecute Conspirator Who Was Not In State At Time Of Substantive Criminal Act, For Offense Committed Pursuant To Conspiracy*, 5 A.L.R. 3d 887 (1966).

41. Minn Stat., § 609.025(3).

42. *Warning to All Internet Users and Providers*, Office of the Minnesota Attorney General, published at http://www.state.mn.us/ebranch/ag/memo.txt.

43. State law in this area is likely to take a back seat to federal law enforcement efforts because readily applicable federal statutes already exist. See, for example, 18 U.S.C. § 1984, which prohibits the transmission of bets or wagers by use of a wire communication.

44. The case is *United States v. Thomas*. The convictions were recently affirmed by the Sixth Circuit Court of Appeals. *United States v. Thomas* Nos. 94-6648 and 94-6649 1996 U.S. App LEXIS 1069 (6th Cir. January 29, 1996). The defendants were prosecuted under 18 U.S.C. § 1465, which makes it a crime to transport obscene images by a "facility or means of interstate commerce."

45. For a discussion of the interesting issues that can be expected to arise in that type of prosecution, see Byassee, *Jurisdiction Of Cyberspace: Applying Real World Precedent To The Virtual Community*, 30 Wake Forest L. Rev. 197 (Spring 1995).

46. Wanda Ellen Wakefield, Annotation, *Judgment of Court of Foreign Country as Entitled to Enforcement or Extraterritorial Effect in State Court*, 13 A.L.R.4th 1109, at 1112 (1982).

47. *Rocke v. Canadian Auto. Sport Club*, 660 F.2d 395 (9th Cir. 1981); *See* Beverly L. Jacklin, Annotation, *Service of Process by Mail in International Civil Action as Permissible Under Hague Convention*, 112 A.L.R. Fed. 241; *Bellante Clauss Miller & Partners v. Alireza*, 634 F. Supp. 519 (M.D. Pa. 1985) (same principles governing the exercise of long-arm jurisdiction also apply in suits against foreign nationals, in this case an individual and a corporation who are residents of Saudi Arabia).

48. Sheldon H. Shapiro, Annotation, *Valid Judgment Of Court Of Foreign Country As Entitled To Extraterritorial Effect In Federal District Court*, 13 A.L.R. Fed. 208, and Anno., supra, n. 46, 13 A.L.R. 4th 1109; and *Corporacion Salvadorena de Calzado, SA v. Injection Footwear Corp.*, 533 F. Supp. 290 (S.D. Fla. 1982).

49. *Intellectual Property and the National Information Infrastructure*, The Report of the Working Group on Intellectual Property Rights, Sept., 1995.

50. *See also Blackmer v. United States*, 284 U.S. 421 (1932) (U.S. citizen residing abroad is subject to punishment in U.S. court for violations of U.S. laws through conduct abroad); *Rivard v. United States*, 375 F.2d 882 (5th Cir. 1967) (U.S. court has jurisdiction to try Canadian nationals for conspiracy to smuggle heroin into the U.S.).

51.   Thus, a British court recently agreed to extradite to the United States a hacker alleged to have broken into a Citicorp computer and transferred funds electronically. The Wall Street Journal, Sept. 21, 1995, p. B8. See also Beverly J. Westbrook, Annotation, *Extradition Of Federal Criminal Defendants Based On Comity Of Nations*, 24 A.L.R. Fed. 940 (1975), and *United States v. Verdugo-Urquidez*, 939 F.2d 1341 (9th Cir. 1991), which addressed the United States' forcible taking of Mexican nationals for criminal prosecution in California.

24
Taxation of Online Commerce

Lorijean G. Oei and Jonathan E. Strouse

24.1 Introduction

Who has the power to tax online activity? and What types of taxes apply? are key concerns of anyone doing business electronically. The answers are frequently not readily apparent.

The power of a state (or a country) to tax an online transaction depends on whether there is a sufficient "nexus" or connection between the transaction or the person engaged in that transaction and the jurisdiction seeking to impose the tax.

Being a resident or having salespeople or an office physically in a jurisdiction are traditional bases for nexus. Electronic commerce, however, transcends physicality and geography, thus raising new issues about when the imposition of a tax is appropriate.

This chapter begins by examining how to determine whether an online activity is subject to the tax laws of a particular state or country. The chapter then discusses the types of taxes that apply to online activity and how they vary depending on the nature of the online activity and the specifics of the tax laws of each jurisdiction that has the power to tax that activity.

24.2 Nexus: The Basis of the Power To Tax Online Transactions

24.2.1 The Power of a State To Tax

Before a state may impose a tax, there must be some connection between the taxpayer or the taxpayer's activities and the state that is sufficient to allow the state to exercise jurisdiction over the person. This connection is called *nexus*.[1] Nexus is required before a state may impose transactional taxes, such as sales and uses taxes, or other taxes, such as income tax. Nexus is similar to personal jurisdiction; however, unlike the facts that are sufficient to confer upon a court's jurisdiction over a person (see Chapter 23), the law generally requires in some areas of state taxation, such as sales and use tax, that a person be "physically present" in a state before nexus is established. What follows is a discussion of nexus for transaction and income tax purposes with an emphasis on this additional "physical presence" requirement.

24.2.1.1 Transaction Taxes. Many states seek to tax online transactions such as the sale of goods or a license to use software or other digital content. There is no question that a state may impose such a tax on a buyer residing within the state (see Section 23.2.1). But the logistics of ensuring that each and every buyer remits such a tax to the state is unmanageable. Consequently, states usually seek to require the vendor to collect the tax from the buyer and then pay it to the state. If the vendor is also located within the state (such as a retail store), this presents no problem. But when a buyer engages in an online transaction with an out-of-state vendor, the question becomes: Under what circumstances does a state have the power to require an out-of-state vendor to collect and pay tax on transactions with its residents?

The answer depends on whether there is a sufficient nexus between the vendor and the state seeking to impose the tax. But determining whether a company's activities within a state are substantial enough to trigger a tax obligation is one of the most complex issues that businesses face. When those activities occur online, the issue becomes even more complex.

In 1992, the U.S. Supreme Court addressed the issue of whether a state (in that case it was North Dakota) could require an out-of-state vendor to collect tax on mail-order sales made to its residents.[2] In that case, the vendor sold office products through mail order and over the telephone. The vendor refused to collect tax on its sales to customers in North Dakota because the vendor had no retail outlets or sales representatives in North Dakota, and thus it felt it did not have a sufficient nexus with North Dakota. North Dakota argued that the vendor did have a sufficient business connection because it was taking full advantage of the business market that the state had nurtured.

The Court sided with the vendor and ruled that states may impose a duty to collect use tax on an out-of-state vendor only if the vendor has a "physical presence" in the state.[3] That is why a nationwide mail-order company such as L.L. Bean, which is located in Freeport, Maine, collects tax from Maine residents only.

The requirement of "physical presence" suggests that most online transactions involving out-of-state vendors will not be subject to the state's taxing jurisdiction. However, "physical presence" can be established in a number of ways, some of which may apply to online transactions with an out-of-state vendor. The most common forms of physical presence are the most obvious: having an office or equipment, employees or independent contractors, or agents or affiliates in a state. But, surprisingly, this requirement is often satisfied by those who do business in the decidedly nonphysical world of cyberspace.

"Physical presence" can be established by having an office or equipment in the state.[4] Many online vendors also currently maintain sales offices or retail establishments in several states. If Sears or K-Mart, for example, were to sell their merchandise online, they would certainly be subject to the taxing jurisdiction of any state in which they also had a store or office. But even vendors doing business solely online may be surprised to learn that they have a physical presence in another state. This could occur, for example, by leasing access to an Internet Web server located in another state. Thus, if an online service provider located in New York were to maintain a bank of servers in Georgia to provide local access to its subscribers there, this might be sufficient to establish a physical presence. Consequently, Georgia may be able to require the New York–based provider to collect taxes from its Georgia subscribers.[5]

It is important to note that it makes no difference whether the vendor owns or leases the servers. Either way, it constitutes "physical presence."[6]

Physical presence can also be established, for example, if a vendor sends employees or other representatives into a state.[7] It makes no difference whether the person is the company's employee or independent contractor or sales representative working on its behalf.[8] Moreover, the employees need not be permanently located in the state. Mere visits often are enough.

The number of visits to a state that will be required before a vendor has established a physical presence varies by state. In practice, a business's contacts with a state can be relatively minor, yet still satisfy the threshold for finding a nexus sufficient to trigger a duty to collect use tax. For example, a New York court recently found that a Vermont company that sold customized software and services in New York had sufficient contacts with New York for the state to require the Vermont company to collect use tax even though the Vermont company's only contact with New York was that its employees periodically entered the state to install and maintain the software. The Vermont company had no offices or employees regularly in New York, and did not advertise or actively solicit business in New York.[9]

Even if a vendor does not have any direct physical presence in a state, nexus can be found to exist by attributing the presence of an affiliate or agent back to the vendor.[10] For example, if an online service provider in Utah also operates an affiliated company that designs and maintains Web pages in Nevada, the affiliate's physical presence in Nevada may be attributed to the service provider in Utah. Even if the service provider has no physical presence in Nevada, the service provider may nonetheless be found to have sufficient nexus with Nevada by virtue of the presence of its affiliate, so that the service provider will have an obligation to collect use tax from its subscribers in Nevada. Similarly, business conducted by an agent physically present in a state may create nexus for its principal.[11] For example, if a vendor sets up its electronic storefront through an enhanced online service provider, the presence of the service provider as an agent may create nexus for the vendor as its principal. Whether such affiliate or agent nexus will be deemed to constitute physical presence depends on the state.

Factors that are considered in attributing the presence of one corporation to another include:

• Common control of finances, policies, and business practices;
• The number of common corporate officers, directors, and employees;
• Common telephone numbers;
• Whether the corporations operate independently, hold themselves out to the public as separate entities, and use different company names;
• Common ownership of stock; and
• Whether one entity caused the incorporation of the other.[12]

The more a company observes corporate formalities and keeps the entities separate and distinct, the less likely a state will be to succeed in attributing the physical presence of one affiliate to another.

A company doing business electronically should be sensitive to whether its activities are sufficient to create a nexus with a particular state. For example, if a vendor delivers to Maryland via common carrier glassware that a customer ordered from an electronic storefront, this should not trigger any nexus with Maryland. If, however, the vendor has an agent in the state who maintains a bank of servers for it, and the customer placed the order through one of those servers located in Maryland, this may be sufficient to establish a nexus that would subject the vendor to a duty to collect use tax from the customer and remit it to the Maryland Department of Revenue. Similarly, if a software publisher is located in Massachusetts but its technical support is conducted through a phone bank in Colorado, this may be sufficient to create a nexus with Colorado even though the technical support function is not directly related to the software publisher's sales efforts.[13]

24.2.1.2 Income Tax. Many states also seek to tax income. There is no question that a state may tax the income of its residents. Many states, however, also seek to tax income that nonresident companies derive from sources within the state. A state's power to tax the income of nonresident companies turns on whether there is a nexus between the state and the activities of the nonresident company.[14] In the income tax context, the nexus analysis is analytically similar to the personal jurisdiction analysis as both are based on Due Process requirements (see Chapter 23). In general, nexus may be established where the nonresident company:

1. Has an office, warehouse, or other place of business or owns property located in the state;
2. Has employees or other representatives in the state; or
3. Is doing business in the state.

The clearest basis for nexus is if a nonresident maintains an office or owns property in a state.[15] The property can be real estate or personal property, such as goods. For example, a vendor that stores inventory in a public warehouse in New York from which it fills orders for goods that it sells online may be required to pay income tax in New York on sales of those goods in New York.[16]

Nexus can also be established if a nonresident has employees in a state.[17] Continuous, systematic, or regular contacts of an employee with a state are more likely to be found to establish sufficient nexus than are isolated or minimal contacts. It does not matter that the person is not technically an employee. The presence of an agent or other representative may be sufficient.[18]

Many companies today find that technology permits them to have employees in states in which they do not maintain an office. With a company doing business electronically, telecommuting from another state may be even more common. Telecommuting employees may establish nexus with a state. A company in North Carolina with an employee who works from his or her home in Virginia may be surprised to learn that the presence of that employee makes it subject to Virginia's corporate income tax.[19]

Finally, nexus may be established if a company is doing business in a state. Doing business generally requires that a company be selling goods or services in the state. It does not require physical presence. The rules about what activity will create sufficient nexus vary depending on whether goods or services are being sold.

With services, almost any activity that results in a sale of services creates nexus. Maintaining an office or sending employees into a state will create nexus. Telephone sales and sales that result from advertising, direct mail, or catalogs sent into a state generally will not, unless an employee goes into that state to perform the services. In general, if the services can be performed electronically, this should not create nexus for income tax purposes. Note, however, that this may not always be the case.[20] In one instance, a data processing company that did not own or lease any property or have any employees in Massachusetts was subject to that state's income tax because it provided the service of entering data into computers (located outside Massachusetts) for use by customers in Massachusetts and transmitted data into the state through the phone lines and magnetic tape.[21] Thus, even if services can be delivered online without sending an employee into the state to perform those services, they may nevertheless be sufficient to create nexus.

With sales of tangible personal property, the power of a state to tax a nonresident's income is more limited. Federal law provides that a state has no power to impose income tax on income derived from the interstate sale of goods if the company's only business activities in the state are soliciting (but not accepting or filling) orders in the state.[22] The federal law does not define what "soliciting" means; therefore, states are free to interpret it as they wish.[23] Some states interpret it narrowly so that any activity beyond the mere soliciting of orders subjects the company to income tax. Some states interpret it more broadly.[24] In cases where states find that a vendor is engaged in more than mere solicitation, the vendor's activity usually involved some physical connection to the state. For example, activities that states have found sufficient to create nexus include:

- Soliciting orders with authority to accept them.[25]
- Providing training classes or seminars for customer personnel.[26]
- Repairing and maintaining the company's products.[27]
- Maintaining inventory and setting up displays.[28]

For a vendor selling goods online, if the goods are delivered from outside the state, there should be no nexus. If, however, the vendor maintains an inventory of goods in the state from which it fills orders, or if the vendor sends repair or other personnel into a state to perform any post-sale service, these activities are likely to subject the vendor to that state's income tax.

With licenses of intangibles, the state's power to tax income may be quite broad, as is illustrated by a recent case involving the licensing of valuable trademarks and trade names including the TOYS 'R' US trademark.

In that case, Geoffrey, Inc. (Geoffrey), a wholly owned subsidiary of Toys 'R' Us, Inc. (Toys 'R' Us), was incorporated and had its principal offices in Delaware. Geoffrey had no employees in South Carolina and owned no tangible property there. Geoffrey owned TOYS 'R' US and several other valuable trademarks and trade names, which it licensed to Toys 'R' Us.

As consideration for the licenses, Geoffrey received a royalty of one percent of the sales of Toys 'R' Us. The royalty payment was made annually by wire transfer from a Toys 'R' Us account in Pennsylvania to a Geoffrey account in New York. The net effect of this corporate structure was to produce so-called nowhere income that escaped all state income taxes.

The royalty payments to Geoffrey that were based on sales by Toys 'R' Us stores in South Carolina were deducted from the South Carolina taxable income of Toys 'R' Us, but Geoffrey was required to pay South Carolina income tax on the royalty income. Geoffrey, claiming that it did not do business in South Carolina and that it did not have a sufficient connection with the state for its royalty income to be taxable there, paid the taxes under protest and filed an action for refund. The South Carolina Supreme Court found a sufficient connection with South Carolina, even though Geoffrey had no physical presence in that state, because the corporation had intentionally directed its activity to the state's economy. The court ruled that an out-of-state licensor of intangible property was liable for state income taxes when its licensee used the property in South Carolina and paid a royalty for the privilege.[29]

Other states that have followed South Carolina's lead include Alabama, Florida, Massachusetts, New Jersey,[30] North Carolina, Tennessee, and Wisconsin. Each state has regulations in place that make income earned from the licensing of intangibles taxable. The practical effect is that anyone licensing software, digital content, or other intangibles, online or otherwise, may be obligated to pay state income taxes to each state where it has licensees. Therefore, the stakes are enormous for companies that license intangible property online into other states.

24.2.2 The Power of a Country To Tax

Companies engaging in electronic commerce operate today in a global economy. Therefore, it is important for businesses to anticipate that doing business online may subject them to the taxing jurisdiction of a country that has some connection to the transaction or the company.

Although international taxing systems differ dramatically from country to country, there are some basic similarities. In general, a country will not attempt to tax income or transactions with which it has no connection. For example, the United States will normally not tax the income of a Spanish corporation that has no assets or any other connection to the United States and whose sales are made exclusively outside of the United States.

As in the state context, there must be a sufficient connection between the country and the parties to provide the jurisdiction necessary to impose a tax. Generally speaking, there are two types of nexus that can trigger the taxing jurisdiction of a particular country. First, income or a transaction may be taxable by a particular country because of a nexus between that country and the activities or underlying transactions. A jurisdictional claim based upon such a nexus is commonly referred to as *source jurisdiction*.[31] *All countries imposing tax exercise source jurisdiction.*[32] For example, if a French entity, through its branch located in Boston, Massachusetts, electronically sells champagne to customers on a worldwide basis, the United States would be entitled to tax the income generated by that Boston branch as a result of source jurisdiction because of a nexus between the United States and the underlying transaction. In addition, Massachusetts may be entitled to impose sales tax on each sale made to residents of Massachusetts because of the nexus between Massachusetts and the transaction.

Second, income may be taxable by a particular country because of a nexus between that country and the person or entity earning the income. A jurisdictional claim based upon such a nexus is commonly referred to as *residence jurisdiction*.[33] The United States is one among a number of nations that exercise residence jurisdiction in that it taxes its citizens and resident aliens on their worldwide income, regardless of the country in which it was earned (that is, regardless of its "source").[34] For example, if a citizen of the United States provides, for a fee, access to an online database stored on a computer located in Greece, to customers situated in the Pacific Rim, that U.S. citizen would be required to report any income generated from such online business even though the only nexus, or connection to the United States, was that the person is a U.S. citizen.[35]

When a U.S. citizen living in Boulder, Colorado, earns transactional income, the claim of the United States to tax that income based on residence jurisdiction may overlap with the claim of a foreign country to tax all or part of that income based on source jurisdiction. Similarly, the claims of foreign governments to tax income based on residence jurisdiction may overlap the jurisdiction of the United States to tax a particular transaction based on its source in the United States.[36] To reduce the likelihood of double taxation, many countries, including the United States, will generally allow the country with source jurisdiction to tax the transaction so that the taxpayer only pays a single, and not a double, tax. For example, the Internal Revenue Code achieves this result by granting a dollar-for-dollar tax credit to U.S. residents for income taxes paid to foreign governments.[37] Most other countries make similar accommodations, either through their taxing statutes or through bilateral tax treaties.[38]

24.3 Types of Tax

Once you have determined that a state or another country has the power to impose a tax obligation on your electronic business activities, you must then determine whether your activities are subject to tax. The different types of taxes that are most likely to apply to online commercial activities include sales and use taxes, excise tax, and customs duties.[39]

24.3.1 Sales Tax and Use Tax

24.3.1.1 What Is a Sales Tax? What Is a Use Tax? *Sales tax* is a tax imposed by states on the sale of tangible personal property and certain services.[40] Sales tax is imposed on *intra*state transactions in which the goods or services are purchased and destined for use in the same state.[41] *Use tax* is a tax imposed by states on the use, storage, or consumption of tangible personal property and certain services.[42] Use tax is imposed on *inter*state transactions in which the goods or services are purchased in one state and destined for use in another state.

A state's use tax complements its sales tax in that it is intended to catch the buyer who purchases goods or services from outside the state and uses them in the state. If those same goods had been purchased within the state, the sale would have been subject to sales tax. Accordingly, a sales tax or a use tax may apply to a particular transaction, but not both.[43]

It is important to note that a "sale" for sales and use tax purposes includes not only sales, but also licenses and leases of tangible personal property.[44] For example, if an online furniture store offers its customers the option of either purchasing or leasing furniture, sales tax will be due regardless of whether the customer buys or rents the furniture. Or, for example, an online software "warehouse" may offer some software products for sale, while other software products are licensed. If a customer acquires two software packages, one that is a true sale and one that is a licensed sale, tax may be due on both.

Because they are complementary, sales tax and use tax share some key similarities. Both increase the cost of goods to end-users, share the same tax rate, and generally are imposed on the same categories of taxable goods and services.[45]

24.3.1.2 What Is Taxed? Most states[46] impose a sales or use tax on sales of "tangible personal property." Although the definition of *tangible personal property* varies from state to state,[47] in essence, it means any personal property that may be seen, weighed, measured, felt, touched, or otherwise perceived by the senses.

Practically, in those states imposing a sales/use tax, almost every physical good bought or sold online will be subject to tax as "tangible personal property." For example, an online department store that sells luggage, clothing, bath towels, perfume, and gourmet chocolates to a customer may be required to charge the customer a sales or use tax on these purchases.

Beware, however, that sometimes states will expressly include an intangible within its definition of "tangible personal property," or states will simply indicate that a particular intangible is taxable anyway. Software is a good example.[48]

When a transaction involves products that exist in a digital form (such as software, sound recordings, or photographs), and that can be delivered either in a tangible form (such as on a diskette or CD-ROM) or electronically online, the method of delivery may have an impact upon whether or not the transaction is taxable. Some states tax computer software, for example, only when it is delivered in some physical form, such as diskette or CD-ROM. If it is delivered electronically, these states consider the software to be an intangible and therefore not taxable.[49] Other states, however, do not rely on the tangible-intangible distinction and simply tax all software regardless of how it is delivered.[50]

It is likely that, when confronted with the question of the taxability of other goods that can take either a physical or digital form—such as books, music, photos, and artwork—states will apply the rules they have developed for software to these other types of digital goods. Thus, for an online vendor that sells digital goods, such as music or software, whether a transaction is subject to sales or use tax may depend on how it delivers the digital goods. If the online store delivers them embodied in a physical medium, such as on a CD or diskette, there is likely to be a tax due on the sale. If, however, it delivers them electronically, there may or may not be a tax due depending on the state.

Many states also impose a sales and use tax on services. However, there is much more variation from state to state regarding the taxation of services than there is for tangible personal property. Moreover, although the tax laws for tangible personal property provide that all such property is taxable unless there is some exception, the tax laws for services generally do not provide that all services are taxable. Rather, they specify each particular service that is taxable.

In several states, computer access and other online services may be subject to tax.[51] However, as is true with software and other digital content, it is often unclear what services are subject to tax. There are three reasons for this.

First, the sales and use tax area is complicated by inconsistent treatment among states. Some states tax "information services," while other states tax "automatic data processing services" or "computer services." Even if states use the same term, they may define it to include different services.

In one case, for example, Reuters America provided three types of information services to its subscribers in Ohio and Texas. First, it furnished news and other information to the media. Second, it provided information about a variety of financial and general topics. Third, it supplied a telecommunication network (essentially e-mail).[52] At issue in Ohio was whether these services were "automatic data processing and computer services,"[53] which were taxable, or "personal and professional services,"[54] which were not taxable under Ohio law. The Ohio court concluded that because the company was providing more than simply access to a computer where information was stored, that is, it was providing "personal and professional services," it was not required to collect use tax.[55] However, this same company, providing essentially the same services, was required to collect tax on the "information services"[56] it provided in Texas.[57]

This example illustrates how a company engaged in the same activities in several states can be required to collect tax in one state, but not in another state. Each state defines differently what is subject to tax. In Ohio, it is "automatic data processing and computer services," and in Texas, it is "information services."

Second, the definitions of taxable services are not always contained in a state's tax statute. Some states define these terms in their regulations, and some states leave it to the courts to determine whether a particular service falls within the definition of a taxable "information service." It is also important to note that, even without a specific statute or regulation on the subject, some states have developed a policy regarding taxing information services through publications of their tax departments. Consequently, a company must examine the tax statutes, regulations, publications, and case law in each state with which it has a nexus in order to determine whether a sale constitutes a "taxable service" for which it must collect sales or use tax.[58]

Third, this area is complicated by the constant and rapid innovation in computer and telecommunications technology. Tax laws do not keep pace; consequently, it is a perennial struggle to determine whether and how an outdated tax statute should be interpreted to cover a new service that the legislators did not contemplate when they enacted the tax statute.

A good example of how a state may interpret a tax statute to cover an online service that is not clearly taxable under the language of that statute is a recent ruling by the Texas Comptroller of Public Accounts. Texas defines "taxable services" to include tele-communication services.[59] The Comptroller of Public Accounts recently determined that monthly access fees for Internet facilities were taxable as telecommunications services.[60] The Comptroller also ruled that monthly fees charged for putting company catalogs online are taxable if customers can place orders by accessing the electronic bulletin board or online catalog.[61]

A recent ruling in Connecticut provides another example. Connecticut taxes information services as part of "computer and data processing services, including, but not limited to, time."[62] "Computer and data processing services" are defined in a Connecticut regulation to include "providing computer time, sorting and filing of information, retrieving or providing access to information."[63] In an administrative ruling, the Connecticut Department of Revenue found that a company's service of providing its customers access via computers to a database of the state Department of Motor Vehicles (DMV) was taxable as a data processing service. The Department of Revenue reasoned that the object of the transaction was for the customer to obtain information with the convenience, speed, and accuracy that was possible only through access to the DMV's database.[64]

24.3.1.3 Who Pays? The ultimate end-user of the good or service pays the applicable sales or use tax.[65] In most states, the tax is actually imposed on the vendor in exchange for the privilege of making sales in the state. Practically, however, the end-user pays the tax because most states allow vendors to pass the tax through to the end-user.

24.3.1.4 Who Collects? In the case of sales tax, the vendor has the duty to collect the sales tax, file the return, and remit the tax. In the case of use tax, the end-user is generally required to report purchases subject to use tax and to remit the tax.

As a practical matter, end-users rarely pay use tax. To avoid the difficulty of collecting use taxes from countless consumers, many states seek to impose a duty to collect use tax on out-of-state vendors. As discussed in Section 24.2.1, whether a state can require an out-of-state vendor to collect such a use tax depends on whether the vendor has a nexus with the state.

24.3.2 Excise Tax

An excise tax is a tax imposed upon specific products or transactions. For example, an excise tax is imposed on the sale or use of fuels,[66] telecommunications services,[67] gasoline,[68] tires,[69] and sport fishing equipment.[70] An excise tax may be imposed by the federal government or by a state government.[71]

For example, there is a three percent federal excise tax on "communications services."[72] "Communications services" include toll telephone service (long distance and WATS) and local telephone service.[73] Similarly, Illinois, under its Telecommunications Excise Tax Act,[74] places a five percent tax on the gross receipts of all interstate calls originating or terminating within the state, and that are charged to a service address in Illinois. The law also places a five percent service tax on intrastate communications.[75]

The obligation to pay or collect an excise tax should not change because the good or service is sold or delivered electronically. For example, if an outfitter also sells sport fishing equipment that is subject to an excise tax when sold through its physical storefront, the fact that the outfitter also sells the equipment online will not relieve the outfitter of its obligation to collect the excise tax.

The person or entity that purchases or uses the goods or services is required to pay the excise tax. However, the person or entity that sells the taxable product or service to the end user will be responsible for collecting the excise tax and remitting it to the government. For example, a local telephone company in Illinois is required to collect the federal and Illinois excise tax on the communication services it sells, file the proper excise tax returns, and remit the excise tax.[76]

24.3.3 Customs Duties and Tariffs

Customs duties are taxes that are levied by the U.S. government on the importation of specific commodities.[77] A tariff is a schedule that specifies the amount of the duty, or rate at which it is calculated, for various commodities. Duties vary by commodity. Duties are also affected by the country of origin and applicable international treaties. In the United States, rates of duty, country of origin, and treaty information are collected for different types of commodities in tariff schedules called the *Harmonized Tariff Schedules*.[78]

To determine whether a particular commodity is duty free or subject to a customs duty, it is necessary to consult the customs law and its voluminous regulations.[79] For example, if a computer software vendor located in Japan delivers the software online directly to the purchaser located in Los Angeles, that transaction would be exempt from customs duties because it would be deemed to be a telecommunication. Telecommunications are exempt from the *Tariff Schedules*.[80] This result is in stark contrast to a situation where a purchaser in Los Angeles orders copies of the software on diskette from a Japanese software developer, or other foreign manufacturer, who then ships the software on CD-ROM to the customer in Los Angeles. In this case, the transaction is subject to duty upon entry into the United States.[81] Thus, in some cases, there may be a planning advantage to sending such products electronically.

In other cases, the method of delivery might not matter. In general, according to the *Harmonized Tariff Schedules*, printed sheet music, original art work, paintings, and books are duty free. Thus, whether such items are delivered electronically or in tangible form makes no difference for customs purposes.

The importer of goods is the person primarily liable for the payment of customs duties.[82] An *importer* is defined as the actual owner of the goods, the importer of record, the consignee, or the transferee of the goods.[83] The importer may pay the Customs Service directly or through a licensed customhouse broker.[84] The United States maintains a lien on the imported merchandise in the event that duties are not paid.[85]

The U.S. Customs Service is responsible for assessing and collecting customs duties.[86]

24.4 Conclusion

Tax laws and the concepts underlying them are grounded on geography—where is a company located or doing business—and on physicality—what tangible things are being sold or services are being performed. In many respects the activities of a company doing business electronically transcend geography and physicality. Consequently, taxing authorities are having a difficult time applying their tax laws to electronic commerce, especially when it comes to sales tax on electronic sales or customs duties on the importation of digital goods. Anyone doing business electronically is confronted with the task of reviewing the statutes, regulations, rulings, and case law of each jurisdiction to determine whether it has nexus with that jurisdiction and whether its activities are subject to tax. This is a substantial undertaking. Furthermore, tax laws frequently change and expand. It is the "folk wisdom of tax historians that every available tax is eventually used."[87] Given the complexity and frequent changes in tax laws, the assistance of a knowledgeable tax advisor is indispensable to anyone doing business electronically.

Endnotes

1. The concept of nexus was first introduced by the U.S. Supreme Court in *Wisconsin v. J.C. Penney Co.*, 311 U.S. 435, 444–45 (1940), which focused on the Due Process Clause underpinnings of the nexus requirement, and was further developed in *Miller Bros. Co. v. Maryland*, 347 U.S. 340 (1954), and *Moorman Mfg. Co. v. Bair*, 437 U.S. 267 (1978). The Commerce Clause underpinnings of the nexus requirement are discussed in the seminal case of *Complete Auto Transit, Inc. v. Brady*, 430 U.S. 274 (1977). The Supreme Court's most recent pronouncement on the Due Process and Commerce Clause's limits on the power of a state to tax came in *Quill Corp. v. North Dakota*, 504 U.S. 298 (1992).

2. *Quill Corp. v. North Dakota*, 504 U.S. 298 (1992).

3. *Quill Corp. v. North Dakota*, 504 U.S. 298, 314–319 (1992).

4. *See, e.g.*, S.D. Codified Laws Ann. § 10-46-20 (1995); W. Va. Code § 11-15A-6a (1995); *see also Nelson v. Sears, Roebuck & Co.*, 312 U.S. 359 (1941).

5. *See Northwestern States Portland Cement Co. v. Minnesota*, and *Stockham Valves & Fittings, Inc.*, 358 U.S. 450 (1959) (business location in the state). *See, e.g.*, Tenn. Code Ann. § 67-6-102(6)(F) (1995). *See generally* Gail Bronson, *The Tax Man Cometh, Even to the Net*, Interactive Age 34 (Jul. 31, 1995); Mitch Betts, *Internet Renews Tax Battles*, Computerworld 64 (Jun. 19, 1995).

6. Thomas Dunst, *Activities Creating Nexus for Income Tax Purposes*, 6 J. St. Tax'n 279, 282–84 (Table) (1987).

7. *See Scripto, Inc. v. Carson*, 362 U.S. 207 (1960); *see also Tyler Pipe Indus., Inc. v. Washington St. Dep't of Rev.*, 483 U.S. 232 (1987) (single independent contractor who solicited sales for taxpayer created nexus); *Felt & Tarrant Mfg. Co. v. Gallagher*, 306 U.S. 62 (1939); *see, e.g.*, W. Va. Code § 11-15A-6a (1995).

8. *See Scripto, Inc. v. Carson*, 362 U.S. 207 (1960); *Tyler Pipe Indus., Inc. v. Washington St. Dep't of Rev.*, 483 U.S. 232 (1987) (single independent contractor who solicited sales for taxpayer created nexus); *Felt & Tarrant Mfg. Co. v. Gallagher*, 306 U.S. 62 (1939).

9. *In re Vermont Information Processing, Inc.*, No. 139 (N.Y. Ct. App. Jun. 14, 1995), *reported in Computer Company Must Pay Taxes in New York, Court Rules*, 12 Computer L. Strategist 7 (Jul. 1995).

10. *See generally* Robert C. Bricker, *Agency and Affiliate Nexus for Sales and Use Tax*, 13 J. St. Tax'n 61 (1995).

11. *See Scholastic Book Clubs, Inc. v. State Bd. of Equalization*, 207 Cal. App. 3d 734, 255 Cal. Rptr. 77 (1989) (teachers who solicited book orders from students were agents of taxpayer and created nexus even though teachers received only bonus points for merchandise as compensation); *see generally* Robert C. Bricker, *Agency and Affiliate Nexus for Sales and Use Tax*, 13 J. St. Tax'n 61, 62–64 (1995).

12. Robert C. Bricker, *Agency and Affiliate Nexus for Sales and Use Tax*, 13 J. St. Tax'n 61, 65 (1995).

13. *See Nat'l Geographic Soc'y v. California Bd. of Equalization*, 430 U.S. 551 (1977).

14. The nexus rules for federal income tax purposes are generally discussed in section 24.2.2.

15. *Northwestern States Portland Cement Co. v. Minnesota*, 358 U.S. 450 (1959); *Williams v. Stockham Valves & Fittings, Inc.*, 358 U.S. 450 (1959); *Wisconsin Dep't of Rev. v. William Wrigley, Jr., Co.*, 505 U.S. 214 (1992).

16. *See Klopman Mills, Inc.* [1968–1971 Transfer Binder] N.Y. St. Tax Rep. (CCH) ¶ 99–237 (N.Y. St. Tax Comm'n 1970); *see also American Refrigerator Transit Co. v. State Tax Comm'n*, 238 Or. 340, 395 P.2d 127 (1964).

17. *See Standard Pressed Steel Co. v. Washington Dep't of Rev.*, 419 U.S. 560 (1975); *International Shoe Co. v. Washington*, 326 U.S. 310 (1945); *Mark Andy, Inc. v. Director, N.J. Div. of Tax'n*, 8 N.J. Tax 593, [1979–1989 Transfer Binder] N.J. St. Tax Rep. (CCH) ¶ 200-483 (N.J. Tax Ct. 1987).

18. *See Geldermann & Co. v. Oregon Dep't of Rev.*, 10 OTR 249, (Ore. Tax Ct. 1985); Letter Ruling No. 1981-41, [1977–1989 Transfer Binder] Mass. St. Tax Rep. (CCH) ¶ 195–235 (Mass. Dep't of Rev. May 27, 1981).

19. *See* Ruling of Comm'r, P.D. 170, [1986-1994 Transfer Binder] Va. St. Tax Rep. (CCH) ¶ 201–774 (Va. Tax Comm'n May 22, 1989).

20. *See National Bellas Hess, Inc. v. Dep't of Rev.*, 386 U.S. 753 (1967) (sending catalogs into state and shipping goods into state by common carrier are not sufficient to create nexus), *rev'd in part*, *Quill Corp. v. North Dakota*, 504 U.S. 298 (1992).

21. Letter Ruling No. 1981-41, [1977–1989 Transfer Binder] Mass. St. Tax Rep. (CCH) ¶ 195–235 (Mass. Dep't of Rev. May 27, 1981).

22. 15 U.S.C.A. § 381 (1976) (overruling *Northwestern States Portland Cement Co. v. Minnesota*, 358 U.S. 450 (1959), and *Williams v. Stockham Valves & Fittings, Inc.*, 358 U.S. 450 (1959), as to the sale of goods only).

23. *See* 1 Jerome R. Hellerstein & Walter Hellerstein, *State Taxation* § 6.13 (1993) (discussing interpretation of "solicitation").

24. *Compare Hervey v. AMF Beaird, Inc.*, 250 Ark. 147, 464 S.W.2d 557 (1971) (inventory checks and receipt of orders in state exceeded narrow definition of solicitation) *with In re Petitions of Nat'l Tires, Inc.*, [1980–1983 Transfer Binder] N.Y. St. Tax Rep. (CCH) ¶ 250-085 (N.Y. St. Tax Comm'n 1980) (calling on customers, arranging displays, and assisting customers to increase sales were within definition of solicitation).

25. *Beistle Co. v. Commonwealth*, 640 A.2d 483 (1991), *aff'd*, 536 Pa. 160, 638 A.2d 943 (1994).

26.   Thomas Dunst, *Activities Creating Nexus for Income Tax Purposes*, 6 J. St. Tax'n 279, 282–84 (Table) (1987).

27.   Thomas Dunst, *Activities Creating Nexus for Income Tax Purposes*, 6 J. St. Tax'n 279, 282–84 (Table) (1987).

28.   *National Tires, Inc. v. Lindley*, 68 Ohio App. 2d 71, 426 N.E.2d 793 (1980); *see also U.S. Tobacco Co. v. Martin*, 304 Ark. 119, 801 S.W.2d 256 (1990) (making inventory checks, swapping products, selling products for cash from stock in vehicles of marketing representatives, and buying stock from wholesalers exceeds scope of "mere solicitation").

29.   *Geoffrey, Inc. v. South Carolina Tax Comm'n*, 437 S.E.2d 13, *cert. denied*, 114 S. Ct. 550 (1993). *See also Amway Corp. v. Director of Rev.*, 794 S.W.2d 666 (Mo. 1990) (license of distributorships created nexus).

30.   The Division of Taxation in New Jersey recently promulgated proposed income tax regulations that would trigger nexus with New Jersey for income tax purposes if a licensor were to license software to a user in New Jersey. *See* 27 N.J. Reg. 3913 (1995). These proposed regulations appear to be a direct reaction to *Geoffrey*.

31.   *See generally* Michael J. McIntyre, *The International Income Tax Rules of the United States* § 1/A (1989).

32.   *See generally* Michael J. McIntyre, *The International Income Tax Rules of the United States* § 1/A (1989).

33.   *See generally* Michael J. McIntyre, *The International Income Tax Rules of the United States* § 1/A (1989).

34.   *See* Treas. Reg. § 1.1-1(b) (1995).

35.   There are certain exceptions. An American living and working abroad will still be required to *report* his or her income on a federal tax return, but he or she may not be required to pay tax on such income under section 911 of the Internal Revenue Code of 1986. *See* 26 U.S.C.A. § 911 (1988).

36.   Two countries may even attempt to assert residence jurisdiction based on the overlapping residence of a particular person. A U.S. citizen living in Germany would have a nexus with both Germany and the United States; however, some efforts have been made to prevent such overlaps through tax treaties. *See, e.g.*, U.S. Model Tax Treaty, Art. 4; *see also* Michael J. McIntyre, *The International Income Tax Rules of the United States* § 1/A (1989).

37.   The provisions of the foreign tax credit are codified largely in 26 U.S.C.A. §§ 901–908 (1988 & Supp. 1995); *see also* Michael J. McIntyre, *The International Income Tax Rules of the United States* § 1/A (1989).

38.   *See, e.g.*, Income Tax Treaty signed on August 31, 1994, between France and the United States (Article 24 provides relief from double taxation); *see also* Michael J. McIntyre, *The International Income Tax Rules of the United States* § 1/A (1989).

39.   Income tax is another type of tax, but this tax is addressed in Section 24.2.1.2.

40.   Walter Hellerstein, *Significant Sales and Use Tax Developments During the Past Half Century*, 39 Vand. L. Rev. 961, 964 (1986).

41.   Paul J. Hartman, *Federal Limitations On State and Local Taxation* § 10:1 (1981).

42.   Herman C. McCloud, *Sales and Use Tax: Historical Developments and Differing Features*, 22 Duq. L. Rev. 823, 824 (1984).

43.   For a historical perspective and analysis of sales and use taxes, see Diane Carpenter, *State Sales Tax on Services: A Perspective on the "New" Old Tax*, 2 Det. C.L. Rev. 561 (1992); and Herman C. McCloud, *Sales Tax and Use Tax: Historical Developments and Differing Features*, 22 Duq. L. Rev. 823 (1984).

44.   *See* 2 Jerome R. Hellerstein & Walter Hellerstein, *State Taxation* § 13.06 (1992).

45. Ann Morse and Christopher Zimmerman, *Efforts To Collect Sales Tax on Interstate Mail-Order Sales* 1 n.4 (Legislative Fin. Paper No. 73 Nat'l Conference of State Legislatures 1990).

46. Alaska, Montana, New Hampshire, and Oregon have no sales or use taxes. Delaware has no sales tax although it does impose a use tax on leases of tangible personal property. ITAA, *Software & Serv. State Tax Report* xiv, 6, 28, 99, 107, 141 (1993).

47. *See, e.g.*, Ariz. Rev. Stat. § 42-1301(16)(1995) ("personal property which may be seen, weighed, measured, felt or touched or is in any other manner perceptible to the senses"); Md. Tax-Gen. Code Ann. § 11-101(h) (1995) ("corporeal personal property of any nature"); Wis. Stat. § 77.51 (1994) ("all tangible personal property of every kind and description").

48. 86 Ill. Admin. Code 130.1935 (Dec. 31, 1994).

49. *See, e.g.*, Ruling of Comm'r, P.D. 95–68 (Va. Dep't of Tax'n Mar. 30, 1995) (although charges for information provided electronically via telephone lines were not subject to Virginia sales tax, charges for the transfer of this information through magnetic tapes were taxable because conveying information through such means constituted a sale of tangible personal property); Cal. Code Regs. tit. 18, § 1502(f)(1)(D) (prewritten programs transferred by remote telecommunications when purchaser does not obtain possession of any tangible personal property are not taxable).

50. *See, e.g.*, *South Central Bell Tele. Co. v. Barthelemy*, 643 So. 2d 1240 (La. 1994) (electronically transmitted computer programs are tangible personal property and thus subject to tax).

51. For a compilation and comprehensive discussion of state sales and use tax law treatment of information services, see J. Elaine Bialczak, *Sales and Use Taxes: Information Services*, 1320 Tax Management Multistate Tax (BNA 1994 & Supp. 1995).

52. *Reuters America, Inc. v. Tax Comm'r*, No. 92-H-1414 (Use Tax), 1994 Ohio Tax LEXIS 1951 (Bd. of Tax Appeals Nov. 28, 1994).

53. "Automatic data processing and computer services" were defined under Ohio law as follows: "Providing access to computer equipment for the purpose of processing data or examining or acquiring data stored in or accessible to such computer equipment." Ohio R.C. § 5739.01(Y)(1) (1994).

54. "Personal or professional services" were defined as "all services other than automatic data processing and computer services." Ohio R.C. § 5739.01(Y)(2) (1994).

55. *Reuters America, Inc. v. Tax Comm'r*, No. 92-H-1414 (Use Tax), 1994 Ohio Tax LEXIS 1951, at *37 (Bd. of Tax Appeals Nov. 28, 1994).

56. The Texas sales/use tax law defined "information services" as follows: "(1) furnishing . . . news or other current information, including financial information, . . . or (2) electronic data retrieval or research." Tex. Tax Code § 151.0038 (since amended).

57. *Reuters America, Inc. v. Sharp*, 889 S.W.2d 646 (Tx. Ct. App. 1994).

58. For a compilation and comprehensive discussion of state sales and use tax law treatment of information services, see J. Elaine Bialczak, *Sales and Use Taxes: Information Services*, 1320 Tax Management Multistate Tax (BNA 1994 & Supp. 1995).

59. Texas' Tax Code defines "telecommunications services" as: "the electronic or electrical transmission, conveyance, routing, or reception of sounds, signals, data, or information utilizing wires, cables, radio waves, microwaves, satellites, fiber optics, or any other method now in existence or that may be devised, including but not limited to long-distance telephone service." Tex. Tax Code Ann. § 151.0103 (1995).

60. Letter from the Comptroller of Public Accounts, Microfiche No. 9412L1329C01 (1994).

61. Letter from the Comptroller of Public Accounts, Microfiche No. 9412L1329C01 (1994).

62. Conn. Gen. Stat. § 12-407(2)(i) (1994).

63. Regulations of Connecticut State Agencies, § 12-426-27(b)(1) (1991).

64. Letter Ruling No. 95-2 (Conn. Dep't of Rev. Servs. Jan. 31, 1995). Under Connecticut law, the taxability of computer-related services is determined by analyzing whether the true object of a transaction is for a customer to obtain data processing services.

65. States generally allow a vendor, such as a retailer, to provide to the manufacturer a resale certificate number so that the retailer will not be required to pay sales tax to the manufacturer when the vendor purchases goods for resale. This prevents the sales tax or use tax from being paid twice—once by the retailer and once by the end-user. *See, e.g.,* Va. Code Ann. § 58.1-602 (1995); Tex. Tax Code Ann. § 151.054 (1995).

66. 26 U.S.C.A. § 4041 (1989 & Supp. 1995).

67. 26 U.S.C.A. §§ 4251–4254 (1989 & Supp. 1995).

68. 26 U.S.C.A. § 4081 (Supp. 1995).

69. 26 U.S.C.A. § 4071 (Supp. 1995).

70. 26 U.S.C.A. § 4161 (1989).

71. *See, e.g.,* 26 U.S.C.A. §§ 4251–4254 (1989 & Supp. 1995); Illinois Telecommunications Excise Tax Act, 35 ILCS 630/1-630/21 (1995).

72. 26 U.S.C.A. § 4251 (Supp. 1995).

73. 26 U.S.C.A. § 4252(b) (1989).

74. 35 ILCS 630/1-630/21 (1995). The United States Supreme Court found Illinois's Telecommunications Excise Tax Act to be constitutional in *Goldberg v. Sweet*, 488 U.S. 252 (1989). The statute broadly defines "telecommunications" as follows:

     [I]n addition to the meaning ordinarily and popularly ascribed to it, includes, without limitation, messages or information transmitted through use of local, toll and wide area telephone service; private line services; channel services; telegraph services; teletypewriter; computer exchange services; cellular mobile telecommunications service; specialized mobile radio; stationary two way radio; paging service; or any other form of mobile and portable one-way or two-way communications; or any other transmission of messages or information by electronic or similar means, between or among points by wire, cable, fiber-optics, laser, microwave, radio, satellite or similar facilities. 35 ILCS 630/2(c) (1995).

75. 35 ILCS 630/3 (1995).

76. *See* 26 U.S.C.A. § 4254 (1989); 35 ILCS 630/5 (1995).

77. 19 C.F.R. § 141.4 (1995).

78. 19 U.S.C.A. § 1202 (1978 & Supp. 1995). (The *Harmonized Tariff Schedules* are a two-volume set of tariffs and rules published annually by the Department of the Treasury.)

79. 19 U.S.C.A. §§ 1202 *et seq.* (1978 & Supp. 1995).

80. *See Harmonized Tariff Schedules,* General Note 16(b) (1995).

81. *Harmonized Tariff Schedules,* Heading No. 8524.90.40.50.

82. 19 C.F.R. § 141.1(b) (1995).

83. 19 C.F.R. § 101.1(l) (1995).

84. Payment of customs duties is governed by 19 C.F.R. § 24.1 (1995).

85. 19 C.F.R. § 141.1(c) (1995).

86. 19 U.S.C.A. §§ 1202 *et seq.* (1978 & Supp. 1995).

87. Carolyn Webber & Aaron Wildavsky, *A History of Taxation in the Western World* 388 (1986).

25
Export Controls and Transnational Data Flow

Thomas J. Smedinghoff

The flow of certain types of information, software, and other forms of digital content from one country to another may be subject to governmental regulation. In the United States, software, encryption technology, and technical data, among other things, cannot be transmitted to another country without implicit or explicit authorization from the U.S. government.[1] This includes electronic communications as well as exports of physical media. Many other countries, particularly in Europe, regulate the online export of data relating to individuals (often referred to as *transnational data flow*).

Both the U.S. export regulations and the European transnational data flow regulations are undergoing significant change as of the date of this writing. Accordingly, this chapter will lay out the fundamental premises of each, but will not seek to address the details of their implementation.

25.1 Overview of U.S. Export Controls

In the United States, Congress has granted authority primarily to the State Department and the Commerce Department to adopt regulations that restrict the export of goods and technology. The primary purpose of these regulations is to further our national security and foreign policy objectives.[2]

In general terms, the stated goal is to balance the benefits to the United States of exporting American goods and technology against the risks of that export to national security and foreign policy goals. As a consequence, both the Commerce Department and the State Department have adopted regulations that restrict the export of technical data, software, encryption technology, and other types of information in digital form.[3] The nature of the technology, product, or information to be exported determines which agency has jurisdiction.

The Commerce Department's Export Administration Regulations[4] control the export of (1) goods, and (2) information and know-how, whether in tangible or intangible form, that can be used to manufacture, utilize, or reconstruct goods, including computer software and technical data.[5] However, the export of some forms of software and information, particularly those involving encryption, may also be controlled by the International

Traffic in Arms Regulations (ITAR)[6] issued by the State Department under the Arms Export Control Act.[7]

Generally, the State Department ITAR regulations control the export of (1) "defense articles"[8] (such as military equipment, firearms, guidance and control equipment, and auxiliary military equipment), and (2) "technical data" (such as information required for the design, development, manufacture, or operation of defense articles and software directly related to defense articles).[9] The *United States Munitions List* sets forth all of the categories of items controlled by the State Department ITAR Regulations.[10]

It is perhaps obvious that technical data, software, and other information related to defense articles are subject to State Department export restrictions. But it is also important to understand that the category of "auxiliary military equipment" includes information security systems, cryptographic (including key management) systems, and software with the capability of maintaining secrecy or confidentiality of information or information systems (subject to some exclusions).[11] It is under this category that the State Department's export controls on encryption software and encryption technology find their source. Of course, these export controls have a significant impact on the use of encryption technology for purposes of privacy and confidentiality, as well as for digital signatures, document integrity, and authentication.

The potential penalties for failing to comply with the export regulations are steep. Civil penalties can be as high as $100,000 per transaction. Criminal penalties can be as high as $250,000 and 10 years in prison for each criminal violation by an individual (and as much as five times the value of the exports, or $1,000,000—whichever is greater—for an entity other than an individual).[12]

In a 1993 decision that highlights the importance of complying with the export regulations, a federal court of appeals upheld the criminal conviction of an individual found guilty of illegally exporting computer software.[13] The defendant had helped to develop computer programs to predict the effects on spacecraft of contamination emitted from rocket nozzles. Early versions of the program were in the public domain, but, according to the government, later versions were subject to export control via the United States Munitions List. The court found the defendant guilty of agreement to transfer the technology through Germany to South Africa in violation of the Arms Export Control Act.[14]

25.2 What Is Regulated?

Any transmission of software, technical data, or other controlled information out of the United States is considered an export.[15] An export of information also occurs when the information is transmitted or otherwise disclosed to a foreign national, even if the foreign national is in the United States.[16]

The general approach taken by the export regulations is to prohibit the export from the United States of all commodities and all technical data, and then to grant permission to export certain commodities and data by virtue of various types of licenses.[17] As discussed in Section 25.3, licenses may be general or specific.

While the U.S. export laws govern all types of goods, from grain and computers to arms and ammunition, it is also clear that they directly apply to much of the digital information, software, and content that is communicated electronically. Software is specifically covered by the export regulations.[18] Likewise, the export of numerous forms of information and content in a digital form is regulated as "technical data."

The Commerce Department regulations indicate that technical data may take many forms, including blueprints, plans, tables, manuals, and instructions. They may be on paper or recorded on media such as disk, tape, or read-only memories.[19] Most data satisfies one of these forms, including everyday business data (e.g., accounting or inventory records).[20] The State Department ITAR regulations are similarly broad, and specifically list software directly related to defense articles.[21]

Based on these definitions, it is clear that there are numerous instances where "technical data" might be communicated electronically out of the country in a way that is subject to the export regulations. In addition to the online communication of software, technical information relating to numerous other goods or products might be communicated electronically to customers in other countries to facilitate a sale or assist in providing post-sale support or maintenance.

However, it is also important to understand that just because data is subject to the export regulations does not necessarily mean that its export is prohibited. In fact, in many cases, export will be allowed, provided that the regulations are complied with. In some cases, this may require obtaining a specific export license. In other cases it will simply require a determination that the export is authorized under existing regulations.

For example, data or information under Commerce Department jurisdiction may be freely exported to many countries if it is generally available to the public in any form, including information published in periodicals, books, print, electronic, or any other media available for general distribution to the public.[22]

25.3 Export Licenses

The export licensing system is extraordinarily complex. Generally, export controls are determined on the basis of the nature of the item to be exported, the country of destination, and the end use or end-user involved.

25.3.1 Commerce Department Commodity Control List

Within the Commerce Department, the Bureau of Export Administration (BXA) maintains a commerce control list (CCL) that includes all items (commodities, software, and technical data) subject to BXA export controls. The CCL does not, however, include those items whose export is exclusively controlled by another department or agency of the U.S. government.

The CCL is divided into ten categories, covering materials, materials processing, electronics, computers, telecommunications and cryptography, sensors, avionics and navigation, marine technology, propulsion systems and transportation equipment, and "miscellaneous." Each of these categories includes software and technology relating thereto.[23] The CCL specifies the conditions under which the export of certain articles and related software and technology are controlled. The level of control depends upon the nature of the software or technology, its proposed export destination, and its end use.

Each entry on the CCL describes the commodities covered by it, lists the necessary or permitted licenses under which the commodity may be exported, specifies particular country group destinations that are permitted or prohibited, and may also describe other commodity specific controls.

The CCL is the key for analyzing the level of export control for software and technology. An exporter must locate its technology or software on the CCL to determine what license is available. However, the CCL is often difficult to use because it is very detailed and fact-specific. The software or technology in question may also fall under more than one CCL category. In these cases, the highest level of control applies.

If desired, an exporter can obtain confirmation from the BXA that it is exporting pursuant to the proper license. The BXA will respond to properly submitted requests for verification of the proper license within 10 working days after receipt of the request. The procedure is useful when an exporter is not sure where its commodity, software, or technology fits on the CCL.[24]

The export regulations simplify the task of determining the controls imposed on a particular transaction by dividing the world into "Country Groups." A country is placed in a particular group according to its geographic location or the degree of disdain with which the United States regards its government. These groups will determine where the commodity may be exported, as specified in the CCL. As a practical matter, however, the use of Country Groups has often caused confusion because the regulations do not treat every country within a group identically in all respects.

25.3.1.1 General Licenses. All exports from the United States of any "commodity" (including software) must be made pursuant to either a general license (which requires no application) or a validated license (which does).

A *general license* permits the exporter to send commodities or technical data out of the United States without obtaining formal Commerce Department permission. The availability of a general license depends on the location of the consignee, the type of item to be exported, and the use to which it will be put. As noted above, the applicable entry on the CCL will indicate what general license, if any, is available for the specified commodity.

A general license comes into being by operation of law. No application is required and the BXA does not issue a license document. It is, in effect, a waiver of the application requirements that is granted by the BXA for specific types of transactions. If a transaction is eligible for a general license, the exporter need only take certain steps required by the regulations.

25.3.1.2 Validated Licenses. A validated license is required for the export of software and technology when one of the general licenses is not available.[25] A *validated license* is a formal authorization issued by the BXA after an application has been submitted by the exporter. The license permits the exporter to ship a specific amount of a specific item to a specific importer in a specific country for a specific designated use. A validated license represents a higher level of export control. The highest level of control is the denial of an export by the BXA or pursuant to the EAR.

The application for a validated license provides the BXA with the opportunity to scrutinize the details of a proposed transaction to determine whether it would harm national security or foreign policy interests. Approval of a validated license application is based on the following considerations:

- The reason for the control (i.e., national security, foreign policy, short supply);
- The type of commodity;
- The ultimate destination;
- The dollar value;
- The intended use;
- Whether the commodity has other potential uses and what those uses are;
- Whether the circumstances suggest the possibility of a diversion to an unauthorized destination; and
- Whether the particular commodities are available from other countries.

It is important to note that BXA will not accept a validated license application without evidence that the exporter has a valid order for the commodity.

In addition to checking the identified commodities, software, or technology and country of destination against the CCL, BXA regulations promulgated pursuant to the Enhanced Proliferation Control Initiative (EPCI) require the exporter to analyze a third element—the end-use or end-user—to determine whether a validated license is required. The EPCI controls originate from an executive order issued by President Bush in 1990 as a consequence of the Persian Gulf War. Under the EPCI, exports of even such seemingly innocent items as paper clips, which would otherwise be freely exportable under a general license, are controlled if destined for facilities or activities involving nuclear, chemical, or biological weapons, or related missile delivery systems in named countries or regions. Specifically, the EAR requires a validated license if the exporter *knows* that the commodities, software, or technology are destined for specifically identified weapons facilities, or for end-users involved in these prohibited weapons activities in countries or regions specifically identified in the regulations, or if the BXA informs the exporter that a validated license is required due to an unacceptable risk of weapons-related use.

25.3.2 State Department Munitions Control List

The Department of State also administers export controls under the authority of the Arms Export Control Act, pursuant to which it has promulgated the International Traffic in Arms Regulations (ITAR). Included in those regulations is the *United States Munitions List* (USML), which sets forth all of the categories of items controlled by the State Department ITAR.[26]

If software or technical data falls under a category of the USML,[27] authority to export the information must be obtained from the State Department's Office of Defense Trade Controls. If it fits under *both* a specific Commerce Department CCL category and a particular section of the USML, the exporter may submit a commodity jurisdiction request to the Office of Defense Trade Controls to determine if the State Department will defer jurisdiction to the Commerce Department.[28] If it is concluded that a particular commodity is on the USML, a State Department export authorization under ITAR must be obtained before the software or technical data can be legally exported and the exporter must register with the State Department as a "Munitions Producer" before applying for a license to export to a specific customer.[29]

25.4 Export Controls on Encryption Software

Perhaps the most controversial of all export regulations are those relating to encryption technology. U.S. businesses are currently prevented from exporting software and hardware that incorporates certain types of encryption technology. This is due to an export licensing system developed over the last 50 years that is designed to limit proliferation of encryption technologies that could hinder efficient intelligence gathering and effective law enforcement.[30]

The U.S. government considers cryptographic technology to pose a potential threat to national security. Thus, encryption software is classified with munitions, missiles, and other military products included on the United States Munitions List,[31] and is subject to the State Department's strict ITAR regulations, which prohibit its export to foreign countries in most cases.

The State Department Office of Defense Trade Controls (DTC) has primary jurisdiction over encryption software and related technology. However, the State Department has transferred jurisdiction over certain types of cryptographic software to the Commerce Department in cases where the encryption features are used only for certain limited functions, such as decryption for copy-protected software, bank or money transactions, certain personalized smart cards, data authentication, and fixed data compression or coding techniques. The DTC also now has expedited procedures for transferring jurisdiction over certain mass-market software to the Commerce Department, provided that the encryption features do not use key lengths that exceed forty bits. However, this has been generally perceived as unacceptable by industry.

The seriousness with which the government views the export controls on encryption software was demonstrated by its investigation of Phil Zimmerman, the author of an encryption program called *Pretty Good Privacy* or *PGP*. Zimmerman made the program available to anyone who wanted a copy, at no charge. In September 1993, a federal grand jury in San Jose, California, began an investigation to determine Zimmerman's role in placing the PGP program on the Internet, and thereby exporting the encryption program overseas. Apparently, the software was placed on the Internet by an undisclosed friend of Zimmerman's, and exported from the United States without an export control license from the State Department. The grand jury investigation ended in January 1996 with a decision not to prosecute Mr. Zimmerman.

Yet cryptography, and its ability to protect data, has begun to assume a major role in electronic commerce. Encryption has become important for protecting the privacy of sensitive data, such as an individual's medical records and the trade secrets of a business. It is also vital to the protection of other property rights. "Copyright owners will not use the NII [National Information Infrastructure] or GII [Global Information Infrastructure] unless they can be assured of strict security to protect against piracy. Therefore, encryption technology is vital because it gives copyright owners an additional degree of protection against misappropriation."[32]

Cryptography also plays a critical role in creating digital signatures—a critical security mechanism required to facilitate electronic commerce over public networks (see discussion in Chapter 4). This dual role of cryptography in electronic commerce—privacy and security—has become very important, and the prohibitions on its export threaten to stifle international commerce.

In early 1995, a suit was filed against the government seeking a ruling that the regulations restricting the export of cryptographic software violated the First and Fifth Amendments of the U.S. Constitution.[33] The case was filed by a graduate student seeking to publish a paper discussing algorithms and software relating to cryptography. The complaint alleged that the regulations prohibited him from publishing or publicly discussing or circulating his paper, algorithms, and computer program, and that the net result was to prevent and inhibit speech protected by the First Amendment. This case may provide some indication of the viability of these export restrictions.

At present, industry is pressing for a relaxation of export controls on encryption. It is unclear, however, whether the government is willing to accept what it perceives to be the national security and law enforcement risks that will flow from such relaxation.

25.5 Overview of Transnational Data Flow Laws

Attempts to control the electronic communication of information over computer networks takes a variety of forms. One form is the so-called transnational data flow laws passed in several countries. These laws primarily regulate the communication of information about individuals—that is, personal data. In many respects they are an attempt to balance the concern over human rights against the desire for the free flow of information. At the same time, however, they can have a significant inhibiting impact on the electronic communication of business-related data.

25.5.1 United States Policy

The United States does not have a single omnibus data protection law that covers the privacy of both public- and private-sector records. Instead, data protection is addressed by numerous federal and state statutes as well as constitutional and common law protections that focus on the privacy interests of individuals in certain limited situations.[34]

Thus, these laws do not address transnational data flow, *per se*, but address issues such as the rights of data subjects (for example, right to notification or access); or obligations of processors of personal data (for example, limits on collection, use or disclosure); data quality and security (for example, accuracy of data and mechanisms to prevent inappropriate disclosures); and accountability, sanctions, and remedies.[35] There is no central governmental body responsible for formulating a comprehensive national policy or regulations on the subject in the United States.[36]

25.5.2 Privacy and Data Protection in Other Countries

Unlike the United States, several other countries have developed omnibus privacy and data protection laws. These include: Australia, Austria, Belgium, Canada, Denmark, Finland, France, Germany, Iceland, Japan, Luxembourg, the Netherlands, New Zealand, Norway, Portugal, Spain, Sweden, Switzerland, and the United Kingdom.[37] Generally, these laws establish administrative data commissions; require registration of data banks; and impose constraints on the use, storage, and transmission of personal data.[38] The scope of these laws varies widely; consequently, each country's law must be examined to determine its applicability to a particular situation.

One significant limitation on these laws is that they seek to protect only persons who can be specifically identified from the data. If the data is such that a person cannot be identified, or if the data is scientific, economic, or technical, the privacy laws do not apply.

To the extent that persons can be identified from the data that a business is transferring (for example, personnel records or customer lists), the privacy laws may impede the transfer of such information. In one case, for example, a Swedish county government was denied permission to transfer personal information regarding its residents to a company in England for processing on the ground that England's data protection law did not provide adequate protection.[39] The Swedish Commission also refused to allow a Swedish subsidiary to transmit personnel information to the parent company in Germany because it determined that German law did not provide adequate privacy protection.

The differences in the various national laws regarding data protection can create particular problems for multinational corporations seeking to transfer information between establishments located in different member countries. Banks and insurance companies processing large quantities of highly confidential information on the financial situation of their customers may run into trouble.

Most countries recognize the importance of the free flow of data and, like Sweden, provide that data may be transferred to countries having adequate privacy protection laws. Generally, this means that the transferee country's law must be at least as stringent as the transferor country's. This is the approach taken in a recent Directive of the European Economic Community.[40]

In October 1995 the European Parliament and the Council of the European Union formally adopted the Directive on the Protection of Personal Data. This directive, which member countries have three years to implement formally through appropriate legislation, seeks to protect individual privacy by prohibiting the improper use of data relating to the individuals. In doing so, the Directive seeks to protect certain fundamental rights of individuals (see Section 17.3.7), while at the same time ensuring the free flow of personal data within countries comprising the European Union. To accomplish this goal, the Directive seeks to regulate the collection and use of data relating to individuals and the electronic communication of such information[41] across country borders.

According to the Directive,[42] personal data may not be transferred to a country outside of the European Union unless the country to which the data is sent ensures an adequate level of protection. Whether the recipient country has laws ensuring an adequate level of protection for personal data is determined by a number of factors, including the nature of the data, the purpose and duration of the processing, the rules of law enforced in the recipient country, and the security measures that are effectively complied with in the recipient country. The final decision as to "adequacy" rests with the individual member states.

The Directive also allows a member state to authorize a transfer of personal data to a third country that does not ensure an adequate level of protection in certain situations, such as where the data subject has consented, it is required on public interest grounds, or the data controller has taken steps to guarantee the effective exercise of the data subjects rights.[43] For transborder data transfers that are internal to a multinational corporation, this might be accomplished through the adoption of internal corporate policies that comply with the Directives provisions. For online communications of data between businesses, contractual guarantees provided by the recipient may also be sufficient to satisfy the requirements of the Directive. It is unclear what specific contractual guarantees would be required, but presumably the recipient would have to provide individuals who are the subject of the data the ability to exercise the rights granted to them under the Directive freely, quickly, and at minimum expense.

Endnotes

1. The export of virtually all goods, software, technology, and data from the United States is regulated by the Department of Commerce under the Export Administration Act of 1979, as amended by the Export Administration Amendments Act of 1985 (50 U.S.C. App. §§ 2401–2420, hereafter EAA) and the Export Administration Regulations (15 C.F.R. Parts 700 *et seq.* hereafter EAR), or in some cases by the State Department under the Arms Export Control Act, 22 U.S.C. § 2778 *et seq.*, and the International Traffic in Arms Regulations (ITAR), 22 C.F.R. Part 120 *et seq.*

2. 50 U.S.C. App. § 2402(2).

3. The Commerce Department Export Administration Regulations (EAR) can be found at 15 C.F.R. §§ 768–799. The State Department's International Traffic in Arms Regulations (ITAR) can be found at 22 C.F.R. §§ 120-130.

4. In mid-1995, the Commerce Department's Bureau of Export Administration proposed the first comprehensive revision and reorganization of the Export Administration Regulations in 30 years. A 200-plus page draft of the proposed changes was published in the Federal Register on May 11, 1995.

5. EAA § 16(4). Tangible forms of information include models, prototypes, drawings, sketches, diagrams, blue prints, and manuals. Intangible forms include training and technical services.

6. 22 C.F.R. § 120 *et. seq.*

7. 22 U.S.C. § 2778.

8. 22 C.F.R. § 120.1(a).

9. 22 C.F.R. § 120.6 (definition of "defense article"), and § 120.10 (definition of "technical data").

10. 22 C.F.R. § 121.

11. 22 C.F.R. § 121.1, category XIII(b).

12. 50 U.S.C. App. §§ 2410 (a)–(c).

13. *United States v. Hoffman,* 1993 U.S. App. LEXIS 30604 (9th Cir. Nov. 12, 1993).

14. 22 U.S.C. § 2778(c).

15. 22 C.F.R. § 120.17(a)(1) (*export* means "sending or taking a defense article out of the United States in any manner"); 15 C.F.R. § 779.1(b) (*export of technical data* means "an actual shipment or transmission of technical data out of the United States").

16. 22 C.F.R. § 120.17(a)(4) (*export* means "disclosing . . . or transferring technical data to a foreign person, whether in the United States or abroad"); 15 C.F.R. § 779.1(b)(ii) (*export of technical data* means "any release of technology or source code to a foreign national" other than persons admitted for permanent residence in the United States).

17. 15 C.F.R. § 770.3(a). On May 11, 1995, the Commerce Department proposed making a fundamental change in this approach. Under the proposed rules, no license or other authorization will be required for any transaction under BXA jurisdiction unless the regulations affirmatively state the requirement for an export license. The approach taken under the current regulations, which states that all exports are prohibited unless an applicable general license has been established or a valid license or other authorization has been granted, would be dropped.

18. 15 C.F.R. § 799.1, Supp. 3 (software is specifically included, and defined as "a collection of one or more 'programs' or 'microprograms' fixed in any tangible medium of expression."); 22 C.F.R. § 121.8(f) ("software includes, but is not limited to, the system functional design, logic flow, algorithms, application programs, operating systems and support software for design, implementation, test, operation, diagnosis and repair").

19. 15 C.F.R. § 799.1, Supp. 3. Other forms include diagrams, models, formulae, and engineering designs and specifications.

20. 15 C.F.R. § 799.1, Supp. 3.

21. 22 C.F.R. § 120.10(a)(4). The ITAR regulations include information in the form of blueprints, drawings, photographs, plans, instructions, and documentation.

22. 15 C.F.R. § 779.3.

23. 15 C.F.R. § 799.1.

24. 15 C.F.R. § 799.1(g).

25. 15 C.F.R. § 779.4(f).

26. 22 C.F.R. § 121.

27. Set forth at ITAR § 121.1 (hereafter, the USML).

28. ITAR § 120.4.

29. ITAR § 122.1(a).

30.   *Intellectual Property and the National Information Infrastructure: The Report of the Working Group on Intellectual Property Rights,*" Information Infrastructure Task Force (Sept. 5, 1995) at 223.

31.   22 C.F.R. § 121.1.

32.   *Intellectual Property and the National Information Infrastructure: The Report of the Working Group on Intellectual Property Rights,* Information Infrastructure Task Force (Sept. 5, 1995) at 224–225.

33.   *Bernstein v. United States Dept. of State,* No. 95-0582 (N.D. Cal., filed Feb. 21, 1995).

34.   R. Plesser and E. Cividanes, *Privacy Protection in the United States* 5–6 (1991).

35.   *Id.* at App. 2. Examples of these statutes include the Cable Communications Policy Act of 1984 (47 U.S.C. § 551); Video Privacy Protection Act of 1988 (18 U.S.C. § 2710); Fair Credit Reporting Act (15 U.S.C. § 1861); Equal Credit Opportunity Act (15 U.S.C. § 1691 and 12 C.F.R. § 202.9); Family Educational Rights and Privacy Act (20 U.S.C. § 1232g); Electronic Communications Privacy Act of 1986 (18 U.S.C. § 2701 *et.seq.*).

36.   J. Eger, *The Global Phenomenon of Teleinformatics: An Introduction,* 14 Cornell Int'l L.J. 203, 235–236 (1981).

37.   J. Eger, *The Global Phenomenon of Teleinformatics: An Introduction,* 14 Cornell Int'l L.J. 203, 212 and n.34 (1981) [citing 3 Transnat'l Data Rep. No. 2, at 15 (1980)].

38.   H. Lowry, *Transborder Data Flow: Public and Private International Law Aspects,* 6 Houston J. Int'l L. 159, 167 (1984).

39.   G. Grossman, *Separating the Privacy Interests of Individuals and Corporations,* 4 Nw. J. Int'l L. & Bus. 1, 23 (1982).

40.   Directive 95/46/EC of the European Parliament and of the Counsel on the protection of individuals with regard to the processing of personal data and on the free movement of such data, October 24, 1995. The Directive provides that: "the Member States shall provide that the transfer to a third country of personal data which are undergoing processing or are intended for processing after transfer may take place only if, without prejudice to compliance with the national provisions adopted pursuant to the other provisions of this Directive, the third country in question ensures an adequate level of protection." Article 25, Section 1.

41.   It is important to note that the Directive's recitals contain an exception for processing of sound and image data carried out for "the purposes of journalism or the purposes of literary or artistic expression . . . in particular [in] the audiovisual field. . . ."

42.   Directive 95/46/EC of the European Parliament and the Council of 24 October 1995 on the protection of individuals with respect to the processing of personal data and on the free movement of such data, at Article 25.

43.   Directive 95/46/EC of the European Parliament and the Council of 24 October 1995 on the protection of individuals with respect to the processing of personal data and on the free movement of such data, at Article 26.

26
E-Mail in the Workplace

Ruth Hill Bro

Endnotes

26.1 The Issues

Today, about 20 million Americans use electronic mail (e-mail) to conduct business.[1] Worldwide, there are an estimated 35 million e-mail users[2]; it is projected that there will be 40 million e-mail users by the year 2000.[3] As the use of e-mail becomes widespread, new legal issues emerge. This chapter focuses on the legal issues faced by businesses providing e-mail for their employees.

Unlike the purchase of a new computer, the installation of a company's e-mail system carries far greater risks than the possibility of underuse. Attached to every e-mail system are significant issues and considerations, including:

- Whether business monitoring of employee e-mail violates employee privacy rights and thereby exposes the employer to liability;
- The scope of employer liability stemming from an employee's use of the company's e-mail system to defame, harass, or engage in other offensive speech;
- The scope of employer liability resulting from an employee's use of e-mail to infringe on another's copyright, misappropriate another's trade secret, send or receive obscenity or child pornography, or violate other statutes;
- The risk that carelessly written e-mail messages (even if the messages have been deleted) may someday have to be produced in response to a discovery request made by the company's opponent in a lawsuit;
- The need to ensure adequate compliance with recordkeeping requirements imposed by government regulatory agencies;
- The risk of employer liability from an employee's cavalier use of the company's electronic "letterhead" to engage in Internet discussions or communications that may commit the company to a particular position or acceptance of a contract; and
- Whether e-mail messages are "secure," such that they can be properly authenticated, the integrity of the messages is protected, and their confidentiality preserved.

Issues relating to the security and confidentiality of e-mail messages are discussed in Chapters 3 and 4, respectively. Recordkeeping issues presented by e-mail are discussed in Chapter 5. This chapter addresses legal issues relating to employer monitoring of e-mail messages, employer liability for employee e-mail messages, and e-mail as evidence in litigation.

26.2 Employer Monitoring of E-Mail

Employers seek to monitor employee e-mail messages for many reasons. They range from legitimate concerns that an employee is engaged in illegal conduct, about to compromise valuable company trade secrets, or harassing another employee, to clearly improper motives, such as delving into an employee's life outside of the workplace. Although the appropriateness of monitoring is not clearly resolved, employers seeking to monitor employee e-mail must consider both an employee's right to privacy and an employee's expectation of privacy created by the circumstances.

26.2.1 Overview

As a general matter, courts view e-mail as a tool provided by employers to employees for work-related communications. As such, the employer generally has the right to access and monitor employee e-mail messages, as long as the employer does it for legitimate business purposes.

In the leading employer-monitoring case,[4] the Supreme Court rejected a government psychiatrist's claim that his privacy rights were violated by his employer's search of his office (including his desk and filing cabinets, from which the employer seized a Valentine's Day card, a book of poems, a photograph, and billing documents regarding a private patient). The Court emphasized that the search was conducted for work-related reasons and was based on reasonable suspicion.[5] The Court also noted that even an employee's reasonable expectation of privacy, which must be determined on a case-by-case basis, should be balanced "against the employer's need for supervision, control, and the efficient operation of the workplace."[6]

Thus, two conflicting interests—the employee's reasonable expectation of privacy and the employer's business justification for the monitoring—must be considered in determining whether employer monitoring of e-mail is permitted. Challenges to employer monitoring of e-mail (as well as voice mail) have centered on an employee's right to privacy. Where there is no clear-cut employee "right" to privacy in the workplace, many cases have been filed on the basis of an employee's "expectations" of privacy based on the circumstances involved. For example, employees given the right to select their own personal password to access their messages on a company e-mail system frequently assume that the password confers absolute privacy. Employers may dispel such expectations, however, by issuing an appropriate e-mail policy. See Section 26.5 for a discussion of company e-mail policies.

26.2.2 Federal Law Governing Employer Monitoring

The Electronic Communications Privacy Act (ECPA)[7] is currently the only federal statute that addresses the privacy of electronic communications such as e-mail, voice mail, fax, cordless phone, and cellular phone communications.[8] The ECPA generally prohibits any-one—other than the sender and the intended recipient of the message—from:

- Intercepting an electronic communication,[9]
- Accessing a stored electronic communication,[10] or
- Disclosing the contents of an electronic communication.[11]

The ECPA applies to both the government and private citizens and provides for criminal as well as civil penalties.

26.2.2.1 Employer Interception of E-Mail Messages. Although the ECPA prohibits interception of e-mail messages during the communications process, two exceptions appear to authorize employer monitoring of employee e-mail messages. They are known as the *prior consent exception* and the *business use exception*. Under these two exceptions, the ECPA provides private employers with considerable, almost unlimited, latitude in monitoring the electronic communications of their employees.

26.2.2.1.a Prior Consent. Under the prior consent exception, it is not unlawful to inter-cept electronic communications when *one* of the parties to the communication has given prior consent to the interception.[12] Thus, if employees give their consent to employer monitoring, there is no question that the monitoring is lawful. Employee consent can take many forms, including an employee's signature on an e-mail policy statement that notifies the employee that all e-mail communications may be subject to monitoring.

An employee's consent can also be implied from the circumstances. For example, in the closely analogous case of workplace telephone monitoring, implied consent can come from informing employees that solicitation calls will be monitored as part of a company's regular training program to improve sales techniques.[13] Similarly, when an employee knows that personal calls on monitored phone lines are not permitted, the employee has no reasonable expectation that such calls will be protected from an employer's intrusion.[14] In the online context, implied consent may occur when an onscreen message, which warns that there is no guarantee of privacy in e-mail messages and conditions the use of the company system on acceptance of this policy, appears each time that the employee uses the company system.

The courts, however, have tended to interpret implied consent narrowly. For exam-ple, a court refused to apply the consent exception to an employer who had taped 22 hours of telephone calls made by an employee, including personal calls of a sexual nature, because the employer had only hinted that it might monitor calls.[15] In another case, a court held that although employees had been informed and had impliedly con-sented to the monitoring of business calls, they had not impliedly consented to all mon-itoring, such as the monitoring of personal calls.[16] Moreover, courts have held that the consent exception does not include *constructive consent*, that is, situations in which the party to the communication *should have known* that monitoring was a possibility.[17] Distribution of, and adherence to, a written monitoring policy can help to ensure that the appropriate employee consent has been given and thereby legitimizes some employer monitoring that might otherwise violate the statute.

26.2.2.1.b Business Use. Even where employees have not consented, the business use exception will normally allow employer monitoring. Under this provision of the ECPA, the entity that provides the electronic communication service through which the messages flow is authorized to intercept messages.[18] This provision permits access by the communications service provider, and thus gives employers—as the provider of the e-mail system in the workplace—great latitude in monitoring company-owned electronic communications systems, including e-mail and voice mail.

The business use exception of the ECPA does not limit the method or degree of employee monitoring, nor does it require employers to provide employees with notice. It does, however, require that the employer's monitoring be "within the ordinary course of its business"[19] and that the subject matter of the intercepted communication is one in which the employer has a "legal interest."[20]

Courts have broadly construed the business use exception, and have generally held that an employer may listen in on, or monitor, an employee for as long as the communication involves business-related information. But once the employee's communication moves on to personal matters, the employer should stop monitoring.

For example, when an employer exceeded its stated monitoring policy by intercepting a personal call in which the employee discussed a job interview with a prospective employer, the court emphasized that the phrase "in the ordinary course of business" is not so broad as to include everything about which an employer is curious.[21] Conversely, when an employer taped a telephone conversation between two employees in which one employee criticized supervisors, the court held the communication to be a business call because (1) it occurred between employees during office hours and involved remarks about a supervisory employee, *and* (2) because the employer had a legal interest in potential contamination of the work environment.[22] Similarly, an employer's monitoring of business calls, based on particular suspicions of confidential information being disclosed to a business competitor, was found to be in the course of business and thus permissible; moreover, the employer's listening-in was limited in purpose and time.[23]

It should also be noted that the business use exception is more likely to apply to employers who provide their employees with written policies regarding such issues as monitoring.[24] In one case, for example, an employee filed suit under the statute preceding the ECPA (which prohibited oral communications and wire interceptions) based on his employer's monitoring of personal calls; the suit failed because the company had a written policy stating that some phones would be monitored for quality control and that personal calls were prohibited on those lines. The employer's monitoring was therefore held to be in the ordinary course of its business, even though the employer ended up monitoring an employee's personal call.[25]

26.2.2.1.c Monitoring External E-Mail. The ECPA prohibits unauthorized interceptions by outside third parties. The question thus arises whether an employer is permitted under the ECPA to monitor an employee's communication with an outside third party who does not work for the employer. Although the courts have not really addressed this issue in the electronic mail context, the above-cited telephone monitoring cases suggest that monitoring of employees' external e-mail communications may not be problematic.

26.2.2.2 Employer Access to Stored E-Mail Communications. In most cases, employer monitoring of e-mail messages will probably involve access to stored communications that reside on the system, rather than the interception of communications in transit.[26] The ECPA provides an even broader exception for employers in regard to access to *stored* communications: specifically, such conduct that is authorized by the person or entity providing the electronic communications service is exempt from the statute's prohibitions.[27] This provision has major implications for e-mail messages that are stored on the employer's system. Even when an employer does not have a right to intercept a message in transit, it may have a right to access and review a "stored message" residing on its system.

26.2.2.3 Other Considerations. Aside from the legal implications, employers may also want to evaluate their decisions to monitor employee e-mail from practical and ethical standpoints. In general, monitoring of employees may turn co-workers into adversaries, strain relationships between workers and management, harm morale, and increase stress-related health problems that, in turn, decrease productivity.[28]

26.2.3 State Law Governing Employer Monitoring

In addition to the federal ECPA, all states, except South Carolina, have adopted wiretapping statutes that address unauthorized access to, and interception of, electronic communications.[29] Although most of these statutes are modeled after the ECPA and include the ECPA's "prior consent" and "business use" exceptions, some states provide more privacy protection than the ECPA provides. A few state statutes—such as those of Arkansas, Kansas, New Hampshire, and Rhode Island—do not contain a prior consent exception.[30] In the statutes of several other states, including California, Delaware, Florida, Hawaii, Illinois, Louisiana, Montana, Pennsylvania, and Washington, the consent of all parties to the conversation is required, but courts have interpreted some of these statutes (including the Delaware and Illinois statutes) to require the consent of only one of the parties.[31] Some states also require that employees be notified in advance regarding the practice of monitoring.[32] Other state statutes allow employers to monitor work-related electronic communications but require them to stop listening when the conversation turns to personal matters.

Most state constitutions incorporate the Fourth Amendment proscriptions regarding search and seizure,[33] but such provisions protect only those employed by government entities. Thus, a private employee could not claim that his employer's "search and seizure" of his e-mail at work violated the Fourth Amendment. Some states—including Alaska, Arizona, California, Florida, Hawaii, Illinois, Louisiana, Montana, South Carolina, and Washington—provide constitutional guarantees of privacy that exceed those of the U.S. Constitution,[34] but California is the only state in which a court has recognized a constitutional right to privacy for both private and public employees.[35] Under California law, although an employer has the heavy burden of demonstrating a "compelling interest" in violating an employee's reasonable expectation of privacy, an employee will usually have a hard time establishing a reasonable expectation of privacy in most cases of employer monitoring of job performance, such as pure service observation and computerized work measurement (as opposed to employer monitoring of more personal areas, such as an employee restroom or an employee locker room).[36] Even though it is far from clear what is "reasonable" from state to state in an electronic communications context, an employer can increase its chances of prevailing by warning employees in advance that their e-mail and voice mail may be monitored, thereby minimizing any reasonable expectation of privacy.

Although state laws tend to cover a wider range of privacy issues than federal laws do, employee suits still often fail, even in states such as California, which has among the strictest state privacy laws. In one case, a California employer without a written e-mail policy allegedly systematically intercepted, copied, and read its employees' e-mail; when confronted with it by one of the company's e-mail administrators, the company terminated that employee for gross insubordination.[37] Despite California's constitutionally guaranteed right to workplace privacy, the court held that the California legislature did not intend to protect electronic communications such as e-mail under the state penal code, and that because the employer provided the e-mail equipment, the employer's actions fell under the business use exception of the ECPA. The employee also failed in a wrongful termination claim.

In another case filed under California law, two employees who had been hired to set up and run their employer's e-mail network were fired after their employer intercepted e-mail containing inappropriate jokes, soft-core pornography, and language that included disparaging remarks about the supervisor and the company.[38] The California trial court refused to extend privacy rights to e-mail.

Because laws and court interpretations can vary widely from state to state, employers should review all applicable state laws before monitoring their employees' e-mail. Most state statutes provide for both civil damages and criminal penalties, but some courts refuse to use the state penal code to protect e-mail communications, as discussed previously in this chapter.[39] Employers should remember, however, that statutes are not the only source of claims made by workers regarding invasion of privacy in the workplace; workers have also made common law privacy claims, which are discussed in Chapter 17.

26.2.4 Improper Use of Monitored E-Mail

Even in situations where employer monitoring of employee e-mail is permitted, an employer's misuse of the information it learns from such monitoring may expose it to liability. For example, if an employer fires an employee after discovering through the employee's e-mail that the employee has AIDS or takes medication for depression, the employee may have a claim under the 1990 Americans with Disabilities Act,[40] which prohibits discrimination against people with various mental and physical impairments.[41] Likewise, disciplinary actions based on information obtained about an employee's sexual orientation, social life, or other activities outside the workplace can also be legal minefields.

Both federal and state law can come into play when employers act on information learned about an employee through e-mail monitoring. Under New York law, for example, employers cannot discharge or otherwise discriminate against an employee because of his or her "legal recreational activities pursued outside work hours, off of the employer's premises and without use of the employer's equipment or other property. . . ."[42] This law has now been tested in both state and federal court. A woman sued Wal-Mart in state court for allegedly violating this statute when it fired her and a fellow worker for violating the company's fraternization policy, which prohibited dating between a married employee and another employee, other than that person's own spouse; the woman was legally separated at the time and was dating a single employee.[43] The New York court held that dating was not a "recreational activity" protected under the statute and dismissed the claim.[44] A federal court, however, recently rejected that state appeals court's analysis when it held that cohabitation is a protected "recreational activity" under the statute and cannot be grounds for discharge.[45] In that case, a woman claimed that she was forced to quit her job for continuing to cohabit with her boyfriend, a former vice president of the company who had been fired two days before she was demoted; the woman was able to file in federal court because she claimed sexual harassment under Title VII (discussed in Section 26.3) in addition to her claim alleging violation of the New York labor law.[46]

The implications of the federal court decision are significant, because many large companies have fraternization policies similar to Wal-Mart's.[47] Other companies have already been successfully sued for interfering with an employee's legal activities outside of the workplace.[48] Moreover, employee lawsuits have already been filed alleging discharge based on non-work-related information learned about the employee through an employer's e-mail monitoring. For example, an employee filed a lawsuit claiming that he was fired after the employer used a message content search and discovered e-mail messages that revealed that the employee had worked as a professional stripper.[49] In short, although employers have great latitude in monitoring their employees' e-mail, they must be careful in using the information they obtain.

26.3 Employer Liability for Employee E-Mail

Employers are generally liable for the conduct of their employees, at least when such conduct occurs within the scope of the employment relationship.[50] Thus, whenever an employee uses e-mail in a way that violates a statute or infringes the rights of others, the employer may find itself liable for the employee's conduct. Examples include the following:

- **Copyrights**. Using e-mail to send or receive material that infringes the copyright of another (such as pirated software, articles, photographs, advertisements, and the like) (see Chapter 10);
- **Trade Secrets.** Using e-mail to send or receive trade secrets in violation of the rights of the owner of the trade secrets (see Chapter 12).

- **Defamatory Materials.** Using e-mail to publish defamatory statements (see Chapter 21).
- **Sexually Explicit Materials.** Using e-mail to send or receive obscenity or child pornography (see Chapter 20).
- **Committing the Company.** Using e-mail to make statements or enter into contractual commitments that may bind the company to a particular viewpoint or contractual obligation. Employees should be cautioned to use the same care in preparing e-mail messages that they would in drafting a letter on paper; a promise made in an e-mail message regarding what the company will do for a customer is just as binding as one made in a letter on paper (see Chapter 6).
- **Harassment.** Using e-mail to harass other employees within the organization, such as by sending messages that contain offensive statements of a sexual or racial nature.

E-mail provides an ideal medium in which to harass others in the workplace. The almost limitless possibility for anonymity in such communications encourages people to act in ways that they might not otherwise act face-to-face, and to do so with greater frequency. Employers who encourage or allow such harassing e-mail communications, or who simply fail to stop such harassment when it is called to their attention, run the risk of potentially significant liability to employees harassed by such messages.

Employees can file harassment claims against their employers under Title VII of the Civil Rights Act of 1964, which prohibits discrimination and differential treatment in the workplace on the basis of a person's race, color, religion, sex, or national origin.[51] For example, if an employee is subject to sexual harassment that is "so pervasive that it had the effect of creating an intimidating, hostile, or offensive work environment,"[52] the employer may be liable. Such a claim does not require that the harassment take the form of sexual advances, but rather can be based on "harassment or other unequal treatment of an employee or group of employees that would not occur but for the sex of the employee or employees . . . if sufficiently patterned or pervasive."[53] Harassment—sexual or otherwise—can easily occur via e-mail.

In such a case, if the employer actually or constructively knew that a sexually hostile working environment existed and failed to correct it, the employer will be liable.[54] This can be established by proving that complaints about the harassment were filed with the employer, who did little or nothing about them, or that the harassment was so pervasive that the employer must have known about it.[55] An official policy against harassment is not enough; employers must act promptly and sufficiently to remedy the harassment to avoid liability.[56] Although Title VII does not require employers to fire all of their "Archie Bunker" employees, it does require that employers act swiftly to prevent such persons from airing their views in a way that is offensive to their fellow workers.[57] Of course, if the employer created the sexually or racially hostile work environment, rather than merely condoning it, the employer can also be held liable under Title VII.[58]

Pervasive use of derogatory and insulting terms relating to women in general and targeted to specific female employees can constitute evidence of a hostile environment.[59] The use of obscene language and communication of pornographic pictures can also create a hostile work environment.[60] Similarly, pervasive use of racial slurs, jokes, and comments can cause a racially hostile work environment.[61] Whether this conduct occurs in traditional office settings or through company e-mail systems, it can create a hostile environment that can trigger employer liability.

Sometimes it can be difficult to tell what kind of e-mail messages constitute harassment. What is merely an off-color joke to one person can be harassment to another. For example, members of the Premier's office for the Canadian province of British Columbia (including the head of the government's public issues and consultation department) circulated an e-mail chain letter that promised "great sex" to all who did not break the chain and instructed recipients to send "copies of the letter to people who need to get laid within 96 hours."[62] In addition to lewd testimonials, the offensive language included: "Hubert Pudstrom received the chain in 1953. He asked his secretary to make 10 copies and send them out. A few days later he encountered her in a red-light district making more than he had ever paid her at work."[63] The Premier claimed that the letter fell short of sexual harassment, but he did reprimand known participants in the chain letter and promised to discover the remaining perpetrators.[64] As one Canadian commentator noted, however, "[t]hat type of e-mail doesn't contribute to a workplace where people feel free from harassment. It makes people nervous and uncomfortable and that type of thing should be dealt with very severely."[65]

Several major corporations have already been the subject of lawsuits based on claims of sexual harassment related to e-mail. For example, in 1995, Chevron Corp. settled a lawsuit filed by four female employees who claimed that they had been sexually harassed through electronic mail and in other ways; although Chevron denied all charges, the settlement cost the company $2.2 million plus legal fees and costs for both itself and the plaintiffs.[66] Similarly, a division of Calsonic International, Inc., in Shelbyville, Tennessee, was sued for $2.5 million by a female employee who claimed that her supervisor had subjected her to various forms of sexual harassment, including lewd remarks to her via the company's e-mail system.[67] Microsoft Corp. was sued by a former employee who was fired in 1990 and claimed that she was not promoted by her manager because of her gender; she claimed that her manager sent e-mail messages to her and other employees that were offensive to women, including innuendo about male genitalia and other sexual references.[68]

One of the key ways an employer can protect itself is to act swiftly when informed of such abuse. Another key means of protection is the formulation, distribution, and enforcement of an e-mail policy that emphasizes that all e-mail and computer bulletin board communications are for business purposes and that sexual harassment and other offensive communications are strictly prohibited (see Section 26.5).

Employees who do sue over electronic harassment may play the final trump card: the offensive e-mail messages, even those that have been deleted, will be subject to discovery. The plaintiffs may themselves have already printed out the harassing messages they received or may request (through a court order) the archival or backup copies that are automatically made and remain long after the original message has been deleted.

Because e-mail harassment provides such tangible, easily-gotten proof, many such workplace suits settle.[69]

26.4 Discovery Requests: E-Mail as Evidence

Discovery[70] requests for electronically stored information, including e-mail messages, are becoming increasingly routine in lawsuits. Companies should remember this when creating e-mail that could end up being subject to an adversary's discovery motion. Last-minute attempts to avoid discovery by destroying electronic mail can result in motions for issue preclusion, judgment, and even criminal spoliation charges.[71] Such destruction may also violate electronic recordkeeping requirements, which are discussed in Chapter 5.

Litigants now make document discovery requests that ask not only for "electronically stored information," but also for "hidden files," which are deleted documents that might still be retrieved from electronically-stored fragments or through court orders that allow access to an entire computer system.[72] In one case, a company claimed that its e-mail had been purged and no longer existed, but the deposition of that company's head of computer services revealed that the company maintained e-mail messages on a backup tape for three years before the company reused the tape; as a result, the company was forced to produce about 750,000 e-mail messages that were then searched by key words to produce damaging evidence regarding the plaintiff's wrongful discharge.[73]

E-mail can be a treasure trove of information for a litigant's diligent attorney. Due to the perception that e-mail is transitory in nature, businesses tend to use it like a telephone and say things they shouldn't because they think the message will disappear by pressing the delete key.[74] In fact, most e-mail messages are not deleted for six months to a year.[75] Even when they are deleted, as indicated above, new technology increasingly is allowing experts to recover some or all of the old data.

Careless e-mail messages increasingly figure prominently in litigation. For example, investigators used advanced technology to recover e-mail from backup tapes that Oliver North had attempted to erase.[76] E-mail messages also contributed to Siemens's decision to seek $146 million in damages from Atlantic Richfield's sale of its solar energy subsidiary to Siemens; the damaging e-mail message from an employee at Atlantic Richfield stated, "'We will attempt to finesse past Siemens the fact that we have had a great amount of trouble in successfully transitioning technology from the laboratory to the manufacturing floor. . . . As it appears that [ARCO's solar technology] is a pipe dream, let Siemens have the pipe.'"[77] Lawrence Powell, one of the Los Angeles police officers accused of beating Rodney King when he was arrested, carelessly broadcast an e-mail message on the Los Angeles Police Department system following the beating: "Oops, I haven't beaten anyone so bad in a long time."[78]

A company can best decrease the potential damage that e-mail may do in future litigation by raising awareness among employees about the need for care in composing e-mail messages and the often long-term retention of such messages despite deletion. Appropriate record retention and destruction policies (see Chapter 5) are also critical.

Key to raising employees' awareness is the distribution of a company e-mail policy, which is discussed in Section 26.5. Indeed, it may be wise for employers to issue a policy statement regarding all communications—including voice mail—because e-mail is not the only type of communication on which an employee could base an invasion of privacy claim.

26.5 Employer E-Mail Policies

26.5.1 How E-Mail Policies Protect Employers

Fewer than one in five U.S. companies currently has an e-mail policy, and many of those who do are probably not adequately communicating them to their employees.[79] Indeed, as the law now stands, companies are not required to announce a policy in order to monitor and read their employees' electronic mail.[80] Yet it may be risky for companies to wait until they have problems before formulating such a policy.

Creating and distributing a policy statement on e-mail monitoring can help reduce the risk of liability in an employee-initiated lawsuit by decreasing employees' expectations of privacy in their e-mail communications. Decreasing actual expectations of privacy may also discourage employees from filing suit against their employers in the first place. Moreover, by informing employees about the proper use of the employer's e-mail system, a written policy statement may help to limit the company's liability to third parties for copyright infringement, defamation, and other related e-mail claims. Such a policy statement may also discourage employees from using e-mail for careless and damaging communications that could later be used against the company in a lawsuit.

Before drafting e-mail policies, employers should examine the applicable federal and state laws, as well as their own union rules, to determine what employer practices are permitted.

26.5.2 What Every E-Mail Policy Should Contain

26.5.2.1 Business Purpose of E-Mail System. Every e-mail policy statement should make clear that the company e-mail system is company property that is to be used for company business. Whether the e-mail system can be used for personal business is another matter.

Some companies adopt strict policies that forbid employees from using the system for personal, nonbusiness-related communications. Such policies emphasize that e-mail use costs the company money and that the employer will monitor the system to prevent abuse. The employer thereby achieves two desirable results: (1) employees are less likely to abuse the system, thereby resulting in cost savings, and (2) the employer has shown the courts that its interest is in protecting its property, not in invading its employees' privacy.[81]

Such strict policies are also compatible with a high level of monitoring. Yet active monitoring of employee e-mail can be extremely expensive, hinder productivity (by undermining employee morale and trust), and inhibit use of the e-mail system.[82] To diminish employee resentment, employers with strict e-mail policies might choose to create bulletin boards that employees can use to send personal messages; the employer should, however, still warn employees that the company retains the right to intercept e-mail messages for maintenance and trouble-shooting purposes.[83]

More liberal policies allow some personal use of the company e-mail system while reserving the employer's right to monitor e-mail in specified circumstances and in accordance with defined procedures. Adhering to such procedures can be more time consuming and costly than a stricter policy that permits monitoring at any time. On the plus side, such policies may foster more trust between employees and employers and thereby promote productivity while still allowing the employer to intervene to protect its rights or duties. The employer's failure to comply with the expected procedures, however, may give rise to an employee complaint.[84]

26.5.2.2 Notification of an Employer's Right to Monitor. In general, employers can better protect themselves by notifying employees in advance and in writing of their policy regarding both the nature and the extent of the company's monitoring practices (if any). Such policy statements may include a justification for the monitoring (legitimate business purposes) and may enumerate reasonable procedural safeguards regarding the use and disclosure of information gathered via monitoring. To minimize privacy expectations, an employer may warn its employees that their e-mail is capable of being monitored at any time, despite system features—such as passwords, blind copies, and the power to delete messages—that give the appearance of privacy.

E-mail policy statements that enumerate the instances in which e-mail monitoring will occur, and that specifically confine employer monitoring to work-related surveillance, will probably be favorably viewed by courts. In evaluating an employer's actions, a court will generally consider: notice to and consent by the employee regarding monitoring (in some cases consent can be implied by the circumstances and need not be express); the scope of the intrusion into the employee's private matters; and the employer's justification for examining the employee's private messages (i.e., was the employer's access unreasonable at its inception or in its scope?).[85]

Employers can better protect themselves if they limit their review to transactional data whenever possible and read the message content only when a narrower search will not accomplish the employer's purpose. Legitimate reasons for employer monitoring include evaluations of individual employee productivity; analysis of overall organizational performance; and investigation of theft, bad conduct, illegality, or fraud.[86] Employers also have a legitimate interest in ensuring the appropriate use of all computer resources and access to business records; safeguarding and protecting proprietary information; monitoring to ensure that employees are not disruptive, offensive to others, or harmful to others (including acts of sexual harassment); routing messages; conducting system maintenance; troubleshooting; and maintaining quality control.[87]

Employers may want to emphasize in their e-mail policy statements that employees do not have a legitimate expectation of privacy in company files and correspondence generated by the employees during work time and using company equipment.

If employer policy statements notify employees regarding the substantive and temporal limitations of the monitoring, the employer should operate within the boundaries of that policy.[88] An employer's potential litigation stance may be enhanced if the employer notifies an employee in advance of particular instances of monitoring (beyond telling the employee that he or she may be subject to random monitoring) in situations where it is appropriate and compatible with the reasons for the monitoring. For example, it would be self-defeating to notify an employee suspected of using e-mail to disclose the employer's trade secrets that his or her e-mail may be monitored. Network supervisors, managers, and other people involved with the security of the system should be trained regarding the pertinent legal restrictions discussed earlier in this chapter.

26.5.2.3 Guidelines for Proper Use. Employers should emphasize in their policy statements that any reference made by an employee to a person's race, color, religion, sex, age, national origin, disabilities, or physique is prohibited: thoughtless running commentary can constitute harassment. For that matter, employers should strongly discourage personal attacks, gossip, and jokes, all of which could constitute harassment and, at the very least, could undermine the work environment.

Companies should also include guidelines in their policy statements for proper use of the e-mail system. Toward that end, companies should adopt and publicize policies regarding the backing up, archiving, and ownership of electronic messages. Employees should also be warned that deleting a careless and damaging message does not eliminate it: an opponent in litigation may someday request such hidden messages to use against the company. Of course, employers should remind employees that failure to keep certain electronic records may also violate the law. Moreover, employers should make clear that other violations of the law—including copyright infringement, disclosure of trade secrets, and sending and receiving obscenity and child pornography—could subject the employee to disciplinary action and possibly to criminal prosecution.

Endnotes

1. Rosalia J. Costa-Clarke, *Workplace Technology Creates Pitfalls for Employers,* Penn. L. Wkly., Dec. 5, 1994, at 6.

2. Doug van Kirk, *Unraveling the Internet Hype,* InfoWorld, Dec. 26, 1994/Jan. 2, 1995, at 52.

3. John K. Keitt, Jr. and Cynthia L. Kahn, *Cyberspace Snooping,* Legal Times, May 2, 1994, at 24.

4. *O'Connor v. Ortega,* 480 U.S. 709.

5. *Id.*

6. *Id.* at 718–720.

7. 18 U.S.C. §§ 2510–2711.

8. The Communications Act of 1934 (47 U.S.C. § 605 *et seq.*) pertains to the unauthorized disclosure of wire or radio communications, but, unlike it did with the wiretap law, Congress never amended the Communications Act to include electronic communications. It therefore is unlikely that a court would sustain a cause of action under that Act for a disclosure that was otherwise permitted by the ECPA. Julia Turner Baumhart, *The Employer's Right To Read Employee E-Mail: Protecting Property or Personal Prying?* 8 Lab. Law. 923, 939 (1992).

9. 18 U.S.C. § 2511 (1995).

10. 18 U.S.C. § 2701 (1995).

11. 18 U.S.C. §§ 2511, 2702 (1995).

12. 18 U.S.C. § 2511(2)(d) (1995).

13. *Watkins v. L.M. Berry & Co.*, 704 F.2d 577, 579 (11th Cir. 1983).

14. *Simmons v. Southwestern Bell Telephone Co.*, 452 F. Supp. 392, 394 (W.D. Okla. 1978).

15. *Deal v. Spears*, 980 F.2d 1153 (8th Cir. 1992).

16. *Watkins v. L.M. Berry & Co.*, 704 F.2d 577 (11th Cir. 1983).

17. *Deal v. Spears*, 980 F.2d 1153, 1157 (8th Cir. 1992); *Watkins v. L.M. Berry & Co.*, 704 F.2d 577, 581 (11th Cir. 1983). *See also* Julia Turner Baumhart, *The Employer's Right To Read Employee E-Mail: Protecting Property or Personal Prying?* 8 Lab. Law. 923, 934 (1992).

18. 18 U.S.C. § 2510(5)(a) (1995). This exception functions independently of the prior consent exception.

19. 18 U.S.C. § 2510(5)(a) (1995).

20. Kenneth A. Jenero and Lynne D. Mapes-Riordan, *Electronic Monitoring of Employees and the Elusive "Right to Privacy,"* Employee Relations L.J., 71, 90 (Summer, 1992).

21. *Watkins v. L.M. Berry & Co.*, 704 F.2d 577, 582–583 (11th Cir. 1983).

22. *Epps v. St. Mary's Hosp. of Athens, Inc.*, 802 F.2d 412, 416–417 (11th Cir. 1986).

23. *Briggs v. Am. Air Filter Co.*, 630 F.2d 414, 420 (5th Cir. 1980).

24. Rosalia J. Costa-Clarke, *Workplace Technology Creates Pitfalls for Employers,* Penn. L. Wkly., Dec. 5, 1994, at 6. *See also* Julia Turner Baumhart, *The Employer's Right To Read Employee E-Mail: Protecting Property or Personal Prying?* 8 Lab. Law. 923, 926–928 (1992).

25. *Simmons v. Southwestern Bell Telephone Co.*, 452 F. Supp. 392 (W.D. Okla. 1978).

26. *See, e.g., Steve Jackson Games, Inc. v. United States Secret Service*, 816 F. Supp. 432 (W.D. Tex. 1993).

27. 18 U.S.C. § 2701(c) (1995).

28. Julie A. Flanagan, *Restricting Electronic Monitoring in the Private Workplace*, 43 Duke L.J., 1256, 1277 (April 1994).

29. Kenneth A. Jenero and Lynne D. Mapes-Riordan, *Electronic Monitoring of Employees and the Elusive "Right to Privacy,"* Employee Relations L.J., 71, 94 (Summer, 1992). *See, e.g.,* 720 I.L.C.S. 5/14-1 et seq. *See also* Illinois' Right to Privacy in the Workplace Act, 820 I.L.C.S. 55/1 *et seq.*

30. Kenneth A. Jenero and Lynne D. Mapes-Riordan, *Electronic Monitoring of Employees and the Elusive "Right to Privacy,"* Employee Relations L.J., 71, 94 (Summer, 1992).

31. *Id.* at 95. *See People v. Beardsley*, 115 Ill. 2d 47, 503 N.E.2d 346, 350 (Ill. 1986).

32. Deborah L. Jacobs, *Are You Guilty of Electronic Trespassing?* 83 Mgmt. Rev. 21 (April, 1994).

33. *See, e.g.,* Ill. Const. Art. I, § 6.

34. Kenneth A. Jenero and Lynne D. Mapes-Riordan, *Electronic Monitoring of Employees and the Elusive "Right to Privacy,"* Employee Relations L.J., 71, 80 (Summer, 1992).

35. Julie A. Flanagan, *Restricting Electronic Monitoring in the Private Workplace,* 43 Duke L.J., 1256, 1265 (April 1994).

36. *Id.* at 1265–1266.

37. James J. Cappel, *Closing the E-Mail Privacy Gap: Employer Monitoring of Employee E-Mail,* J. of Systems Management, Vol. 44, No. 12, at 6 (Dec., 1993), *citing Alana Shoars v. Epson America, Inc.,* No. SWC 112749 (L.A. Super. Ct.).

38. James J. Cappel, *Closing the E-Mail Privacy Gap: Employer Monitoring of Employee E-Mail,* J. of Systems Management, Vol. 44, No. 12, at 6 (Dec. 1993), *citing Bourke v. Nissan Motor Co.,* No. YC 003979 (L.A. Super. Ct.).

39. Deborah L. Jacobs, *Are You Guilty of Electronic Trespassing?* 83 Mgmt. Rev. 21 (April, 1994).

40. *Id.*

41. *Id.*

42. N.Y. Labor Law § 201-d(2)(c) (Consol. 1994).

43. *State v. Wal-Mart Stores, Inc.,* 621 N.Y.S.2d 158 (N.Y. App. Div. 1995).

44. The statute defines *recreational activities* to mean "any lawful, leisure-time activity for which the employee receives no compensation and which is generally engaged in for recreational purposes, including but not limited to sports, games, hobbies, exercise, reading and the viewing of television, movies and similar material." N.Y. Labor Law § 201-d(1)(b) (Consol. 1994).

45. *Sex Discrimination: Cohabitation Protected Outside Activity under New York Law, Federal Court Says,* Daily Law Report (Aug. 24, 1995), *citing Pasch v. Katz Media Corp.,* DC SNY, No. 94-Civ-8554 (RPP), Aug. 4, 1995.

46. *Id.*

47. Wal-Mart has since abandoned its former policy and now ignores dating except when there is a direct supervisory relationship. Mary Loftus, *Frisky Business; Romance in the Workplace,* Psychology Today, Vol. 28, No. 2, at 34 (March, 1995).

48. For example, IBM was held liable for firing a female employee who refused to stop dating a man who worked for a competitor. Similarly, a jury awarded millions to two lovers who were fired by Rohr Inc. for cohabiting. Aaron Epstein, *Big Brother Watches for Workplace Sins: Employee Privacy Getting Harder to Find,* The Arizona Republic, at A1 (July 9, 1995).

49. Corey L. Nelson, *Is E-Mail Private or Public?* ComputerWorld, at 135 (June 27, 1994), *citing Thomasson v. Bank of America.*

50. *Burger Chef Systems, Inc. v. Govro,* 407 F.2d 921 (8th Cir. 1969), *citing Restatement of Agency* § 219.

51. 42 U.S.C. § 2000e *et seq.* (1994). It is an unlawful employment practice for an employer "to fail or refuse to hire or to discharge any individual, or otherwise to discriminate against any individual with respect to his compensation, terms, conditions, or privileges of employment, because of such individual's race, color, religion, sex, or national origin." 42 U.S.C. § 2000e-2(a)(1) (1994).

52. *Andrews v. City of Philadelphia,* 895 F.2d 1469, 1482 (3d Cir. 1990). *See also* 29 C.F.R. § 1604.11(a) (1995).

53. *Hall v. Gus Constr. Co.,* 842 F. 2d 1010, 1014 (8th Cir. 1988), *citing McKinney v. Dole,* 765 F.2d 1129, 1139 (D.C. Cir. 1985). *See also Andrews v. City of Philadelphia,* 895 F.2d 1469, 1485 (3d Cir. 1990).

54. *Katz v. Dole,* 709 F.2d 251, 255 (4th Cir. 1983).

55. *Id.*

56.   *Id.* at 256; *Bennett v. Carroon & Black Corp.*, 845 F.2d 104, 106 (5th Cir. 1988); *Andrews v. City of Philadelphia*, 895 F.2d 1469, 1486 (3d Cir. 1990).

57.   *Andrews v. City of Philadelphia*, 895 F.2d 1469, 1486 (3d Cir. 1990), *citing Davis v. Monsanto Chem. Co.*, 858 F.2d 345, 350 (6th Cir. 1988), *cert. denied*, 490 U.S. 1110 (1989).

58.   *Ways v. City of Lincoln*, 871 F.2d 750, 755 (8th Cir. 1989).

59.   *Andrews v. City of Philadelphia*, 895 F.2d 1469, 1485 (3d Cir. 1990).

60.   *Bennett v. Carroon & Black Corp.*, 845 F.2d 104, 106 (5th Cir. 1988).

61.   *Ways v. City of Lincoln*, 871 F.2d 750, 755 (8th Cir. 1990).

62.   Justine Hunter, *Lewd E-Mail Not Harassment, Premier Says,* The Vancouver Sun, April 11, 1995, at A3.

63.   *Id.*

64.   *Id.*

65.   *Id., quoting* Liberal critic Gary Farrell-Collins.

66.   Amie M. Soden, *Protect Your Corporation from E-Mail Litigation: Privacy, Copyright Issues Should Be Addressed in Policy,* Corporate Legal Times, May, 1995, at 19.

67.   Mitch Betts and Joseph Maglitta, *IS Policies Target E-Mail Harassment,* ComputerWorld, Feb. 13, 1995, at 12.

68.   Stephanie Stahl, *Dangerous E-Mail: Companies Are Finding that E-Mail Indiscretions Can Leave Them Legally Vulnerable,* InformationWeek, Sept. 12, 1994, at 12.

69.   Mitch Betts and Joseph Maglitta, *IS Policies Target E-Mail Harassment,* ComputerWorld, Feb. 13, 1995, at 12.

70.   *Discovery* in trial practice is defined as "the pre-trial devices that can be used by one party to obtain facts and information about the case from the other party in order to assist the party's preparation for trial." *Black's Law Dictionary* 466 (6th ed. 1990).

71.   John K. Keitt, Jr. and Cynthia L. Kahn, *Cyberspace Snooping,* Legal Times, May 2, 1994, at 24. *Spoliation* means the "intentional destruction of evidence and when it is established, fact finder may draw inference that evidence destroyed was unfavorable to party responsible for its spoliation." *Black's Law Dictionary* 1401 (6th ed. 1990).

72.   Vera Titunik, *Collecting Evidence in the Age of E-Mail,* Am. Lawyer, July/Aug. 1994, at 119, *citing* John Jessen, managing director of Electronic Evidence Discovery.

73.   *Id.*

74.   *Id.*

75.   *Id.*

76.   John K. Keitt, Jr. and Cynthia L. Kahn, *Cyberspace Snooping,* Legal Times, May 2, 1994, at 24.

77.   *Id.*

78.   *Id.*

79.   Commentators differ somewhat in their estimates of the number of companies with e-mail policies. One source estimates that fewer than 10 percent of companies have e-mail policies on privacy and security. John K. Keitt, Jr. and Cynthia L. Kahn, *Cyberspace Snooping,* Legal Times, May 2, 1994, at 24. Another commentator found that only about 16 percent of the respondents to a June 1993 survey published in *PC Week* had a privacy policy regarding e-mail monitoring, and many of those 16 percent may not have been adequately communicating those policies to their employees. James J. Cappel, *Closing the E-Mail Privacy Gap: Employer Monitoring of Employees' E-Mail,* J. of Systems Management, Vol. 44, No. 12, at 6 (December, 1993).

80. John K. Keitt, Jr. and Cynthia L. Kahn, *Cyberspace Snooping*, Legal Times, May 2, 1994, at 24.

81. Julia Turner Baumhart, *The Employer's Right to Read Employee E-Mail: Protecting Property or Personal Prying?* 8 Lab. Law. 923, 935 (1992).

82. Kimberly Patch, *Proposed E-Mail Bill Offers Balance*, PC Week, Sept. 6, 1993, at 24.

83. Deborah L. Jacobs, *Are You Guilty of Electronic Trespassing?* 83 Mgmt. Rev. 21 (April, 1994).

84. *See* David R. Johnson and John Podesta, *Privacy Tool Kit: Access to and Use and Disclosure of Electronic Mail on Company Computer Systems* (Electronic Messaging Association 1994) (lists sample e-mail policies and suggests guidelines for formulating an employer e-mail policy); Rosalia J. Costa-Clarke, *Workplace Technology Creates Pitfalls for Employers*, Penn. L. Wkly., Dec. 5, 1994, at 6 (lists key provisions for employer e-mail policy); Kenneth A. Jenero and Lynne D. Mapes-Riordan, *Electronic Monitoring of Employees and the Elusive "Right to Privacy,"* Employee Relations L.J., 71, 97–100 (Summer, 1992) (article lists suggested provisions for employers to include in policy statements to minimize exposure to liability while promoting fairness in employer monitoring practices).

85. Julia Turner Baumhart, *The Employer's Right To Read Employee E-Mail: Protecting Property or Personal Prying?* 8 Lab. Law. 923, 947 (1992).

86. Kenneth A. Jenero and Lynne D. Mapes-Riordan, *Electronic Monitoring of Employees and the Elusive "Right to Privacy,"* Employee Relations L.J., 71 (Summer 1992). *See also Smyth v. Pillsbury Co.*, 1996 U.S. Dist. LEXIS 776 (E.D. Pa. January 18, 1996), in which the court held that the company's interest in preventing inappropriate and unprofessional comments or illegal activity over the company e-mail system outweighed any privacy interest the employee may have had in the comments, even though the company had assured its employees that such communications would not be intercepted or used as grounds for reprimand or termination.

87. Joel P. Kelly, *Whose E-Mail Is It Anyway?* 1 Empl. L. Strategist, Feb., 1994, *reprinted in Business and Legal Aspects of the Internet and Online Services*, 831, 832 (Law Journal Seminars Press, 1994).

88. Kenneth A. Jenero and Lynne D. Mapes-Riordan, *Electronic Monitoring of Employees and the Elusive "Right to Privacy,"* Employee Relations L.J., 71, 92 (Summer, 1992).

27

Contracts for Making the Online Connection

Larry M. Zanger

27.1 Overview

All online activity begins with a connection to a network capable of carrying electronic messages. In most cases, this involves entering into a contract with an internet access provider, an online service provider, a value-added network, or some other entity that provides the capability of carrying messages and/or the online content desired.

Online connections are initiated to engage in a variety of activities. These include sending and receiving electronic mail (e-mail), accessing the Internet, establishing and operating Internet Web sites, accessing online content made available by the various online services, engaging in electronic commerce, engaging in electronic data interchange (EDI) transactions, and engaging in electronic funds transfers (EFT).

In EDI or EFT transactions, electronic commerce can be conducted directly between trading partners. However, many forms of electronic commerce, such as business-to-business EDI trading partner relationships, and business-to-bank EFT relationships, are conducted through one or more intermediary computer networks generically referred to as *third-party service providers* or *value-added networks* (*VAN*s). VANs provide a variety of services for EDI trading partners, such as translation services for EDI documents communicated in incompatible formats, a relatively high level of system security, and certain recordkeeping and audit functions.

In addition, a number of online services have been established that permit users to access an enormous amount of information from newspapers and magazines, to court opinions and advertising, and to participate in "chat rooms" and access bulletin board services and the Internet and World Wide Web.

The discussion that follows addresses the contract issues that arise in the various agreements that document the provision of these services. Although online agreements frequently involve a unique combination of facts, circumstances, and issues, there are a number of basic issues that are common to most agreements. Although this book cannot evaluate all of the unique problems and circumstances that may arise in the wide variety of online commerce situations that exist today, it attempts to provide a general overview of the basic issues that can be expected to arise most frequently.

Keep in mind, however, that it may not be necessary for a given online provider agreement to address all of the issues raised here. Alternatively, other issues not addressed here, may be relevant. Every agreement must be structured to meet the needs of the particular transaction, and, to the extent possible, should reflect accurately the needs of the service user. Many online service agreements are standard form contracts often presented on a non-negotiable basis. Even in such cases, it is important to understand the issues in order to evaluate the potential benefits and risks of the relationship fairly. In analyzing online service agreements, the issues raised in this chapter should be considered, although the extent to which they are relevant, and the way in which they are handled, will vary depending on the particular situation, the type of contract involved, and the relative negotiating strength of the parties.

27.2 Value-Added Network Agreements

27.2.1 Checklist of Drafting Issues

To introduce the contract issues involved with agreements between value-added networks and a customer for EDI transactions, we begin with a checklist of basic questions—an overview of the types of questions that should be raised when preparing or reviewing an agreement with a value-added network service provider.

1. **Scope of Services.** What are the services that are included in the agreement? What are the rights of the customer?
2. **Customer Operating Environment.** What minimum equipment configuration is required for the VAN to provide its services? How is the VAN to verify the existence of that configuration? What happens if the VAN changes its systems during the term of the agreement?
3. **EDI Standard.** Which EDI format and protocols will be used in connection with the services?
4. **Materials Provided by the VAN.** What software and other products will be provided by the VAN? What, if anything, may the customer retain after termination?
5. **Commencement of the Service.** Is a defined commencement date provided for in the agreement? Is there a penalty for late commencement?
6. **Fees, Charges, and Payment Terms.** What are the current fees and charges for the services that the customer might require? What increases will be permitted in these charges during the life of the agreement and any renewals?
7. **Term.** Is the agreement for a fixed term, or does it renew automatically? What is the notice needed to terminate the agreement? Is there a termination charge?
8. **Termination.** What other events will cause the agreement to terminate? Is there a "cure" period?
9. **Confidentiality and Protection of the Proprietary and Intellectual Property of the Parties.** What intellectual property is considered to be owned by each party? What is the undertaking of each party with regard to the intellectual property of the other? What is the confidentiality standard that is imposed on the VAN? What exclusions from confidentiality will the parties permit?

10. **Security Procedures.** What are the required security systems that must be in place at the VAN's location and at the customer's location?
11. **Reliability, Availability, and Capacity of the System.** What percentage of "uptime" is the network required to maintain? Will the VAN be required to provide its own disaster-recovery site? What volume of transactions is the system required to handle? Which party is responsible for errors in communication and processing of transactions?
12. *Force Majeure.*[1] What is the VAN required to do in the event of a failure of its system for reasons "beyond its control?" What redundancy in the system should the VAN be required to maintain?
13. **Indemnification.** What indemnification will each party demand from the other? What are the remedies if there is a breach of the indemnification?
14. **Warranties.** What warranties, if any, are made by the VAN?
15. **Limitation of Liabilities.** To what extent is the VAN responsible for damages that the customer might suffer as a result of using its network and services? Is there a limit on the nature or the extent of the VAN's liability?

27.2.2 Scope of Services

Most VAN agreements, utilized in EDI and EFT transactions, very broadly state the scope of the services provided. These services include the communication, storage, and translation of data; the time-stamping and receipt verification of the messages themselves; and recordkeeping. This list should be amended to delete the services that the customer is not going to use and to add services that the customer expects the VAN to provide.

It is important for the parties to agree on the specific additional services that the VAN is expected to render. VANs generally provide the equivalent of a "mailbox" service, according to which the VAN will accept and store the EDI transactions that the customer may access from time to time. The VAN may be required to "time-stamp" or otherwise validate the transactions that it processes.

VANs differ widely in the scope of the services they will provide to a customer. Some VANs supply few services beyond the provision of the communications connection, while others are full-service providers furnishing a vast array of consulting and technical advice. The contract should specify the availability of ancillary professional services and the hourly charges that the VAN will assess for services provided by its technical assistance personnel.

27.2.3 Customer Operating Environment

Since EDI requires a precise configuration of equipment, both parties must ensure that the equipment used by the parties is compatible. Such requirements may be so extensive that they will be attached to the agreement as a referenced exhibit. The customer may be obligated to obtain special telecommunications equipment or computers and peripherals of a certain size or configuration. The customer will want assurance that if it provides the required computers and data communications equipment, the VAN will not be able to blame the customer for any deficiencies in the provision of services.

The VAN will want the opportunity to verify that the equipment that the customer proposes to use complies with the VAN's specifications, and will provide the customer with a written evaluation of any deficiencies, in much the same way as a computer service company evaluates the condition of the machines it is being asked to service before the contract begins. The customer would then have to remediate the operating environment if, as installed, it does not comply with the requirements of the VAN.

Once the customer has installed the operating environment, changes may occur in the system requirements or services provided by the VAN. Such changes may have a substantial negative impact on the customer. Therefore, the customer may want to obtain a substantial notice period if such changes are planned. In addition, the customer may want to seek an undertaking from the VAN that the level of services provided for in the agreement will remain unchanged for the term of the agreement or longer.

27.2.4 EDI Standard

All EDI transactions require the use of standard EDI formats and protocols. The customer and its trading partners will designate the format and protocols that they will be using in their transactions. The customer and its VAN should agree on the extent to which modifications may be made in the originally specified formats and protocols. The customer should also understand that modifications that it makes in the EDI standard or protocol that it uses will result in the VAN charging additional fees.

27.2.5 Materials Provided by the VAN

The agreement should list the specific software programs (including the version numbers and operating system required), user manuals, and other documentation, as well as proprietary hardware that the VAN is providing to the customer. These programs would be those that are necessary to access the VAN's system. If there is an undertaking to update the software and user documentation, it should be recited, together with any fees that are related to the update. The customer should be certain that it will have the necessary updates for as long as the customer intends to be on the VAN.

Most VAN agreements require the return of all listed material at the end of the agreement. Therefore, the customer will either want to negotiate a different provision or will, at least, want to guaranty that the VAN retains copies of all of the materials that the customer used during the term of the agreement. This could be necessary to a customer if its auditor requires the ability to verify the contents of its transactions, or if such verification is required in an income tax audit or in connection with litigation. If the customer does not have access to the VAN's proprietary software, it may not be able to verify its transactions.

27.2.6 Commencement Date for the Service

If a trading partner of the customer requires it to commence its use of EDI on a specified date, the customer should seek to include a deadline for the commencement of the

VAN's services. The customer will want to seek a penalty from the VAN if the services are not operational, without the fault of the customer, by the agreed deadline.

27.2.7 Fees, Charges, and Payment Terms

The rates that a VAN charges should be clearly defined. The section that describes the fees and charges of the VAN generally includes its basic monthly charges (for a defined number of transactions), fees for transactions in excess of the base number, the charge for electronic mailboxes, applicable state and municipal taxes, provision for telephone expenses, and license fees for the use of computer software or for the use of proprietary hardware of the VAN. In addition, this section might provide for off-peak discounts that are tied to evening, weekend, or holiday usage.

Finally, the parties must agree on the level of increases that the VAN will be permitted to make in these charges during the life of the agreement and any renewals. It is important to remember that once the customer has begun to use a given VAN, the customer loses some of its bargaining power because it has already incurred the costs of the initial implementation.

The billing cycle in the typical VAN agreement is monthly, with payment generally due within 30 days following the date of the invoice. Although most of the billing for EDI services uses conventional paper invoices, some VANs are themselves implementing electronic billing using EDI. The customer should seek to ensure that the VAN agreement delineates the billing procedures and requires advance written notice before finance charges are added.

27.2.8 Term

Customers usually want to guarantee the continuation of the services of the VAN. Consequently, most VAN agreements include a clause that provides for automatic extension or renewal. Such provisions eliminate the possibility that the agreement will be inadvertently terminated. Such provisions typically provide for 30, 60, or 90 days' written notice to terminate the agreement. The customer should determine whether there are any termination charges, as well as whether any of the VAN's services can be terminated without the customer's permission.

27.2.9 Termination

Customers should be certain that their VAN agreement permits the customer to terminate the agreement at any time with or without cause. This is advisable in case the VAN's service deteriorates or becomes unavailable, or in case the customer needs to change the VAN to satisfy one or more of its trading partners.

VANs themselves often retain the right to terminate the agreement at any time and without cause. A provision such as this should be a concern to a customer regardless of the length of the notice period. The exercise by a VAN of a right such as this could be a disruption to the customer's ability to transact its business. One solution would be to require the VAN to give the customer sufficient notice (three to six months) if it intends to terminate its service, and to obligate the VAN to assist the customer in obtaining substitute service and in completing the migration to that service.

If the VAN agreement contains a provision terminating the agreement due to the bankruptcy or insolvency of the customer, the customer will prefer that if the bankruptcy is involuntarily instituted, it have a "cure period," a period during which the customer may have the bankruptcy filing dismissed. If the breach of the agreement is the nonpayment of uncontested invoices from the VAN, a shorter cure period would be typical.

The occurrence of various other events will also be considered to be a breach of the agreement, which, if uncured, would lead to its termination. For example, use of the services and instrumentalities of the VAN for illegal purposes would result in immediate termination of the agreement.

27.2.10 Confidentiality and Protection of the Proprietary and Intellectual Property of the Parties

Each of the parties to the agreement exposes certain of its intellectual property to the other. For example, the VAN brings its proprietary computer software, user documentation, and proprietary hardware to the contract. In addition, the VAN also has the copyrights, service marks, trademarks, patent rights, and trade secrets related to such property. The VAN will preclude the customer from infringing on its copyrighted software and from any use of the VAN's marks.

The VAN should undertake to protect the confidentiality of sensitive customer information and to protect such information from infiltration or alteration from outside or inside by the installation of security procedures.

The VAN will be exposed to a considerable amount of confidential information regarding the customer's business transactions and regarding the customer's trading partners. A VAN agreement should require that all of the customer's communications be treated as confidential. VAN agreements are affected by the Electronic Communications Privacy Act of 1986.[2] The ECPA specifically authorizes electronic communications services to view communications passing through their network. Since this result would probably not be what the customer wants, the customer should attempt to negotiate a contractual revision to it.

27.2.11 Security Procedures

Security is a significant factor in the operation of every EDI communication network. It is necessary to guaranty the reliability of the system, to protect the customer's data, and to protect the integrity of the transactions sent over the system. Since the operation of any security scheme is primarily the responsibility of the VAN, the VAN agreement should define the requirement of the VAN in that regard.

The customer is very concerned that its transactions and business data are protected from disclosure to outsiders and to unauthorized changes in content. The customer must determine that the VAN implements specific security procedures to protect data against disclosures and changes. If the VAN will not agree to specificity, the customer should expect the VAN to assure that "commercially reasonable security procedures" have or will be implemented.[3]

Such issues as whether the VAN or the customer generates the passwords, whether the VAN knows the passwords, and how frequently the passwords may be changed should be described in the contract.

In addition to passwords, which relate to system access, security procedures also relate to authentication, document integrity, document confidentiality, audit trails, time stamping, and recordkeeping. A detailed review of these issues in contained in Chapters 3, 4, and 5 of this book.

27.2.12 Reliability, Availability, and Capacity of the System

Perhaps the most important provision of any VAN agreement is the amount of time that the network will be available to process the customer's transactions. Any disruption in the operation of the system is potentially devastating to any customer. Disruptions can result in lost orders or orders that are transmitted incorrectly, deterioration of customer relations, the additional expense of providing alternative communications, and the potential additional expenses of operating a paper-based system. While the VAN may be reluctant to guarantee any level of up-time, a customer with sufficient bargaining power may be able to obtain such a commitment. Customers may also want to obtain an undertaking that the VAN's system will be able to accommodate a stated volume of transactions.

Because the use of VANs in connection with a customer's business transactions can be so important, many VANs undertake to provide their own disaster-recovery sites for customer mailboxes and often provide redundancy in their communications network. Redundant sites provide cut-over capabilities if the VAN's primary network has a problem. These so-called hot sites necessarily involve the duplication of all of the customer's data and the retention of all operational programs in two locations. Since the operation of disaster-recovery sites is not typical to VAN agreements, customers should determine whether the VAN is going to provide such services and what expectations customers may have regarding the resumption of services following such an emergency.

The VAN agreement should state how much liability the VAN is willing to accept for errors in communications and in the processing of transactions, or what remedial efforts the VAN will undertake if errors occur.[4] In this regard, the agreement should consider whether the correction of an error is intended to take the place of the assessment of damages, how long the VAN has to correct errors, how the source of errors is determined, and the effect of an error that cannot be corrected.

The parties should also agree on whether the VAN will store the customer's data. Although most VANs have the ability to store data, the specifics of such storage—including the duration of storage, the location of storage, the medium on which the storage will take place, the protocols for deletion of stored data, and the requirement to respond to audit requests from the customer's certified public accountants or to sub-poenas and court or administrative orders seeking disclosure of the customer's data—should be considered.

27.2.13 *Force Majeure*

Closely tied to the disaster-recovery undertaking is the *force majeure* provision. Without an agreement, there is no legal obligation for a VAN to provide any redundancy or plan for disruption. Must such redundant networks be activated in the event of a failure of its system for reasons "beyond its control"? The agreement must define those occurrences. If there is no such undertaking, a standard *force majeure* clause would be expected.

27.2.14 Indemnification

Each party will seek indemnification from the other party. The VAN will seek an indemnification from the customer to protect itself from any liabilities that result from the customer's improper use of the VAN's services or communications system, including violations of privacy, copyright, or proprietary rights.

   The customer will demand similar indemnification protection from the VAN. Though it may be concerned about patent or copyright violations by the VAN (especially if infringing software is installed by the VAN on the customer's computer), the customer is more concerned about indemnification by the VAN for improper disclosures of customer data, misdelivery of data, and deletion or alteration of data.

   If the indemnification provisions are invoked, the party seeking protection must promptly notify the indemnifying party, and provide the indemnifying party with necessary information and assistance and cooperation in defending the claim.

27.2.15 Warranties

Although general warranty disclaimers are standard in most VAN agreements, customers with bargaining leverage may be able to obtain some warranty protection. The customer would reasonably want or expect warranties from a VAN regarding the provision of security for the communications network, the amount of time that the network is available for use, the proper translation of EDI data, and the maintenance of agreed EDI formats and protocols.

27.2.16 Limitation of Liabilities

VANs are typically involved in transactions where the value of the information transmitted far exceeds the charge that the VAN receives for the service provided. Consequently, most VAN agreements provide for a general disclaimer of damage, except for direct damages. In one case, for example, the plaintiff's bank telexed a wire transfer to a Swiss bank to secure a European ship charter for the plaintiff.[5] The Swiss bank, which did not know the purpose of the wire transfer, lost the wire transfer. The plaintiff consequently lost the charter and had to contract at a higher price for another, resulting in a loss of

$2.1 million. The plaintiff sued the Swiss bank to recover its damages—the difference between the original and replacement charter prices. The court refused to find for the plaintiff in part because the defendant could not have anticipated that its failure to complete a wire transfer would result in such an injury. However, the court implied that the bank could have been liable if it had been aware of the special circumstances surrounding the transfer.

There are three types of contract damages: direct, incidental, and consequential. *Direct damages* result immediately from a breach of the contract. In EDI transactions, these might be the cost of retrieving or processing lost or damaged data. The customer would seek to guarantee that the contract with the VAN grants the customer recovery of direct damage, including a credit for the cost of any faulty service and all of the expenses incurred to reconstitute lost data. *Incidental damages* include reasonable charges or expense incurred by the customer as a result of a breach by the VAN. Such expenses might include the cost of contracting with another VAN.

Consequential damages are those that result from the remote effects of the breach and can include such items as the profits lost from not being able to transact through the network during a disruption of service. Common law generally provides that a party breaching a contract can be held liable for consequential damages that it could reasonably foresee as resulting from the breach.[6]

Caps on damages typically limit the VAN's exposure to the lesser of actual damages or fees paid by the customer or some other liquidated sum.

27.3 Online Service Agreements

Online services include generalized services such as America Online, CompuServe, Prodigy and the fledgling Microsoft Network, and such specialized services as LEXIS Counsel Connect and Law Journal Extra. These services are generally computer online, interactive information, communication, and transaction services.

27.3.1 Checklist of Drafting Issues

To introduce the contract issues involved with agreements between online service providers and a customer, we begin with a checklist of basic questions—an overview of the most important types of questions that should be raised when preparing or reviewing an agreement with an online service provider. The complete list of topics covered in Section 27.2.1 may also be consulted.

1. **Commencement of the Relationship.** What method does the online service use to begin the relationship with the member? What services are included with the monthly membership fee and what services will be provided at an extra cost?
2. **Responsibility of the Member.** Which party is responsible for the telephone connection? How are membership and extra-charge services paid for?
3. **Conduct of the Member Online.** What conduct of the member is restricted while online?

4. **Rights of the Online Service.** What rights does the online service have with respect to the member?

5. **Treatment of Copyrighted and Proprietary Materials.** What restrictions exist with respect to copyrighted and proprietary materials that are available online? What rights do members have to utilize such materials?

6. **Third-Party Sales and Services.** What limitations exist for products and services obtained online from third parties?

7. **Limitation of Liability and Disclaimers of Warranty.** How is the rendition of the online services limited by disclaimers contained in the agreement?

8. **Software Licensing.** How does the online service agreement cover the licensing of software used to operate on the system?

27.3.2 Commencement of the Relationship

Online services facilitate the commencement of their services by dispensing with the use of signed paper contracts. Rather, these services typically require only that a member click the "yes" box on a sign-up screen that appears when the member initially accesses the service. The complete terms of the agreement with the online provider are usually written out as part of the materials that accompany the "trial membership" package.

Online services operate through the concept of membership accounts. These accounts are necessary for the billing of charges to the member for online hours in excess of the number that are included with the basic monthly membership, for Internet access charges, and for the use of various extra-cost services that are designated in the online agreement or in the membership manual. These extra-cost services may include databases, publications, discussion forums, and other services that are not included in the monthly charge.

27.3.3 Responsibilities of the Member

The use of an online service presumes that the member has a modem and a telephone line with which to connect to the service. The member is also responsible for all charges related to making the initial connection to the online service. The largest online services have arranged for telephone numbers around the country so that the initial connection is a local call, but the agreement does not guaranty the availability of a local access number.

The member is responsible for the choice of a password and for maintaining the confidentiality of the password. The member is also responsible for the consequences of that password being disclosed.

The member must represent to the online service that he or she is an individual and at least of legal age. If the member is a minor, special arrangements have to be made with the minor's parents or guardian.

The member's account is, in effect, a charge account for the use of online services, in much the same way that a telephone number is a charge account for long-distance and 900-number billings. Therefore, the member undertakes to pay all charges made to his or her account. To secure the payment, the online service typically obtains a credit-card number to charge or a checking account to debit for services on a monthly basis.

27.3.4 Conduct of the Member Online

Online services typically seek to prohibit conduct by one member that restricts or inhibits another member from using or enjoying the service. Members agree to use the service only for lawful purposes, and further agree not to post or transmit through the service any unlawful, harmful, threatening, abusive, harassing, defamatory, vulgar, obscene, profane, hateful, racially, ethnically, or otherwise objectionable material of any kind.

However, a case that arose from activities on the Prodigy online service may have changed the rigor with which online services review the activities of their members. In that case, a court determined that Prodigy, which operates a large computer network, could be held liable for the damages caused by its users posting defamatory messages on one of the bulletin boards on its online service.[7] As a result of the *Prodigy* case, online service providers, though they will continue to retain the right to review the postings made by their members, may be less likely to use that power.

27.3.5 Rights of the Online Service

The online service usually retains the right to monitor the chat rooms, message boards, and file upload areas to determine that its rules prohibiting unlawful, harmful, threatening, abusive, harassing, defamatory, vulgar, obscene, profane, hateful, racially, ethnically, or otherwise objectionable material of any kind are being followed. The online service also reserves the right to add to its list of prohibited conduct additional activities that it considers, in the exercise of its sole discretion, to be harmful to the service or its members.

The online service retains the right to terminate its agreement with the member at any time if the member has violated any provision of the service agreement. The online service also retains the right to change the operation of the service, the charge levied for the use of the service, or the content that is available through the service. Many online service agreements provide that if the member is not satisfied with such changes to the service, its only recourse is to terminate service.

27.3.6 Treatment of Copyrighted and Proprietary Materials

Online services contain a tremendous amount of copyrighted, trademarked, and proprietary materials that is referred to as *content. Content* includes the magazines and databases, software, photographs, video, graphics, music, and sound effects, available through the service, each of which is protected either by statute or by common law proprietary rights law. Members are prohibited from publishing, transmitting, or creating derivative works[8] from content or exploiting such materials in any way unless the service has obtained permission for its members to make copies of portions of the content for their own personal use.

Members may also upload to the service software and other materials that are either the member's own creation, that are considered to be public domain materials, or that are the property of third parties who have given the member the right to upload such materials to the system. Member agreements contain language that reminds the member that they and not the service are liable for damages that result from the uploading of such materials. Given the litigation that has arisen in this area, online services are understandably cautious of being considered to be contributory infringers.[9] In addition, due to the holding in the *Prodigy* case,[10] online service providers are beginning to include language that states their status regarding third-party content. One service has included the following statement:

> AOL, Inc. is a distributor (and not a publisher) of Content supplied by third parties and Members. Accordingly, AOL, Inc. has no more editorial control over such Content than does a public library, bookstore, or newsstand.[11]

27.3.7 Third-Party Sales and Services

Online services also act as intermediaries between their members and third-party merchants and service providers. However, since the online services are not directly involved with providing those goods and services, the service agreements contain a complete disclaimer of warranties and liability with respect to products or services the member may order over the online service.

27.3.8 Limitation of Liability and Disclaimers of Warranty

Contracts provided by online service providers typically contain extensive disclaimers. First, there is clear language that the services are used by the member at the member's risk, and that the online service provider makes no warranty that the services provided will be uninterrupted or error-free. In addition, there is language that the services are provided on an "as is" and "as available" basis, without any warranty of any kind. A standard contractual disclaimer of warranties is also frequently included.

The disclaimer of the implied warranty of merchantability or fitness for purpose that is usually associated with sales of goods[12] rather than services is included in contracts provided by online service providers, since courts often look to the Uniform Commercial Code for direction in connection with service contracts.

As was the case with VAN agreements, online service provider agreements contain extensive disclaimers of liability regarding direct, indirect, incidental, special, or consequential damages. This disclaimer includes losses due to use or inability to use the services; or because of the deletion of any of the members' files; or due to errors, defects, or any failure of performance of the system, including failures due to acts of God. Finally, if any claim for damages may be successfully argued in the face of all of the disclaimers, the online service agreement limits the liability of the service provider to a sum equal to the prior 12 months' fees paid to the service provider.

27.3.9 Software Licensing

Since the use of an online service involves the use of a computer and modem, each online service must provide the member with software to access the system and navigate through it. Either as a separate document, or included in the service agreement, are typical licensing terms that relate to the service provider's proprietary software.

27.4 Internet Access Agreements

Internet access providers (IAPs) permit individual and business users of the Internet to connect through their auspices. Many providers are local services; however, a few national firms (such as Netcom and UUNet) are beginning to take advantage of the growth of interest in the Internet. Most of the contracts we have reviewed in connection with IAP services are very short and cover very few of the issues that one would expect to be addressed in such agreements.

27.4.1 Checklist of Drafting Issues

To introduce the contract issues involved with agreements between an IAP and a customer, we begin with a checklist of basic questions—an overview of the types of questions that should be raised when preparing or reviewing an agreement with an IAP. The complete list of topics covered in Section 27.2.1 may also be consulted.

1. **Conduct of the User.** What conduct of the user is restricted while using the IAP's service?
2. **Rights of the IAP.** What rights does the IAP have with respect to the user?
3. **Treatment of Copyrighted Materials.** What restrictions exist with respect to copyrighted materials that are available online? What rights do users have to utilize such materials?
4. **Limitation of Liability and Disclaimers of Warranty.** How is the rendition of the Internet access services limited by disclaimers contained in the agreement?
5. **Software Licensing.** How does the online service agreement cover the licensing of software used to operate the system?
6. **Service Options.** What are the service options that the IAP offers?
7. **Availability of the System.** What percentage of "up time" is the IAP required to maintain?

27.4.2 Conduct of the User

IAPs typically seek to prohibit unlawful conduct by the user. Members agree to use the service only for lawful purposes and further agree not to use the service for any purpose in violation of state or federal regulations.

27.4.3 Rights of the IAP

The IAP retains the right to monitor any and all communications through the IAP's service to the extent necessary to correct system errors and malfunctions. The IAP retains the right to monitor messages to determine that its rules prohibiting unlawful, harmful, threatening, abusive, harassing, defamatory, vulgar, obscene, profane, hateful, racially, ethnically, or otherwise objectionable material of any kind have been obeyed. The IAP also reserves the right to add to its list of prohibited conduct additional activities that it considers, in the exercise of its sole discretion, to be harmful to the service or its other users.

The IAP retains the right to terminate the user's rights at any time if the user has violated any provision of the service agreement. The IAP also retains the right to change the operation of the service or the charge levied for the use of the service.

27.4.4 Treatment of Copyrighted Materials

IAPs permit users to access an enormous amount of copyrighted, trademarked, and proprietary materials. The user agrees not to transmit any material that is copyrighted; adjudged to be illegal, threatening, or obscene; or material that is protected by trade secret law.

27.4.5 Limitation of Liability and Disclaimers of Warranty

Contracts provided by IAPs, like those provided by online service providers, typically contain extensive disclaimers, including disclaimers of the accuracy or quality of information obtained through the use of the service. First, there is clear language that the service is accessed by the user at the user's risk, and that the IAP does not warrant that the services provided will be uninterrupted or error-free. In addition, there is language that the connection service is provided on an "as is" and "as available" basis, without any warranty of any kind. A standard contractual disclaimer of warranties is also frequently included.

The disclaimer of the implied warranty of merchantability or fitness for purpose that is usually associated with sales of goods[13] rather than services is included in these contracts, since courts often look to the Uniform Commercial Code for direction in connection with service contracts.

As was the case with VAN agreements and online service provider agreements, IAP agreements contain extensive disclaimers of liability regarding direct, indirect, incidental, special, or consequential damages. This disclaimer includes losses due to use or inability to use the services; or due to errors, defects, or any failure of performance of the system, including failures due to acts of God. Finally, if any claim for damages may be successfully argued in the face of all of the disclaimers, the IAP agreement limits the liability of the IAP to a sum equal to the prior 12 months' fees paid to the IAP.

27.4.6 Software Licensing

Since the use of an Internet access service involves the use of a computer and modem, each IAP must furnish the user with software to access the system and navigate through it. Either as a separate document, or included in the service agreement are typical licensing terms that relate to the IAP's proprietary software.

27.4.7 Service Options

Internet access providers frequently offer different service options. For example, the user can choose between what is called a "shell" account that provides access to Internet electronic mail, and a full-access account. The latter provides access to such services as file transfer protocol (FTP) and gopher.

27.4.8 Availability of the System

One provision that may be important to the user is the amount of time that the Internet will be available to the user. The IAP will not volunteer to guaranty any level of up-time, and in fact will disclaim any such guaranty. However, a user with sufficient bargaining power may be able to obtain such a commitment. The IAP agreement typically states that the IAP will accept no liability for errors in communications, and a commercial user of the Internet will want to negotiate an undertaking by the IAP for such liability.

Endnotes

1. *Force majeure* is a Latin term that is used in contracts to signify "acts of God" or other circumstances beyond the control of the parties.

2. 18 U.S.C. § 2510 *et seq*. Section 2511 prohibits the intentional interception of any wire, oral, or electronic communication and provides for imprisonment for up to five years and the imposition of a fine, or both. The definition of *electronic communication* contained in section 2510 includes "any transfer of signs, signals, writing, images, sounds, data, or intelligence of any nature transmitted in whole or in part by a wire, radio, electromagnetic, photoelectronic, or photooptical system that affects interstate or foreign commerce."

3. See a detailed discussion of security procedures in Chapter 3.

4. *See Shell Pipeline Corp. v. Coastal States Trading, Inc.,* 788 S.W.2d 837 (Tex. Ct. App. 1990). In this case, Shell operated a computerized oil pipeline, through which various oil suppliers and refiners traded oil. Employees of Shell made an error in the transmission of a quantity of oil, resulting in a loss to Coastal. The court imposed liability on Shell for negligence in setting up and maintaining that system. It was an informal industry practice for pipeline operators to keep track of buyers and sellers of oil in the pipeline and sometimes to warn parties of inconsistencies in their transactions. In this case, there was confusion about who was to receive one large unit of oil through the pipeline, and Shell's employee failed to program its computer to warn of the confusion. According to the court,

    > [Shell was negligent] in failing to warn members of the public . . . that the system Shell designed for implementing online transfers was susceptible to error and thereby lulling the public into the erroneous belief that those participating in the online transfers need only follow its own procedures [and was also negligent] in designing a system that depended upon such an inherently unreliable process. 788 S.W.2d at 845.

5. *Evra Corporation v. Swiss Bank Corporation,* 673 F.2d 951 (7th Cir, 1982), *cert. denied,* 459 U.S. 1017 (1982).

    Section 4A-305 of the Uniform Commercial Code, governing electronic funds transfers, provides that if a receiving bank accepts but fails to properly execute a funds payment order, it may be liable to the originator of the order, and sometimes to the beneficiary, for (1) its expenses in making the order, (2) its incidental expenses, (3) any loss of interest it might suffer, and (4) its attorney's fees if it had to sue the bank. However, Section 4A-305 excludes the bank's liability for consequential damages (unless the bank expressly agreed to be liable for those damages).

    Official Comment 2 to Section 4A-305 maintains that the *Evra* rule should not apply to modern, high-speed funds transfer systems. Banks should not be responsible for consequential damages, the comment argues, because banks must process funds transfers very quickly and at a low price. The imposition of consequential damages would force banks to increase their transmission fees. Banks would then have to vary their fees from one transaction to the next depending on the amount of money being transferred. This would slow the processing of transactions.

6.   *Restatement (Second) of Contracts,* § 351 (1982).

7.   *Stratton Oakmont, Inc. v. Prodigy Services Co.,* No. 31063/94, (N.Y. Sup. Ct. May 25, 1995). *Prodigy* is the first case in which a court held that a commercial online computer service can be treated as more than a passive conduit of information, and, therefore, subject to the same liability standards for defamation as any other "publisher" of news or information.

   The court accepted Prodigy's argument that computer bulletin boards should generally be regarded in the same context as book stores, libraries, and TV network affiliates, and should not be liable for what they make publicly available, because they have no control over the editorial content of the messages. The court concluded that Prodigy was different, however, because it attempted to exert editorial control over the content of messages posted by its users.

   Specifically, the court cited the fact that when Prodigy commenced business in 1990, it enunciated a policy that it was a family-oriented computer network. As such, Prodigy held itself out as an online service that exercised editorial control over the content of messages posted on its computer bulletin boards, thereby expressly differentiating itself from competing online services and expressly likening itself to a newspaper. Prodigy insisted that its policies had changed and evolved since 1990 and that the latest published memorandum on the subject, dated February, 1993, did not reflect the policy of Prodigy in effect in October, 1994, when the allegedly libelous postings were made.

   The court also cited the fact that Prodigy had promulgated "content guidelines" for messages posted on its network, employed a software screening program that automatically prescreens all bulletin board postings for offensive language, and appointed a group of "board leaders" whose duties include enforcement of the content guidelines. The Prodigy system also included an "emergency delete function" that allows a Prodigy board leader to remove offensive notes quickly.

   The judge in *Prodigy* distinguished the earlier case of *Cubby v. CompuServe, Inc.,* 776 F. Supp. 135 (S.D.N.Y. 1991), where the court held that CompuServe was not liable for a defamatory message posted by one of its subscribers. CompuServe did not exercise editorial control over the messages posted on its service, and the court held that CompuServe was more like a bookstore or newsstand than a publisher, and therefore it could not be held liable for defamatory messages posted on its service. On October 24, 1995, in exchange for an apology of sorts by Prodigy, Stratton Oakmont agreed to drop the libel suit against Prodigy.

8.   *Derivative works* are defined by the Copyright Act (17 U.S.C. § 101) as "work based upon one or more preexisting works, such as a translation, musical arrangement, dramatization, fictionalization, motion picture version, sound recording, art reproduction, abridgment, condensation, or any other form in which a work may be recast, transformed, or adapted. A work consisting of editorial revisions, annotations, elaborations, or other modifications, which, as a whole, represent an original work of authorship, is a "derivative work."

9.   *See Playboy Enterprises, Inc. v. Frena,* 839 F. Supp. 1552 (M.D. Fla. 1993); *Sega Enterprises, Inc. v. Maphia,* 30 USPQ 2d 1921 (N.D. Cal. 1994); and *Frank Music Corporation v. CompuServe, Inc.,* 93 Civ. 8153 (S.D.N.Y., filed Dec. 1993) settled Nov. 7, 1995 without admission of liability.

10. See discussion at note 7.

11. America Online Services Agreement, § 2.7.

12. See sections 2-314 and 2-315 of the Uniform Commercial Code.

13. See sections 2-314 and 2-315 of the Uniform Commercial Code.

28
Unfair Competition and Deceptive Trade Practices

Elizabeth S. Perdue

28.1 Introduction

The terms *deceptive trade practices* and *unfair competition* refers to extremely broad concepts, covering a wide range of improper business activities, including trademark infringement, false advertising, trade libel, false endorsements, and trade dress infringement. The law of unfair competition is the umbrella for all causes of action arising out of business conduct that is contrary to honest practice in industrial or commercial matters.[1]

Unfair and deceptive practices are likely to be as common in the online world as they are elsewhere. Indeed, because information can be easily manipulated, combined, and transmitted online, the potential for deception may even be greater. In addition, when individuals and small businesses unfamiliar with the law have greater access to public means of communication, violations will occur.

A major source of unfair competition law is section 43(a) of the federal Lanham Act, which generally prohibits false or misleading descriptions of fact and designations of origin.[2] Other federal and state laws that affect this area include state uniform deceptive trade practices acts and consumer fraud acts, anti-dilution laws, state common law, the Federal Trade Commission Act and related regulations, and a variety of industry-specific laws relating to trademarks and labeling.[3]

Because of its breadth, a complete treatment of unfair competition is beyond the scope of this work.[4] This chapter will outline some of the more traditional types of unfair business practices that may impact activities online.

28.2 Trademark and Trade Name Infringement

Trademark and trade name infringement are forms of unfair competition, which can occur in many online activities.[5] For example, online bulletin board operators have faced trademark infringement claims for using others' trademarks to promote computer games and photographs.[6] Similarly, setting up a Web site containing someone else's trademark or trade name would be a violation of unfair competition laws, if the public is likely to be confused. Trademark infringement is discussed in detail in Section 13.4, and many of the same basic principles apply to infringement of trade names.

28.3 False Advertising and Trade Libel

False advertising means making false or misleading representations about one's own product or service. *Trade libel* or *product disparagement* is similar to false advertising, except that it involves misrepresentations about *someone else's* products, services, or commercial activities.[7]

False advertising and trade libel can take very subtle forms, as businesses attempt to influence the public by indirect representations and attacks on competitors. For example, say an online advertisement depicted a polar bear throwing a can of Coca-Cola into a trash can labeled "Keep the Arctic Pure" and picking up another drink. Coca-Cola would be able to enjoin this advertisement, based on the fact that it disparages the "purity and quality" of Coke.[8]

Whenever goods and services are promoted, whether through print, television, or online, false advertising and trade libel will follow. These issues are discussed in Chapter 22.

28.4 Unfair Practices in Connection with Creative Works

Unfair competition laws have been used to combat a variety of deceptive activities in connection with literary and other creative works. Online technology offers great opportunities for manipulating and disseminating text, music, videos, and artworks. Thus, this area of the law is likely to become increasingly important in online situations.

The following sections illustrate typical kinds of prohibited conduct.

28.4.1 False or Misleading Copyright Notices

What happens if a copyright infringer puts his or her own copyright notice on an infringing work? Not only is it a copyright violation, but it is also a violation of unfair competition laws. That is because the notice falsely implies that the infringer owns the copyright.[9] It can even be a violation to put a copyright notice on an unoriginal work in the public domain, since the public is deceived into thinking the work is copyrightable.[10]

Other deceptive wording in copyright notices should also be avoided. For example, using a phrase such as "exclusive original" in a copyright notice can be misleading, if the work is not in fact original.[11]

All of these situations can easily occur online. Indeed, because it is relatively easy to change copyright notices on works and transmit them online, particular care should be taken to avoid violations.

28.4.2 Improper Credit or Attribution

Online works, just like those in traditional media, can include false or misleading statements about an author's or artist's involvement in the work. Such actions can result in liability under unfair compensation laws.

For example, using false credits, such as by deleting the correct name and substituting another, can be a violation.[12] Even incomplete credits can be misleading; in one case, a record company was found liable because it listed only a single composer in the credits when in fact there was more than one.[13]

Overattribution can be another form of unfair competition. When an artist's level of participation in a work is exaggerated by the promoter, it can mislead the public. For example, the makers of the movie *The Lawnmower Man* referred in the movie credits to the author of the book on which the movie was loosely based. The court found this to be an improper attempt to deceive the public into thinking that Stephen King had been involved in making the movie.[14]

United States law is not generally interpreted to require that a creative artist be given credit—merely that when credit is given, it must be accurate.[15] However, in other countries, creative artists have certain "moral rights" that entitle them to receive proper credit for their works.[16]

28.4.3 Misrepresentations About the Currency of a Work

What if an older work is published using a current picture of the artist? This is often done by music publishers in an attempt to increase sales of older recordings. However, this type of activity has been held to violate the Lanham Act, since it misrepresents the currency of the work.[17] Performing artists sue in such cases because their style of performance may have changed over time, and they do not wish the public to associate their current reputation with an older style.

Because music and pictures can easily be combined and transmitted online, these issues can be expected to arise in the online context.

28.4.4 Unauthorized Modifications or Editing

Computer technology can easily be used to modify or edit creative works in a way that makes it almost impossible to detect the changes. However, merely because manipulation is technically possible does not mean it is legal.

If a modified work is attributed to the original artist, the public can be deceived into thinking the artist authorized it.[18] For example, when ABC severely edited a Monty Python film to avoid offending the U.S. public, the comedy group sued, claiming the edited version was a mutilation that impaired the integrity of the original. The court found the public could be deceived into thinking the edited version was the product of Monty Python, when it was in fact a "mere caricature of their talents."[19]

In addition to editing, computer technology provides great opportunities for combining different types of works—graphics, photographs, text, and sounds. However, care should be taken in such activities. Using an author's name on a work that has been overdubbed or unacceptably combined with other elements has been held to violate the Lanham Act.[20] However, where the credit indicates that the author's original has been altered, there may not be deception.[21] Minor changes are less likely to trigger liability,[22] although there could still be a separate copyright violation.

As noted above, foreign countries recognize "moral rights" in creative works. In addition to requiring proper credit, these rights entitle artists and authors to prevent their works from being distorted or mutilated.[23]

28.5 Use of Titles and Characters

28.5.1 Titles

It is a well-recognized principle of copyright law that titles of single works—such as book, song, or record titles—cannot be copyrighted.[24] Nor can these titles be registered as trademarks in most cases.[25]

However, if a title has acquired "secondary meaning"—that is, if it has become associated in the public's mind with a single source—it may be protected under the unfair competition laws.[26] Violations may occur when titles are used for the same type of work (using a book title for another book), or for different types of works (using a book title for a play, or a movie title as a trademark for a children's toy).[27]

Those who operate in the online world are also subject to these prohibitions. For example, using a well-known movie title as the title of a Web site or an online computer game could expose one to liability if the public is likely to be confused as to source, sponsorship, or approval.

28.5.2 Characters

Characters may be protected under the Lanham Act.[28] Examples include Conan the Barbarian, the Peanuts cartoon characters, and the Dr. Seuss figures.[29]

The unfair competition law prohibits only those uses that are likely to confuse or deceive the public.[30] However, the public has become accustomed to seeing comicbook and movie characters promoting a wide variety of goods and services, including clothing, toys, food, and even insurance. Because of this growth of character-related merchandising, almost any unauthorized use of a famous character is likely to be an infringement. Thus, although it may be tempting to use a famous (or not-so-famous) character in an online publication or to promote an online service, such activity is likely to produce a successful objection from the owner.

28.6 False Endorsements

Endorsements by celebrities or organizations can be very valuable marketing tools. However, one cannot falsely state or imply that a person or entity has endorsed a product or service. This would be a violation of the unfair competition laws, as a false representation of source, sponsorship, or approval.

Some try to avoid liability by using subtle suggestions rather than explicit statements. However, false implied endorsements are just as actionable as false direct ones. The ultimate test is whether consumers are likely to be confused into thinking the product was endorsed or approved when it was not.[31]

One common technique is to use a celebrity's picture or name on a product or advertisement without expressly stating that the celebrity endorses it. The courts usually find these uses to be an improper attempt to mislead the public into believing the celebrity endorses the product.[32] Thus, merely using a picture of Johnny Carson on a Web page for a shopping service can be an implied endorsement—it may be no different than directly saying "Johnny Carson shops here, so should you."[33] Although conspicuous disclaimers can sometimes help avoid liability, they do not always work.[34]

Another technique is to use celebrity lookalikes and soundalikes. However, unless there is a sufficient disclaimer, these can constitute implied endorsements. For example, when a video store used a Woody Allen lookalike and soundalike to promote its services, Mr. Allen succeeded in enjoining the activity.[35] In another case, a well-known entertainer successfully sued when his unique style of vocal delivery was imitated in a television commercial.[36]

The law of unfair competition has even been extended to cases involving robotic imitations of celebrities. In one case, the court held that a robot dressed in a blond wig, standing next to a game wheel, would be sufficiently identified with Vanna White that the public would believe she had authorized the commercial.[37] In another case, the actors who played "Cliff" and "Norm" in the *Cheers* television show brought a false endorsement claim against a bar that used animatronic figures of their characters.[38]

Online technology presents numerous opportunities for false endorsement, both intentional and inadvertent. Thus, for example, it may be easy to combine a celebrity's picture or voice with other material and transmit it online. A picture or voice can even be digitally created or manipulated. These activities will continue to be subject to unfair competition analysis; as discussed above, if the usage falsely implies an endorsement, liability can result.

28.7 Confusion Arising from Web Page Links

One online practice that will raise unfair competition issues is the hypertext link. Hypertext is one of the outstanding features of the World Wide Web; it is what makes it possible to link one Web site to another, so that the reader can pass seamlessly from site to site. The reader clicks on a highlighted word at one site, and the hypertext link takes the reader to another site. But the linked site may not necessarily be affiliated with the original site.

The practice of linking Web sites is universal and widely encouraged. However, this same facility can be misused and can result in unfair competition claims such as false advertising, trade libel, and false suggestions of sponsorship or approval.[39] Examples might include:

- A law firm Web site stating: "We offer comprehensive legal services to our valued clients." When one clicks on the word *clients*, the hypertext link takes the reader to the Web site for General Motors. Unless General Motors is indeed the law firm's client, this would be a violation of the Lanham Act, as a false or misleading representation.

- An online shopping mall[40] containing links to various retailers' Web sites. It includes a link to a retailer who did not consent to being in the mall. The retailer could claim that the link falsely implies that it sponsors, approves, or is otherwise associated with the mall. Some Web pages address this issue by including a disclaimer that states there is no endorsement of any other Web pages which may be linked from the site.
- A Web site for a product including a (truthful) statement that "studies prove our product works 10 times faster than the Acme brand." When the reader clicks on the word *Acme*, the hypertext link takes the reader to an obscene site, or to one with degrading or derogatory pictures. While the statement by itself would have been undeceptive and truthful, the link could create a trade libel.

Most hypertext links require the reader to click on the highlighted word to see the next site. However, some commands will cause one Web site to pull up material from another's Web site, with no action required on the part of the reader.[41] For example, a Web site owner might use a command to pull up and display someone else's syndicated cartoons on his page automatically. In that case, the cartoon owner should be able to claim a violation of the unfair competition laws.[42]

28.8 Reverse Passing Off

Trademark infringement, false credits, and false endorsements are all different forms of the historical concept of *passing off*. *Passing off* occurs when one person passes off his or her goods or services as those of another.

Reverse passing off occurs when someone takes another person's goods and rebrands them as his or her own, or sells them unbranded.[43] Thus, for example, when Illinois Bell attempted to advertise phone books under its name, without giving proper attribution to the co-publisher, it committed reverse passing off.[44] Similarly, a bulletin board operator was guilty of reverse passing off when it made *Playboy* photographs available online, deleting *Playboy*'s name and substituting his own information.[45] In another case, the court found that a software marketer could be liable when it sold software under its own trademark, rather than under the manufacturer's mark.[46]

Digital technology makes reverse passing off easy. One can copy text and distribute it online, under a different name or without attribution. However, such activities can be illegal under the unfair competition laws.

28.9 Trade Dress Infringement

Trade dress is a broad term covering the design of a product or the packaging or presentation of a product or service. When one person copies another's trade dress and it causes a likelihood of confusion, this can be unfair competition. Examples of trade dress that have been protected include:

- The decor, menu, and style of a Mexican restaurant.[47]

- The package and bottle design of Chanel perfume.[48]
- The distinctive design of the Dallas Cowboys cheerleaders' costumes.[49]
- *People Magazine*'s cover format.[50]
- Rubik's Cube puzzle design.[51]
- The appearance of a video game console.[52]
- The distinctive design of the automobile used on the *Dukes of Hazzard* TV show.[53]

Trade dress issues will certainly arise online. For example, an online game program might place a character in a setting that imitates someone else's trade dress, such as the setting of a famous restaurant or TV show. A computer game's distinctive "game universe" might even be found to constitute protectable trade dress.[54] A Web site that imitates another's distinctive magazine or Web site design would also be subject to attack.[55]

28.10 Anti-Dilution Laws

Another concept under the broad umbrella of unfair competition is known as *dilution*. Trademark infringement law is based on the likelihood of confusion between goods or services; it does not protect against nonconfusing uses. Many states therefore have anti-dilution laws prohibiting the use of a trademark (or trade dress) when it would "dilute the distinctive quality" of another's mark, even if no confusion was likely. As of January 16, 1996, a new federal trademark dilution statute also came into effect.[56]

Courts have described the rationale behind anti-dilution laws in a number of ways, including: protection against "a gradual whittling away" of the distinctiveness or unique character of a mark; protection of the "selling power" of a distinctive mark; or protection against "blurring" of a distinct mental image.[57]

A typical dilution case involves a nonconfusing use of a famous mark on unrelated goods or services that is found to dilute the distinctive quality of the famous mark. For example, Polaroid succeeded in stopping use of the mark *Polaraid* on heating systems, and *Hyatt Hotels* succeeded in a suit against *Hyatt Legal Services*, despite the lack of competition or confusion.[58] Other famous marks that have prevailed in anti-dilution cases include *Trivial Pursuit, Tiffany,* and the shape of a Coke bottle.[59]

Those who are tempted to use a famous trademark in an online context (or otherwise) should be aware of the potential for violating anti-dilution laws. Unlike trademark infringement, a dilution action can be brought even if there is no competition or confusion. Thus, for example, use of a famous mark as an Internet domain name might be challenged under the anti-dilution laws, even if no likelihood of confusion is found under trademark laws.[60] Similarly, one would not be wise to set up a Web site called "Tiffany's," even if it is unrelated to jewelry.

28.11 Other Practices

The above sections describe only some typical examples of activities that can lead to unfair competition liability—the breadth of potential unfair trade practices is limited only by the creativity of wrongdoers.

Courts' views of what constitutes appropriate business conduct will also shift over time. As Judge Learned Hand stated (in 1925), "There is no part of the law which is more plastic than unfair competition, and what was not recognized an actionable wrong twenty-five years ago may have become one today."[61] Thus, while new technologies can inspire new types of unfair practices, the laws of unfair competition will likely continue to be flexible enough to provide a remedy.

Endnotes

1. The term *unfair competition* is something of a misnomer. One does not have to be a competitor to be subject to the unfair competition laws.

2. 15 U.S.C. § 1125(a). Briefly summarized, this section prohibits using a word, term, symbol, or device or any false or misleading description or representation, on or in connection with goods or services, that (1) is likely to cause confusion or mistake, or to deceive others as to source, sponsorship, or approval, or (2) in commercial advertising, misrepresents the nature, qualities, or geographic origin of goods, services, or commercial activities.

3. See, for example, the list of statutes contained in International Trademark Association, *U.S. Trademark Law and Practice* (November 1989).

4. For a good treatment of unfair competition in general, see J. Thomas McCarthy, *McCarthy on Trademarks and Unfair Competition* (3d ed. 1992).

5. A *trademark* or *servicemark* is a name or device used to distinguish the source of goods or services. A *trade name* is used to identify a business. In many cases, the same word will be both a trademark and a trade name—for example, the word *Microsoft* is used as a trademark to identify a certain brand of software, as well as a trade name for the company that makes it.

6. See *Sega Enterprises, Ltd. v. Maphia*, 30 U.S.P.Q.2d 1921, 1928 (N.D. Cal. 1994) (unauthorized *Sega* games made available online; *Sega* name shown on programs and file names); *Playboy Enterprises, Inc. v. Frena*, 839 F. Supp. 1552 (M.D. Fla. 1993) (unauthorized *Playboy* photographs made available online; *Playboy* names used for file names).

7. *Product disparagement* is a statement about a competitor's goods that is untrue or misleading and that is made to influence or tends to influence others not to buy the competitor's goods. *Aerosonic Corp. v. Trodyne Corp.*, 402 F.2d 223, 231 (5th Cir. 1968).

8. *Polar Corp. v. Coca-Cola Co.*, 871 F. Supp. 1520 (D. Mass. 1994). (Same facts as cited in main text, for television commercial).

9. *FEL Publications, Ltd. v. Catholic Bishop of Chicago*, 214 U.S.P.Q. 409 (7th Cir. 1982). At least one court has rejected this view, on the grounds that all copyright claims should not be converted to Lanham Act claims. *Kregos v. The Associated Press*, 937 F.2d 700 (2d Cir. 1991).

10. *EFS Marketing, Inc. v. Russ Berrie & Co.*, 836 F. Supp. 128 (S.D.N.Y. 1993) (both parties were enjoined from using copyright notices on a standard public domain "troll" doll, because neither had made sufficient modifications to entitle it to copyright).

11. *Eden Toys, Inc. v. Florelee Undergarment Co.*, 697 F.2d 27 (2d Cir. 1982) ("[t]his deception can mislead consumers into believing that the [product] they purchased is a unique novelty instead of a common copy"); *Greeff Fabrics, Inc. v. Spectrum Fabrics Corp.*, 217 U.S.P.Q. 498 (S.D.N.Y. 1981).

12. *Smith v. Montoro*, 648 F.2d 602 (9th Cir. 1981)(substituting another actor's name on credits).

13.   *Lamoth v. Atlantic Recording Corp.*, 847 F.2d 1403 (9th Cir. 1988).

14.   *King v. Innovation Books, Inc.*, 976 F.2d 824 (2d Cir. 1992) (Although the court permitted the movie to be promoted with truthful statements that it was "based on" the King novel, the parties subsequently settled the case with an agreement that King's name not be used at all.) *Also see Nice Man Merchandising, Inc. v. Logocroft Ltd.*, 23 U.S.P.Q.2d 1290 (E.D. Penn. 1992); *Wyatt Earp Enterprises, Inc. v. Sackman, Inc.*, 157 F. Supp. 621 (E.D.N.Y. 1958).

15.   *Morita v. Omni Publications Int'l Ltd.*, 741 F. Supp. 1107 (S.D.N.Y. 1990), vacated on other grounds, 760 F. Supp 45 (S.D.N.Y. 1991). There is some disagreement on this issue, however. See J. Thomas McCarthy, *McCarthy on Trademarks and Unfair Competition*, § 10.08[5][b] (3d ed. 1992). In addition, authors of certain types of fine artworks must be given proper credit under the Visual Artists' Rights Act, which covers paintings, sculptures, and limited editions of graphic works.

16.   *See generally* 2 *Nimmer on Copyright* § 8.21 (1993). In addition, at least 11 states have enacted laws protecting moral rights for visual artists. *Id.* at 8-282.5 and n.51.

17.   *CBS, Inc., v. Springboard International Records*, 429 F. Supp. 563 (S.D.N.Y. 1976).

18.   *Gilliam v. American Broadcasting Cos.*, 538 F.2d 14, 24–25 (2d Cir. 1976) (modification of Monty Python film); *Granz v. Harris*, 198 F.2d 585, 588 (2d Cir. 1952) (deletion of eight minutes of music from phonograph recording of plaintiff's performance). *See also Bonner v. Westbound Records, Inc.*, 49 Ill. App.3d 543, 364 N.E.2d 570 (1st Dist. 1977) (claim by recording artists against record company for release of album attributed to the recording artists that contained songs subsequently interpreted, edited, and substantially altered by persons other than the recording artists without their consent). The artist may have a section 43(a) claim, whether or not he or she owns the copyright in the work. *Schatt v. Curtis Management Group Inc.*, 764 F. Supp. 902 (S.D.N.Y. 1991).

19.   *Gilliam v. American Broadcasting Cos.*, 538 F.2d 14 (2d Cir. 1976). One of the interesting aspects of this case was the fact that ABC had a contract with the BBC authorizing it to make modifications. However, the BBC did not have the right to permit changes without the consent of Monty Python. Had ABC reviewed the underlying contracts, it could have avoided an expensive lawsuit.

20.   *National Bank of Commerce v. Shaklee Corp.*, 207 U.S.P.Q. 1005 (W.D. Tex. 1980) (inclusion of advertising material in *Hints from Heloise* book); *Benson v. Paul Winley Record Sales Corp.*, 452 F. Supp. 516 (S.D.N.Y. 1978) (overdubbing sexually explicit sounds).

21.   *See e.g., Geisel v. Poynter Products, Inc.*, 295 F. Supp. 331, 354 (S.D.N.Y. 1968).

22.   See *Considine v. Penguin U.S.A.*, 24 U.S.P.Q.2d 1947 (S.D.N.Y. 1992) (book excerpt in magazine; changes not extensive enough to trigger liability).

23.   *See generally* 2 *Nimmer on Copyright* § 8.21 (1993).

24.   See Section 9.4.2.1.

25.   For example, although a single book title cannot be registered, a name for a series of books can be. *See Trademark Manual of Examining Procedures* § 1202.

26.   J. Thomas McCarthy, *McCarthy on Trademarks and Unfair Competition* § 10.02. See discussion of "secondary meaning" in Section 13.3.2.

27.   *See Brandon v. Regents of the University of California*, 441 F. Supp. 1086, 1091 (D. Mass. 1977) (film title); *Hospital for Sick Children v. Melody Fare Dinner Theatre*, 516 F. Supp. 67, 73 (E.D. Va. 1980) (use of name Peter Pan); *Orion Pictures Co. v. Dell Publishing Co.*, 471 F. Supp. 392, 396 (S.D.N.Y. 1979) (film title); *National Lampoon, Inc. v. American Broadcasting Cos.*, 376 F. Supp. 733, 746 (S.D. N.Y. 1974), *aff'd*, 497 F.2d 1343 (2d Cir. 1974) (use of word "Lampoon" in the title of a television pilot); *Dawn Associates v. Links*, 203 U.S.P.Q. 831, 834 (N.D. Ill. 1978) (film title).

28. As discussed in Section 9.3, characters are also protected by copyright.

29. *Conan Properties, Inc. v. Conans Pizza, Inc.*, 752 F.2d 145 (5th Cir. 1985) (pizza parlor prohibited from using Conan the Barbarian character); *United Feature Syndicate v. Sunrise Mold Co.*, 569 F. Supp. 1475 (S.C. Fla. 1983) (Peanuts characters); *Geisel v. Poynter Products, Inc.*, 295 F. Supp. 331 (S.D.N.Y. 1968)(Dr. Seuss characters).

30. *See Universal City Studios Inc. v. Nintendo Co.*, 746 F.2d 112 (2d Cir. 1984) (owners of *King Kong* movie could not stop use of Donkey Kong character; public not likely to be confused).

31. *Storball v. Twentieth Century Fox Film Corp.*, 30 U.S.P.Q.2d 1394, 1395 (C.D. Cal. 1993); *New West Corp. v. NYM Co. of California, Inc.*, 595 F.2d 1194, 1201 (9th Cir. 1979).

32. *See Allen v. National Video, Inc.*, 610 F. Supp 612, 629 (S.D.N.Y. 1985) ("[w]hen a public figure of Woody Allen's stature appears in an advertisement, his mere presence is inescapably to be interpreted as an endorsement.").

33. Whether the use of a name or picture is an implied endorsement will depend on the facts and the context. Thus, for example, a book publisher might be able to display pictures of actual book covers at its Web site, without necessarily implying any endorsement by those whose pictures are shown on the covers.

34. *See M'Otto Enterprises, Inc. v. Redsand, Inc.*, 831 F. Supp. 1491 (W.D. Wash. 1993) (disclaimer ineffective).

35. *Allen v. National Video, Inc.*, 610 F. Supp. 612 (S.D.N.Y. 1985). The court required a very clear disclaimer of any endorsement by Mr. Allen.

36. *Lahr v. Adell Chemical Co.*, 300 F.2d 256, 259 (1st Cir. 1962) (Burt Lahr's voice).

37. *White v. Samsung Electronics America, Inc.*, 23 U.S.P.Q.2d 1583, *rehearing denied*, 26 U.S.P.Q.2d 1362 (9th Cir. 1993).

38. *Wendt v. Host International*, Nos. 93-56318 and 93-565510 (9th Cir. 1995) (in an unpublished opinion, the court held that issues of material fact precluded summary judgment for the defendant). In this case, the makers of the *Cheers* television show gave permission to the bar to use the show's name and format; however, the individual actors were still entitled to assert false endorsement claims when their personal images were imitated.

39. Because hypertext links do not involve technical copying, Web site operators may not realize the potential for violating the law. However, physical copying is not a prerequisite to an unfair competition claim.

40. An *online shopping mall* is a Web site that has links to various retail sellers' sites. Typically, the retail providers pay a fee to the mall provider for the privilege of being included.

41. The command is "img src," which causes the reader's Web browsing software to go to the referenced site and pull up the image onto the original Web site.

42. A Web site publisher using this approach might believe that it is avoiding copyright infringement, since using a hypertext link to pull in an image is not the same as copying it. However, this practice could also violate the copyright owner's exclusive rights to public display and to make derivative works. It may also constitute contributory copyright infringement: the Web site's imbedded command automatically causes the user's computer to copy the image.

43. *Smith v. Montoro*, 648 F.2d 602 (9th Cir. 1981) (substitution of actor's name on credits); *Marling v. Ellison*, 218 U.S.P.Q. 702 (S.D. Fla. 1982) (improper credit on infringing cookbook); *R. H. Donnelley Corp. v. Illinois Bell Telephone*, 595 F. Supp. 1202 (N.D. Ill. 1984) (improper credit for directory); *Dodd v. Fort Smith Special School Dist. 100*, 666 F. Supp. 1278 (W.D. Ark. 1987) (substituting credit). *But see Morita v. Omni Publications Intern'l, Inc.*, 741 F. Supp. 1107 (S.D.N.Y. 1990) (no credit required for sculptor).

44. *R. H. Donnelley Corp. v. Illinois Bell Telephone*, 595 F. Supp. 1202 (N.D. Ill. 1984).

45. *Playboy Enterprises, Inc. v. Frena*, 839 F. Supp. 1552 (M.D. Fla. 1993).

46. *Classic Font Corp v. Fontbank, Inc.*, No. 97 C 607, 1994 U.S. Dist. LEXIS 4647, CCH Computer Law Cases ¶47,040 (N.D. Ill. 1994) (plaintiff was likely to prevail on the merits, supporting a preliminary injunction).

47. *Taco Cabanna Int'l Inc. v. Two Pesos, Inc.*, 932 F.2d 1113, 19 U.S.P.Q.2d 1253 (5th Cir. 1991), *aff'd*, 112 S. Ct. 2753, 23 U.S.P.Q.2d 1081 (1992) (the infringer, who had copied the design of a competing restaurant, was ordered to pay damages of $1.9 million plus $900,000 in attorneys' fees).

48. *Chanel, Inc. v. Suttner*, 109 U.S.P.Q. 493 (S.D.N.Y. 1956).

49. *Dallas Cowboys Cheerleaders, Inc. v. Pussycat Cinema, Ltd.*, 604 F.2d 200 (2d Cir. 1979).

50. *Time, Inc. Magazine Co. v. Globe Communications Corp.*, 712 F. Supp. 1103 (S.D.N.Y. 1989).

51. *Ideal Toy Corp. v. Plawner Toy Mfg. Corp.*, 685 F.2d 78 (3d Cir. 1982).

52. *M. Kramer Mfg. Co. v. Andrews*, 783 F.2d 421 (4th Cir. 1986).

53. *Warner Bros., Inc. v. Gay Toys, Inc.*, 658 F.2d 76 (2d Cir. 1981), on remand 553 F. Supp. 1018 (S.D.N.Y. 1983); *Processed Plastic Co. v. Warner Communications, Inc.*, 675 F.2d 852 (7th Cir. 1982).

54. *Cf. FASA Corp. v. Playmates Toys, Inc.*, 869 F. Supp. 1334 (D.C. Ill. 1994)(issues of fact exist with respect to trade dress infringement claims for copying of plaintiff's computer game characters).

55. For example, a magazine Web page that copied the format of *People Magazine*'s cover would likely be a trade dress violation. *See Time, Inc. Magazine Co. v. Globe Communication Corp.*, 712 F. Supp. 1103 (S.D.N.Y. 1989).

56. The Federal Trademark Dilution Act of 1995 added a new Section 43(c) to the Lanham Act, to prohibit the use of trademarks and trade names that dilute the distinctive quality of a famous mark. The federal act may provide less protection against dilution than state laws, since it expressly applies only to "famous" marks, although many state law cases have implied such a standard.

57. *See* J. Thomas McCarthy, *McCarthy on Trademarks and Unfair Competition* § 24:13 (3d ed. 1992).

58. *Hyatt Corp. v. Hyatt Legal Services, Inc.*, 736 F.2d 1153 (7th Cir. 1984), on remand 610 F. Supp. 381 (N.D. Ill. 1985) (case settled); *Polaroid Corp. v. Polaraid, Inc.*, 319 F.2d 830 (7th Cir. 1963).

59. *Coca-Cola Co. v. Alma-Leo, USA, Inc.*, 719 F. Supp. 725 (N.D. Ill. 1989) (bottle shape diluted by bottle for bubble gum powder); *Horn Abbot Ltd. v. Sarsaparilla Ltd*, 601 F. Supp. 360 (N.D. Ill. 1984) (*Trivial Pursuit* diluted by use of mark on book); *Tiffany & Co. v. Boston Club, Inc.*, 231 F. Supp. 836 (D.C. Mass 1964) (*Tiffany* diluted by use on restaurants).

60. See Chapter 14 for a discussion of trademark issues as they relate to Internet domain names.

61. *Ely Norris Safe Co. v. Master Safe Co.*, 7 F.2d 603 (2d Cir 1925). *Also see Electronic Data & Sales v. Electronic Data Systems Corp.*, 954 F.2d 713 (Fed. Cir. 1992).

29
Liability for Conduct of Others

Thomas J. Smedinghoff

Messsages communicated electronically can cause harm in a variety of ways. They can constitute copyright infringment; they can be defamatory; they can be obscene, harassing, or otherwise illegal; or they can be part of a fraudulent scheme. In most cases, the originator of such messages will clearly be liable for the harm caused. But in many cases the originator will be anonynous, cannot be found, or may be judgment-proof. Accordingly, there has been a tendency to try to hold third parties liable for the harm done. Thus, online service providers, systems operators, Internet access providers, employers, and other third-party intermediaries are brought into lawsuits because of harmful messages posted on their systems or via their services.

For example, when defamatory material was published via Compuserve, the plaintiff sued Compuserve instead of the original author of the defamatory message.[1] Similarly, when a defamatory message appeared on Prodigy, and the originator of the message could not be identified, the injured party sued Prodigy.[2]

The result has been similar in cases involving copyright infringement. When copyrighted MIDI files began appearing on Compuserve, the owners of the copyrights in the musical works sued Compuserve, not the many individuals who uploaded the files.[3] When an affiliate of the Church of Scientology brought suit against one of its former members for allegedly distributing copyrighted materials via the Internet, it sued not only the former member, but also the computer bulletin board system used by the member to post the material on the Internet, and the Internet access provider used by the bulletin board system to transmit data to the Internet.[4]

Trademark and unfair competition claims have been similarly handled. Thus, when Playboy discovered that a number of its copyrighted photographs bearing its trademarks had been uploaded to a computer bulletin board and made available for subscribers to download, it sued the sysop of the bulletin board, rather than those who had uploaded the photographs.[5] When Sega Enterprises learned that its computer games were being uploaded to a computer bulletin board for distribution to subscribers, it sued the sysop of the computer bulletin board, rather than those who did the uploading, for copyright and trademark infringement.[6]

To date, most attempts to hold third parties liable for the conduct of others online have centered around copyright infringement or defamation claims. Accordingly, this chapter focuses on these types of claims. In reviewing the following material, however, keep in mind that two very different standards of liability are applied. Thus, whether the action involves copyright infringement or a claim of defamation can have a significant impact on the potential liability of the third party being sued.

29.1 Direct Copyright Infringement

Copyright law imposes different standards of liability for *direct, contributory,* and *vicarious* forms of infringement. As discussed below, because of the nature of copyright laws, certain third parties—such as employers or operators of online services—can be exposed to liability under all three theories, even if the harmful activity originated with an employee or a subscriber.

Direct infringers are held to a standard of strict liability—they are liable for copyright infringement without regard to their intent or knowledge. Contributory or vicarious infringers are not held to such a strict standard.

Can the operators of computer bulletin boards, online services, and the like can be liable for direct copyright infringement as a result of the activities of their subscribers? According to one court, the answer is yes. That is, if one subscriber uploads an infringing work, and it is made available to other subscribers of the system for downloading, the system operator can be liable for direct infringement because the operator is "distributing" infringing copyrighted materials. It can be liable even though it had no role in uploading the materials in the first place, and even though it had no knowledge that the materials were infringing.

This conclusion was reached by the court in a case involving infringing Playboy photographs that were uploaded to a computer bulletin board.[7] The court held the sysop of the BBS liable for direct infringement that resulted when his subscribers downloaded the infringing photographs. The court found that the sysop had directly infringed Playboy's exclusive rights to distribute and display its photographs. As the court noted:

> There is irrefutable evidence of direct copyright infringement in this case. It does not matter that defendant Frena [the sysop of the BBS] may have been unaware of the copyright infringement. Intent to infringe is not needed to find copyright infringement. Intent or knowledge is not an element of infringement, and thus even an innocent infringer is liable for infringement.[8]

In late 1995, however, the second court to consider this issue expressly disagreed with the position taken by the court in the *Playboy* case. The second case involved a claim for copyright infringement brought by the Religious Technology Center, an affiliate of the Church of Scientology, based on the activities of Dennis Erlich, a former Church member who was allegedly posting copyrighted Church documents to a UseNet news group on the Internet.[9] The claim was brought both against Erlich, the bulletin board system to which he subscribed in order to post the documents on the Internet, and Netcom Communications Services, the Internet access provider used by the bulletin board system to transmit the documents to the Internet.

It was undisputed that when Erlich posted the allegedly infringing documents to the Internet UseNet news group they were transmitted to the BBS computer, and then subsequently transmitted onto Netcom's computer and onto other computers on the UseNet. They were maintained for eleven days on Netcom's system and made available to Netcom's customers and UseNet neighbors who could download the messages to their own computers. There was no question that the Netcom system made temporary copies of the Church's copyrighted works, but the court noted that these copies were automatically made on the Netcom computers, using software provided by Netcom, as part of a process initiated by a third party. Netcom did not take any affirmative action that directly resulted in copying the Church's works other than by installing and maintaining a system whereby software automatically forwards messages received from subscribers onto the UseNet and temporarily stores copies on its system.

Unlike the court in the *Playboy* case, this court felt that the mere fact that Netcom's system incidentally makes temporary copies of plaintiff's copyrighted works does not mean Netcom has caused the copying. Rather, the court compared Netcom's acts of designing and implementing a system that automatically and uniformly creates temporary copies of all data sent through it to the acts of the owner of a copying machine who lets the public make copies with it. To hold Netcom liable for copyright infringement, the court felt, would, carried to its natural extreme, lead to unreasonable liability. It would result in liability for every single UseNet server in the worldwide link of computers transmitting Erlich's messages to every other computer.

Thus, the court held that the storage on Netcom's system of infringing copies of the plaintiff's work and retransmission of those copies to other servers was not a direct infringement *by Netcom* of the copyright owner's exclusive right to reproduce the work where such copies were uploaded by an infringing user.

The court also expressly disagreed with the *Playboy* opinion, stating that it was not convinced that the mere possession of a digital copy on a bulletin board that is accessible to some members of the public constitutes direct infringement by the bulletin board operator of the copyright owner's right of public distribution. Only the subscriber to the system should be liable for causing the distribution of the plaintiff's work, as the contributing actions of the bulletin board provider are automatic and indiscriminate. Where the bulletin board system merely stores and passes along the messages sent by its subscribers and others, the bulletin board should not be seen as causing these works to be publicly distributed or displayed. And as the court concluded, "it does not make sense to adopt a rule that could lead to the liability of countless parties whose role in the infringement is nothing more than setting up and operating a system that is necessary for the functioning of the Internet."

29.2 Secondary Liability for Copyright Infringement

Although the Copyright Act does not expressly hold a person liable for infringement committed by another,[10] the Supreme Court has made it very clear that a person may be held liable for copyright infringement even if that person did not actually do the copying or distributing.[11] Two theories are applied: *contributory infringement* and *vicarious liability.*

- **Contributory Infringement.** A person may be held liable for infringement committed by another where the person:
  1. Had knowledge of the infringing activity; and
  2. Induced, caused, or materially contributed to the infringing conduct of another.[12]
- **Vicarious Liability.** A person may also be held liable for infringment committed by another where the person:
  1. Had the right and ability to supervise the infringing activity, and
  2. Had a financial interest in exploitation of the copyrighted materials.[13]

Liability for contributory copyright infringement turns on the defendant's relationship to the direct infringement. If the defendant took some act in furtherance of the direct infringement, courts will hold the defendant liable for contributory copyright infringement. Vicarious liability rests not on the defendant's relationship to the direct infringement, but, rather, on his or her relationship to the direct infringer; a financial interest in and an ability to control the direct infringer's conduct form the basis for liability.

Thus a defendant will be liable for contributory infringement if he or she knew of, and contributed to, the direct infringement, even though the defendant could not control and had no financial interest in the acts of infringement. A defendant will be vicariously liable if he or she could control the infringer and had a financial interest in the infringement (such as with an employee), even though the defendant did not know of it or contribute directly to it.

29.2.1 Contributory Infringement

29.2.1.1 Knowledge. To establish liability for *contributory infringement,* a plaintiff must establish that the defendant had knowledge of the infringing activity of a third party. This knowledge may be either actual or constructive,[14] that is, did the defendant know or have reason to know of the infringement?

This question is more difficult to answer than it might initially appear. In the *Netcom* case discussed in Section 29.1, representatives of the copyright owner had notified Netcom of their claim that Mr. Erlich was sending infringing materials through the Netcom system. The court held that once it was on notice, Netcom's refusal to remove the infringing materials could subject it to liability for contributory infringement.[15]

For an Internet access provider that transmits billions of bytes of messages per day, the concept of "notice" raises some interesting issues. For example, the Church of Scientology claimed that the material was infringing, but Mr. Erlich claimed that he had the right to post that material under the doctrine of fair use. Was Netcom obligated to believe the copyright owner merely because it made the accusation? Was Netcom entitled to rely on the statements made by Mr. Erlich in his defense?

The court was clearly troubled by this issue, noting that:

The court is more persuaded by the argument that it is beyond the ability of a BBS operator to quickly and fairly determine when a use is not infringement where there is at least a colorable claim of fair use. Where a BBS operator cannot reasonably verify a claim of infringement, either because of a possible fair use defense, the lack of copyright notices on the copies, or the copyright holder's failure to provide the necessary documentation to show that there is a likely infringement, the operator's lack of knowledge will be found reasonable and there will be no liability for contributory infringement for allowing the continued distribution of the works on its system.

However, because Netcom did not even look at the postings once they were given notice, but simply refused to remove them, the court held that there was a question of fact on this issue that would have to be resolved at trial.

29.2.1.2 Materially Contributes to the Infringing Conduct. A plaintiff must also show that the defendant induced, caused, or materially contributed to the client's infringing conduct. A secondary infringer may "induce, cause or materially contribute to the infringing conduct of another" through either (1) direct participation that forms part of or furthers the infringement, or (2) contribution of materials or equipment that provide the means to infringe.[16]

Under the "direct participation" approach, the defendant's conduct is a material element in furthering the direct infringement. Examples include an operator of an electronic bulletin board soliciting users to upload (i.e., copy) copyrighted video games to the bulletin board,[17] a radio station broadcasting advertisements and a shipper shipping infringing records for a direct infringer,[18] and a licensor who authorized a licensee to make copies without the right to do so.[19]

In one case, for example, the defendant was the sysop of a computer bulletin board service that was used to exchange copies of Sega's copyrighted computer video games.[20] The defendant actively advertised that Sega programs were available on the service, and sold users equipment specifically designed to facilitate the copying. Accordingly, even though the defendant had not placed copies of Sega's programs onto the system himself, the court found that he had engaged in copyright infringement: "even if defendants do not know exactly when games will be uploaded to or downloaded from the Maphia bulletin board, their role in the copying, including provision of facilities, direction, knowledge and encouragement, amounts to contributory infringement."[21]

In the *Netcom* case discussed above, the court found that Netcom could be substantially participating in infringing conduct simply by allowing infringing messages to remain on its system and be further distributed to other UseNet services worldwide.[22] It reached this conclusion, in large part, because Netcom could have simply canceled the infringing messages, and thereby stopped the infringing copy from being distributed.

Under the "contribution of machinery or goods" approach, regardless of who uploads the content, a BBS sysop or online service could still be held liable for providing the means to infringe. In one case, for example, the court held that the defendant who commercially operated sound recording duplication facilities was liable for contributory infringement. Not only did it operate the facility, it lent copyrighted tapes to customers for purposes of duplication, and also sold them the blank tapes to make the copies. The defendant was not immunized by the fact that the actual duplication process was done by the customers on a self-service basis.[23]

In the case of *Sony v. Universal City Studios*, however, the Supreme Court limited the scope of secondary liability based on contribution of machinery or goods.[24] According to the *Sony* Court, merely providing the means by which others can make later infringements does not make the third party liable, even if the provider knew that such infringement is likely to occur, as long as there is a substantial non-infringing use for the product:

> the sale of copying equipment—in this case, VCRs—like the sale of other articles of commerce, does not constitute contributory infringement if the product is widely used for legitimate, unobjectionable purposes. Indeed, it need merely be capable of substantial non-infringing uses.[25]

The Court then applied the modified test to hold that the manufacturer of Betamax video cassette recorders and tapes could not be held liable for infringement since the equipment was capable of substantial, non-infringing use.

It is unclear when *Sony* applies in an online context. In *Sony*, the defendant had no contact with the direct infringers and did not encourage or induce their copying. It simply manufactured and sold the equipment used to make unauthorized copies. The Court pointedly emphasized that there was no on-going relationship between the direct and contributory infringers.[26] Thus, *Sony*'s modified test of contributory infringement could be limited to these facts.

29.2.2 Vicarious Liability

As noted above, *vicarious liability* is a separate theory on which third parties can be held liable for direct infringement by others. Unlike contributory infringement, knowledge and means are not vital. Rather, the defendant must have the right and ability to supervise the infringing activity, and must also have a financial interest in exploitation of the fruits of the infringement.

29.2.2.1 Right and Ability To Supervise. For vicarious liability, a plaintiff must show that the defendant had the right and ability to supervise the infringing activity. This means the defendant had control over the direct infringer with regard to the infringing activity, or control over the operation of the place where the activity occurs.[27]

This right of control over the infringer must be fairly extensive. The defendant must have the right and ability to stop the direct infringer from engaging in the infringing activity.[28] For example, a department store owner was found liable because it contractually had the right and ability to stop its concessionaire from selling infringing records.[29] Similarly, a radio station that could prevent a disc jockey from playing infringing music had the right and ability to supervise.[30]

Courts have found control over the place of infringement, where, for example, the defendant was the manager of the establishment where the infringement occurred;[31]

where the defendant had responsibility for the day-to-day operations of a club and, in fact, had refused to purchase a music license;[32] and where a defendant radio station had "ultimate authority" to control use of air time, whether or not it exercised such authority.[33] In the *Netcom* case, the court felt that there was a genuine issue of fact as to whether Netcom had the right and ability to exercise control over the activities of its subscribers, since the evidence indicated that with an easy software modification Netcom could identify postings that contain particular words or come from particular individuals, and that Netcom could have limited the access of the allegedly infringing subscriber to the UseNet without affecting any of the other subscribers of the system.

29.2.2.2 Financial Interest. To establish vicarious liability, a plaintiff finally must also show that the defendant had a financial interest in the exploitation of the copyrighted work. Such an intent may be either a direct monetary benefit[34] or an indirect benefit.[35]

For example, in one case, the operators of a lounge in an apartment complex showed a bootleg copy of the film, *Coalminer's Daughter*.[36] The owner of the complex and the management company that ran the complex (but not the lounge) were sued for vicarious liability. They claimed that they had no direct financial interest in the exploitation of the film, and moved for summary judgment. The court denied the motion, because the rent paid by the lounge operator was based on a percentage of the lounge's gross receipts. The court noted that the indisputable purpose for showing the film was to stimulate business; that the defendants stood to benefit by receiving higher rent.

By contrast, in the *Netcom* case, the court concluded that Netcom did not receive any direct financial benefit from the infringing postings of its subscriber since it received a fixed fee from the subscriber for access to Netcom's system.

29.3 Secondary Liability for Defamation

When online defamation is involved, the secondary liability of bulletin board operators, online service providers, and access providers will be examined under one of three major legal models. Potential liability will vary depending upon whether the third party is considered to be a publisher, distributor, or common carrier.

If an entity is considered a *publisher,* the law presumes that it controls the contents of the messages that it publishes, and therefore, that it is liable for any resulting harm.[37] The problem with this approach in the online world is that it presumes that the publisher has direct control over the materials it distributes. Although this may be true for print publishers, such as newspapers and magazines, and even some online publishers, there is a real question as to whether the operator of an electronic data communications system can exert such control.[38] It appears, as a practical matter, virtually impossible for a third-party service provider to monitor, in real time, all of the messages flowing through its system, much less to detemine whether they constitute defamation. In recognition of this fact in an analogous situation, many states have enacted statutes requiring that some degree of fault on the part of a broadcaster exist before liabiilty can be imposed for third-party statements.[39]

Alternatively, an online service might be considered a *distributor*. Because a distributor typically does not control the content of a publication, it is liable for harm created by the distribution only if that harm is brought to his or her attention.[40] Thus, newsstands, bookstores, and libraries typically do not exert any control over what they transmit. However, they often reserve the right (and in some cases have the duty) to exclude harmful content after they learn of it.

A third approach is to consider online service providers as *common carriers*. A business may be a common carrier if it holds itself out as serving all clients indiscriminately.[41] Other factors frequently cited as determining common carrier status include whether the carrier has any direct or indirect control over the content or selection of the transmission, whether it merely passively retransmits every message that gets sent through it, and whether transportation of information is its primary business.

Unlike publishers and distributors, common carriers have a duty to carry all content, without discrimination.[42] But, as a consequence, common carriers have immunity from liability for the content they carry. The telephone system and the post office, for example, are not usually liable for what is transmitted via their systems.

However, common carrier status may not be appropriate for online services, since it would then obligate them to serve all customers, may subject their charges to government approval, and may bar certain types of conduct with respect to the market. Moreover, online services do more than just provide the wires and conduits. Further, they are not natural monopolies that are bound to carry all the traffic that one wishes to pass through them, as with the usual common carrier.

What is the status, for liability purposes, of the providers of interactive online services? Should they be subject to liability for infringements committed by their users?

In *Cubby v. Compuserve, Inc.*,[43] the Compuserve online service was sued for libel on the basis of allegedly false and defamatory statements contained in an electronic newsletter available in Compuserve's Journalism Forum. The newsletter was published by a third party with no connection to Compuserve, and the Forum itself was moderated by an independent contractor who was responsible for its contents. Neither Compuserve nor the moderator had an opportunity to review the contents of the newsletter, which became available to Forum members as soon as the publisher uploaded it onto Compuserve's computer system.

The court found Compuserve not liable for defamation that takes place on its system in the absence of knowledge and an effective means of control:

> [Compuserve] is in essence an electronic, for-profit library that carries a vast number of publications and collects usage and membership fees from its subscribers in return for access to the publications. . . . While Compuserve may decline to carry a given publication altogether, in reality, once it does decide to carry a publication, it will have little or no editorial control over that publication's contents. . . .

> Compuserve has no more editorial control over [the publication at issue] than does a public library, bookstore, or newsstand, and it would be no more feasible

for Compuserve to examine every publication that it carries for potentially defamatory statements than it would for any other distributor to do so. . . .

Given the relevant First Amendment considerations, the appropriate standard of liability to be applied to Compuserve is whether it knew or had reason to know of the allegedly defamatory statements.[44]

A similar case, *Auvil v. CBS "60 Minutes,"*[45] involved a defamation claim against a TV station based on a network broadcast that it had transmitted. Citing *Cubby,* the court refused to hold the station strictly or vicariously liable:

With the possible exception of re-run movies, the content of which is already widely known and/or cataloged, plaintiff's construction would force the creation of full-time editorial boards at local stations throughout the country which possess sufficient knowledge, legal acumen, and access to experts to continually monitor incoming transmissions and exercise on-the-spot discretionary calls or face $75 million lawsuits at every turn. That is not realistic. . . . More than merely unrealistic in economic terms, it is difficult to imagine a scenario more chilling on the media's right of expression and the public's right to know.[46]

A contrary holding, however, was announced on May 25, 1995, in the case of *Stratton Oakmont Inc. v. Prodigy Services Co.* There, a New York state court ruled that Prodigy can be held liable for defamatory messages posted by users of its online service. Prodigy argued that it cannot be held responsible for what its subscribers post on its bulletin boards, any more than a bookstore or newsstand can be liable for what they make publicly available, because they have no control over the editorial content of the messages. The court found that Prodigy did not fall into this category.

The court agreed that "Computer bulletin boards should generally be regarded in the same context as bookstores, libraries and network affiliates," but concluded that Prodigy was different. Unlike a bookstore, it attempted to exert editorial control over the content of messages posted by its users. Specifically, Prodigy has promulgated "content guidelines" for its postings, employed a software program to prescreen all bulletin board postings for offensive language, and appointed a group of "board leaders" to enforce the guidelines. The Prodigy system also includes an "emergency delete" function that allows Prodigy to remove offensive notes quickly. According to the court, "it is Prodigy's own policies, technology and staffing decisions which have altered the scenario and mandated a finding that it is a publisher. . . . Prodigy's conscience choice, to gain the benefits of editorial control, has opened it up to a greater liability than CompuServe and other computer networks that make no such choice."[47]

This precedent-setting decision is the first time a U.S. court has held that a commercial online computer service can be more than passive conduits of information, and thus be subject to the same standards of liability for defamation (and perhaps also for invasion of privacy) as any other publisher of news or information.

Cubby and *Auvil* recognize that it is not feasible to examine the contents of every file. The result in *Prodigy*, on the other hand, was dictated by the court's conclusion that

Prodigy attempted to (and did) control content thereby making its actions more like those of a publisher. Unfortunately, this suggests that as long as a service provider or bulletin board operator does not adopt a monitoring policy like Prodigy's, it can avoid liability for defamation by its users.

This decision was legislatively overruled on February 8, 1996, when the Communications Decency Act of 1996 (CDA) was signed into law as part of the Telecommunications Act of 1996 (S .652). Section 509 of the CDA (47 U.S.C. § 203(c)(1)) helps to shield access providers such as Prodigy from defamation liability in a section called "Protection for 'Good Samaritan' Blocking and Screening of Offensive Material." The provision states that no provider of an interactive computer service shall be treated as the *publisher* or speaker of any information provided by another information content provider (i.e., any person responsible for the creation of information provided through the service). It also states that no provider of an interactive computer service shall be held liable on account of any voluntary action taken in good faith to restrict access to or availability of material that the provider or user considers to be obscene, lewd, lascivious, filthy, excessively violent, harassing, or otherwise objectionable." It is still too early to tell, however, how broadly or narrowly this provision will be interpreted by the courts.

Endnotes

1. *Cubby, Inc. v. Compuserve, Inc.*, 776 F. Supp. 135 (S.D.N.Y. 1991).

2. *Stratton Oakmont, Inc. v. Prodigy Services Co.*, No. 31063/94 1995 N.Y. Misc. LEXIS 229 (N.Y. Sup. Ct. May 24, 1995).

3. *Frank Music v. Compuserve, Inc.* No. 93-Civ. 8153 (S.D.N.Y. filed Nov. 29, 1993).

4. *Religious Technology Center v. Netcom On-Line Communications Services, Inc.*, No. C-95-20091, 1995 U.S. Dist. LEXIS 18173 (N.D. Cal. Nov. 21, 1995).

5. *Playboy Enterprises, Inc. v. Frena*, 839 F. Supp. 1552 (M.D. Fla. 1993).

6. *Sega Enterprises, Ltd. v. Maphia BBS*, 30 U.S.P.Q.2d 1921 (N.D. Calif. 1994).

7. *Playboy Enterprises, Inc. v. Frena*, 839 F. Supp. 1552 (M.D. Fla. 1993).

8. *Id.* at 1559.

9. *Religious Technology Center v. Netcom On-Line Communications Services, Inc.*, No. C-95-20091, 1995 U.S. Dist. LEXIS 18173 (N.D. Cal. Nov. 21, 1995).

10. *Sony Corp. v. Universal City Studios, Inc.*, 464 U.S. 417, 434, 104 S. Ct. 774, 784 (1984) ("[t]he absence of such express language in the copyright statute does not preclude the imposition of liability for copyright infringements on certain parties who have not themselves engaged in the infringing activity").

11. *Id.* at 435, 104 S. Ct. at 785.

12. *Gershwin Publishing Corp. v. Columbia Artists Management, Inc.*, 443 F.2d 1159, 1162 (2d Cir. 1971).

13. *Shapiro, Bernstein & Co. v. H.L. Green Co.*, 316 F.2d 304 (2d Cir. 1963).

14. *See Cable/Home Communications Corp. v. Network Prods., Inc.*, 902 F.2d 829, 836 (11th Cir. 1990) (defendants had actual or apparent knowledge that computer program was copyrighted); *Screen Gems-Columbia Music, Inc. v. Mark-Fi Records, Inc.*, 256 F. Supp. 399 (S.D.N.Y. 1966) (allegations that direct infringer had "the well-known indicia of the fly-by-night operator" held "sufficient to permit a finding that [the contributory infringer] had either actual or constructive knowledge of [the direct infringer's] infringement" and "may be held liable as one who knowingly participated in or furthered the tortious conduct.)"

15. *Religious Technology Center v. Netcom On-Line Communications Services, Inc.*, No. C-95-20091, 1995 U.S. Dist. LEXIS 18173 (N.D. Cal. Nov. 21, 1995).

16. *See Cable/Home Communications Corp. v. Network Prods., Inc.*, 902 F.2d 829, 845–847 (11th Cir. 1990).

17. *Sega Enterprises, Ltd. v. Maphia*, 857 F. Supp. 679 (N.D. Cal. 1994).

18. *Screen Gems-Columbia Music, Inc. v. Mark-Fi Records, Inc.*, 256 F. Supp. 399 (S.D.N.Y. 1966).

19. *Universal City Studios, Inc. v. Nintendo Co.*, 615 F. Supp. 838 (S.D.N.Y. 1985), *aff'd* 797 F.2d 70 (2d Cir. 1976).

20. *Sega Enterprises, Ltd. v. Maphia*, 30 U.S.P.Q.2d 1921 (N.D. Cal. 1994).

21. *Id*. at 1926.

22. *Religious Technology Center v. Netcom On-Line Communications Services, Inc.*, No. C-95-20091, 1995 U.S. Dist. LEXIS 18173 (N.D. Cal. Nov. 21, 1995).

23. *Elektra Records Co. v. General Elec. Distribs., Inc.*, 360 F. Supp. 821 (E.D. N.Y. 1973). *See also RCA Records v. All-Fast Systems, Inc.*, 594 F. Supp. 335 (S.D.N.Y. 1984)(defendant commercially operated sound recording duplication facilities for unauthorized copying of recordings and was found liable for contributory copyright infringement even though the customers themselves furnished the copyrighted tapes to be duplicated); *Accord Columbia Pictures Indus., Inc. v. Aveco, Inc.*, 800 F.2d 59 (3d Cir. 1986) (video shop that rents screening booth to customers liable for authorizing public performance, even if customers furnish their own videocassette of another's copyrighted motion picture); *Telerate Systems, Inc. v. Caro*, 689 F. Supp. 221 (S.D.N.Y. 1988) (computer program used by purchasers to copy copyrighted database onto personal computer has no substantial non-infringing uses and infringes plaintiff's copyright).

24. *Sony Corp. v. Universal City Studios, Inc.*, 464 U.S. 417 (1984).

25. *Id*. at 442.

26. *Id*. at 437–438.

27. *Polygram Int'l Publishing, Inc. v. Nevada/TIG, Ltd.*, 855 F. Supp. 1314, 1328 (D. Mass. 1994).

28. *Id*. at 1326.

29. *Shapiro Bernstein & Co. v. H.L. Green Co.*, 316 F.2d 304 (2d cir. 1963).

30. *Boz Scaggs Music v. KND Corp.*, 491 F. Supp. 908, 913 (D. Conn. 1980).

31. *Broadcast Music, Inc. v. Larkin*, 672 F. Supp. 531, 534 (D. Me. 1987).

32. *Fermata Int'l Melodies v. Champions Golf Club*, 712 F. Supp. 1257, 1262 (S.D. Tex. 1989), *aff'd*, 915 F.2d 1567 (5th Cir. 1990).

33. *Realsongs v. Gulf Broadcasting Corp.*, 824 F. Supp. 89, 93 (M.D. La. 1993).

34. *See, e.g., Shapiro*, 316 F.2d at 307 (defendant had a direct financial interest in exploitation of copyright works because defendant received a percentage of sales of such works by direct infringer).

35. *See, e.g., Superhype Pub., Inc. v. Vasilou*, 838 F. Supp. 1220, 1225 (S.D. Ohio 1993) (restaurant owner had "direct" financial interest because he received benefit of music played in his restaurant); *Realsongs v. Gulf Broadcasting Corp.*, 824 F. Supp. 89, 93 (M.D. La. 1993) (radio station has direct financial interest even though it was paid a flat fee for rental of air time unrelated to content of infringing performance); *but see Artists Music, Inc. v. Reed Publishing, Inc.*, 31 U.S.P.Q.2d 1623 (S.D.N.Y. 1994) (trade show operator had no direct financial benefit in that its revenues were based on booth rentals, not on whether or not copyrighted music was played).

36. *Universal City Studios, Inc. v. American Invsco Management, Inc.*, 217 U.S.P.Q. 1076 (N.D. Ill. 1981).

37. *See Loftus E. Becker, Jr., The Liability of Computer Bulletin Board Operators for Defamation Posted by Others*, 22 Conn. Law Review 203, 222, and n. 89 (1989).

38. *But see Stratton Oakmont, Inc. v. Prodigy Services Company*, 1995 N.Y. Misc. LEXIS 229 (N.Y. Sup. Ct. May 24, 1995).

39. *See* Loftus E. Becker, Jr., *The Liability of Computer Bulletin Board Operators for Defamation Posted by Others*, 22 Conn. Law Review 203, 226, and n. 111 (1989).

40. *Restatement (Second) of Torts* § 581(1) ("one who delivers or tansmits defamatory matter published by a third person is subject to liability if, but only if, he knows or has reason to know of his defamatory character").

41. *See, e.g., National Association of Regulatory Utilities Commissioners v. F.C.C.*, 533 F.2d 601, 608 (D.C. Cir. 1976).

42. 47 U.S.C. § 202(a) ("it shall be unlawful for any common carrier to make any unjust or unreasonable discrimination and charges, practices, classifications. . . ."; *See also MCI Telecommunications Corp. v. F.C.C.*, 765 F.2d 1186, 1192, (D.C. Cir. 1985) ("practices [must] be just, fair, reasonable and nondiscriminatory") (quoting *AT&T v. F.C.C.*, 572 F.2d 17, 25 (2d Cir. 1978).

43. *Cubby v. Compuserve, Inc.*, 776 F. Supp. 135 (S.D.N.Y. 1991).

44. *Id.* at 140–141.

45. *Auvil v. CBS "60 Minutes,"* 800 F. Supp. 928 (E.D. Wa. 1992).

46. *Id.*

47. *Stratton Oakmont, Inc. v. Prodigy Services Company*, 1995 N.Y. Misc. LEXIS 229 (N.Y. Sup. Ct. May 24, 1995).

30
Criminal Online Conduct

Ruth Hill Bro

30.7 Unauthorized Possession of Passwords

30.8 State Computer Crime Statutes

Endnotes

30.1 Overview

As more and more companies do business online, the opportunities for computer crime expand accordingly. Unlike traditional modes of crime, which are largely constrained by physical limitations (for example, robbing a bank requires traveling to an actual street address and carrying away bags of paper and coin to a getaway car), computer crime involves intangible data that can be accessed from anywhere (for example, robbing a bank online can be as simple as altering or transferring data by a few keystrokes in a matter of seconds from the privacy of one's own home or office).

Yet online crime is not an activity reserved solely for the self-proclaimed hackers who engage in malicious or destructive acts or for traditional criminals who have merely found a new arena in which to commit their crimes. What may seem like innocent behavior on the part of a computer user, such as accessing a private online database or borrowing a friend's password without permission, could trigger criminal and civil liability.

Computer crime can include almost any type of activity directed against, or involving the use of, a computer. With some forms of online crime, information stored on the computer itself is the target: the perpetrator wants to access, copy, alter, or destroy data resident on a computer. With other forms of online crime, the computer is merely the most efficient tool by which to perform other criminal acts, such as committing a fraud or conducting a scheme to steal property from its rightful owners.

30.1.1 Legislation

Every state except Vermont has now passed computer crime legislation.[1] Some states have enacted comprehensive computer crime statutes; others have simply modified existing criminal statutes to fit computer crimes better. At the federal level, two statutes specifically target online computer-related offenses: the Computer Fraud and Abuse Act (CFAA)[2] and the Electronic Communications Privacy Act (ECPA).[3] These statutes were enacted to respond to a perceived escalation in computer crime and the inability of traditional criminal statutes to cover all possible computer-related crimes.[4] By better defining the types of online activities that are prohibited, these statutes have greatly assisted prosecutors in filing charges for computer-related crimes and have freed them from having to stretch existing laws to fit offenses for which they were not designed.

In many states, computer crimes can also be prosecuted under more traditional criminal statutes, including those concerning trespass, theft, destruction of property, misappropriation of trade secrets, false pretenses, larceny, and embezzlement. Moreover, some computer crime may be prosecuted under federal criminal statutes governing wire fraud, mail fraud, credit-card fraud, transfer of electronic funds, interstate transportation of stolen property, receipt of stolen property in interstate commerce, and copyright and trademark infringement.

This chapter focuses on the statutes specifically aimed at computer crime. Statutes that prohibit other criminal offenses online are discussed in other chapters, including copyright infringement (discussed in Chapter 10) and child pornography (discussed in Chapter 20).

30.1.2 Prohibited Conduct

The activities most commonly prohibited by computer crime statutes include:

- Unauthorized access to, or use of, a computer,
- Alteration or destruction of data without authorization,
- Theft of computer services,
- Computer fraud (using a computer to commit other crimes),
- Denial of another's access to a computer, and
- Unauthorized possession of passwords.

Although each state's computer crime statutes use different language and definitions, they generally follow a similar pattern. Prohibition of unauthorized access to, and alteration of, data constitutes the core of most states' laws.

30.2 Unauthorized Access/Use

30.2.1 State Law

Virtually every state prohibits unauthorized access to a computer, and almost any online contact with a computer will be considered "access." In Illinois, for example, "access" means "to use, instruct, communicate with, store data in, retrieve or intercept data from, or otherwise utilize any services of a computer."[5]

Access to a computer is unauthorized if (1) it is without the permission of the owner or someone else allowed to give permission, or (2) it exceeds the permission originally granted.

Access can exceed authorization in a number of ways. For example, permission to access a few select files does not include permission to access restricted files. Thus, a subscriber with a valid account on a bulletin board system or online service who discovers how to exceed the granted scope of access may be violating a state computer crime statute. Likewise, permission to use another's computer does not constitute permission to use that person's password, network, or software, and permission to use another's computer or password on one particular occasion does not entitle the user to unlimited future access. Use beyond the scope of permission granted may violate the law.

In one case, an arraignment clerk for the Cuyahoga County Court of Common Pleas in Ohio was convicted of unauthorized access to a computer system for accessing—for personal reasons—information from a special database regarding the criminal record of her brother's friend (who turned out to be an undercover cop); the employee had been told at her training classes that the use of such data was restricted.[6] In another case, a Florida public service aide for a local law enforcement agency was convicted for exceeding her authorization to use the agency's computer for official business when she used the computer to see if her boyfriend had a criminal record.[7]

The few states that do not specifically ban unauthorized *access* typically ban unauthorized *use*. For example, Colorado,[8] Montana,[9] New York,[10] South Dakota,[11] and Virginia[12] all ban the unauthorized use of a computer. The meaning of these two terms can often be very similar; in fact, as the Illinois statute above indicates, some state statutes actually define "access" as "make use of."[13]

Most state computer crime statutes prohibit the accessing of a computer without authorization only if it is done willfully or intentionally. Thus, if an employee accidentally deletes or negligently modifies a program while trying to fix a problem, he or she has not committed a crime because the requisite intent is missing. By the same token, when an employee erases an obsolete program or modifies a program at the employer's bidding, the employee has not committed a crime because he or she is acting with the authorization of the employer. Conversely, when a payroll employee uses his or her position to gain access to the company payroll system and add 25 percent to his or her weekly paycheck, these actions constitute a crime because they are both intentional and exceed authorized access.

One author has described the process of obtaining unauthorized access to a computer system as the "cyberspace equivalent of breaking and entering a real world home or business."[14] Once the online intruder has unlawfully entered, the level of his destructive intent (or recklessness) and the property available to be stolen, destroyed, or deleted determine what happens next.[15] Mere access, without more, is typically classified as a misdemeanor[16] under state law.

It should be noted that unlawfully accessing another's computer may violate more than one state's laws. For instance, a person who uses a computer in California to access a computer in Iowa may be committing the crime of unauthorized access in *both* jurisdictions and may be held criminally and civilly liable in both jurisdictions.[17]

30.2.2 Computer Fraud and Abuse Act

Unauthorized access to a computer is also a crime under federal law. The Computer Fraud and Abuse Act (CFAA) prohibits unauthorized access to:

- A government computer,[18]

- A computer containing classified or restricted government information (e.g., data regarding national defense or foreign relations),[19]
- A financial institution's computer (to obtain financial records),[20]
- A computer of a credit-card issuer (to obtain credit-card information),[21]
- A computer of a consumer reporting agency (to obtain credit information),[22] and
- A federal interest computer.[23]

Unauthorized access alone triggers liability under the CFAA if the computer accessed is used exclusively by the government.[24] Liability for unauthorized access to other computers requires some extra element, such as the obtaining of information,[25] an intent to defraud or cause damage,[26] or transmitting a harmful component of a program that causes damage exceeding $1,000.[27] The criminal penalties vary depending on the offense, but typically include a fine and/or a maximum prison term ranging anywhere from one year to ten years; subsequent offenses can carry maximum prison terms of ten or twenty years, depending on the offense committed.[28] Civil causes of action allow compensatory damages, injunctive relief, and other equitable relief.[29]

Because the CFAA is primarily limited to crimes involving federal interest computers, the statute has not been used as frequently as the various state computer crime statutes. Since it was enacted in 1986, however, cases involving charges under the CFAA have included the following:

- In 1989, a defendant pled guilty to five counts, including a CFAA count of unauthorized accessing, with intent to defraud, of a federal interest computer in connection with the embezzlement of $47,000 from a federally insured bank.[30]
- In 1990, charges were brought under the CFAA (and under the federal wire fraud and interstate transportation of stolen property statutes) against two defendants who had allegedly defrauded Bell South Telephone Company by stealing a computer text file that contained supposedly proprietary information (valued at $80,000) regarding the company's emergency 911 system and by publishing that information in one of the defendants' computer newsletters.[31] The CFAA charges were dropped when it was disclosed that the general public could purchase the "proprietary" information for under $15.[32]
- In 1991, the CFAA[33] was used to prosecute and convict Robert Morris, a Cornell graduate student, who had released a self-replicating computer program that he claimed was designed to explore the Internet and compile information regarding the inadequate security of the national computer network.[34] A programming error, however, transformed Morris' Internet "worm" into a relentless virus[35] that infected thousands of computers—including installations at leading universities, military sites, and medical research facilities—within a matter of hours.

30.2.3 Electronic Communications Privacy Act

The Electronic Communications Privacy Act (ECPA)[36] prohibits a third party from intercepting or disclosing electronic communications, in the same way that the federal wiretapping law prohibits the interception of telephone calls. The ECPA also prohibits unauthorized access to, and disclosure of, stored electronic communications, including both voice mail and electronic mail.[37] For example, accessing another person's electronic mail without his or her permission could constitute a criminal violation of the ECPA. Nevertheless, conduct that is authorized by the service provider (often an employer) *or* by a user of that service with respect to the user's own communication, or one intended for that user, is not a crime under this statute.[38]

For example, in a highly publicized case,[39] an employee of Sega (a computer video game company) collected evidence against a computer bulletin board that was suspected of allowing users to upload and download copyrighted Sega video games. The Sega employee gathered evidence by gaining access to the board under a pseudonym, using information supplied by an informant who was an authorized user. A key issue in the case was whether the Sega employee's access was authorized under the ECPA.

The court held that Sega's access was authorized because the board was open to the public and was normally accessed by means of an alias or pseudonym.[40] Moreover, the court noted that Sega's access was authorized directly or indirectly by a bulletin board user whose authorized access was undisputed, thereby complying with the ECPA, which allows access that is authorized by a user of the service with respect to a communication for that user.

As this case makes clear, there is no problem under the ECPA in infiltrating a bulletin board by using an informant's (i.e., an authorized user's) identity and password with his or her permission. Moreover, there would be no adverse repercussions in answering "no" to the bulletin board's question at the sign-on stage as to whether the user has any connection with the government or with computer watchdog organizations; such failure to identify oneself would not provide the party being investigated with a defense to copyright or trademark infringement if accurate identification would have defeated the investigation.[41]

Criminal sanctions under the ECPA can range from prison terms of up to five years and fines of up to $10,000, depending on the violation.[42] Civil remedies may include preliminary and other equitable relief, actual damages, or profits of up to $10,000 per violation, as well as reasonable attorneys' fees and litigation costs.[43]

30.3 Alteration or Destruction of Data

Most states make it a felony[44] to alter, destroy, delete, or modify another's computer data without authorization.

In one case, a New York court ruled that merely *activating existing instructions* that command a computer to shut down constituted unauthorized alteration of computer data or a computer program.[45] The defendant was convicted of computer tampering (that is, unauthorized and intentional alteration or destruction of a computer program or computer data) for intentionally *altering* two computer programs designed to provide uninterrupted telephone service; the defendant had disconnected the application programs and commanded the computers to shut down, thereby *altering* the programs in some manner.[46] The court emphasized that there was no legal distinction between the defendant using existing instructions to direct the phone system offline and inputting new instructions to accomplish the same thing. Lacking a definition from the state legislature, the court indicated that the term *alter* must be given its ordinary meaning, which is "to change or modify;" the court also noted that the statute contained the expansive language that alterations "in any manner" would constitute a crime.[47]

Conversely, a Florida court held that a new accounts credit analyst did not modify computer data, programs, or supporting documentation when he added information to a computer by bypassing a feature that would automatically send the prospective credit-card customer's information to a credit bureau to check on the person's credit rating; there was no modification or alteration because the defendant's use of an existing computer function did not change the form or properties of the detailed information residing in the computer or the system.[48] Instead, the court observed that the defendant's acts, though fraudulent, appeared instead to be unauthorized use of a computer or accessing a computer without authorization, but the defendant had not been charged under such a statute.[49]

The unauthorized deletion of computer data is unlawful, even if the deleted data may still be retrieved. A Texas court rejected a defendant's defense that the records he had erased were not "physically" deleted but rather only "logically" deleted in that they still existed but were inaccessible to the computer in question for processing the payroll file.[50]

If someone, without authorization, uses a computer used in interstate commerce or communications to cause damage to, or to deny the use of, another computer (whether the damage is caused knowingly or with reckless disregard as to the consequences), that person may also be guilty of a federal crime under the CFAA if:

1. It causes aggregate loss or damage of $1,000 or more to one or more persons during a one-year period; or
2. It modifies or impairs the medical examination, medical diagnosis, medical treatment, or medical care of one or more individuals.[51]

Such a crime carries a penalty of a fine and/or imprisonment of up to five years (for *knowingly* causing) or up to one year (for *reckless disregard* in causing); a subsequent offense can carry a prison term of up to ten years.[52]

30.4 Theft of Computer Services

Most states explicitly prohibit the theft of computer services. New Hampshire's definition of *computer services* is fairly typical of those states that define the term: computer service "includes, but is not limited to, computer access, data processing, and data storage."[53] New Mexico's definition is a little more detailed: computer service "includes computer time, the use of the computer system, computer network, computer programs or data prepared for computer use, data contained within a computer network and data processing and other functions performed, in whole or in part, by the use of computers, computer systems, computer networks or computer software."[54]

Depending on the wording of the state statute, the crime of theft of computer services may require that the obtained service was actually available only for compensation. For example, although a woman was properly convicted under Pennsylvania's unauthorized computer use statute for appropriating voice mailboxes, she was judged to be not guilty under the Pennsylvania theft of services statute, because outsiders were not expected to pay a price for leaving messages in the voice mailboxes nor could outsiders pay for the right to use the voice mailbox system for themselves.[55]

Because commercial access providers charge a fee for supplying computer services, any attempt to use such services for free could amount to theft of services. When a state does not specifically prohibit the theft of computer services, a person stealing such services could possibly be prosecuted under the state's general theft statute.

30.5 Computer Fraud

In general, if something is a crime to begin with, it is no less a crime when it is done online; the conduct can still be prosecuted under traditional crime statutes. Some states, however, have taken the extra step of specifically prohibiting the use of a computer to fraudulently obtain money, services, or property. Under the Virginia Computer Crimes Act, for example, a person commits computer fraud when he or she uses a computer or computer network without authority and with the intent to:

1. Obtain property or services by false pretenses,
2. Embezzle or commit larceny, or
3. Convert another's property.[56]

In Virginia, if the value of the property or services obtained is $200 or more, the crime is punishable as a felony; otherwise, the crime is a misdemeanor.[57] It is irrelevant under the statute whether any property or services were actually obtained; the intent to obtain is sufficient to trigger criminal liability.

Such schemes to swindle others are particularly well-suited to the online context: the identity of the defrauder is more easily concealed (there is no voice or face to identify), and unlimited numbers of victims can be recruited simultaneously and at a greatly reduced cost and time investment.

30.5.1 Telephone Cases

Several persons have been convicted under state computer crime statutes for improperly "reaching out and touching someone." For example, a defendant was convicted in New Mexico of computer access with intent to defraud for his scheme in which he called New Mexico residents, using a telephone receiver in Florida, and falsely told them that he was a Nevada attorney awarding money from a lawsuit to customers of a fraudulent telemarketing company and that they would have to send 10 percent of the amount owed to them to cover fees and court costs.[58] The court held that the switching involved in a long-distance call constituted accessing a computer network.[59] Moreover, the court emphasized that under the statute the intent to defraud that accompanies access need not be directed against the owners and operators of the computers.[60]

In Washington, a defendant used a home computer to dial repeatedly and randomly, a different six-digit access code at 40-second intervals in an attempt to obtain valid long-distance telephone codes from telephone company computers; such computer "hacking" led to his conviction on three counts of computer trespass and four counts of possession of a stolen access device.[61] In Illinois, a defendant was convicted of unlawful use of a computer for participating in a similar computer hacking scheme involving long-distance telephone access codes.[62]

A Pennsylvania court affirmed the conviction of a *phone phreaker* (one who illegally markets telephone calling card numbers) on two counts of unauthorized use of a computer for ousting authorized users from a company's voice mailbox by altering the mailbox's secret password and leaving messages for other phone phreakers who left lists of illegally obtained credit- and calling-card numbers in the voice mailbox.[63]

30.5.2 Credit Fraud Cases

A prime form of crimes involving unauthorized computer access involves fraudulent credit schemes. For example, a defendant was convicted in California of three counts of illegal computer access for gaining access to the confidential computer files of various credit bureaus and deliberately entering false information that he knew would result in the bureaus' subscribers extending credit to individuals with bad credit ratings that the companies would otherwise refuse.[64] The defendant was also convicted of grand theft by false pretenses for his false representations to clients that he could legally clear their bad credit.[65]

A credit counselor in Tennessee committed a fraud upon her employer when she skimmed large amounts of money from the company by taking partial utility payments from delinquent customers, calling up the customer account and printing a duplicate bill, and then entering the account number on the computer as a bad debt that the utility company would write off without further investigation. The defendant was convicted under a state statute that prohibits the knowing and willful accessing of a computer for the purpose of (1) devising or executing any scheme or artifice to defraud or (2) obtaining money, property, or services by false or fraudulent pretenses, representations, or promises.[66]

Fraudulent credit schemes are perpetrated not only by those in the credit business. For example, in February, 1995, the FBI arrested Kevin Mitnick, a computer hacker who infiltrated dozens of corporate and government computers over a period of 12 years.[67] Mitnick was charged with access device fraud and computer fraud for taking approximately 20,000 credit cards from Netcom Communication in San Jose, California, although apparently he did not do so for material gain.[68] Mitnick pled guilty and agreed to serve eight months in prison for one count of possessing stolen telephone numbers; the other twenty-two charges were dismissed under the terms of the plea bargain.[69]

Accessing a credit-card company's computer and trying multiple combinations of numbers in an attempt to discover a valid account is strictly prohibited by the Credit Card Fraud Act and by many state statutes. For example, a defendant was convicted under the Credit Card Fraud Act for violating the unauthorized access device provision when he gained access to American Express's computer system, tried out various combinations until he found some that the computer would accept, and then charged goods to the credit cards using fictitious names.[70]

30.5.3 Other Schemes

The crime of accessing a computer for fraudulent purposes can take many other different forms. For example, in Georgia, a defendant was convicted on 69 counts of accessing a computer for fraudulent purposes for using her position as a payroll clerk to issue computer-generated checks made out to other supermarket employees and then forging them herself.[71]

30.6 Denial of Another's Access

Florida, the first state to enact a computer crime statute, goes further than most other states by making it a crime to interfere with another person's access to a computer. The statute makes it a felony to "willfully, knowingly, and without authorization den[y] or cause the denial of computer services to an authorized user of such computer system services. . . ."[72] If such denial of access is done to defraud or obtain property of any kind, the offender is guilty of a felony in the second degree.[73] Conversely, in South Carolina, denial of computer service to an authorized user is a crime only if it is done to defraud or commit another felony.[74]

Even if it is not specifically prohibited by a state statute, the denial of another's access can serve as evidence of unauthorized access. For example, a court concluded that a defendant knew that her access was unauthorized because the exclusive control and use of the plaintiff's voice mailboxes was necessary if she were to successfully reroute the contraband information that she was attempting to disseminate. By such usage, the defendant knew that she would be preventing authorized users from using the plaintiff's messaging systems and thereby would disturb normal operations.[75]

30.7 Unauthorized Possession of Passwords

Some states prohibit knowing attempts to identify any valid access codes without authorization[76] or the knowing taking or disclosure of such computer passwords.[77] Such statutes allow prosecutors to press criminal charges on those who "traffic" (trade or deal) in passwords that allow access to various credit-card accounts, for example, without having to prove any other element such as actual access to the account or actual trafficking.

Several states prohibit one person from providing another with the means or the information needed to illegally access a computer. For example, under Georgia law, a person can be guilty of the crime of computer password disclosure if he or she knows that the disclosure[78] is without authority *and* the disclosure results in damages to the computer's owner exceeding $500 (including the fair market value of any services used and victim expenditure).

It is also a federal crime to knowingly, and with an intent to defraud, traffic in any password through which a computer may be accessed without authorization if such trafficking affects interstate or foreign commerce or if the computer is used by or for the U.S. government.[79] Although Congress primarily designed this provision to attack pirate bulletin boards,[80] this provision also applies when the trafficking affects interstate commerce.[81] The provision, however, does not apply to any lawfully authorized investigative, protective, or intelligence activity of a government law enforcement or intelligence agency.[82]

30.8 State Computer Crime Statutes

Alabama Code of Alabama
  Sections 13A-8-100 to 13A-8-103
Alaska Alaska Statutes
  Section 11.46.200(a)
  Section 11.46.484(a)(5)
  Section 11.46.740
  Section 11.46.985
  Section 11.46.990
Arizona Arizona Revised Statutes Annotated
  Section 13-2301
  Section 13-2316
Arkansas Arkansas Code Annotated
  Sections 5-41-101 to 5-41-107
California West's Annotated California Penal Code
  Section 502
  Sections 1203.047 to 1203.048
Colorado Colorado Revised Statutes
  Sections 18-5.5-101 to 18-5.5-102
Connecticut General Statutes of Connecticut
  Section 52-570b
  Sections 53a-250 to 53a-261
Delaware Delaware Code Annotated, Title 11
  Sections 931 to 939
Florida Florida Statutes Annotated (West)
  Sections 8.15.01 to 8.15.07
  Sections 934.01 to 934.43
Georgia Official Code of Georgia Annotated (Michie)
  Sections 16-9-90 to 16-9-94

Hawaii Hawaii Revised Statutes
  Sections 708-890 to 708-896
Idaho Idaho Code
  Sections 18-2201 to 18-2202
Illinois Illinois Compiled Statutes (Michie), Chapter 720
  Section 16D-1 to 16D-7
Indiana Burns Indiana Statutes Annotated
  Section 35-43-1-4
  Section 35-43-2-3
Iowa Iowa Code Annotated (West)
  Sections 716A.1 to 716A.16
Kansas Kansas Statutes Annotated
  Section 21-3755
Kentucky Kentucky Revised Statutes Annotated, Official Edition (Michie/Bobbs-Merrill)
  Sections 434.840 to 434.860
Louisiana West's Louisiana Revised Statues Annotated, Title 14
  Sections 73.1 to 73.5
Maine Maine Revised Statutes Annotated (West), Title 17-A
  Section 357
  Sections 431 to 433
Maryland Annotated Code of Maryland, Art. 27
  Section 45A
  Section 146
Massachusetts Massachusetts General Laws Annotated (West), Chapter 266
  Sections 30, 33A
Michigan Michigan Statutes Annotated (Callaghan)
  Section 752.791 to 752.797
Minnesota Minnesota Statutes Annotated (West)
  Sections 270B.18
  Sections 609.87 to 609.89
Mississippi Mississippi Code Annotated
  Sections 97-45-1 to 97-45-13
Missouri Missouri Revised Statutes
  Section 537.525
  Sections 569.093 to 569.099
Montana Montana Code Annotated
  Section 45-2-101
  Section 45-6-310
  Section 45-6-311
Nebraska Revised Statutes of Nebraska
  Sections 28-1341 to 28-1348
Nevada Nevada Revised Statutes Annotated (Michie)
  Sections 205.473 to 205.491

New Hampshire New Hampshire Revised Statutes Annotated
    Sections 638.16 to 638.19
New Jersey New Jersey Statutes Annotated (West)
    Title 2A, Sections 38A-1 to 38A-6
    Title 2C, Sections 20-23 to 20-34
New Mexico New Mexico Statutes Annotated (Michie)
    Sections 30-45-1 to 30-45-7
New York McKinney's Consolidated Laws of New York Annotated (Penal Law)
    Sections 156.00 to 156.50
    Section 165.15
North Carolina General Statutes of North Carolina
    Sections 14-453 to 14-457
North Dakota North Dakota Century Code
    Section 12.1-06.1-01(3)
    Section 12.1-06.1-08
Ohio Ohio Revised Code (Page's)
    Sections 2901.01(J)(1),(2)
    Sections 2913.01(E),(F),(L)-(R)
    Section 2913.02
    Section 2913.04
    Section 2913.42
    Section 2913.81
Oklahoma Oklahoma Statutes Annotated (West)
    Sections 1951 to 1958
Oregon Oregon Revised Statutes
    Section 164.125
    Sections 164.345, 164.354, and 164.365
    Section 164.377
Pennsylvania Purdon's Pennsylvania Consolidated Statutes Annotated (Crimes and
Offenses)
    Title 18, Section 3933
Rhode Island General Laws of Rhode Island
    Sections 11-52-1 to 11-52-8
South Carolina Code of Laws of South Carolina Annotated (Law. Co-op.)
    Sections 16-16-10 to 16-16-40
South Dakota South Dakota Codified Laws Annotated
    Sections 43-43B-1 to 43-43B-8
Tennessee Tennessee Code Annotated
    Section 3-10-109
    Sections 39-14-601 to 39-14-603
Texas Vernon's Texas Codes Annotated
    Title 6, Sections 143.001 to 143.002 (Civil Practice and Remedies)
    Title 7, Sections 33.01 to 33.04 (Penal Code)
    Art. 13.25 (Criminal Procedure)

Utah Utah Code Annotated
Sections 76-6-701 to 76-6-705
Section 76-10-1801
Vermont
No computer crime statute
Virginia Code of Virginia Annotated
Sections 18.2-152.1 to 18.2-152.14
Washington Revised Code of Washington Annotated
Section 9A.48.100
Sections 9A.52.110 to 9A.52.130
West Virginia West Virginia Code
Sections 61-3C-1 to 61-3C-21
Wisconsin West's Wisconsin Statutes Annotated
Section 943.70
Wyoming Wyoming Statutes
Sections 6-3-501 to 6-3-505

Endnotes

1. Florida, in 1978, was the first state to enact a specialized computer crime statute. *Newberger v. State*, 641 So.2d 419, 422 (Fla. Dist. Ct. App. 1994).

2. 18 U.S.C. § 1030 (1995).

3. 18 U.S.C. §§ 2510–2711 (1995).

4. For example, Florida is one of several states that includes a statement of legislative intent in its computer crime statutes. It says:

    The legislature finds and declares that:

    (1) Computer-related crime is a growing problem in government as well as in the private sector.

    (2) Computer-related crime occurs at great cost to the public since losses for each incident of computer crime tend to be far greater than the losses associated with each incident of other white collar crime.

    (3) The opportunities for computer-related crimes in financial institutions, government programs, government records, and other business enterprises through the introduction of fraudulent records into a computer system, the unauthorized use of computer facilities, the alteration or destruction of computerized information or files, and the stealing of financial instruments, data, and other assets are great.

    (4) While various forms of computer crime might possibly be the subject of criminal charges based on other provisions of law, it is appropriate and desirable that a supplemental and additional statute be provided which proscribes various forms of computer abuse. Fla Stat. Ann. § 815.02 (West 1994).

5. 720 I.L.C.S. 5/16D-2(e) (Michie 1994).

6. *State v. Lebron*, 97 Ohio App. 3d 155, 646 N.E.2d 481 (Ohio Ct. App. 1994).

7. *Gallagher v. State*, 618 So.2d 757 (Fla. App. 1993) (only dissenting opinion published).

8.   Colo. Rev. Stat. §§ 18-5.5-101(10), 18-5.5-102 (1986).

9.   Mont. Code Ann. §§ 45-6-310, 45-6-311 (1993).

10. N.Y. Penal Law § 156.05 (McKinney 1988).

11. S.D. Codified Laws Ann. §§ 43-43B-1 (1994), 43-43B-3 (1994), 43-43B-4 (1994), 43-43B-5 (1988), 43-43B-6 (1988).

12. Va. Code Ann. § 18.2-152.2 *et seq.* (Michie 1988).

13. *See also State v. Rowell*, 119 N.M. 710, 895 P.2d 232 (N.M. Ct. App. 1995), *citing* N.M. Stat. Ann. § 30-45-2(A).

14. Robert L. Dunne, *Deterring Unauthorized Access to Computers: Controlling Behavior in Cyberspace Through a Contract Law Paradigm*, 35 Jurimetrics, J. 3 (Fall 1994).

15. *Id.*

16. A misdemeanor triggers less punishment (fine and/or imprisonment under one year) than a felony does.

17. According to Cal. Penal Code § 502(j) (West 1994), "[f]or purposes of bringing a civil or a criminal action under this section, a person who causes, by any means, the access of a computer, computer system, or computer network in one jurisdiction from another juris-diction is deemed to have personally accessed the computer, computer system, or com-puter network in each jurisdiction."

18. 18 U.S.C. § 1030(a)(3) (1995).

19. 18 U.S.C. § 1030(a)(1) (1995).

20. 18 U.S.C. § 1030(a)(2) (1995).

21. 18 U.S.C. § 1030(a)(2) (1995). *See also* 15 U.S.C. § 1602(n) for the definition of "card issuer."

22. "Credit Information" means information contained in a file of a consumer reporting agency on a consumer as defined in the Fair Credit Reporting Act, 15 U.S.C. § 1681. *See* 18 U.S.C. § 1030(a)(2) (1995).

23. 18 U.S.C. § 1030(a)(4) (1995). A "Federal interest computer" includes a computer that: (1) is operated by or on behalf of the U.S. government or a financial institution, or (2) is used along with at least one other computer from another state to commit the offense. 18 U.S.C. § 1030(e)(2) (1995).

24. 18 U.S.C. § 1030(a)(3) (1995).

25. 18 U.S.C. §§ 1030(a)(1), 1030(a)(2) (1995).

26. 18 U.S.C. §§ 1030(a)(4), 1030(a)(5), 1030(a)(6) (1995).

27. 18 U.S.C. § 1030(a)(5) (1995).

28. 18 U.S.C. § 1030(c) (1995).

29. 18 U.S.C. § 1030(g) (1995).

30. Robert L. Dunne, *Deterring Unauthorized Access to Computers: Controlling Behavior in Cyberspace Through a Contract Law Paradigm*, 35 Jurimetrics J., 1, 7 (Fall, 1994), *citing United States v. Lewis*, 872 F.2d 1030 (6th Cir. 1989), 1989 WL 40125 (unpublished disposition in table; text in WESTLAW).

31. *United States v. Riggs*, 739 F. Supp. 414 (N.D. Ill. 1990). *See also United States v. Riggs*, 743 F. Supp. 556, 559–560 (N.D. Ill. 1990) (court held that the First Amendment does not prevent prosecution of the individual because his criminal conduct happens to involve speech, which in this case was the publication of the "911" information).

32. Robert L. Dunne, *Deterring Unauthorized Access to Computers: Controlling Behavior in Cyberspace Through a Contract Law Paradigm*, 35 Jurimetrics J., 1, 7 (Fall, 1994).

33. 18 U.S.C. § 1030(a)(5)(A) (1995).

34. *United States v. Morris*, 928 F.2d 504 (2d Cir. 1991), *cert. denied*, 502 U.S. 817 (1991).

35. *Virus* has become a catch-all term for a potentially harmful computer program that is passed from one computer to another.

36. 18 U.S.C. § 2510 *et seq.* (1995).

37. 18 U.S.C. §§ 2701, 2702 (1995).

38. 18 U.S.C § 2701(c) (1995).

39. *Sega Enterprises, Ltd. v. Maphia*, 857 F. Supp. 679 (N.D. Cal. 1994).

40. *Id.* at 689.

41. *Id.* In support of this proposition, the court cited two cases: *Olan Mills, Inc. v. Linn Photo Co.*, 795 F. Supp. 1423 (N.D. Iowa 1991), *rev'd on other grounds*, 23 F.3d 1345 (8th Cir. 1994) (court held that the defense of unclean hands was unavailable even though the plaintiff had deceived the defendant, who probably would not otherwise have unlawfully reproduced the copyrighted photographs); *Reebok Int'l Ltd. v. Jemmett*, 6 U.S.P.Q.2d 1715 (S.D. Cal. 1988) (court held that the fact that the copyright infringement plaintiff's investigator may not have identified himself as such to the defendant, and may have led the defendant to believe that he was someone other than an investigator for the plaintiff, was not sufficient to make the plaintiff guilty of unclean hands so as to deny discovery). A pirate bulletin board would not be able to use a copyright owner's failure to identify himself as a defense to the infringement, because such identification by the copyright owner would defeat its investigation of the pirate bulletin boards.

42. *See* 18 U.S.C. §§ 2512, 2701 (1995).

43. *See* 18 U.S.C. §§ 2520, 2707 (1995).

44. A *felony* is a major crime punishable by a fine and/or a prison term exceeding one year.

45. *People v. Versaggi*, 83 N.Y.2d 123, 629 N.E.2d 1034 (N.Y. 1994).

46. *Id.*

47. *Id.*

48. *Newberger v. State*, 641 So.2d 419 (Fla. Dist. Ct. App. 1994).

49. *Id.*

50. *Burleson v. State*, 802 S.W.2d 429, 436–437 (Tex. Ct. App. 1991).

51. 18 U.S.C. § 1030 (5)(A),(B) (1995).

52. 18 U.S.C. § 1030 (6)(c)(3) (1995).

53. N.H. Rev. Stat. Ann. § 638:16 IV (1986).

54. N.M. Stat. Ann. § 30-45-2 F (Michie 1989).

55. *See, Commonwealth v. Gerulis*, 420 Pa. Super. 266, 616 A.2d 686 (Pa. Super. Ct. 1992).

56. Va. Code Ann. § 18.2-152.3 (Michie 1988).

57. *Id.*

58. *State v. Rowell*, 119 N.M. 710, 895 P.2d 232 (N.M. Ct. App. 1995).

59. *Id.*

60. *Id.*

61. *State v. Riley*, 121 Wash.2d 22, 846 P.2d 1365, 1371–1372 (Wash. 1993) (some of these convictions were overturned, however, because the search warrant violated the Fourth Amendment guarantee against unreasonable searches and seizures because it failed to specify the crime under investigation).

62. *People v. Casey*, 225 Ill. App. 3d 82, 587 N.E.2d 511 (1st Dist. 1992).

63. *Commonwealth v. Gerulis*, 420 Pa. Super. 266, 616 A.2d 686 (Pa. Super. Ct. 1992).

64. *People v. Gentry*, 234 Cal.App.3d 131 (Cal. Ct. App. 1991). The defendant was convicted under former Cal. Penal Code § 502 (West 1987), which prohibited intentional access for the purpose of devising or executing a scheme to defraud or extort or for the purpose of obtaining money, property, or services with false or fraudulent intent; the law changed in 1988 and added to the access provision the requirement of alteration, destruction, deletion, damage, or other use of data or a computer for the purpose of devising or executing a scheme to defraud or for the purpose of wrongfully controlling or obtaining money, property, or data.

65. *Id.*

66. *State v. Joyner*, 759 S.W.2d 422 (Tenn. Crim. App. 1987).

67. Mitch Betts and Gary H. Anthes, *FBI Nabs Notorious Hacker*, ComputerWorld, Feb. 20, 1995, at 4.

68. Charles Babcock, *A Hacker's Lines of Attack*, ComputerWorld, March 6, 1995, at 8.

69. Bruce Haring, *Computer Hackers' Biggest Backer*, USA Today, Sept. 14, 1995, at 8D; *The MacNeil Lehrer NewsHour*, October 4, 1995, Transcript #5368.

70. *United States v. Taylor*, 945 F.2d 1050 (8th Cir. 1991).

71. *Gordon v. State*, 206 Ga. App. 450, 425 S.E.2d 906 (Ga. Ct. App. 1992).

72. Fla. Stat. Ann. § 815.06 (West 1994).

73. Fla. Stat. Ann. § 815.06(2)(b) (West 1994).

74. S.C. Code Ann. § 16-16-20(3)(b)(i) (Law. Co-op. 1994).

75. *Commonwealth v. Gerulis*, 420 Pa. Super. 266, 616 A.2d 686, 694–695 (Pa. Super. Ct. 1992).

76. *See, e.g.*, Md. Crimes and Punishments Code Ann. § 146 (1992).

77. *See, e.g.*, Mo. Ann. Stat. § 569.095 (Vernon 1994).

78. Ga. Code Ann. § 16-9-93(e) (Michie 1992).

79. 18 U.S.C. § 1030(a)(6) (1995).

80. According to the Senate Report, "[t]he new subsection 1030(a)(6) to be created by the bill is a misdemeanor offense aimed at penalizing conduct associated with 'pirate bulletin boards,' where passwords are displayed that permit unauthorized access to others' computers. It will authorize prosecution of those who, knowingly and with intent to defraud, traffic in such computer passwords." S. Rep. No. 432, 99th Cong., 2d Sess. 13 (1986).

81. *See* H.R. Rep. No. 612, 99th Cong., 2d Sess. 7 (1986).

82. 18 U.S.C. § 1030(f) (1995).

PART VI
APPENDICES

31
Primer on Cryptography

Lorijean G. Oei

31.6 The Legal Status of Cryptography

Endnotes

31.1 Basic Concepts

31.1.1 Cryptography

Cryptography is the art and science of keeping communications secure.[1] *Cryptanalysis* is the art and science of defeating such security.[2] There are two kinds of cryptography; conventional or symmetric and public-key or asymmetric cryptography.

31.1.2 Encryption

Encryption is the process of disguising, that is, encrypting, a readable communication into an unintelligible scramble of characters according to some code or cipher. The readable communication is called *plaintext*. The encrypted communication is called *ciphertext*. *Decryption* is the process of converting the ciphertext back to its original, readable form.

Communications are encrypted according to some predetermined code or cipher. For example, a simple, albeit easily breakable, cipher is A = 1, B = 2, and so on, so that "2-21-25 6-15-18-20-25 19-8-1-18-5-19 15-6 2-12-21-5 3-8-9-16 9-14-3" is the ciphertext of "Buy forty shares of Blue Chip, Inc."

Modern encryption[3] does not rely upon such simple ciphers, but instead relies on algorithms. These algorithms are complex mathematical functions for converting plaintext to ciphertext and vice versa.

A person wishing to encrypt a communication uses special software or hardware that incorporates one of these algorithms.[4] The person must also supply certain variables. One variable is the communication itself. (A digital communication is, after all, a very long binary number, that is, a long string of zeros and ones.) Another variable is called a *key*. A key is also a long number. When the communication and the key are plugged into the encryption algorithm, the software or hardware executes the algorithm and the result is the encrypted communication.

The unique value of the key causes the algorithm to produce ciphertext that is different from the ciphertext that would result if the same electronic communication were encrypted using a different key. Similarly, the same key will produce different ciphertext if a different communication is encrypted.

31.1.3 How Is the Algorithm Applied?

Encryption algorithms are incorporated into software and hardware products.[5] The algorithms work in the background of most modern applications, and the end user is led through the necessary operation by a user-friendly interface.

31.1.4 Who Needs a Key?

Anyone who wants to send or receive encrypted communications must have a key. People as well as entities need a key. Computers and facsimile (fax) machines may even need keys. In many implementations of EDI, a computer will automatically solicit bids and place orders electronically if inventory is low. Some fax machines encrypt documents before they are sent.

A person or entity may have more than one key. A person may have one key for use when communicating in his or her capacity of vice president for an employer, another for use when in the capacity of treasurer of his or her homeowners' association, and another for personal business. Similarly, a business entity may have one key for general business purposes and others for each of its different departments.

31.1.5 Where Do You Get the Key?

In most cryptosystems, the software or hardware product that contains the encryption algorithm generates the key. The person who wants a key initiates the key-generation process by entering the appropriate commands on a computer keyboard, or, in the case of hardware, a special key pad or module.

For example, generating a key using Pretty Good Privacy (PGP), widely available encryption software, is a five-step process. A user:

1. Types the command to begin the key-generation process.
2. Enters a pass phrase that will protect the secret key while it is not being used. (A pass phrase is similar to a password, only longer.) PGP stores the secret key on the computer's hard drive, and the user must type the pass phrase every time he or she wants to use the key.
3. Selects the desired key size. The longer a key, the more secure it is. Longer keys, however, slow the encryption process.
4. Specifies a user ID to be associated with the key, such as the name of the person, company, or department that is to use the key.
5. Types some random text. The software measures the intervals between the user's keystrokes and uses these to derive large, random numbers from which the key is then generated.[6]

In some cryptosystems, however, the user selects the key, which is much like selecting a password. When a user selects a cryptographic key, it is important that he or she avoid choosing easily guessed keys such as common words, the name of a spouse, or birthdays. These types of keys are very insecure and susceptible to cryptanalytic attack.[7]

31.1.6 Where Do You Keep the Key?

Keys, because they are nothing more than very large numbers, can be stored as data on the hard drive of the user's computer. (It is a good idea not to store the key on a drive that others may access through a network connection.) Keys can also be stored on a floppy disk. In either case, they should be password or pass-phrase protected.

Keys can also be stored on a magnetic-stripe card, plastic key with an embedded ROM chip, or special smart card. A *smart card* is a plastic laminated card, about the size of a credit card, that contains a computer chip. The key and password are programmed into the chip. The contents of a smart card, unlike the contents of a hard drive or floppy disk, are not susceptible to direct copying. This makes it difficult for anyone to defeat the password protection and read the key. When a user wants to encrypt a communication, the user inserts the smart card into a special reader or built-in slot in the computer.

31.2 Conventional (Symmetric) Cryptography

In *conventional* or *symmetric cryptography,* a single key is used to encrypt and to decrypt a communication.[8] Both the sender and the recipient must have a copy of the same key. If the sender wants to send a message to a recipient and keep it confidential, the sender encrypts the communication using her copy of the key and transmits the encrypted communication to the recipient. When the recipient receives the communication, he decrypts it using his copy of the key, which transforms the ciphertext into readable plaintext.

Because only the sender and recipient have a copy of the key necessary to encrypt and decrypt the communication, the encrypted communication can be sent over an insecure network. It does not matter that someone has seen the communication along the way because it will appear as an unintelligible scramble.

31.2.1 Different Kinds of Conventional Cryptography

There are a number of different conventional cryptosystems. Each is based on a different algorithm. All, however, use a single key to encrypt and decrypt communications.

One such algorithm is the Data Encryption Standard (DES). DES is the current U.S. government standard.[9] The financial services industry depends heavily upon electronic funds transfers and uses DES to facilitate these transfers. It is an aging algorithm, however, having been designed by IBM with the help of the National Security Agency in 1975. DES is not considered to be secure. Its short 56-bit key has been broken through brute-force attacks, and one cryptanalyst has even developed a computer chip that can crack a DES key in an average of 3.5 hours.[10] It can, however, be very secure when implemented using a technique known as *triple encryption.*[11]

Another algorithm is the International Data Encryption Algorithm (IDEA).[12] IDEA is used in the Pretty Good Privacy (PGP) cryptosystem.[13]

31.2.2 The Problem with Symmetric Cryptosystems

For symmetric cryptography to work, the sender and recipient must generate, share, and store the key in secret and in advance. This is not realistic for electronic commerce for four reasons. First, electronic commerce is often conducted between parties who do not have an established relationship. Necessarily, they cannot agree on and share a key in advance.

Second, electronic commerce is conducted in real time. Having to exchange keys in advance eliminates this advantage of electronic commerce by introducing a time delay.

Third, electronic commerce is conducted over insecure networks, such as the Internet or over value-added networks of varying security. If the network is not sufficiently secure, so that the sender and recipient are not willing to send a plaintext message, they necessarily cannot communicate the secret key over this network. If anyone intercepts the key while it is in transit, that person can encrypt and decrypt messages using that key. Consequently, the sender and recipient must exchange keys through some secure channel. If the sender and recipient are in separate physical locations, they must trust a courier or some other secure transmission system to communicate the key. Sending key-carrying couriers around the globe is not practical for the average company that wants to use cryptography with distant trading partners or customers.

Fourth, a company would need to have a different key for each correspondent with whom it wished to exchange communications. Keeping track of a different key for each correspondent would be unmanageable. Although it may be possible to exchange keys in secret and in advance for small-scale communication among a limited number of trusted business partners and customers, it is not workable for electronic communications over open networks.

In addition, for symmetric cryptography to work, only the sender and the intended recipient may know the secret key. Both must trust each other to keep the key secure. Both parties must also trust each other not to repudiate a previously sent communication by claiming that the shared secret key was compromised so that anyone could have forged the communication.

Thus, conventional cryptography has serious key management problems.[14] A solution to these problems came in 1976 with the development of public key cryptography.[15]

31.3 Public-Key (Asymmetric) Cryptography

In *public-key cryptography,* a pair of complementary keys are used.[16] Each person who wishes to communicate securely has a key pair. One key is kept secret. This is the private key. The private key is never shared; consequently, the person who holds the private key is solely responsible for keeping it secure. This solves the problem that exists with conventional cryptography of having to trust someone else to keep the key secret.

The other key is shared with anyone with whom the person may want to communicate securely. This is the public key. The public key may be widely disseminated, because it is computationally infeasible to determine the private key even if a person knows the algorithm and the public key. Consequently, the public key can be shared across an open, insecure network. This solves the key distribution problem of conventional cryptography.[17]

Either of the two keys can be used to encrypt a communication, with the other key used to decrypt the communication. When a communication is encrypted using the public key, it can be decrypted only using the private key. Conversely, when a communication is encrypted using the private key, it can be decrypted only using the public key.

31.3.1 Different Kinds of Public-Key Cryptography

There are a number of different public-key cryptosystems. Each is based on a different algorithm. All, however, use a pair of keys to encrypt and decrypt communications.

One such algorithm is *RSA*, which is named after its inventors, Rivest, Shamir, and Adelman. Another is the *Digital Signature Algorithm* (DSA), which the government has adopted as a Federal Information Processing Standard for public-key encryption.[18] Despite the government's efforts, the industry has focused its attention and implementation efforts on RSA-based applications of public-key cryptography. One reason for this is that RSA can be used for both encryption and digital signatures, whereas DSA can be used only to create digital signatures.[19]

31.3.2 The Problem with Public-Key Cryptography

The algorithms used in public-key cryptography perform lengthy and complex mathematical calculations when they encrypt and decrypt communications. As a result of this "computational overhead," public-key cryptography is very slow, and the resulting files become unwieldy. A solution to these problems is to use a public-key algorithm in conjunction with another type of algorithm called a *hash function.*

31.4 Hash Function

A *hash function* is a function that takes a variable-length communication and converts it to a fixed-length string of characters, called a *hash value* or *checksum.*[20] If the function cannot be reversed to work backward from the hash value to the original communication, it is called a *message-digest function* or *one-way hash function,* and the result is called a *message digest.*[21] Examples of a few well-known hash functions are MD4, SHS, and Snefru.

A message digest has some useful qualities. A message digest concisely represents the communication from which it was computed. It is also unique to that communication. No two communications should have the same hash value. This makes it possible to substitute the message digest for the communication in certain cryptographic applications. For example, when the fixed-length message digest is used in place of the communication in public-key cryptography, this solves the computational overhead problem. It is much quicker to encrypt the message digest when the input, the message digest, is short because the computations are fewer. The resulting files are also necessarily shorter.

Another quality is that the contents of the communication or even the type of communication it is (e.g., letter, contract, or graphics) cannot be discerned from the message digest itself. This is useful because a message digest can be date/time stamped[22] without revealing the contents of the communication.[23] Because the message digest represents the communication, the result is the same as if the communication itself had been stamped.

When public-key cryptography and a hash function are used together, the technique is called a *digital signature*.[24] Digital signatures can be used to establish the authenticity and integrity of a communication and to prevent a sender from falsely denying that he or she sent a communication or any part of its contents as discussed in detail in Chapter 4.

31.5 Cryptosystems Can Be Broken

Cryptography is a tool, and like any tool, it has its limits. It is important to realize that cryptography is not a guarantee of absolute security. Cryptosystems can be broken through a cryptanalytic attack.

Cryptanalytic attacks may be directed either at the algorithm or at the key. In an attack on the algorithm, the cryptanalyst relies on the nature of the algorithm to try to deduce plaintext from ciphertext or to deduce the key. In an attack on the key, the cryptanalyst tries every possible key on a piece of ciphertext until one works to translate it into plaintext. Such an attack on the key is known as a *brute-force attack*. Recently, for example, the encrypted portion of a commercial transaction conducted using the export version of Netscape's World Wide Web browser was cracked using a brute-force attack. It took a French student eight days using 120 computer workstations, or approximately $10,000 worth of computing power, to crack the 40-bit key.[25]

Although this example illustrates that cryptography does not provide absolute security, it also illustrates the power of cryptography. The student expended substantial time, effort, and computing resources to decrypt a single message. Many messages will not be worth the effort. Unless a person independently knows or suspects that a message he or she has intercepted is valuable, the person would have to break many messages before finding one that contained valuable information. There are millions of messages passing through open networks. The small chance of "hitting paydirt" makes it very unlikely that any given message will be cracked. When based on tested algorithms and implemented using nonobvious keys of sufficient length, cryptography is very, very strong, and is capable of providing more than adequate security for most electronic commerce needs.

31.6 The Legal Status of Cryptography

There is currently no general prohibition on the use of encryption in the United States.[26] The federal government is trying, however, to control its use in part through export controls. Except for certain mass-marketed encryption products and products that use key lengths of 40 bits or less,[27] cryptography cannot be exported unless the State Department first issues a license permitting such export. In this way, the federal government is trying to slow the spread of strong encryption.

It is important to note, however, that these export controls have been interpreted to permit the export of encryption tools used for digital signatures and digital date/time stamping. It is only encryption designed to keep information confidential that is subject to export controls.[28]

The federal government is also trying to control the development and use of cryptography through its Capstone project. Capstone is the U.S. government's project to develop a set of standards for publicly available cryptography.[29] The Clipper Chip, designed for encrypting voice, fax, and low-speed data communications, and the Capstone chip, designed for encrypting digital communications necessary for secure electronic commerce, are the backbone of the government's controversial project. There are four functions the government seeks to establish as standards:

1. A data encryption algorithm known as *Skipjack;*
2. A digital signature algorithm known as DSA;
3. A public-key exchange protocol, as yet unspecified; and
4. A hash function known as *SHA.*

While DSA and SHA have been approved as the standards for use by the federal government and its contractors,[30] widespread criticism from the computer industry, Internet community, and civil libertarians[31] have caused the government to abandon its original approach of trying to make these de facto commercial standards as well.

The criticism stemmed from the practical concerns raised by the fact that Skipjack is classified. First was a concern about how secure it is. The best way to test how secure an encryption algorithm is, is to try to break it. When an encryption algorithm withstands attacks by cryptanalysts, confidence in its strength grows. Necessarily, before an encryption algorithm may be subjected to such cryptanalysis, it must be disclosed. Skipjack, however, is being kept secret. The government had disclosed Skipjack only to a small group of independent cryptographers who tested it at the government's invitation. This group believes it to be secure, but has stopped short of making a definitive conclusion because its study was too limited.

Second was the concern that Skipjack cannot be implemented in software which would necessarily require that Skipjack be disclosed. This means that Skipjack must be hardware-based and programmed into a computer chip known as the *Clipper Chip.* Only government-authorized manufacturers to whom Skipjack was disclosed could produce the Clipper Chip.

Third was the concern that the private encryption key was to be held not only by its user, but also by one or more escrow agents. The intent behind key escrow is to balance the needs of the public for secure communications and of law enforcement for access to the communications of suspected criminals. The idea is that each person who wants to communicate confidentially would have and use a key pair, just as in any public-key cryptosystem. If, however, law enforcement had probable cause to suspect that someone was engaged in illegal activity, upon securing and presenting a warrant to the escrow agents, law enforcement would be given access to the key necessary to decrypt the communication. The private key is divided in two parts, with each part held by a different escrow agent. Both parts would be required in order to decrypt a communication, in much the same way that a safe deposit box requires both the box holder's and the bank's keys to be opened. The key is divided to make it more secure. It is more difficult for someone to trick or bribe two people into disclosing the private key than it is to trick or bribe one. Despite the split-key precaution, many did not trust the government to hold these keys securely or to avoid abuse of them.[32]

In part in response to public criticism and outcry, the government has now proposed a new key encryption standard that would not rely on Skipjack and the Clipper Chip but on existing encryption algorithms and would permit users to generate and store their own keys and to choose their own escrow agents provided that such agents can be served with a search warrant. To help ensure that the computer industry will build software with the key escrow capabilities that the government wants, the government is proposing to grant export licenses for such products which may use a 56-bit key, rather than a 40-bit key which is the maximum key length that may now be exported. The industry has rebuffed the proposal and pejoratively dubbed it "Clipper II" and "son of Clipper."[33]

Despite the efforts of the federal government to control the use of cryptography, its use is moving into the mainstream of global electronic commerce, and many are using cryptographic products based on algorithms other than those advanced by the government. It is doubtful that the government will be able to slow or change the direction of this commerce-driven momentum.

Endnotes

1. Bruce Schneier, *Applied Cryptography: Protocols, Algorithms and Source Code in C* 1 (2d ed. 1996) [hereinafter *Applied Cryptography*].

2. *Applied Cryptography* 1.

3. For an introduction to modern cryptography, see R. L. Rivest, *Cryptography in Handbook of Theoretical Computer Science* (1990). For a history of cryptography, see David Kahn, *The Codebreakers: The Story of Secret Writing* (1967).

4. *See Applied Cryptography* 223–25.

5. *See Applied Cryptography* 223–25.

6. Philip Zimmermann, *The Official PGP User's Guide* 21–22 (1995).

7. *See Applied Cryptography* 171–73.

8. *Applied Cryptography* 4; Paul Fahn, *RSA's Frequently Asked Questions About Today's Cryptography* (May 5, 1995).

9. National Institute of Standards and Technology, FIPS Publication 46-1: Data Encryption Standard (Jan. 22, 1988).

10. *See* Philip Zimmermann, *The Official PGP User's Guide* 76 (1995). It would cost $1 million to build a computer that could break a DES key in 3.5 hours. A significant price tag, no doubt, but well within the budget of a large corporation or government bent on espionage.

11. *See* Philip Zimmermann, *The Official PGP User's Guide* 76–77 (1995).

12. X. Lai & J. L. Massey, *A Proposal for a New Block Encryption Standard*, Advances in Cryptology: Eurocrypt '90, 389-404 (1991).

13. Philip Zimmermann, *The Official PGP User's Guide* 77–78 (1995).

14. *Applied Cryptography* 29.

15. Whitfield Diffie & Martin E. Hellman, *New Directions in Cryptography*, IT-22 IEEE Transactions on Information Theory 644–54 (1976).

16. *Applied Cryptography* 31–32.

17. *Applied Cryptography* 31–32.

18. National Institute of Standards and Technology, FIPS Publication 186 (effective Dec. 1, 1994).

19. *Applied Cryptography* 17. For discussion of digital signatures, see Chapter 4.

20. *Applied Cryptography* 30; Paul Fahn, *RSA's Frequently Asked Questions About Today's Cryptography* (May 9, 1995).

21. *See Applied Cryptography* 30; Paul Fahn, *RSA's Frequently Asked Questions About Today's Cryptography* (May 9, 1995).

22. Date/time stamping is discussed in Chapter 4.

23. *See* Paul Fahn, *RSA's Frequently Asked Questions About Today's Cryptography* (May 9, 1995).

24. For a discussion of digital signatures, see Chapter 4.

25. Tom Abate, *Student Cracks Netscape Code: Firm Downplays Frenchman's Stunt*, The San Francisco Examiner, Aug. 17, 1995, at B1.

26. There are certain limited prohibitions. Federal law prohibits disclosure of information about governmental cryptography. *See* 18 U.S.C.A. § 798 (1976 & Supp. 1995). The Federal Communications Commission's regulations prohibit use of encryption for amateur radio communications. 47 C.F.R. § 97.113(a)(4) (1994).

27. Note that a computer capable of trying one million keys per microsecond can defeat a 56-bit key in approximately ten hours. William Stallings, *Protect Your Privacy: A Guide for PGP Users* 14 (Table 2.1) (1995).

28. *See* International Traffic in Arms Regulations, 22 C.F.R. §121.1(vi)(1995). For a discussion of export controls, see Chapter 25.

29. The Capstone project was authorized by the Computer Security Act of 1987, Pub. L. No. 100-235, 101 Stat. 1724 (codified as amended in scattered sections of 15 U.S.C. and 40 U.S.C.). Paul Fahn, *Capstone, Clipper and DSS* in *RSA's Frequently Asked Questions About Today's Cryptography* (May 5, 1995).

30. *See* Federal Information Processing Standard (FIPS) Publication 186 (DSA); FIPS Publication 180 (SHA).

31. For a discussion of constitutional issues raised by key escrow, *see* Michael Froomkin, *The Metaphor Is the Key: Cryptography, the Clipper Chip, and the Constitution*, 143 U. Penn. L. Rev. 709 (1995).

32. *See* Michael Froomkin, *The Metaphor Is the Key: Cryptography, the Clipper Chip, and the Constitution*, 143 U. Penn. L. Rev. 709 (1995).

33. The government's proposal and related commentary and materials can be found at http://www.epic.org.

32
Glossary

Adaptation Right. The *adaptation right* refers to the exclusive right granted to the owner of a copyright to prepare derivative works of the work in which he or she owns the copyright. 17 U.S.C. § 106(2). (See Section 10.2.) See also Derivative Works.

Article 4A. *Article 4A* refers to the section of the Uniform Commercial Code that defines the rights and obligations that arise in connection with nonconsumer electronic funds transfers.

Assign, Assignment. An *assignment* is the transfer or sale of property or of rights granted by a contract. For example, if a user licenses the right to use content from the copyright owner, and then transfers his or her right to use the content (granted in the license agreement) to another person, he or she will have *assigned* the license agreement.

Asymmetric Cryptography. *See* Public-Key Cryptography.

Audiovisual Works. *Audiovisual works* are copyrightable works that consist of a series of related images that are intrinsically intended to be shown by the use of machines or devices such as projectors, viewers, or electronic equipment, together with accompanying sounds, if any, regardless of the nature of the material objects, such as films or tapes, in which the works are embodied. 17 U.S.C. § 101.

Authenticity, Authentication. *Authenticity* refers to the business and legal requirement that a recipient of an electronic communication be able to ascertain or establish that the communication comes from the purported source and is what it purports to be.

Brute-force Attack. A *brute-force attack* is a type of cryptanalytic attack in which all possible keys are tried until one decrypts the ciphertext.

507

CA.   *See* Certification Authority.

CD-ROM.   Acronym for *Compact Disc Read-Only Memory*.

Certificate.   A *certificate* is a computer-based record that documents that a particular public key belongs to an identified person. A certificate is issued by a certification authority after that authority has ascertained the identity of the person, called a *subscriber*. The certificate usually includes the following information: (1) the name of the certification authority issuing it, (2) the name of the subscriber, (3) the subscriber's public key, and (4) the digital signature of the certification authority.

Certificate Revocation List (CRL).   A *certificate revocation list*, or *CRL*, is a list of certificates that have been revoked by the issuing certification authority. A CRL is maintained by the certification authority and lists only certificates issued by that certification authority.

Certification Authority (CA).   A *certification authority* is a person or entity that ascertains the identity of a person and issues a computer-based record known as a *certificate* that associates that person with a public-private key pair used to create digital signatures (see Section 4.2).

Checksum.   *See* Hash Value.

Child Pornography.   *Child pornography* is any visual depiction involving the use of a minor (usually under the ages of eighteen) engaging in sexually explicit conduct. Child pornography is illegal and is not protected under the First Amendment (see Section 20.3).

Ciphertext.   *Ciphertext* is the encrypted version of a communication.

CISG.   The term *CISG* refers to the United Nations Convention on Contracts for the International Sale of Goods, which is a multinational convention governing transactions in sales of goods between parties who have places of business in different countries. The Convention was prepared by the United Nations Commission on International Trade Law (UNCITRAL).

Collective Work.   A *collective work* is a copyrightable work, such as a periodical issue, anthology, or encyclopedia, in which a number of contributions, constituting separate and interdependent works in themselves, are assembled into a collective whole. 17 U.S.C. § 101.

Commission on New Technological Uses of Copyrighted Works.   This commission was established by Congress on December 31, 1974, to analyze the impact of the computer on copyrighted works. This commission, generally referred to as *CONTU*, collected data and held hearings over a period of three years. On July 31, 1978, it issued its final report, entitled *Final Report of the National Commission on New Technological Uses of Copyrighted Works, 1978*. In this report CONTU recommended amendments to the Copyright Act designed to deal with the issues raised by software. CONTU's recommendations were enacted with minor modifications in the Computer Software Copyright Act of 1980.

Common Law.   *Common law* is the law established through the decisions of our courts. It is to be distinguished from statutory laws enacted by the Congress or state legislatures.

Compact Disc Read-Only Memory.   *Compact disc read-only memory* (or *CD-ROM*), is 4.75-inch laser-encoded optical memory storage medium similar in appearance to compact audio discs. CD-ROMs can hold about 550 megabytes of data.

Compilation.   A *compilation* is a copyrightable work formed by the collection and assembling of preexisting materials or of data that is selected, coordinated, or arranged in such a way that the resulting work as a whole constitutes an original work of authorship. The term *compilation* includes collective works. 17 U.S.C. § 101 (see Section 9.3).

Computer Fraud and Abuse Act (CFAA).   The prime federal statute to combat "hacking" and "computer crime," the *CFAA* prohibits users from gaining unauthorized access to, exceeding authorized access to, and damaging, altering, or destroying information on certain computers. Computers covered by the CFAA include those used by or for the government, financial institutions, credit card issuers, and consumer reporting agencies as well as those used in interstate commerce (computers in two different states) (see Chapter 30).

Computer Program.   Under the Copyright Act, a *computer program* is defined as "a set of statements or instructions to be used directly or indirectly in a computer in order to bring about a certain result." 17 U.S.C. § 101.

Confidentiality Agreement.   A *confidentiality agreement* is an agreement that secret information disclosed by its owner to an individual or organization will be kept confidential and not disclosed to anyone else. This agreement is a binding contract that places the person to whom the information has been disclosed under a legal obligation not to use the information in a manner not authorized by its owner, and not to disclose the information to anyone else.

Content.   The term *content* is used to refer to the various types of data that can be displayed by a computer, such as text, sound, images, photographs, and motion pictures. Content should be contrasted with *software*, which is the set of computer programs used to make the content available to the user.

CONTU.   *See* Commission on New Technological Uses of Copyrighted Works.

Conventional Cryptography.   *Conventional cryptography*, also known as *symmetric cryptography*, refers to a type of cryptography in which the same key is used both to encrypt and to decrypt communications.

Copy.   A *copy*, as that term is used in the Copyright Act, is any material object, other than phonorecords, in which a work is fixed by any method now known or later developed, and from which the work can be perceived, reproduced, or otherwise communicated, either directly or with the aid of a machine or device. 17 U.S.C. § 101. *See also* Phonorecord.

Copyright.   *Copyright* is the exclusive right granted "to authors" under the U.S. Copyright Act to copy, adapt, distribute, publicly perform, and publicly display their works of authorship, such as literary works, databases, musical works, sound recordings, photographs and other still images, and motion pictures and other audiovisual works. Copyright is further explained in Chapters 9, 10, and 11.

Copyright Act of 1909.   The *Copyright Act of 1909* was the statute that governed copyright protection for works created between 1909 and December 31, 1977. On January 1, 1978, the Copyright Act of 1909 was superseded by the provisions of the current Copyright Act, known as the *Copyright Act of 1976*.

Copyright Act of 1976.   The *Copyright Act of 1976* is the current statute governing copyright protection for works of authorship. It became effective on January 1, 1978, and can be found at 17 U.S.C. § 101 *et seq.*

Creation.   A copyrightable work is *created* when it is fixed in a copy or phonorecord for the first time; where a work is prepared over a period of time, the portion of it that has been fixed at any particular time constitutes the work as of that time, and where the work has been prepared in different versions, each version constitutes a separate work. 17 U.S.C. § 101.

CRL.   *See* Certificate Revocation List (CRL).

Cryptanalysis.   *Cryptanalysis* is the art and science of defeating encrypted communications.

Cryptography.   *Cryptography* is the art and science of keeping communications secure.

Cyberspace.   The term *Cyberspace* was originally coined by science fiction author William Gibson in his novel *Neuromancer* (Ace Books, 1984), to refer to the virtual world created by a computer system. The term *Cyberspace* is currently used to refer to the world of electronic communications over computer networks.

Data Encryption Standard (DES).   See DES.

Date/Time Stamp.   To *date/time stamp* means to append or attach to a communication, digital signature, or certificate a digitally signed notation indicating at least the date, time, and identity of the person appending or attaching the notation. A *date/time stamp* also refers to the notation thus appended or attached.

Decryption.   *Decryption* is the process of converting ciphertext back to its original, readable form.

Defamation. *Defamation* is any communication that is false and injurious to the reputation of another. Defamation can take two forms: (1) *libel*, which is written and visual defamation, and (2) slander, which is oral and aural defamation (see Chapter 21).

Defendant. The *defendant* is the individual or business entity being sued in a lawsuit.

Derivative Works. As defined in the Copyright Act, "a *derivative work* is a copyrightable work based upon one or more preexisting works, such as a translation, musical arrangement, dramatization, fictionalization, motion picture version, sound recording, art reproduction, abridgment, condensation, or any other form in which a work may be recast, transformed, or adapted. A work consisting of editorial revisions, annotations, elaborations, or other modifications which, as a whole, represent an original work of authorship is a derivative work." 17 U.S.C. § 101. For example, a movie based on a book is a derivative work of the book, a French translation of an English novel is a derivative work, and a sound recording of a copyrightable musical work is a derivative work (see Section 10.2).

DES. *DES*, also known as *Data Encryption Standard*, is a conventional encryption algorithm.

Digital Content. The term *digital content* is used to refer to any information that is published or distributed in a digital form, including text, data, sound recordings, photographs and images, motion pictures, and software.

Digital Signature. A *digital signature* is a transformation of a communication using a public-key cryptosystem such that a person having the communication and the signer's public key can accurately determine (1) whether the transformation was created using the private key that corresponds to the signer's public key, and (2) whether the communication has been altered since the transformation was made.

Digital Signature Algorithm (DSA). *See* DSA.

Digital Signature Guidelines. *Digital Signature Guidelines* refers to a publication of the Information Security Committee, Electronic Commerce and Information Technology Division, Section of Science and Technology of the American Bar Association, which sets forth a set of general, abstract statements of principle intended to serve as long-term, unifying foundations for the development of sound law and practice regarding digital signatures. The *Digital Signature Guidelines* were released in draft form for comment on October 5, 1995. Release of the final version is expected in 1996.

Digital Signature Verification. *Digital signature verification* is the process of checking a digital signature by reference to the original communication and a public key, and thereby determining whether the digital signature was created for that same communication using the private key that corresponds to the referenced public key.

Display. To *display* a copyrighted work means to show an original work or a copy of it, either directly or by means of a film, slide, television image, or any other device or process or, in the case of a motion picture or audiovisual work, to show individual images nonsequentially. 17 U.S.C. § 101.

Distribution Right. The term *distribution right* refers to the exclusive right granted to the owner of a copyright to distribute copies of his or her copyrighted work publicly by sale, rental, lease, or lending (see Section 10.3) 17 U.S.C. § 106(3).

Domain Name. A *domain name* is a mnemonic corresponding to a numeric Internet network address that uniquely identifies a host computer on the Internet.

DSA. *DSA*, also known as the *Digital Signature Algorithm*, is an algorithm approved as a U.S. government standard for use in generating and verifying digital signatures using public-key cryptography.

ECPA. *See* Electronic Communications Privacy Act (ECPA).

EDI. *See* Electronic Data Interchange (EDI).

EFT. *See* Electronic Funds Transfer (EFT).

Electronic Commerce. *Electronic commerce* refers to the end-to-end, all electronic performance of business activities. Electronic commerce includes EDI, but it also includes the use of electronic mail, electronic transfer of digital content, electronic purchasing and payments, and the business process re-engineering necessary to implement the broad capabilities of online technology.

Electronic Communications Privacy Act (ECPA). The *ECPA*, a federal statute, prohibits a third party from intercepting or disclosing electronic communications as well as unauthorized access to, and disclosure of, stored electronic communications, which include e-mail, voice mail, fax, cordless phone, and cellular phone communications. It applies to both government and private citizens and imposes both criminal and civil penalties (see Sections 17.4, 26.2.2, and 30.2.3).

Electronic Data Interchange (EDI). *Electronic data interchange* (or *EDI*), refers to the online exchange of routine business transactions in a computer-processable format, covering such traditional applications as inquiries, purchasing, acknowledgments, pricing, order status, scheduling, test results, shipping and receiving, invoices, payments, and financial reporting. The data is exchanged directly between computers, utilizing standardized formats, so that the data can be implemented directly by the receiving computer. EDI is used in a wide variety of business contexts, including transactions involving sales of goods and services, insurance claims processing, tax filings, and exchanges of inventory information.

Electronic Funds Transfer (EFT). An *electronic funds transfer* refers to the series of electronically communicated transactions, beginning with the payment order of the originator (such as a buyer making payment to a seller), made for the purpose of making payment to the beneficiary of the payment order (such as the seller).

Electronic Mail.   *Electronic mail* (or *e-mail*) is the computer-to-computer exchange of messages, usually written in free text, rather than a structured format.

Electronic Mail Policy.   An *electronic mail policy* is a policy statement issued by an employer to its employees outlining the business purpose of the company electronic mail system, the scope of the employer's right to monitor e-mail messages, and guidelines for proper usage. Such policies are a key means of reducing an employer's potential liability stemming from employee-initiated lawsuits and third-party lawsuits based on an employee's copyright infringement, defamation, and other related claims based on an employee's use of e-mail (see Chapter 26).

E-Mail.   *See* Electronic Mail.

Encryption.   *Encryption* refers to the process of disguising a readable communication into an unintelligible scramble of characters according to some code or cipher.

Fixed.   A copyrightable work is *fixed* in a tangible medium of expression when its embodiment in a copy or phonorecord, by or under the authority of the author, is sufficiently permanent or stable to permit it to be perceived, reproduced, or otherwise communicated for a period of more than transitory duration. A work consisting of sounds, images, or both, that are being transmitted, is fixed if a fixation of the work is being made simultaneously with its transmission. 17 U.S.C. § 101.

Harmonized Tariff Schedules.   *Harmonized Tariff Schedules* are a collection of lists of rates of duty, country of origin, and treaty information for different types of commodities that govern customs duties and tariffs.

Hash Function.   A *hash function* is an algorithm mapping or translating one sequence of bits into another, generally smaller set (the hash value) such that (1) a communication yields the same hash result every time the algorithm is executed using the same communication as input, (2) it is computationally infeasible that a communication can be derived or reconstituted from the hash result produced by the algorithm, and (3) it is computationally infeasible that two communications can be found that produce the same hash result using the algorithm. Hash functions are also referred to as *one-way hash functions* or *message digest algorithms.*

Hash Value.   A *hash value* is the output produced by a hash function upon processing a communication. A hash value may also be referred to as a *hash result, message digest, manipulation detection code, integrity check value,* or *checksum.*

H. R. Rep. No. 94-1476.   This refers to the U.S. House of Representatives' *Report on the Copyright Act of 1976,* dated September 3, 1976. This document is, in essence, the legislative history of the current Copyright Act, and is frequently referred to by courts seeking to interpret the various provisions of the Copyright Act.

HTML.   *See* Hypertext Markup Language.

Hypertext Markup Language. Hypertext markup language (often referred to as HTML) is the coding language used to create hypertext documents for use on the World Wide Web. HTML looks a lot like typesetting code, where a block of text is surrounded by codes indicating how the text should appear on a computer screen. HTML also allows linking to another file on another computer on the Internet. HTML files are meant to be viewed using a World Wide Web browser, such as Netscape or Mosaic.

IDEA. *IDEA*, also known as the *International Data Encryption Algorithm*, is a conventional encryption algorithm.

Indecent Materials. *Indecent materials* are sexually explicit materials that are not obscene (*see also* Obscenity). Indecent materials are legal and protected by the First Amendment, but they may be regulated (see Section 20.4).

Indemnification. An *indemnification* agreement is an undertaking by one party to reimburse a second party for payments that the second party is required to make to a third party. An insurance policy is a classic example of an indemnity agreement. The indemnity clause typically found in a license agreement obligates the copyright owner to indemnify the licensee for any loss or expense incurred by the licensee as a result of a lawsuit filed by a third party against the licensee over ownership of the content.

Information Security. *Information security* refers to measures that a business can take to protect information itself while it is passing through an outside network or while it resides on a computer system beyond the business's control. Examples include digital signatures and encryption.

Infringement. The concept of *infringement* arises in patent, copyright, or trademark law. When someone copies software without permission of the copyright or patent owner, or uses a trademark without the permission of the trademark owner, he or she has committed an act of infringement, that is, he or she has infringed on the rights of the copyright, patent, and/or trademark owner.

Injunction. An *injunction* is a court order directing a party to a lawsuit to do or refrain from doing something.

Intangible Asset. An *intangible asset* is a property right having no physical substance, such as patent rights, copyrights, trademark rights, and trade secret rights.

Integrity. *Integrity* refers to the business and legal requirement that a party be able to verify that a communication or record has not been changed while in transit or storage.

Integrity Check Value. *See* Hash Value.

International Data Encryption Algorithms. *See* IDEA.

Internet.   The *Internet* is a worldwide network of networks, made up of approximately 7 million computers interconnected through 60,000 networks, all sharing a common communications technology. It is decentralized in that there is no central hub through which information must be routed and no central governing body. Started as a project by the Department of Defense, the Internet has expanded to include universities, government agencies, and commercial enterprises. There are currently over 25 million users worldwide accessing the Internet, and the numbers are growing exponentially. Users of the Internet can access such services as e-mail, usenet use group, file exchanges, and the World Wide Web, a distributed hypertext information service, accessed using a Web browser.

Key.   A *key* is a secret value used in an encryption algorithm. A key may consist of letters and numbers, alphanumeric characters, printable characters, or ASCII characters. The key may be known by one or both of the communicating parties. It is analogous to a combination number for a safe.

Key Management.   *Key management* is the process by which keys are generated, distributed, used, stored, updated, and destroyed. Key management is a significant vulnerability of cryptography.

Key Pair.   In public-key cryptography, a *key pair* is a private key and its corresponding public key, having the property that the public key can decrypt ciphertext that was encrypted using the private key and vice versa.

Libel.   *See* Defamation.

Licensee.   The *licensee* is the party who acquires permission to exercise certain rights in software or content, subject to the terms and conditions imposed by the licensor, in a license agreement. A licensee obtains no ownership rights in the copy of the content that he or she receives.

Licensor.   The *licensor* is the party who grants to another certain limited rights to possess and use software or content.

Literary Works.   *Literary works* are works, other than audiovisual works, expressed in words, numbers, or other verbal or numerical symbols or indicia, regardless of the nature of the material objects, such as books, periodicals, manuscripts, phonorecords, film, tapes, disks, or cards, in which they are embodied. 17 U.S.C. § 101.

Manipulation Detection Code.   *See* Hash Value.

Message Digest.   A *message digest* is a condensation or summary of a communication in the form of a fixed-length, unintelligible string of characters that results from applying a hash function to a variable-length communication. A message digest is unique to the communication on which it is based. Because the message digest is derived from the variable-length communication, a change in that communication will result in a change to the resulting message digest.

MIDI Files. *Musical instrument digital interface files,* or *MIDI files,* are computer files that contain instructions controlling how and when devices such as digital synthesizers produce sound. They can be stored in a digital form on computer-readable media such as disks and CD-ROMs and later recalled to play back the music work that is the subject of the MIDI recording.

Misappropriation. *Misappropriation* refers to the theft or other improper use or disclosure of the trade secrets of one party by another.

Moral Rights. *Moral rights* are a form of copyright rights granted to the author. These generally include the right to prevent distortion, mutilation, or destruction of the work (right of integrity); the right to attribution and the right against misattribution, and to prevent others from using the work or the author's name in such a way as to prejudice the author's professional standing (right of attribution); the right to control the work's publication (right of disclosure); and the right to withdraw, modify, or disavow a work after it has been published (right of withdrawal).

Morphing. *Morphing* (short for *metamorphosis*) is a process that involves a transition of two documents (such as pictures) into a third; a dynamic blending of two still images creating a sequence of in-between images that, when played back rapidly, metamorphose the first image into the last.

MPEP. Manual of Patent Examining Procedure.

Musical Works. A *musical work* is a copyrightable work of authorship that typically consists of a musical composition (that is, the notes) and, in some cases, corresponding lyrics.

Nexus. *Nexus* refers to the requirement imposed by the Due Process and Commerce Clauses of the U.S. Constitution that there be a certain connection between a taxpayer and a taxing authority before the taxpayer can be subject to the taxing authority's power.

Nonrepudiation. *Nonrepudiation* means that a party to a communication cannot falsely deny having sent the communication or its contents or disclaim a duty or obligation imposed by that communication.

Obscenity. *Obscene* material is any material that, when considered as a whole, has as its dominant theme or purpose an appeal to the prurient interest in sex, as judged by community standards; describes or depicts in a patently offensive way conduct specifically defined by the applicable state law; and lacks serious literary, artistic, political, or scientific value. Obscenity is generally illegal and is not protected under the First Amendment (see Chapter 20).

One-way Function. *See* Hash Function.

Patent. A *patent* is a grant of exclusive rights issued by the U.S. Patent Office that gives an inventor a 20-year monopoly on the right to "practice" or make, use, and sell his or her invention.

Payment Order. A *payment order* is an instruction of a sender to a receiving bank, transmitted orally, electronically, or in writing, to pay, or to cause another bank to pay, a fixed or determinable amount of money to a beneficiary if (1) the instruction does not state a condition to payment to the beneficiary other than time of payment, (2) the receiving bank is to be reimbursed by debiting an account of, or otherwise receiving payment from, the sender, and (3) the instruction is transmitted by the sender directly to the receiving bank or to an agent, funds-transfer system, or communication system for transmittal to the receiving bank.

Permanent Injunction. An *injunction* issued by the court at the conclusion of a lawsuit. *See* Injunction and Preliminary Injunction.

Phonorecord. *Phonorecords* are material objects in which sounds, other than those accompanying a motion picture or other audiovisual work, are fixed by any method now known or later developed, and from which the sounds can be perceived, reproduced, or otherwise communicated, either directly or with the aid of a machine or device. 17 U.S.C. § 101. Thus, a compact disc is a phonorecord.

Plaintext. *Plaintext* is the readable form of a communication.

Plaintiff. The *plaintiff* is the person who brings suit against someone, the defendant, whom the plaintiff believes is responsible for doing him or her harm.

Preliminary Injunction. A *preliminary injunction* is a temporary injunction entered at the beginning or during the course of a lawsuit that lasts only until a trial is held and a decision reached. Its purpose is to preserve the status quo pending the conclusion of the lawsuit. The preliminary injunction will either be terminated or converted into a permanent injunction after the trial is over.

***Prima Facie* Case.** A *prima facie case* is evidence introduced during the trial of a lawsuit that, if unrebutted, would entitle the person having the burden of proof to the relief he or she is seeking. Stated another way, it is enough evidence to require the opponent to introduce evidence in his or her defense or risk losing the case.

Private Key. In public-key cryptography a *private key* is the key of a key pair kept secret by its holder and used to create a digital signature.

Product Disparagement. *Product disparagement*, also known as *trade libel,* is a statement about a competitor's goods that is false or misleading and that is made to influence others not to buy the competitor's goods (see Section 28.3).

PTO. U.S. Patent & Trademark Office.

Public Display Right. The term *public display right* refers to the exclusive right granted to the owner of a copyright to display (and to authorize others to display) his or her work publicly. 17 U.S.C. § 106(5).

Public Key.   In public-key cryptography a *public key* is the key of a key pair publicly disclosed by the holder of the corresponding private key and used by the recipient of a digitally signed message from that person to verify the digital signature.

Public-Key Cryptography.   *Public-key cryptography* is a form of cryptography in which two keys are used: one to encrypt a message and the other to decrypt the message. One key is kept secret, and the other is made available to recipients of encrypted communications. Public-key cryptography generally can be used to encrypt data and to attach a digital signature to a communication.

Public Performance Right.   The term *public performance right* refers to the exclusive right granted to the owner of a copyright to perform (and to authorize others to perform) his or her work publicly. 17 U.S.C. § 106(4).

Public-Private Key Pair.   *See* Key Pair.

Published, Publication.   *Publication*, under the Copyright Act, is the distribution of copies of a copyrighted work to the public by sale or other transfer of ownership, or by rental, lease, or lending. The offering to distribute copies to a group of persons for purposes of further distribution, public performance, or public display also constitutes publication. A public performance or display of a work does not of itself constitute publication. 17 U.S.C. § 101.

Repository.   A *repository* is a system for storing and retrieving certificates or other information relevant to digital signatures.

Reproduction Right.   The term *reproduction right* refers to the exclusive right granted to the owner of a copyright to make (and authorize others to make) copies of his or her work. 17 U.S.C. § 106(1).

Residence Jurisdiction.   *Residence jurisdiction* refers to the basis on which a taxing authority relies in imposing tax on its residents.

RSA.   *RSA* is a public-key encryption algorithm named after its inventors—Rivest, Shamir, and Adelman.

Sales Tax.   *Sales tax* refers to a tax imposed by states on the sale of tangible personal property and services. Sales tax is imposed on intrastate transactions in which the goods or services are acquired and destined for use in the same state.

Sampling.   *Sampling* is the conversion of analog sound waves into a digital code. The digital code that describes the sampled music can then be reused, manipulated, or combined with other digitized or recorded sounds using a machine with digital dataprocessing capabilities, such as a computerized synthesizer. Sampling also refers to the process of copying a portion of a sound recording in a digital form for subsequent editing and/or incorporation in a new work.

Scan. *Scanning* is the process by which an image (such as a photograph, drawing, or text) is digitized—that is, converted into a digital form. The resulting digital image is also called a *scan.*

Secondary Meaning. *Secondary meaning* is a trademark term that refers to a mark that is initially merely descriptive but that over time acquires a meaning over and above the meaning ordinarily ascribed to it (see Section 13.3.2).

Shrinkwrap License. Technically, a *shrinkwrap license* is a software license agreement that appears on the outside of a software package, visible through the clear plastic shrinkwrap covering the package, that states that the user is deemed to accept the terms of the license by opening the package or using the software. More broadly, this term is often used to refer to any license contract that purports to be accepted by conduct such as opening a package or using the item.

Signed, Signature. *Signed* or *Signature* refers to any symbol made or adopted with an intention, actual or apparent, to authenticate the writing as that of the signer. U.C.C. § 1-201(39).

Slander. *See* Defamation.

Smart Card. A *smart card* is a plastic laminated card, similar in appearance to a credit card, that contains a computer chip. Smart cards can be used to generate and/or store passwords and encryption keys.

Software. *See* Computer Program.

Sound Recordings. *Sound recordings* are copyrightable works that result from the fixation of a series of musical, spoken, or other sounds, regardless of the nature of the physical medium, such as disks or tapes, in which they are embodied. 17 U.S.C. § 101. However, the soundtrack of a motion picture is not considered a sound recording, but rather is considered to be part of the copyright in the motion picture.

Source Jurisdiction. *Source jurisdiction* refers to the basis on which a taxing body relies in imposing tax on income that has its source within the taxing authority's geographic borders.

Statute of Frauds. The term *Statute of Frauds* is a common designation for statutes that have been adopted in nearly all states of the United States and provide that certain classes of contracts cannot be enforced in court unless they are documented in writing and signed by the party against whom the contract is sought to be enforced.

Statutory Damages. In situations where the plaintiff is unable to prove the actual damages that he or she sustained as a result of the wrongful acts of the defendant, some statutes allow a court to award what are called *statutory damages* in any event. One such statute is the Copyright Act, which provides that the plaintiff may recover between $500 and $100,000 for each copyrighted work infringed by the defendant, regardless of whether he or she is able to prove in court that he or she has actually been damaged. 17 U.S.C. § 504.

Subscriber.   A *subscriber* is a person who is identified in a certificate and who holds a private key that corresponds to a public key listed in the certificate.

Symmetric Cryptography.   *See* Conventional Cryptography.

System Security.   *System security* refers to the measures that a business can take to protect its computer systems and the records and other information they contain from attack from outside (e.g., hackers, viruses, and natural disasters) and inside (e.g., disgruntled, dishonest, or snooping employees).

Tangible Personal Property.   *Tangible personal property* refers to any personal property that may be seen, weighed, felt, touched, or otherwise perceived by the senses.

Temporary Restraining Order.   A *temporary restraining order* is an injunction issued by the court for a very short period of time (usually no more than 10 days) in order to prevent some immediate harm from occurring before the court can have a hearing on a motion for a preliminary injunction. For example, if a defendant in a lawsuit is about to destroy the only copy of the source code for software over which the ownership was in dispute, a court might issue a temporary order prohibiting such destruction for 10 days until it had time to hold a hearing into the dispute.

Time Stamp.   *See* Date/Time Stamp.

TMEP.   Trademark Manual of Examining Procedure.

Tort.   A *tort* is a wrong for which the injured person has a right to recover damages under the common law. Examples include negligence, fraud, theft, and defamation.

Trade Libel.   *See* Product Disparagement.

Trademark.   A *trademark* is any word, name, symbol, or device, or any combination thereof, adopted and used by a manufacturer or merchant to identify his or her goods and distinguish them from those manufactured or sold by others (see Chapter 13). 15 U.S.C. § 1127.

Trade Secret.   Any secret formula, pattern, device, or compilation of information that is used in one's business and that gives an advantage over competitors who do not know or use it is considered to be a *trade secret* (see Chapter 12).

Trading Partners.   The parties to an electronic data interchange transaction, that is, the sender and recipient of EDI data, are commonly referred to as *trading partners*.

Trading Partner Agreement.   A *trading partner agreement* is the master written agreement entered into between trading partners in an electronic data interchange transaction, which governs their relationship with respect to EDI matters.

Transaction Set.   Each set of formatted data exchanged via electronic data interchange, such as requests for quotation, purchase orders, and invoices, is referred to as a *transaction set*.

Transborder Data Flow.   *Transborder data flow* refers to the electronic communication of data (usually data relating to individuals) across national borders.

TRO.   *See* Temporary Restraining Order.

Trusted Third Party.   A *trusted third party* is a disinterested person who has no vested interest and no allegiance to either of the primary parties involved in a communication and who is trusted by both of the primary parties to perform some act honestly and correctly.

U.C.C.   *See* Uniform Commercial Code.

Uniform Commercial Code.   The *Uniform Commercial Code* is a body of law governing the sale of goods, banking transactions, and security interests, among other things, that has been adopted (with minor variations) in all states except Louisiana. All sales of goods, such as the sale of computer hardware, are governed by the Uniform Commercial Code.

Use Tax.   *Use tax* is a tax imposed by states on the use, storage, or consumption of tangible personal property and certain services. Use tax is imposed on interstate transactions in which the goods or services are purchased in one state and destined for use in another.

Value-Added Network.   A *value-added network*, or *VAN*, is an intermediary computer network that provides a variety of services to its customers, including translation services for EDI documents in incompatible formats, a secure network over which information can be sent, and recordkeeping and audit functions.

VAN.   *See* Value-Added Network.

Verify a Digital Signature.   To *verify a digital signature*, with respect to a given digital signature, message, and public key, means to determine accurately that (1) the digital signature was created by the private key corresponding to the public key, and (2) the message has not been altered since its digital signature was created.

Work Made for Hire.   A *work made for hire* is a copyrightable work of authorship that is either (1) a work prepared by an employee within the scope of his or her employment; or (2) a work specially ordered or commissioned for use as a contribution to a collective work, as part of a motion picture or other audiovisual work, as a translation, as a supplementary work, as a compilation, as an instructional text, as a test, as answer material for a test, or as an atlas, if the parties expressly agree in a written instrument signed by them that the work shall be considered a work made for hire. 17 U.S.C. § 101 (see Section 9.5).

World Wide Web.   The *World Wide Web* is a nickname for a collection of information resources (both commercial and noncommercial) available on the Internet using a protocol known as "http." These resources (or *Web sites*) contain text, graphic, audio, and video files organized using a set of instructions called *hypertext markup language* ("html"). Web sites can be accessed by Internet users who have the proper software (or browser).

Writing.   *Writing* refers to letters, words, numbers, or their equivalent, set down by handwriting, typewriting, printing, photostatting, photographing, magnetic impulse, mechanical or electronic recording, or other form of data compilation.

Index

Addison-Wesley Developers Press publishes high-quality, practical books and software for programmers, developers, and system administrators.

Here are some additional titles from A-W Developers Press that might interest you. If you'd like to order any of these books, you can use one of the following ordering methods:

FAX us at: 800-367-7198

Call us at: 800-822-6339
(8:30 A.M. to 6:00 P.M. eastern
time, Monday through Friday)

Write to us at:
Addison-Wesley Developers Press
One Jacob Way
Reading, MA 01867

Reach us online at:
http://www.aw.com/devpress/

International orders, contact one of the following Addison-Wesley subsidiaries:

Australia/New Zealand
Addison-Wesley Publishing Co.
6 Byfield Street
North Ryde, N.S.W. 2113
Australia
Tel: 61 2 878 5411
Fax: 61 2 878 5830

Southeast Asia
Addison-Wesley
Singapore Pte. Ltd.
15 Beach Road
#05-09/10 Beach Centre
Singapore 189677
Tel: 65 339 7503
Fax: 65 338 6290

Latin America
Addison-Wesley Iberoamericana S.A.
Blvd. de las Cataratas #3
Col. Jardines del Pedregal
01900 Mexico D.F., Mexico
Tel: (52 5) 568-36-18
Fax: (52 5) 568-53-32
e-mail: ordenes@ibero.aw.com
 or: informaciona@ibero.aw.com

Europe and the Middle East
Addison-Wesley Publishers B.V.
Concertgebouwplein 25
1071 LM Amsterdam
The Netherlands
Tel: 31 20 671 7296
Fax: 31 20 675 2141

United Kingdom and Africa
Addison-Wesley Longman Group Limited
P.O. Box 77
Harlow, Essex CM 19 5BQ
United Kingdom
Tel: 44 1279 623 923
Fax: 44 1279 453 450

All other countries:
Addison-Wesley Publishing Co.
Attn: International Order Dept.
One Jacob Way
Reading, MA 01867 U.S.A.
Tel: (617) 944-3700 x5190
Fax: (617) 942-2829

If you'd like a free copy of our Developers Press catalog, contact us at: devpressinfo@aw.com

The Software Publishers Association Legal Guide to Multimedia

Thomas J. Smedinghoff
ISBN 0-201-40931-3, $44.95 w/disk

The Software Publishers Association Legal Guide to Multimedia is a straightforward, plain-English guide to the multimedia legal jungle, written for multimedia developers, publishers and marketers, owners of media content, and any professional involved in the multimedia industry. This book will give you a command of multimedia software legal principles, including copyright, trademark and unfair competition, right of publicity, right of privacy, defamation, trade secrets, and patents.

The Software Developer's and Marketer's Legal Companion

Gene K. Landy
ISBN 0-201-62276-9, $34.95 w/disk

This book provides down-to-earth, real-world legal information in plain English for anyone who needs to understand how the law affects a software business. Topics covered include software copyright law, trade secret law, trademark law, patent law, liability issues, and software distribution in foreign markets. There are eight chapters covering the common types of software contracts.

The LEXIS® Companion

Jean Sinclair McKnight
ISBN 0-201-48335-1, $19.95

The LEXIS® Companion is a practical guide to efficient and cost-effective searching for busy attorneys, paralegals, and others who need current and complete legal information. It provides step-by-step instructions on how to use LEXIS with a minimum of effort for a maximum return on your time and money. Written in everyday English by a tried and true teacher of LEXIS classes, this book makes the business of serious legal research friendly—if not downright funny.

The Internet Business Companion: Growing Your Business in the Electronic Age

David Angell and Brent Heslop
ISBN 0-201-40850-3, $19.95

The Internet Business Companion tells you how to harness the Internet's competitive business advantages and explosive market opportunities without bankrupting your business. It succinctly explains how to develop and implement a cost-effective Internet business strategy. Whether your business is a small start-up or an established corporation you'll learn all the information you need to establish an online presence.

Online Market Research: Cost-Effective Searching of the Internet and Online Databases

John. F. Lescher
ISBN 0-201-48929-5, $19.95

Online Market Research provides you with a thorough grounding in contemporary market research and online searching. You will learn what kind of data is available online; how to determine what your needs are, develop research strategies, and formulate a market plan; and how to acquire and sharpen online searching skills. Most importantly, you will learn how to conduct efficient and economical research about market information using the vast spectrum of online databases and archives available today.

Web Weaving: Designing and Managing an Effective Web Site

Eric Tilton, Carl Steadman, and Tyler Jones
ISBN 0-201-48959-7, $24.95

Covering UNIX®, Windows®, and the Macintosh®, *Web Weaving* shows you how to install and configure Web servers, use authoring tools, implement security, and build structured, well-organized Web sites. The authors, experienced Webmasters, include tips for planning for growth, building in maintenance schemes, catering to your users' needs, and creating a logical, underlying infostructure.

defamation, trade secrets, and patents.

The Internet Publishing Handbook For World-Wide Web, Gopher, and WAIS

Mike Franks
ISBN 0-201-48317-3, $22.95

The Internet Publishing Handbook takes you through the process of Internet publishing from beginning to end, using examples and advice gathered from Internet publishers around the world. You'll learn how to assess hardware and software server needs for your site; choose server setup options and features for World-Wide Web, Gopher, and WAIS; design HTML documents; implement digital cash, digital checks, charging, and more.

Hooked on Java™: Creating Hot Web Sites with Java Applets

Arthur van Hoff, Sami Shaio, and Orca Starbuck, Sun Microsystems, Inc.
ISBN 0-201-48837-X, $29.95 w/CD-ROM

Written by members of Sun's Java development team, *Hooked on Java* is a concise and practical introduction to using applets to add interactive capabilities to World-Wide Web sites.The CD-ROM contains a wealth of cool Java applets ready to plug into your home pages, examples of HTML pages that are already Java-enabled, Java source code, the Java Developer's Kit for Windows® 95, Windows NT, Solaris 2.x, and more.

Planning and Managing Web Sites on the Macintosh®: The Complete Guide to WebSTAR and MacHTTP

Jon Wiederspan and Chuck Shotton
ISBN 0-201-47957-5, $39.95 w/CD-ROM

This book, written by two acknowledged experts in the field, teaches you everything you need to know about using WebSTAR, the best known Mac HTTP server software and its shareware predecessor MacHTTP, as well as about writing CGI applications for your server. A special version of WebSTAR, plus tons of useful software are on the CD-ROM.